THEATRE, CHILDREN and YOUTH

Jed H. Davis

and Mary Jane Evans

anchorage press

This book is dedicated with love to our families, whose patience and support were unwavering.

Thank you

BETTY   ROB

          JOHN   DAVID

                    BRIAN   HAZEL

                    JULIE

FOREWORD

The world of theatre is one world. The purpose of theatre is one purpose: to make experiential through an emotional and/or intellectual transaction the nature of being human. It has always been so. From earliest times to latest, theatre has been the mirror of the society which produced it, reflecting the hopes and fears, the desires and needs of any given social group by the selection and ordering of ideas, actions and characters into a semblance of virtual life (or, as Aristotle says, "an imitation of life") intended to convey some perceptions about life. It is the mutually enjoyed experience of performers and audience, the living together of an ordered existence not always otherwise available, the interchange of spoken or unspoken thoughts, ideas, emotions, actions. Because of its nature, no art form other than theatre is so apt to foster an understanding of man and his world.

Theatre for children and youth is no different in its basic form and purpose from theatre in general. However — and here is where this volume is particularly valuable — the perceptions, the emotions and the intellectual capacities of children are in a continuum of development which grows in specific ways from year to year. If the theatre experience for children is to be life-enhancing and helpful in that growth, it must be cognizant of the stages of development from early childhood to adolescence. In other words, the materials, means and effects of theatre (when the audience participants are children or youth) must be structured with the child view in mind and with a clear perception of audience profiles at the various age levels.

To the material contained in their earlier book, Jed H. Davis and Mary Jane Evans have here added — in clear and compelling form — the implications of recent discoveries in developmental psychology for children's theatre. Begin with the child, they say. And as you progress through the selection of materials for presentation and the decisions about staging, return always to the child. Theatre for children is important, not because they are a *future* audience, but because they are a *present* one.

The book is sequential and comprehensive. Its concern is serious and insistent but gracefully and delightfully presented. That concern is good theatre for children: where it started, where it is now, how to make it and how to evaluate it. In addition, there are a number of useful appendices. It is a work not only essential to the worker in the field of children's theatre, but it is also useful to workers in the theatre in general because of its clear analysis of dramatic structures and its sensible progression through the essentials of play production.

For the totality of their careers, the authors have been devoted to theatre for children and youth. They have been "movers and shakers" in the development of that field. Their professional careers, if combined, would cover more than half the length of years in which there has been a focus on theatre for children and youth in this country. Obviously, they speak with the voice of authority. Over the years, I have learned much from them, and this book teaches me more. I thank them.

— Vera Mowry Roberts
HUNTER COLLEGE
City University of New York

PREFACE

On a brisk November day in 1960 — the same day that John F. Kennedy was elected President of the United States — we received the first copies of our new book, *Children's Theatre: Play Production for the Child Audience*. Twenty years later we thumb through those same volumes, now dog-eared and long consigned to the shelf, and are struck by the prophetic quality of the opening sentences of Chapter I: "What an age we live in! What a breathless era, in which civilization moves at breakneck speed from one milestone to the next!" Little did we know how many milestones would be set in the path of history within a few short years, nor could we predict the breakneck speed with which the world view of the theatre for children and youth would change. At mid-century-plus-ten we knew our profession had passed beyond the stage of lusty infancy, but it was closer to the brink of a rebellious adolescence than either of us realized.

That book was addressed to a field that had found a measure of stability. The form and content of productions were rather narrowly prescribed and quite consistently observed in the mainstream. Producers at least paid lip service to a set of agreed-upon standards. We were justly proud of all that had been achieved, even as we were painfully aware of many glaring discrepancies between qualitative and quantitative growth. We called for excellence and a forward look, never dreaming how far that look would carry us. In the intervening years, yesterday's prevailing practices have been largely set aside. Having labeled them "traditional," many view them with scornful affection; others view them only with scorn, if they accord them any attention at all. Diversity of approach is the order of the day, and it is difficult to chart the mainstream, so complex is its network of tributaries.

This present volume is about today, but every today has its roots in a yesterday, and we make frequent reference to what used to be. This is not because we yearn for the "good old days." Rather we believe that familiarity with the past puts the present in perspective and provides a frame of reference for judging the future. Students need to know what groundwork has been laid over the years and to be aware that those years are not even a century in number. Young as it is, the theatre for children and youth has a rich and colorful history. To neglect it is to deprive students of acquaintance with people, programs and practices that shaped the field. In passing, we might also observe that history and movements and fashions all have a way of repeating themselves. Attempts to create something completely new often lead to rediscovery of the old.

Some aspects of the "old" are eternally unchanging, however. No matter how far our dynamic profession deviates from past practice, we must constantly reassert our adherence to certain eternal verities: unending concern for standards in whatever dramatic idiom we may find to express ourselves; an ongoing obligation to consider the growth and well-being of children and youth in all we do; and a continuing consciousness of the important function theatre should fulfill in transmitting our multi-faceted cultural heritage to upcoming generations. This book places heavy emphasis on all three.

The international children's theatre movement has been instrumental in broadening our world view of the field and has profoundly affected American thought and practice. While influences from abroad are taken into account throughout our work, this is a book about theatre for children and youth in the United States. Therefore no attempt has been made to provide detailed accounts of theatre programs in countries other than our own.

We also have had to limit our references to American producing groups, specific productions, playwrights and plays. As we recall the past, we make mention of only a representative few of the organizations, many now non-existent, that have left their mark. It has been equally impossible to acknowledge by name all the individuals whose vision, leadership and artistic talent have shaped the field. We honor them all, and our respect for their legacy is implicit in all that we have written. As we examine the contemporary scene, we provide only a sampling of theatre organizations which are doing exemplary work. At the moment all of them are thriving, and we wish them long life. Knowing the past as we do, however, it is almost certain that some of them will have changed their status by the time this book is printed.

We recognize, too, that many innovative programs have been made possible through a vast variety of funding patterns for the arts. Since funding from the public and private sectors is dependent upon the economy and the political and social climate, these patterns are anything but stable. They change as rapidly as do the groups they support, and there is no assurance that the flow of money will continue unabated. In these and other matters, we can only write of what is and use restraint in speculating about what may occur in the future.

When we determined the scope of this book, we decided to eliminate all detailed treatment of the procedures that design and technical artists follow in making their contributions to the production process. We acknowledge the vital role they play and set forth standards for their work. However, we have assumed that students of the theatre for young audiences also are students of theatre who have prior knowledge of the fundamentals of production practice which are common to all theatre.

Further, our focus is on the live performance. Therefore we have eliminated any discussion of puppetry or mass media drama. Much of what we say, however, is directly applicable to those art forms.

We have made a conscientious effort to continue the growth of theatre for children and youth as a respectable academic discipline. Our research and reporting represent an attempt to correct many errors and eliminate many misconceptions that have been perpetuated over the years. We also have tried to relate our work to thinking outside our narrow field by establishing connections with psychology, communications, adult theatre and drama, education and any other fields of study having something to contribute to a fuller understanding of what we do.

The material covered in this book is cumulative and interdependent. Its subject matter develops sequentially, and after presenting an overview of the field in Chapter I, we have written each subsequent section assuming that the reader has absorbed the content of those that have come before. Chapter II lays a foundation for all that follows as it provides definitions of prevalent theatrical styles and sets forth standards for all production activity. There follows an in-depth examination of contemporary developmental theory and how perceptions of childhood apply to the work we do.

Chapter IV reviews the script repertoire and examines the content and thematic values of an extensive body of dramatic literature currently available for production. In Chapter V, we show how the director finds production values in each of the several performance styles, with an emphasis on scripted material. Next we outline the steps the director follows in preparing for production activity. Chapter VII carries the production from tryout through post-performance evaluation.

Business matters occupy our attention in Chapter VIII, and because so many organizations now choose to sponsor rather than produce plays for children and youth, we have seen fit to devote a separate chapter to their concerns. Finally, in Chapter X, we bring theatre into the schools. When they read this chapter, we trust that students will recall all that has been written about the child as performer in preceding sections of the book.

At the conclusion of the text, readers will find a series of Appendices containing a variety of materials which have been included with our hope that they will serve a useful purpose.

No book can be written in isolation, nor can its ideas come from the authors alone. To list all the individuals whose lives and work have influenced our own would be a task so formidable as to beggar description. Through the years we have learned from our teachers, our colleagues on several college campuses and, more than we can say, from our students. We have had the active support of administrators who have given us room to grow. Our long and intimate involvement in the American Theatre Association, and especially in the Children's Theatre Association of America, has extended our list of valued mentors and colleagues, broadened our knowledge and widened our horizons. Above all, it has put us in contact with a body of like-minded people who affirm our belief that there can be unity in diversity.

We acknowledge our debt to all the artists and scholars whose works we cite, and to all the producers and directors who have generously provided pictorial material to enliven the text. Our thanks to Vera Mowry Roberts, a great lady of the American educational theatre, not only for contributing the Foreword to this book, but for the active, enlightened support she unfailingly lends to the cause of theatre wherever she finds it.

Finally, we raise our glasses to Orlin Corey, who said it could be done and, with gentle nudges, motivated us to put our thoughts on paper. His patience and perception have been notable, his editorial work invaluable. If our efforts to make some small contribution to the theatre for children and youth prove successful, the field must thank him, for he alone made this book possible.

JHD
MJE

PREFACE TO THE REVISED PRINTING

The five years since this volume first was published have seen no radical or substantive changes in the philosophical foundations or practical aspects of producing plays for young audiences. Nonetheless, time does not stand still. As we predicted in 1982, each season sees the disappearance of some producing units and, on the positive side, further development of established programs and the inception of promising new ones. The field is increasingly committed to research and to publication of scholarly findings. Our repertoire of scripted material is enhanced each year.

Most recently, the demise of the American Theatre Association and the concomitant disbanding of its several divisions, including the Children's Theatre Association of America, stimulated leaders in the field to take stock and seek other channels for their interactions. For something more than a year, the newly-established American Association of Theatre for Youth dedicated itself to continuing CTAA's commitment to the betterment of theatre art and education for the young; and, even as we go to press, AATY's merger with the equally new American Association of Theatre in Secondary Education appears a certainty, promising a vastly enlarged agenda for the professional society that comes into being. The fledgling organization will be afforded the luxury of a fresh start even as it draws upon the richness of the two societies' heritage.

In light of these developments we have undertaken a revised printing of *Theatre, Children and Youth*, making no claim to a total revision of our earlier work. Rather we have scrutinized it with particular attention to updating sections presenting factual material about organizations and events of significance to the field, and changes appear sporadically throughout the text. The Bibliography has been revised, as has the annotated listing of playscripts in the Appendix.

This modest effort is our way of expressing gratitude to a profession that has nurtured us and given us the privilege of sharing what it has taught us.

JHD
MJE

TABLE OF CONTENTS

APPENDICES

CHAPTER I
EXAMINING THE CONTEMPORARY SCENE

Come with us on a very special journey.

Busloads of fifth grade children jostle and laugh as they file into the beautifully appointed lobby of the University of Texas-Austin's B. Iden Payne Theatre. They have come to see the world premiere of a new Aurand Harris play about death — *The Arkansaw Bear* — but no hint of sadness dampens their jocular arrival. Inside, the theatre fills with the five hundred invited audience members, and the play begins.

A little girl enters a pool of light. She is carrying a wilted bouquet of pink flowers to give her dying grandpa, but he is too ill to see her. She is sent away, crying, to seek her private solace beneath a favorite tree. Soon an aged, panic-stricken Dancing Bear arrives, trying vainly to outrun Death in the person of the Great Ringmaster. The children laugh delightedly at the Bear, in contrast to the subdued hush of the deathbed scene.

The arrival of the Ringmaster revives the hushed apprehension, but it is soon relieved by delighted shrieks as the character of Star Bright (the first star I've seen tonight) enters from the flies on a trapeze, ready to grant the girl's and the Bear's wish that Death should hold off until they learn how to face the ultimate end of things with dignity and resignation. Each time Star Bright makes his spectacular entrance from the flies, the children cheer; but they know that soon will come the dawn, and with the dawn all wishes vanish: the reality of death must be faced.

But the highest level of delight to the children is reserved for the arrival of Little Bear, pert and sassy, charming in her innocence, ready to take on the task of learning all the old Bear's dances, providing the continuity into the future — the very meaning of life and the solace of the dying.

An audible gasp is heard as the old Bear takes his last bow and collapses. And the adults have a hard time suppressing a sob as the dying Bear allows his faithful Mime friend to release the balloon of his life.

As they leave, these fifth graders give every sign of having had a truly meaningful experience in theatre for young people.

And on another day in another city:

A vitalized group of two hundred youngsters of mixed ages sits down front to keep them separate from the critical children's theatre specialists attending the state festival in St. Louis. The Metro Theater Circus is playing in their home city, but as a touring group their home is where their hats hang. A huge brown blob occupies most of the thrust stage at Washington University's Edison Theatre, but to stage right is a collection of keyboard instruments and percussion. It is with music the performance gets under way, and as the rollicking beat of the piano and synthesizer is picked up by increasingly massive undulations of the brown blob, we are drawn in to the imagistic charm of *Mudweavings*.

The talented company of seven alternates functions as storyteller, actor, musician, dancer, or prop-shifter as the succession of childhood sensations rolls forward. Ordinary, unthreatening, fun things that all children know and respond to in their lives are given special meaning and importance in these skilled, sympathetic, respectful hands. They sing about sunlight and secrets and rain. Delightful original music, expertly played, propels the fast-moving performance through dozens of sights and sounds we take for granted in our humdrum lives. How do you love a mountain? How do you physicalize macaroni? Or ocean waves?

Mud, the most ordinary of ordinary substances, is made the focus of a delightful piece of theatre and capitalizes on the special talents the performers bring to their work. The ensemble piece is arranged in upward sequence by a sensitive artist, and after it both children and adults feel better about being alive in this marvelous world.

San Diego:

The group calling itself the Yellow Brick Road is about to perform its story theatre version of Andersen's *Nightingale* before delegates to the national meeting of the Children's Theatre Association of America. A mixed crowd settles in, savoring the intimate atmosphere of the performance arena while the four actors chat with audience members, especially the children seated on the floor close to the action. Setting elements are few: a prop stand on a small level at one end of the elliptical playing space, and a cloth backing for a throne at the other. Costuming is limited to suggestive Chinese shirts and headpieces added to contemporary clothing.

Almost imperceptibly the chatting blends into the opening speeches of the narrator character. With stylized Oriental gestures and rhythmic movement the storyteller delivers needed exposition and calls our attention to the musician-sound effects person who will accompany the action on a collection of instruments at the side. We are told that everything the Emperor valued gets taken away by the gods, even his favorite "imperial blue cat's eye marble," won from him by a rival ruler. Sticks with cloth strips are waved violently about to suggest the winds that come to destroy the vain Emperor's garden or a devastating fire. But since music can cheer him from his depressed state, the accompanist plays a simple melody. Still unsatisfied, the Emperor asks for more ornamentation, adding more instruments, until, as a last resort, we in the audience become a massed orchestra, divided and trained in sections — violins, trumpets, drums, and tubas. Start and stop signals are carefully prearranged by the narrator-conductor. We all rise and bow as the Emperor enters to conduct us himself; but, alas, we cannot play elaborately enough to please him.

During this participation, we note several children in the front row who hold back. They watch other children and the performers but they do not take part — and the actors wisely make no special effort to coerce them or make them feel conspicuous.

At last the Nightingale appears — a free spirit of the forest with a simple, true song. An actress with a subtly expressive face and delicate hand movements portrays the bird's flying or perching to our complete satisfaction; and when she is captured by the Emperor, fettered, and adorned with a heavy ornamental robe which stifles her song our hearts go out to her. When she is banished from the kingdom for failing to please the Emperor, the guilty ruler is visited by Death, an actor carrying a large conventionalized mask; and his sins of thoughtlessness and selfishness are danced in ritualistic form. How can the Emperor be saved from Death? We have been prepared, and as we place our hands over our hearts (even those of us who were previously reluctant), the repentant ruler does likewise. The Nightingale heeds the call, returning from banishment to cheer the Emperor and his people for a long time to come.

The play ends on a quiet note of inner satisfaction, a celebration of love and the caring life.

The place: Minneapolis, Minnesota.
The time: Spring.

Parking spaces are hard to come by. Yellow buses drive in and out of the entranceway crowded with children and adults. Despite the rain, colorful clowns greet the arriving throngs. The Minneapolis Institute of Arts is awash with people, for this is the all-arts festival for children, and colorful handbills outline the day's agenda: a richness of gallery tours, musical events, mummers, mimes and puppets. Balloons, popcorn, confusion — but confusion that has its own order as smiling docents answer questions, give directions, and help lines to form. One of those lines patiently awaits admission to the Minneapolis Children's Theatre Company production of *The 500 Hats of Bartholomew Cubbins*. The production has been sold out for weeks, and enthusiasm is high.

From the noise and commotion of the lobby, the audience moves into a dimly lighted, comfortable and special space — a theatre designed just for them — and are immediately captivated by the larger-than-life, dimensional work of art that greets them. Here, framed in a glowing arch and shrouded in mist and mystery is the Kingdom of Didd, straight out of the pages of Dr. Seuss. High on the hill, and seemingly far away, King Derwin's castle looms over the village giving promise of adventures to come. The lights change, the music begins, a hush falls over the house, and there is magic.

Characters in costumes absolutely faithful to the Seuss illustrations proclaim in song the excitement of the day: the King is coming to town. The muted colors of the set and costumes stand in sharp contrast to the red of Bartholomew's hat as he enters the square to sell his cranberries and to join in paying homage to the King. The familiar favorite story unfolds, faithfully recreating each moment of Bartholomew's adventure. Hats appear as if from nowhere as his efforts to remove them become ever more frustrating. The scenes move from place to place magically and before our eyes. Music and song carry the story along. No matter that everyone knows the outcome, there is a hush of suspense as Bartholomew ascends the tower, taunted by the brattish Grand Duke Wilfred and accompanied by the relentless counting of the Keeper of the King's Records. And a gasp of relief and wonder accompanies the appearance of the 500th hat, a miracle of ostentation. A shout of joy fills the air when Wilfred receives his spanking.

Music, graceful movement, high style, vivid characterizations, technical magic all have combined to provide a feast for the eye, the ear, and the spirit. Shining eyes, smiling faces and excited chatter mark the departure of several hundred happy theatre-goers.

The train-car-plane returns you to your city, but really the journey has just begun. The world of theatre for children and youth is far-flung and rich in its diversity. If this is your first look at it, things may seem energetic, enthusiastic, but somewhat chaotic. Groups appear to be going their own ways. There appears to be little agreement as to where, how, or why, at least on the surface. If you bring with you the impression that here is a pretty stodgy art form, steeped in tradition and virtually without prestige in the great theatre world, perhaps a place where actors work when they can't find real work, or where amateurs play at making theatre for kiddies who won't know the difference, then we hope you will pay close attention along the way and will ultimately arrive at your destination with some new attitudes and perhaps a commitment to become part of the new image.

A LOOK BACKWARD

Before going any farther into the present, let us step into our time capsule and take a brief trip backward, to see where we've been. We won't have very far to go because prior to 1900 there just wasn't much to see. Since this information is given in much detail elsewhere,[1] we won't have to stay very long, and we can just pause a moment at the landmark stations.

It is October, 1903. New York City, at Jefferson Street and East Broadway.

It is an occasion long awaited in this immigrant section of town. Inside the auditorium of the Educational Alliance Building, the area's main settlement house, the Children's Educational Theatre is about to open its first production, *The Tempest,* with a cast of community children. For weeks shops have been sold out of books containing this Shakespearean play. Every family has a copy, eager to become familiar with the sounds of English at its best. We are all much aware that this is the opening of the first ongoing children's theatre in the United States; and its new director, Alice Minnie Herts, is intent on making it into a vital community force that will help ease the transition into American life, and interest youngsters in better examples of English drama than are found at the corner Nickelodeon or at the Vaudeville down the street. Fully set and costumed, this production will establish a precedent for careful staging that will characterize Miss Herts' plays and, six years later, will be a cause of her theatre's demise. After all, tickets are only a nickel; and how far will that go, even in 1903?

November 6, 1905. The Empire Theatre on Broadway, New York City.

Maude Adams is opening in *Peter Pan,* Mr. Barrie's new play that was such a hit in London last December. Advance word is that the show is sure to be revived regularly as a holiday treat, so perfectly does it suit one ideal of a play for children. And glory of glories, Peter flies like a bird, and teaches other kids to fly, too — right there on the stage! There have been a few professional productions of other plays before in town, but none had the star attraction that this one has. Yes, *Peter Pan* promises to be around for years to come!

On the same whirl about Broadway we catch an elaborate staging of *The Blue Bird* at the New Theatre in October, 1910, freshly arrived from successful runs in Moscow and London; the deForest version of *Little Women* in October of 1912; *Snow White and the Seven Dwarfs* at Winthrop Ames' Little Theatre in December, 1912; *Racketty-Packetty House,* by the famous Mrs. Burnett, at our very own children's theatre on top of the Century Theatre, newly opened in 1913; a new *Alice in Wonderland* in March, 1915, after a short run in Chicago; and, finally, a spectacular *Treasure Island* at the Punch and Judy the following December where we marvel at the fully rigged *Hispaniola* tossing and lurching on the "high seas." Oh, it's been glorious; but as we look far ahead through our magic perspective we can see no other period when Broadway is blessed with such richness of plays for children.

It is still 1915, and a young man with a dream is about to begin a most innovative venture. His name is **Stuart** Walker, and his dream will be called the "Portmanteau Theatre." Here at Christadora House in New York City, he had hopes that the unique portable theatre he has built will be the center of drama activities for his young settlement house charges. But he now has engaged a group of talented young professionals to act his original plays for family audiences. The theatre can be packed away in manageable crates and transported by the performers from one hall to another, wherever they book engagements. The structure with its modest size and three playing levels is one of the very first theatres for children to implement a director's desire for close physical ties between actors and spectators; but once again we look ahead and see the end of the project in 1919.

Two years later — 1921 — another first; the Junior League of Chicago is about to introduce theatre for children into its local program, and from thence into League programs all over the country. The play is *Alice in Wonderland,* by Alice Gerstenberg, co-directed by the author and Annette Washburn, at the Fine Arts Building Playhouse. The Leagues, organizations of young women of means, are beginning with elaborate downtown productions at high ticket prices, but gradually they will change their emphasis to bringing more manageable plays to children in the schools, using their own members as cast and crew. And farther yet down the road, into the 50's, 60's, and 70's, they will shift their emphasis to sponsorship and service as pivotal agencies in community arts programs.

It is still 1921, and another landmark appears in New York City. It is the beginning of Clare Tree Major's Threshold Players, soon to be relocated in the "most beautiful children's theatre in the world," the Heckscher Foundation's building at 105th Street and Fifth Avenue. There her company of young professionals will play such favorites as *Treasure Island, Hansel and Gretel* and *Pinocchio,* next expanding her operations to the Princess Theatre for performances of plays for high school students, and finally, by 1928, into the first nation-wide touring program and Academy. It is the system of financially successful touring for which Mrs. Major will be chiefly remembered. As many as six companies will troupe from coast to coast until her death in 1954, using her own adaptations of favorite stories such as *Little Women, Aladdin* and *Robin Hood* to reach literally millions of children.[2]

It is the mid-Twenties, and at Northwestern University Winifred Ward is about to establish the Children's Theatre of Evanston, Illinois. It is to be a joint program with the Northwestern School of Speech and the Evanston school system sharing responsibilities. As we look ahead we see Miss Ward as a prime mover of the field of theatre and drama with and for children, who maintains preeminence and exerts an influence far beyond Evanston until her death in 1975.[3] From these beginnings, many programs tied to colleges and universities will comprise a pattern unique in the world.

Again in 1925, in nearby Chicago, the Goodman Theatre is establishing its own series of plays for children; but it will not be until 1931 when Charlotte B. Chorpenning, beginning her third career at age sixty, joins the staff that an intensive playwriting and production program for child audiences will reach significant stature. With Mrs. Chorpenning's death in 1955. the program at the Goodman will continue, even through the transfer of the Goodman School of Drama from the Art Institute of Chicago to DePaul University.[4]

At this stage in our journey we can see many islands of activity — so many we cannot count them all in this quick survey. The numbers of groups in each established category (professional, settlement house and recreation, educational, Junior League, and community theatres) are growing. There in New York is the unusual King-Coit School which annually produces a magnificent and exotic play derived from the culture of some foreign land using children in the school in a way never really duplicated by another organization.[5] Elsewhere, at Cain Park in Cleveland Heights, Ohio, is a children's outdoor drama program of rich dimensions evolving from 1938 to the early 1950's under Dina Rees Evans; and out west in Palo Alto is an exemplary theatre established in 1932 as part of the city's recreation program for child participants but moving into its own special building in 1936, all under the guidance of its dynamic leaders, Hazel Glaister Robertson and Caroline Fisher. For a time it looks as if even the federal government will get into the act when, from 1936 to 1939, the Federal Theatre Project, a program of the Works Progress Administration (WPA), begins producing special plays for children in selected cities. But the total Project closes in a morass of political invective; and there is no further federal involvement until the establishment of the National Endowment for the Arts in 1965.[6]

Another important landmark emerges in 1936. It is called Junior Programs, Inc., and it is being initiated by Mrs. Dorothy McFadden and her group in Maplewood, New Jersey, particularly to sponsor children's entertainment in their own community. But the idea of sponsorship catches on, and similar Junior Programs are set up across the country to act as intermediaries between professional performers and the communities they serve. By the Fifties, the hiatus in travel occasioned by World War II is over, and most of the existing professional children's theatres are touring under sponsorship or direct commission by Junior Programs and similar community agencies.

Our hasty trip revealing highlights of the past ends as our time capsule dissolves and we find ourselves face-to-face with the present.

THEATRE FOR YOUNG AUDIENCES TODAY

By the time World War II ended, important groundwork had been laid for a national children's theatre movement that was awe-inspiring in its diversity. The term "children's theatre" encompassed anything from a commercial enterprise to a person who conducted classes in "dramatics" in a private studio, and no two of them were very much alike.

Among the evolving types of organizations a set of purposes for engaging in the activity of producing or sponsoring theatre for young audiences began to emerge.

Purposes

Whether stated or unstated, these purposes permeate every facet of a theatre's operation, determine what is done, with whom and for whom, and what the ultimate effect is presumed to be.[7]

The commitment to provide *entertainment* of a meaningful sort is almost always a stated objective. Those to be entertained are identified as children, perhaps children and youth, or even the family, including senior citizens. The entertainment (or enjoyment) of the participants in the process of making theatre is not always stated, but it is certainly implied in activities focused in a community or recreation setting.

The intention to provide an *opportunity for learning* may either be stated or implied; but the degree of emphasis placed on learning or on the selection of matters to be learned is subject to great variation from group to group. Children or youth audience members, through identifying with the performance in a role modeling process may learn behavior patterns, moral concepts, and attitudes as well as facts. Learning experiences may be structured for those young people involved in the production as cast, crew or staff members. Learning the various aspects of the art form may be a stated objective for children or youth who study at theatre academies, or for teenagers in active junior or senior high school drama programs. In leisure-time settings (recreation, art centers, youth centers, Y's, etc.) opportunities for learning as well as pleasure are usually offered youthful participants. College students study and take part in productions in order to learn theatre processes, often to learn particularly about theatre for young audiences. Other adults, such as Junior League members or community theatre and recreation workers, generally admit they are happily engaged in a valuable learning process in many respects.

In some groups, the opportunity to learn is amplified into a commitment to *teach*, to promote a particular cause or philosophical stand. In recent times concepts of peace, love of fellow human beings, equality of sexes and races, anti-pollution, use of metric measurements, and physics have been quite frankly taught in the theatre for young audiences. Of course, religious beliefs have been taught quite candidly for decades. Such teaching could well apply to both audience and participants.

Contributing to the *mental health* of youthful audiences as well as production participants most often is an implicit rather than a stated purpose. Through encouragement of emotional involvement in the material of the performance, producers promote a controlled release of hostile feelings, or at least provide a pleasant relief from sordidness, pressures and tensions.

Enriching the lives of children and youth through emotionally satisfying submersion in the theatre art form is often stated as an objective, but the specific ways in which this is to be accomplished tend to remain rather vague. It is assumed, however, that enrichment occurs as learning and emotional satisfaction occur, brought about by the particular magic of theatre, both on stage and in the house.

Making a significant contribution to *artistic growth* of young audience members, as well as of all participants is a readily acknowledged purpose of most organizations in this field. The statement is often supplemented with declarations that only performances of the highest quality will have this effect.

The following purposes for establishing or maintaining a program in theatre for young audiences are seldom stated but are nonetheless frequently operative. It should be noted that nothing pejorative is neccessarily implied in such purposes, but they do tend to be more pragmatic than idealized.

Providing a living for the participants is an obvious reason to engage in any theatrical venture. Theatre for young audiences is no exception.

A desire to *increase a theatre's income* will sometimes lead an established adult theatre program to add a young audience dimension. Increasing the possibilities for *obtaining grant money*, with accompanying "overhead" margins, is also a possible operative purpose.

Enhancing an existing theatre's public image in a community by establishing ties to the local school system, to parents, or to other community organizations may be one of the more common purposes for engaging in theatre for young audiences. As the threads of financial support become increasingly intertwined in a complex society, few theatres can afford to overlook avenues of potentially favorable image construction.

Helping to ensure that adults who have spent satisfying hours in the theatre as children will *continue to elect the living theatre* over more popular media is a purpose sometimes denounced as too crass and commercial to consider seriously; but for those of us who believe in the theatre's unique power to affect people's lives in countless favorable ways, this purpose can be seen more as a desire to share good fortune.[8]

In functional terms, a major distinction can be made between theatre organizations that produce and those that sponsor productions by others.

Types of Producing Organizations

A clear sign of the growing maturity of theatre for young audiences is the increase in numbers of professional groups serving the field. Efforts to document that growth culminated in the publication of a two-volume directory of some sixty-five theatres that regularly offer a season of plays, that support a paid staff and at least a nucleus of paid performers, and that have a minimum annual budget of $50,000.[9]

The highest level of professional company consists of those that not only meet these expressed criteria, but also set and maintain high production standards which take them beyond the level of commercialism and stop-gap employment which has sometimes characterized our field.

Occupying a prominent place in the top echelon of professional groups is The Children's Theatre Company of Minneapolis, whose founding artistic director was John Clark Donahue. Performers are professional actors employed by the theatre as well as children who take part in the theatre's educational program. The theatre plant is specially built to accommodate the elaborate productions for which this program is justly famous world wide.

The Nashville Academy Theatre, established in 1931 as the Nashville Children's Theatre with Junior League roots, is now a professional company operating out of its own theatre plant named for long-time volunteer leader, Ann Stahlman Hill. The latest step in the development of this remarkable organization is the addition of the Academy offering accredited training in theatre arts and crafts on the secondary level.

One of the most prestigious groups was the Everyman Players of New Orleans, guided meticulously by producer Orlin Corey from 1957 to 1980. Everyman's staging of classics such as *Reynard the Fox, The Tortoise and the Hare,* and *Don Quixote of La Mancha,* with designs by Irene Corey, are widely known through published photos of the costumes and make-up. A similar fame extends to their productions of religious pieces such as *The Book of Job.* Through appearances at festivals and tours on four continents, it became one of the best known American theatres in international circles.

The Little Theatre of the Deaf, the children's theatre component of the much acclaimed National Theatre of the Deaf, was founded in 1968. Masterminded by David Hayes, this group is headquartered at the O'Neill Foundation in Waterford, Connecticut. Its touring program has brought nationwide recognition to the unique and excellent work it does. Besides setting a high performance standard for ensemble treatment of original and adapted material, this company is in the forefront of the national movement to bring hearing impaired populations into the mainstream of American artistic life.

Under Judith Martin's leadership, the world famous Paper Bag Players have been "in residence" at various New York City locations since they formed in 1958; but basically the group has remained a touring operation. Noted for a distinct production style involving sketches full of music and mime with costumes and props of cardboard cartons and shopping sacks, this talented group has achieved an enviable reputation for high artistry.

On the West coast, the Improvisational Theatre Project operates out of the Mark Taper Forum of the Los Angeles Music Center, performing there and on tour. With a production style based on the Paul Sills *Story Theatre* concept, the ITP keeps audiences actively involved by building short plays from audience suggestions, conducts workshops in classrooms, and with a writer-in-residence develops longer plays through company improvisation.

Sometimes limited to a single yearly production but nevertheless welcome as an entry from the professional sector are other children's theatre adjuncts to adult repertory companies. The Guthrie Theatre of Minneapolis usually stages an annual production for child audiences. The Imaginary Theatre of the Loretto-Hilton Repertory Theatre tours regularly in the St. Louis area and beyond. The ACT (A Contemporary Theatre) of Seattle does excellent work on two plays for children and youth as part of the regular season, touring them to local schools and throughout the region.

Other worthy and comparatively long-lived professional groups are THEATREWORKS/USA (formerly PART Foundation, Inc.), Periwinkle Productions, Inc., and Maximillion Productions, Inc., all of New York City. Each has an individual area of specialty, each its unique performance style. Comparatively new to the scene, yet establishing solid reputations, are Stage One: The Louisville Children's Theatre, ArtReach Touring Theatre of Cincinnati, the Nebraska Theatre Caravan of Omaha and the California Theatre Center of Sunnyvale.

A uniquely American phenomenon which has developed in recent years is the addition of a professional children's theatre component to educational theatre programs. As a rule, these companies are relatively small and consist of salaried non-Equity members who may either be students or recent graduates. Most confine their scope to regional touring or summer resident productions; however, the Empire

State Youth Theatre Institute, funded by the State of New York with ties to the State University system, maintains a teaching and production program of unusual dimensions at its impressive home site in Albany. The Creative Arts Team (CAT) of New York University, which performs productions and works directly with students in classes using theatre-in-education methodology, is building yet another framework for cooperation between the profession and the campus.

Professional performer/teachers who work with special child populations in dramatic modes appear ready to emerge in significant numbers. One such group, CLIMB, Inc., of Minneapolis, utilizes a mixture of performance and creative drama techniques designed to involve exceptional children physically, intellectually and emotionally, adding a revolutionary new dimension to the field of drama therapy.

Theatre for young audiences first connected to academia in 1919, when children were involved in plays under student supervision at Emerson College in Boston. In 1926, a similar program using child casts was set up at the University of Tulsa. From 1925, Winifred Ward's program at Northwestern functioned as a cooperative venture between the University and the Evanston Public Schools. A unique feature of this arrangement was the inclusion of creative drama, both as an area of study on campus and as an in-class program in the schools. The practice of offering courses in children's theatre and creative drama and of producing plays for child audiences has been widely adopted in colleges and universities following Northwestern's lead.

No one really knows how many academic children's theatres actually exist in the United States. Directories published in the 50's, 60's and 70's variously tallied from one hundred fifty to three hundred fifty programs attached to colleges and universities. Their scope ranges from a single production under advanced student direction to prestigious undergraduate and graduate curricula and production activities leading to bachelor's, master's and doctoral degrees. Opportunities for conducting meaningful research are, of course, better in an academic setting than anywhere else.[10]

Curriculum ranges from a single all-purpose course in children's theatre and creative drama to many courses in which the full philosophical and practical dimensions of the two fields are explored. At several institutions, specified courses in the field are required of students preparing for elementary teacher certification. Whether the program is located in a school or department of fine arts, liberal arts, communication arts or education, there are almost always strong ties with the campus agency responsible for training teachers.

Since most college children's theatres began with the simple addition of a play for young audiences to the regular performance schedule, it is not surprising that many have limited their emphasis to production. Some have instituted touring to help serve community or area cultural needs. These days it is common to offer academic credit for production involvement, and if touring extends student commitments beyond the scope of laboratory experience credits, financial compensation may be added. Many university groups became professional or semi-professional in just this way.

In order to give their students as broad a "hands on" experience as possible, academic programs in theatre for young audiences have employed a wide variety of production styles. Published scripts in the traditional mode are used by many. Others collaborate with playwriting classes to try out new scripts as they are developed. Still others tie their productions to classes in improvisation or ensemble acting, actually evolving a theatre piece from class activity. Performance modes introduced by experimental groups are quickly adopted by these voracious explorers. In these ways the theatre education of the college student is immeasurably enriched, and the numbers of well-trained practitioners available to the profession is increased.

While we rarely find a course in children's theatre below the college level, schools frequently produce plays for young audiences. Many senior high schools do plays for children, sometimes inviting elementary students to their auditorium, sometimes trouping their performances to the lower schools. As we examine many senior high school drama programs we notice that today these enthusiastic and well-trained Thespians do more and better work than many college theatres did a generation back. Facilities and student support often are adequate to handle large-scale, big cast productions. When they are properly indoctrinated to positive attitudes toward playing for children, and when they are carefully and skillfully directed, high school actors are able to inspire an unusually satisfying level of audience identification.

Many junior high or middle schools now present performances for parents, peers and the general public. The repertoire suitable for young teenagers is not yet adequate to satisfy the demand, but the dedication they display under knowledgable leadership seems to justify the unending search for material that will interest and challenge them.

As creative drama has gained more acceptance and teachers better trained in creative drama methods have infused school systems, drama work in elementary grades has increasingly taken the form of in-class demonstrations rather than public performances. Even so, many schools regularly schedule productions of formal plays for the student body and the public, often charging admission. Production standards vary greatly at this level.[11]

Theatre for young audiences commonly appears under the auspices of community agencies, notably departments of recreation, parks and playgrounds, community arts centers, youth activity centers, singly or in combination, and sometimes in collaboration with the school system. Financial and facility needs often dictate alliances among agencies. One major purpose of engaging in production is to give opportunity for meaningful and satisfying creative endeavor for the participants; but bringing joyful theatre experiences to large community audiences at no charge or for a low admission fee is another strong incentive. A few groups that began this way — the Honolulu Theatre for Youth is a notable example — climb the ladder to professional status, changing their focus from recreation for participants to satisfaction of child or family audiences.

Traveling trailer stages, tents, open-air spaces as well as more traditional performance settings are utilized by such groups. As more cities convert old libraries and railroad stations into art centers, adequate performance areas are provided and theatre activity can be centered in an identifiable home. One such group, the Davenport, Iowa, Children's Theatre, capitalized on its community reputation of many years' standing to garner support for its own theatre building. Some municipalities, such as Palo Alto and Waterloo, Iowa, provide the buildings. The lovely Wichita Children's Theatre, attached physically and administratively to the Wichita Art Association, was built privately through the solicitations of its founder, Irene Vickers Baker.[12]

Many community children's theatres have no direct affiliation with any other agency. The Emmy Gifford Children's Theatre, originally the Omaha Junior Theatre with Junior League roots dating from 1949 and named for its best known mentor and designer, has its own broadly based board of directors to oversee its expansion into a professional program. Now occupying an imaginatively converted movie theatre with a building addition housing rehearsal and production spaces, the theatre's staff is rapidly augmenting the program to include an academy. Junior Leagues in other cities such as Cedar Rapids, Lincoln and Kansas City are often at the center of these independent organizations, providing impetus and leadership for their evolution, and marshalling support for their activities. Increasingly, these theatres are employing directors and other staff in efforts to upgrade productions which rely almost entirely on child and volunteer adult casts and crews.

A unique organization known as the Children's Theatre Association, Inc., of Baltimore, came into being in the early 1940's. Originally a laboratory for a teacher training course at Johns Hopkins University, it came to be listed as a private (unfunded) agency of the Recreation and Education division of the Baltimore Council of Social Agencies. In addition to ticket income and membership fees from child and teenage participants who took creative drama classes and were cast in plays, CTA relied heavily on private donations to sustain operations. Productions staged in area high schools often evolved from creative drama class work. Adult community members also acted in them. Its Showmobile performed in county parks and playgrounds with business and industry sponsorship. Through much of its history its founder, Isabel Burger, continued her teacher training classes in workshops and college courses both there and abroad.[13]

Community theatres often are parents of children's theatres, which may develop as an expansion of the regular bill or as separately organized adjuncts to the program. Whether plays are cast from the adult talent pool or with children, they bring a new level of contact with the community. In Michigan, the Kalamazoo Junior Civic Theatre is a joint venture of the community theatre and the city school system. Participants in its comprehensive after-school theatre training and production program are first screened by their teachers and finally chosen by the director and selected advisors. The director is a board of education employee who must be certified to teach. The theatre provides facilities, technical instruction and production support.

The development of programs such as these exemplifies the ingenuity, vitality and extreme adaptability of people who have been responsible for the unusual diversity of nonprofessional children's theatre in the United States.

Sponsoring Units

Sharing responsibility with producers for bringing theatre to children and youth are many sponsoring groups that work diligently and conscientiously to connect productions to audiences. In the past, a committed individual might singlehandedly arrange all the details of an appearance of a touring company such as Clare Tree Major's. Even today, when this complex responsibility is undertaken by a sponsoring group, we frequently find one dedicated and inspiring individual who serves as its prime mover.

As we have seen, one such person was Dorothy McFadden who was responsible for setting up the most extensive sponsoring organization ever to exist: Junior Programs, Inc. Not only did she organize a local effort to bring professional musical and theatrical entertainment from New York to appear in Maplewood, New Jersey, she also helped organize similar Junior Programs series elsewhere. Junior Programs of California is a direct descendent in this line. It screens and books professional and nonprofessional performing groups to appear under its sponsorship in a number of locations in the Los Angeles metropolitan area.

As part of a general commitment to community service, Junior Leagues are often involved in sponsorship activities. The same motive also brings Parent-Teacher Associations (PTA's) or chapters of the American Association of University Women (AAUW) into the sponsorship business, although these groups are more likely to feel obliged to enrich educational programs by setting up fine arts experiences not ordinarily available otherwise. Groups such as these often form consortia, establishing specially constituted Children's Theatre or Performing Arts Series committees to plan and arrange many different kinds of arts experiences over a period of years. Arts Centers, Y's and similar organizations are known to sponsor youth theatre productions as part of their total arts support programs in the communities they serve.

Not all organizations, of course, are committed to a broad or long-lasting involvement in sponsorship. Some are there for one time only, perhaps sponsoring a production for children as a quick money-maker for some unrelated project. Most, however, hope to accomplish the dual purpose of satisfying a local cultural need and achieving their private goal. Newspapers and radio-TV stations may sponsor performances in conjunction with promotion campaigns. A department store may tie them to advertising or to bring crowds to shopping centers. Even a service group such as Jaycees, Lions, Kiwanis, or Rotary may be more concerned with creating a favorable community "image" for business purposes than with bringing in theatre for its own sake. The contemporary trend, however, is toward pooling commercial resources and committing them to support of arts programs for the greater good of the community.

With ever more effective aids to sponsorship provided by national, state and local agencies, the work of sponsor committees is becoming increasingly efficient. A local group that wishes to bring in a theatre troupe, music group or individual artist has many channels to pursue not only to locate the right talent but to help organize for action. In the past decade, state arts commissions or associations of community arts councils have become effective agencies ready to supply information about available companies, dates, and fees, often by means of "approved" lists. They distribute publications outlining problems to anticipate and solutions to try. They conduct sponsorship workshops, and they can even put one in touch with other groups engaged in similar efforts or with experts willing to serve as consultants. Local arts councils often have their beginnings in a group that has banded together to sponsor an event in a community and has realized the need for continuation on a regular basis.

One other kind of sponsorship occurs in the contemporary scene. It is the support by business or industry which underwrites productions or pays for a facet of a program such as touring. At present the McDonald Corporation totally or partially sponsors a number of children's theatres. It provides underwriting in exchange for program credit and other promotion. Considering the amount of money this company invests, its demands on producers are startlingly modest.[14] WCBS-TV has been the official sponsor of a professional children's theatre in New York City. Local businesses and industries as well as branches of nationwide corporations frequently finance individual performances for particular groups of children or those given in parks or playgrounds away from a producer's home base. Sponsorship in such cases is entirely financial, not administrative. The producer is responsible for all other sponsorship functions such as those described in Chapter IX.

Funding Patterns

Theatres and other cultural and artistic groups are particularly vulnerable in periods of high inflation. Those which survive do so because of the ingenuity they display in reshaping their product to reduce costs and in reconstituting their financial base to take advantage of whatever funding opportunities exist. At the present time it is widely recognized that almost no performing arts groups are able to survive on ticket sales alone. Estimates by federal funding agencies indicate that anywhere from thirty to seventy percent of costs have to come from sources other than admissions.

Theatre groups producing for child audiences have long recognized the need to reach an admission price "balanced" between one so high potential customers would be turned away and one so low that discerning patrons would be prone to undervalue the product itself. Pricing psychology operates geographically as well, indicating that patrons accept the need to pay up to $45 for a child's admission to *Annie!* on Broadway while viewing a much lower charge as an outrage elsewhere in the country. An "average" admission price today appears to be somewhere between $2.50 and $5.00.

Income from ticket sales is frequently augmented with fees charged for touring performances, workshop or residency tuition or charges, fees for supplementary classes, and donations subscribed by members of the community being served by the group. Some organizations charge annual membership fees. The Emmy Gifford Children's Theatre is sustained by a family movie series shown on week nights in its versatile facility.

Businesses and local industries have traditionally contributed to theatres through the time-honored practice of taking out ads in the printed programs. This form of subsidy, still widely provided, is now being augmented by more substantial support given to underwrite either an aspect of a group's operation or sponsorship of certain performances. Business frequently underwrites the costs of tickets for selected groups of children in a community, or may pay the costs of transporting them to the theatre. Through the energetic Business Committee for the Arts,[15] groups in need of support are put in touch with businesses that are committed to help arts organizations, usually in a local or regional area. Fast food chains and oil companies appear to be entering this realm of support on a rather large scale. Tax advantages as well as recognition that businesses and industry share the responsibility for a community's cultural climate are happily leading more of them into the support columns each year.

Private grants may also come from other agencies in a community. Service clubs, the Junior League, local private foundations, the chamber of commerce, the tourism promotion group, even the school system may make a grant for a general or special purpose. Producers who approach them are sometimes pleasantly surprised to discover the rich resources the community really possesses.

Theatres that include academies may, of course, increase their funding base substantially through tuition charges. If the school is accredited for theatre arts training at the secondary level, as is the case in Nashville, enrollments can be accompanied by commensurate appropriations from the board of education.

Subsidy from various levels of government provides the greatest amount of support for all types of producers and sponsors beyond ticket sales income. Even groups that are financed mostly by private donations rely on the tax deduction incentive in their fund drives. Tax money reaches theatres through many channels. A program attached to a recreation department receives appropriations from a municipality, perhaps supplemented by the county if service extends beyond city limits. Parks and Playgrounds may also receive some funding from state arts councils which, in their turn, are supported by the National Endowment for the Arts and by state appropriations. Other state and federal agencies may also be involved, allocating grants for service to special populations such as underprivileged, handicapped, non-English speaking, or "impacted populations" near federal installations.

University, college, and secondary school children's theatres are most usually funded as constituent budgetary units within a departmental, divisional, college or school structure through which appropriations gradually filter down to those who spend the money. Private and church-related school and college theatre programs rely to some extent on tax exempt status to solicit contributions from donors. Children's theatres in academic settings may also receive allocations from student activity fees. Groups which receive direct government funding from whatever source are usually considered ineligible for grants from federal or state arts endowments.

Since the National Endowment for the Arts has produced such an impact on the financing of professional theatres in this country since 1965, its programs are worth special note. Large and small professional companies producing for child audiences and conducting tours and residencies are eligible to apply for various size grants on a matching basis; that is, they may ask for up to fifty percent of a budget figure, agreeing to raise the other fifty percent elsewhere. Money has been available under "expansion arts" to bring theatre to populations not normally served otherwise. Companies may be supported in performance oriented residencies under an "artists-in-the schools" program which enjoys the cooperation of the Department of Education (DOE). Even though much of NEA funding is administered through state arts councils, there is a category of "chairman's discretionary funds" that may be tapped for very special projects that arise as unusual opportunities. Since the NEA's emphases are refocused annually, it is important for potential applicants to send for up-to-date information and to keep abreast of changing priorities. Eligibility for NEA grants is partly determined by the fact that a group pays Equity or comparable wages to its company members.

The states' arts councils through which large amounts of NEA money are channeled make grants both to producers and sponsors of theatre for young audiences. In some cases certain amounts are set aside for almost automatic disbursal to sponsors requesting partial funding to bring in "approved" productions. In others, the request is addressed to the council and decided on an individual basis. These state agencies are fast becoming the eye of the arts hurricane, stimulating more and better arts experiences for all segments of the population to an extent no one thought possible fifteen years ago.

Theatre for young audiences may be the recipient of funding from local arts councils as well. These groups, spawned in the last decade, assume leadership for requesting, receiving and disbursing state or federal arts funds according to a locally-determined set of priorities. Nonprofessional groups ineligible for other support may receive a sympathetic hearing from such an arts council. More and more frequently the work of these councils is focused on a total arts program in an arts center which relates closely to the people of the community. A theatre for or by children and youth may well be a constituent part of this total program.

It must be noted that all nonprofit groups receiving funding from any federal source are subject to regulations set forth in Section 504 of the Rehabilitation Act of 1973. In brief, Section 504 stipulates that no persons shall be denied access to arts programs, either as spectators or participants, because of physical or mental handicaps. To comply with the law, theatres are altering their physical plants to accommodate wheelchairs in backstage as well as public areas. As a special service to hearing-impaired audiences, sign language interpreters are engaged for performances. Braille synopses and program materials are made available to the blind. It is common for theatres to enlist an advisory committee of handicapped persons who help define needs and determine a course of action designed to give special populations direct access to the artistic life of the community.

While the Arts and Humanities division of the Department of Education generally does not fund theatre production *per se,* it does engage in much inter-agency cooperation to conduct innovative arts-in-education programs. These may well include theatre components which in turn might consist of performances by the children themselves or by adult companies. Similarly, the National Endowment for the Humanities does not make grants for production work, but, through its state affiliates, it may fund adjunct educational and cultural projects in some ways linked to the production of a specific theatrical piece. For instance, seminars dealing with the subject matter or historical context of a play might receive Humanities Endowment support.

In some ways, the grant programs of large private foundations in the 1960's may well have provided the impetus for government support of the arts. The increase in numbers of professional repertory companies made possible by the Ford Foundation and the Rockefeller Foundation is well documented. Involvement of the JDR III Fund in arts-in-education programs is also well known. But efforts of small private foundations to sustain existing theatres, provide needed facilities and staff, and improve quality of performances for young people has not been generally publicized. Hundreds of such foundations exist, some connected to individuals or families, some to businesses; and each has its special interests and emphases. In aggregate, private foundations continue to be an important source of support for theatre for young audiences. Foundation directories which provide comprehensive information about current granting practices and procedures are available in many libraries.

Finally, special note must be taken of many ingenious funding projects that enthusiasts have devised over the decades to keep their theatres afloat on turbulent seas. Many communities now conduct annual fine arts drives similar to the United Fund campaigns, with arts groups sharing in the total collection. Some communities levy a special tax to support their arts groups. One state has a lottery for the arts. Art fairs and carnivals, bake sales, car washes, even rummage sales are organized to supplement arts budgets. Season ticket sales are sometimes coupled with contests, complete with prizes and honors. Few devices for raising money have escaped the attention of those hardy folks involved in theatre for the young. Announcements about special conferences, institutes and workshops on identifying fund sources, writing grant proposals, and managing resources are arriving with increased frequency. It appears that funding for the arts is itself becoming big business!

THE PROFESSION TAKES STOCK

Since World War II, important progress has been made in raising the level of professionalism attained by workers in theatre for young audiences. Overcoming an amateur image with which the field was early identified has not been easy, nor is it yet completely eliminated. This section will call attention to the most important agents that have nudged practitioners up the ladder toward higher attainments in the art form.

A NATIONAL ASSOCIATION EMERGES

Winifred Ward, chief mentor of the field for much of its history, was the first to act on the need to establish a communicative link among the few people who were engaged in theatre and drama for and with children in the 1940's. In the summer of 1944, and despite the formidable inconveniences of war-time travel, a venturesome crowd assembled in Evanston for the first children's theatre conference. Then a student at Northwestern, Mary Jane Evans recalls that Miss Ward's students were expected to attend, and attend they did to listen, awestruck, as they encountered the "who's who" of the field. The eighty delegates voted to become the Children's Theatre Committee (CTC), and allied themselves with the American Educational Theatre Association (AETA), itself only eight years old at the time. Hazel Glaister Robertson of Palo Alto was elected its first chairman.

From then on, development was rapid. CTC changed from a committee to the first full-fledged Division of its parent Association, changed its name to the Children's Theatre Conference, and committed itself to an education and advocacy program stressing stringent self-evaluation even as it broadened the scope of its activities and influence. Its membership consisted of representatives of professional groups, educational theatre at all levels, recreation programs, community theatres and, most notably, of Junior Leagues. Annual meetings featured productions and critiques, workshops, demonstrations and discussions of all aspects of creative drama and play production for young audiences, and formal speeches and papers that helped establish a philosophical base for all the practical work that went on in the field. By the early 1950's, an active regional structure began to flourish, and CTC became the voice of a growing profession.

During its early years, CTC had a great need to reinforce a spirit of community effort and to exchange information about programs and projects in the field. Sara Spencer of the Children's Theatre Press was one of the organization's staunchest leaders, and she undertook to edit the "Children's Theatre Newsletter," which met that need and became the chief record of work being done across the country. In time she passed the reins to Campton Bell of the University of Denver. From these beginnings the publication metamorphosed into the *Children's Theatre Review*. As the activities of CTC became more complex, its name was changed to the Children's Theatre Association of America; and, reflecting the growing stature of the field, the *Review* began publishing substantive articles and extensive reports which earlier had appeared in the *Educational Theatre Journal*, the scholarly publication of the parent organization.[16]

Such material now appears in the *Youth Theatre Journal*, originally published by CTAA's successor, the American Association of Theatre for Youth, which was formed in 1986. Having seen virtually continuous publication from 1949 to the present, the "Newsletter," *Review* and the *Youth Theatre Journal* constitute a principal source of research material for scholars in the field.

Responding to ever-changing needs and conditions which were reflected in various structural and name changes, the national children's theatre association remains a fully professional society serving a diversified membership, promoting the field in theatrical, educational, governmental, economic and cultural circles here and abroad.[17] Through its projects and committees it encourages innovative scholarly and creative research. Association archives housed at Arizona State University provide a repository for its records and those of producing organizations, as well as significant personal papers as further inducement. A prestigious scholarship for graduate study in the field is awarded annually through the independent Winifred Ward Memorial Fund, Inc.

The association's programs and projects are as diverse as its constituency. Through its Professional Presenters and Producers Program and other agencies, it encourages festivals and showcases at national, regional and state levels. An unpublished play reading project screens new and promising scripts, awarding prizes and distributing information to prospective producers. The affiliate National Conference of Youth Theatre Directors meets annually to support the work of theatres using children and youth in their casts. Another project promotes study of and involvement in drama and theatre with and for the handicapped. Under its direction, and with frequent financial assistance from the Children's Theatre Foundation, specialized conferences and symposia have been held in an effort to reach consensus regarding drama and theatre in the contexts of child development and education.

Although most association programs function on a year-round basis, as with CTAA, the highlight of its life is its annual meeting, where the membership gathers to seek renewal, reinforcement and challenge, and to honor outstanding workers in the cause of theatre for children and youth.

The Status of Research

The growth of theatre for young audiences is rooted in practical research. In the beginning, Ward, Chorpenning, Major and other pioneers had no precedents to guide them. They had experience in theatre, and some of them may have worked with children in classrooms or recreation centers. But staging productions especially devised for children and bringing large numbers of children into the theatre for those special performances was such a new idea that there was little dust of past experience on the clean slates where they composed their scenarios and strategies. All they could do was experiment. A production was written and staged, and, with carefully tuned eyes and ears and sensitive hearts, they recorded what happened.

At the Goodman Theatre Mrs. Chorpenning conducted extensive observational studies of her plays as they were received by the children. Her students were assigned to sit in different parts of the house during performance after performance. There they recorded responses to key scenes in the play. Subsequently the script was amended and the cast re-rehearsed to make desired adjustments, sometimes only minutes before the curtain opened on the next performance.[18] Unfortunately, the actual data gathered in her studies are lost to us, but the format has been widely adopted, and variations on this research scheme are operative in every theatre each time a show is presented.

The *Children's Theatre Review* regularly carried updates on research in progress, completed studies and research challenges. The *Youth Theatre Journal* continues this practice. A research committee established by CTC in 1956 prepared the first master list of graduate theses that same year. A second list appeared in 1964. In 1975, ATA published the Klock and Van Tassel Bibliographies, which brought research listings up to that date.[19] The present generation of children's theatre practitioners is keenly interested in research which not only will record, but will also validate, the work we do. With their leadership, association-sponsored studies soon may become a reality.

The first master's degree in children's theatre was awarded in 1932. Eight years later, Geraldine Brain (Siks) wrote and directed *Marco Polo* as a creative thesis at Northwestern. The first doctorate in the field was conferred on Kenneth L. Graham by the University of Utah in 1947. The names of institutions currently offering specialized graduate training have already been listed (Note 10), but other colleges and universities not appearing on that list also have awarded graduate degrees for work in this field.[20] Studies have been of the standard types. Close to half the total number have been *creative*, principally in playwriting and directing. There have been a number of *historical* theses and dissertations, several of which are cited in this text. *Descriptive* studies have drawn from a variety of fields to arrive at philosophical conclusions about a number of aspects of children's drama. Other types have been *critical*, involving minute examination of playscripts and productions for discovery and evaluation, and *empirical* studies which involve experimental research using controls and statistical analyses to draw conclusions. Throughout this book we draw upon studies that relate to our discussions.

Doctoral dissertations have been done on the work of many, but not all, of the pioneers in the field. There is need for additional historical studies to complete the account of the early trend-setting years. Although several important theatre programs have been the subject of thorough study on the doctoral level, many more have been accorded only a paragraph or two in some larger work. They, too, deserve fuller examination by careful scholars.

As Jed Davis noted in a 1961 article, the greatest need, however, is for well designed empirical studies. Some progress has been made in finding answers to the questions posed twenty years ago, but many of them remain unresolved. These questions have to do with what actually happens to children in the theatre experience. Are concepts and attitudes changed in any way? To what other aspects of the child's life — intelligence, personality, environment — do these changes relate? How permanent are they? Does a child's personality change in any way after he experiences a theatre performance? How is identification involved in what happens to the child? What age, sex, racial or socio-economic differences exist in identification with characters portrayed by children? By adults? How do acting and staging affect identification, conceptualization and attitudes? Does the theatrical method hold any advantage over other methods of imparting knowledge or developing attitudes? These are only a sample of the questions for which the field needs to find answers. Perhaps they can be discovered by graduate students. More likely, however, a team of specialists in child drama and experts in experimental methodology might have greater success in dealing with these and other complex questions. This type of research really requires substantial funding through such agencies as the National Institute of Education (NIE) or the Department of Education.

Each answer we discover will lead to more questions. That is the nature of research. As we reach our maturity as a scholarly field, we become increasingly conscious of our need. Two generations of children's theatre specialists have stressed the creative and artistic aspects of our work. We have relied on intuition and have tended to be suspicious of empirical thought. This problem is not unique to the theatre for the young, but to theatre in general. Surely the academician in our specialized field has a place in the laboratory. That laboratory is not limited to the theatre. It also includes the computer terminal. When the two are joined, we will be able to find some answers to our seemingly eternal questions. While a respectable body of creative, historical, descriptive and critical research has been accumulated in the field, we must recognize that the time has come to expand our studies to include empirical methodology.

An International Perspective: ASSITEJ

Early overseas ambassadors from American children's theatre, among them Campton Bell, Winifred Ward, Rose Robinson Cowan and Isabel Burger, returned from their European travels to instill in their colleagues an interest in what was happening abroad and envy for the status the theatre for young audiences had achieved. World War II forced Americans to become internationally minded, and the establishment of the United Nations with its many agencies, especially UNESCO, continued to impress us with the fact that concern for theatre for the young was not exclusively ours. Congresses of the International Theatre Institute (ITI), which had been formed under UNESCO in 1948, attacted many U.S. children's theatre leaders to distant countries during the early fifties; and some of these meetings stressed theatre for young audiences. Rosamond Gilder, head of the United States ITI Center, was instrumental in guiding the international organization in this direction. The longevity and stature of East European children's theatre especially attracted the admiration of our own leaders, and many sessions at CTC conferences were devoted to sharing information about those programs.

When the invitation arrived for CTC to send delegates to the first "Overseas Children's Theatre Conference" to be held in May, 1964, at the Commonwealth Institute in London, Director Agnes Haaga set about composing a delegation. Michael Pugh and Gerald Tyler of the British Children's Theatre Association (BCTA) and Leon Chancerel of France were three of the prime movers to begin the development of an international organization, and there was support from representatives of all forty countries present in London. Sara Spencer, editor of the Children's Theatre Press, was appointed the U.S. delegate to a constitutional committee which presented the document for adoption at a meeting in Paris, June, 1965. Memberships in the Association Internationale du Theatre pour l'Enfance et la Jeunesse (ASSITEJ) were limited to national centers which each country was required to establish. Each national center was entitled to three votes in the General Assembly, two votes for its professional theatres and one vote for its nonprofessional groups. The focus was on theatre in performance, and creative drama as a discipline was pointedly excluded. And so, in an atmosphere of expectation and east-west suspicion, the first regular Congress of ASSITEJ was called for Prague, June, 1966.[21]

Early congresses were biennial events held successively in The Hague, Venice, and Albany, New York. Since Albany, they have been scheduled every three years — in East Berlin, Madrid, Lyon, Moscow, and Adelaide. Each congress is an incredibly complex operation, and United States delegates to early meetings were overwhelmed to find sessions being translated into five languages and to discover first hand the realities of east-west power maneuverings, even in this small corner of the world of the arts. American influence has been felt, however; and in 1972, Nat Eek of the University of Oklahoma, rose to the presidency of ASSITEJ.

Through their participation, Americans have absorbed much of what is desirable and duplicable in other countries' youth theatre programs. They have discovered the sense of commitment, urgency and importance of those programs in other countries.[22] Children's theatre *mattered* to their governments! Their treasuries poured millions in scarce currency into a massive effort to ensure the right atmosphere and orientation for their children. We may have scorned efforts at political indoctrination and manipulation through the theatre, but we could not help but admire the degree of honor they laid at the feet of their children's theatre artists.

The U.S. national center existed as a committee of CTC/CTAA from 1965 until 1981 when it became independent, changing its name to ASSITEJ/U.S.A., Inc. The numbers of citizens influenced by ASSITEJ and its programs increased rapidly in those years. The Center collected dues in order to print a Newsletter (now called *Theatre for Young Audiences Today)* as well as distribute the international *Bulletin* issued by the Czech Center, and the *ASSITEJ Review* published by the international headquarters in Paris. The Center approved official delegations to congresses and encouraged greater representation from professional groups to balance the always formidible numbers from nonprofessional organizations. ASSITEJ can be credited with the careful nurturing of U.S. professional groups and a strong effort to draw them into association with others in a common effort.

When the 1972 Congress met in tandem at Montreal, Canada, and SUNY-Albany, New York, some two hundred fifty U.S. representatives were able to see the work of the Moscow Central Theatre for Children, the Ion Creanga Theatre of Bucharest, the Moscow Opera Theatre for Children, under its dynamic director, Natalia Sats, as well as that of the five U.S. companies selected on the basis of nationwide adjudication by a panel of experts.[23]

We also began hearing about periodic national festivals of children's theatres in many countries including England, Wales, Yugoslavia, Germany, USSR, Roumania and Italy. ASSITEJ Executive Committee meetings were often scheduled in connection with these festivals, and our people traveled abroad in ever greater numbers officially and unofficially to see productions by such famous groups as the Jiřiho Wolkrá of Prague, the Leningrad Theatre for Young Spectators (TIUZ), the Theatre der Freundschaft of East Berlin, the Bosko Buha of Belgrade, or to experience the great wealth of professional puppetry throughout the civilized world.

The forum established by ASSITEJ provided U.S. professionals and nonprofessionals with a massive international theatre education in a very short time. Whatever our political differences, we found that we could advantageously exchange production ideas, share criticism and philosophy, compare research, and get to know our colleagues from other lands and cultures in ways we never experienced before. An "International Bibliography of Plays in Translation," complied and distributed by Michael Pugh of the BCTA, provided early encouragement for production of each other's plays. Similar efforts by ASSITEJ/U.S.A. culminated in 1984 with the first volume of Patricia Whitton's *Outstanding Plays for Young Audiences,* a list of the best plays of each center's repertoire, along with appropriate rights and production information. Our own publishing houses stepped up efforts to supply U.S. producers with translations of worthy scripts from abroad. Overseas tours by U.S. companies began to be arranged, both inside and outside the ASSITEJ framework. As the U.S. Center was asked to recommend companies to be invited to perform at congresses, we were obliged to find systems for identifying our best.

Since ASSITEJ is concerned only with theatre for child audiences, preferably at the professional level, some U.S. practitioners have begun to shift their allegiance to the International Amateur Theatre Association (IATA/AITA) in order to promote work in creative drama. Still others, primarily interested in puppetry, cultivate an alliance with the Union Internationale de la Marionnettes (UNIMA). Both of these organizations are affiliates of UNESCO, and work cooperatively with ITI and ASSITEJ.

By focusing our attention on the problems and dreams shared by a whole world of peers, these international bodies have provided our children's theatre people a new sense of purpose and a fresh perspective.

Showcases, Festivals and Celebrations

The custom of bringing several plays or theatre pieces for young people to a central location has been part of the contemporary scene since the early meetings of CTC. Committees planning national, regional and state conferences are universally motivated by a desire to expose participants to exemplarly productions.

By 1955 another motive for bringing a number of productions to a central location came to fruition when CTC Region 14 decided to provide a service for sponsors and producers by scheduling a showcase at the 92nd Street YM/YWHA in New York City. Sponsor groups desiring to see before they bought, appeared from a variety of communities to select their seasons from the smorgasbord spread before them by professional children's theatre companies based in New York. This showcase became so popular with sponsors and producers that the volunteers who organized and ran it were obliged to substitute excerpts for complete performances. By 1969 the showcase was able to include the services of professional critics. At about the same time, however, the professional companies formed their own association to promote their interests through a Preview. They called their organization the Producers Association of Children's Theatre (PACT), and their Preview replaced the regional showcase. PACT's purposes are frankly commercial, and the organization does not apply quality control to its Preview scheduling.

Still another showcase made its appearance in 1979; only this one served a much larger geographical area. The first National Showcase of Performing Arts for Young People was staged at the National College of Education, Evanston, Illinois. The seventeen companies selected to perform came mostly from the eastern half of the country, and they travelled at their own expense in anticipation of the opportunity to perform before potential sponsors from all over the United States. The organization responsible for this momentous achievement was the Professional Presenters and Producers Committee of CTAA under its chairman, Carol Jeschke. Recurring annually, the event, under CTAA and, later, under AATY's auspices, fulfilled at least a double-barreled function: a service to sponsors in showcasing the best available for nationwide or regional touring, and to help the producers get wide exposure to those who do the booking. The committee exercises quality control in the selection of companies invited to perform.

An increasing number of festivals have presented yet another rationale for bringing shows to a central spot. The occasion becomes a joyous celebration of the theatre art form in its many varieties. Children, families, professionals in the field and even adults who arrive alone assemble in a congenial, exciting atmosphere to share the fun. Usually the productions are reviewed by "respondents," experts in the field who hold post-performance discussions with the performing groups. The setting is non-competitive, and evaluation sessions are characterized by an atmosphere that encourages mutual learning.

Festivals highlighting the work of producers in a limited area have been growing in popularity ever since one of the earliest, held in Bellingham, Washington, was organized by Gayle Cornelison in 1970. Elaborate festivals have been staged since 1973 by the Southern California Children's Theatre Association, later by the Southern California Educational Theatre Association (SCETA) which usually takes over a college or university campus, scheduling continuous performances throughout two days, using every conceivable performance space. The region is unusually blessed with a wide variety of groups and individuals that perform in every known style, and the festival highlights this diversity. For a time a special feature was a panel of "junior reviewers," a carefully selected group of children who systematically recorded their reactions, sometimes in interview form, thereby providing yet another valued perspective on every performance.

Southern California's lead was followed shortly in Northern California; and soon festivals were occurring under regional or state association auspices in the southeast, midwest, and Great Lakes areas as well as in many states. These festivals, composed either by invitation or on an open-entry basis, all flourish in their own ways, leaving an important impression on the contemporary scene.

Probably the most ambitious of such events in recent years was the World Festival of Theatre for Young Audiences, held in conjunction with the New Orleans World's Fair in June of 1984. Sponsored by ASSITEJ/U.S.A., with Ann M. Shaw as Director and Orlin Corey as Producer, the celebration featured productions by eleven companies from eight nations, selected on the basis of a two-year on-site evaluation tour. A World Theatre Symposium and commentaries by a panel of professional critics were allied features.

Yet another kind of festival first appeared on the U.S. scene in 1982, although it had precedents in Great Britain. It is known as the Young Playwrights Festival, and it features workshop productions of the plays of young people between the ages of eight and eighteen. With the youthful authors' full participation, professional directors and actors rehearse and perform for peer audiences, generally engaging in the same creative process as that used by professional authors. The system, deriving from Gerald Chapman's initiatives at the Royal Court Theatre in London, was transposed to America by the Dramatists Guild at Stephen Sondheim's behest, reaching fruition at the Circle Repertory Theatre in New York under Chapman's direction. The system has been acclaimed for its educational as well as cultural values, and shows signs of being adopted in cities other than New York.[24]

The prospect of holding a full scale national festival of theatres for young people has intrigued leaders of the field ever since the 1972 ASSITEJ world congress in Albany. The method of selecting companies for that event—professional critics who toured the country to view previously screened productions—showed promise for a future effort. An alternative system may be devised which relies on a pyramid of state and regional festival selections, much like that which leads to the Kennedy Center performances of the American College Theatre Festival (ACTF).

Even though a national festival is still only a dream, a nationwide "Imagination Celebration" has been presented each spring since 1977 by Programs for Children and Youth of the John F. Kennedy Center for the Performing Arts. Under the program's Producing Director, Carole C. Sullivan, the Celebration features exhibits, workshops and performances of musical and theatrical events, some specially commissioned for the occasion. An aspect of the total agenda of the Center's Alliance for Arts Education (AAE), headed by Jack Kukuk, the Celebration takes place not only in the nation's capital but in many "outreach" locations across the land.[25] By showcasing the arts for children in influential Washington circles and by demonstrating successful outreach capabilities, the celebrations have contributed greatly to increasing our stature in governmental as well as artistic circles.

An AAE affiliate program called Very Special Arts is of interest here. Organized in 1974 as the National Committee, Arts with the Handicapped, the project, in part, consists of a festival occurring in model sites across the country in which eligible children demonstrate acting, singing, dancing, instrumental music, and display their art work. All concerned express much enthusiasm for this effort to enrich the lives of these very special children.

Critics and Criticism

Professional critics have not overwhelmed theatre for young audiences with their attention. It is true that in the early years of the movement, when productions by or for children were a novelty or newsworthy from some special point of view, there was quite complete coverage, at least in metropolitan centers such as New York. The Broadway performances of *Peter Pan, Alice in Wonderland,* and especially *The Blue Bird* were fully analyzed by top newspaper and magazine reviewers. One of the notable things about the King-Coit Theatre of the 1920's and 30's was the veritable adulation espoused by columnists of the calibre of John Mason Brown, who acclaimed "the first art theatre for children in America." But gradually press accounts merely chronicled rather than analyzed these events; and it seemed as if most of the actual coverage in periodicals was provided by directors and producers rather than by critics. Of course there were some communities where a local press gave regular support, often on the social page; but for the most part, between 1930 and 1960, reviewing plays for children was considered unworthy of professional theatre critics' time or the newspaper space.

In the 1960's two first-line critics began to write serious criticism of theatre for children and youth: Dan Sullivan of the *New York Times,* later of the *Los Angeles Times,* and Norman Nadel of the Scripps-Howard syndicate. Both were uncompromising in their expectations and demands. No cuteness or good intentions passed for acceptable art. At several meetings of CTC they urged respect for the children as the essential starting point for all who wanted to work in this field. For many years Sullivan applied rigid criticism to the Region 14 Showcase and some of his commentaries were reprinted in the *Children's Theatre Review.* On the west coast he brought the same level of serious concern to work being done in that area, as did his distinguished *Los Angeles Times* colleague, Sylvie Drake. Currently the *Times* regularly publishes critic Lynne Heffley's insightful reviews of productions for youth.

The expertise of professional critics contributed greatly to the Albany ASSITEJ Congress, and, later, to the World Festival in New Orleans. Clara Hieronymus of the *Nashville Tennessean* took part in both events. She traveled the country selecting performances for the Albany Congress in the company of Dan Sullivan and Orlin Corey, then President of CTA. Mike Steele of the *Minneapolis Tribune* joined her and Norman Nadel in critiquing performances at the Congress itself. Hieronymus' evaluations of World Festival productions were added to those of Ernest Schier of the *Philadelphia Bulletin* and Linda Winer of *USA Today,* providing an unusually challenging dimension to the New Orleans celebration.

Critical commentary on productions seen at festivals, conferences, overseas visits, or other occasions regularly appeared in the *Children's Theatre Review,* and continues in *Youth Theatre Journal.*[26] Festival productions are usually reviewed by invited experts whose evaluations often appear in festival newsletters. A coterie of knowledgeable evaluators is becoming quite skilled at providing astute insights and reactions without destroying the collegial atmosphere nor the central purpose of mutual learning for which festivals were created. In a true sense they can be described as respondents rather than critics, since they receive the production in its own terms, then reflect back what they saw, allowing the group to decide whether or not the reviewer saw what was intended.[27] Standards and value judgments form the basis of the discussion.

National, regional and state professional associations are reasserting the need and desire for knowledgeable evaluative comment on productions. As professionalism in the field itself grows, so does the need for more and better criticism. The associations now are providing convenient forums through numerous showcases and festivals, and the seriousness of our intent should be obvious. A model partnership has been demonstrated. It remains only to be duplicated many times over all across the country.

STATUS OF THE PROFESSION

For purposes of discussion, a "professional" is anyone who is paid a living wage for work involving some aspect of theatre for young audiences. A person contemplating a life in this field has a right to know what sorts of positions exist and what to expect by way of compensation. While we cannot quote actual figures (they would be outdated overnight) we can at least speculate as to levels of adequacy.

People are working at one or any combination of the following jobs; or their jobs may entail dividing their time between theatre for children and theatre for adults.

Playwrights have long been regarded central to the play production process, and several of the well-established authors with a number of popular scripts in the active repertoire are able to make a substantial supplementary income from them. It must be pointed out, however, that children's plays generally carry a lower royalty payment than plays for adult audiences, and that some producing companies develop original dramatic material primarily to avoid the payment of even that small royalty.

Managing Directors of their own companies have a chance to build a reasonably good financial base for themselves. Nowadays, even those who are hired by established theatres, earn quite respectable salaries, with some options for additional income built in for classes, workshops and special services to the community.

Directors function in many production contexts, and salary levels vary widely. Some are hired for a single production, others for a season or more. Many are able to command respectable salaries, especially after they have established good credentials. Directors are hired by community theatres, some of which are climbing close to professional status, by recreation programs, by community children's theatres and by art centers.

Performers are paid whatever local circumstances dictate. Actor's Equity first introduced a children's theatre contract in 1969, and companies working under that contract guarantee the "going minimum" plus fringe benefits. Some non-Equity companies pay that same rate. Of course, many professional groups cannot operate at this level and must hire performers for less compensation. For the actor or actress, this often means taking additional jobs wherever they are offered. Sometimes additional compensation can be earned within a company by doing extra tasks such as bookkeeping or company management. Some ensemble groups operate on a share basis, with the head of the company and principal performers receiving multiple shares. Thus the income of members is tied to total company fortunes. Whatever the arrangement, income for performers is usually not princely, and many companies change personnel regularly as each member, as a free agent, charts a course to his own economic advantage. In all fairness it must be pointed out that employment and income facts for Equity members as a whole are not much better. As a profession we treat our performers rather shabbily, but always that distant prospect — becoming a star — spurs many to enter the profession in spite of the odds.

Designers, stage managers, and *technicians* who plan, construct, and operate all the technical aspects of production are much in demand, and some are paid quite well while they work. Some are free lance. Others are identified with particular companies on a continuing basis. Needless to say, designers looking for employment with professional groups should seek out the ones that still place a high priority on physical production. The field of special effects provides a good living to a select few who manage to keep busy helping Peter Pan fly. Technical-design talents coupled with performance abilities still make a salable combination in today's tight marketplace.

Teachers at all educational levels may have directing and management duties assigned as part of the job. Elementary teachers understandably have less responsibility along this line than secondary school drama/theatre teachers. Special training leading to teacher certification (or credential) is, of course, required in all states, although in some circumstances certification can be granted temporarily to someone with qualifications to do a particular job in a public school.[28] Many children's theatre manager/directors functioning today are *professors* operating from a college or university base. They are subject to all the qualifications listed for professorships, including advanced degrees and professional growth and achievement that make them eligible for tenure and promotion in rank within a faculty structure. Income figures are tied to rank, longevity, and individual qualifications, often specified in scales and steps by state regulations. Many college and university programs employ *assistants,* graduate students seeking advanced degrees who earn stipends at a barely livable level while helping with the children's theatre program. *Actors who can also teach* children and teenagers are especially needed for the growing number of academies.

Recently an employment category known as *educational director* has appeared with the larger professional children's theatre operations. Such a person performs liason functions with schools and manages the academy and outreach operations. Income potential is comparable to that of academic appointments.

While this function is frequently performed by the educational director or some other company member, employment as *dramaturg* looms as a possibility in the future. The dramaturg has charge of script analysis, selection of seasons, and composition of teachers' materials.

As we saw in the last section, professional *critics* are highly prized and probably also well paid if they work for major periodicals. They come to their positions by various routes, often through journalism, and of course none exclusively reviews the theatre for young audiences.

In rare instances, persons with a children's theatre background have found their way into the *publishing business* where their expertise enables them to exert considerable control over the materials, books and plays the nation's producers will be dealing with in the years ahead. While very few such firms are devoted exclusively to turning out children's theatre materials, several have this field as a part of their total concern. Publishing is, of course, an extremely competitive business, as some playwrights have found when they set out to publish and market their own scripts.

People with experience in theatre for children, especially those who work in management, are prime candidates for positions with arts councils at local, state, even national levels. A few have found their way to employment with the National Endowment for the Arts, the Kennedy Center, and other agencies concerned with arts for children. Employment opportunities have increased as government arts agencies proliferate. Salaries for positions with these agencies often are determined by the civil service formula. Several universities now offer specialized training in arts management, providing the best preparation for such positions.

Lest this listing of job opportunities sound discouraging, we would like to point out that the situation is vastly improved over what it was a generation ago. If one starts a professional theatre for children today there are many more places to look for funding than before. With improved training and more realistic practical experience in universities and internships, with better models of successful management practices and a better perspective on national and international models of high artistic quality, with local and state arts agencies standing by with advice and funding, and with more effective regional and national showcasing possibilities to help in marketing, the chances of success are infinitely greater than ever before. In fact it must be said that there never was a better time to consider entering this profession.

Our journey began with some present-day theatre experiences for children and youth, went backward in time for a brief exposure to our heritage, and then took us step by step into a look at some of the components of the complex and promising contemporary scene. If it has shown us one thing we can clearly identify it is that many talented and dedicated people have been attracted to the cause. Together they have built the systems and structures we have today. Some of them are good and deserve continued life. Others need to be revised. Perhaps some should be discarded. In any case, change is inevitable. Our pioneers would be the first to advise us to continue taking stock, always setting new goals, and, above all, never to become self-satisfied.

Our sights need only be kept on the children we serve to remain faithful to those who began it all.

NOTES

[1]Nellie McCaslin, *Theatre for Children in the United States: A History* (Norman, Oklahoma: The University of Oklahoma Press, 1971).

[2]Michael W. Gamble, "Clare Tree Major: Children's Theatre, 1923-1954," Diss. New York University 1976.

[3]Jan A. Guffin, "Winifred Ward: A Critical Biography," Diss. Duke 1976; memorial issue of *Children's Theatre Review*, XXV, 2 (1976); Ruth Beall Heinig, ed., *Go Adventuring! A Celebration of Winifred Ward: America's First Lady of Drama for Children* (New Orleans: Anchorage Press, 1977). See also the Bibliography for titles of books by Winifred Ward.

[4]Roger L. Bedard, "The Life and Work of Charlotte B. Chorpenning," Diss. Kansas 1978; Janet E. Rubin, "The Literary and Theatrical Contributions of Charlotte B. Chorpenning to Children's Theatre," Diss. Ohio State 1978.

[5]Ellen Rodman, "Edith King and Dorothy Coit and the King-Coit School and Children's Theatre," Diss. New York University 1979.

[6]For an extended account of the Federal Theatre's program in children's theatre, see Lowell Swortzell, ed., *Six Plays for Young People from the Federal Theatre Project (1936-1939)* (New York: Greenwood Press, 1986).

[7]Some of these statements are based on Kenneth L. Graham, "An Introductory Study of the Evaluation of Plays for Children's Theatre in the United States," Diss. Utah 1947.

[8]So far research has failed to prove a relationship between child theatre-going and attendance later as adults, but that does not necessarily mean a relationship does not exist.

[9]Lin Wright, ed., *Professional Theatre for Young Audiences,* Vol. I (1984) and Vol. II (1986) (Tempe, AZ: Department of Theatre, Arizona State Univ.).

[10]The Winifred Ward Memorial Fund, Inc., has certified the graduate programs in children's drama at which Winifred Ward Scholars may study. The approved programs are at Emerson College; Hunter College; Universities: Arizona State; Brigham Young; California State-Northridge; Eastern Michigan; Hawaii at Manoa; Illinois State-Normal; Kansas; New York (NYU); North Carolina-Greensboro; Northern Iowa (Cedar Falls); Pennsylvania State; Texas at Austin; Utah; Virginia Tech; Wisconsin-Madison; and the Empire State Institute for the Performing Arts.

[11]Readers who do or plan to work with children in the elementary grades are referred to Chapters II, V, and X for relevant discussion of standards and making choices for drama with this age group and how productions fit into a total scheme of drama/theatre education.

[12]*The Wichita Children's Theatre: The First Thirty Years* (Wichita, KS: The Wichita Children's Theatre Guild, 1975). Available from Anchorage Press.

[13]P. Donna Burbank, ed., *The First Twenty Years: 1943-1963* (Baltimore: Children's Theatre Association, 1963); Joanna Halpert Kraus, "A History of the Children's Theatre Association of Baltimore, Maryland from 1943-1966," Diss. Columbia 1972.

[14]An account of one such sponsorship is given by Susan Pearson, "Goldberg, The Golden Fish and the Golden Arches: PAF/McDonald's Youth Theatre," *Children's Theatre Review*, XXVI, 3 (1977), 2-3. McDonald's underwrites the Great American Children's Theatre of Milwaukee and probably others at various times.

[15]Address: 1700 Broadway, New York, NY 10019.

[16]The periodical, now called *Theatre Journal,* is published by Johns Hopkins University Press, for the Association for Theatre in Higher Education.

[17]From 1951 until 1972, the organization was called the Children's Theatre Conference. When the parent AETA was restructured into the American Theatre Association (ATA), CTC became the Children's Theatre Association (CTA), a name it retained until 1975 when it became CTAA. In 1986, ATA and all its divisions ceased operations; very shortly thereafter AATY was organized to continue CTAA's mission. Chief executive officers of CTC were known as "Directors." Those of CTA, CTAA and AATY are called "Presidents." Presently under discussion is a proposal to merge AATY and the American Association for Theatre in Secondary

Education into a single organization serving the interests of theatre art and education for students in grades K-12.

[18]Charlotte Chorpenning, *Twenty-One Years with Children's Theatre* (Anchorage, KY: Children's Theatre Press, 1954. (Now New Orleans: Anchorage Press)

[19]Jed H. Davis, "A Partial List of Research in Children's Theatre, 1956-1960," (CTC Research Committee files, mimeographed); James E. Popovich, "A Bibliography of Research in Child Drama (1926-1964)," (Distribution 1964 CTC Annual Meeting, mimeographed); Mary E. Klock, ed., *Bibliography of Creative Dramatics* (Washington, D.C.); Wesley Van Tassel, ed., *Children's Theatre Bibliography* (Washington, D.C.); Carol Jean Kennedy, "Child Drama: A Selected and Annotated Bibliography, 1974-79" (A project of the Theatre Department, Arizona State Univ.), (Washington, D.C: Children's Theatre Association of America, 1981).

[20]Colleges and universities, other than those mentioned in Note 10, accepting theses in the field number about ninety. The largest number of degrees were earned at Adelphi, Baylor, Boston, Catholic, Teachers College-Columbia, Denver, Florida State, Illinois, Michigan, Michigan State, Minnesota, Northwestern, Ohio State, Oklahoma, San Francisco State, Southern Illinos, Texas Women's, and Washington Universities, in addition to those named in Note 10.

[21]Frederick Scott Regan, "The History of the International Children's Theatre Association from its Founding to 1975," Diss. Minnesota 1975.

[22]As of 1986, there were ASSITEJ national centers in forty-three countries: Algeria, Argentina, Australia, Belgium, Brazil, Bulgaria, Canada, Cuba, Czechoslovakia, Denmark, Ecuador, Federal Republic of Germany, Finland, France, German Democratic Republic, Great Britain, Greece, Hungary, Iran, Iraq, Israel, Italy, Japan, Republic of Korea, Mexico, Netherlands, Norway, Paraguay, Peru, Poland, Portugal, Romania, Spain, Sri Lanka, Sweden, Switzerland, Turkey, Union of Soviet Socialist Republics, United States, Venezuela, Vietnam, and Yugoslavia.

[23]Orlin Corey, "As I Saw Them: A 12,000 Mile Quest for Quality," *Theatre for Children — Kid Stuff, or Theatre?* (Anchorage, KY: Anchorage Press, 1974) pp. 50-68.

[24]Lowell Swortzell, "Special Report: The Young Playwrights Festival—1982," *Children's Theatre Review,* XXXII, 1 (1983), 25-26; Kay Print Janney and Marian Galbraith-Jones, "The Young Playwright's Festival: Another Perspective," *Children's Theatre Review,* XXXV, 1 (1986), 10-12; Carol M. Tanzman, "The Young Playwrights' Festival: Serious Beginnings," *Children's Theatre Review,* XXXI, 3 (1982), 9-11.

[25]The AAE numbers among its many projects the American College Theatre Festival and programs in every state encouraging innovative arts in the schools.

[26]One of the regular contributors to this column, Muriel Broadman,, is a veteran reviewer of the Region 14 Showcase, and author of an important book of critical insights into stage, television and movies called *Understanding Your Child's Entertainment* (New York: Harper and Row, 1977).

[27]This system for responding to productions was developed by Ronald Willis particularly to serve adjudication needs of the American College Theatre Festival with which he is closely associated.

[28]Artists-in-the-schools may thus be provided with temporary certification in school systems where it would be required.

THE DREAM FISHER (Donahue) — Children's Theatre Company and School, Minneapolis, 1977.

Irene Corey's classic designs for REYNARD THE FOX and Noble the Lion (Fauquez) — Everyman Players, 1962.

CIRCUS MAGIC, an improvisational theatre piece — University of Wisconsin-Madison, 1973.

THE ICE WOLF (Kraus) — CSU-Hayward, 1972.

A LANCASHIRE LAD (Kennedy) — Empire
State Youth Theatre Institute-SUNY, 1980.

THE ARKANSAW BEAR (Harris) — University of
Texas at Austin, 1980.

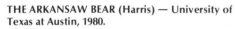

A Time For Dying Comes to THE ARKANSAW BEAR (Harris) —
University of Texas at Austin, 1980.

THE PIED PIPER (Bernhardt) — CSU-Hayward,
1970.

A MEMORABLE ACCOUNT OF MARK TWAIN IN
THE SANDWICH ISLANDS (Colwell) — Honolulu
Theatre for Youth, 1980.

An Environmental Audience Configuration for
JACK AND THE BEANSTALK (Chorpenning) —
San Jose State University, 1980.

Greek Gods and Voyagers in a New ODYSSEY (Falls and Beattie) —
Young ACT, 1977-79.

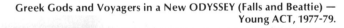

STEAL AWAY HOME (Harris) — Kansas University
Theatre for Young People, 1977.

Chorus Characters in WILEY AND THE HAIRY MAN (Zeder) — Everyman Players, 1979-80.

(Top Right): REYNARD THE FOX (Fauquez) — CSU-Northridge, 1971-72.

(Second From Top Right): THE MAN IN THE MOON (Cullen) — Goodman School of Drama, 1969.

(Second From Bottom): Aboard Captain Ahab's Ship in MOBY DICK - REHEARSED (Melville) — Nashville Academy Theatre, 1979.

(Bottom Right): TWO PAILS OF WATER (Greidanus) — CSU-Northridge, 1967-68.

18

(Top Right): Flying High: PETER PAN, with Sandy Duncan — Bufman and Nederlander Production, 1979-80.

(Middle Right): A CHRISTMAS CAROL at the Guthrie — Guthrie Theatre, Minneapolis, 1979.

(Bottom Left): THE MEN'S COTTAGE (Goldberg) — Stage One, The Louisville Children's Theatre, 1978-79.

(Bottom Right): GOLLIWHOPPERS! (Atkin) — CSU-Northridge, 1977-78.

19

20

21

BEANS (Sheffield) — Sheffield
Ensemble Theatre, 1979-80.

JOHNNY MOONBEAM AND THE SILVER ARROW
(Golden) — Kansas University Theatre for Young
People, 1965.

TALES FROM HANS CHRISTIAN
ANDERSEN (Evans, Anderson,
Archer) — CSU-Northridge, 1978-79.

(Top Left): THE SNOW QUEEN (Browne) — Children's Theatre Company and School, Minneapolis, 1976.

(Top Right): THE CLOWN OF GOD (dePaola, Olson) — Children's Theatre Company and School, 1981.

(Bottom Left): Aboard the Hispaniola enroute to TREASURE ISLAND (Mason) — Children's Theatre Company and School, 1979.

(Bottom Right): THE 500 HATS OF BARTHOLOMEW CUBBINS (Seuss, Mason) — Children's Theatre Company and School, 1980.

31

29

30

(Top Left): ALICE IN WONDERLAND (Flatt): The Caucus Race. (L to R) Two Crabs, a Water Rat, a Duck, a Dodo, a Parrot, and Unnamed Bird — Dallas Theatre Center MimeAct, 1980.

(Top Right): ALICE IN WONDERLAND (Flatt): Alice is terrified by the Knave of Hearts in the presence of the King and Queen of Hearts — Dallas Theatre Center MimeAct, 1980.

(Bottom): ALICE IN WONDERLAND (Flatt): Alice meets the Red Knight and the White Knight — Dallas Theatre Center MimeAct, 1980.

32

CHAPTER II
A POINT OF VIEW

> I remember (I think everyone does) the first time I ever went to a real theater. Not the grammar school Christmas play but a play that had real actors and strangers in the audience except for my sister and my mother. The play was *Jack and the Beanstalk* at the Goodman Theatre in Chicago and I was scared out of my mind. No one could convince me that the giant wasn't real and I cried and screamed until my mother led me out of the theatre just before the end of the first act.
>
> My mother, a wise woman, knew exactly what to do. She marched me to the stage door and took me right in to meet the giant in his dressing room. 'He's not a giant and he's not going to really eat Jack,' she said, 'he's just an actor pretending — now go and shake the man's hand.' I did as I was told and something deep inside me, deeper than I had ever felt before, opened up and felt wonderful. It was my first magical experience and it had happened in a theatre.[1]

The world and the theatre have seen countless changes since that day an experience at a play left its lasting impression on a young boy. Yet every individual, every group involved in presenting theatre for young audiences clings steadfastly to the goal of creating that special moment of magic. This book has been written to help in achieving that goal. It also is designed as a guide for those who observe this theatre and form judgments about it. It is a book about magic, but it also is intended to be used in college classrooms, by producing units, by anyone who cares about what happens when children and young people come to see a play.

It reveals the way two people think and feel about the theatre for children and youth and unabashedly presents our point of view. While we acknowledge and applaud the venturesome and count ourselves among the supporters of any production style that generates excitement and freshness, we strongly believe in preserving the integrity of the magic world of the stage.

This chapter charts the course for those that follow, first by taking note of some of the social and artistic forces that brought about the rapid and significant changes in philosophy and practice that mark the progress of the field since 1960. We examine how those changes compelled the profession to redefine the terminology we use to describe what we do in theatres and classrooms. Numerous variations in approach to production and performance mandate more definitions to establish a basis for subsequent discussions of styles. These styles will be examined and reexamined as we discuss the intrinsic nature and qualities of playscripts and their production values, the potential and the pitfalls of non-scripted performance, and the complex process of conceptualizing and staging the performance.

Certain standards apply to all we do in the theatre for children and youth. The ones we set forth here become the hallmarks of excellence for playscripts, establish criteria for selecting the style and material for productions, and, most important, provide benchmarks against which we can test our attitudes and work in any assignment we may undertake. The words of this chapter will echo and re-echo through those that follow — intentionally and for good reason. Whatever our gifts, however refined our skills, however dedicated we may be, each one of us needs constant reminders of the obligations we assume when we commit ourselves to this art form.

If we are to dedicate ourselves to preserving the integrity of the magic world of the stage, we first need to understand what theatre for young audiences is and where it stands in relationship to other types of dramatic activity. Peter Slade, whose work in England has profoundly influenced drama and theatre for the young, has said it better than we:

> Theatre is a civilized, wonderful, artificial thing. It's like a bubble that floats on the sea of civilization. We made it. Man created theatre as a sort of mirror of life,

a poetic mirror, if that's not mixing metaphors too much. Drama in education is totally different in that it really is for the child a voyage of discovery, a proving of events and learning of life, in fact. I do, I struggle is the great drama. This is life. Only when you piece selected bits of life together, formalize it, if you like, script it, improvise around it, gather it up, polish certain things like speech and footwork and pause and relationship, you arrive at something you call theatre. For the most part there is a differentiation, though less so these days, between actor and audience. In the drama — the doing of life — everybody takes part, all at the same time. Although there isn't always a division between actor and audience, the two things are entirely different.[2]

Slade here shares his conviction that drama and theatre are different, expressing a view that has been held since the ancient Greeks defined drama as "a thing done" and theatre as "to gaze upon." Fundamentally, the field continues to respect those distinctions. Our literature increasingly uses drama/theatre as a term which properly differentiates the two while affirming their commonalities.

In contemporary practice two kinds of drama/theatre experiences are provided for children and youth. Creative drama, first called creative dramatics in this country, is an expressive activity, informal in nature but purposeful in method. Engaging its participants in the processes of dramatic creation and expression, it is not intended to prepare a group for performance. It is analogous to Slade's drama in education. Theatre for children and youth, on the other hand, provides the opportunity "to gaze upon."

To some, however, these are arbitrary distinctions, and, as Slade suggests, "these days" those distinctions are increasingly blurred in the theatre. This melding of forms is only one manifestation of a changing viewpoint toward the theatre for young audiences. Several factors leading to this change require examination.

ROOTS OF CHANGE

First let us consider television. Never before in history has instant entertainment been immediately available to virtually everyone living in the United States. The full impact of this phenomenon has yet to be measured, though it is scrutinized and evaluated by everyone from research scholars to the man on the street. To date, systematic studies have provided information about its effects on children's cognitive, linguistic and moral development, their interests and behavior, and the relationships between violence in entertainment and in society. All of these are relevant to our present discussion and will be examined in some detail in the next chapter. Even without these studies, however, theatre practitioners are keenly aware of the influence television has had on their audiences and have themselves been influenced by it in production practice.

Television, however, is only one of a spectrum of developments and events that have influenced theatre for children and youth in this country.

The second half of the Twentieth Century has been a period of ferment when, for a multitude of reasons, all the value systems of our society have been subject to scrutiny and change. The Vietnam War and all its associated civil turmoil, generated considerable challenge to constituted authority and recognition that all levels of the citizenry have responsibility for decision making.

As the civil rights movement gathered momentum, a situation which had long pricked the conscience of the nation erupted into street battles and mass marches and culminated in enlightened legislation and affirmative action.

Assassinations of important public figures focused attention on psychological stress and aberrations of power and spurred anew the debate over firearms legislation. Tense international relations and power struggles among nations, acts of atrocity, hostage taking, the energy crisis — all these continue to create a climate of dis-ease. Political scandals have highlighted questions of power and privilege that reach the very roots of the American value system.

Women's liberation gained momentum and began to exert its influence on literature for the young, television programming, clothing styles, and child rearing.

In a very real sense science fiction became reality as man landed and walked on the moon, forcing reexamination of concepts of fantasy. The advance of computerization into almost every aspect of life challenged people to find new ways to discover and reassert their humanity.

And all this came to pass in full view of the television audience.

Today, as in every dynamic period of human history, the arts reflect and, in fact, often influence, thought and feeling, frequently taking vanguard positions in the process of revolutionary change. Because the theatre is unique among the arts in that it uses the human condition as its subject and the human being as its expressive medium, it can be a potent force in reflecting, commenting upon and questioning society and in influencing cultural change.

Theatre presents and represents human life symbolized through live persons engaged in live action, allowing direct exploration of human experience. It deals with people in action, making decisions and living with the consequence of their choices. It asks questions for which there are no answers. It universalizes even as it particularizes.[3]

In its quest for expression, the theatre, as the other arts, seeks new and useful means of reflecting, commenting and questioning. Even as society as a whole questions its traditions and value systems, so does the theatre as it breaks connection with conventions and traditions that are felt to constrict and inhibit communication. Thrust stages, arena stages, open spaces and myriad variations of performance placement in relation to the audience have been adopted as alternatives to the proscenium. In fact, almost any spot where players and audience can assemble is regarded as appropriate for performance.

Economics also plays a part. As the cost of mounting full-scale productions soared, producers were forced to seek alternative ways to bring theatre to the public. The challenge to create low-budget performances has had some gratifying side effects, providing a new stimulus to creativity and finding audience acceptance.

Artistic priorities change as continuous experimentation with non-standard dramatic forms breaks all established conventions. Playwrights create scripts that bear no resemblance to familiar and comfortable styles. In many cases the work of the playwright is set aside altogether as companies originate and shape material to suit their own purposes. In collaborative group theatre the role of the director as the central figure in determining and realizing a unifying production concept may be minimized or ignored altogether. Indeed, some companies involve the audience in the playmaking process, relying on their suggestions to shape the performance and determine its outcome. Many production styles place little stress on visual spectacle and theatrical realism and a great deal of emphasis on the actor, who, instead of being cast in a single role, is involved in a continuous series of transformations according to the needs of the drama. This list is by no means exhaustive, but it gives some indication of the artistic ferment that keeps the theatre vitally alive.

While it is true the adult theatre always has influenced the theatre for young audiences, early indications of those influences were relatively unspectacular. If musicals were popular on Broadway, a surge of musical performances soon found its way into the repertoire for the young. After 1960, however, trends in the adult theatre were reflected almost immediately in its youthful counterpart. Perhaps it was due to the fact that so much of the new theatre was essentially child-like in conception and performance, borrowing from childhood the exuberance of game playing, of frank engagement in make-believe, the charm of instant transformation, all in an atmosphere unencumbered by traditional stage trappings. Indeed, Paul Sills' landmark *Story Theatre* used familiar folk tales in very literal translation, and, although social comment was the motivating force behind that production, its charm and style immediately captivated youthful audiences. Adults responsible for presenting theatre to young audiences quickly saw its possibilities, and a trend had begun.

Although this was not the first sign of rebellion in children's theatre ranks, it seemed that all of a sudden the fairly standardized body of philosophy, principles and practices that had guided the field almost since its inception was called into question. Creative drama, which always had been clearly understood to mean a special form of process-centered expression for the benefit of the participant alone, was clearly related to the theatre games Viola Spolin had devised for actor training and which now were being used by companies to generate theatre pieces. Furthermore, many adult theatre troupes were having great success working spontaneous audience involvement into their performances. Anyone who had ever observed a child audience knew that the urge to enter the drama is strong. And more questions were raised.

It no longer seemed valid to believe that creative drama and theatre for children were mutually-exclusive, though complementary, components of a single art form. Conventionally-structured scripts began to seem dated and unappealing. Producers wondered whether realistic settings and fully-executed period costumes were absolute requisites to successful production.

Needless to say, attributing what might be termed the children's theatre revolution to adult theatre and mass media influences alone is simplistic and unfair. Economics always has played a part in experimentation and innovation. Too often the theatre for children has been subject to budgetary restrictions that would have made its adult counterpart close its doors. In fact, it might be claimed that Grotowski did not invent the "poor theatre." We found it first!

Economics aside, our field always has had its experimenters and innovators whose creative energies demanded new modes of expression, who found themselves frustrated with constricting conventions and rebelled against them, who devoted themselves to exploring fresh ways to reach their audiences. But in earlier times they usually functioned apart from the mainstream, and their work often was viewed with doubt and suspicion - even disdain - by their more conservative colleagues. It is a sad commentary on the profession that innovation on the adult level has seemed to carry more credibility than it has in the theatre for young audiences.

International influences also have played a part. Theatre pieces which actively engage the audience seem to have emerged simultaneously in adult theatre and the theatre for young audiences. In the latter case, the style was adopted from the British. We have seen how additional influences from abroad have come through ASSITEJ as Americans became involved in its affairs and traveled to its congresses. As our representatives became cognizant of theatre as it was presented to young citizens in countries throughout the world, they brought a new dimension to their own work and, in so doing, influenced the field as a whole. An important by-product of these international exchanges has been publication of scripts that might not otherwise have been available in the United States.

Finally, the field of theatre for children and youth no longer needs to rely on a body of assumptions and intuitive assessments of childhood in planning and evaluating what we do. In recent years a burgeoning body of important research related to how children develop, perceive, learn and respond has become accessible to us. Enlightened producers are utilizing this information to bring increasingly sophisticated understandings to their work in theatre. We regard that research and its potential for helping shape the future of our theatre as so important that we devote the next chapter to it and use it ourselves as a foundation for all the discussions that follow.

NATIONAL PROFESSIONAL ASSOCIATIONS: A UNIFYING FORCE

While it may seem that the theatre for child audiences has lacked form, focus and the courage of its convictions, one must remember that this relatively young art form, like its youthful patrons, needs to try its wings. Further, its practitioners come from widely diverse practical and philosophical backgrounds; and they practice their art in situations so varied that they beggar description. In the preceding chapter we introduced the Children's Theatre Association of America as the pioneering authoritative voice of the profession in the United States. In its early years as CTC, it attempted to bring stability to a growing field by disseminating its 1956 statement, "Drama With and For Children: An Interpretation of Terms,"[5] which drew the clear distinctions between creative drama (then creative dramatics) and children's theatre to which reference is made throughout this chapter. Those definitions and accompanying statements of principle reflected the philosophy and practice of the time and provided guidance for the field for a number of years.

As the field flourished, however, it outgrew its definitions, and in 1977 CTAA adopted a new "Terminology of Drama/Theatre With and For Children: A Redefinition,"[6] which is reprinted in its entirety in Appendix 1. It established a continuum beginning with drama in its natural state, moving to guided drama, participation drama/theatre, to theatre. Drama in its natural state refers to unguided, spontaneous dramatic play. Guided drama means creative drama or child drama. Although creative drama is the commonly-used term in the United States, child drama, the preferred term in England, is increasingly finding its way into our professional vocabulary.

Creative drama is defined as "an improvisational, non-exhibitional, process-centered form of drama in which participants are guided by a leader to imagine, enact, and reflect upon human experiences."[7] Terms that apply to theatre will be defined as the discussion proceeds. Additional definition and clarification of the relationships and distinctive qualities of creative drama, participation theatre and children's theatre will be found in a statement developed at a conference in Attleboro, Massachusetts, in 1976. The full text is found in Appendix 2.

Though its annual convention provided opportunities for CTAA members to share ideas and keep abreast of the field, crowded programs allowed little time for the reflective thought and quiet dialogue so critical to the health of any profession. Thus, CTAA was grateful when, in 1977, the Johnson Foundation responded favorably to its appeal to provide the facilities, amenities and support staff of Wingspread, its handsome, secluded conference center in Racine, Wisconsin, for a forum allowing selected leaders in the field to deliberate on matters related to the role of drama/theatre in the education of children and youth. The summary report of that conference is reprinted in Appendix 3.[8]

For over forty years CTAA functioned as a stabilizing force, thoughtfully responding to the changing needs of its constituency. It laid a firm foundation for the new generation of leadership emerging in its successor organization, an association committed to new beginnings based on the best of what has gone before. While by no means all of the individuals and organizations producing for young audiences are members, the national association is sufficiently representative to claim leadership in the field.

PRODUCTION AND PERFORMANCE STYLES IN THE THEATRE FOR CHILDREN AND YOUTH

As we turn our attention to the actual making of theatre, we must first consider the several styles in which it is produced. We have drawn from a number of sources — our personal involvement in countless conferences and festivals, our reading and our personal experiences as producers and teachers of theatre — to formulate a series of definitions of styles currently popular in the theatre for children and youth. Out of this collage may come words and thoughts that are not original with us, but which we unwittingly repeat.

Children's Theatre is a global, non-specific term that refers to the field as a whole. Because it encompasses a form of theatre designed for audiences ranging in age from early childhood to early adolescence, and because at a certain age a child no longer wishes to be called a child, *theatre for young audiences* is an increasingly popular substitute for the traditional appellation. Other frequently-encountered terms are theatre for the young, for young spectators, children and youth; youth theatre, young people's theatre, junior theatre and recreational drama — the last a term describing performances by children.

Whatever its designation, this is a form of theatre in which living actors present a performance which has been especially prepared for a young audience. When the performance is intended for youngsters between the ages of five to approximately twelve years, it is properly called "theatre for children." Performances specifically designed for young persons typically of junior high school age are appropriately designated as "theatre for youth."[9] In this volume children's theatre, theatre for young audiences, theatre for children and youth and their variants will be used interchangeably, simply for variety of expression. When a specific age level is important to the discussion more precise terminology will be employed.

Family Theatre is sufficiently different from children's theatre to deserve special mention. It can be defined as a performance for adults with a broad enough appeal to interest children. *Story Theatre* (the original production, not the style that derived from it), various ballets (*The Nutcracker* comes immediately to mind), many musicals such as *You're a Good Man, Charlie Brown, Li'l Abner* and *Oliver!* among them; and straight dramas such as *The Miracle Worker* and *Mrs. McThing* are typical of productions that fit this category. It also must be noted that adults who attend children's theatre with their youngsters will enjoy it, not only through sharing their children's pleasure, but on their own level as well — if it is good.

Theatre for children and youth includes many styles of production, each sufficiently unique to warrant individual attention. Interestingly enough, the mode that until fairly recently was universally accepted as *the* way to present plays to young audiences now requires its own category in a growing list of production styles.

Traditional productions are those in which a fully-rehearsed cast presents on stage a play, written by a playwright, most often developing a single story line, with full settings, costumes, make-up, lighting, sound and special effects. The production has been conceptualized by a director, who also has shaped the performance. There is physical separation of actors and audience, and direct interaction between actors and audience is minimal or non-existent. This definition refers directly to *production* style. In the recent script literature we find many plays written in the traditional dramaturgical mode which lend themselves to non-traditional staging practices.

Story Theatre is a method of dramatizing narrative literature, while retaining the narrative. Some portions of the story, or stories, are narrated by the actor as storyteller; others are translated into dramatic dialogue and action, requiring the actor to assume a variety of characterizations as the story progresses. Actors may transform into animals, inanimate objects or environmental elements according to the needs of the presentation. Although scripts written in this mode are increasingly available, many companies develop their own adaptations through improvisation, finally setting performance pieces which remain relatively stable from one showing to the next. As a footnote, we must observe that transformational acting is not unique to story theatre pieces, but is found in other plays that are conceived without the distinguishing feature of story theatre, retention of narrative.

Improvisational Theatre is a style in which a company working closely together over an extended period prepares a performance developed through experimentation and exploration. The process begins with an idea or series of ideas gleaned from a variety of sources, which may or may not include literary works. Through constant reiterative experimentation in thought and action, performance pieces emerge. They may or may not be set, but characteristically they do follow a predetermined scenario. They may unfold as planned, or they may depend on ideas solicited from the audience for direction and resolution. Even when the audience is involved in shaping the performance, the company has engaged in careful prior preparation with regard to content and format.

Instant Theatre, on the other hand, is just what the term implies. It is improvisational exercises performed before an audience. The company asks the audience to feed them ideas to which they then respond spontaneously, attempting to create characterizations, environment and story line, complete with resolution. Nothing is predetermined. This type of performance requires a company long used to working together as an ensemble. It demands quick wits, creative prowess and rare interactive abilities. Moments of instant theatre sometimes are injected into a performance that previously has been shaped through improvisation. In the theatre for young audiences, companies are known to use this technique to warm the audience and develop a direct relationship with them before beginning the actual performance.

Participation Theatre emerges from the work of Peter Slade and Brian Way in England. Way and his disciples have been particularly influential in the spread of this style in the United States. "Participatory theatre involves a *play,* a total aesthetic experience with a structure and thematic content shaped by an artistic consciousness. . . . The goal of participatory theatre is to bring children *into* a play, one shaped by a playwright, and give them a vital part, under the guidance of skilled performers, in fulfilling his design."[10]

Theatre in Education (TIE) is a term describing a program of taking theatre to schools and classrooms and working with children either as participants in the performance or in pre- and post-performance drama experiences or both.

Readers Theatre is a form of group oral interpretation in which narrative, lyric or dramatic literature is presented, conventionally with script in hand. The material is presented as written. Narrators become dramatically involved, but not to the point of enactment. Staging may vary from the simple use of stools and lecterns to modes sufficiently elaborate to approach the visual completeness of a fully-staged production.

Opera for children is a steadily-growing specialized field, enlisting the interest of composers and producers alike. An opera is a story told entirely or almost entirely through music.

Musical Theatre indicates a story told with spoken dialogue and musical numbers mixed in varying proportions. A play *with music* denotes that the proportion of dialogue is considerably greater than would be true of a musical.

THEATRE FOR SPECIAL POPULATIONS

While it is not a special form or style,[11] theatre for special populations must be mentioned here. Society's concern for special populations — those who through accident or by birth are functionally impaired and those who are not native English speakers — is reflected in the arts. Theatre is responding to this challenge and increasingly devotes itself to preparing performances for these groups, both as audiences and participants. This theatre is being used effectively to enlighten the general population. We earlier made mention of the Little Theatre of the Deaf. Through its example and the example of its parent organization, sign language theatre has become a highly developed art form with broad general appeal. The highly visual nature of sign language performance has made it especially attractive to young audiences.

THEATRE BY CHILDREN AND YOUTH

"Theatre by Children and Youth" is a particular variant of "Theatre for Young Audiences" in which the performers are children and/or teenagers rather than adults.

Preferably the performers are no younger than ten years old and have been well schooled by a director in their primary task of bringing dramatic material to life for the audience. Organizations engaged in "Theatre by Children and Youth" ordinarily plan their productions to focus on audiences of children younger than the performers plus interested adults.[12]

Children

This book finds its focus in the theatre *for* children and youth. Its emphasis is on adult work in that theatre and on standards that adults who are knowledgeable, skilled and truly professional in attitude are more capable of achieving than are children and young teenagers. Nevertheless, we recognize that play production with child casts is a pervasive practice in the United States, despite the fact that the field has long held that non-exhibitional creative drama is the mode of choice for developing and channeling the expressive capacities of children. We agree that engaging them in the processes of drama without subjecting them to the pressures associated with production and performing for an audience is more important to children's development than is play production, at least until they are well into middle childhood.

Having expressed our reservations, we readily acknowledge that many theatre programs are exclusively devoted to producing plays with child casts and that children are widely involved in play production in schools, recreation programs, churches and temples, and in other organizations promoting group activities for the young. The best of these programs provide experiences of both kinds. Classes in creative drama are offered and valued for their own sake, allowing children who prefer not to perform in public opportunities to limit their participation to low-pressure, non-competitive group-centered dramatization. Others may view these classes as stepping stones toward eligibility to participate in production, and indeed creative drama does develop sensibility, confidence, creative skills and other personal qualities that are great assets to youngsters who wish to be in plays.

Some organizations set a lower age limit for eligibility to be cast or work on production. Many insist that children must not be permitted to develop a one-sided view of theatre and organize their production program so that youngsters participate behind the scenes as well as on stage. Whatever its format, the worthy child-centered production program is non-exploitive and nurturing. When it is guided by adults whose motives are pristine and whose understanding of childhood is balanced by considerable theatrical skill, the theatre with children can make a positive contribution to the personal and artistic growth of its participants and its audiences.

Theatre with children, as all theatre that falls within the global definition of children's theatre, is *for* the child audience. In working with a child cast the director has to deal with two sets of values. He must be ever concerned for the well-being of the performers while still keeping his focus on end product and its effect upon the audience. Not only must he understand children, he must know how to work with them. He must know the limitations of their concentration ability. He must be aware of and respect the natural limitations of their ability to interpret dramatic material, to grasp and sustain character, to master technique and to retain consistency in performance. He must develop realistic parameters for his expectations without compromising his own standards, and this is difficult to do.

It is generally agreed that the child-to-child performance provides the audience with an experience quite different from the one they have when actors are adults. The difference rests largely in the way they identify. With adult actors, we believe the audience becomes empathically involved with characters. When children act, we believe identification rests more strongly with the actors and that a large measure of enjoyment derives from seeing other children in a play. This, many believe, is valuable in and of itself.

Youth

Young people of junior high school age usually are not content to limit their experiences with drama/theatre to the classroom or studio. They can be expected to demand opportunities to perform. Production work can provide a fine channel for their boundless energies. The director must realize, however, that their self-control is limited and understand that their performance abilities will not have progressed far beyond those found in younger children. If they are carefully nurtured and trained and handled with the right degree of firmness, they may be capable of a somewhat more polished and sustained performance which may prove quite convincing to younger audiences.

STANDARDS

In our examination of the contemporary scene we observed that every group undertaking theatre for young audiences has its own reasons for doing so. One universally-expressed motivation is a firm belief in the power of the theatre to affect the individual in countless desirable ways. Often, however, there is a vast discrepancy between expressed and private motives, and stated goals obscure the real ones. For example, many choose theatre over the other arts because of their great need to share while still retaining a controlling position. Others have a strong personal need to express themselves in this way, perhaps only to receive favorable attention and response. Each of us should be challenged to probe the surface of what we *say* we do and examine why we *really* do it.

From the beginning the children's theatre has espoused a set of audience-related goals that includes providing the child (1) the joy of believing in an illusion as a story comes alive upon the stage; (2) standards of taste which improve with true art experience; (3) the understanding and appreciation of life values drawn from human experiences as portrayed on the stage; and (4) the basis for becoming a discriminating adult audience of the future.[13]

Those goals, of course, assume excellence in production. In speaking of excellence, the field has tended toward global statements: "Children's theatre is good theatre." "The best is none too good for children." These are worthy slogans, but their very non-specificity gives one no concrete assistance in their realization. Early purpose and value statements have been scrutinized and refined as the field develops, but it is realistic to observe that whatever goals we verbalize, they are too often honored more in their breach than in their observance.

In 1975, the Johnson Foundation sponsored a conference at Wingspread which enabled leaders of the American Theatre Association to reflect upon the status of theatre in the United States and determine directions for its continued growth. Prior to the conference participants received several papers which had been prepared to stimulate and focus their thinking. One of those papers was written by Arthur W. Foshay of Teachers College, Columbia University, and was titled, "The Future Audience is in School."[14] While its purpose was to outline principles to guide theatre educators, there is common agreement that all theatre unquestionably has an educational dimension no matter how or where it is experienced. Thus Foshay's principles apply as directly to producers and sponsors of theatre for young audiences as they do to classroom teachers. The first obvious connection is found in his assertion that the theatre educator must be an unusual person who not only is expert in his art, but who also possesses an effective theory of the student, at least to the point of being able to make educated guesses.

He then poses a series of questions related to why theatre experiences are undertaken, not why they should be; what substance should be offered for attention and what are the odds that any given substance will be understandable; what is the nature of understanding; how what is offered relates to the personal past of the individuals for whom the experience is designed; what kind of response is being promoted; and the nature of the reward that comes from the experience. Among his more telling remarks were these: "The quality of the response to the theatre experience . . . dictates future responses (hence audience behavior) to theatre;" and "If the experience seems unpleasant . . . one can be certain that he [the student, in our case the theatregoer] will not repeat it voluntarily, yet it is just such voluntary theatre-going and theatre participation that we seek as the ultimate consequence of our efforts."

Consideration of standards was central to that 1975 Wingspread Conference. It pervades any discussion of goal-oriented activity. In a sense, standards are elusive, and unanimity of opinion is rarely found, even among people who hold common interests and concerns. In the arts, unanimity of vision and practice would be stultifying. The theatre for children and youth certainly has benefited from its growing diversity, and no one would presume to say that any given form, style or mode of expression is inherently superior to another. On one thing we all agree, however, and that is on pursuit of excellence. But what is excellence? Dictionary definitions notwithstanding, value judgments vary according to each individual's background, taste, bias, expectations and perceptions.

Is it possible, then, to develop a set of uniform standards for a diverse field? We believe it is. While each form or style of theatre for young audiences will have its unique goals and individualized standards, which we will consider in proper context, certain universals apply. We agree with John Allen: "...I believe that the theatre...is an art, and an art has certain laws and disciplines. Art is concerned with a certain area of human existence and sensibility. And however much the artist or the teacher of genius may seek to extend the expressive frontiers of that art it is necessary from time to time for him to remind himself of the basic nature of the art he is using."[15]

All theatre involves process, product and perception. The basic premise of this book is that theatre-making has but a single objective: creating, through process of whatever kind, a viable product — performance — which is worthy of the perceiver — the young audience. Consideration of process focuses on how it is best applied to making theatre with implicit acknowledgement that engaging in it is valuable to the player. Standards for the product also are audience-related. Ultimately, all standards derive from the four classic components of all criticism: intent, structure, effectiveness and worth. These components establish a framework for determining a universally-applicable set of standards for all theatre for children and youth.

The difficulty of creating discrete categories is self-evident. Intent obviously relates to worth, worth derives from structure as well as intent, and so on. Nevertheless, an attempt has been made to develop a practical yardstick by which to measure and test process, product and effect on audience.[16] Standards for *intent* deal with motivations for doing theatre for the young and attitudes toward that theatre and its audiences. Standards for *structure,* the "how" of making theatre, focus on stylistic decisions reached in the process of conceptualizing productions in order to realize intent. Technical and artistic excellence in execution of product are essential to *effectiveness. Worth* is the quality of the product. Was it worthy of the time spent on it? Was it worthy of the time the audience spent with it?

Intent

Every individual, every group engaged in producing theatre for the young should have clear-cut and valid motives related to the audience and uncontaminated by selfishness and self-service.

Every producing unit must have a clearly-understood and agreed-upon objective or set of objectives for each of its productions. Objectives should be specific rather than globally-conceived. "To bring good theatre to children" — "To provide an aesthetic experience" — these are worthy goals, but precise thought about how these goals are to be achieved is necessary to their fulfillment. "You cannot be imaginative unless you are exact."[17] Clear objectives channel and focus and thus free the imagination.

When it is part of a comprehensive production program, theatre for young audiences must have equal status with every other production, and equal access to talent, facilities and funding.

By its very nature theatre addresses the childlike in every human being. No group should take the narrow view that it is producing for a child audience rather than a theatre audience. The only difference is that youngsters are not interested in everything that interests adults. Decisions about what will interest the young audience cannot be made arbitrarily. An educated understanding of childhood is the only basis for choice.

Producers should aim to introduce young audiences to a wide variety of production styles and dramatic material.

In some measure difficult to define, performers undertake responsibility for the well-being of young audiences which extends well beyond the in-theatre encounter. They must be willing to fulfill that responsibility by presenting work that is aesthetically sound and psychologically honest.

Aesthetic sensibility and taste are essential attributes in all theatre-makers and providers. Simply stated, aesthetic sensibility is the faculty to distinguish between art and trivia. Taste is born of aesthetic sensibility and respect, which is not earnest sobriety, that inhibitor of joyful exuberance. Rather, respect arises from belief and seriousness of purpose. It is discipline and self-control and the willingness and ability to stand aside and take a hard, cold look at the realities of any given situation.

Everyone engaged in our theatre must have respect for the act being undertaken and for himself as an artist with sufficient insight to realize that any portion of content, any action, any verbal reference that demeans the actor is equally demeaning to the audience. Likewise any costume that feels tacky to the wearer, any technical element that creates a sense of unease or discord, diminishes artistry.

"Is our theatre addressed to an audience of the arrested, locked in the land of never-never?"[18] It should be unnecessary to develop a case for respect for children and youth, yet an affirmative answer to

Orlin Corey's question is implicit in countless productions even in this enlightened age. If there is one overriding standard to govern the work of playwrights, producers, directors, actors, design and technical artists, house staff, sponsors — everyone in any way involved in this form of theatre — it is respect for the young and their ability to understand with every fibre of their being and to grow accordingly.

Finally, there is respect for material. In writing about children's literature, C. S. Lewis, whose fantasy stories are universally captivating, provides insight of great relevance to theatre practitioners. He cautions against regaling the child "with things calculated to please him but regarded by yourself with indifference or contempt" and notes that "a children's story which is enjoyed only by children is a bad children's story. . . . I think we can be sure that what does not concern us deeply will not deeply interest our readers, whatever their age."[19] Respect for material also means willingness to examine the literature of our heritage to discover the meanings it has for today and to present that literature honestly rather than to manipulate and distort it in a futile, even spurious attempt to enhance its contemporary appeal.

Structure

No single way of creating theatre, no single form or style, is, in and of itself, superior to any other. Therefore, it is as foolish to reject the playscript as unnecessary as it is to assert that the script is the exclusive vehicle for successful production.

While no one would insist that realistic settings and the full panoply of technical support are essential to appreciation and understanding, it would be short-sighted to relegate traditional production styles to history in favor of exclusive use of fragmentary sets and costumes and pantomimed props.

Stylistic decisions must be based on intent and a careful assessment of the potential of a style to realize it.

A given style is valid only insofar as it is given consistent treatment for creation of a unified effect — a coherent image — for the audience to work with. Effective image requires more than theatrical device. Most importantly it derives from meticulous attention to all the elements of drama and theatre.

Novelty should not be valued for its own sake, and popularity is no valid basis for uncritical acceptance of any break-away mode. Decisions to adopt the unusual must be based on the ability to discriminate between fad and substantive innovation.

An understanding of theatre, its conventions and dramaturgy, is essential, no matter how far one chooses to deviate from tradition. It has been rightly said that to create an anti-play one must first have some concept of a play.[20]

Every production requires a point of focus and a through-line to give it coherence and clarity of intent. Whether it is conceptualized and shaped by a director or reached through group consensus, a unifying point of view is an absolute necessity.

The style and scale of the production must suit the size and configuration of the playing space, theatre size and audience seating in relation to playing space.

Effectiveness

Playscripts and other literary material must be thoughtfully analyzed for substance. Surface simplicity should be probed for buried meanings giving richness which may not immediately be discerned. Only through working with substance can a company give dimension and texture to a performance.

An effective production is the product of systematic preparation by a group of individuals possessed of artistic vision, technical skill and a willingness to submit to the disciplines of the theatre and who are prepared to dedicate themselves singlemindedly to bringing a finished performance to an audience.

All artists in the theatre for young audiences should certainly find joy in their work, but they must take that work seriously, ever mindful of the fine line that separates exuberance and self-indulgence.

Excellence and discipline are inseparable. Creativity and freedom are not synonymous. The act of creation requires self-control and mental discipline.

Adequate preparation time must be allowed, taking into account the nature, structure and style of production.

A performance will be effective only to the degree that it has been shaped with meticulous attention to detail.

Visual elements must be consistent with production and performance styles, each contributing to a unified, harmonious effect. They must be imaginatively conceived and precisely executed. The quality of all visual and technical elements must be uniformly superior.

Physical action must be motivated, arresting, precise in definition, clear, and imaginative in conception.

Dialogue must be literate, vivid, rich in vocabulary, economical but cogent, and free of anachronism and cliche.

Actors must be proficient, possessed of refined technique, physical flexibility and control, vocal variety, clarity of speech and the ability to project.

Strong ensemble work is critical to effectiveness.

Believable characterizations require that actors identify with the characters they portray and care about their problems.

The skill with which the actor visualizes, conceptualizes and makes transformations, including transformation of self, objects and environments, will determine how well the audience grasps the essence of those transformations and imaginatively completes them.

In deference to the relative brevity of attention span in the young, the performance must be shaped to provide sufficient variety of stimulus in rhythmic alternation to modulate tension without breaking the thread that holds the performance together.

Worth

> We all want children's theatre to be good; we are concerned when it isn't. All of us are seeking for quality, hoping for honesty . . . What dismays me most is the lack of regard for the intelligence of even small children. It is a grievous mistake, for example, to limit the play to what a child knows — has experienced so far. If all childhood experience were limited to what was already familiar, he'd never learn. Life would be static . . . Let the play have a point of reference to his own experience — or several such — but let it progress from there to something new. Give the child something to discover. (Often) he is treated not as the quick, curious, experience-hungry creature he is, but as a small moron. There is a vast difference between a young mind and a stupid mind.
>
> — Norman Nadel[21]

The content of a performance should be chosen and shaped to make contact with the audience on its present level and carry it forward, if even a short step. It should let them experience something new or gain fresh insights into things already known.

Audience members should be able to find something of themselves, their problems, interests and aspirations in characters they see portrayed. Themes should provide something the audience can carry away and apply to the process of daily living.

Themes need not be limited to simplified moral concepts of "good" and "bad." Theatre for young audiences can treat the moral ambiguities of human existence. It can and should pose questions without invariably providing answers.

Theatre for young audiences no longer claims to perpetuate the heritage of any single race or culture. It speaks to many populations and has an obligation to speak for and about them, creating shared experiences among diverse groups.

Young audiences bring a sense of wonder with them when they come to the theatre. In return they deserve sincerity in performance, richness of thought and feeling, eloquent expression and visual excitement. The greatest offense is to underestimate the audience and so to condescend through insincere performance and haphazard staging.

The company's belief in the value of what they are doing is as important · as their artistic skills. A performance becomes honest and real through the integrity of those presenting it.

There is no place for a blasé attitude in adult actors. Each performance must have the freshness of the first time.

Performances should have the warmth and charm of genuine make-believe. There is a world of difference between child-like charm and insincere "cuteness."

Adult humor, company in-jokes, and double entendre and self-indulgence have no place in the theatre for young audiences. Anachronisms and spoofs of favorite stories and characters should be approached with caution and generally avoided for audiences of young children.

Children's overt responses are part of the reward of playing for them. It is unethical to manipulate and exploit spontaneity in service of the ego needs of the company.

If we continue to claim that theatre provides an experience profoundly different from television, there is no justification for stooping to the "cheap tricks" for which television often is criticized. On the other hand, there is no point in attempting productions that film and videotape are technically equipped to do better.

Provocative material should be presented with sufficient clarity to ensure communication, but without overt explanation or admonition.

Concern for worthiness of outcome must pervade the entire process that culminates in performance. Worth means more than diversion and an hour spent away from home. It means more than giving adults good feelings about having brought youngsters to the theatre — more than giving an actor the satisfaction of having "strut and fret his hour upon the stage."

The parent freed for an hour, the bored child given a change of scene, the actor given opportunity to vent his creative urge all could say, "It was worth it." The critic seeking a kindly phrase to express his reservations might write, "It was a worthy effort." If "worth" carries these connotations for the reader, let him substitute *value, validity* and *depth.*

Children do not set their own standards for the theatre. Standards are set for them until they have had rich opportunities to draw comparisons, and their tastes are sufficiently developed to establish their own. The entertainment provided them will play a part in shaping taste.[22] Could this be why the group we classify as young people is frequently lost to us?

NOTES

[1]Kenneth Brecher, "On Stage," *Westways*, Nov. 1979, p. 58.

[2]Helane S. Rosenberg, "An Inverview with Peter Slade," *Children's Theatre Review*, XXIV, 4 (1975), 9.

[3]Lin Wright, "CTAA at Wingspread," *Children's Theatre Review*, XXVI, 2 (1978), 1.

[4]See Viola Spolin, *Improvisation for the Theatre* (Evanston: Northwestern University Press, 1963).

[5]Ann Viola, "Drama With and For Children: An Interpretation of Terms," *Educational Theatre Journal*, VII, 2 (May 1956), 139-142.

[6]Jed H. Davis and Tom Behm, "Terminology of Drama/Theatre With and For Children: A Redefinition," *Children's Theatre Review,* XXVII, 1 (1978), 10-11.

[7]Davis and Behm. This definition was adapted from the work of Ann Shaw, Frank Harlan and Ann Thurman for the 1972 ASSITEJ Congress.

[8]In August, 1983, ASSITEJ/USA had Johnson Foundation support for a Wingspread Conference entitled "The Role of Theatre for Young Audiences in the American Regional Theatre, and in International Cultural Exchange." A report of that conference was distributed by ASSITEJ/USA, 42 Riverside Dr., New York, NY 10024, in September, 1984.

[9]Davis and Behm.

[10]Pat Hale, ed., *Participation Theatre for Young Audiences: A Handbook for Directors* (New York: New Plays for Children, 1972), p. 1.

[11]For a comprehensive treatment of the subject, see Ann M. Shaw and CJ Stevens, eds., *Drama, Theatre, and the Handicapped* (Washington: American Theatre Association, 1979). A practical study of directing sign language theatre, "A Procedure for Directing a Sign-Language Theatre Production for a Child Audience," by Darlene Kaye Allen, Thesis California State University, Northridge, 1977, is available through SCA: ERIC/RCS, No. CS 501778.

[12]Davis and Behm.

[13]Viola.

[14]Arthur W. Foshay, "The Future Audience is in School," unpublished paper prepared for the American Theatre Association Wingspread Conference, 1975.

[15]John Allen, *Drama in Schools: Its Theory and Practice* (London: Heinemann Educational Books, 1979), p.9.

[16]Readers who are abreast of the field will recognize that these standards derive from a variety of sources.

[17]Ralph G. Allen, "The Uses of Theatre," unpublished paper prepared for the American Theatre Association Wingspread Conference, 1975.

[18]Orlin Corey, *Theatre for Children - Kid Stuff, or Theatre?* (Anchorage, KY: Anchorage Press, Inc., 1974), p. 49.

[19]C.S. Lewis, "On Three Ways of Writing for Children," reprinted by permission, *Hornbook Magazine*, Oct. 1963, pp. 459-469.

[20]Ralph G. Allen.

[21]Norman Nadel is a theatre critic. This quotation is found on p. 19 of Corey.

[22]For extensive treatment of this subject, see Muriel Broadman, *Understanding Your Child's Entertainment* (New York: Harper and Row, 1977).

CHAPTER III
CHANGING VIEWS OF CHILDHOOD

"The children loved it!"

Such a straightforward observation! And quite possibly correct, however difficult to verify. In this business of presenting dramatic works for children and youth audiences we could all wish for this direct evaluative statement to be truly said of all our efforts.

Yet we also know the complexity of what is actually implied when we attempt to select dramatic material, shape it into appropriately intriguing and meaningful form, help actors and actresses bring stage life to it through the analytical and imaginative processes of their art and craft, design and construct its physical environment, and manage the theatre-going experience in such a way as to ensure pleasure and acceptance of the premises of the performance. If indeed "the children loved it," then our work has been well done and all the effort has been worthwhile.

It is unfortunately true of our profession, however, that we have tended to indulge in considerable wishful thinking about evaluating our efforts. A solicited answer from a child as he leaves the theatre may or may not provide valid insight about the performance's overall effectiveness. Years of sitting in the midst of audiences of children can provide some information to a producer who needs to understand children's reaction patterns, likes and dislikes, and apparent involvement. Teacher post-performance assessments can also help give another perspective on the production's apparent effect. It seems, through many of these efforts, an assessment of a kind of general effectiveness has been sought, but we have too often been satisfied with less than specific outcomes of the process.

In some future book on this subject it will be possible for a chapter or more to be devoted to research findings focusing on the major problems we producers encounter. But until such a body of research has been accumulated, we may profitably construct a base for our work in the research of closely allied fields.

The function of this chapter, then, is to present information gathered about children and youth that seems to have particular relevance to their theatre. From the vast body of literature available we have selected items that appear to have application to choosing materials appropriate to certain ages in terms of content, form, and manner of presentation. To develop this child view we have drawn upon theories of cognitive, affective, and moral development, theories of social learning, and upon writings in the fields of psychiatry, anthropology, literature, and education. Included is discussion of children as audience members, and our child view concludes with some observations about dangers of implied censorship of playwrights and producers when our child view is unnecessarily restrictive.

PERCEPTIONS OF CHILDHOOD

The main currents of contemporary thought on children and childhood from the psychological perspective are identified as behaviorism and neo behaviorism, developmental psychology, social learning theory, and, of course, extensions of Freudian psychology. Writings by the principal representatives of these disciplines such as B. F. Skinner, Jean Piaget, Albert Bandura, Erich Fromm, Bruno Bettelheim, Karl Menninger, Lawrence Kohlberg and their many explicators have revealed much change in methodology and theoretical base since the Twenties and Thirties when child psychologists working in institutes of child welfare laid important groundwork. They also reveal that there is no let-up in the conceptual battle between the internal motivator proponents and the environmentalists as to which is the chief determinant of behavior.

At the present time, social learning theorists are vigorously challenging many of the basic assumptions of the behaviorists and the developmentalists. Building upon study of observable changes in behavior brought about through exposure to models seen on television and film, the social learning advocates postulate that children do what they do because of the "continuous reciprocal interaction" of personal and environmental forces, not because they are exclusively driven by one or the other.[1]

Those who agree with B. F. Skinner that behavior is entirely a matter of learned responses to one's environment, except for that which is accounted for by one's genetic make-up, also support the premise that one need only seek out what reinforcements tend to shape behavior, then apply these reinforcements in order to engineer society's most desired behaviors.[2] A society so engineered will, say Skinnerians, approach a Utopian condition, finally free of what presently appears to be mankind's headlong plunge toward self destruction through overpopulation, atmospheric pollution or nuclear holocaust and redirected toward humanity's best potentials. For those who find such a vision of society somewhat Orwellian and frightening, comfort can be taken in the social learning premise that environments themselves are not static. They undergo change rather continuously; and part of that change is brought about by individuals who are reacting to both inner and outer incentives to alter the conditions in which they live. So while it is true that behavior is "regulated by contingencies, the contingencies are partly of a person's own making."[3]

The ways in which the child's inner forces are developed would be the chief concern of those of us who work in the theatre. Making a contribution, however small, to the reinforcement of desirable personal resources seems a worthy focus to our efforts. Because we believe in the many values of the theatre-going experience in the lives of children and young people, we are anxious to make use of valuable knowledge to help us succeed in reaching their inner lives. To do this, we must try to understand the processes involved in growing up, to see the world as children see it, to share their eagerness to increase in physical and mental powers, to gain control over emotions, to make sense out of the morass of contradictions between right and wrong, and to develop resources that will help them recognize and resist attempts at manipulation by vested interests.

The key to this success lies in our ability to evoke *identification*. Unless the child's cognitive capacities are sufficiently developed so that he sees himself in the person of a character in the play, unless that character exhibits some traits he sees in himself, unless that character arouses in him an emotional sympathy through a shared problem or interest, unless that character exemplifies something of the child's aspirations and visions of his ideal self, there is likely to be little interest in the play. Freudians have defined identification as either primary (an infant's inability to distinguish between self and the outside world) or secondary (instigated by anxieties about love for the opposite sexed parent or hatred, fear and jealousy of the same sexed parent). More relevant to us are amplifications of these ideas that define identification as the child's ability to subsume into his own action patterns those of people with whom he associates.[4] Social learning theory places great stress on the power of observed models to exert vicarious influence on the behavior patterns of others. The extent to which we as producers can elicit such identification with dramatic material will no doubt determine the degree of influence we will have on shaping the child's personal, inner being.

Developmental Stages

Any producer who invites a mixed audience of adults, teenagers and children into the performance area knows that his actors actually will be presenting many performances in a single one. Each person there will see something a little different from his neighbor. Depending on the unique qualities and perceptions which each audience member brings along, one may see a humorous parody; another may see a very moving story of inner struggle and heroism; still another may see or remember very little about it. At least part of what is experienced by different audience members is reflected in their particular developmental level.

Jean Piaget, the noted Swiss child psychologist, has described three main stages of intellectual development which children generally seem to follow during their growing years. Several substage designations are also used to identify important differences within the three main headings. The age designations are approximate only:

Stage I: the period of *Sensori-Motor Intelligence* (0 to 18 months)
Through six substages, development proceeds through simple "reflex" actions and hand and eye coordinations, associating voices and faces, imitation of simple actions, repetition of pleasurable actions, looking for dropped objects (permanence), discovery of the constancy of objects' size and shape (basic perspective), game behavior involving others, appreciation of an order of events, into the stage where sensori-motor exploration is replaced by mental combinations of predictive value. Thinking is almost entirely *egocentric*.

Stage II: the period of *Concrete Operations* (18 months to 11 or 12 years)
In this stage children progress in ability to plan for and achieve goals that are distant in time and space through manipulation of classes, relations, and numbers.

II A: *Pre-operational* (18 months to 7 years)
Substage 1: *Pre-conceptual* (18 months to 4½ or 5 years)
Acquisition of language makes it possible for children increasingly to substitute thinking for action. Symbolic use of words, drawings, and play extends the range of experience beyond activity, but true concepts cannot yet be formed.

Substage 2: *Intuitive* (4½ to 7 years)
Children begin to ascribe reasons for actions and beliefs, and begin to form concepts. Judgments are made on the basis of perception, however, not logic. Thinking is not "reversible;" i.e., judgments may differ each time the problem is encountered.

II B: *Concrete Operations* (7 to 11 or 12 years)
When children reach this stage they are able to substitute mental actions for physical actions. Size, shape, and color differences are easily fathomed, groupings are correctly made, systems of classification are taking shape. Egocentricity decreases. They still have trouble dealing with verbal problems, perceiving general rules, and solving problems by other than trial and error means.

Stage III: the period of *Formal Operations* (11 or 12 to 15 years)
This level allows children or adolescents mentally to survey many possibilities, to explore many points of view, to hypothesize and test solutions to problems. Several instances of a phenomenon prompt the supposition of a general rule (induction). They are sufficiently detached so that they can observe happenings objectively, without involving the ego.[5]

Developmental psychologists emphasize that regardless of the exact age at which an individual child reaches any of these stages, he must first have acquired the necessary neurological maturity to make it possible, and he must have sufficient environmental stimulation to propel him on a regular course from one stage to the next. The order is presumed to be constant, even though special environmental factors could well have a profound delaying or accelerating effect on the actual age at which each is achieved.

It should be noted, however, that such regularity of progression is suspect from a social learning viewpoint. And the behaviorists point out that it is possible, through intensive directed practice, to accelerate what is thought to be normal development.[6]

Development of Logical Thinking

The ability to reason logically, that is, to perceive a problem and, by applying analysis from all appropriate perspectives, arrive at a solution, is not readily achieved. Indeed, it can be said that many people achieve it only imperfectly regardless of their years.

By Piaget's framework, the stage of *formal operations* is usually reached by the age of eleven or twelve in normal children. What does this mean? What are the characteristic thought patterns along the way? Surely it is not simply a matter of a stairway to perfection. Child thought and logic have their own special characteristics at each level, and these should be understood by producers who hope to make their dramas meaningful.

Piaget makes a distinction between thought which is internalized and private (often expressed in monologues) which he calls *egocentric,* and thought which is shared with others, *communicated intelligence.* The egocentric logic of the child in the preconceptual substage is apparent as he readily links unrelated things and immediately perceives relationships according to some comprehensive scheme which makes sense only to him. It is a global perception which ignores details. He is able to connect everything with everything else (syncretism).[7] Ascribing characteristics of life to elements such as wind or water is also common as a reason things move (animism). Argument is neither inductive nor deductive at this age (or, indeed, for some time to come) but rather moves from particular to particular — a system Piaget calls *transductive.*[8]

Not much before seven is the average child able to perceive that pouring liquid from a short fat container into a tall thin one makes no difference in the quantity of liquid *(conservation).* As children share with others their thoughts about presumed causality they increase their powers of objectivity and decrease tendencies toward syncretism, animism, and transduction. Yet a child of six or seven may still think that stars or fire have a life of their own and have the power to move or change position. In addition, four- to seven-year-olds will assert their belief that many natural occurrences are made and controlled by people.[9] The sun rises because someone pushes it up; or, also characteristically for children this age, the sun rises because "it wants to." An internal motivation is assumed. Piaget calls such thinking *precausality.*[10]

With increasing social contact through school and other social groups, children of seven or eight increase noticeably in ability to engage in genuine argument. Precausal thinking declines after age seven. While Piaget found that children of seven or eight did not expect nor want logical causation answers to their "why" questions, this could be an observation no longer viable in an era of extensive exposure to television teaching. Bandura asserts, for instance, that young children are able to adopt linguistic forms well beyond their current grammatic usage simply through modeling.[11] It may well be that children now progress earlier into answer-demand patterns identified as "justifications" (rules, customs) and "logical reasons" (classification and connection of ideas) than had previously been supposed. A question such as "Why do I have to go to bed at eight?" calls for justification in terms of rules of the household, health principles, and the like. A question such as "Why does the car stop when you press the brake pedal?" calls for an involved explanation of the mechanisms and their interrelated functions.[12] Highly motivated learning through attractive television programming might even be affecting the age at which most children understand conservation.

During the sub-period of concrete operations (age seven to eleven or twelve) children are reaching toward a mature reasoning power. Yet it takes time for them to accept premises and to reason from them. They may easily mistake a premise, or refuse to accept it, or even fail to acknowledge its importance to the problem. Such a failure can cause them to miss the point completely. They will frequently treat each instance of a phenomenon as a separate case, apparently not yet able to induce the presence of a general rule.[13]

The transition from concrete to formal operations is signalled by a child's ability to survey many possibilities and to theorize about outcomes of specific actions. "If I (did this), then (such and such) would happen." The young adolescent looks for general properties from which he can extract definitions and general laws. Relationships are especially interesting to explore, and he is conscious of his own thought processes, taking delight in logical manipulations.[14] Chess may become a favorite game because of the mental exercise involved. Hypothetical reasoning reaches its peak at fourteen or fifteen.[15]

For most teenagers discovering the full dimensions of causality is a continuing and delightful challenge. Mechanical explanations can become intricate, since physical laws are understood and spatial relationships can be visualized. At last the person is able to engage in deductive and inductive reasoning, relying on a realization of classes, individuals, and relationships which makes such thinking possible. At no previous stage of development has he been able to do this consistently. The fact that young adolescents do not always reason this way is merely a reflection of their human condition, deficiencies in their native equipment, or deprivations in their environment, including education.

If social learning proponents are correct, future generations can expect to reach advanced levels of abstract thinking much sooner than has previously been possible. While accepting the rather hard and fast limitations of deliberate and slow neurological development, more efficient systems of education will no doubt evolve, helping youngsters go farther faster in this important aspect of intellectual growth.[16] Continuous scrutiny of research findings in this area is clearly warranted.

Development of Spatial Concepts

During the sensori-motor period, the infant engages in a multitude of behaviors that result in allowing him to be oriented in space, to differentiate himself from other objects, and to realize that objects possess permanence. Moving a toy close to the eyes, then away again, demonstrates a fundamental rule of perspective. Crawling and later walking expand the field of spatial experience, introducing relationships of his person to physical laws of motion, momentum, gravity, centrifugal force, and balance. Muscles and concepts are equally involved in helping the child relate to the space of his environment.

The clear relationship between children's ability to understand spatial concepts and their intelligence has been noted in connection with conservation of quantity. Children younger than seven rather typically believe that the quantity of liquid will change when it is poured out of one large glass into several smaller glasses, or they readily believe that the mass has changed when shape or appearance has changed. The appearance of things is of paramount importance.[17] The familiar "Draw-a-Man" test devised by Florence Goodenough and improved by Dale Harris has been used as both a projective technique and a measure of intelligence. Perception of parts of the body and their relationship to the whole are mastered by age seven, as shown in children's drawings.

During the intuitive substage (age 4½ to 7), children appear to be especially sensitive to things or creatures that are inside of other things. Their drawings show chicks inside eggs, food in the stomach, people inside houses. This transparency concept which Piaget calls *intellectual realism* extends to drawings that show two eyes on the profile of a face or both arms projecting from one side of a profile body.[18] At this age children tend to concentrate on a single feature in their field of vision. The center of the field is of paramount importance, and since this center is frequently the largest area, smaller features tend to be underestimated in importance.[19] Distortions of proportion, as in gross enlargements of tiny articles or creatures, can be bewildering to young children who are trying to deal with the reality of size, shape, and perspective.[20]

What children draw has been used as an indicator of their spatial orientation. Piaget has outlined a stage by stage "System of Horizontal-Vertical Coordinates" which is characteristic of his meticulous methodology:

Stage I: Up to age 4 or 5, inability to distinguish surfaces or planes, either liquid or solid.
Stage II A: Age 5 or 6, water level was parallel with the base of a jar, and trees were perpendicular to the mountain side.
Stage II B: Age 5, 6, or 7, water in the jar may be on a curved line surface; the sand mountain had trees and people perpendicular to the base, but drawings showed trees and people perpendicular to the slope.
Stage III A: Age 7 to 9, a transition to full understanding of horizontal and vertical.
Stage III B: By age 9, full understanding.[21]

Obviously the ability to draw these objects according to a naturalistic scheme is not just a matter of drawing skill, not just a matter of hand and eye coordination. Since it takes most children to the age of nine to interrelate principles of parallels, angles, directions, and distances, such skills must be based on a comprehensive insight reflecting intellectual growth.[22]

Children's sense of correct perspective appears to follow much the same line of development. When asked to select the picture the doll would see when placed at various spots in relation to three cardboard mountains that could be moved on a template, children demonstrated that at an early age the doll's view is the same as their own; after age seven the view progresses into "genuine but incomplete relativity," and achieves an accurate sense of perspective sometime after nine years old.[23]

Emotional Development

Understanding the emotional climate in which children normally function is important for the theatre person because *empathy,* a process central to the theatre experience, is the vicarious arousal of an emotional state in the viewer as he imagines the situation happening to himself, not just to the character(s) on stage.[24] Since the human being is a functioning totality from the very beginning of conscious life, it is difficult to separate emotional from intellectual behavior. Obviously there is much overlap, much interdependence between right brain and left brain functioning. A child who is continually in an upset emotional state will not develop his intellect at a normal rate. Abnormal emotional functioning is cause for much concern among parents, teachers, and companions, and, of course, gives rise to an entire specialized branch of psychiatric medicine.

Emotion may be described as a state of generalized arousal with overtones of feeling. Emotions possess valence in that they are positive and pleasant or they are negative, unpleasant, disturbing. They possess degree or intensity; for instance, they can be vague, indefinite and calming, or violent, all-consuming, and unbearably strong. Emotions possess the quality of activity as well. They may arouse one only slightly, either to perpetuate or dispel their effect, or they may arouse one to vigorous effort. These features, interrelated and infinitely variable as they are, indicate the ability of the human being to adapt to the actual circumstances giving rise to the emotion, to respond to the specific need of the moment. The body prepares one to adjust and act by supplying glandular secretions, adjusting heart and breathing rates, and putting the organism "on alert" in the case of the more intense and life-supporting emotions.[25]

Early emotional expression is characterized by a generalized, all-body response. The infant cries, screams, waves its hands and feet and rolls around in its crib; or it gurgles and giggles, waving its hands, kicking its feet with equally consuming happiness. As age and experience increase, more particularized adaptation occurs, and children's emotions become more discriminating, more focused, less generalized. With an increase in age, cognitive mechanisms and modeling also qualify the expression of emotions, telling the child that a given emotion produces desirable consequences, that overt expression of another is forbidden in society, or that yet another has severe sanctions attached. Displacement, control, modification all tend to regulate expression of emotions as experience increases. Emotions combine with needs and desires into behavior motivations that become the driving forces behind people's lives.

It was once thought that there were only three basic emotions: love, fear and rage. Since drama deals in such a wide range of emotions, we may find it more useful to consider a number of variations and refinements in these general classifications.

Joy probably is the most pleasant and attractive emotion. Younger children identify joyful occasions as those when they receive special attention — holidays or birthdays, for example. Older children identify times when they are especially satisfied with personal attainments or discover special qualities in themselves. Pride, triumph, and self-actualization appear to be strong correlaries to joy, if they are not, indeed, separate emotions.[26] Pleasurable excitement can also be joyful.

Laughing can be a sign of joy, of course; but humor, or what children find funny, is far more complex than a simple emotion, even though it can culminate in similar laughing behavior. In the fashion of Piaget, Roy Tamashiro has identified five stages of the development of humor. While he does not specify ages at which these stages occur, he does equate them with other developmental conditions, and points out their sequential nature. The first, during infancy, notes laughing responses to bodily contact and tickling. The second, which he calls "impulsive," reflects consciousness of growing control over bodily functioning and an emerging sense of self in relation to environment. Humor at this stage is related to noises of bodily functions (burps, hiccoughs, passing gas, yawns, snores, etc.), as well as to physical dysfunctions such as falling down, silly and slapstick accidents and actions. The third phase is identified as "self-protective." Practical joking is common as a source of humor, and insults and put-downs replace teasing as a method of indicating a child's superiority. In the fourth stage the child is identifying strongly with a group, and humor is "conformist." Conventional humor in the form of cliché jokes (moron, elephant, knock-knock, racial and ethnic) emphasize belonging to the "in" crowd. Late in adolescence one enters the "conscientious" stage in which personal assessment of values is paramount. Satire enters the picture, as do parody and advanced forms of verbal humor.[27]

Martha Wolfenstein, another analyst of children's humor, points to a general conclusion that much joking is aimed at poking fun at the bigness and powers of others, mainly adults, making them ridiculous and powerless.[28] She explains the appeal of moron jokes as the child's delight in the moron's extravagant use of energy and his disdain that he does things the child himself would never do.[29] The exaggerated disasters of much television cartoon fare are funny because there is no time to mobilize sympathetic distress. The suddenness of a violent death on stage may arouse laughter in children, even in adults, as a kind of protective detachment is triggered within them.[30] At certain ages, incongruity, superiority, misnaming, or miscalling one's sex; absurdities, the discomfort of other people, and gross deformities and disproportions all may arouse laughter.[31] Sexual innuendos become funny at surprisingly early ages.

For centuries dramatists have used these devices to arouse the sense of humor and provoke laughter in the audience. Yet children sometimes miss the signal that they are intended to be humorous rather than tragic. Much adult humor relies on cognitive maturity for appreciation, and not until adolescence will children consistently recognize verbal humor. The line between joking and serious behavior is not perceived very clearly by children younger than nine or ten. Unless the stimulus is clearly unreal, the hero's deeds quite clearly improbable and his inappropriate behavior quite obvious, the hero might be perceived as tragic and the whole point missed.[32]

Emotions associated with love and nurturing appear very early in life, in some cases with surprisingly little encouragement.[33] Children express love to parents, blankets, toys, pet animals and birds, other persons, furniture and other objects which supply some special comfort. Thus the roots of eventual parenting are established early in a child's life. Sympathy for others, empathic reactions to observed pleasure or pain may well be founded in the love emotion. If a child can say with Archie Bunker, "I don't care," he probably will not be very happy in the theatre, regardless of what is playing!

But any child knows, sometimes quite early, that love is not all sweetness and light. It can have its unpleasant side, sometimes leading to great emotional trouble at any stage in life. Childhood jealousies can be strong and impassioned, especially if an unwise parent appears to favor a sibling or reject the child in other ways. Under those circumstances love is distorted into hatred and anger, often accompanied by guilt and self-recrimination so intense that the child cannot even discuss it in polite company.

Among the unpleasant or disturbing emotions, fear is one that takes on many forms and degrees of intensity. In the theatre, it is potentially one of the most troublesome, since a stage occurrence may inadvertently trigger a child's innermost terrors. Inadequate barriers and repressions may be assailed, and a totally inappropriate response generated.[34] Fear may range from a persistent, vague feeling of apprehension that permeates all a child's interpersonal relationships to an intense, life-preserving mobilization of all the body's resources to escape a present danger. It is interesting to note that after a time self-defense behavior may be automatically pursued without actually being preceded by the fear emotion.[35]

Most theorists accept the biologically adaptive aspect of intense fear emotions. Fear of heights, vicious wild animals, speeding automobiles, tornados (not only in Kansas!) and of wildly tossing ocean waves makes good rational sense. But our society has created another class of fears which are just as real. They are rooted in interpersonal relations, in religion and philosophy, and in the realization of death. They have to do with personal unacceptability, unworthiness and general insecurity. Advertisers exploit these fears cynically and persistently.

According to Bruno Bettelheim and other Freudians, the greatest fear to a child's mind is that of "separation anxiety." The ultimate joy is to be reunited or not to be deserted.[36] Fear of imaginary creatures and even fear of the dark may be traced to a more basic fear of separation from the loved parent. While such fears are obviously observable at the preschool age, they may persist in insidious forms throughout a person's lifetime.[37] Preschoolers may also show fear of novelty or strangeness. How many photos have you seen of crying children on the laps of department store Santas? Fear may be triggered by defects, a dismembered or decapitated doll, a neighbor's artificial leg or glass eye, unusually large lips on a well-meaning relative.[38] Older children, especially adolescents, are afraid of being different from peers, of seeming to possess physical, intellectual or sexual inadequacies.[39] A child's sense of guilt, conscience or, in Freudian terms, his super ego, may be developed by parents who withdraw or withhold love from the wrong-doing child, thus arousing a fear of separation. Through his fear, the child builds an inner control over his impulses toward unacceptable behavior.[40]

Fear and guilt are related in still another way. Knowledge of death comes to children gradually, leading from an inexplicable phenomenon that occurs to flowers, pets, sometimes to remote acquaintances, through an understanding that it happens to all living things, and finally, by about age nine, to the realization that it will indeed happen to them as well. It is not too difficult for a child to get the idea that even so, death is a punishment for one's sins and transgressions rather than a natural occurrence. As if fear of the unknown quantity of death itself were not enough, the guilt that comes from being "bad" is compounded by the fear of punishment after death. In his provocative *Children in Fear,* Stephen Joseph takes parents and teachers to task for frightening children with this "moral theory" of divine punishment and proposes that youngsters be allowed the right to make mistakes. Departing from the subject of death, Joseph also takes strong exception to the notion that preschool children enjoy being frightened by stories, television programs or theatre productions.[41]

The close tie between fear and anger also is interesting to observe. Assaults on one's ego often elicit defensive behavior; but under circumstances in which the recipient feels he has "taken enough," a defensive posture may change to one of aggression and attack. By then fear has given way to anger, perhaps rage. Anger seeks an outlet, however effective the inhibiting mechanisms. If a child does not lash out, he may seethe inside for long periods, possibly erupting inappropriately at some later time.

Anger is aroused in infants when movements are restrained. In children it can be a response to a real or imagined threat to one's person or ego, or to the denial of a request or demand. Temper tantrums, irate outbursts or sulkiness are typical behavior manifestations. Anger in childhood is most usually directed toward parents, playmates, teachers or others in the power establishment. Older children and teenagers become angry when they are teased or treated unfairly, lied to or taken advantage of, or when things generally do not go right. As children grow older swearing is a rather common release pattern. In the past this was particularly true of boys, but the growing equality of women appears to be having its effect, and swearing rather than weeping is permitted as an acceptable female response to anger.[42] The increasing frequency of swearing on television may well lower the age at which swearing is observed as a manifestation of anger in both boys and girls.

Frustration in achieving one's goals often produces anger, especially if one has low tolerance or if the condition has persisted for a long time. Most experiments that attempt to measure the degree to which young children learn aggressive behavior by watching models involve mild frustration as an action stimulus. But fear, boredom or a generalized need for stimulation and excitation, as well as anger, may account for violent, aggressive behavior.

In recent years violence as a behavior pattern has been the subject of an enormous amount of study. Freud believed aggressiveness is an instinct driving man to destroy either himself or others. Konrad Lorenz, a naturalist, asserted that aggression is akin to hydraulics, a vast storehouse of energy, dammed up and waiting. In the case of the coral fish he was studying, the trigger for release was defense to the death of territory. The fish became aggressive when space to flee became too restricted or "when social pressure not to flee was too strong."[43] In both his *Territorial Imperative* and *African Genesis,* Robert Ardrey made virtually the same claims for the human being.[44] It seems more likely, however, that violence and aggressiveness are learned behavior rather than innate reactions. If one has been successful in achieving goals through such behavior, or has seen models succeed through aggressive means, the pattern is likely to be repeated.[45]

Erich Fromm is careful to distinguish between two kinds of aggressive behavior: benign and malignant. He has placed all life-serving violent behaviors in the benign category: defensive/reactive, predatory (killing for food); accidental, playful, self-assertive, conformist (having to obey orders); and instrumental (acts calculated to obtain what is necessary or desirable). He classes as malignant those behaviors that are biologically nonadaptive or not life-serving; lustful destructiveness, cruelty or sadistic control of another person, vengeance (including all forms of punishment); ecstasy (going berserk), mental cruelty, and necrophilia (love for and desire to make all things dead).[46] In these categories, Fromm has accounted for acts of violence differentially, since he feels strongly that it is misleading and a gross oversimplification to assume that all acts of aggression are committed for the same reason or are rooted in the same emotion.

Several ideas have been proposed to reduce mankind's propensity for acting aggressively. Behaviorists such as Skinner wish to create a carefully controlled learning environment for children in which violence is simply programmed out as a possible response to noxious stimuli. Only socially desirable behaviors would be reinforced. Another method assumes the validity of Feshbach and Singer's concept of catharsis, which allows for vicarious reduction of violent tendencies by providing views of such action through sports and games, theatre, movies, and television.[47] Menninger disputes that notion, recommending that games of chess and contact sports be encouraged as direct involvement substitutes for antisocial violence.[48] Bandura and the social learning proponents urge that models of behavior shown to children exemplify non-violent solutions to problems.[49] Fromm admits that while defensive/aggressive behavior probably will never be eliminated, it could be modified by altering social, political, and economic conditions that mobilize it.[50] Each of these ideas has to do with children, their education, their entertainment, their total environment. Theatre for young audiences will either contribute to the problem or assist in its solution.

We began this discussion of emotions with joy; we shall conclude with sorrow. Children grieve in ways that are just as diversified as are adults' ways, ranging from quiet, internalized unhappiness or evasive activity to wildly extravagant crying. In children, crying may be a manifestation of a number of emotions other than grief, however, among them fear, anger and frustration. Physical pain and discomfort probably are the most frequent causes of sorrow in children, but by no means the only ones. Very early in life they register anguish at the departure of either parent, sometimes carrying their sorrow through several unhappy hours. Being deprived of a doll, toy, favorite blanket, or anything that spells security and love may cause simple sorrow or sorrow compounded with fear. At later ages, disappointed expectations, assaults on one's ego, failure in an important task, the injury or death of a loved one, pet or person, will bring on expressions of sadness that vary with each person and each situation.

The entire repertoire of emotions, interlocking, cross-connected, compounded, is available to help a child meet life's situations more or less adequately. As a balanced, dual system, the brain keeps the intellect functioning as a check on the grosser, more primitive emotions. Its two hemispheres work together to further the child's self-interests in relation to a complex social structure full of competing demands. Theatre relies on its ability to tap the child's memory of emotions to encourage his involvement in the dramatic situation, his pleasure and his enlightenment. It is possible that exposure to the problems of others through this medium will lead him a little closer toward achieving emotional maturity — the ability to bear tension and to settle for delayed responses.[51]

Development of Moral and Ethical Systems

Moral development has been described as the gradual internalization of cultural rules involving personality traits such as honesty, service, willingness to sacrifice for the common good, charity, self control, persistence. It is generally assumed to culminate in a strong conscience which governs a child's actions or, at least, causes him to feel guilt and discomfort when he breaks the rules.[52] Moral development closely parallels intellectual progress and is intimately tied to it. While Kohlberg defines moral maturity as "the capacity to make decisions and judgments which are moral and to act in accordance with such judgments,"[53] Bandura cautions that the ultimate development may be the child's (or adult's) ability to rationalize an immoral act in convincing moral terms, thereby avoiding sanctions.[54] While such a cynical outcome of moral education undoubtedly occurs, we prefer to focus our efforts on developing a child's capacity to consider carefully the results of his actions before he commits them and to effect a close tie between what he says is right and what he actually does.

In examining age level trends, Piaget discovered that moral judgments gradually shift from concern for consequences of violating rules *(moral realism)* to a consideration of intentions or motivations behind the transgressive act *(subjective intentionalism)*. The change is believed to take place some time between eight and ten years of age.[55]

In large part, morality is directly imposed on the very young child. Mother or father physically restrains the exploring offspring from injuring himself as he reaches for hot objects, starts down stairs, or puts inedible things in his mouth. As mobility and physical skills increase, restraints are supplemented with verbal "no, no's" when unsafe or unacceptable behaviors are demonstrated. The child is forbidden to hit baby brother with a toy truck, to kick grandma, to pull the cat's tail or to wander into the busy street. Right and wrong are entirely dictated by parents, and conflicts arise over an ever-widening circle of environmental contacts with people, objects and physical laws.

At about five, says Piaget, the child becomes conscious of the rules of games, such as marbles. To him these rules are immutable, "of God," and they may not be broken. Fairness and right are determined by adherence to inherited rules. It is not until he reaches eight or nine years that the child realizes rules of games may be altered by mutual consent of the players.[56] Between age four and seven (the intuitive substage), the child is unable to make distinctions between his own impulses and the rules superimposed from above. Naughtiness is judged by the consequences of one's acts. The bigger the catastrophe, the bigger the crime, regardless of whether the act was prompted by selfish or altruistic motives. Lies are bad because "God punishes them."[57]

By the time a child is in school he already knows most of the basic rules of acceptable moral behavior. As his circle of influence widens, he apparently becomes more conscious of the place of companions in this moral scheme, and he begins to lessen his hold on authority as the root of all right and accepts a socially based definition. Equal treatment emerges as basic justice. On the one hand there is the law; on the other, group loyalty. After reaching seven or eight, one does not snitch on friends, and cheating to help a buddy may be considered good and right, not evil and wrong.[58]

Group identification for moral rightness increases during the sub-period of concrete operations (seven to twelve). One does not lie to friends, and actions are judged increasingly on the basis of motivations. If the reason for the act was wrong (assessed as unworthy of group approval) then it was bad, regardless of insignificant material damage. Mistakes can now be distinguished from intentional wrongdoing.[59] Lying is telling an untruth, and "2 + 2 = 5" is a lie to the child under eight. To the younger child, the bigger the lie the more deserved the punishment. To the older child (over ten) the bigger lie is less likely to be detected and therefore less serious.[60]

The youth in the formal operations stage (twelve to fifteen) is thoroughly into adjustment of rules to effect social good. One needs only to get agreement. Moral absolutism decreases, and he sees both goodness and badness, right and wrong in the same person and the same act.[61]

According to Piaget and his followers, notions of appropriate punishment for breaking moral rules also change with increasing age. Punishment is needed for badness in "Stage I" thoughts of those younger than six or eight in order to expiate, to prevent repetition. And justice is "immanent, automatic, mechanical." Sure as anything it will befall the transgressor like a bolt of lighting! "Stage II" thinking of eight- to nine-year-olds changes to concern for justice, fairness, and "reciprocal" punishment that fits the crime. Impulses toward forgiveness and generosity rather than strict revenge enter a child's thinking at this stage,[62] but not so much as to interfere with a strong conviction that poetic justice extracts an "eye for an eye" in the outcome of favorite fairy tales.[63] The shift from believing in immanent justice to acceptance of reciprocity is gradual, of course, and understanding that evil is not always punished or that innocent people are sometimes mistakenly punished is long in coming. One study reported a drop of 86% of six-year-olds to 34% of twelve-year-olds who believed that punishment would be automatic.[64]

Lawrence Kohlberg has built a tri-level scheme of moral development based on Piaget's stages. Each level contains two types of moral judgments:

Level I. Premoral (rules are obeyed simply to avoid punishment)
    Type 1. (age 6-7)   Punishment and obedience orientation
    Type 2. (age 7-9)   Naive instrumental hedonism (living for pleasure)
Level II. Morality of Conventional Role-Conformity (rules obeyed to avoid guilt produced by censure
        from authority) (age 10-14)
    Type 3. Good boy morality of maintaining good relations, approval of others
    Type 4. Authority maintaining morality
Level III. Morality of Self-Accepted Moral Principles (rules obeyed in terms of individual principles of
        conscience) (age 15+)
    Type 5. Morality of contract, or individual rights, and of democratically accepted law
    Type 6. Morality of individual principles of conscience [65]

Using the Kohlberg system, Longstreth found that from age seven to thirteen, Level I responses diminished but nevertheless persisted throughout the range. By age thirteen, Level II responses had strengthened, but Level III responses remained few indeed.[66]

It is only fair to mention challenges to the neatly-drawn stages concept in the area of moral development even as we question rigid categories for intellectual growth. Quite possibly the stages and levels defined by Piaget and Kohlberg are oriented to Western culture and not universally applicable.[67] Social learning authorities also assert that, in general, research findings do not confirm the presence of distinct stages, that in actual fact children's ideas on moral questions simultaneously bridge several "levels." Furthermore, they challenge the notion that children cannot handle moral concepts too far above their present "stage," claiming that such shifts can be readily effected through role modeling.[68] Obviously we are in no position to settle the argument, but we can profitably account for as much careful thought on the subject as we can possibly find.

A few comments probably should be made about the relationship between the morality that is known, believed and professed, and actual moral behavior. After all, it doesn't matter a great deal what a child can tell his parents and friends about what is right and good if he doesn't practice what he preaches. Many experiments with children of all ages show an almost zero correlation between verbalized and behavior morality when conditions are right for deviation. Moral actions apparently are specific to the actual situation. Cheating in one context does not mean that one will always be a cheater. Carefully nurtured inner control mechanisms — the conscience, the super ego — are not always capable of stopping an immoral act, though they may cause considerable guilt feeling in the offender.[69] According to Kohlberg, increasing, or even establishing, the guilt mechanism is possible only when the child identifies himself with the person who does the punishing.[70]

If conscience is really such a weak and inconsistent control over moral behavior, what then will function as a more effective control? Kohlberg indicates that "ego strength" is emerging as the more likely mechanism. The factors involved include all the cognitive functions that develop with age and that contribute to decision-making based on known conditions and potential outcomes.[71] Bandura proclaims that one good determinant of moral behavior is social learning, through pointed observation of appropriate role models. Moral decisions are social ones, made on the basis of factors such as characteristics of the doer, the nature of the specific act, the immediate and long range consequences, the setting, motivations, remorse potential, and number and type of victims. By observing the consequences of actions committed by a model, children will be able to utilize knowledge of these consequences in making social decisions.[72]

In the theatre the child's sense of what constitutes right and wrong is constantly called upon as a basis for judging the action before him. Under the right circumstances the theatre could become an important part of what Bettelheim calls a "moral education," one that "subtly and by implication only conveys the advantage of moral behavior, not through abstract ethical concepts but through that which seems tangibly right and therefore meaningful."[73]

Preschool Intervention

From time to time in this chapter we have mentioned that cognitive or moral development might possibly be accelerated by the contemporary child's extensive exposure to role modeling and television learning. More systematic efforts to accelerate early intellectual growth have taken on considerable momentum in the past twenty years.

While day care centers, nursery schools, and pre-kindergartens of the Montessori "House" kind have been in operation for decades, it took the sudden appearance of the Russian Sputnik in 1957 to arouse national concern for preschool education and, in fact, to force a reexamination of education at all levels. Nursery schools traditionally focused their programs on developmental activities, stressing unhurried natural maturation, self expression, creativity, and social interaction without undue pressure.[74] Montessori schools were dedicated to more pointed exploration than most, especially in the sciences; but stress was kept on discovery, not instruction. Children who attended these preschools were, for the most part, those of middle and upper class families, whose needs were defined mainly in terms of enrichment and socialization.

With Sputnik came a clamor for serious intervention at the earliest possible moment to identify and accelerate those gifted children who were likely to make the greatest contribution to satisfying national goals of scientific superiority. No sooner had this effort aroused support than a desperate cry arose at the other end of the privilege spectrum: a way must be found to reverse the ever-declining academic accomplishment of minority children, especially the Black populations in urban ghetto settings.[75] Project Head Start, begun in 1965, was a preschool for two- to four-year-olds dedicated to rectifying a multitude of interrelated ills. Not only did Head Start supply education, as variously defined by individual programs, but it compensated for inadequacies in the children's homes by providing physical and emotional nurture, medical and dental services, and nutrition. In 1968, Project Follow Through was instituted in order to extend children's Head Start gains up to the third grade level. Parents were extensively involved in both programs.[76]

Still another factor has entered into the focus on preschool education. World War II brought increasing numbers of women out of the home and into the country's work force. Since that time, social and economic conditions have continued the trend, and more and more mothers are absent from home during the working day. At the same time, family structures have become looser, lending more social sanction to divorce and to nontraditional home environments. All this in turn has necessitated custodial care for preschool age children in all social strata. The role of traditional preschools thus has changed from simple enrichment to one of providing much more comprehensive preparation for entry into regular school.

Head Start and Follow Through, however, proved unable to produce academic achievement gains that held after the children left the period of intensive intervention. Characteristically, gains made by Head Start children subsided, and once again they were behind age norms by the second grade.[77] Except in some Black urban centers, failure could possibly have been due to the program's focus on rectifying many evils rather than on acquisition of behaviorally defined reading and cognitive skills. Other programs such as the Primary Education Project (PEP) of Pittsburgh and similar ones in Nashville and Ypsilanti reported much more stable gains through concentration on helping urban children master very specific, graduated tasks.[78]

Preschool intervention is based on the premise that "any subject can be taught effectively in some intellectually honest form to any child at any stage of development."[79] In other words, "readiness" to learn or to engage in certain kinds of intellectual pursuits is seen as more contingent on teachers' abilities to construct a suitable environment than on the child's physical and neurological structures' having arrived at a certain level of maturation.[80] Furthermore, success in stimulating intellectual progress that persists at later stages might better be expected if efforts were concentrated in one of the two periods of extraordinary mental growth: the one between four and six.[81] Behavior modification techniques have been used as the basic methodology in the more successful preschool programs.

The question of the desirability of a massive national effort in early childhood education certainly is not settled. Strong, methodical opposition to the whole concept of acceleration and intervention, except for disadvantaged children and special populations who are clearly in need of compensatory help, is based on the economic advantage and the generally longer lasting effectiveness of home-based parent nurturing, which preferably continues until the age of eight. Perceptual-neurological mechanisms, say the opposition, are not equipped to handle a concerted onslaught on cognitive functions until that age.[82] And the dangers of taking children out of the protective home environment in their early years may far overshadow any short-term gains.

PERCEPTIONS OF THE AUDIENCE

Let us now turn our attention from children as developing personalities to children as audience members. In this section artists of the theatre — playwrights, producers, directors, designers, actors and sponsors — will find four age-group Profiles of children as audience members, a discussion of value systems as revealed in plays and examined in several audience studies, and some further examination of the apparent influences of television on children as audience members.

Age Group Profiles

The summary of various perspectives on children's intellectual, emotional, and moral development presented earlier in this chapter reminds us that what we do to match the theatre experience to the children for whom it is intended goes much deeper than a concern for playing time, which in most cases is more related to school bus schedules than to children themselves! Included in the Profiles are matters of content such as subjects and character interests, expected levels of comprehension, likely responses to questions of morality and justice, problems associated with perception and art appreciation, attention characteristics, language, humor, emotions, and special cautions that should be observed with each age group. While they may be somewhat arbitrary, the age divisions conform to natural dividing lines used in many school systems: preschool and kindergarten, lower elementary, upper elementary, and junior high school. This discussion proceeds from the premise that children younger than four are not yet ready for theatre.

PROFILE
The Audience with Four- and Five-Year-Olds

Audiences partly composed of four- or five-year-old children (perhaps some even younger) are not uncommon in theatre for young people. Invariably they will constitute some unknown percentage of audiences for "family theatre." Open attendance performances such as Saturday matinees will see many this young accompanying parents, grandparents, or brothers and sisters, although some theatres have house policies that exclude children younger than six. Further, it is not unusual that when smaller school systems bus children to a performance they will bring the entire school population, including the kindergartners, simply because it is politically and economically unwise for them not to. Although this is the age when participation theatre works best, and occasional performances of that kind may be offered them, it is not usual to perform exclusively for children this young. Nevertheless, we have seen the necessity to account for their presence in the audience.

Developmental and Other Bases[83]

Child As Audience Member[84]

(Numbers in left margin match items in right column)

COGNITIVE
Between Piaget's *preconceptual* and *intuitive* substages.

1, 9, 11   *Transductive* reasoning (without logical derivation)

1, 9, 14   Sees world as chaotic.

2, 9, 11, 14   *Precausal thinking (does not seek truly causal explanations)*.

1, 7, 11   *Syncretism* (connecting everything according to some personal, illogical scheme).

9   *Animism* (ascribes life to inanimate objects and forces)

6   Imitation and role-modeling potentials.

5, 10, 11   Language acquisition increasing rapidly, but vocabulary limited, reflecting social group.

7, 14   Discrimination between fact and fantasy is tenuous.

8, 14   Limited concentration, easily distracted.

SPATIAL
7, 13   Pre-conservation.

3, 13   Drawings are *pre-schematic*, reflect *intellectual realism* (transparent views of eggs show chicks inside).

4, 13   Centered perception (focus on small details or areas at one time).

1. Tries to make sense out of what's happening by any scheme available.

2. A thing happens because "it wants to" or because "it does;" not concerned with character motivations.

3. Great interest in enclosures, doors, little houses the characters go into.

4. Visual focus on important happenings needs to be clear.

5. Language of performance may go over his head, convey little, or convey erroneously; may not even be in the same language or dialect child speaks.

6. Can imitate language features beyond his "stage." May imitate aggressive behavior of characters he sees, regardless of characters' motivations.

7. Easily deceived by appearance of things. Believes what he sees. May try to enter the action.

8. Appreciates rapid changes in story progress, or prefers short sketches or variety program. Won't pay much attention when action stops. Has trouble seeing and hearing in spaces designed for adults, and this interferes with his ability to follow sequential action. Concentration on performance easily broken by distractions in the playing area (bells, P.A. announcements, stray light, children or monitors passing).

Four- and Five-Year-Olds

8, 9   Small physical size in relation to adults and environment.

EMOTIONAL

12,14   Fear easily aroused.

8, 9, 10, 11   Joy, pleasure, delight in physical movement, control, accomplishments.

10, 11 Humor on simple, physical level.

11,14   Trying to control expressions of anger and frustration. Tensions surrounding control of bodily functions.

9, 10, 11   Wants size and power of adults to exert control over others.

MORAL/ETHICAL

12 Naughtiness judged entirely by consequences (size or degree of outcome determines enormity of the crime).

12 Right equated with absolute eternal rules derived from parents.

12 *Immanent justice* (retribution visited automatically on wrongdoers).

12 Acts totally right or wrong, no halfway.

9. Interests: little people accomplishing big things: personified, animated familiar objects; reality based, familiar characters in familiar settings; child, small animal, or family characters; spectacle elements if not frightening or uncanny.

10. Pleasure: songs, dancing, making sounds; rhythmic participation; physical involvement (participation theatre); things and people that move; unusual physical skills (acrobatics).

11. Humor: body noises: nonsense (or what is erroneously perceived as such); incongruities (what he sees against what he knows to be possible); silly characters engaged in outlandish behavior who damage themselves; changing sex by changing name or dress; clumsiness, falling, slapstick action; fantasies of size (Tom Thumb, Lilliputians); characters surprised or who have expectations thwarted; can mistake serious events for comic ones and vice versa; may laugh at almost any stage event for unfathomable reason; humorous component of violence.

12. Morality and Justice: happy outcomes mandatory to resolve fears; appropriate rewards, clearly dealt; wrong-doing physically punished; mercy for unjust is unsatisfying; ambiguity of rightness/wrongness likely to be missed; characters' motivations don't count for much.

13. Art Response: prefers a few recognizable elements in uncomplicated, clear arrangements; probably will not detect relationships among elements; sees self as center of all pictures.

14. Cautions: separation anxiety easily aroused by darkness in house or on stage or by characters who are lost or isolated; easily startled by sudden noises, flashes, characters who suddenly intrude on his space (down aisles or inside audience area from behind); does not enjoy being frightened as older children might; allow child to enter into participation activities of his own accord without pressure (some may not wish to take part at all); prolonged suspense may over-excite with unpleasant results; excitement response to chases is easily exploited to detriment of other responses.

PROFILE

The Audience of Six-, Seven-, and Eight-Year-Olds

Almost all theatres for children and youth report that perhaps a majority of their audiences are in this age group. They are delightful to play for since their response is enthusiastic and uninhibited, creating an atmosphere in the theatre akin to that which must have prevailed in Shakespeare's time, or in the music halls and opera houses of the old West. Furthermore, a large part of the repertoire, particularly the older plays, has been written with this age group in mind.

Developmental and Other Bases

Child As Audience Member

(Numbers in left margin match items in right column)

COGNITIVE

Some in the *intuitive substage, some entering sub-period of concrete operations.*

5, 6 — Beginning to make distinctions between physical world and psychical and intellectual world.

1, 3, 9 12 — *Logical justification* (causality) beginning to emerge from *precausal* thinking. Anthorpomorphic explanations of nature still made (physical laws confused with intentions of the Creator or man). Animism may still be present in younger ones.

1, 3, 6, 9, 12 — Thinking does not proceed from acceptance of premises and reasoning from them. Child sees only the specific case before him without need to express a general law. He may refuse to accept the premise and fail to see he has missed the point of the series of events. Thinking is dominated by immediate perceptions.

6, 7 — Intellectual challenges in exercises in classifications, groupings, ascending or descending orders, family trees. Concept of time enters into active consideration for most operations.

2, 3 — Language functions are increasingly important in daily interactions. Becoming quite skilled and familiar with power of words to stimulate response in others.

2 — Susceptibility to modeling influences modified by learning and established inner controls.

5 — World gradually assuming less chaotic, more orderly operation.

1. Follows a story from event to event, but may miss point because of failure to make complete or accurate connections between events and their causes as established through character motivations or dramatic sequences.

2. Can learn advanced linguistic forms through modeling. Not likely immediately to imitate violent behavior seen in performance, but may at some later time.

3. Still needs frequent changes in action sequences, visual picture and emotional tone to maintain attention. Episodic structure or story theatre series is advantageous. Conversations, imperfectly understood, tend to bore him when they stop action.

4. Becomes emotionally involved in the aspirations of story's hero. Delights in his triumphs, is fearful for his danger. If emotions too intense may "turn off" or engage in divergent thoughts.

5. Believes in what is occurring on stage but is able to remember he is in a theatre; able to perceive reality or improbability of stage occurrences by 8.

6. Art response: visual focus in performance still important to keep action clear; while average child prefers realism and wants to identify objects and scenes in terms of familiar experiences, "artistic" child approves unusual, primitive, or experimental aspects of picture. Simultaneous view of inside and outside (i.e., Peter Pan's underground house) easily comprehensible. Post-production drawings may show his recollection of what an event (shown as frozen action) or a sequence (shown as montage) actually looked like, may show an original en-

Six-, Seven-, and Eight-Year-Olds

3   Concentration can be centered longer than at younger age.

5   Distinction between reality and fantasy now quite clear.

10, 11   Concept of death is forming, but it remains puzzling in spite of amount of thought devoted to it; it appears to occur at the whim of life's "inventor."

SPATIAL

6   Perception is still centered (focus on one area or element at a time.) Center of vision field, often the largest area, is overestimated in importance.

1, 6, 7   Drawings may show *intellectual realism* (X-ray view); evolving into *schematic* stage (definite form to objects which are "lined up" across the page or laid out in a simultaneous time-space sequence). Significant details may be exaggerated in size. Child beginning to perceive interrelationships among objects in a painting. "Pilot's view" of maps understood by 8-year-olds.

5, 6   *Conservation* achieved by age 7; thereafter not likely to be deceived by the appearance of things.

6   Plays with a variety of symmetrical patterns.

EMOTIONAL

4, 7   Child's emotions tend to be extreme, completely happy or completely miserable. Little intermediate ground.

4, 5, 7   Able to empathize and sympathize with plight of others. Becomes genuinely aroused.

9, 12   Humor still largely visual, physical and obvious, but now engages in word humor as well: ambiguity of meanings, innuendos, ready-made jokes and riddles; practical jokes; insults and "put downs" used to control others.

4, 5, 7   Fears still tied to separation anxiety; sensitive to signs of fear and pain in others;

vironment he has invented for a described event or scene, may show an interpretation of the scene he saw, or an extension of the experience into a whole new, imaginative realm. Ideas of relative importance may be shown by exaggeration of selected features; sounds and script lines may be added in block letter printing; accuracy of memory frequently amazing and shows degree of attention accorded; may show how "suggested" or conventionalized elements are translated into fully detailed realistic form by active imagination. May reveal degree to which stage magic was actually concealed (Peter Pan may have string attached in drawings).

7. Interests: range of interest topics broadening to include fantasy, legends, myths, fairy tales and other adventurous and realistic stories having clear morality; holidays; TV cartoons and situation comedies; enchantments and magical transformations that put things right (the lost found, rightful heir restored); elements of conflict, danger, potential tragedy. Child protagonists somewhat sex related; family situations.

Melody study: 6-year-olds chose living room or castle as setting for story, 7-8-year-olds chose cave or castle; all told stories about what normally occurs in such settings; story elements were adult characters in violent action, natural disasters, war, destruction, chasing, and death juxtaposed with everyday activities (standard fairy tale motifs absent); boys used boy heroes, girls used boy and girl heroes; animals, kings & queens, monsters.

As at all ages, preference stated for mesomorphic body builds; assigns positive behavior traits to them as opposed to endomorphic or ectomorphic builds.

8. Pleasure: physical involvement as in clap-a-long (in rhythm to stage music); supplying noises, sound cues, singing and other forms. By 8 is less likely to take part enthusiastically in participation theatre designed for younger children. Likes odd sounding words, fanciful names, rhymes, alliteration and imagery in poetic dialogue.

fear and mistrust of opposite sex leading to companionship almost exclusively within own sex; fear of supernatural characters, monsters, and ghosts sometimes deliberately stimulated to prove superiority over it.

4, 5, 7 "Family romance" common: child thinks his real parents are of an exalted family and that he is merely staying with these folks awhile. This explains the "stepmother" fantasy: it is all right to hate this false mother/witch, keeping the true mother inviolate (Bettelheim). May have imaginary companions to play with and share hates and ambitions with.

MORAL/ETHICAL

10   In Kohlberg's *Pre-moral stage* (rules obeyed to avoid punishment).

4, 7, 10   Actions gradually seen to be worse if motives are wrong, not just if material damage is great. Mistakes distinguishable from deliberate wrong-doing by age 8. Middle class children develop concern over motives sooner than lower class children.

10, 11   Importance of social interaction and obligation to friends gradually brings change of allegiance from authority and rules to a more socially mediated base; one does not lie to or snitch on friends.

7, 10, 11   Fairness of punishment now important, based on equality with punishment given others for similar offense; *reciprocity* (something similar done to the wrong-doer) replacing automatic deference to adult authority. Lower class children develop *reciprocity* with peers, dropping adherence to adult authority, sooner than middle class children.

10   Child knows basic moral rules by first grade. Believes moral rules are equated with physical laws, fixed and eternal.

7, 10   While most believe an act is totally right or wrong, some are developing an insight into possible ambiguity, depending on motivations.

9. Humor: falling and other slapstick events; exaggeration of hero's plight and ineptitude of his reactions assure his being perceived clearly as comic rather than as serious; increasing vocabulary allows child to appreciate some verbal humor if amply supported by visible means. Jokes on stage can misfire easily if verbal constructs are beyond his experience. Surprises, chases, excitement if not too serious arouse laughter. Incongruity, superiority, and deviations from normal increase as reasons for laughter. Practical jokes played on villains especially delightful.

10. Morality and Justice: characters' motives begin to affect judgment of rightness and wrongness of actions for an older or advanced child. Being true to friends, protecting them, supporting them, become a principal moral obligation. Justice occurs if evil characters receive what they wished to inflict on hero. Outcomes most satisfactory if standard poetic justice is served. Ultimate consolation is not to be abandoned, to find a rightful place.

11. Death of evil characters is seen as part of a reciprocal justice scheme, and as such is acceptable and satisfying. Death of sympathetic characters or those not deserving punishment forces a deeper, more inclusive concept of death to be dealt with.

12. Cautions: negative responses probable to extended scenes of romantic love. Failure of protagonist may be difficult to understand and distressing. Though he knows occurrences on stage are fantasy, child can become genuinely frightened if the situation touches an exposed nerve, a situation close to his own inner fears; but there may be satisfaction later in being able to say "I wasn't scared when such-and-such happened." Child does not understand irony or sarcasm, takes parodies of fairy tales as the real thing. It is unethical to pass off such dishonest "camp" dramas as genuine versions of the fairy tales he loves and expects (see Chapter IV). Child may be upset when musical numbers interrupt story progress.

PROFILE

The Audience of Nine-, Ten-, Eleven- and Twelve-Year-Olds

Another significant portion of the script repertoire is written to serve this age group. It is a crucial age for children's and youth theatre because today the child's rapid development and increasing sophistication lead him into mature interests earlier and earlier, it seems. The possibility that a play will appear childish is high unless producers and performers are conscious of the young person's need for challenge and respect. By now he is genuinely able to follow the dialogue and dramatic premises of the play — a fact which makes this age delightful to play for.

Developmental and Other Bases

Child As Audience Member

(Numbers in left margin match items in right column)

COGNITIVE

Most are in sub-period of *concrete operations*. A few will have entered the stage of *formal operations*.

1, 2, 3
6, 9
Prior to entering *formal operations* at about 12, child cannot reason from given specific instances to a general law; however, is proceeding to differentiate reasons from justifications (customs or rules); answers to "why" questions now more frequently understood if they contain information about mechanical functions, spatial contacts, life phenomena, psychological motivation, and even logical explanation (classification and connection of ideas).

1, 2, 3,
9
As a child enters *formal operations* he can develop hypotheses and proceed to test them, state general laws derived logically from separate instances. Language can be used as substitute for physical manipulation of concepts; he can reason in propositions and argue by implication.

1, 2, 3,
6
Interest in studying and testing mechanical relationships in increasingly complex model building and operation grows during this period. He will find intellectual challenge in problems and ideas that are momentarily beyond him.

1, 2, 3
Challenge in games and collections demanding classifications, groupings, labeling, arrangements of numbers.

4, 5, 8,
10
Knows by 9 that death will occur to him as well as to all living things.

1. Intellectually able to follow a sequential story with ease; attention span no longer a serious problem; is able to concentrate for considerable length of time if material is appropriate and interestingly presented; causal reasoning sufficiently developed to tie motives to actions or characters.

2. More of the story can be carried by the dialogue since his linguistic development is proceeding rapidly and he is able, by 11, to project possible consequences from information verbally presented.

3. More fully drawn characters with strengths and weaknesses will be understood; admires heroes of the past, present and future; space adventurers challenge both imagination and mechanical/scientific curiosity.

4. Empathic responses to characters' emotional states can be quite intense if situation elicits full attention; but he may guard his social image by rejecting the stage event or diverting his attention if scene is too arousing.

5. Able to appreciate moral complexity of characters' actions, to account for intentions and motives, and to discern the greater guilt among several characters.

6. Enjoys speculating about the "how" of stage occurrences; enjoys elements of spectacle, including those that are startling or uncanny.

7. Art response: post-production drawings generally show the same kinds of treatments of the viewed action as the 7-8-year-olds with more complexity and detail drawn with greater accuracy; will depict actual view of "suggested"

Nine-, Ten-, Eleven- and Twelve-Year-Olds

SPATIAL

2, 3, 6, 7   As child enters *formal operations,* he can visualize physical relationships that are not immediately tangible, finite, or familiar.

6, 7   *Conservation* firmly established, allowing child to structure what is seen into accurate relationships that follow natural laws.

6, 7   Gradually mastering concept of topological features of maps and concept of perspective in drawings.

6, 7   Preferences in art works slowly evolving from simplistic and symmetrical to the more complex and mature.

6, 7   Drawings demonstrate period of *dawning realism* (Lowenfeld): objects still symbolized, not represented in naturalistic sense; drawings now smaller with objects related to each other rather than merely lined up on the paper. By 11 or 12 child can interpret what is happening in a picture. By 10 or 11 child is concerned for representational values in his own drawings (light and shade, atmospheric effects and graduations of color). By 12 drawings become a representation of space and objects within it. Likes paintings of clear realistic representation and more complexity than at earlier ages.

EMOTIONAL

3, 4, 8, 9   Forms strong attachments to friends; attachments may be consolidated in groups, cliques, gangs, that are mutually supportive and occasionally aggressively exclusive. Boys shun girls, seek their own companionship. Girls' friendships may be very close.

8   Need for excitation and stimulation; increasing independence of actions opens more possibilities for satisfaction. Vicarious excitement sought in sports, games, movies, television, theatre, and reading.

4, 8   May deliberately court fearful situations, tell ghost stories at slumber parties or

scenic units, or views extended to reality dimension, or both kinds in the same picture; may depict entire action sequence in one drawing using a time-space scheme that may be lateral or circular. Satisfaction apparently achieved either by a literal or an amplified creation in which he indicates the degree to which the art work he saw stimulated a reality image.

8. Interests: an age of division of interests by sex, but there is some overlap. Mystery, suspense, dogs, horses, stories of realism and adventure appeal to both boys and girls. Girls have interest in boy and girl heroes; boys will reject "girls' books," and do not use heroines in their own stories. Violence and aggressive action, a strong attraction for boys, brings a negative response from girls. "Ideal" persons, say boys, are those heroes associated with war, politics, sports, and space exploration; for girls the "ideal" is one likely to be associated with humanitarian causes, religion, royalty, or the movies. Scenes of romantic love will be enjoyed by girls but rejected by boys, although boys will tolerate brief encounters if not too mushy. Adult characters and situations now more acceptable than at earlier ages, but respond most favorably to heroes their age or a little older. Family situations interesting to both sexes.
Melody: castle and cave settings chosen by 4th and 5th graders for their stories; cave, forest, and mountains chosen by 6th graders; both sexes told stories of realistic or adventurous content, with fantasy told mostly by girls; idealism appeared in boys by 4th grade; boys and girls related far-out occurrences in settings far removed from daily experience: explorations, lost and found, and rescues; boys told of natural disasters, destruction, war, boy heroes, cavemen, monsters, and historical figures; girls told stories containing death, work, boy and girl heroes, princes and princesses.

9. Humor: now can be more situation related, building sequentially through the drama, since child retains the earlier premises on which later humor depends; still strong physical and visual components; verbal humor less likely to be misunderstood than formerly, but joking

around scout camp fire, watch monster movies, explore dark caves or old houses. Genuine fear aroused by concern for accidental injuries and incapacities or death, of seeming different or strange; very conscious of any physical handicaps. Angry outbursts or withdrawal may result from ego assaults.

4, 8   Great pleasure in personal achievements which support child's ideal self image or solidifying friendship.

4, 8   Empathizes deeply with pain, sorrow, fear, joy, and love of characters in stories that are within interest range and which do not violate his taboos.

1, 2, 9   Humor still mostly visually and physically based, but jokes and riddles with a verbal, intellectual component, are increasingly popular; incongruity, superiority, deviations from normal, discomfort of others are stimuli to laughter; an element of in-groupness to some racial, ethnic, or deviant humor that purposely excludes outsiders. Making fun of human imperfections and frailties can have sadistic edge. Difference between joking and seriousness now quite clearly understood; off-color, scatological and sexually oriented humor growing within closed groups.

MORAL/ETHICAL

5, 10   Most are still responding at Kohlberg's Level I: *Premoral* (rules obeyed to avoid punishment); some now operate at Level II: *Conformity* (obeys rules to forestall guilt when censured).

1, 5, 10   Motives for actions increasingly comprehensible and become important in assessing degree of rightness or wrongness of an action; admits others may make different assessments. In Piaget's terms, *subjective intentionalism* evolves from *moral realism* by about age 10.

1, 3, 5   Moral obligations to companions replace those to adult authority; rules may be changed by consent of those involved.

1, 2, 10   Able to see ahead to potential outcomes and judge advisability of doing harmful

can still misfire; comic heroes will be accurately perceived with less obvious comic cues than[a] needed for younger child; parody and irony only vaguely understood, seldom appreciated.

10. Justice and death: resolutions, outcomes, and justice in plays may include ideas of reform or forgiveness of wrong-doers; death of protagonist or other sympathetic characters may now be perceived as a kind of ultimate tiumph by metaphysical extension.

11. Cautions: whether sex differences in interests will begin to recede or increase with decline in sex role stereotyping in society and literature remains to be seen. Because boys now appear able to tolerate brief romantic sequences without audible rejection, some increase in such scenes might be expected; however with the media tending to "hurry" sexual contact through modeling there is some question whether TYA should augment the problem. Desire to attenuate gory details should be generally resisted in deference to child's need for vicarious experiences too often prohibited in other contexts. Spoofs are still likely to be misinterpreted and are generally to be avoided until a later stage. Because this age child's artistic development is so important in terms of ultimate expectations it is mandatory that art works presented to him exemplify the highest possible quality, to help develop his taste and appreciation for beauty.

acts; intent to do harm is basis for censure.

10, 5   Justice is largely a question of fairness; it is all right to give back the blows one has received; *reciprocity* as basis for punishment is established firmly; some (by 11) can see the view of the other party and attenuate demands for reciprocal punishment; milder, less painful punishments, reform of wrong-doers and even forgiveness become more acceptable to older children.

10   With increasing age comes consciousness that wrong doing often goes unpunished in the real world and that the innocent are sometimes wrongly punished. Yet, in one study (reported by Longstreth), 54% of 9-10-year-olds and 34% of 11-12-year-olds still believed in *immanent justice.* Obviously this idea dies hard!

PROFILE

The Audience of Young Teenagers

Young persons in the early teen years are, unfortunately, the most neglected in the present repertoire of plays. In their eagerness to avoid the stigma of doing "kid shows" junior high teachers will sometimes try adult theatre material quite unsuited to their young charges. But when one of the growing body of plays for young teens is presented we find there is no more enthusiastic and appreciative group in the entire spectrum. Teenagers' level of understanding of dialogue, character motivation and moral complexity provides for a breadth of responsiveness encountered in no other age group in this survey.

Developmental and Other Bases

Teenager as Audience Member

(Numbers in left margin match items in right column)

COGNITIVE

Now in Piaget's stage of *formal operations.*

1, 5   Increases in ability to formulate propositions and argue from them. Tests hypotheses in a variety of ways against a growing body of experience and increased reasoning powers. Errors in reasoning can be recognized and corrected.

1, 4, 5   A period of intellectual expansion in which basic processes have been

1. Intellectually able to understand some adult drama and will try to hurry his identification as an adult by preferring it over "kid shows." Materials appealing to his special interests and accounting for his developmental level must be packaged totally in ways that avoid the stigma of childishness. A good age to discover Shakespeare, William Gibson, Mary Chase as well as growing repertoire of plays for the young teen set.

2. Response to spectacle: the more discerning capable of appreciating artistic base for non-

AGE: THIRTEEN, FOURTEEN, FIFTEEN

achieved and the vast world of intellectual possibilities opens up. The young person's mental capacities will never be much greater than they are in this period.

1, 4, 5   Imperfections in formal, logical reasoning and differentiation of causal explanations make continued effort and stimulation through this period especially important. The fact that education in the years of junior and senior high school and college seems able to produce few perfect thinkers should not be cause for discouragement, only a challenge for us to find ways to involve the young person totally in the excitement and the joy of learning.

SPATIAL

2, 4   Able to perceive himself in relation to the infinitely small (which he can see in science class microscopes) and infinitely large (which he can glimpse in telescopes or televised views from interplanetary Voyagers).

4   Understands mechanical/spatial interactions which he can manipulate in model building and other experimentation.

2   Perspective drawing technique of 13-year-olds improves with training. Drawings demonstrate *pseudo-naturalistic* stage (Lowenfeld): concern for proportion and depth; much detail in human figures, clothes, and hair styles; gradations of color. Cartooning may reflect satirical comments. Although art classes may or may not improve general skills or judgment of art works, by 14+ youth is capable of developing a real interest and individualized skill that carries into adult life.

EMOTIONAL

3, 4, 5   Feelings are intense and, for some, easily aroused; potential for extremes of emotional depression to lead to suicidal actions; everything seems to be most glorious or the worst possible. Much private, uncommunicated suffering. Empathizes

realistic sets, actually stating preference for imaginative stimulation.

3. Difference between boys' and girls' assessment of factors contributing to peer prestige may be diminishing as sex-role stereotyping is reduced in society. In earlier survey athletic prowess, boisterousness and fearless assertiveness were associated with male prestige, while neatness, attractive appearance and demureness were seen as female prestige factors. Personal qualities such as friendliness, expansiveness, enthusiasm, humor and self assurance probably replace more exclusive "boy" or "girl" traits from past eras; but for teenagers who do not fit the "prestigious" mold, plays that point out compensation possibilities such as excelling in art fields or special skills will have unusual appeal. Girls are especially attracted by physical attributes of performers. Both boys and girls express preference for mesomorphic body builds, but since a certain number of teenagers will have ectomorphic or endomorphic builds, they will appreciate plays that recognize their needs for compensation.

4. Interests: detective stories, mysteries, adventure, **the supernatural, tragedy, romanticized/idealized love stories, comedy, parody, ani**mals (especially dogs and horses), science, nature, historical adventure, contemporary teen literature. Characters their own age who have inner doubts about their appearance or their worth; outlaws and others who defy conventions and rules; contemporary social issues (teenagers' family troubles, alcoholism, drugs, divorce), teenage pregnancy, abortion, nuclear power, treatment of deprived and handicapped populations, environmental pollution, and political corruption. May still enjoy fantasy if not at "childish" level (i.e., space stories, game of Dungeons and Dragons, *Lord of the Rings)*. Chivalric deeds or idealistic stories of great sacrifice, heroism, romance, and martyrdom.

Kilmer study (media preferences): boys read comic books and sports magazines, girls read youth magazines and comics; books listed by these authors: Carol R. Brink, Frances Hodgson Burnett, Jack London, Shakespeare, Alfred Lord Tennyson, Charles Dickens, Herman

Young Teenagers

intensely with romanticized models in plays and movies. For girls it is an age of wild crushes on rock stars, singers, actors, athletes, teachers, attractive politicians or others in public view.

3, 4   Emotional state has much to do with peer interaction and response. Is usually more sensitive to peer opinion and approval than to adults', although wants adult approval as well.

3, 4, 5   Physical changes with maturation produce fears and distress associated with awkwardness, lack of mature beauty, skin problems, feelings of difference or unacceptability, male voice change, and the image projected to others. Girls are generally taller and more mature than boys, leading to a high degree of segregation by sex in 7th and 8th grades; groups blend more by 9th grade. Girls are ready for heterosexual social occasions sooner than boys, leading to unequal pressures.

3, 4   Models behavior on that of person most admired. Tries to decide who he really is and tries several "personalities" in a brief time.

1, 3, 4   Anger is stimulated by conflicts with or perceived slights by other people; being teased, people being unfair or bossy, taking things, being lied to. Fears are primarily of social situations at which he will appear disadvantageously. Love object at age 12 is usually peer of the same sex; after puberty it changes to a peer or older person of the opposite sex.

4   This is an age of rebellion and desire for increased independence; much energy is expended figuring ways to avoid adult-imposed rules and sanctions or to assert independence.

1, 4, 5   Youth are increasingly aware of sex as a basis for humor. Innuendos, jokes, or almost any casual remark may be so interpreted. Verbal humor takes on more complex dimensions: puns, hyperbole, satire and parody (*Mad* Magazine). In-group focus leads to making fun of those who are different or are "outsiders."

Melville, Robert Louis Stevenson, J.D. Salinger, Lloyd Douglas, Mary Mitchell, Alex Haley, J. R. R. Tolkein, H. G. Wells, Asimov; they preferred mysteries, adventures, romances, and science fiction. Favorite TV programs were "Saturday Night Live," situation comedies, police dramas, and family dramas. Cinema preferences by both sexes for comedies, adventures, and mysteries; girls expressed preference for musicals and animated features, boys for science fiction.

It must be stressed that any list of teenager interests will vary according to the specific teenage population referred to; economic and environmental factors will shape the subculture in which activities and interests function.

5.   Humor: still responding to visual, physical humor (slapstick perennially popular). Verbal humor now quite sure to be understood as well, so youth is likely to enjoy a performance in a whole new way when he reaches this age; he may hear sexual overtones in dialogue where none were intended.

MORAL/ETHICAL

1   Mostly responding at Kohlberg's Level II: *Conformity* (obeys rules to forestall guilt when censured); very few are responding at Level III: *Principles* (obeying rules to satisfy individual conscience).

1, 4   Rules may be changed by application of democratic processes and are not carved in stone.

1, 3, 4   Idealism is revealed by intense questioning of rules and practices he is forced to follow. He is quick to point out adult inconsistencies. He challenges authorities to defend the rules logically. Is frequently impatient to have the rules changed quickly to accommodate his need.

3, 4, 5   Sexual maturation (average in girls 12-13, in boys 14-15) brings a whole new set of ethical problems: how to reconcile physical urges with social or religious prohibitions and continuing economic dependence.

1, 4   An acute sense of justice and fairness. Indignation against unfairness runs high when punishment is administered to the innocent. Knows wickedness often goes unpunished if one is clever enough not to get caught. Getting caught produces resentment for all those who "got by" with the same offense.

1, 4   While in general the young person feels it is fair to give back the blows one has received, one study found this not true of 13-14 year olds (Graham).

1, 4   Forgiveness, milder punishments, or restitutions to victims and reform of wrongdoers are advocated by those 13 and over who can put themselves in another's place.

The up-to-date student of theatre for children and young people will, of course, never infer from the preceding Profiles that the last word has been said about developmental and other factors that relate to theatre practices. Fortunately, we are in an era of rapidly expanding knowledge in these areas. The Profiles are intended to be only a base line, a body of assumptions, mostly research based, against which additions and alterations may conveniently be made. Nor are the traits and abilities associated with certain ages to be regarded as so definitive that one is absolutely obligated to observe them in selecting dramatic material. Young people enjoy challenges that fall beyond their present abilities. Possibly the profiles can best be used to get an indication of what the present abilities of an age group are presumed to be and how far beyond them one might propose to go in any given production.

Examining Value Systems Inherent in the Plays

What the child or young person gets out of a performance is to a large extent dependent on his stage of physical and intellectual development, the degree of identification and empathy he accords the performers, and the level of attention he is able to give. We must stress that in all probability the young audience member will not be able to verbalize his inferences, nor would we advocate drilling him on the moral of the story either before or after he has seen it in order to ensure that inferences are indeed made. For the audience, meanings are derived naturally through action, story line and distribution of rewards and then lived with, privately if that is the child's wish.

For the producer, however, meanings are an entirely different matter. Only when he is sure what a play is intended to say can he take steps to help youngsters at whatever stage they may be absorb its meanings. If he is to make appropriate choices as he shapes the theatrical work, it is essential that he understand the meanings inherent in it. The following discussion is important for the producer, director, actors, designers and anyone else who needs to understand what a play is all about before proceeding to produce it.

Every play makes thematic statements. As Kenneth Graham pointed out long ago, probably no themes are incomprehensible to children if they are told in terms they can understand and identify with. Themes are likely to be the main unifying principle in imagistic productions presenting material in collage form. In traditional plays the story carries the meaning.

Allegorical Interpretations

All plays are allegorical in that the story represents the working out of a universal principle. Broadly stated, goodness triumphs over evil in most plays for children and young people; and a basic need to experience the workings of justice on a rather obvious level is thereby served. An encouraging development in recent years is the willingness of playwrights to challenge their viewers, particularly the older children, with less simplified or obvious morality concepts. In other words, goodness and rightness are not all that clear cut in the plays with which we more frequently deal today. Since this is true, it is even more essential that we bring a rather acute sense of thematic analysis to our task in order that we will know what we really are saying to the children attending our performances.

Allegory in drama is most clearly shown in the medieval morality plays. In the most famous of these, "Everyman" is faced with the prospect of death, and he pleads with his friends, Beauty, Discretion, Strength, and the Five Wits, to save him. In the appeal process, Everyman discovers some potential allies he never knew he had: Knowledge and Good Deeds; but in the end only his Good Deeds accompany him into the grave. Allegory may be perceived as a battle in which mankind is the field and his soul is the prize. The seven deadly sins — Pride, Gluttony, Greed, Lust, Envy, Wrath, and Sloth — are shown in battle against seven variously identified virtues, such as Humility, Peace, Charity, Benevolence, Temperance, Chastity, and Industry. In pure allegory these forces of good and evil are usually personified as characters in the drama, but seldom with any dimension at all. They possess "tag names" as well, a practice that persists in contemporary drama as a quick identification of the chief trait of each character. In earlier times such plays were literally animated sermons presented to help an illiterate public understand the moral principles the producers (the church and the trade guilds) were trying to impart.

Allegory may also be thought of in terms of a journey or quest. The Everyman character takes leave of his or her home in search of some goal which is equated with a higher plane of existence, however it may be defined in any particular story. The vices and virtues are forces influencing the protagonist's progress. Vice is usually the attractive force, tempting man to give up his eternal soul in exchange for pleasures and indulgences. John Bunyan's *Pilgrim's Progress* is the obvious prototype. Maeterlinck's famous play, *The Blue Bird,* may be seen in the light of such a journey taken by two children, Tyltyl and Mytyl, in search of the blue bird that represents happiness. The episodic nature of this form of allegory is apparent as they encounter a different set of characters at each stop, while a few companions continuously serve as reinforcement and challenge. As in all true allegories of this type, the children return home at the end, wiser, fulfilled, ready to enter a new and higher state of being.[85]

Meanings in plays for children may sometimes be described allegorically as myths of nature. What in religious terms is an exalted state of existence or even life after death may, in a naturalistic interpretation, become the arrival of spring after winter, or dawn after the long dark night. An antagonist in such plays sets out to prevent the reappearance of light or life to this realm of darkness, coldness or apparent death; but a determined protagonist armed with a clearly defined set of virtues and strengths and sometimes aided by some intermediary force manages at the crucial hour to defeat the powers of darkness. A familiar example is the story of the Sleeping Beauty in which an evil fairy representing night or death strikes down the day (in some versions called Princess Aurora) when she reaches her maturity. After a long sleep in which death is only feigned the Princess is awakened by her Prince's kiss to a life of fullness and light. The dawn has arrived after darkness, spring after winter, life after death.

Some plays are capable of sustaining a further extension of allegory into what medieval scholars termed an "anagogical" level of meaning. From this point of view, a quest is always toward "eternal glory," and usually proceeds through a period of intense trial and tribulation, perhaps even to a kind of death and purgatory during which time the Everyman character awaits the intercession of a messianic person, one who performs the required act which brings the hero into a state of grace. Usually one character performs the function of the Devil who seeks the soul of man by whatever devious means. The better versions of Rumpelstiltskin clearly identify Rumpel as a devil figure, conniving to get the soul of man (the first-born of the hapless Miller's daughter and the King); and the Devil is defeated in his infernal plan only when the daughter can call the Devil by his true name. Her purgatory is the suffering that follows Rumpel's demand for the fulfillment of her promise to hand over her child in exchange for spinning the straw into gold; and the servant who chances upon Rumpelstiltskin vainly shouting his name to the skies is the messiah who supplies the Miller's daughter with the answer to the eternal riddle.

In *Steal Away Home* Aurand Harris has written: "My name is Amos Carpenter. On free land is my location, and Heaven is my destination." Having survived the hardships of the underground railroad journey from South Carolina to Pennsylvania, the runaway slave boy could well exult in his deliverance from hell by the intercession of many willing hands. His courage and his cunning as well as the faith and support of his little brother who accompanied him on the journey demonstrate the worthiness of his victory. Rich in allegorical and anagogical meaning, this play begins with a "leavetaking" and ends with a "homecoming;" and it is accompanied throughout by a choir singing spirituals which have always shown a unity between the quest for glory in the hereafter and the struggle for freedom in the here-and-now.

A Freudian View of Fairy Tales

In earlier sections of this chapter we made several references to the work of Bruno Bettelheim whose book, *The Uses of Enchantment,* provides an important stimulant to our thinking about fairy tales. Coming at a time when the fairy tale was, once again, under attack as a dangerous form of literature, when many educators, psychologists, and librarians were stepping up their objections to the violence and gore contained in them, Bettelheim seemed somehow to vindicate the children's theatre repertoire that had from the beginning drawn so heavily upon them. While he undoubtedly had in mind the one-to-one relationship of reading parent to listening child rather than a literal enactment on a stage in the physical presence of the child, with all the means producers have to make the experience immediately alive,[86] it still seems that the basis of his defense of the fairy tale is one we have all felt every time we see a group of children responding enthusiastically to a production. For those of us with a perspective of some years that pleasure never diminishes.

However, Bettelheim is an advocate of the Freudian view; and some of the Freudian implications of dreams and fantasies startle, even shock, many of our colleagues. Intellectually we may be able to entertain the idea that even in very young children sexuality is at the root of many troublesome emotions. But when a similar interpretation is given to fairy tales — well, that goes too far! Surely such thoughts were not intended by the good housewives who told and retold these tales in years gone by!

According to Bettelheim, the whole point of fairy tales is that they concern themselves at base with unmentionable subjects, those deep, guilt-filled wishes and fears which a child dare not discuss with anyone — the things that make a child a monster to himself, a hateful creature, undeserving of the love and care he receives. That, of course, is precisely why reading or seeing these tales enacted can be reassuring and helpful, supplying despicable thoughts with form and substance where the child can see them as well as observe how such problems have a way of working themselves out. Nebulous guilt in a seven-year-old is a traumatic thing, and for generations the fairy tales have quietly served their function of vicarious expiation.

While it is not our purpose to detail the Freudian interpretation of fairy tales that Bettelheim includes in this important work, we shall at least recount the most common motifs contained in such stories as one more insight into analysis of themes.

Rites of passage, or initiation rites, symbolize the death of the former, inadequate self and rebirth of the individual on a higher, more mature plane. Note how similar this idea is to previously described anagogical themes in a religious frame.

A small person who is clever can outwit stupid giants who are too slow, however big and powerful they may be.

By forming a true interpersonal relationship with someone on a mature level one is in a sense avoiding separation anxiety. The ending reunion is not accomplished as the child hoped it would (never to be separated from mother) but it is accomplished in a different way.

One should not expect instant gratification of wishes or desires for revenge. One must learn to be patient. Maturity comes slowly. Persistence is ultimately rewarded. It is all right to dream of getting even some day, but don't kill your rival today.

One can safely feel anger toward, even despise, one's transformed mother (who is now a wicked stepmother or witch) without blame, keeping one's true mother, the essence of kindness and goodness, "inviolate."

The Simpleton or youngest child is the "ignorance of childhood" which is replaced with cleverness and success.

Animal characters represent the animal nature of human beings (i.e., the wolf in Little Red Riding Hood; in Freudian terms, the id). White doves represent the conscience (super ego).[87]

As Bettelheim points out, fairy tales may be read and enjoyed at many stages of one's development, from early childhood to adulthood. Most theatres will produce these tales primarily for the younger set, the six-seven-eights; but all producers know how accompanying adults seem to delight in the play's happenings. Are they merely reliving their childhood, or are they discovering something new?

Studies of Morality in Children's Plays

In 1964, William Kingsley wrote that American authorities of theatre for child audiences customarily encouraged a traditional poetic justice in which obvious right triumphs over obvious wrong, advocated that all endings be happy ones, and recommended that all characters be simplified because children would supposedly be discontented and frustrated by the plays if things were otherwise. Authorities expressed conviction that such playwriting principles guaranteed a safe escape mechanism from real life for the children and would ensure that no harm would come to their growing sense of morality nor to their natural idealism.[88]

Even so, there were already on the boards a few plays for young audiences that did not exactly fit that pristine view. Some rogue protagonists had, in fact, been romping about for some time. Tom Sawyer, Huck Finn, Zar and Zan, and Pinocchio all demonstrated some degree of imperfect behavior. When Reynard the Fox first appeared in the repertoire in 1962, [89] he represented to children a sympathetic, attractive figure who flattered his adversaries shamelessly, "played on their predatory instincts, greed and vanity" to involve them in unpleasant situations, enjoyed playing pranks that were occasionally painful to the victims, and managed to save his life by playing on their gullibility. Furthermore, he was never punished.[90]

An important research study on this play was conducted by Dorothy Edna Aldrich shortly after it was published. About one thousand children of lower socio-economic status from the fourth, fifth and sixth grades of Pittsburgh, Pennsylvania, schools, constituted the experimental group. They were given a pretest to determine their natural attitudes toward prankish behavior performed by a mythical bad boy named Johnny X. After seeing the play, Reynard the Fox, they were tested similarly to determine their attitudes toward the prankish behavior of Reynard. Two months later the children who had seen the play were asked once again to answer the same attitude questionnaire on Johnny X's and Reynard's pranks.

From the data gathered, Aldrich concluded that children's strong tendency to disapprove of bad behavior and to expect such behavior to be punished is reduced somewhat by seeing these actions performed by a sympathetic and attractive character; yet it does not disappear. Disapproval is strongest among younger children and girls. The children had much stronger admiration for Reynard, whom they found likable and attractive, than for Johnny X, whom they did not know personally; and even though a strong majority admired Reynard, they did not want to be like him. Over time the children's sympathy for Reynard diminished sharply; so it appeared as if no important or lasting attitude change occurred as a result of seeing the play.

A marked divergence of opinion occurred between teachers and children regarding the morality of events in another play with a controversial protagonist.[91] Martha Hershey Rhea conducted a study of responses to a production of Dean Wenstrom's Big Klaus and Little Klaus using seventy-five middle grade teachers and one hundred fifth and sixth grade children in Lawrence, Kansas, as subjects.

Analysis of responses to the forty-item questionnaire which utilized a modified semantic differential scale[92] revealed that the early events in the play were judged by both test groups quite evenly in terms of rightness and wrongness; but as the play progressed the teachers applied increasingly traditional moralistic judgments to the actions of Little Klaus, giving them less and less approval. His "pretend" actions at the beginning of the play were transposed into "lying" actions at the end. Teachers approved his "cleverness" early in the play, but were not nearly as supportive of his actions at the end which saved his life. Children, on the other hand, retained their judgment of Little Klaus' lying, both at the beginning and at the end. They consistently approved his positive points. They identified Big Klaus as a bully, and felt he got what he deserved when Little Klaus pushed him over the bridge to his doom. It was on incidents of death that teachers disagreed most sharply with the children. Teachers registered strong disapproval of the "murderous" action by Little Klaus when he switched places in the weighted sack with a Drover who wished to die and go to Heaven; and even though they felt Little Klaus was acting in self defense and that Big Klaus deserved it, he should not have been pushed into the river. Rhea concluded that teachers' responses reflected an ambivalence of judgment which can occur when what one wishes is in conflict with what one has learned is right and proper and just. The children's responses were more definite, clear-cut and consistent. They recognized that what Little Klaus did was not right or proper, but they liked him anyway and realized he was acting in the only way he could to save his own life.[93]

While the characters in Aurand Harris' *Rags to Riches* could hardly be termed controversial, they were, along with an added character, a Street Singer, subjected to scrutiny on moralistic grounds in a study by Robert Landy. The production was given an epic theatre slant at California State University, Northridge, by showing the central action of the Horatio Alger-inspired play through the eyes of an ex-slave who commented upon the themes as they developed.

Landy used a clinical interview technique in the Piaget manner, asking selected questions of his subjects immediately following performances of the play. Ninety-eight audience members took part: seventy-two children between age four and eleven, and twenty-six adults over eighteen years old. The questions were designed to elicit clues about identification with characters (to what extent did the subjects like and/or want to play the role of a certain character?), and about the subjects' interpretation of the action in the scenes.

Identification appeared to occur in four stages, roughly corresponding with Piaget's sensori-motor, pre-operational, concrete operations, and formal operations stages of intellectual development, and with Kohlberg's stages of moral development. Children displaying Stage I development (40% of the four to five-year-olds) typically were unable to relate causes and effects or to interpret scenes, or interpreted them incorrectly. Stage II, representing some 60% of four to seven-year-olds, pointed to identification on the basis of external appearance, acting ability, or carrying out some basic action sequence. Identification at Stage III, 40% of the ten to eleven-year-olds involved in the study, tended to be with characters similar to themselves, those who exhibited conventional adherence to laws of right and wrong "not necessarily related to intentions." Only at Stage IV were the subjects, mostly the adults, able to identify on the basis of "the moral and dramatic validity of a character's actions and intentions." The most difficult scenes for the children to interpret were those involving irony.[94]

Such results, tentative as they are, should certainly encourage more students to work for the broadening of knowledge in these directions. The variety of methods used by Aldrich, Rhea, and Landy demonstrate a range of research techniques that could be expanded and refined. More particularly, such results should give us confidence in our audiences' abilities to see a play of some complexity of character and with some moral ambiguity without racing from the theatre to become criminals. Though they only scratch the surface, these studies have at least focused on the questions raised by Sharon Scoville in her investigation of the rogue protagonist: (1) Do the children identify with him? (2) Do they like him and what he does? and (3) Would they have acted the same way in certain circumstances?[95]

Apparent Influences of Television Viewing

Even when it doesn't try, television is an enormously effective teacher. Throughout much of this chapter we have pointed out influences of television viewing on rates of cognitive, linguistic, and moral development as well as on interests and behavior which could be far advanced from what would normally be expected for a given age. When a deliberate effort is made to educate, and millions in federal and foundation funds are infused in the project, television proves to be even more successful. "Sesame Street," "The Electric Company," and "Mister Roger's Neighborhood" have been thoroughly studied and found to have a positive effect on young children's cognitive development and on growth of desirable social skills such as task persistence, rule obedience and tolerance of delay.[96] These programs have proved the medium capable of breaking down racial stereotypes as well; and other studies have demonstrated that specially produced programs can break down stereotypic ideas related to sex-appropriate occupations.[97] However, less attention seems to have been paid to matters of attitudes, concentration patterns, and appreciations which probably have a carry-over effect into other audience situations.

There is some speculation that children who see a great deal of television expect the same degree of visual focus on significant happenings and the same time segmentation when they come to a theatre performance. The camera's ability to zoom in for a close-up view of a face, a hand action, or even a significant object in the setting is an advantage the theatre does not possess as a means of centering attention. As we know, young children's perceptions of art objects, whether in the gallery or in the theatre, tend to focus naturally on the big areas or possibly on insignificant details simply because they are attractive in some way. There is less chance of that happening in a well directed television program. And, of course, advertisers and others are well aware of how long at an interval children of various ages will focus their attention on something before showing signs of distraction. Episodes in programs such as "Sesame Street" are carefully timed to retain concentration for a brief period, then switch to something deliberately contrasting. "Releases" are built in as well, allowing for a calculated interval of squirming and readjusting. This pattern, adapted successfully by many children's programs, has spawned a counterpart on our stages through the many kinds of theatre events that do not tell a single sequential story. Children appear to recognize the format and feel perfectly at home with such programs. Producers who continue to present the more traditional plays increasingly remark on the need to account for television-induced attention spans.

In spite of the generally realistic environment created for most young children's television — "Sesame Street" looks like a street; "Mister Roger's Neighborhood" is centered in a living room — shows for older children introduce them to theatricalized environments, abstract settings and stylized production. Whether or not they actually prefer these modifications of realism, children certainly get acquainted with them early, and this is an advantage when they encounter them in the theatre.

Television presents another challenge to theatre producers. Literally nothing by way of marvelous, magical or extra-terrestrial effect is impossible through video technology. When children come to see *Starman Jones* in the theatre, they may expect to see the *Star Wars* epic reenacted in all its billion dollar screen wizardry. Producers may choose to invite comparison by designing a show with similar sensational effects, or they may choose to emphasize the unique and advantageous features of theatre, especially the proximity of actor and audience. If they are tried, tricks of staging must be technically flawless to be anything but laughable to today's children.

Large investments have been made in this country and elsewhere to try to ascertain the relationship between violence in society and violence portrayed in the media, especially television. As the average child watches television three or four hours a day, he may witness an unreasonably high number of violent and aggressive acts which, according to social learning theorists, teach him that these are the ways people solve their problems. In experiments, children were placed in situations comparable to a model where they were given a mild frustration stimulus and opportunity to respond. Bandura's now classic studies demonstrated that young children imitated the models' aggressive acts almost exactly.[98] As the 1972 Report to the Surgeon General conceded, "Imitation of observed violence is assumed to be already established experimentally."[99]

Diligent research has refined our knowledge of conditions regulating imitation of observed aggression. Children already rated high in aggression are more susceptible to aggressive modeling. Preschoolers observed by Friedrich and Stein demonstrated that initially high aggressors exposed to "natural" programming of violent content failed to produce exact imitation, although they exhibited less tolerance of delay, less task persistence, and less rule obedience as well as showing more aggressiveness toward their peers.[100] It has been more difficult to show a clear relationship between modeled aggression and actual aggressive behavior in older children, although there is an apparent tie between a child's preference for violent programs and his own aggressiveness.[101] Bandura has proposed that children imitate aggressive models because they have been shown how to do it and because identification with the aggressive model tends to break down tenuously established inhibitions. Unless environmental conditions or fear of punishment intercede, the child is likely to repeat the newly learned action.[102]

Apparently it makes little difference to a young child what the reason for the violent action is. The action itself is what is imitated.[103] Seeing the aggressor character punished seems to reduce the tendency to imitate, although there is also some evidence that the child may have succeeded in learning the very act for which the aggressor was punished.[104] Still unresolved are questions of the roles of *catharsis* and consciousness of unreality. Does viewing televised violence reduce inner tensions and aggressive tendencies resulting in less aggressive behavior as Feshbach and Singer reported with institutionalized teenagers? And do those programs which are unreal in a recognizable way produce less aggressive imitation as maintained by Himmelweit and Oppenheim?[105]

Extensive research being conducted at such places as Harvard University's Project Zero and Kansas University's Center for Research on the Influences of Television on Children (CRITC) is producing a sizable literature that goes far beyond the matter of TV violence. It focuses on such general questions as apprehension of content, comparative strength of auditory and visual stimuli in determining retention, and attention patterns and comprehension as affected by formal features such as pace, movement, change, novelty, cuts and zooms. According to Jeanne Klein, much of this research has potential application to theatre for children in its methodology as well as in its substantive conclusions.[106]

Even larger questions are raised by Neil Postman in his provocative work, *The Disappearance of Childhood*. For example, is television in effect doing away with the necessity to regard children as a separate class of human being, and, if so, can anything be done to arrest the move?[107] Since we are in no position to supply answers, we shall only ponder the premises, continuing to apply our best efforts to keep the living theatre a vital part of children's total cultural milieu.

DE FACTO CENSORSHIP

Playwrights, producers, and sponsors have seemed to engage in a tug-of-war as to whose work was more susceptible to a *de facto* censorship. Playwrights appeared to be working from a list of restrictions, subjects they must not treat, words they must not use, motivations they must not suggest. Producers refused to mount certain plays because audiences or school systems would object if this concept or that action were actually shown on stage. Sponsors carefully checked out scripts and actual productions for objectionable material, sometimes making absence of potentially offensive material their sole criterion for selection of a company.

Several conditions contribute to an absence of complete freedom for all who work in this field. We exist as part of a social and educational system that is undergoing constant change as it is shaped by new discoveries and responds to a multitude of political pressures. Our own wish to be unhampered by economic necessities may suddenly be set aside when a sponsor cancels bookings because of a play's content. A formidable public outcry against showing children scenes of violence may cause a producer to change his plans in midstream. Pressures from feminist groups, the NAACP, the Native American Society, or any number of other organizations advocating worthy causes may affect what playwrights write and producers produce. Sensitivity to the total social-political ambience of the community will certainly determine what sponsors will sponsor. None of us is really free of this kind of influence on our work, and it does constitute a form of censorship.

Potential censors can appear from any quarter at any time, as we well know. We are familiar with what was done to fairy tales by publishers in the Thirties, and how writers such as Pickard and Joseph have continued the attack into our own time. Very vocal these days are groups advocating the abolition of sexism in all of children's literature and children's television programs. A few years back great advances were made in elimination of racial stereotypes in the same media. Environmentalists, Zero Population Growth, and many other groups seek ways to get their messages across and their principles adopted by those who have influence on children and their developing attitudes. However valid the causes may be, we must be alert to ensure that wholesale adoption of them does not lead our productions into the abyss of didacticism.

We would suggest that in our child view the best interests of the art form are served by playwrights and creators who dare to push back horizons, assailing ancient restrictions in the light of an intimate knowledge of contemporary children's actual environment and cultural melieu. They are served by producers who dare to stage the challenging play or theatre piece, using good taste and informed artistic judgment as their main restrictions, again from the baseline of a thorough knowledge of children derived from observation, study, and never-ending personal research. Finally they are served by sponsors who are willing to be part of this new atmosphere in children's and youth theatre, anxious to assail old barriers and chart new courses in their communities rather than just holding the line. Quality must be assessed in many ways, the least of them being the degree to which a production is unlikely to ruffle feathers.

And if this discussion of children can tell us anything at all, let it be that we have a mandate to err on the side of stretching rather than on the side of underestimation.

NOTES

[1]Albert Bandura, *Social Learning Theory* (Englewood Cliffs, NJ: Prentice-Hall, 1977), pp. 11-12.

[2]B. F. Skinner, *Beyond Freedom and Dignity* (New York: Alfred A. Knopf, 1971); Erich Fromm, *The Anatomy of Human Destructiveness* (New York: Holt, Rinehart and Winston, 1973), p. 34.

[3]Bandura, p. 203.

[4]Langdon E. Longstreth, *Psychological Development of the Child,* 2nd ed. (New York: Ronald Press, 1974), pp. 323-24.

[5]Ruth M. Beard, *An Outline of Piaget's Developmental Psychology* (New York: Basic Books, 1969), and Molly Brearley and Elizabeth Hitchfield, *A Guide to Reading Piaget* (New York: Schocken Books, 1966), furnished the basis for this compendium.

[6]Bandura, p. 20; Joachim F. Wohlwill, *The Study of Behavioral Development* (New York and London: Academic Press, 1973), p. 295; Milly Almy, *Young Children's Thinking* (New York: Teachers College Press, 1966), p. v. The advisability of such acceleration is seriously questioned by Raymond S. Moore, Dorothy N. Moore *et al., School Can Wait* (Provo, Utah: Brigham Young University Press, 1979).

[7]Beard, pp. 64-65; Jean Piaget, *The Language and Thought of the Child,* trans. Marjorie Cabin of 2nd ed. (1930) (New York: New American Library, 1974), p. 148.

[8]Beard, p. 63.

[9]Beard, p. 77.

[10]Piaget, p. 188.

[11]Bandura, pp. 42, 175.

[12]Piaget, pp. 178-80.

[13]Beard, p. 105.

[14]Douglas Graham, *Moral Learning and Development* (London: B. T. Batsford, Ltd., 1972), pp. 118-19.

[15]Brearley and Hitchfield, p. 118.

[16]Bandura, p. 183.

[17]Almy, p. 9.

[18]Beard, p. 89.

[19]Beard, p. 75.

[20]Brearley and Hitchfield, p. 71.

[21]Brearley and Hitchfield, p. 74.

[22]Brearley and Hitchfield, p. 99.

[23]Beard, p. 108; Brearley and Hitchfield, p. 10.

[24]Bandura, p. 66.

[25]Arthur T. Jersild, "Emotional Development," in *Manual of Child Psychology,* ed. Leonard Carmichael (New York: John Wiley & Sons, 1954), pp. 833-34. Skinner (p. 16 *et passim*) emphasizes "contingencies" in the environment rather than "feelings" as a behavior determinant.

[26]Jersild, p. 902

[27]Roy T. Tamashiro, "A Developmental View of Children's Humor," *Elementary School Journal,* 80 (Nov. 1979), 68-75.

[28]Martha Wolfenstein, *Children's Humor* (Glencoe, Ill.: The Free Press, 1954), p. 12.

[29]Wolfenstein, p. 93.

[30]Wolfenstein, p. 127. Such a response to the death of Joe in Harris' *Steal Away Home* may be explained in this way.

[31]Wolfenstein, pp. 64, 66; Jersild, p. 903.

[32]Wolfenstein, pp. 13, 52, 196, 201.

[33]Jersild, p. 893.

[34]P. M. Pickard, *I Could a Tale Unfold* (New York: The Humanities Press, 1961). p. 5.

[35]Bandura, p. 62. Skinner (p. 26) describes avoidance of "aversive" treatment entirely without reference to the fear emotion. It is simply an explainable behavior.,

[36]Bruno Bettelheim, *The Uses of Enchantment: The Meaning and Importance of Fairy Tales* (New York: Alfred A. Knopf, 1976), p. 145.

[37]Jersild, pp. 865-66.

[38]Jersild, p. 863.

[39]Jersild, p. 867.

[40]Lawrence Kohlberg, "Development of Moral Character," in *Review of Child Development Research*, eds. Martin L. Hoffman and Lois Wladis Hoffman (New York: Russell Sage Foundation, 1964), p. 385.

[41]Stephen M. Joseph, *Children in Fear* (New York: Holt, Rinehart and Winston, 1974) pp. xii, xiii, xv.

[42]Jersild, pp. 883-87.

[43]Konrad Lorenz, *On Aggression,* trans. Marjorie Kerr Wilson (New York: Harcourt, Brace and World, 1963), p. 28; Fromm, pp. 1, 2, 16. Skinner, too (p. 27), acknowledged man's tendency to attack "those who crowd us or annoy us" or who are unwanted "controllers."

[44]Robert Ardrey, *African Genesis* (New York: Atheneum Publishers, 1961) and *The Territorial Imperative* (New York: Atheneum Publishers, 1966); Fromm, p. 114.

[45]Fromm, p. 42.

[46]Fromm, p. 4 *et passim.*

[47]Seymour Feshbach and Robert D. Singer, *Television and Aggression: An Experimental Field Study* (San Francisco: Jossey-Bass, 1971).

[48]Karl Menninger, *The Crime of Punishment* (New York: The Viking Press, 1969), pp. 267-70.

[49]Aletha Huston Stein and Lynette Kohn Freidrich, *Impact of Television on Children* (Chicago: University of Chicago Press, 1975), p. 6.

[50]Fromm, p. 216.

[51]Jersild, pp. 860-61.

[52]Kohlberg, pp. 384, 387.

[53]Kohlberg, p. 425.

[54]Bandura, p. 43.

[55]Graham, p. 207.

[56]Longstreth, p. 529; Kohlberg, p. 395.

[57]Beard, p. 80; Graham, p. 210.

[58]Brearley and Hitchfield, pp. 132-38.

[59]Beard, p. 107.

[60]Longstreth, p. 532.

[61]Beard, p. 118.

[62]Graham, p. 221.

[63]Bettelheim, pp. 143-44; 147.

[64]Longstreth, pp. 533-34; Beard, p. 81; Graham, p. 14; Brearley and Hitchfield, pp. 120-21, 128.

[65]Kohlberg, p. 400, with modifications from Longstreth, p. 537.

[66]Longstreth, p. 537.

[67]Longstreth, p. 538.

[68]Bandura, pp. 42-44.

[69]Longstreth, p. 542; Bandura, p. 155; Graham, p. 15; Kohlberg, pp. 386, 392, 408.

[70]Kohlberg, p. 413.

[71]Kohlberg, pp. 391-92. Skinner (p. 65) generally supports this premise, but he would add the condition of consciously restructuring "contingencies" to support desired behavior.

[72]Bandura, pp. 42, 46, 49.

[73]Bettelheim, p. 5.

[74]David Elkind, "Preschool Education: Enrichment or Instruction?" in *Early Childhood Education*, ed. Bernard Spodek (Englewood Cliffs, N.J.: Prentice-Hall, 1973), p. 110.

[75]Kenneth B. Clark, *A Possible Reality* (New York: Metropolitan Applied Research Center, 1972), p. 7.

[76]Moore and Moore, pp. 18-20.

[77]Clark, p. 74; Longstreth, p. 240.

[78]Clark, pp. 68-75.

[79]Jerome S. Bruner, *The Process of Education* (Cambridge, Mass.: Harvard University Press, 1962), p. 33.

[80]Elkind, p. 113.

[81]Moore and Moore, p. 129; Longstreth, p. 251.

[82]Beard, p. 55; Moore and Moore, p. 24.

[83]The "Developmental and Other Bases" sections of these Profiles are compiled from the sources cited in the previous discussions of cognitive, spatial, emotional and moral development. We drew most heavily on the works by Almy, Bandura, Beard, Bettelheim, Brearley and Hitchfield, Graham, Jersild, Kohlberg, Longstreth, Piaget, Tamashiro, Wohlwill, and Wolfenstein. In addition, acknowledgement is made to the following works: Viktor Lowenfeld and W. Lambert Brittain, *Creative and Mental Growth,* 6th ed. (New York: Macmillan Publ. Co., 1975); Gordon S. Plummer, *Children's Art Judgment* (Dubuque, IA: Wm. C. Brown Co., 1974).

[84]The "Child As Audience Member" sections of these Profiles are developed from the works mentioned in Note 83 plus the following sources: Patricia Melody, "Children's Interests in Story Content for Children's Theatre," Thesis Kansas 1967; Mariam Alexanian Duckwall, "Children's Interests in Stories," Michigan State University, n.d. (mimeographed); Paulette Kilmer, "Theatre and Self-Esteem in Teenagers," Thesis Kansas 1980; Thomas Behm, "Elements of Style in Scene Design," Thesis Kansas 1967; Gayle Cornelison, "Preferences of Children for Saturated Colors and Tints," Thesis Kansas 1965; Clayton Crenshaw, "Color Association in Costume Design," Thesis Kansas 1967; Gayle Cornelison, "Death and Childhood," Diss. Kansas 1975; *Television and Growing Up: The Impact of Televised Violence,* Report to the Surgeon General, United States Public Health Service (Washington, D.C.: GPO, 1972).

[85]Sellina Machiach, "Allegory in Children's Theatre and Drama," Diss. Kansas 1975. In addition to *The Blue Bird* she discusses allegorical implications in four contemporary children's plays.

[86]Suzan L. Zeder, "The Misuses of Enchantment: Another Look at Bettelheim," *Children's Theatre Review,* 27 (Spring 1979), 4-5.

[87]Bettelheim (motifs in order), pp. 35, 179; p. 27; p. 11; pp. 33, 52; p. 69; pp. 76, 102.

[88]William H. Kingsley, "Happy Endings, Poetic Justice and Strength of Characterization in American Children's Drama: A Critical Analysis," Diss. Pittsburgh 1964, p. 85.

[89]Pickard, p. 104, notes that the story of Reynard was already centuries old when it was first published in 1481. The script referred to here is by Arthur Fauquez (New Orleans: Anchorage Press).

[90]Dorothy Edna Aldrich, "A Study of Child Audience Reaction to a Controversial Character in a Children's Play," Thesis Pittsburgh 1965, p. 14.

[91]This play was later withdrawn from the Anchorage Press catalogue.

[92]In a pilot study conducted on a production of *Peter Pan* at the University of Kansas the semantic differential showed considerable promise as a measuring tool to determine attitude shifts of upper grade children. For basic information on the semantic differential see Charles E. Osgood, et al., *The Measurement of Meaning* (Urbana: University of Illinois Press, 1957), and R. G. Smith, "A Semantic Differential for Theatre Concepts," *Speech Monographs* 28 (1961), 1-8.

[93]Martha Hershey Rhea, "A Comparison of Children's and Adults' Attitudes Toward an Imperfect Protagonist in a Children's Play," Thesis Kansas 1970.

[94]Robert J. Landy, "Measuring Audience Response to Characters and Scenes in Theatre for Children," *Children's Theatre Review,* XXVI, 3 (1977), 10-13; Robert J. Landy and Luis Joyce-Moniz, "A Developmental Study of Dramatic Identification," TS, n.d.

[95]Sharon L. Scoville, "The Rogue as a Children's Theatre Protagonist," Thesis Kansas 1963.

[96]Lynette Kohn Friedrich and Aletha Huston Stein, "Aggressive and Prosocial Television Programs and the Natural Behavior of Children," *Monographs of the Society for Research in Child Development,* Serial N. 151, 38 (August 1973), 57; Jan Perney *et al.,* "TV Viewing and Early School Achievement," *Phi Delta*

Kappan 59 (May 1978), 637.

[97]"Attitude Shaping: Kiddie TV Keeps Women Workers in Their Place," *Human Behavior,* 7 (Dec. 1978), 46; Frederick Williams, Robert LaRose, and Frederica Frost, *Children, Television, and Sex-Role Stereotyping* (New York: Praeger Publishers, 1981).

[98]Albert Bandura, Dorothea Ross, and Sheila A. Ross, "Imitation of Film-Mediated Aggressive Models," *Journal of Abnormal Psychology,* 66 (1963), 7.

[99]*Television and Growing Up,* p. 10; a five-volume supplement contains the research reports on which the report to the Surgeon General is based.

[100]Friedrich and Stein, pp. 56, 58.

[101]Aletha Huston Stein and Lynette Kohn Friedrich, "Television Content and Young Children's Behavior," in *Television and Social Behavior*: Reports and Papers, Vol. II (A Technical Report to the Surgeon General), (Washington, D.C.: GPO, 1972), p. 203.

[102]Stein and Friederich, *Impact of Television . . .,* p. 6; Bandura, *Social Learning Theory,* p. 39.

[103]Stein and Friederich, *Impact of Television . . .,* pp. 35-38.

[104]Bandura, *Social Learning Theory,* p. 122; Longstreth, p. 550.

[105]Hilde T. Himmelweit, A.N. Oppenheim, and Pamela Vince, *Television and the Child* (London: Oxford University Press, 1958), p. 38; Feshbach and Singer.

[106]Jeanne Klein, "Understanding Your Audience from Television Research with Children," paper, Kansas Conference on Theatre for Young Audiences: Principles and Strategies for the Future, Lawrence, 17 Oct. 1986.

[107]New York: Delacorte Press, 1982. Postman's address: "The Disappearance of Childhood," was the Sara Spencer Event at the 1982 CTAA convention and was subsequently published in *Children's Theatre Review,* XXXII, 1 (1983), 19-23.

(Left): Participation Theatre for Young Children: MAGICAL FACES (Way) — University of Wisconsin-Madison, 1978.

(Top Right): THE LEGEND OF SLEEPY HOLLOW (Gaines) — Eastern Michigan University Theatre of the Young, 1975.

84   (Bottom Right): THE 500 HATS OF BARTHOLOMEW CUBBINS (Seuss, Mason) — Children's Theatre Company and School, Minneapolis, 1980.

(Top): THE ICE WOLF (Kraus) — CSU-Hayward, 1972.

(Bottom Left): RIP VAN WINKLE (Ruthenburg) — Arizona State University, 1975.

(Bottom Right): The Grasshopper from THE BUTTERFLY (Mofid) — Everyman Players, 1978-80.

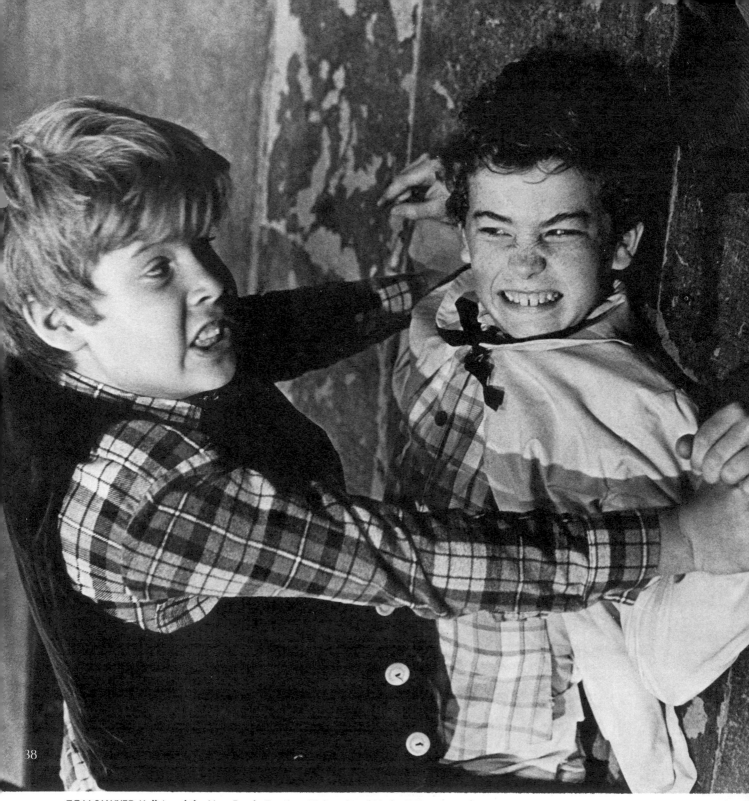

TOM SAWYER (Adix) and the New Boy in Town — University of Utah, 1969.

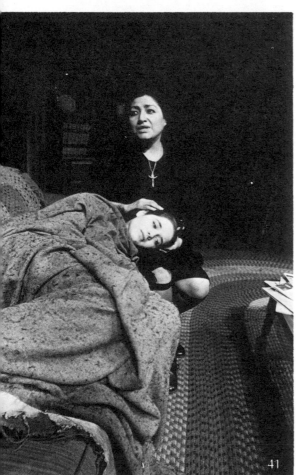

(Top Left): MAGGIE MAGALITA (Kesselman) at the Kennedy Center — Carole Huggins production for Kennedy Center, 1980.

(Top Right): STEP ON A CRACK (Zeder) — University of Wisconsin-Madison, 1980.

(Bottom Left): MAGGIE MAGALITA (Kesselman) — Carole Huggins production for Kennedy Center, 1980.

(Bottom Right): THE MIRACLE WORKER (Gibson) — Empire State Youth Theatre Institute, SUNY, 1980.

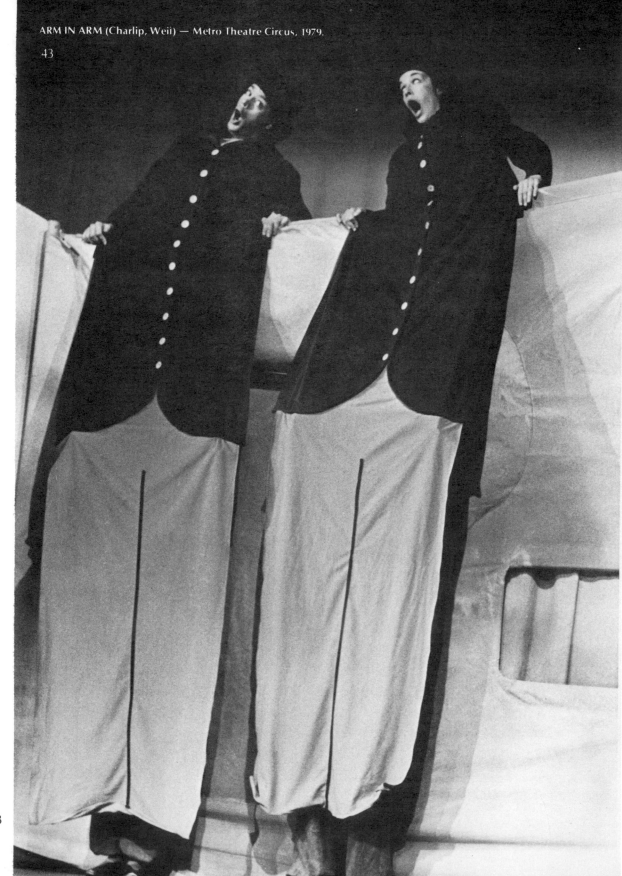

ARM IN ARM (Charlip, Weil) — Metro Theatre Circus, 1979.

43

44

45

89

PREVIOUS PAGE

(Top): Children's Theatre Festivals in Southern California Settings: CARNIVAL OF THE ANIMALS — Betsy Brown Puppeteers, Los Angeles Festival, 1976.

(Bottom): PETER PAN (Barrie) — Theatre for Young People, University of North Carolina-Greensboro, 1976.

(Top Left): Audience Participation with Yellow Brick Road Shows' THE HUMBLE KING (collaboratively adapted), 1976-77.

(Top Right): Classic Comedy, THE BIRDS (Aristophanes, Biroc), adapted to environmental theatre — CSU-Northridge, 1977.

(Bottom Left): Yellow Brick Road Shows' Participatory FOOL OF THE WORLD (Urquhart and Grossberg), 1980.

(Bottom Right): Yellow Brick Road Shows' Participatory NIGHTINGALE (Urquhart and Grossberg), 1980.

(Top): GOOD MORNING, MR. TILLIE (Donoahue) — Children's Theatre Company and School, Minneapolis, 1979.

(Bottom Left): Children's Theatre Festivals in Southern California Settings: KID'S WRITES (Mairs) — Magic Carpet Theatre Co., Los Angeles Festival, 1976.

(Bottom Right): Authentic Period Costume as Principal Visual Element: A BOY CALLED TOM SAWYER (Schneider) — CSU-Northridge, 1980.

91

CHAPTER IV
AN EXPANDING REPERTOIRE

Theatre for young audiences is growing up.

Like most growth, its patterns are not entirely consistent. All limbs are not maturing at the same rate. Some arms are still playing at being bunny rabbits and writing "new scripts" to support themselves; others are playing with advanced ethical concepts and value systems that even adults have some trouble accepting. *Pinkie and the Fairies* is still with us, of course; but so is *Special Class*. In addition to the "camp" plays and musicals that seek to parody familiar children's stories and dramas there are the delicious romps of Alan Cullen, Nicholas Stuart Gray, and Mary Melwood. The producer of today surely has quite a respectable storehouse on which to draw for his scripts and there is good reason for optimism.

GREATER FREEDOM FOR PLAYWRIGHTS

Happily for children everywhere, a new freedom has been proclaimed throughout the profession. Less and less we hear that certain things must never be done for children. Playwrights have increasingly asserted their prerogative to write plays reflecting their own critical powers and sensibilities rather than dramatic exercises conforming to an unstated but nonetheless operative list of rules.

The new freedom appeared to be asserted simultaneously by playwrights, publishers and producers. The Sixties heard a general cry for a repertoire of plays worthy of young people — one that would in some way contribute to their preparation to meet the great social, humanitarian and scientific challenges of the complex and demanding decades ahead.

Many plays written in the last twenty years are recognizable by their apparent faith in children to comprehend and handle a wider scope of subjects treated in a much greater range of styles than we previously thought possible. We have seen how an experimental spirit prevailed as the Sixties and Seventies unfolded in a social climate of violence, hypocrisy and distrust on an unprecedented scale. Writers and producers realized that children who lived through the gory details of this upheaval every evening in front of their television sets, if not, indeed, on their own streets, could philosophically cope with plays of considerable depth. They would need help sorting out many sides of big questions, help to see degrees of rightness and wrongness, help to keep perspective on the apparent disruption and chaos all about them. Even the matter of death, seemingly forever banished from young audience stages, called out for reconsideration and treatment. Challenges to a morality structure thought to be sacrosanct by earlier generations began to present our playwrights with a whole new set of questions requiring answers.

The complex roots of the ideological changes accompanying the new wave of playwriting for children and youth have been examined in Chapter II. While some of those influences gave rise to experimentation in non-scripted theatrical styles beyond the scope of the present chapter, plays written by playwrights appropriately continue to be central to the life of the theatre for children and youth. They are the literature of the field. The new spirit of freedom, generated in all experimental forums, has had a highly desirable effect on the published repertoire; and it is the existing repertoire that we propose to examine in this chapter.

TYPES OF SCRIPTS

Classifying anything as complex as playscripts is always fraught with problems. Still, it seems that some terminology could be useful if it allows us to identify and discuss characteristics such as content and style.

In addition to the traditional categories of *tragedy, comedy, melodrama, farce,* and their many subdivisions, plays for young audiences are usually identified with terms indicating general subject matter, relative longevity and status, and style of presentation.

Subject Matter

Early publications in the field popularized a classification scheme that identified a play primarily according to its story content. A play was a *fantasy or fairy tale,* an *adventure,* a *romance,* a *historical* play or a *modern* (sometimes a *modern realistic*) play. Another early designation was a *favorite story,* signifying that the play was based on a published and popular work of literature and that its content was very likely one of the types mentioned. A subdivision of the first grouping called *original fantasy* was introduced in the Sixties to distinguish traditional fairy tale adaptations from plays not derived from other sources. A further subdivision occurred later with the category of *animal play,* a term that gained some credence even though one so classified could have found itself in at least one other category as well. The term *today play,* inherited from the Russian children's theatre during the Sixties, was used interchangeably with *modern* to denote everyday, real characters encountering contemporary problems.

Longevity and Status

The term *classic* in the repertoire of theatre for young audiences has been used in various ways. Presumably a classic is a work of art that has withstood the test of time and exemplifies the first rank of quality. It has been applied, perhaps most accurately, to adaptations of Greek comedies; but it has also been applied to plays of Shakespeare, Moliere, the medieval farces and other plays of the classic adult repertoire that are finding their way in shortened and edited form into the young people's theatre.

Classic is also beginning to mean scripts that have arrived in some special way into that exalted state. Landmarks recognizable from at least a three-quarter century's perspective are such plays as Barrie's *Peter Pan,* Maeterlinck's *The Blue Bird,* Goodman's *Treasure Island,* White's *Snow White and the Seven Dwarfs,* Chorpenning's *The Emperor's New Clothes,* Miller's *The Land of the Dragon,* and even such recent candidates as Fauquez' *Reynard the Fox* and Harris' *Androcles and the Lion.* Such plays have been known and loved by millions of young people and continue to be produced regularly.[1]

Styles of Presentation

Another set of terms describing the young people's theatre repertoire developed as the inadequacies of the old set became apparent. These terms denote style of presentation rather than content. They include such designations as *traditional scripts, opera, musicals, participation theatre or drama* (sometimes called *involvement drama*), and *story theatre.* Throughout our discussion of those styles, and indeed, throughout this chapter, our listing of plays and playwrights is intended to be illustrative rather than inclusive.

A STYLISTIC EXPLOSION

Not too many years ago, Sara Spencer, the late editor of the Anchorage Press, wrote that there were perhaps a hundred good plays for young audiences in print. At that time her remark had to apply only to playscripts of the traditional kind — those developing a single dramatic story line that were meant to be presented on proscenium or arena stages where audiences were expected to respond vicariously rather than actively — for those were just about all that existed. While today's repertoire is vastly augmented with the addition of other styles, there has been a sufficient increase in the number, quality and dimensions of traditional scripts to let us know that the form continues to flourish.

Traditional Scripts

The playscripts of Charlotte Chorpenning can be perceived as the core of the early traditional repertoire for young audiences. Chronologically, her work at the Goodman Theatre signaled the end of the beginning phases of development. From her pen came a body of scripts, over thirty in number, that served the growing field and provided impetus for a newer generation of playwrights to try its wings.

Earlier in the century a handful of playscripts served the need. *The Forest Ring* by deMille and Bernard was an early favorite, as were Frances Hodgson Burnett's familiar *Racketty-Packetty House* and *The Little Princess*. Another Burnett classic, *Little Lord Fauntleroy*, enjoyed a recent television revival that belied its 1880's origins. Pirated and authorized versions of *Tom Sawyer* and *The Prince and the Pauper* forever established Mark Twain's identification with the movement. Constance D'Arcy Mackay's *The Silver Thread* and Cornelia Meigs' *Helga and the White Peacock* were both produced regularly. Jules Eckert Goodman's *Treasure Island*, Alice Gerstenberg's *Alice in Wonderland*, Marian DeForest's *Little Women*, and Jessie Braham White's *Snow White and the Seven Dwarfs*, all achieved popularity before 1920. Stage versions of the Oz stories began appearing in 1904 with L. Frank Baum's own musical *Wizard*; but Elizabeth Fuller Goodspeed's *The Land of Oz*, published in 1928, was more widely presented by amateur groups. By the time Clare Tree Major began adding her adaptations of fairy tales and favorite stories to the existing repertoire in the 30's there was a recognizable body of scripts available for producers to select from.

But it was Chorpenning who really produced the base for the repertoire of the 30's, 40's and 50's. Such plays as *The Emperor's New Clothes, Cinderella, Jack and the Beanstalk, The Sleeping Beauty, The Adventures of Tom Sawyer, The Indian Captive* and *Hansel and Gretel* are a reminder of how conscious she was of the drawing power of familiar titles. Many, of course, are still produced. In fact one, *Rumpelstiltskin*, continues to enjoy great popularity. A summary of this play should serve to exemplify the older traditional repertoire.

At the beginning Rumpelstiltskin is seen dancing diabolically around his pot at "The Edge of the World," shouting his name and displaying consummate vanity, arguing with Mother Hulda about how he can get control of the hearts of men and rule the world. To succeed he must have a king's baby to put in his pot, but to get one he must trick some unwary maid into making an unlikely promise. Opportunely a Miller's Daughter is about to be put into an impossible situation by her proud father and mother who brag to the King that their daughter can spin straw into gold. The greedy King promises that she shall marry his Son if this is indeed true. If not, she dies. In Act Two the evil dwarf twice exacts tokens in exchange for spinning the gold from straw, but the third time a promise is demanded: her first born child after she is Queen. This too is given and the gold is once more spun. In Act Three a year has passed and the court is busy tending the new-born prince when Rumpel arrives to collect his promised child. To her tearful pleading he strikes another bargain. If she can guess his name he will release her from the promise. In the final moments of a world-wide search the Daughter herself chances upon the evil man shouting his name to the skies. Over the innocent baby's cradle, the Daughter calmly asks, "Is your name, perhaps, Rumpelstiltskin?" Enraged, the dwarf flies to pieces, and the play ends.

Chorpenning's collaborations introduced additional playwrights such as Nora McAlvay *(The Elves and the Shoemaker)* and Anne Nicholson *(The Magic Horn of Charlemagne)*, both of whom provided more scripts on their own. Several close associates were probably influenced by her as well. James Norris, her son-in-law, gave us popular versions of *Hiawatha, Robin Hood* and *Aladdin and the Wonderful Lamp*. Geraldine Brain Siks' *Marco Polo* and *The Nuremberg Stove*, among others, established her as an important contributor to the field. Martha Bennett King's output, begun in the 40's, includes such titles as *A Christmas Carol, The Snow Queen and the Goblin, Peter, Peter, Pumpkin Eater, Riddle Me Ree* and *Space Harp*.

But a growing number of plays in the traditional mold continued to flow from the pens of contemporaries and near-contemporaries quite independently of Mrs. Chorpenning. Rosemary Musil, almost alone in treating modern subjects, gave us "Hurricane Island," *Five Little Peppers, Mystery at the Old Fort,* and *The Ghost of Mr. Penny.* Sara Spencer used her own *Tom Sawyer* as one of the four original titles on which the Children's Theatre Press, now the Anchorage Press, was founded in 1935, later adding her *Little Women* to an expanding playlist. *Tom Sawyer* remained in the "top ten" as of 1978. Margery Evernden, actively writing since the 50's, has contributed a large body of scripts to the repertoire including *The King of the Golden River* and *King Arthur's Sword.* William Glennon, a prolific playwright, has authored versions of many of the famous tales including *Aladdin, Beauty and the Beast* and *The Pied Piper.* Original fantasies such as *Greensleeves' Magic* and *Timblewit* combine with fresh adaptations of traditional tales such as *Beauty of the Dreaming Wood* in the total offerings of Marian Jonson. Faye Parker is best known for her lively accounts of the childhood and youth of famous personages in such plays as *Young Ben — Franklin's Fight For Freedom, Young Stephen Foster* and *Tom Edison and the Wonderful "Why".* Kristin Sergel's *Winnie-the-Pooh* is at the top of most popularity lists.

Two well known playwrights, Madge Miller and Aurand Harris, hold special places in the annals of American theatre for young audiences since their work demonstrates a bridge from the older traditional modes to the new.

Like Chorpenning, Madge Miller had the opportunity to test her scripts in actual production. Working closely with the Pittsburgh Children's Theatre and the Knickerty Knockerty Players, she composed her well known versions of *Pinocchio, Puss in Boots, Robinson Crusoe* and *Snow White and Rose Red,* all called Miniature Plays, and appearing in a single volume under that title. She also wrote popular versions of *The Pied Piper of Hamelin* and *The Princess and the Swineherd.* But her greatest successes were with *Hansel and Gretel, The Unwicked Witch* (her most recent publication), *Alice in Wonderland,* and above all, *The Land of the Dragon,* her first published play (1946). Had she never written anything but *The Land of the Dragon* her fame would be assured. Its popularity was established early and continues undiminished. Its unusual dramatic mode, its fluid style with bare Oriental stage and action flowing freely from scene to scene mark it as a pioneering work. Her *O.P.Q.R.S., Etc.* is a remarkable play because of its thematic examination of dictatorships using such devices as colors, letters of the alphabet and behavior patterns children can understand. Innovative structure, high style and challenging subject matter are Miller trademarks. Precursors of things to come, her plays are universally popular with producing groups.

Aurand Harris' work prior to 1977 is documented in Coleman Jennings' edition of *Six Plays for Children by Aurand Harris.*[2] His total canon of published plays for children now numbers thirty. His early output, appearing in the mid-40's, belongs in the older traditional mode; but the plays were quickly recognized for their structural precision and sensitivity to child values in character, dialogue, and humor distilled from years of teaching. With *Buffalo Bill, Junket,* and *Simple Simon* he was already displaying a determination to search out untried material to dramatize. Publication of *The Brave Little Tailor* (1961) with its fresh, unconventional style put his work in the vanguard of the movement to free playwrights from unwritten restrictions about naturalism for child audiences. His most popular works, all musicals, explored commedia style in *Androcles and the Lion,* Nineteenth Century melodrama in *Rags to Riches,* and "dark comedy" with a puppet stage setting in *Punch and Judy.* With *A Toby Show,* he reached into American theatrical history to find the wise-cracking fix-it-all country bumpkin character popular on tent show circuits in the early 1900's. His versatile output includes a bicentennial revue (*Yankee Doodle*), a three-story musical (*Just So Stories*), two adaptations of classics (*Robin Goodfellow* and *A Doctor In Spite of Himself*), and a dramatization of C.S. Lewis' popular story, *The Magician's Nephew.* Two non-musicals, *Steal Away Home,* about two boys traveling the underground railroad, and *The Arkansaw Bear,* about death, exemplify expansions of stylistic treatment and subject matter for which Harris and the newer traditionalists are recognized. Responding to commissions, he revised his earlier fantasy of India, *The Flying Prince,* and composed the lyrical, free-flowing *Ride a Blue Horse* on the early life of Hoosier poet, James Whitcomb Riley. The combination of all his plays makes Harris "the most produced children's theatre playwright in America."

With notable exceptions, the above examples of traditional plays demonstrate that much stress was laid on familiar titles, on adaptations of favorite stories and fairy tales, that only a few historical subjects were treated, that precious few contemporary subjects, and practically no controversial matters, were dramatized. A close examination of this repertoire would further reveal that most stories were handled straightforwardly, in the well-made play tradition, frequently in three-act form. They were more or less realistic in style, requiring full staging in a traditional manner and, except in a few instances, without much stylistic invention. Characters were quite intentionally less than three-dimensional. Children could perceive and understand what happened without much stretching or use of the imagination, for abstraction was generally avoided. Serious themes were treated, however, and some playwrights did develop distinctive styles in structure and dialogue. It can be safely said that playwrights were feeling their way through unexplored territory, balancing many factors, including children's expectations, desires, and levels of theatrical sophistication, as well as adult social and educational attitudes that were quite restrictive about what was suitable for children. Obviously, the majority of the plays was aimed toward the lower to middle age groups, leaving the upper grades slighted and the young teens almost totally unserved.

But we must remember that it was from this base that the newer playwrights gained impetus to launch forward. Perhaps in an attempt to prove the inadequacy of the old, perhaps as a direct challenge to children who were being seen in a whole new light by the 1960's and 70's, innovative scripts began to appear in greater numbers. Many, of course, explored a range of unconventional styles of theatrical performance, but many American playwrights also persisted in writing plays in the traditional way.

Newer plays of the traditional style reflect one or more recognizable characteristics. On the surface, for one thing, their titles often show some disdain for the old clichés about marketability. Titles tend to be evocative, but not necessarily familiar; and even when they sound familiar they often contain a new twist.

Characters with very real dimensions are appearing in greater numbers. In Suzan Zeder's *Step On a Crack*, not only is the girl protagonist, Ellie, a fully blown not-so-readily-lovable sort, but the other two principals, Max and Lucille, are unusually complex for fathers and stepmothers in plays for children and youth. Ed Graczyk's *Courage!* depicts a boy who is at first atttracted by the trappings and promised glories of Civil War army life, but who soon finds that the horrors of actual battle dispel this childish view and stir an inner conflict that tests his true character to the limit. Anatou, the fair-haired Eskimo girl in Joanna Halpert Kraus' *The Ice Wolf*, is portrayed as a mild, humble girl who is pushed into uncontrollable vengeance by the rejective behavior of the villagers. And in her *Circus Home*, Kraus has given us a circus "giant," an enormous boy with a big heart and even bigger sensitivities, who more than anything longs for open acceptance by his family and friends. At least in some plays for older children and youth three dimensional characterizations are challenging a rather widely accepted premise of the older tradition.

Expectations about comprehending more mature themes and subject matter are also implied in some works of the genre. In Brian Kral's "One to Grow On," a boy's feelings of rejection and loneliness when his parents divorce are the main concern. A similar theme is explored in Suzan Zeder's *Doors* and *Other Doors*. All three plays stress the need to recover and get on with life in changed circumstances. Zeder's *Ozma of Oz* depicts Dorothy's resentment of her aging, irascible Uncle Henry which is dispelled only when he proves by heroic actions that he still has much to give and deserves respect. Wendy Kesselman's "Maggie Magalita," a cross-cultural landmark, examines how a girl learns to accept her Latino grandmother with pride rather than shame. Brian Kral's *Special Class* asks us to empathize with the disappointment of a junior high boy whose impendng operation will prohibit his transfer from the class of handicapped youngsters into the "mainstream" of his school. Nicholas, in Julian Wiles' *The Boy Who Stole the Stars*, acts out a natural wish to delay his beloved grandfather's deterioration and death by his own heroic effort. Moses Goldberg delves into Margaret Mead's accounts of primitive rites of passage and provides a model for American teenagers in *The Men's Cottage*. Young people existing in a world of computerized control are principals in Pauline Conley's provocative *The Code Breaker*. Paul Maar's charming *Noodle Doodle Box* expects audiences to see beneath the characters' clownish actions and sense the danger of international disasters rooted in petty jealousies, inconsideration and manipulation by vested interests. Advanced themes often incorporate advanced morality concepts; but these will be discussed in a later section.

Fluidity of action is a feature of many newer plays. Terms such as "cinematic" or "free form" have been used by playwrights to describe the effect of continuous performance without breaks for changes of location or even shifts in time. *Step On a Crack* alternates scenes of Ellie's real life with Max and Lucille and scenes of her fantasy life with Lana and Frisbie, her imaginary companions. "One to Grow On" is structured so that the boy's earlier life is depicted in episodes perceived by himself in later years. In *Circus Home* incidents in Benjie the giant's life with the circus and those depicting his frustrations as a boy trying to relate to family and companions are juxtaposed in a frankly theatrical way. Gregory Falls' adaptation of *The Odyssey* is characterized by a free form structure in which Odysseus and his men traverse the known and unknown Greek world using only the most theatrical, unrealistic means. The action of Falls' *The Forgotten Door* is kept fluid as actors become scenic elements and provide narrative for the story of Jon, the boy from another world who roams the countryside in search of a way home. Freely flowing action between a Victorian teahouse where Grandfather is telling the story to his grandchildren and a neutral ground where the multi-location story is being enacted in Kabuki style is an unusual feature of Richard Shaw's adaptation of *Sleeping Beauty* as performed by the Children's Theatre Company of Minneapolis. The same group's script of *The Legend of Sleepy Hollow*, by Frederick Gaines, requires cinematic fluidity without scene changes to accommodate the several locales and the time span. It can be seen that such requirements contained in the scripts themselves would have a profound effect on all the choices a director must make in staging them. But this, of course, is a different chapter.

Some scripts specifically call for a neutral playing space modified in the Shakespearean manner to accommodate fast moving action. Such a play is Jonathan Levy's *The Marvelous Adventures of Tyl*, which calls for a few useful geometric forms or blocks that can become different scenic elements in a nonliteral way. Goldberg's *The Outlaw Robin Hood* calls for five locale changes executed in suggestive Shakespearian fashion by the players themselves as action proceeds. For *Marco Polo and the Prince Timur*, Marie Starr and Lisa Merkl specify an uncluttered stage space in the tradition of Peking Opera, with locales shaped suggestively by actors who place blocks, bamboo poles and banners using mime, dance and T'ai-chi-ch'wan movement.

Frankly using the devices of the theatre to help tell the story indicates increasing confidence of today's playwrights in children's ability to transpose, recognize, and understand what is intended. Conventions associated with the Oriental theatre are employed by Coleman Jennings in *The Honorable Urashima Taro*. The hero's stylized trip to the ocean floor with the Turtle, the "blue billowing fabric" that is waved to suggest the scene underwater, and the formalized fight with the Sea Scorpion emphasize theatrical values as well as introduce children to elements of another culture. Judith Kase's adaptation of *The Emperor's New Clothes* sets the action on a Kabuki or Noh platform which is tended by a "Keeper of the Stage" and two "Protectors of Properties." Similarly, customs and beliefs of the Navaho Indians are shown as people become animals by donning their skins in Joy Harvey's *Antelope Boy*; and the frank use of a chorus of actors to make sounds, become trees, swamp creatures and objects of terror in Suzan Zeder's *Wiley and the Hairy Man* introduces children to that ancient theatrical device. In Michael Brill's *The Masque of Beauty and the Beast* the scenes are kept moving by a corps of "grotesques" who place props and perform other functions in this cinematic version of the familiar story. The eerie effect should be somewhat Gothic, even though the author admits the origin of the device is the Oriental propmen, those now familiar functionaries who were introduced to children at least as far back as *The Land of the Dragon*.

A strong, pervasive style which is nonrealistic and nonliteral yet with elements that remain recognizable characterizes some of these plays, and it is the style which indicates considerable faith in the abilities of children to stretch beyond the artistic limitations of realism for enjoyment and understanding. One such play is Suzan Zeder's "In a Room Somewhere." Five characters are confined between mysterious, dreamlike walls with no doors; and events of their past lives are intermixed with efforts to find the way out. The acting style called for in Marie Starr's *Old Silent Movie* asks children to visualize another time and another art form with which they may or may not have had previous acquaintance in order to appreciate the zany happenings during a day at an old-time movie studio.

These examples of the evolving maturity of traditional scripts encourages us to watch for further developments within that genre. Now, however, it is time to turn our sights on plays and playwrights that have expanded the repertoire in other stylistic directions.

Opera

Opera versions of favorite stories and fairy tales have been staged for well over a century, and the venerable art form is alive and well today. Rossini's *La Cenerentola* (Cinderella) and Humperdinck's *Hansel and Gretel* were joined as standard holiday fare in 1952 by Gian Carlo Menotti's *Amahl and the Night Visitors* on both professional and amateur circuits. The story of Amahl, a crippled shepherd boy and his mother who shelter three kings on their way to Bethlehem, was initially presented on television; but despite formidable technical requirements, Menotti's *Help, Help, the Globolinks!* was meant for the stage. Globolinks are space creatures who subsist on electronic music but are vulnerable to the sounds of the standard instruments played by the children they have captured. A more recent Menotti opera, *A Bride from Pluto*, premiered at the Kennedy Center, tells the story of a tailor's son who ultimately rejects the chance to marry an exotic space visitor when he understands he must first give up his heart and soul.

Seymour Barab is establishing a reputation as one of the most productive composers in this field. His *Little Red Riding Hood* is a delightful version of the familiar tale. *Chanticleer*, a musically exquisite setting of Chaucer's "Nun's Priest's Tale," lists M.C. Richards as a collaborator. Other works by Barab include an operatic *Ransom of Red Chief*, a Christmas story called "Only a Miracle," *The Pink Siamese*, a charming tale of prejudice conquered by understanding, and *The Toy Shop*.

Quite a stir was created in the operatic world recently when Maurice Sendak's *Where the Wild Things Are* first appeared on English stages. Composed by Oliver Knussen, the opera version of Sendak's 1963 controversial children's book follows the naughty Max from a fiesty encounter with his mother to his room in disgrace. There, of course, he brings his fantasy to life: a forest transforms into an ocean with a raging sea monster, and a mysterious island produces the gigantic Wild Things who are tamed and crown him their King.

An operatic treatment of de Brunhoff's tale, *Babar the Elephant*, composed by Nicolai Berezowsky, brings the familiar characters of Babar, Celeste, and the Old Lady to life in refreshingly new dimensions. Douglas Moore, a successful composer of standard adult operatic works, was one of the earliest to give some attention to children and youth with his *Emperor's New Clothes*, *The Greenfield Christmas Tree*, *The Headless Horseman* and *Puss in Boots*. From the number of original works premiering each year it is quite clear that a growing interest in opera has a steadily developing repertoire to sustain it.[3]

Musicals

Since the 1920's, the musical production has held a special place in the American theatre, spreading its conventions and pleasures throughout the world. It is no wonder that its applicability to child and youth audiences was so soon recognized. It seems to possess so many of the features known to attract and hold interest: song, dance, spectacle, in fact, infinite variety. Its enormous popularity is evident on every hand, even though an occasional note of caution is sometimes sounded regarding children's actual preference for it.[4]

No one knows how many musical Tom Sawyers, Cinderellas, Rumpelstiltskins or Brementown Musicians actually exist. Producers have a wide choice of almost all the popular titles in several musical versions. These vary in their degree of adherence to the original source, quality of musical treatment, and scale of production mandated by the text.

We can mention only a few examples of this vast repertoire. Children of a wide range flock to and enjoy family musicals that have had commercial success, among them *Peter Pan, Annie, Oliver!, You're a Good Man, Charlie Brown,* and its companion, *Snoopy!!* Even *Bye, Bye, Birdie* has a strong appeal to young teens because of its rock star motif. The classic MGM film *The Wizard of Oz* has spawned many stage counterparts, only one of which legally includes the familiar tunes we all associate with that story.[5]

Rock musicals especially enjoyed by junior high and upper grades have proved popular as developed by Ed Graczyk in collaboration with various composers. *Aesop's Falables* (probably the most successful of the genre), *To Be, Imagine That, Electric Folderol* and *Runaway,* utilize a contemporary musical idiom with combo accompaniment. These works explore such topics of concern to older children and youth as discovering one's identity. For the younger set, a series of *Magic Theatre* pieces by Saundra Mathews-Deacon asks energetic young casts to play theatre games and enact sketches of everyday life set to infectious rhythms provided by a modest ensemble.

Eleanor and Ray Harder's *Sacramento Fifty Miles,* a version of the "Brementown Musicians" set in the American west; *Good Grief, a Griffin,* which takes place in a respectable village near the Dreadful Wilds; and *The Near-Sighted Knight and the Far-Sighted Dragon* with its most unconventional Princess, together comprise an imaginative and musically worthy addition to the literature. David Woolcombe's *Peace Child* is noted for much more than its contemporary music, being a plea to halt the international arms race before a nuclear catastrophe. In a similarly serious tone but on quite a different subject unusual for musicals is one by Pat Hale and Al Bahret, *The Little Mermaid,* which follows the Andersen original closely. An increasingly popular genre of science fiction and space fantasy in musical form is represented by Frank Leary and Hank Beebe's *Captain Billy.*

Musical and story theatre idioms appear to blend naturally in the oft-produced *Golliwhoppers!, Skupper Duppers, Tarradiddle Tales* and *Tarradiddle Travels,* all by Flora Atkin, and all containing several culturally oriented folk tales. Requiring similar versatility of performers is Mary Jane Evans, Deborah Anderson and Ed Archer's *Tales from Hans Christian Andersen.* Calling for a small ensemble, but no less talented and capable of engaging in total theatre, are the musical sketches from the Paper Bag Players repertoire, *Dandelion, Christmas All Over the Place, The Runaway Presents, Wiggle Worm's Surprise, The Lost and Found Christmas, Everybody, Everybody,* and *Reasons to Be Cheerful,* with music by Donald Ashwander and book by Judith Martin. Other composers and playwrights have also deemphasized story line, utilizing instead a thematic thread that ties selected nursery rhymes, poems, sketches or "bits" together in almost a vaudeville fashion. Such a work is Carol Pearson's *Don't Count Your Chickens Until They Cry Wolf,* a fresh look at Aesop's fables, or *Flashback!,* Alice Wilson's revue of childhood events in a vein more humorous than nostalgic. The versatile form takes yet another turn with *My Days As a Youngling,* full of the folk songs of John Jacob Niles and using Johnnie himself at several different ages to tell the story of his early life and work.

A word of caution seems appropriate here. The worst excesses connected with musicals have arisen with regard to intent. Often they seem to present to authors and composers an irresistible temptation to be cute and "campy," that is, to make condescending adult commentary on the situation behind the backs of trusting children.[6] The prime example in our memory is that of an "Emperor's New Clothes" in which an inane Empress went about constantly blasting on a bugle, and which introduced a totally irrelevant courtship between two minor personages who were thereby catapulted into principal status to the unnerving distortion of the story. Special care should be exercised to detect this unfortunate quality in many musicals presently available.

Even so, the versatility of the musical form is being proved over and over as newer approaches are explored with each passing season. Its popularity with producers is beyond question.

Participation Plays

As we have seen, the name most closely associated with the genre of participation theatre is Brian Way, an Englishman who has spent several years in the United States conducting workshops, lecturing, and generally promoting his special philosophy about children, education and the drama. The canon of his plays is now available through Baker's. It is divided into scripts suitable for family audiences, for grades K through three, four through six, and secondary school age.

In his plays for family viewing, participation is limited to things the audience can do without leaving their seats, such as helping Pinocchio learn to brush his teeth or wash his hands. The family audience scripts include *Pinocchio, A Christmas Carol, Sleeping Beauty* and *Treasure Island,* all of which can be performed either in proscenium or open staging facilities, although even in proscenium Way requests that audiences be limited to five hundred. He requests an even lower number, two hundred, to be exact, for plays he writes for the youngest audience. His oft-produced *Mirrorman* encourages a more active level of involvement as the young audience helps Toyman, Mirrorman and the doll, Beauty, to defeat the witch. This play, as well as *The Hat, The Bell* and *The Wheel,* require open staging so that youngsters can easily enter the action.

For upper grades, participation becomes more crucial to the progress of the drama itself. For instance, *On Trial* asks four groups of twenty selected young people to become teams on an expedition in search of a medicinal herb that will stop an epidemic; and their participation is continuous. Other plays in this age category require small group participation or total group involvement from the seated audience. These titles include *Crossroads, The Ladder* and *The Decision.* The plays listed for teenagers — *Grindling Gibbons and the Plague of London, The Struggle* and *Angel of the Prisons* — call for improvised participation as members of crowds or even for sequences in which members of the audience have been previously rehearsed. Because of their subject matter, these last plays are more popular in England than they are in this country.

The style developed by Brian Way has served as inspiration if not a model for plays by other authors. Moses Goldberg's *Hansel and Gretel* and *Aladdin* evolve in a framework showing the performers as people and family members. They ask the children chiefly to support the protagonist through sounds and actions without leaving their seats. Bernice Bronson's *Canterbury Tales, In the Beginning* and *The Most Powerful Jujus* were all developed by the Looking Glass Theatre and demonstrate a general premise that the best participation is through a kind of group identity such as a tribe or community. *Creation, Tribe* and *Sunsong,* by Saphira Barbara Linden and her associates grew from experiments at the Om Theatre Workshop of Boston and stress children's physical involvement in play situations leading to their awareness of environmental pollution, human injustice, and productive family relationships.

The work of Claire Jones and Robert Varga at the University of Oklahoma City, called Involvement Dramatics, has contributed such scripts as *Have a Grumpish Holiday, The Magic Pouch* and *Take Me to the Treasure.* Jack Stokes' *The Incredible Jungle Journey of Fenda Maria* calls for limited participation of individual children as well as group interaction to effect the outcome. Betty Jean Lifton's *Kap the Kappa* asks mostly for vocal help from the children in evolving the story of the legendary Japanese trickster, but at the end invites children and all kappas to dance together in the playing space. A group of Canadian participation plays on Native American themes will be discussed later in a different context.

Except for the titles mentioned in Brian Way's teenage category, it is clear that American participatory dramas are most appropriate for children eight years old and younger. Producers who work extensively in this style have developed systems of promotion and audience management that allow the dramas to work as intended with the children engaging in the degree and kind of involvement specifically structured into each script.

Story Theatre

While musicals in story theatre style have achieved special prominence in the contemporary repertoire, nonmusical story theatre, similarly calling for effective ensemble playing, is represented both by scripts telling a single story and those telling several shorter stories. The narrator's *persona* ranges from a single impersonal, detached storyteller to one or all of the involved characters momentarily assuming the function.

A "conteur" describes the settings and makes transitions in the sequencing of Dennis Scott's *Sir Gawain and the Green Knight*, developed for the National Theatre of the Deaf. An intricate pattern of transformations into characters, animals, and birds is worked out, requiring of a versatile company skill to suggest place, weather and all conditions of the heroic tale without recourse to stage mechanics. The plays evolved by the Yellow Brick Road company are also of the single story kind. *Nightingale* and *Fool of the World*, folktales adapted by John Urquhart and Rita Grossberg, require audience participation as well, indicating the further versatility of the story theatre idiom. In *Nightingale* it is the Servant who functions as narrator; in *Fool* it is Peter the Magician. Atkins' scripts, identified with the Adventure Theatre's In-School program, also include some limited audience participation at selected points, with narration passing among the cast members in their various roles. Robin Hall assigns narration to a different character in each of the *Three Tales from Japan* — a Storyteller for "The Magic Fan," a Fisherman for "The Princess of the Sea," and the Old Man for "Little Peach Boy." In still a different format the function of narrator is passed among most of the characters at one time or another to tell the several stories of Shirley Pugh's *In One Basket*.

John Baldwin has introduced still another example of the adaptability of story theatre techniques. In his *Metrics Can Be Fun* Baldwin has demonstrated a frank educational usage for the drama, capitalizing on the presentational, direct contact aspects of this production style.

The Paul Sills production by that name may have started story theatre on a development journey whose end cannot be foreseen. Its usefulness to children's and youth theatre playwrights already has been amply demonstrated.

With all the advances made in the traditional modes as well as the expansion into new styles and dimensions, the American repertoire has been enriched even further by the influx of scripts from abroad.

INTERNATIONAL DIMENSIONS

The world's literature has always been fair game for playwrights who adapt for young audiences. Folk and fairy tales, epics, short stories, novels, legends and myths from almost every culture have flourished in the young people's theatres around the globe. Heroism, large or small, knows few national boundaries.

With the development of ASSITEJ an effective system has been set up for the exchange of the best scripts from member countries. Today's children experience a steadily increasing likelihood of seeing good plays from a much broader range of cultures than any previous generation, and each country has the opportunity to measure its best against the repertoire from abroad. Sharing the best of that repertoire was facilitated for a time by regular editions of the "International Bibliography of Plays Recommended for Performance to Children and Young People," by Michael Pugh of the British Center. A worthy successor, Patricia Whitton's *Outstanding Plays for Young Audiences*, published by the U.S. Center, describes several scripts recommended by each member country, names the languages in which each is available, and tells where rights to production may be obtained.

In addition to ASSITEJ efforts, publishers in the United States continue to make special efforts to locate and distribute selected works from the international repertoire. As they negotiate translation and production rights, they increase the availability of scripts from abroad, and quite a number of these plays have already become favorites with American producers.

It is just and right that Belgium, home of *The Blue Bird* and Arthur Fauquez, be listed first. When speaking of the "new repertoire" in young people's theatre we almost always begin with Fauquez' *Reynard the Fox*, a play that has in its brief life achieved a near-classic status and has opened many doors to subsequent playwrights. Other Fauquez scripts which are currently available are *Ambrosio Kills Time* (or *The Man Who Killed Time*), *The Golden Apples* and *Don Quixote of La Mancha*.

For some years, Canada was the chief North American center for promotion of Brian Way's plays and participation theatre techniques. His style continues to predominate much work coming from our northern neighbor. However, Canada's output of plays on American Indian themes is an especially valuable contribution to the literature. Some of these, as well as many others on a wide range of subjects, are distributed by the Playwrights Union of Canada. English translations of two plays from Le Theatre de la Marmaille in Montreal have become available. *Crying to Laugh*, by Marcel Sabourin, centers on a child's need to balance reason with emotions; and the Marmaille's collective creation, *Umiak*, depicts crises in the lives of Inuit people of the far north. Also from Canada comes Beth Lambert's *The Riddle Machine*, a space age Noah's ark story. The Canadian repertoire is growing, and luckily for us, most of it is in English.[7]

A few scripts are currently available from the Czech repertoire, and perhaps this number will increase as interest grows. Jan Jilek's *The Sun King, the Moon King and the Wind King*, the same author's *The Firebird and Trixie the Vixen*, and Sasa Lichy's *The Tin Soldier* are all fairy tales, the last based on Hans Christian Andersen's original. Miloslav Stehlik's *Life, Here We Come* is an adaptation of the Russian novel about life in a Soviet colony for homeless children and juvenile delinquents.

Leon Chancerel and Jean de Brunhoff's *An Adventure of Babar* from the French repertoire, presents on stage the same popular Babar the Elephant that American composer Nicolai Berezowsky adapted as an opera. Also available in English translation is the tender and mystical *The Violin of Passing Time*, by Aristide-Christian Charpentier. Recently a translation of *Where To, Turulu?*, by Degoutin, Vedienne and Hugues, has appeared, making available to American children the charming adventures of the naive Turulu who encounters the evil influences of his world for the the first time.

Probably one of the most provocative offerings from abroad comes from West Germany. A series of plays produced in Berlin by a company called Grips, under Volker Ludwig's leadership, has been published here in a volume titled *Political Plays for Children*, translated and edited by Jack Zipes.[8] The plays, *Mugnog, Bizzy, Dizzy, Daffy and Arthur* and *Man oh Man* generally espouse the cause of "kid power." Similarly, Friederich Karl Waechter's *School With Clowns* is a caricature of life in strict German schools. Paul Maar's delightful *Noodle Doodle Box*, translated and adapted by Anita and Alex Page, tells a simple story that, in effect, traces the very origins of all international conflict.

As might be expected, a major influence from abroad is exerted by Great Britain. Long before the appearance of ASSITEJ, English scripts by James Barrie, A.A. Milne, and the many adapters of Lewis Carroll's Alice stories were jumping the Atlantic and becoming major components of the budding repertoire here. Even the prolific Frances Hodgson Burnett was born in England!

Our debt to Great Britain has not diminshed in recent years. The Brian Way scripts mentioned earlier originated there, of course. Since the Fifties a goodly stream of scripts from the pen of Nicholas Stuart Gray has enchanted thousands of children. *Beauty and the Beast* has been one of the most popular, and *The Tinder Box, New Clothes for the Emperor, The Marvelous Story of Puss in Boots* and *The Imperial Nightingale* also are available in this country. Plays by Alan Cullen have been extremely popular as well, especially *Niccolo and Nicollette, Trudi and the Minstrel, The Beeple* and *The Man in the Moon*.

Another Englishman, Alan Broadhurst, gave us *The Great Cross-Country Race*, the ever-popular account of the competition between a hare and a tortoise, with some embellishments on Mr. Aesop's original. He also gave us a version of *Young Dick Whittington* whose famous cat won her master a fortune. Two from the pen of Mary Melwood, The *Tingelary Bird* and *Five Minutes to Morning*, from Carol Jenner's Unicorn Theatre in London, add absurdist dimensions to young people's theatre. Robert Bolt's *The Thwarting of Baron Bolligrew* has become well established as a play for older children, presenting a mock-heroic quest in almost a Brechtian style. Joan Aiken, turning her hand from children's stories to plays, has given us the mystical, enigmatic *Winterthing* and the more conventional *The Mooncusser's Daughter*. Jackson Lacey's *The Prince, the Wolf, and the Firebird*, thoroughly British even though on a Russian folktale, is another of a somewhat absurdist character. All signs indicate that the British influence on our repertoire will continue to expand stylistic and content horizons.

The children's theatre of Holland is represented here chiefly by plays emanating from the former Toneelgroep Arena company, notably Aad Greidanus' very popular *Two Pails of Water* and two by Erik Vos,

The Dancing Donkey and *Professor Filarsky's Miraculous Invention.* All reflect the commedia and folk orientation of this remarkable but modest size theatrical troupe.

An almost gossamer film overlays a predatory viciousness that never really prevails in the Iranian fantasy, *The Butterfly*, by Bijan Mofid. An allegory set in the insect world of beetles, lightning bugs and spiders, *The Butterfly* is an unusual challenge both to producers and child audiences.

From Norway comes Thorbjorn Egner's *People and Robbers of Cardemon Town,* a folk tale of considerable musical stature that is achieving a world-wide audience.

Sweden has provided us a fresh look at a familiar story. *Medea's Children,* by Per Lysander and Suzanne Osten, retells the Greek tragedy from the perspective of the children whom Medea slays in revenge for her husband's treachery.

Poland has given us a musical "Tom Thumb" by Tadeusz Kierski and Julia Hartwig, featuring an invisible Tom who appears and grows to the height of several men in the last moments.

Scripts from the U.S.S.R. are increasingly becoming available here. Evgeny Schwartz is represented by five highly respected plays, *The Dragon, Little Red Riding Hood, The Naked King* (story of the Emperor's New Clothes), *The Shadow* (also based on Andersen), and *The Two Maples* (after Russian folklore). In addition, his version of *The Snow Queen* was the basis for the British Young Vic production adapted by Suria Magito and Rudolf Weil. Schwartz' scripts are noted for their subtextual political satire.

Latvia, one of the Soviet republics, is the point of origin for Brigadere's *Spriditis,* a musical of operatic proportions, which uses native folk melodies to support a boy's quest for maturity.

The poet Pyotr Ershov's famous *The Little Humpback Horse,* the play that was originally staged by Briantsev in 1922 for the Leningrad Theatre for Young Spectators (TIUZ), has been recently translated by Lowell Swortzell. Samuel Marschak's *The Little Animal House,* an anti-war satire and an adaptation of the Czech fairy tale, *Twelve Months,* concerning a poor step-daughter who is sent out to pick snowdrops on New Year's Eve, represent the work of this highly regarded playwright. Of special interest is the publication of a volume of *Russian Plays for Young Audiences,* five plays from the modern repertoire translated and edited by Miriam Morton.[9] The volume contains Schwartz' *The Two Maples,* Lev Ustinov's *City Without Love,* Anatoly Aleksin's *The Young Guard,* Gennadi Mamlin's *Hey There — Hello!,* and *The Young Graduates* by Victor Rosov, perhaps Russia's foremost playwright for the adolescent audience.[10]

"Captain John Peoplefolks," by Dusan Radovic and Miroslav Belovic, is a favorite with Yugoslavian children, proving again the universal appeal of comedy interwoven with adventure.

While obviously not all countries are represented in this listing and in all probability all these listed scripts are not of equal quality from the best of standards, it is clear that the availability of scripts from other lands is much broader than has been generally supposed. With such a beginning we can look forward to a shared repertoire, at least with other ASSITEJ countries.

RESTRICTIONS FADE

Before proceeding, we must point out that experiments in theatrical style have received more ready acceptance from sponsors than have explorations into unconventional subject matter. Educators especially welcomed participation plays, even though they placed restrictions on audience size. Innovative styles, such as musicals and story theatre, were accepted because they held audience attention, allowed for shorter attention spans, and often substituted various kinds of physical involvement for silent spectatorship. These were attributes to be encouraged.

However, sponsors and their constituents have not greeted all efforts to venture into broader, more mature subject matter, deeper philosophical concepts and actual, rather than verbalized, morality systems with unbridled enthusiasm. In the early days of this era it took considerable courage to write, publish, produce or sponsor some of the door-openers, the pacesetters, or the controversial scripts; and it will be some time before the battlefield is entirely safe.

Rogue Heroes

The rogue hero, defined by Sharon Scoville Ellis as a rascal or scamp who does not follow the codes of conduct established by his society but is not an evil character, has been part of folk tradition, literature and the stage repertoire since the beginning. He is found in every known culture. Nor have we discovered anything new in recognizing his popularity with children. For he is the very essence of childhood. He is good and bad, generous and selfish, lying and truthful, a cheat, a mischiefmaker and one who helps us keep our sense of humor. He is recognized as Huck Finn, Pinocchio, Tom Sawyer, Tyl Eulenspiegel, Toad of Toad Hall and all their cousins.

But then a new breed of rogue began to appear on stage. Not that he hadn't been in the wings all along, but in the Sixties he dared to venture into view. The first of these was Fauquez' *Reynard,* that ancient and infamous Fox who shamelessly tricks the whole animal community into destroying its crime records on himself, who embarrasses the King, who ridicules the clergy and shows up the hypocrites of his society. His pathway is littered with the remnants of little acts of violence, and in the end he not only escapes a promised death but he avoids punishment completely. And we are glad! Everyone who registers a complaint about Reynard in performance in effect reveals the thing about himself that is most vulnerable.[11]

Dean Wenstrom's *Big Klaus and Little Klaus* caused such a stir the publisher eventually withdrew it from distribution. The Klaus brothers are also ancient indeed, deriving from who knows where before they were finally captured on paper by that venerable storyteller, Hans Christian Andersen. Here is a tale of a clever little man's ability to turn disaster into victory, to turn a bully's greed and baseness into weapons that implode. Little Klaus was fighting for survival in a harsh, deadly environment. The people, including big brother, went to church and sang hymns; and when big brother emerged he was able to toss what he thought was little brother into the river with the off-hand line, "Well, that's what comes of saying your prayers, it lightens your burdens . . . Yes, it does."

And that was not the worst. Not only do we have a hint of promiscuity involving a Sexton and a farmer's wife, but we have a play that ends in a rather blatant murder. Little Klaus complies with his big brother's request to tie him in a weighted sack and dump him in the river so he can go get that herd of cattle Little Klaus had described to him. As he goes kersplash, Little Klaus casually remarks, "I'm afraid he won't get any cattle, I'm afraid;" and he walks away puffing on his pipe!

Now here was a play to curl the hair of the traditionalists. It seems to contain everything they had ever been taught was forbidden in plays for children. It shook their foundations. It seemed to attack capitalism and organized religion. It condoned murder. Not only was Little Klaus not punished for killing Big Klaus, he was allowed to keep all the profit he had made in his questionable enterprises. Feedback from one production revealed that at least some children wondered why the episodes with the grandmothers had been left out! (You might just have to go to your Andersen to read about the grandmothers.)[12]

Even the immortal Punch has found his way back to the children's theatre stage after being effectively banished for decades. A popular vehicle by Aurand Harris, *Punch and Judy* starts the familiar characters off as puppets, then brings them to life as actors. Punch effectively does away with all his adversaries with a swat of his slapstick and a merry song. All his traditional impudence is there as well as the usual list of crimes against society. "You hit a dog. You smacked your wife. You cracked a professor. You whacked a doctor. You threw a baby out the window." Worst of all, Punch causes the Hangman to hang himself; then in the final battle all men must wage, he conquers the Devil. "There will always be a Punch and Judy," sing the characters. It is as if the new freedom in children's theatre has given assurance of that.

Jonathan Levy's *The Marvelous Adventures of Tyl* begins with an unusual sight: Tyl is born, emerging apparently from the "exaggerated profile" of his mother's swollen belly. Immediately he bites the doctor, insults his grandmother, and smears jam on his cousin. No, Tyl will be no ordinary well-behaved child! From birth his mischief centers on mocking stupidity (the school teacher, no less), conformity (the army), cruelty (the butcher), hypocrisy (the doctors) and greed (a rich man). But it all catches up with him, and his outraged victims lead him to the execution block. One last trick and he not only escapes death but ends up with a wife, an estate, and great wealth. When the citizens think he is dead, their lines echo our view of a typical rogue: "He was wild but he wasn't all bad. I liked him." "At least he was honest. He said what he thought." "Can't be too honest in this world and live to be old."

The weavers in *New Clothes for the Emperor*, Nicholas Stuart Gray's version of the Andersen tale, are noted for their particularly roguish treatment. Piers and Perkin lie, cheat, and throw a kingdom into turmoil with zest and irresistible good humor. Unlike the endings of Punch, Reynard, and Tyl, this ending shows a slight attenuation. Piers and Perkin have a bothersome twinge of conscience about their roguery, and the final scene finds them once again in the stocks as direct punishment for their misdeeds.

A necessary ingredient for appreciating the rogue hero is a sense of humor. To enjoy Harris' *Peck's Bad Boy* or Wendy Gray's "Adventures of Coyote," we need to be able to laugh at outrageous behavior, chuckle as human foibles are exposed, or delight in the fall of the pretentious and mighty. Apparently not all adults can keep perspective and realize the necessary place such characters have in a balanced repertoire for the young people's theatre. We see their inclusion as a progressive sign.

Ethnic Cultures

The appearance of even a few scripts with Black, Indian, or Hispanic protagonists sympathetically portrayed is a gigantic step forward. Hailed as a significant advance in several respects was Joanna Halpert Kraus' *The Ice Wolf*. The story of Anatou, the light-skinned, blond Eskimo girl is one of hardly concealed racial prejudice ending in tragedy. Superstition and hatred drive the orphaned girl from her tribe to take up a life of vengeance as an ice wolf, killing and marauding, forcing her oppressors into lethal countermeasures. It is an allegory of our times, set in the Canadian wilderness among a primitive people who, perhaps not surprisingly, act just like us.

The story of Phillis Wheatley, a Black woman who rose above her status as a slave in colonial Boston to win acclaim as a poetess respected both in America and abroad, is told in Martha Hill Newell's *Phillis*. Two scripts depicting experiences on the pre-Civil War "underground railroad" made their appearance almost simultaneously. Joanna Halpert Kraus' *Mean to Be Free* tells the story of the great Negro leader, Harriet Tubman, who applied strong psychology and inspired management to bring two young children from slavery to freedom in Canada through a series of hairbreadth escapes. In Aurand Harris' dramatization of Jane Kristof's *Steal Away Home*, two boys, Amos and Obie, are brought out of slavery by a succession of helpers who eventually lead them to their father and freedom in Pennsylvania. Closely related is Ozzie Davis' *Escape to Freedom*, about young Frederick Douglass' life as a slave and his ultimate realization that reading would lead the way to freedom.

A sign that Americans have gained some perspective on racial relations between Blacks and Whites is the renewed acceptance of plays based on Uncle Remus tales such as Ed Graczyk's *Livin' de Life*, Eugene Jackson's *Brer Rabbit's Big Secret*, or The *Adventures of Brer Rabbit* by Pat Hale (Whitton), whether the character of Uncle Remus is included or not. A few short years ago they might have been thought demeaning and condescending to Blacks, but now they are received as views of an important American culture.

Indians, too, are more frequently finding sympathetic treatment on the stages of theatres for young audiences. The American Indian movement has brought a new consciousness of heritage, culture and future aspirations to the rest of the citizenry; and the "Hollywood Indian" syndrome is rapidly fading as an acceptable view to perpetuate on the younger generation.

Charlotte Chorpenning's *The Indian Captive* was one of the earliest (1937) to break with tradition and accord Indians sympathetic treatment on stage. James Norris followed suit in 1953 with *Hiawatha, Peacemaker of the Iroquois*. Joseph Golden's popular *Johnny Moonbeam and the Silver Arrow* provided yet another look at Indian culture, this time focusing on a hypothetical rite of passage into adulthood. While all three of these may present some problems to contemporary producers, they reflected a heightened consciousness that there are many discrete Indian cultures, not just one.

The character of Coyote, a trickster sometimes malicious, sometimes just mischievous like Brer Rabbit or Reynard, has been the focus of several plays emanating from legends of Southwest Indian tribes. Joy Harvey's *Antelope Boy* from Navaho culture depicts Coyote on a deadly hunt for Cloud Girl of the Antelope people, but his evil magic is defeated in the last moments. Coyote is shown in a more mischievous light in Wendy Gray's "Adventures of Coyote" based on Hopi legend. Lin Wright's student company at Arizona State University evolved a pair of plays from Pima stories: "Coyote and His Brothers" and "The Great Hunters," which centered on the famous trickster.

But in a different tone, *Tribe,* an environmental piece by Barbara Linden, involves children literally in the disruption of culture and life as three tribes — Sioux, Navaho and Muskogee — are driven from their lands by the U.S. government.[13] In a rare view showing the modern problems of existing in two cultures simultaneously, Saul Levitt's musical *Jim Thorpe, All-American,* allows family audiences to experience his triumph as "the world's greatest athlete" and his heartbreaking fall from the heights of worldly acclaim.

Earlier in this chapter we mentioned some Canadian contributions to understanding Indian cultures. More deserve mention here. In Paddy Campbell's *Chinook,* three children and the storyteller, with the help of everyone in the "story circle," foil the Ice Woman's efforts to hold the earth in her icy grip, permitting the annual triumph of Fire Woman and her warmth. The magic transformation is supplied by the Chinook wind created by the audience.

Isabelle Foord's *A Dream of Sky People* is a myth about how Nazabo and his nagging wife, Nacha, left their comfortable home in the sky and learned to accept the trials and glories of pursuing life on earth. In *Shaman* the same author reveals the conflict of the wise old Eskimo medicine man with his counterpart, the "Dark Shaman," Ooktah, who wants to establish eternal cold in the Arctic territory.

Even though it is not based on authentic Eskimo lore, Henry Beissel's *Inook and the Sun* captures a true folk flavor in this ambitious tale of Inook who carries his search for the life-giving sun to the great hall of the Spirit of the Ice. There he finds and releases the sun so it can return to warm the frozen wastes of his land.

While each of these plays has its own quality, the authors all make a clear effort to give honest treatment to nature myths in form and language contemporary children can understand and appreciate. In many of these plays children take part in the ritual, thus becoming more than watchers as they share in the ancient magic.

Kesselman's "Maggie Magalita" introduces what we all hope will be a welcome series of plays on Latino themes, providing a view of the special problems Spanish speaking minorities encounter in communities across the U.S. As we widen our horizons we are increasingly aware of the need for scripts depicting Black, Chicano, Oriental, and Native American protagonists dealing with the problems they face in contemporary society.

Death

Many generations of children's theatre playwrights have adhered to general dicta tacitly accepted years ago: death best belongs to antagonists; if death happens to protagonists, it is not final; if it must occur, it belongs somewhere in the middle of the play; if it has to be treated, it must seem as remote as possible, preferably occurring offstage. These were rather confining rules. Presumably they were based on a desire to protect children from harsh reality as long as possible and to avoid upsetting them emotionally during a performance. Since very few plays for children violated accepted taboos about death, opportunities to observe actual audience reaction to it were limited or non-existent. Thus adult sensitivity rather than actuality appears to have been the major reason for skirting the issue.[14]

And skirt the issue we did. If death was not actually ignored in plays for young audiences, it was held at arm's length, so to speak. Tinker Bell and Beauty's Beast "almost die," but are revived at the last instant.[15] Snow White, King Midas' daughter Tyra, Sleeping Beauty, Kay in *The Snow Queen,* and Prince Ivan in *The Prince, the Wolf and the Firebird* all suffer symbolic deaths, only to be revived before the play ends. Villains melt, fly to pieces, turn to stone or disappear in flashes and puffs of smoke. They leave no traces. They are simply "gone."

Various dramatizations of Oscar Wilde's *The Birthday of the Infanta* for many years were the sole examples of plays for the young that concluded unhappily. Whether the death of the dwarf toward the end of the play could actually be considered a tragic event, or whether it could be interpreted on another level, it certainly aroused sympathies. For the most part, however, dramatists simply avoided adapting those stories from Andersen, Grimm, Perrault, Pushkin and Colum that prominently depicted death, either symbolically or actually, nor did they go out of their way to write original scripts that put death in a prominent position as a subject to be dealt with seriously. Television and contemporary children's literature helped put an end to the necessity of protecting children from harsh realities in their theatre. Thus recent years have seen fundamental change in playwriting, as our dramatists have dared to show the death of a sympathetic character, finally and irrevocably, on stage.

The death of the good Don at the end of Fauquez' *Don Quixote of La Mancha* broke rather new ground in 1967. Confused as he is, the Don is a character we grow to like as we travel with him through fourteen scenes. When he dies, says William Birner in his introduction to *Twenty Plays,* "it is not a sad or unhappy ending. It is a natural ending." The same could be said of the ending of *Appleseed,* in which Johnny's life ends on a soft note of content and fulfillment. But in quite a different key, Anatou, in Kraus' *The Ice Wolf,* pursues her path of vengeance, actually killing one of the Eskimos on stage, until inevitably she is herself killed by a hunter's arrow. The pathos of her death is increased by her self sacrifice in saving the life of her childhood friend, Tarto. In Harris' *Steal Away Home,* Joe, a runaway slave and traveling companion to the principals, Obie and Amos, is shot to death by bounty hunters while dashing across the stage in a frantic escape bid. Joe's death, too, is a shattering experience in the stark reality of the historic situation.

The sacrificial death of Will Scarlet at the hands of the Sheriff in Mason's *Robin Hood: A Story of the Forest* appears naturally motivated from previous character exposition. In Kral's "One to Grow On," Timmy's Grandpa leaves behind a heartbroken but strengthened boy when, in a scene reminiscent of Willie Loman's funeral, Tim comes to accept the exigencies of his life. When the wicked Hyena attacks Noah, threatening to push him off the ark into the floodwaters, it is the Great Auk who intercedes, giving her life—and that of her species—to extinction in the climactic moments of Bix Doughty's *Noah and the Great Auk.* "Outside In," by George Nelson, clearly aimed at young teens, depicts a boy's attempt to cope with the untimely death of his best buddy; and Nicholas, in Julian Wiles' *The Boy Who Stole the Stars,* realizes he must seek alternatives rather than engage in vain, if heroic, attempts to prevent the inevitable, when his best friend moves away and his beloved grandfather dies.

The Pardoner's story in Bernice Bronson's *Canterbury Tales* recreates the medieval personification of Death as a shrouded figure, a skeleton perhaps, who can be encountered at any crossroad and who cannot be outwitted no matter how clever one is. Led by the Pardoner, the children actually take part in the Dance of Death. We already have described the tender, reassuring treatment of the subject Harris has given in *The Arkansaw Bear;* and any accurate adaptation of Andersen's *The Little Mermaid,* such as Hale and Bahret's or the one given by the Children's Theatre Company of Minneapolis, would have to conclude with the mermaid's sacrifice of her own life so that her beloved Prince could be happy with his new bride.

Beissel's *Inook and the Sun* provides a view of death as peace and rest after a life of hard struggle. Inook's father is killed by a polar bear, on stage, early in the play, and in turn the bear is killed by the boy, Inook. As the father dies, he tells his son, "Don't grieve. Ayorama. All is decreed. I'm not sorry to leave the world. I'm tired of struggling. In the Land of the Dead I shall find peace at last. Perhaps the sun shines there forever. Warmth and peace." Later in the play, Inook finds the soul of his father encased in ice where the sun also is held prisoner. As Inook tries to release him, the father stops him with the words, "It is decreed my struggles are over."

Not all practitioners will agree that the present trend toward including various realistic and romantic views of death in plays for young people is a desirable one. There have been times when children's stories, songs and sermons were filled with allusions to death, threats of eternal fire, and frightening images, sometimes purported to keep them from the wayward path or perhaps just to bring tears to the eyes. We hope that the present trend is more positive, assigning death its natural place in the scheme of things as we realize that at least for children over the age of nine, there is little point in banning its occurrence from the stage.

Violence and Aggression

In the last chapter we discussed the application of violence and aggression studies in television programming to young people's theatre. These studies are of considerable importance to us in that they represent a massive effort to ascertain what role aggressive action patterns in entertainment media play in determining violent behavior in life situations. Violence — at least "action" or "conflict" — has been part and parcel of the drama since the dawn of time. It is difficult to imagine the drama from which violence has been barred. Yet, since we accept our role as artists in a social and educational context, it behooves us to look to our repertoire and constantly evaluate what behavior models we present to children.

In the wake of these studies and the consequent nationwide attention to the problem, we may expect to see considerably more caution on the part of playwrights toward inclusion of violence. Granted, no discernible trend in this direction is yet evident in playwriting. In fact, the greater freedom we have talked about through much of this chapter has encouraged playwrights to think in terms of fewer, not more, restrictions.

Obviously, if a more realistic picture of functioning morality systems is being drawn, a certain amount of violent and aggressive behavior must be shown. Violence is almost certain to occur when rogue heroes tread the stage. If commedia dell 'arte forms are adapted to theatre for young people, slapstick and physical contact humor go right along with them. If a bear kills an Eskimo, or a bounty hunter shoots a runaway slave boy, violent as it is, the event cannot be excised without doing damage to the cultural or historical truth being expounded by the playwright.

Much of the present repertoire evolved in a less sophisticated age, one less troubled by the questions we raise today. Certainly the original sources and most dramatizations of many childhood favorites reflected a naive acceptance of the inevitability of violence. *Treasure Island, Robin Hood, William Tell* and countless other adventure stories are alive with it. But the ultimate disposition of Grandmother, Red Riding Hood and the Wolf became something of a dilemma as soon as authors began to be conscious of opposition to violence in stories for children. Dramatists, too, were caught up in this growing philosophy of attenuation, especially as it related to fairy tales. Alternative outcomes were invented. While this practice will probably continue, we must admit that all efforts to attenuate have not been equally successful from a dramatic point of view.

Some modern playwrights have managed to avoid violence completely or have written their way around it, perhaps couched it stylistically. *Two Pails of Water* and *The Dancing Donkey*, both from the Dutch repertoire, come as close as possible to being violence-free while retaining dramatic interest. Aurand Harris' *The Brave Little Tailor* at one point has two dead Giants on stage, but their fight-to-the-death occurred behind a cloth screen. We saw only the energetic bumping of the curtain, the flying shoes and clubs. According to Golden's stage directions, Johnny Moonbeam's fight with the gods of Rain, Fire and Earth is a virtually choreographed affair. Joy Harvey has Antelope Boy and his people exorcise the evil powers from the nearly dead Cloud Girl and send them mystically to attack and kill Coyote, thus returning evil to its perpetrator. Thistle and Nettle in Kierski and Hartwig's "Tom Thumb" dance a ritualized attack on the friendly flowers in an effort to capture Tom.

Playwrights make conscious decisions regarding the appropriateness of violence or violence-substitutes for each dramatic situation, basing each decision on a knowledge of the educational potential of the theatre. We feel that such decisions are safer in their hands than in any actual or *sub rosa* board of censors. Here, as elsewhere, we favor freedom, an enlightened freedom, as of course all freedom should be.

Sex Roles

Theatre for young people is making an effort to free itself from one tradition that has held it captive for decades. From the perspective of feminists of the late Sixties and Seventies, our plays shared with children's literature and school textbooks a narrow view of vocational roles, occupational models, and behavior patterns appropriate to girls and women. One response to the challenge was a marked increase in the number of non-scripted theatre pieces, quite characteristically and pointedly free from sexism. Another was the appearance of more plays in various styles that presented women and girls on a more equal footing from a contemporary point of view.

A look at the playscripts we have discussed thus far reveals that male protagonists outnumber females more than two to one. This fact no doubt is rooted in the generally accepted premise that girls and boys both will be interested in the doings of boy protagonists, whereas boys, especially at certain ages, will reject stories and plays with girl protagonists. The phenomenon no doubt is culturally based and may well change as boys are encouraged by their entire unbringing to accept the equality of girls in all matters. Almost one-third of these same plays has a pair of protagonists, a boy and a girl, or a human or animal protagonist of indiscriminate sex. Coincidentally, about two-thirds of the playwrights and composers we have mentioned are men.[16]

Charges against the plays from a feminist perspective would appear to be justified. Those based on traditional literature, no doubt reflecting a historical societal view of women's servility and inferiority to men, usually depicted females aspiring to marriage or a state of protective security for self fulfillment. Plays in the modern idiom most often showed girls whose role in their families is to support the men and boys. As one of a pair of protagonists the girl almost always is the follower, not the leader. She watches the boy do things. In situations of stress, she is likely to cry while the boy solves the problem.[17]

Girls, women, princesses who rebel against their traditional lot in life are usually "straightened out" by their prospective husbands, as in the various versions of "The Princess and the Swineherd." In some dramatizations of "Hansel and Gretel," an effort is made to soften the stigma of the witch's murder by having Hansel share in, or even perform, the act which in Grimm belongs exclusively to Gretel. While the Andersen story of "The Little Mermaid" remained for many years without a dramatization, it now stands in at least two versions as the very antithesis of an acceptable relationship between men and women from a feminist perspective, however charming and mystical it may be in other respects.

But there is a more positive side to the picture. Back in 1948 Charlotte Chorpenning in collaboration with Rose Hum Lee published a play called *Lee Bobo, Detective for Chinatown,* which was ahead of its time in terms of female sex roles. Lee Bobo, a girl oscillating between her ancestral Chinese and her adopted American cultures, displays an unusual dedication to adventure and to unmasking a robber. A protagonist such as Ellie Murphy in *Step On a Crack,* advances further along the anti-sugar-and-spice path, for Ellie is a highly imaginative, determined young girl who keeps her room in a mess and enjoys all sorts of non-girl activities such as sports and playing war. *Molly Whuppie,* by Joella Brown, lives an imaginative life that brings her into contact with the creatures and people of her fantasies, requiring great courage to confront the giant. All the Grips plays from West Berlin make a point of the fight for equality of the sexes, both on the part of the children who are the protagonists and that of the adults whose shortcomings in this regard figure prominently in the plots. Such plays as these emphasize that there is a wide range of acceptable behaviors for girls — that they can do anything boys can with just as broad an acceptable character base.

Another kind of play shows women and girls engaging in acts of heroism. Marian Jonson's *Green-*

sleeves' Magic concerns the determination of Princess Miranda to learn the frightening secret that alone can defeat the diabolical Grand Duchess and to muster the courage to do what must be done. Gerda, the little girl in the various versions of "The Snow Queen," undertakes a fearful journey through many harrowing adventures, arriving finally in the Queen's icy realm where she rescues her friend Kay. Vasilisa the Hard Worker encounters hardship and fearful confrontations with that most wicked of witches, Baba Yaga, and accomplishes impossible tasks to rescue her sons who have been turned into *The Two Maples*. The well known heroism of Harriet Tubman, called Moses, who led her people in small groups out of slavery into Canada on the underground railroad, is depicted in Kraus' *Mean to Be Free*. Nicollette goes on a virtual Odyssey to rescue Prince Niccolo from the spell of the evil Magnus, and Trudi displays great courage and inventiveness as she and the Minstrel destroy the power of the Baroness in two popular plays by Alan Cullen. Thus women are shown to be capable of heroic actions on a par with men in a number of scripts available today.

In some older plays women who followed professional careers were either subjects of ridicule or were so myopic that they became antagonists in pursuit of their own goals. One may of course point to all those dramatizations of *Little Women* in which Jo aspires to a career as a writer, or to Brian Way's *On Trial,* in which one female is the doctor accompanying the expedition in search of a medicinal herb, as examples of suitable occupational models. Unfortunately, these are exceptions to a general pattern of neglect or avoidance. One recent script, Harders' *The Near-Sighted Knight and the Far-Sighted Dragon*, depicts a princess-heroine who aspires to be an engineer and carries a slide rule which she occasionally uses as a sword; but even this one seems to put such aspiration into an incongruous, humorous context that is part of the total ambience of the musical.

As Bettelheim says, whether the protagonist in a fairy tale is depicted as male or female makes little difference to children. They will perceive either sex in that role as they visualize themselves in the action, for the central conflict is a human matter applicable to both sexes equally. Yet it would seem that plays with contemporary themes and settings are badly needed to help girls see the options open to them now that our social view has expanded and lost a great deal of its sexist constriction.

Thus one more dimension of freedom opens for our playwrights.

Morality and Poetic Justice

Implied in much of the discussion of fading restrictions on the young people's theatre playwright is an undercurrent of increased willingness to introduce to children — especially older children and youth — a more complex code of morality than was previously thought suitable.

As soon as we permit rogue heroes to arouse our sympathies or we allow the virtuous to die on stage, we have said at least two important things. First, we have admitted that right and wrong are not absolutes but rather are relative to the character and the situation. The greater right or the greater wrong needs to be perceived in making judgments. Second, we admit that virtue does not always triumph, that good does not always win. It is true in life and it can be true on the stage. There comes a time when childlike reasoning patterns of absolutes, of easily recognized good-bad morality codes, necessary as they may be for a base of idealism, do not satisfy the needs of the developing intellect.

An allegory of children's evolution into adult morality is Isabelle Foord's *A Dream of Sky People*. The Indian husband and wife leave the peace, security, moral simplicity and perfection of their heavenly home. They journey to earth. There they encounter Lynx and other predatory animals seeking their lives. They are frightened by dangers and threats. Gradually they come to learn naturalistic laws, that life and death, good and evil exist side by side. As Lynx says, he too lives in this world. "What is good? What is pretty? Good is a kill; pretty is a full stomach;" and after performing a simple good deed his friend the grizzly echoes, "My heart is soft, but sometimes an empty stomach speaks louder than the heart." The husband and wife decide to stay and coax their sustenance from the reluctant earth; and to remind them of their beginnings in perfection, they are allowed to keep the small piece of sky the wife had tucked away.

Many of the plays we have previously mentioned in connection with rogue protagonists, death and violence ask children to make increasingly mature moral judgments. Individuals can have both evil and good within them, and sometimes a single act can have both good and bad aspects. Instead of innumerable variations of the maxim that "good always triumphs over evil," some of the new repertoire is daring to say some things that come closer to a functioning (if not verbalized) morality system. "Might makes right." "Possession is nine points of the law." "It's not what you know, it's who you know." "A fool and his money are soon parted." "Revenge is sweet." "Opportunity knocks but once." "Win. I don't care how, but win." "Survival of the fittest." "All's fair in love and war."

Ted Hughes in his thought-provoking play, *The Tiger's Bones,* tells of a distinguished but addle-brained scientist who teaches a primitive African tribe to replace its natural jungle food supply with flowing wheat fields. When the wheat burns he teaches them to build automobile factories, to make cars to sell for food. An apparent good deed has brought on disaster, leading surely to starvation. When a concept such as "an evil good," one symbolizing genocide, appears in the repertoire, surely we must take note of the occasion.

Poetic justice, the principle that evil is punished and good rewarded, gets more complicated when goodness and badness are not represented in absolute terms by the characters.

Reynard, Punch, and Little Klaus, to name three, are not ultimately punished for their misdeeds. Don Quixote, the Little Mermaid, Johnny Appleseed, and Anatou the Ice Wolf are sympathetic protagonists who die, violating the axiom of the happy ending. Rewards in such plays do not exemplify poetic justice in a simple, obvious sense. Naturalistic laws are also working, and decisions about justice require a broader frame of reference than is usually required for children's plays.

Undoubtedly a majority of the repertoire for young audiences will continue to demonstrate an obvious poetic justice. Most plays, especially those for the younger ages, will continue to end with the triumph, not the death, of the protagonist. We would not advocate abolishing the precedent. But we would encourage playwrights to recognize the needs of older children to wrestle with more mature and complex moral problems, and to admit that simple justice is not always present in the real world. By nine or ten a child already knows these things. Sometimes the wrong wins. Sometimes the good die. Here is one way that an expanded repertoire can give children something to grow on.

Love and Sex

For a time Pat Hale's dramatization of *The Little Mermaid* and her unrequited devotion to her Prince was the sole example of a play for children pointedly on the subject of romantic love. Then the Honeybee rather shyly declared his love for *The Butterfly* within the thinly veiled disguise of an insect world metaphor. In quick succession came a Lady Alison who attempts to seduce *Sir Gawain* and a Beast who speaks to Beauty of bending her to his will. Soon Europe provided us two plays of young love, both acknowledging sexual attraction, yet emphasizing tenderness and respect. *Hey, There — Hello!* comes from the Soviet repertoire, and *What Do You Call Love Here?* originated in West Germany.

While none of these indicates that plays for children are soon to become X-rated, they do suggest an important shift in thinking. The previously tight doorway has been opened even further by society's increasing concern for matters of sexual abuse and the general topic of sex education. Plays such as *Bubbylonian Encounter* by Gene Mackey, achieved wide distribution through a Theatre for Young America tour, production rights and videotape in an effort to make young children aware that they have a right to protest "forced sexual touch." Changes in society's attitudes may well be attributed to increased attention to sexually related problems among children and teenagers or to acknowledgement that television programming seems to negate the need to be protective, since wide exposure to the subject of sex is unavoidable.[18]

Most plays for children, however, continue to emphasize dispassionate love and admiration, friendship, if you will, between partners destined for marriage; affection between friends and members of families; and impassioned love for institutions such as home, freedom and justice.

HALLMARKS OF EXCELLENCE

Criteria for judging the worth of scripts are obviously undergoing some change. In the past one could accept or reject them largely according to their adherence to the restrictions assumed to be operative in the form itself. But now that so many of those prohibitions have dissolved or at least lost their potency, we are faced with the need to reassert what we feel are desirable qualities inherent in scripts themselves.

A Genuine Relevance

That much overused term, relevance, in its best sense means a recognizable applicability or pertinence. Plays should in some meaningful way arouse in the audience a recognition that the characters and situations are speaking to them directly, that they have meaning in their lives. When it is used this way, we have no quarrel with the term.

There has been, however, an unfortunate tendency for some playwrights and groups to incorporate a cheap and easy relevance in their plays in an obvious effort to capitalize on a contemporary market. In some cases we need not worry about such scripts because their so-called relevance disappears shortly after the plays are published. Others, however, hit upon a subject that continues in the public eye and makes their scripts superficially attractive for some time. Preventing forest fires, the simpler aspects of ecology, conserving energy or television pop-culture are all capable of being exploited on the cross of relevance.

The only test for true relevance, aside from an instinctive revulsion of phoniness, is that of ensuring that the theme in question is integral to the progress of the total story. It must not be superimposed. If it can be excised without harming the main plot line, perhaps cutting it out is the simplest way to save an otherwise good script.

Respect for Children

A genuine, positive respect for the intelligence and emotional integrity of young people in the audience has always been regarded a prime qualification for our playwrights. Presumably such respect will be reflected in the scripts themselves. And so will its opposite, which takes the form of exploitation for cheap laughs, of easy, unmotivated solutions, of topical quips and funny gags that set the company (seldom the children) into paroxysms of hilarity. The tendency toward this kind of fault has been increasing instead of decreasing.

Respect is shown in the fact that the deeper meanings of the script are integral to the story and its characters, not gratuitously tacked on as a preachy moral. It means that the jargon and jingle of television commercials are left to the exclusive use of that medium. Language in plays needs to be conscientiously created, not hastily thrown together with clichés and slang in abundance.

Respect means that humor is characterized by a genuine sense of childlike fun rather than tongue-in-cheek adult jokes. This kind of humor, at children's expense, is the worst sort of "camp" and has no place in our playscripts.

There also appears to be a distinction between freedom to adapt traditional stories and desecration of those stories. Children are anxious to recognize the play version of the story they come to see. Often they cannot, it has been so changed, so updated, so infused with pseudo-relevance. This seems to be especially true of musicals. Respect for children should act as a deterrent for those playwrights who might be tempted to destroy a familiar story for the sake of what they believe to be freshness.

A similar problem exists in the category of "spoofs." A delightfully honest spoof of old time vaudeville is suggested in the routines of Toby the dog and Hector the dancing horse in Harris' *Punch and Judy*. But enjoyment of those brief routines does not depend on having seen vaudeville in its heyday. Spoofs and parodies of fairy tales, film westerns or old-time melodramas, however, often miss the mark for children. Perhaps the critical evaluation is this: if children need to be familiar with the original reference, the art form, the story or institution being spoofed for the humor or enjoyment of the situation, then the chances of failure are great indeed. Children accept what they see at face value until they have acquired a frame of reference to interpret otherwise. That is the beauty — and the vulnerability — of childhood. We have no business violating it for our own amusement.

Pleasurable Theatre

As we have discussed maturation in subject matter, themes, morality judgments, disappearing stereotypes of race and sex, and increasing freedoms for playwrights we are aware that readers' expectations of the repertoire may shift undesirably toward didacticism. Nothing could be farther from our intentions. There are few things worse than a play that deliberately sets out to teach something, anything, however worthy.[19]

While teaching *per se* is to be avoided, we can expect that learning will take place, and it will take place largely through role-modeling, a process which was discussed at some length in the preceding chapter. Scripts, then, should reflect an enlightened view toward nationalities, races, cultures and social classes, toward sex-appropriate behaviors and career expectations, toward violence and aggression as a method of solving problems. This obligation must not be construed to mean that a playwright should distort history in a non-contemporary play to conform to later attitudes, nor does it require that such a point of view be anachronistically incorporated into tales derived from different cultures. *Escape to Freedom* could not very well show white masters holding respectful attitudes toward their slaves. *The Ice Wolf* must be told in the context of a society that put girl babies out to perish in the snow in times of short food supply.

Plays teach because an idea is embodied in an action. The main thing a play does, however, is to involve young people in an engrossing experience. Above all, our playscripts must be arresting, seizing attention and sustaining interest in a developing sequence of incidents that leads to emotional satisfaction and a sense of fulfillment.

Logical Outcomes

The new freedom for playwrights has given them the chance to allow the denouement to be a true and natural outgrowth of the characters and situation. As more complex issues are treated in children's plays, the tendency toward simplistic solutions must be resisted.

The difference between the honest and the simplistic outcome was demonstrated to delegates at two different ASSITEJ Congresses. In 1968, at The Hague, an Amsterdam ballet company presented a dance drama about an American Negro girl who was going to a white school on the first day of the term. She was new in the area. She was shy. The other students rejected her. As problems multiplied, a kind and understanding teacher told the white children they should accept the new girl into their games. And they did. Everything ended happily. A phony poetic justice, if not logic, was served. By contrast, at the 1972 Albany Congress, "The Georgia Tour Play" as presented by the Academy Theatre of Atlanta, depicted sympathetically, theatrically and honestly the complicated efforts of two high school boys, one white and one black, to remain friends in spite of the pressure of parents and peers in an atmosphere of racial conflict. At the end, an edgy truce substituted for the friendship that had been. It was not a pretty ending, but it was an honest one.

Plays for younger children should demonstrate a similar truth and logic. As Ilse Rodenberg pleaded at the Hague Congress, "the theatre must not pretend a social harmony or show a misleading picture of the world."

114

Meaningful Involvement

Scripts calling for audience participation have had less time to demonstrate what constitutes excellence than some other styles of production; yet from our brief perspective it appears as if much participation has been cheap and easy, like relevance. Almost any perfunctory excuse has been sufficient for a playwright to ask children for some direct response: a sound effect, a magic word at the right moment, to stand up, turn around and sit down. Some scripts give one the feeling that a series of pantomimic exercises has been loosely strung together in a semblance of plot in order to keep children busy for an hour.

If a participation drama is a sequential story, then a set of characters creatively and interestingly conceived by the playwright is engaged in a struggle of some significance. As in any script, characters and plot must be devoid of inconsistencies and unfulfilled expectations. Children should not be asked to give their loyalties and their labors to pointless and really fruitless causes. The children's participation should arise naturally and needfully from the premises of the drama itself, not be tacked on at odd moments when they might otherwise be getting restless. In addition to giving clear cues for generating and stopping the participation, dialogue written for the actors needs to exemplify as high a literary standard as any other play for children.

Even though a participation play is by nature incomplete until performed with the help of children in the audience, the center of the experience is the play as conceived by a playwright; and it needs to be just as good as — if not better than — any other play if the children are to take part in it.

Artists laboring to develop an improved and expanded repertoire for the theatre for children and youth continue to breach the boundaries, moving in an almost bewildering number of directions. The hardy band of playwright-pioneers includes some whose output is prodigious, others with only one or two works to their credit. While a single innovative script does not necessarily set a trend, each one is important, and every playwright who blazes a new trail deserves notice. In the aggregate, their work suggests directions we might choose to follow.

The plays mentioned in this chapter represent only a sampling of the number of scripts currently available for production. We have attempted to choose representative works which reveal the diversity characteristic of the contemporary repertoire. We have noted that many of yesterday's barriers are crumbling, but we hasten to add that they are by no means gone. Many of the faults we tolerated in the scripted literature of an earlier time are still very much with us. Much of our growth is slow and painful, and there always are those who remain resistant to change.

But change we will, and our playwrights will continue to serve as instruments of that change. Their plays reflect trends, often set them. We rely on them for the material around which we shape our art. Their work is the record of the field, and as we examine it, we gain needed perspective.

NOTES:

[1]Descriptions of most of the plays mentioned in this chapter will be found in Appendix 11.

[2]Austin: University of Texas Press, 1977.

[3]For catalogues and other information about operas and music dramas for children, contact Opera for Youth, Box 219, Route 2, Athens, Ohio 45701.

[4]Claire Jones, "What Do Children Want in Children's Theatre?" *Children's Theatre Review*, XXII, 4 (1973), 11.

[5]Book adapted from L. Frank Baum by Frank Gabrielson, score by Harold Arlen and E.R. Harburg (New York: Tams-Witmark Music Library, Inc., 1938, 1939, 1978).

[6]Dan Sullivan, " 'Camp' and Children's Theatre," Speech to the 12th Annual Showcase of Professional Children's Theatre, New York, May, 1967. Reprinted in *Children's Theatre Review*, XVI, 3 (1967), 7-9; Dan Sullivan, "Children's Theatre in New York: Some of it is Good." New York *Times*, April 10, 1967.

[7]See Joyce Doolittle and Zina Barnieh, *A Mirror of Our Dreams: Children and the Theatre in Canada* (Vancouver, B.C.: Talonbooks, 1979).

[8]St. Louis: Telos Press, 1976.

[9]Rowayton, Connecticut: New Plays Books, 1977.

[10]Two more books for which Miriam Morton is responsible have provided at last an accurate view of children's and youth theatre in the U.S.S.R. *Through the Magic Curtain* (New Orleans: Anchorage Press, 1979) is a collection of essays by prominent artists of the Soviet TIUZ, past and present. *The Arts and the Soviet Child* (New York: Free Press, 1972) gives an overview of arts education in the U.S.S.R., including the place of theatre in the total picture.

[11]See Chapter III for a discussion of Dorothy Aldrich's study of children's reactions to a production of Reynard.

[12]See Chapter III for a summary of Martha Rhea's study of children's and teachers' attitudes toward this play.

[13]During a period of acute sensitivity, the "Sun Snatchers" episode in *Golliwhoppers!* in at least one production was perceived by Native Americans as failing to keep the various Indian cultures sufficiently discrete.

[14]Gayle Cornelison, "Death and Childhood: Attitudes and Approaches in Society, Children's Literature and Children's Theatre and Drama," Diss. Kansas 1975.

[15]In Brill's *The Masque of Beauty and the Beast,* Beast actually dies in Beauty's arms and then returns to life transformed.

[16]What appears as a reversal of the assumed predominance of women playwrights is likely a reflection of the particular segment of the repertoire examined here.

[17]Elizabeth Green, "Female Gender Role Representation in Children's Theatre Literature," Thesis Kansas 1975.

[18]Sex education specials so far have been aired only on eduational television. In West Germany the Rote Grutze attracted considerable attention through its production of "One Doesn't Talk About That," a sex education play using "anatomically correct" costume overlays. See Anita Page, "Some New Aspects of Children's Theatre in West Germany," *Children's Theatre Review*, XXV, 1 (1976), 6-7. An interesting related discussion can be found in Neil Postman's *The Disappearance of Childhood*, cited earlier.

[19]For an extended discussion of this point see Jonathan Levy, "A Theatre of the Imagination," *Children's Theatre Review*, XXVII, 1 (1978), 2-5 ff.

CHAPTER V
MAKING CHOICES

Once again it is time to choose the next show. The director contemplates a colorful array of play-scripts and flips through them in random fashion. There's a good title! But a quick reading of the opening scene turns him off. The discard pile grows . . . wrong style, trivial theme, shallow treatment of story, stereotyped characters, uninspired dialogue. Another arresting title. But will it sell? Here is a script that seems to pass the test. But alas, it can't be considered this year . . . too many practical problems. Off it goes into the future possibilities stack. And the process goes on and on.

Elsewhere a group of performers gathers. Excited over the possibility of creating their own theatre piece, they fill the air with ideas. "Hey, this would be cute!" "Wouldn't it be fun if . . .?" Suddenly someone says, "Wait a minute! Isn't this supposed to be for kids?" And there is silence.

Whether it involves a single person screening and evaluating scripts, or a group probing its collective imagination, selecting material, style or focal point for a production can be the most agonizing step in the entire process of making theatre for young audiences. Ultimately, the success of the entire venture rests in the hands of the one who makes the initial choice. Once it is made, the complex machinery of the producing organization is set in motion. A commitment, once made, leaves no avenue of retreat.

Thus we devote this chapter to developing some guidelines for choosing material and production style. In Chapter VI, we will examine the process of conceptualizing the production and preparing for rehearsal. Chapter VII is focused on bringing concept to stage. Throughout these chapters we assume that the director's understanding of the young audience and his concern for high production standards will influence every decision that is made.

Obviously, choice of style or material is less difficult when the responsible party has a clear sense of purpose and sufficient knowledge of theatre for the young, its literature and the several styles available to him. If he is associated with an established theatre, he has the advantage of being able to review past seasons to analyze successes and failures and to evaluate how effectively the organization is fulfilling its obligation to offer its public a variety of theatre fare.

In years gone by, the path to season planning and play selection was more direct than it is today, in that it quite narrowly focused on the types of scripts available for consideration. Choices were partially governed by the contribution a given script would make to a program designed to provide young audiences a mix of fairy tale, fantasy, realism and hero story from season to season. Production decisions related to whether the play would be staged in proscenium, in the round or in some variant of the arena, and to how much visual elaboration would be necessary to make the characters and settings real to the young. Then, as now, style was thought of as a point of view toward the production as a whole, but particular attention was paid to its comprehensive contribution to making a *story* come alive. Today we work in a broader frame of reference and think of style as a way of making theatre.

As we have seen, a number of professional companies have developed individualized performance styles which have become their trademarks. Free of the need to make stylistic choices, their main area of decision making is in choosing and shaping material in a continuous effort to maintain freshness. The average producer, however, welcomes opportunities to work in a variety of styles.

THE DIRECTOR AS ARBITER OF CHOICE

We advocate that responsibility for making stylistic and content choices, establishing and overseeing implementation of the over-all production plan and general coordination of its processes be vested in a single individual — the director. This chapter develops from his point of view.

Practical considerations should be set aside in the early stages of the selection process. Most directors know full well what limitations ultimately will have a bearing on choice, but they should not become the base line from which one works. The first stages of selection are essentially subjective, and the director lets his imagination range among a number of possibilities related to what he would enjoy doing. He must want to work with the style and the material he chooses, and find a challenge in it. His own need to grow as an artist is not really a self-serving motive. The artistic growth of the entire organization as well as the audiences it serves is at least in some degree dependent upon the director's expanding vision.

First of all, enthusiasm and commitment are infectious. Fresh challenges to their creativity keep designers and technicians interested in and respectful of the work they do for children's theatre. Exploring new ways of working stimulates the best efforts of an established acting company, and opportunity to experience variety is appealing to actors who respond to open auditions. Above all, the young audience deserves opportunities to share in explorations of the richness that is theatre.

The more exposure the director has had to the work and thinking of his colleagues in the field, the broader his vision. An exciting production may introduce him to an unfamiliar script or arouse renewed interest in one already known. Direct observation of performances in new and unfamiliar styles will be more enlightening than any amount of reading. The director is able to be far more objective in assessing the overall quality and effectiveness of a production that has been staged by someone else. He also benefits from what other directors have to say about their artistic decisions and their experiences with dramatic material and styles. A cautionary word, however: no director should adopt a performance style or choose any script simply because it worked for someone else, nor should he let current popularity of any style or title be a primary criterion for choice.

The director's primary motivation should be to provide a rich variety of theatre fare in each season and over a period of several seasons. He particularly wants to avoid giving young theatregoers the false impression that theatre is any single style of production, which he is likely to do if he ignores the options open to him. He continually asks what special experience he wishes the audience to gain from each production and makes his choices accordingly.

In thinking about style the director also considers his personal preferences and his own strengths and weaknesses. With each production he becomes increasingly aware of the approaches and methods that enable him to work with the highest degree of security, effectiveness and pleasure. If the demands of a given style seem overwhelming, if he has reservations about the style itself, or if he feels ill informed about it or doubts he has the special skills it demands of a director, he should leave it alone.

ON CHOOSING A STYLE

The director may choose from among the performance styles defined in Chapter II, or, in this day and age, he may set about inventing his own. We have seen in Chapter IV that an increasing number of scripts place more emphasis on theatrical style than on conventional dramatic form, broadening options for the director who wishes to work in a variety of modes, but who feels more comfortable with a script and wishes to exercise customary directorial control over the production. For many, the published script is the preferred choice, and it certainly can be the safer one. Virtually all play publishers issue only scripts that have been subjected to the test of production and which have been chosen by people who spend a lifetime observing and reading plays. This is not to minimize the importance of innovative original work, merely to point out that there are unquestioned advantages to working with proved material.

Several styles of production and performance were defined in Chapter II and examined as part of the discussion of the contemporary script repertoire in Chapter IV. We now return to them, as we outline some of the characteristics of each one that the director will want to keep in mind as he takes the first steps in deciding what type of play he will do and how he will do it.

Traditional

In recent years some directors as well as other personnel associated with the theatre for young audiences have come to view the traditional style as dated, unnecessarily encumbering and overly confining, and have abandoned it in favor of less representational production modes. Others continue to believe that the traditional production with all its trappings is synonymous with theatre magic. While it would be unreasonable to argue that children require elaborate mounting and sumptuous costumes in order to understand and enjoy a performance, it would be equally shortsighted to reject the traditional production out of hand. If it appears to be the style that will best serve the script, and if its aesthetic and practical requirements can be met, it has considerable merit. It is virtually the only one in which children's theatre actors can create fully-developed and sustained characterizations. For design and technical artists there is the special gratification of being able to create fully-realized spectacle. For the audience there is the satisfaction of surrender to illusion, of empathic involvement in a story brought fully to life through action and spectacle. John Donahue makes a strong case for this style of theatre:

> I think it's possible that adults who are tied to that kind of perception in their own lives — requiring a very specific delineation and articulation — and who don't share the child's ability to make abstract connections may feel purged and freed when they see work done in quite the opposite way. They respond to it as being fresh and childlike. ...But I think that most children, as they make do with a board and a pole, would actually rather be sailing one of the 'tall ships.'
>
> I don't think that naturalistic spectacle is by any means the only way of telling stories to children, and I do not use it exclusively in my own work. But I do know that it is a valid way of making things materialize at one end of a room, in a theatre. People say, 'Oh, it's elaborate. Children don't need it, children don't want it.' I feel that children may not need it, but they certainly do appreciate it when it's offered to them. I don't think everything should be reduced to colored boxes and cardboard circles.[1]

Non-illusionistic Styles

Other styles are more frankly presentational and actor-centered. They are viewed with favor because, as Orlin Corey observes, "The joy of performance is exploited by freeing productions from timber, paint and properties. The theatre's infinite and unique resources for actor-made atmosphere and mood are marshalled, and an imaginative dimension is developed."[2]

As Donahue suggests, many feel that these styles hold particular charm for children because they have some of the characteristics of childhood dramatic play. Whether or not they are invited into direct participation, young audience members are called upon to become co-creators. As actors and audience share in make-believe, the spectators give their own imaginative dimension to characters, non-illusionistic visual elements and non-existent properties. Directors find satisfaction in discovering that the fragmentary, non-linear structure characteristic of so many of these theatre pieces tends to hold audience attention more consistently than does the single-story play.

The frankly presentational production affords actors opportunities to explore varied approaches to characterization and audience interaction. Performances take on a ritualistic quality and encourage strong ensemble playing. The creative resources of actors and designers are challenged as they seek imaginative ways of building a lively dramatic event using only themselves and minimal theatrical trapping.

Story Theatre

Typically, story theatre maintains a degree of audience distancing akin to the traditional style, unfolding before the audience and involving them empathically rather than overtly. A number of fine scripted works are available for choice. Or the director may elect to guide a cast in the collective development of the theatre piece. In the latter case he will have to decide whether he will preselect material or entertain suggestions from the group. Whether it is scripted or group-generated, this style calls upon its actors to tell as well as show the stories.

Improvisational Theatre

Here we think of a performance that is originated and shaped by a company, but brought to polished state before it comes to the audience. Improvisatory exploration may culminate in full-length treatment of a single story, a series of stories in which actors assume individual characters, a story theatre piece, a series of sketches in the manner of vaudeville, a collage of childhood images, impressions and sensations, mood pieces, compendia of rhymes, or even circus acts.

In considering group-generated production, the director must first make a realistic assessment of his own willingness and ability to relinquish the tight control he traditionally holds on the production process. He also must be keenly aware of the delicate boundary that separates democracy from the anarchy of abdicated responsibility. If he sees himself capable of standing aside to let collective creativity shape the performance; if he has a clear sense of what he hopes such a performance will achieve in terms of audience impact; if he can organize realistically to meet the established deadline; if he realizes that at some point improvisation and exploration must stop and feels able to make a smooth transition into his more traditional role, he may well find the experience rewarding.

The director also must decide how much latitude he will give the cast in determining content and form and how much pre-conceptualization he will bring to rehearsal. If design and technical support will be sought outside the cast, he will have to be ready to clarify goals and expectations in a context that, at the outset, is necessarily unclear. Another important decision relates to the presence of a writer. If there is to be one, the director will want to determine precisely how that person will function in relation to the group and to the director himself.

Instant theatre requires such skill and such a strong ensemble that it is best left alone except by a group that has been improvising together over an extended period of time. In any case, the weakness of planning an entire performance in this mode should be immediately apparent.

Participation Theatre

There are more inherent limitations on this style than on any other considered thus far. Even its staunchest advocates warn that its effectiveness depends on intimate playing space and a small audience of common age level. A participatory performance should not be undertaken in a large theatre or in circumstances where the size and composition of audience cannot be controlled. Probably it is most satisfactory when the performance can be taken into a controlled environment, such as a school, rather than attempted for public performance. This style demands that actors be possessed of exceptional skills, for they not only must be able to give a credible performance. They also must be accomplished creative drama leaders.

Theatre in Education

This is not a style, but rather a program. It will be discussed in Chapter X.

120

Readers Theatre

This is not popularly thought of as a style for public performance in the theatre for children and youth, although it is worthy of consideration. It is interpreters' theatre, and although readings from dramatic works have been well received in the adult theatre, narrative and poetry seem to be preferred choices for presentation. Those unfamiliar with readers theatre are inclined to think of it as a static style in which a group of readers are seated on stools with manuscripts spread before them on lecterns. Its exponents have experimented with performances ranging from traditional reading to staged performance, differing from the conventional theatre only because the performance usually is done with script in hand.

The Institute for Readers Theatre in San Diego, California, publishes a newsletter containing information of value to the director wishing to familiarize himself with this style.[3]

Musical Theatre

Opera. We have noted that the director can avail himself of an increasing number of operas especially composed for young audiences. Stylistically, these works range from traditional opulence to artful simplicity in their staging requirements. The variety of available material means that children and young people no longer need be denied opportunities to enjoy operatic performances for budgetary reasons alone. Nevertheless, the decision to produce an opera is contingent upon the availability of an expert music director, singer-actors capable of meeting its demands, competent instrumental musicians and, in many cases, a choreographer.

Musicals. Perhaps no style of theatre is as universally popular as this one, and there are numerous scripts to consider. As with opera, the success of the musical will depend on the quality of the musical direction, singing voices and instrumental support. Dance is integral to most musicals, making expert choreography a must.

ON CHOOSING A SCRIPT

While there is no way of knowing what percentage of the productions staged for children and youth are based on scripted material, it seems reasonable to believe that a significant number are. Not all of them are selected from publishers' catalogues. Many directors write their own or solicit them from a variety of sources. An increasing number of groups have a writer present when they work improvisationally. The writer records material as it evolves and eventually gives it dramatic form. Certain criteria apply to all scripts, whatever their source or style. Throughout Chapter IV, attention is called to qualities and content that contribute to the intrinsic merit of playscripts. The qualities that make them worthy of performance also need to be understood.

For the present we limit discussion of structure, theme, character, dialogue, action and spectacle to guidelines for selection. The director's in-depth analysis of these elements will be a subject for Chapter VI.

Structure — The Single Story

If the script is based upon a single story, the plot line must be clear and uncluttered, with events occurring in logical sequence. The plot begins with a problem that immediately arouses interest and concern. Then it develops in a manner that validates the emotional expenditure of the perceiver, showing the protagonist confronting the problem and struggling to overcome obstacles as they arise. Complications build tension. The resolution of each complication gives rise to another, building rhythmically to a telling climax and an outcome that emerges as a logical result of everything that has preceded. All events of consequence to the plot occur on stage. Even when it comes about through the intervention of a magical force, the resolution never happens to a passive protagonist. He must have been actively involved in finding his own way to overcome his difficulties.

A script based upon a known literary work must be faithful to the original. Though the short story will require amplification, and the novel-length work will be adapted through selection, all choices must be made with sincere respect for the qualities that made the material worthy of adaptation in the first place.

Structure — Multiple Stories

Instead of writing scripts giving sequential treatment to single stories, many playwrights choose to develop a series of stories into performance packages. This has a number of advantages, not the least of them being that it enables an author to give dramatic life to material that does not lend itself to adaptation as a full-length play. These scripts are drawn from a rich variety of sources — ethnic, literary, national, biographical, to name a few. Material may be chosen on the basis of common theme as well.

In this mode, each story becomes a mini-play subject to the same structural criteria applied to a longer work. The effectiveness of the script will depend to large degree on the way it is structured to create a unified theatre piece. Transitions thus become as important as the individual dramatic scenes. A number of imaginative devices are available to the playwright. Songs, dances, narration, choreographed scene shifts, or any of these in combination can be effectively used to unify the material and at the same time keep action flowing smoothly from one story episode to the next. Whatever device is chosen, it must be in harmony with the material and build interest from one segment to the next.

Structure — Participation Theatre Scripts

Only a sophisticated playwright is truly capable of creating a worthy participation theatre script, since he is not just writing a play to be produced for an audience, but also writing for audience as actors. If ever an understanding of the young is required of a playwright, it is when he undertakes this really formidable task. An examination of participation theatre scripts will reveal that many of them presuppose that the contributions of the director and actors should be greater than those of the playwright. In reality, the convention will work well only if the play is well structured. Participatory episodes must be generated in the plot, contribute to it and move it forward in a significant way, arising only when the story reaches a point where it cannot proceed without direct audience intervention. In other words, participation must be so designed that it increases rather than diffuses, defuses if you will, the dramatic focus of the play. It cannot interrupt the mood or be inserted merely to make the play longer or cover an awkward transition.[4] The quality of participation must also be taken into account. Beware the cliché request to clap or shout or say magic words on the count of three. Such shallow and predictable devices only pay lip service to participation and show little respect for the young audience.

Theme

The theatre for young audiences is not the place for sermonizing or polemics. A playwright who begins with a theme unrelated to a good story, either adapted or original with him, tends to shape all the elements of the drama with undue focus, and thus emphasis, on theme. Such an approach mitigates against artistry. No genuinely excellent play for the young deliberately sets out to teach. Certainly the playwright will have a point of view toward his story and characters, but that point of view is communicated implicitly through what happens in the play. The outcome of the drama will make the theme as explicit as it needs to be when the audience sees the results of actions taken by the characters.

Characters

Style has an important bearing on the way a playwright delineates characters. The contemporary repertoire, with its variety of styles, contains many characters written to serve style as well as story. Regardless of style, however, characters must be believable in context, and, in the case of favorite story plays, true to the original. The good script presents a variety of characters, each of whom has a clear relationship to the plot and a function in developing and revealing the dramatic conflict. If the script provides for "chorus" characters (a boon to the director who must find a place on stage for all the youngsters in a theatre group) the need for their presence and the function they will serve should be apparent.

The detail and depth with which individual characters are drawn will depend upon the overall style of the script and also upon character type. Those around whom the plot revolves must be defined, motivated, and of sufficient human dimension to arouse audience identification, and they should be capable of growth and change. The central figures in such plays as *Cinderella* and *The Sleeping Beauty* should be written with these qualities. The supernatural figures in folk and fairy tales, however, are archetypes, symbols of the good and evil forces abroad in the world. Cinderella's fairy godmother, the good fairies in *The Sleeping Beauty* and their counterparts in other stories are finished in form and unwavering in their goodness, and there is no need for them to change. The supernatural antagonist character — Rumpelstiltskin, the evil fairy in *The Sleeping Beauty,* the witch in *Hansel and Gretel,* Baba Yaga in *Vasalisa* come to mind — is unrelentingly evil, inherently incapable of change. Under no circumstances does the playwright destroy the impact of the drama by having one suddenly reform and go forth to lead a new and better life.

In many plays with a more realistic frame of reference the antagonist is equally incapable of change. It is not very likely that the Sheriff of Nottingham is going to undergo character reform when he receives his come-uppance from Robin Hood. In other plays the conflict resolves with an altered point of view in the antagonist, if not in a complete turn-about, at least in some accommodation to circumstances. In those cases the capacity to change must be inherent in the character, change is the logical outcome of the conflict, and the reasons for it have been implicit throughout the play.

Stereotyped characters must be validated by style or function. Sometimes they are purposely written to stand in sharp contrast to other characters. Their predictable reaction patterns deepen the significance of characters who are capable of a variety of responses. They almost always are antagonist figures like Cinderella's stepmother and stepsisters.

Stereotyped, one-dimensional or symbolic characters are an essential component of a number of highly-presentational, conventionalized theatre styles. Playwrights choose these styles to serve their aesthetic purposes as well as to expose young audiences to the variety of their theatre heritage. Truth to style and consistency within style are important criteria for characterization when one evaluates these scripts.

Examples of plays with characters of limited dimension include the Harris *Rags to Riches,* a recreation of old-time hiss-the-villain-cheer-the-hero melodrama where the pure and innocent are pitted against squint-eyed evil. Miller's *The Land of the Dragon* utilizes the conventions of the Oriental theatre to recount the struggles of characters whose names define them. "Jade Pure," victimized by "Covet Spring" and "Precious Harp," among others, is rescued from her plight by "Road Wanderer," who just happens along at the right moment. *Androcles and the Lion* (Harris) employs stock characters from the commedia dell'arte to unfold a tale of young innocence triumphing over materialism.

The character of Punch emerged at a much earlier time, and for generations has been a symbol of man's struggle for identity and for victory over the forces that stifle him. Folk characters in story theatre scripts are primarily symbolic and quickly sketched in conformance with the restrictions of that style.

Characters of narrow dimension have to be artfully conceived and delineated in order to capture the subtle essence of the good line drawing, and avoid the blatant statement of overblown cartooning.

Dialogue

A play is told through dialogue. Unlike the novelist who can write as many descriptive passages as he needs to develop his story, the playwright is limited to dialogue to further plot, reveal character and clarify situations. Knowing its importance, the author of a play for young audiences can easily trap himself in oversimplification, repetition and primer language that diminish his artistry and result in an inferior script. Richness and beauty of language and clarity of expression are not mutually-exclusive qualities in any writing. Youngsters are capable of understanding vocabulary far beyond their reading level, and they readily comprehend the meanings of words they do not themselves use in conversation. This, however, does not give the playwright license to indulge in use of language for its own sake. A talky play is a bad play in any form of theatre, and the author must bear in mind that this is particularly true in the theatre for the young, where audiences are far more interested in what they see than what they hear.

What, then, are some criteria for dialogue? In addition to quality and economy of language, variety in word choice, phrasing and sentence structures, and conversational tone combine to create desirable rhythm. Dialogue must generate and forward action, even as it accompanies it, and action must begin at the opening of the play. Exposition is an ingredient of action. The static expository scene is to be avoided, as are dialogue sequences written to express inner thoughts or state philosophy.

Humor must be neither overly sophisticated nor simplistically childish. While youngsters relish word play and pun, such devices should not be used gratuitously. Great care should be taken that dialect does not demean. Slang and colloquialisms are out of place in any play save the one in which it is suited to characters, period and situation. Dialogue should capture the flavor of a period without being archaic and obscure. If the play is an adaptation, the playwright should preserve the quality of its author's language, his turn of phrase and the way he has characters speak. This often means liberal borrowing and adjusting one's personal writing style.

Some playwrights make extensive use of rhyme in dialogue. We have some reservations about this practice. Much rhymed dialogue seems self-conscious and precious. Rhyme and meter are difficult for actors to handle well, and they are all too likely to fall into a singsong delivery that interferes with communication of thought, meaning and emotional content.

Dialogue individualizes characters. On the stage, as in life, the language and expressive manner of an individual are indicative of station in life, regional or ethnic roots, general background, learning, attitude and over-all personality. The audience will expect characters to speak suitably. Thus the playwright will avoid anachronisms. Members of a royal court do not use contemporary argot. Unless he is most unusual, a street urchin does not speak with professorial literacy.

In story theatre, where the spoken word includes narrative as well as character dialogue, the narration is impersonal, as if being told by someone outside the story. It usually is kept in the third person, always in the past tense. Lines written to invite audience involvement in participation theatre scripts should maintain the quality and tone of the dialogue spoken within the stage action, be suited to character, and, most importantly, be free of invitation to the cliché response.

Emphasis already has been placed on the implicit theme and on the negative quality of explicit statements of lessons to be learned from the play. Except in rare instances where the style or the period being recreated validate a didactic tone, the playwright eschews direct moralizing, and, unless he is deliberately creating prissy, unlikeable characters, he will not give them such lines to speak. Characters in highly conventionalized plays, of course, are legitimate exceptions. Often they are naive and express their thoughts on morals and propriety simply because that is what seems to them the right thing to do, and we find them charming. No one objects to the moralistic statements of Ragged Dick in the Harris *Rags to Riches*. Within the context of the old-time melodrama such dialogue is expected and accepted. The same lines coming from a Huckleberry Finn or a Cinderella, however, diminish those characters and tarnish the image they should create.

Action and Spectacle

The director invokes all his imaginative powers as he reads the script, seeking to visualize its characters, their actions, and the environment in which the action takes place. Some directors choose to ignore all explanatory material and stage directions during the first reading in order to let their own images form. Others will rely heavily on the playwright's suggestions. No matter what the script presents by way of description and explanation, however, the director must discern its production possibilities in light of his own vision of what it might become in performance.

The script should be rich with opportunities to develop interesting and varied physical action to assist in telling the story. As we have stated earlier, all events of consequence to the plot must be shown on stage. As a corollary, all events of no consequence must be kept off it. Unless it finds its source in character, physical action becomes mere activity — randomized, often frenetic, and always arbitrary. Is this chase *really* necessary?

Elements of spectacle in the action — dances, songs, chorus numbers — must derive from the plot and serve a purpose in unfolding, clarifying and forwarding its movement. The director should be able to discern a valid motivation for every action sequence written into the script.

He must also be able to find a source for conceptualizing the visual elements of the production, discovering the possibilities the script presents for imaginative background and costume, for creation of mood and atmosphere. The playwright's style and point of view will, of course, be respected when the director moves into the conceptualizing process. The playwright, in turn, must be realistic in his own visualizing, always guided by his informed understanding of what is possible of realization, given the limitations of the stage.

Operas

Special criteria for the musical theatre purposely have been left to this late point in our discussion of script selection, since all the elements thus far described apply equally to this form. The best operas for young audiences reflect known principles guiding the content and structure of spoken drama. Focus should remain on clarity of story line. While older classical works will usually be opulently melodic, the newer repertoire uses a music idiom that is both simple and sophisticated and more in the contemporary vein. Thus one does not expect to find tuneful melodies to stimulate sing-alongs, but rather music that complements the action and allows for clear communication of the "dialogue" of the work.

Musicals

The score will be charming, simple and direct. It can be lilting, lyrical and witty, but it must be free of adult sophistication or of jarring echoes of mass media commercials and theme songs. Of greatest importance, musical numbers must arise from and advance the story line. The author and composer must bear in mind that young audiences have even more difficulty than adults understanding words that are sung. Preferably, songs will be short, making their dramatic points without unnecessary elaboration. While the adult audience can be expected to applaud long and uproariously at the end of a number that appeals to them, no such response can be automatically assumed when children and young people comprise the audience. Therefore, endless add-ons and reprises are generally to be avoided.

The Director as Playwright

In the early years of the children's theatre movement, a scarcity of worthy published scripts drove many directors to become their own playwrights, and most successful ones. Their works are still to be found in play catalogues, frequently listed as "classics" of the theatre for children. Nowadays, the amount of published material and the number of publishers, both general and specialized, listing plays for young audiences increases each year. Despite this, directors continue to write their own material for production, some of them with considerable success, and the best of these works find their way into the published repertoire. The finest director-written plays come from individuals who have considerable experience in production. Through directing other playwrights' works they have discerned the qualities that make scripts effective in performance, and, combining that knowledge with a gift for writing, have been able to create significant dramatic material.

The average director who wishes to try his hand at playwriting must have a realistic understanding of the complexity of this form. It is better for him to undertake a writing project with no deadline in mind, allowing himself time to experiment, testing and discarding ideas, honing and polishing, until he is satisfied that his script is ready for production. Even then he might be well advised to schedule a longer rehearsal period for his original work to provide time for rewriting and refining the script as the need arises. We emphasize that avoidance of royalty and playscript purchase is the poorest excuse for deciding to write one's own play.

The Play Catalogue

One learns to view the hyperbolic descriptions of "sure fire hits" that are scattered across the pages of many catalogues with a cautious and critical eye. Others will present less effusive and more helpful information about content and theme as well as the standard listings of cast size, number of settings and basic style. No matter how well it is put together, the catalogue provides only a starting point for selecting a play. Each script being considered must be studied *in toto* before the choice is made. Funds should be allocated to purchase individual reading copies of scripts the director wishes to examine. Spending money to build a respectable script library is no extravagance in any theatre.

The non-royalty play or the one carrying what seems to be an unusually low licensing fee is worth only the price one pays for it — precious little. An examination of current play catalogues will reveal what seem to be typical or standard royalty fees, and the producer should expect to pay the going rate. While many stories are in the public domain, copyrighted plays bearing the same titles are not, and to use a script without gaining permission and paying an agreed-upon royalty is unethical and illegal. Copyright laws also forbid unauthorized duplication of playscripts, so the producer should be prepared to purchase them in sufficient quantity to serve the needs of actors and other members of the producing unit.

PRACTICAL MATTERS AFFECTING CHOICE

Season Planning

If the theatre for young audiences is part of a comprehensive producing organization which draws on a common pool of talent, facilities and budget, the size and scale of its productions will necessarily be affected by the overall plan for the season. The children's theatre director should be party to all discussions and decisions related to season planning, and his productions should receive equal consideration in determining how resources will be allocated. Without compromising artistic standards, he will be willing to let the best interests of the organization have bearing on the choices he makes.

When several plays for young audiences will be included in a season, choices are made to provide variety of content and style. All of us know the frustration of trying to implement a program designed to provide productions specifically geared to given age levels, since most of us sell tickets to the general public and have no control over their purchase. Despite all our efforts to educate the public, there is a curious quality in parents that drives them to bring children to the theatre to see enactments of stories they would not consider reading them at bedtime.

This, of course, causes many directors to seek some sort of least common denominator, which no doubt has led to the loss of older youngsters in our audiences. The courageous producing organization will include productions for young people and be prepared for telephone calls from irate parents who claim that *Step on a Crack, Hang onto Your Head, The Magic Horn* or *Robin Hood* are *not* children's theatre because their five-year-olds were restless.

Talent

The material and performance style should be within the grasp and capabilities of available talent. It is perfectly reasonable to have an actor- as well as an audience-oriented purpose for a production, provided that the former does not take precedence. If the theatre serves a training as well as a performance function, choice of style can logically relate to very specific learning goals, but only when the goals are capable of achievement to ensure that the audience partakes of the aesthetic experience that is its right.

The age and experience of performers must be taken into account in choosing a style for public performance. The younger and less experienced they are, the fewer the stylistic demands that can be reasonably placed on them. Child actors have trouble enough developing and sustaining a characterization without being placed in a story theatre piece where they must effect quick character transformations. Teenagers, however, may be able to develop some proficiency in this style. In our opinion, neither group has the maturity to handle participation theatre. Both may be able to work out rather effective improvisatory pieces, but we prefer that such exercises be performed under special conditions which are more appropriately discussed when drama/theatre in the schools is considered in a later chapter.

Time

Few theatre groups have the luxury of unlimited time to prepare a production. An open-ended, generalized concept for creating a performance through group process requires a lengthy rehearsal period. While a scripted production done by adults can be brought to acceptable performance standard in as few as three weeks of intensive rehearsal, it is better to think of months for company-originated work. Whatever the style, the director working with young or inexperienced actors must allow sufficient time to teach as well as to shape the performance.

Time also is a crucial factor in preparing the visual elements of the production. Final decisions on style, scale, elaborateness of sets and costumes — anything that will place demands on shops and technical staff — will not be made without determining whether there is sufficient shop and staff time to execute the designs.

Theatre Space

The conditions of performance must be taken into account. Expectations which would be perfectly justifiable when the play is to be staged in a fully-equipped theatre must be modified when it is to be performed in a standard school auditorium, on an outdoor stage or in a makeshift playing area. If the production is to tour, the need to adapt to various theatres and stages will influence choices.

The style and scale of the production must suit the size and configuration of the playing space, the size of the theatre and audience seating in relation to the playing space. These factors also determine the degree of distancing or involvement possible in performance.

Technical Support

The expected level of technical support is to be considered realistically before conceptualizing begins. If one can draw on the talents of designers and has the advantage of staffed and equipped shop facilities as well as a full complement of lighting and sound equipment and controls, the sky can be the limit. But the director should beware of over-extending his concept in relation to the actualities of the situation in which he works.

He must know who will be responsible for creating and executing designs and take into account their level of artistic and technical skill. If he will have to do most of the work himself, depending on busy volunteers or inexperienced youngsters, or perhaps even his cast, for assistance, he will look at his choices with a very practical eye.

Budget

Dollar figures alone should not be regarded as constricting except as they relate to the scale of a production. We remind the reader that limited funding is no excuse for artistic deficiency. Instead of succumbing to a "make do" philosophy, the theatre artist realistically scales each production to make the best possible use of available resources.

Ticket Sale Potential

Hand in hand with budget goes concern for ticket sales. While young people have at least some measure of freedom to determine whether or not they will attend the theatre, children usually do not. The choice is made by adults, who, for whatever reason, are inclined to look to title first. Producers are well aware of this, and many theatres feel obliged to choose familiar titles exclusively. Records of scripts selected for performance from the catalogue of the Anchorage Press from 1960 through 1978 reveal that favorite story titles, most of them folk and fairy tales, dominate the list of the fifteen scripts most frequently produced every one of those years. *Rumpelstiltskin* (Chorpenning) has been among the top five fifteen times. Despite the definitive treatment the story has been given on film, and its frequent re-runs on television, The *Wizard of Oz* (Thane) appears in the top ranks fourteen times. These and other frequently-appearing titles are scripts written in the traditional manner.

The Land of the Dragon is not based on a familiar story, though the title sounds as if it were. When it first appeared in 1946, its frankly presentational style made it unique among currently available scripts, providing a refreshing change for producers. And it obviously appealed to audiences. The publisher's records have it among the top five choices for sixteen of the nineteen years covered in the file. It should be noted that this script has appeal for youth as well as children, which may contribute to its popularity.

For many years favorite story plays were expected to be written in a traditional manner that had its antecedents in the well-made play, and commitment to producing familiar titles effectively limited stylistic choices. As we have seen, a number of scripts bearing familiar titles now are written in unusual styles. This may account for the remarkable popularity of the Harris *Androcles and the Lion,* which was in thirteenth place in 1966, surged to first the next, and has stayed there except for one year when it dropped to second. Another example is *Aesop's Falables* (Graczyk), a rock musical spoof of the familiar fables, which has been widely selected since 1970.

If there is anything to be learned from this, it is that the known title is a safe title. This should be a factor in making choices when a group has not yet firmly established itself, but once it has developed a following, a vital theatre organization will do well to become more venturesome.

Sponsor Preference

If the production is to be booked by one or several sponsors, their wishes and expectations must be taken into account. Often sponsors' value systems are not clearly defined beyond their desire to bring theatre to young audiences and their hope that they can find excellent productions to show. Needless to say, they keep a close watch on ticket sales and tend to feel safer with familiar titles, although the degree to which an organization is established and respected in the community will have a bearing on how venturesome it will be in booking.

Sponsors who are well informed about child development are likely to be willing to offer the untried as a matter of principle. A producing unit that has developed credibility with sponsors through consistently excellent production should be less limited in its choices than will be one without an established track record.

Most sponsors seek a variety of performances in booking a season, and the director who is negotiating with them will do well to engage in some consultation before making his title choice firm.

Consultation with Colleagues

The foregoing discussion may have left an impression of the director as a dictator who expects his colleagues to bend to his will. That is not our intention. Obviously, no person can produce theatre alone. On the other hand, trying to create a unified work of art when everyone involved has equal voice every step of the way unnecessarily complicates the situation.

Some theatres have a play selection committee. This practice is most commonly found in community theatres, though other groups may also adopt it. When such a committee exists, their working relationship with the director must be clearly defined. Since he is the one ultimately responsible for the success of the production, he must have some freedom of choice. The committee should not be empowered to impose a selection upon the director. As the process of season planning or individual play selection begins, they have every right to suggest the type or types of plays they would like to place on the bill. In return, the director keeps those preferences in mind as he narrows his choices. When it is time to make the final decision, he should have several alternatives ready to submit to the committee, each one a script with which he would enjoy working. They then read them and, in consultation with the director, recommend the play or plays to be produced.

Whether or not his selection will be influenced by an advisory committee, the director will not finalize his decision until he consults all personnel who will have responsibility for the production: the designers and technical artists and, if their services will be needed, the choreographer and musical director. Needless to say, the business manager will be consulted on practical matters related to financial support. The director gives all his artist colleagues opportunity to read and react to a script, or he makes a clear presentation of his goals for and preliminary ideas about a project in group-generated theatre. If their imaginations are stirred and their response positive, the director can feel secure about announcing his choice. If, on the other hand, they do not see the project as one for which they can generate considerable enthusiasm, the director will do well to explore other options.

As we prepare to move into an examination of the production process, we realize that selecting style and material is only the first of many decisions the director will be called upon to make. Each one will be important to the success of the venture, but the first one is crucial. Realizing that, the director uses all the wisdom, critical power, creative thought and good common sense at his command to guide him through this initial step.

NOTES

[1]John Donahue, "Tell Me Things," in *Theatre for Young Audiences,* ed. Nellie McCaslin (New York: Longman, Inc., 1978), p. 86.

[2]Orlin Corey, *Theatre for Children — Kid Stuff, or Theatre?* (Anchorage, KY: Anchorage Press, Inc., 1974), p. 71.

[3]Mailing address: P.O. Box 17193, San Diego, CA 92117. See also Leslie Irene Coger/Melvin R. White, *Readers Theatre Handbook: A Dramatic Approach to Literature,* rev. ed. (Glenview: Scott, Foresman & Co., 1973).

[4]F. Scott Regan, "Creative Involvement in Children's Theatre/Sharing the Magic," *New Ways,* March/April, 1975.

(Top): THE RABBIT WHO WANTED RED WINGS
(McCaslin) — CSU-Hayward, 1968.

(Middle Left): A Bicentennial Celebration at the
University of Wisconsin: HAPPY BIRTHDAY US
(company creation), 1976.

(Bottom Left): ANDROCLES AND THE LION (Harris)
— CSU-Northridge, 1969-70.

(Bottom Right): Scrooge and Tiny Tim at the Guthrie:
A CHRISTMAS CAROL (Dickens, Fields) — Guthrie
Theatre, Minneapolis, 1979.

(Top Left): Mr. Fleet, from THE
TORTOISE AND THE HARE
(Broadhurst) — Everyman Players, 1967.

(Top Right): THE THWARTING OF
BARON BOLLIGREW (Bolt) —
University of Minnesota, 1979.

(Bottom Left): THE ICE WOLF (Kraus)
— Kansas University Theatre for Young
People, 1971.

(Bottom Right): The Paper Bag Players
in EVERYBODY, EVERYBODY (Martin),
1976.

61

(Top): STEAL AWAY HOME (Harris) —
CSU-Hayward, 1973.

(Bottom): JOHNNY MOONBEAM AND
THE SILVER ARROW (Golden) —
University of Minnesota, 1977.

62

63

Fagin in OLIVER! (Bart) — Cabrillo Theatre, 1977.

64

(Middle): BEAUTY AND THE BEAST
(Gray) — Kansas University Theatre for
Young People, 1963-64.

(Bottom): THE HONORABLE
URASHIMA TARO (Jennings) —
University of Texas at Austin, 1969.

65

A CIRCLE IS THE SUN (Donahue and Gaines) — Children's Theatre Company and School, Minneapolis, 1978.

(Top Right): THE LITTLE HUMPBACK HORSE (Swortzell) — New York University, 1980.

(Below): PUNCH AND JUDY (Harris) — Kansas University Theatre for Young People, 1974.

(Top): A WRINKLE IN TIME (L'Engle, Falls) — Young ACT 1979-80

(Bottom): PETER PAN (Barrie) — Arizona State University, 1974.

72

73

Let's meet the actors! CSU-Northridge productions.

CHAPTER VI
IMAGINING AND CONCEPTUALIZING

"... the more public the event the more planning it will require so that 'fitting' things are done."

Dorothy Heathcote[1]

Recall for a moment the forlorn, drab ugliness of an empty stage with its marred walls, nicked floor, exposed rigging, furled drapes, dangling cable, clumsy lighting instruments and harsh work lights. Then conjur an image of the stage completely transformed into a magical locale, vivid and intriguing, ready for a performance. Such transformations regularly occur in every theatre. The arriving audience, basking in the glow of warm lights played upon a closed curtain, or responding to an environment carefully contrived to move them into the play before it ever begins, never will know how much thought and labor went into creating the production they have come to share.

Preparing the performance involves a remarkable mix of the magic and the mundane, of image making and physical toil. In today's theatre for young audiences, it may be scripted or non-scripted, but whatever its source, the effective production requires the collaborative efforts of a team of dedicated, disciplined artists who plan and work with meticulous attention to detail, leaving nothing to chance in their pursuit of a common goal. This is a complicated process that begins long before the production is cast as the director, designers and musical director and choreographer — if the latter services are required — start laying the foundations for their mutual efforts. Although he knows that his responsibility ultimately will be to cast and rehearse the actors, the director is keenly aware that he is equally responsible for determining the production concept and approving all artistic decisions made in the process of its realization. He will seek and value the contributions of every member of his artistic team, but his judgment must prevail to ensure that a unified work of theatre art reaches the stage.

We realize that many directors in the theatre for young audiences also must create their own production designs and rely on their own skills and the assistance of untrained students or volunteers to produce their shows. If they take this into account and set their sights on realistic goals, their productions can be as exciting and aesthetically satisfying as any others. While our discussion of conceptualization assumes that the director will have artistic collaborators, the guidelines we provide are adaptable to any producing situation.

THE SCRIPTED PRODUCTION

"Recognizing the right of the audience to experience the works of dramatists as they were created by their authors, it is the policy of this Association to require of its artists that they adhere to the spirit of truth to the material produced in the theatre."

Code of Ethics of the American
Theatre Association

By the time he has chosen a script, the director is familiar with its content and tone and has general ideas about its production potential, but he realizes that his subjective response and intuitive-imaginative ideas are only a starting point for defining a clear point of view. Aware of his responsibility to present the playwright's work fairly and honestly, he does not commit himself to a production concept until he has scrutinized each component of the script and completed appropriate research, which includes investigation of source materials, period and culture, if they are important to the play, and relevant information on theatrical style. All the artists who will share in the conceptualizing process do comparable preliminary work, but the director's will be particularly thorough.

Every script defines some parameters for conceptualization. The traditional script, the one in story theatre or any fragmented, non-linear mode, participatory plays, the musical and the opera all have unique performance requirements. Within each of these categories, an individual script often prescribes additional conventions that must be observed in performance — the theatrical style of a specific period or culture, for example. More often than not, these "givens" will be more rigidly observed in conceptualizing the performance than in designing the production.

It is important to distinguish between that which is intrinsic to the script and that which is appended to it, either by the playwright or by the publisher, with the playwright's concurrence. Here we refer to the copious design and production notes, floorplans and blocking schemes which are included in many playbooks. This material should be regarded as helpful rather than prescriptive, and the director need not feel obliged to pay attention to it. It either recapitulates the production concept of a director who staged the play according to his own preferences and producing situation, or it suggests the way the playwright might give dimensional life to his script. If he relies too heavily on this information, the director limits his personal vision. Theatre is an interpretative art, and the director should use his own imagination and judgment, realizing that all his artistic decisions must find validation in the script.

The analytical process involves dissecting the script to examine each of its elements. This is an intellectual activity with a creative component, for by the time the director has completed all the steps in the procedure, he will be deeply involved in the life of the play and have a vivid set of images with which to work.

Structure — the Traditional Plot

A play written in conventional form contains a *story,* which is *what* happens, and a *plot,* which is the story arranged and amplified to show *how* events unfold. For example, every worthy dramatization of any classic story tells the original tale, but each bears the mark of the playwright, who shapes and elaborates it to make it stageworthy. When the play is from a longer work, its author selects, highlights and intensifies selected episodes to illuminate his point of view.

If the script presents a single story, the director first reads it to find its overall shape and to discover how well it conforms to conventional structure. If it does, it opens with a scene that establishes the situation, introduces important characters and gives information necessary to understanding the action to follow. It should be brief and vivid. It should lead without delay to the inciting incident which sets the conflict on its way. The body of the play develops the conflict, building suspense through a pattern of obstacles and complications, which are individually resolved, but which give rise to new ones, each more intense than the one preceding, until the crisis is reached. The crisis is that moment when the outcome of the story is most in doubt. It is quickly followed by the climax, or the resolution of the crisis. At that moment the outcome is clear, and the play closes with a brief concluding scene which wraps up any loose ends.

Having studied the general shape of the plot, the director examines its building blocks. This involves going beyond the act and scene divisions established in the script to break the play into small segments for individual analysis. The traditional method for defining these units is to subdivide the play into "French scenes," a scheme in which each scene is said to be defined by the entrance or exit of a major character. The contemporary director may find the method presented by John Dietrich and Ralph Duckwall more useful and adopt their system of isolating motivational units, each of which is a small integral scene, "wherein the motivational pattern is constant."[2] As we borrow their definition, we remind the reader that the Dietrich-Duckwall book and any number of other directing texts are helpful sources of detailed guidance for play analysis as well as all other tasks the director is called upon to perform.

Each motivational unit will be found to have a primary purpose. In the traditional script for young audiences, most of them serve a storytelling function. According to Dietrich and Duckwall, others may have character revelation, character conflict (both inner and outer), or the creation of mood or emotion as focal points. Some sequences may not seem to belong to any unit, or to have any life of their own. These form transitions between the major scenes. Dietrich and Duckwall outline eight steps for analyzing the purpose and meaning of each motivational unit:

1. discovering the relationship of the unit to surrounding units;
2. judging the relationship of the individual unit to the whole play;
3. assessing the significance of the theme or subject;
4. tracing the motivational forces arising from the situation;
5. analyzing the drives motivating the individual characters;
6. tracing the interaction between characters;
7. discovering the individual characteristics of the characters; and,
8. determining the mood of the unit and the effect the unit should have upon the audience.[3]

As he goes through this phase of script analysis the director looks for contrast in action, tone and intensity, for it is through contrast that the rhythm of the play is established.

The Non-traditional Script

The liberated theatre for children and youth no longer restricts the playwright's structural choice. He may ignore plot entirely and deal with impressions. He may present a series of stories which, on surface examination, seem not to bear any relationship to each other. The non-traditional script does not lend itself to rigorous application of the process of plot analysis, although attention to the eight steps for examining motivational units certainly will assist in studying the fragmented theatre piece; for no matter how episodic it may be, each segment has unique qualities and an individual point of focus. Taken as a whole, the worthy script has internal validity and is structured for cumulative effect or coherent image. The director is obliged to discover its through-line and the pattern in which its segments have been assembled to achieve unity and harmony.

Many non-linear plays are given coherence through the use of narrative and song. Instead of opening with an enacted scene which establishes the situation and presents necessary exposition, a singer, chorus or an actor who subsequently will become a character in the play presents introductory information in direct address to the audience. Once established, this convention is consistently observed throughout the performance. Within the relatively loose structure of alternating narrative and enacted story or episode, each segment will have its own integrity and will contribute to the overall effect or message of the play.

In considering this structure, one immediately thinks of story theatre. A brief examination of Flora Atkins' *Golliwhoppers!* will suggest a way of approaching structural analysis for this style of play. It requires no deep examination to discover that the only commonality among the four stories is their American folk origin. However, when the opening song invites the audience to return to earlier days and learn how their forebears entertained one another before the advent of the mass media, common ground is established. Immediately thereafter, the actors set or distribute the properties for the first story, establishing a convention that is observed throughout the performance. Equally consistent is the use of combined instrumental music, song, dance and narrative for transition and introduction. The rhythm and mood of each story are established in the quality of a narrator's speech, through dances suggestive of the region from which the story originated, or, in the case of the more somber Indian legend, through meaured drum beats. The overall rhythm of the performance grows out of the repeated use of these devices.

The heart of the play, however, is found in its stories. Each one has a unique structure and qualities that give it a rhythm of its own, and traditional guidelines for plot analysis will be applied to it.

Harris' *Just So Stories* is not a story theatre piece, since the actors do not alternate between narrators and characters or transform into several characters. It does, however, present three stories linked by narrative device, in this instance a Djinn, who gives the play an aura of magic. This character stands apart from the stories except when his services are needed to cast a spell in "How the Camel Got His Hump." The stories themselves deal with the beginnings of civilization. In "The Cat Who Walked by Himself," the first family unit is established, and the domestication of animals begins. "How the Camel Got His Hump" shows an early cooperative venture in building a society. "How the First Letter was Written" is a humorous recounting of the advent of written communication and interactions among people of different backgrounds.

While the dramatic situation of the second story does not grow out of the first, or the situation of the second does not give rise to the problems encountered and resolved in the third, the play does have a cumulative effect in its progression toward greater human and social sophistication. Again, each story has its own structural integrity and must be subjected to a scene-by-scene analysis.

The Harris *Punch and Judy* is an example of an episodic play recounting the escapades of its central character. The action occurs in a play-within-a-play, which begins and ends with puppets, who come to life and are portrayed by actors. From the beginning, characters step out of the action to speak directly to the audience, providing a continuous reminder that the performance is indeed a play, although in removing themselves from the action they never drop character. This direct address serves an alienation function, keeping the audience aware that Punch's dreadful actions are symbolic, not real. Fragmentary and interrupted as they are, the episodes of the play are linked to a single theme of defiance and rebellion against familial and societal restraints. They are carefully conceived to achieve a cumulative effect as each of Punch's encounters moves to a new level of seriousness, culminating in his struggle with the Devil. Suspense should build, not because there ever is doubt that Punch will win, but because we are caught up in wondering how he will extricate himself from each new confrontation. The play neatly divides into French scenes, each of which also is a clear motivational unit. Each of them will be analyzed to discover its function and tone. The tension-release pattern is obvious, but each scene has a quality that sets it apart from the others. If all of them are given equal tone and value, the rhythm of the play will be monotonous and unvarying.

Whatever its style, every script will be structured from components purposefully included to build the effect the playwright intends to create. As each component is examined and evaluated, the director will make discoveries that will be of invaluable assistance to him in his conceptualization and essential to his subsequent work with actors.

Theme

Thematic analysis is the key to establishing contact with the inner life of the play. It is important in every script, but it takes on added significance when one is aware that theme may well be the sole unifying element in the fragmentary theatre piece. Discovering the overall theme of the play and searching for sub-themes is a crucial step in establishing a solid foundation for the production concept. Theme relates to mood, which in turn is reflected in all the visual elements. When the play is to be scored, its theme will be considered in selecting or composing music. A grasp of the layers of meaning in the play and the manner in which each character relates to or reflects its themes will assist actors in creating genuine and believable portrayals. Though the central source of the play's rhythm will be found in its structure, the thematic import of individual scenes will give it nuance.

Very rarely does a story or a dramatic work for young people lack a theme. The occasional exception might be found in a nonsense story, tall tale or bit of whimsey which has its own intrinsic merit. Any attempt to impose profundity will spoil its fun. In other plays, surface frivolity makes a very serious statement about the human condition, human value systems, human actions and attitudes.

Theme has been considered in some detail in earlier chapters, where we have noted that the contemporary repertoire is moving well beyond the once pervasive theme of good triumphing over evil as it introduces increasingly subtle and complex issues. We have examined the thematic content of plays, old and new, pointing out that significant and durable works exist on a number of thematic levels.

The director who would avoid an inane and simplistic production will devote considerable time to finding the multiplicity of meaning inherent in the script, seeking to go beyond its central statement to the layers that give it substance and texture, thus strengthening the fabric from which the production is woven. Study of source materials can be of immeasurable help in thematic analysis. Knowing the source, significance and dimensions of an original work will enhance understanding of an adaptation. The playwright's intent will be illuminated when the thematic strands of the original are compared to the thematic content of the dramatization to discern how the writer's personal vision has been imposed upon the source material. If the playwright has seemed to slight the themes, the director's knowledge of source will help him find the continuing present which resides in the past.

Character

The surface simplicity with which the characters typically are written does not give license to treat them superficially, either in conceptualization or in performance. By the time he has selected the script, the director will have more than a nodding acquaintance with its characters. Structural and thematic analysis deepens that acquaintance and reveals each character's relationship to the plot and theme. Now the director studies the script to discover each character's internal substance and motivations, attitudes, personality set and relationship to other characters. While the style of the performance may preclude revelation of anything more than the essence of a characterization, each portrayal must have individuality and a human dimension and inner life.

Reference to appropriate background material will assist the director in finding dimension and symbolic significance in characters. If they are written to be portrayed in a specific style, he will visualize them coming to life in that context. Even when they are not, their dialogue, attitudes and behavior may suggest an appropriate style, as we shall see. As he analyzes them, characters cease to be abstractions in the director's mind. He begins to see them as people, and he begins to conceptualize them visually in time, place and action, and it is from this visualization that the costume scheme begins to emerge.

Action and Spectacle

Analysis of the action patterns of the characters also has an imaginative dimension. Again, as he has gone through previous steps in studying the script, the director has begun to see the play coming to life in an environment. When he begins to concentrate on action and spectacle, he will continue to work with images. Practical matters are considered in the next phase of the conceptualizing process. For the present, he thinks of the demands the script makes: the number of settings, and the environment and atmosphere of each as well as how literal the environments should be; the amount and nature of the physical action explicitly required or visualized as growing out of the script; the number of characters who will be on stage at any given time for scenes of spectacle, chorus or dance numbers; which important scenes will require special emphasis and focus. He will become aware of any potential staging problems that might arise from specialized action sequences. He will begin to see what elements will be needed to create the visual framework for the play and to develop some preliminary ideas about the style he will choose for the performance.

Script Problems: Cutting and Editing

Before moving to the next stage of conceptualization, this seems to be the place to answer some questions about script problems. Generally speaking, the primary justification for cutting is to adjust running time. Sixty to ninety minutes seems to be the preferred length for the children's theatre performance, and in many minds no play should run longer than an hour for the child audience. This, of course, is less a problem when the play is addressed to youth. European producers and audiences are conditioned to longer performances, and Americans often find scripts from abroad overly long.

Judicious cutting and minor editing are perfectly legitimate, provided that there is no distortion of the playwright's intent; and obviously no trimming or alteration should be attempted until the script has been thoroughly analyzed. Even then, the director will exercise great care to retain the essential action and thematic qualities of the play. He certainly will not tamper with its outcome.

Many of the older adaptations of classic fairy tales remain viable theatre pieces when their dialogue is honed. Many scripts, in fact, are improved when overwritten, flowery or redundant dialogue sequences are whittled or even excised. Scripts from Britain frequently have word play sequences which may provide great fun for English audiences, but may bewilder the American youngster. Moralizing speeches, lines which do not read easily or naturally, forced rhymes — all these can be cut or amended. Vocabulary and expressions which are out of key with the overall quality and flavor of the dialogue can be changed.

Redundant dialogue sometimes describes actions which are better performed silently, letting the pantomime carry its own message. Songs which in themselves may be charming interludes but which have only tenuous relevance can be eliminated. Any sequence that seems to be imposed upon rather than derived from the play should be carefully scrutinized, for the performance may be better off without it. Chases, processions through the audience, audience contact that seems gratuitous and arbitrary, even participatory episodes, may detract rather than enhance. When this is so, they should be removed.

Some plays are improved with the elimination of an entire scene, though this may not become apparent until the play is in rehearsal, or even in performance. For example, after several performances of *Reynard the Fox,* audience response suggested that the hero's feigned death from poison early in the play diminished the impact of his pretended demise at the climactic moment that ends it. In this situation, the director and company worked together to find a way to eliminate all but the consequence of the first deception, to the betterment of the play.

Thus we see that cutting and editing may occur at any point from conceptualization through performance. The director may do some of this before the play goes into rehearsal, but once actual work begins, he will be sensitive to script problems as they arise and take steps to remedy them.

Investigating Sources

When the play is an adaptation of a known literary or folk work, or recounts the adventures of real or legendary personages or events from history, a search for background material will supplement, or even precede, analysis of the script itself. No one would consider producing *Huckleberry Finn, Winnie-the-Pooh, Alice in Wonderland,* or any play based on a full-length novel or storybook without first becoming intimately acquainted with the entire work. If a play is a compendium of several stories by a single author — Kipling's *Just So Stories, Tales from Hans Christian Andersen* — the collection should be read in its entirety. Other works written by or about the author will provide additional enrichment.

Every available version of a folk or fairy tale should be examined to discover the qualities different folklorists have emphasized in their recorded renditions. If the play is based on episodes in the life of a historical figure, biographical research is in order. A rich tapestry of legend grew up around such half real, half fictionalized characters as Robin Hood, King Arthur, Marco Polo, Davy Crockett, Johnny Appleseed and countless others. Playscripts centered on heroes of whatever origin are necessarily limited to selected highlights, which will be enriched in their presentation when a larger frame of reference surrounds them. This frame of reference includes the social and political conditions that gave rise to apocryphal embellishment of their exploits.

Investigation of the origins of strictly fictional characters from the past will reveal their symbolic significance to the peoples who invented them and safely used them to voice concerns and comment upon society and justice. Among them are the persons of nursery rhyme, Reynard and his cohorts,

Punch, and other rogue heroes. The gods and demi-gods of myth find their source in genuine religious belief. Fairy and folk tales speak of the yearnings and fears of less sophisticated peoples. To ignore the root significance of stories and personages from other times is to do disservice to our heritage and to our young audiences.

Every play worth presenting reflects humanity and society and makes some statement about them. Even when a script is entirely original with the playwright, it illuminates some facet of mankind's eternal struggle, and thus springs from roots that can profitably be examined. Plays addressing issues of contemporary life have their sources in matters of concern to today's youth. There is a context for each of those problems. The director will perceive all dramatic works more sensitively when he understands the human situations around which they are developed.

Investigating Style

We have defined style as a point of view toward the production and as a way of making theatre. In conceptualizing, style can be subdivided into three categories which are interrelated and interdependent, but which can profitably be considered separately. The first is period or cultural, and it, too, can be further subdivided into literal period or culture and the theatrical style of a period or culture. Next is production, which is how the visual elements of the play are shaped. Finally, there is performance, which is how the play is acted. Performance style will be incidental to the present discussion and dealt with in some detail in the next chapter.

Period and Culture. When a play is written to introduce young audiences to the styles and conventions of a specific period in theatre history or of another culture, the director will feel obliged to give it an authentic quality, both in production and in performance. If he is producing *Rags to Riches,* he will familiarize himself with the staging practice and acting style of old-time melodrama. Harris' *Androcles and the Lion* and plays of like style will require investigation of the traditions of the commedia dell' arte. A number of plays for young audiences have been adapted from Moliere's works, and will require understanding of the French neo-classic theatre. *The Land of the Dragon* utilizes production and performance conventions associated with the Oriental theatre. Other plays in the Oriental mode may require observance of conventions of a specific Far Eastern style. Several Kabuki style scripts, the Starr-Jorgensen *Peach Boy,* Shaw's *Sleeping Beauty,* and Kase's *The Emperor's New Clothes* come to mind. In sum, any play written to conform to the theatrical conventions of a specific era or culture will be effective in performance only if it adheres to them.

Other scripts that are not set in time or place may contain inherent qualities that lead the director to believe that the theatrical style of a period or culture will best serve to communicate story or theme. In the traditional repertoire, for instance, Chorpenning's *Cinderella* presents characters who could have been taken from an eighteenth century comedy of manners, and the director might find his conceptualization in that style. Her adaptation of *The Emperor's New Clothes* can be staged in an Oriental setting and performed in the Oriental mode. The characters' names certainly validate that choice. After studying the personalities and motivations of its characters and the thematic content of the script, another director might choose to set it in pre-Revolution France and adapt the conventions of its theatre for an equally striking interpretation. Among more recent plays, *Two Pails of Water* is not set in time or place, but its plot and characters echo qualities of French farce and are more effectively played in that mode.

The script based upon actual or fictionalized history will be brought to life in a production that at least captures the essence of the appropriate period and place. When the director feels that setting a play in time will best serve the author's intent, even though the script may not make specific historic reference, he will consistently adhere to that concept. It should be clear that setting a play in a definite period does not mean that one also will adopt its production or performance style. Only when theatrical conventions of a given era are in harmony with the playwright's treatment of material will this choice be valid.

Many scripts which do not require historical settings are placed in specific geographic locales, and many others will lend themselves to a defined regional setting. For instance, a folk tale may gain from being placed in its country of origin. When the director chooses this course, he will wish to communicate an aura of authenticity through costume and scenic elements. To settle on a cliché "universal peasant" production scheme is to take the line of least resistance. In the Western world there is a surface universality to peasant dress, but the attire of each country or region does have distinguishing characteristics. Certainly the architecture of the peasant house or the village square is markedly different from country to country. Customs, dance, music and art vary from culture to culture.

Stylistic choices find their sources in the script. The production concept will be enriched through examination of source and background information, which includes history and culture, social structures, attitudes, customs and manners, occupations, architecture, dress, the arts — an endless list of subjects to be explored through reading, examining photographs, even listening to music. Theatre source books will provide necessary information on theatrical styles and on recreation of literal period.

The director and every other artist responsible for contributing to the production scheme will find that rich resources make for rich images. Whether or not the information gleaned from preliminary study is made visible in the production, it provides an invaluable starting point for conceptualization, and it certainly will be applied to the performance and the costuming in every production except those in which actors will play multiple roles. Even then, the basic costumes may be designed to capture essential characteristics of a given time or place.

Production Style. The stylistic revolution actually began with producing groups who tired of time-worn conventions and sought fresh and inventive ways to stage their shows. Innovative styles emerged as other groups developed productions from improvised beginnings. Some of them began to experiment with audience interaction and involvement. Through rebellion, experimentation and observation of events in the adult theatre, producers started the new wave that released the theatre for children and youth from hidebound tradition. While some playwrights had previously experimented with departures from accepted norms, the upsurge of non-traditional dramaturgy finds its roots in innovative productions.

No single style dominates the theatre for young audiences today, and directors and scenic artists have unprecedented freedom to conceptualize any production almost any way they wish. More emphasis is placed on capturing essences that stimulate the young imagination. Contemporary productions are daring and eclectic. Conventions are intermingled at will, making it virtually impossible to define neat categories for production styles. Non-illusionistic modes which once were considered avant-garde, even taboo, now are favored over more representational productions. We find much frank use of theatrical device, even of the actors themselves, in creating environments for our productions.

Winnie-the-Pooh has been taken out of the forest and returned to the nursery, where large, colorful cushioned building blocks manipulated and arranged by the actors create changes of scene in a performance staged in arena. Charlie Brown and his friends cavort on specially designed and scaled playground equipment. An individual fragmentary setting for each of the numerous scenes in *Trudi and the Minstrel* is contained in two giant books occasionally augmented by a property or two in a touring proscenium production.

Flexible theatres transform into environments which draw the audience into the performance, whether or not it is a participatory play. The course for *The Great Cross Country Race* is defined by free form grassy hillocks where the children sit as the action swirls around and among them. A setting for each of the stages of the journey recounted in *The Brementown Musicians* is built along the walls and in the corners of the same theatre, and children seated on cushions in the center pivot to follow the action. Wide strips of artificial grass surround a wonderful pile of discards, the setting for Isabelle Foord's participatory *Junkyard,* and colorful signs reading "Please Stay on the Grass" welcome children to sit where they easily can move into the action. The fourth side of an arena configuration is filled with a set of giant books, each a different size, waiting for *Tales from Hans Christian Andersen* to unfold.

Gothic arches set against a lighted cyclorama frame a proscenium production of Chorpenning's *Rumpelstiltskin.* A large unit that looks like a patchwork quilt cut by mischievous hands to spell the title of *Golliwhoppers!* soon transforms into a house, a forest, a mountain top and many other places as it becomes the background for that story theatre play. Cold lights, which change with the mood of the story create a far-northern sky, and abstract set pieces reminiscent of an ice-covered world become the setting for *The Ice Wolf.*

Some directors do not take advantage of the artistic possibilities offered by the new freedom. Others seem to forget that a fine line separates freedom and self-indulgence and, rather than exploiting the potential of scenic art, exploit their audiences instead. The more latitude we have, the more diligent we must be to avoid going to extremes ranging from oversophistication and pointless obscurity to condescending "cuteness," or, even worse, lapsing into careless and lackadaisical conceptualizing — or not conceptualizing at all! No producing group should regard the simplified styles typical of the new repertoire as less demanding than those of an earlier time. This attitude is self-deceiving and extremely unfair to the audience.

While the traditional theatre for children has had its share of uninspired and shoddy productions, its cliché "periodless peasant" approach to folklore and pseudo-Gothic renditions of fairy tales, the new theatre has its own stereotypes. Ladders, which in the past were properly consigned to backstage areas, have become the stock in trade of the liberated theatre. They are too much used as the focal point of the neutral setting, which also features bare boards, barrels, stark platforms and kitchen stools. This is not an attractive convention, nor is it inspired.

The theatre is a wonderful place where wonderful things are possible, and whatever the style of the production, it should be conceived and executed to create an aura of specialness. The visual elements must be attractive, appealing and sufficiently lucid to allow the audience to like and feel comfortable with them. They must make instant communicative connection with the audience, transporting them into the world of theatrical reality and then holding them there through the performance.

To do this, the production must be designed. John Allen puts it succinctly when he says, "To design stage scenery is to conceive a three-dimensional environment which must fulfill at least three requirements: it must be honest to its own visual style; it must be responsive to the conceptual intentions of author and director; and it must provide an acceptable environment for the actors in both practical and imaginative terms. It is the art of visual transformation in its most advanced and sophisticated form. I believe that design is not wholly a matter of an inner vision expressed in two-dimensional pictures, but a visual concept created out of the practicalities of the play, the actors, and the materials available."[4]

The setting that conveys a feeling of a complete locale continues to be a viable production style if the script lends itself to that treatment and if a proscenium stage and the necessary support are available. But even when a play is written in the traditional mode and will be staged in proscenium, the production need not be conceived realistically. Fragmentary units can be designed to communicate the essence of an actual environment. A few realistic set properties placed in a neutral setting of drapes and platforms give the flavor of authenticity to a period or locale and a sense of environment when they are properly defined and accented by light. This concept also offers a practical solution to the problems posed by a script that requires multiple settings.

An abstract or neutral background best serves fragmented, episodic plays, story theatre and imagist pieces with their fluid action, frequent changes of mood and their use of actors as part of the environment. Many plays, even those with linear plots, are enhanced in production when fragmentary scenic elements are stylized and non-illusionistic. Distorted, even exaggerated set pieces can be designed to emphasize a specific quality in the script. The important thing to remember is that the comment they make must be valid. When scenic units are stylized, all properties must be keyed to them.

Lighting. "Light is a very powerful ingredient in visual experience." Again we cite John Allen, who writes about standards for dramas produced in schools. He not only speaks of the power of light but also observes that is *the* element most responsible for the apparent transformation of the stage into the magic environment that it should be.[5] His is a message that every producing group can take to heart. Despite the fact that many producers minimize the necessity for anything more than general illumination, as do many playwrights, who claim that their work can play "anywhere" with little technical support, we insist that the lighting design is as crucial to the production as is any other element.

The less definition provided by the scenic investiture, the more dependent one becomes on lighting to help communicate the play. The ritualistic quality of many performances demands enhancement that lighting alone can provide. In neutral, fragmented and abstract settings, lighting is crucial to defining playing areas and focusing action. As we strip away the dimensional elements of production we increasingly rely on the power of light to create visual excitement and atmospheric and emotional effectiveness.

We realize that a goodly number of productions are trouped to elementary schools and other sites where there is no possible way to control illumination, and we reluctantly agree that they are exceptions. When the play is staged in a theatre, however, lighting will be designed to take full advantage of the potential of modern lighting equipment and controls.

Costumes. The curtain opens to reveal a bare stage. Clear blue light washed over the cyclorama tells us that it is a fine day, but nothing more. Suddenly the gulf is filled by a group of actors. One look and we know we are in nineteenth century mid-America. A glance at the actresses reveals who are children and who are adults. Little girls have short calico dresses puffed out by petticoats, and when they dance and romp, we see that their knees are well covered by white bloomers. Their hair, uniformly parted in the center, either is braided or hangs in tight ringlets beneath stiff-brimmed bonnets. Coarse cotton stockings and stout shoes which lace over the ankles, dark, deep-pocketed pinafores covering the fronts of dresses all speak of no-nonsense practicality and of dust and mud and unpaved walks.

More severely cut, the women's calico dresses have long sleeves, long skirts, cut full but unsupported by frivolous petticoats. Black laced shoes, hair pulled into sleek buns beneath bonnets a bit more ornate than those allowed the girls, somehow make simultaneous comments about virtue and old-fashioned warmth. As we observe the men, some in fine trousers, velvet-trimmed frock coats and tall stiff hats, others in shirt sleeves and thread-bare homespun pants, we know who the community professionals are. Hosed and shod like the girls, the boys are in knee pants and shirts of practical cut and color, but we notice that some wear ties and proper caps. Others are a bit less tidy in their get-up, and we learn something about them even before they speak. As soon as the opening chorus introduces the play, a new boy enters. Dressed in the same basic costume as the other youths, he wears a hat rather than a cap, and there is an air about his dress that separates him from the chorus and lets us know at once that here is the central character of a new musical entitled "A Boy Called Tom Sawyer,"[6] a series of vignettes taken from the novel and selected more to reveal the personality of the boy than simply recount his adventures. As the play unfolds, we await the arrival of Huck Finn, and we are not disappointed when he makes his appearance in tattered pants, soiled shirt, wisps of straw poking forth from the broken brim of his straw hat, and a bandage on the great toe of one of his bare feet.

Although only minimal set pieces ever were introduced, its costumes gave this highly theatricalized production a distinct flavor of time and place. In addition, every costume clearly placed its wearer in perspective. Individuals were separated from the chorus. Central characters were dressed in costumes which highlighted their personalities. It was obvious that the director and costumer had done their homework and the costumer had made extensive use of background information to support her creative contribution to the production.

In the scripted play, the author will have predetermined the framework for conceptualizing performance. If the playwright has chosen to develop his material so that each actor will be assigned a single role, the performance will be conceptualized to clarify and augment the function of each character. If, on the other hand, his script requires members of an ensemble to make instant transformations into a variety of personalities and objects, the approach will be quite different. In the first, it will be necessary to consider characters as individuals; in the second, one's primary focus is on the collective image he wishes to create.

The performance calling for individualized characters is the more traditional, but it no longer is necessary, or even wise, to follow traditional prescriptions for establishing a concept. Formerly, the concept was established through the scene, and the costumes became an extension of it. In present practice, this approach may be followed if the setting is to be realistic or the production and performance are to be uniformly stylized. It becomes questionable, however, when we consider how the style of the production often deviates from the style of the performance in these liberated times. More often than not, costumes are far more definitive than the setting, which may not exist at all. The unified production emerges from the performance, and, as a corollary, through what the actors wear.

Costumes help to establish the country and period in which the action takes place, if that is important. They aid in character delineation by enhancing the actor's stage appearance, by reflecting outstanding traits and by contributing to effective movement. While they must be functional, they also supply beauty through their line, flow and color. They help the actor develop a deeper feeling for his character, and they assist the director in composing attractive and focused stage pictures.

We have dealt at some length with the importance of accuracy when a production is set in a specific period or locale. This does not mean that costumes will adhere to every detail of dress, but rather that period and culture will be reflected through line and silhouette and selected individualizing details. Appropriate footwear, headgear and undergarments are added for authentic effect.

Every costume must aid the actor in projecting a clear-cut character with a specific function in the drama and a relationship to the theme. Costume defines social station and helps clarify each character's relationship or opposition to other characters. Line, fabric, cut, simplicity or elaboration, and color all combine to define, relate and comment upon the characters in the play.

Although costumes should not be designed in stereotypical terms, children, more than teenagers, have certain expectations about how characters in their favorite stories should look. The definitive conceptualization for many of them appears in the original illustrations in literary works, and it is difficult to deviate from them. We think immediately of *Winnie-the-Pooh,* for example. Although we did not mention it earlier, directors and designers can find inspiration in the work of excellent illustrators of children's books. Examination of the richness that is shelved in the juvenile section of any public library will reveal how graphic artists capture images of storybook characters. The discerning theatre artist will learn to discriminate between freshness and charm and unimaginative stereotype in illustrative materials.

Inevitably, the director of plays for children will confront the problem of animal characters, and will have to decide how literally they will be costumed. There is obvious visual benefit to having them padded and dressed to give them individualized form and masked to project facial contour and characteristics. Some directors and designers favor authenticity, others choose to work more with suggestion, both in costume and make-up. To some extent the decision will rest upon how vigorous the action will be, the skill and stamina of the actors, who are greatly encumbered by full animal costume, and the effect of mask on vocal quality and clarity of speech. Excellent ideas about using make-up rather than mask to capture the quality of animal faces are found in Irene Corey's *The Mask of Reality.*[7]

Make-up and hair style are adjuncts to costume and visual elements that cannot be slighted. In stylized productions make-up will be as carefully designed as any other component. Appropriate make-up and hair style for every character will be included in the production and performance concept.

The importance of costume does not diminish when the script requires actors to assume a number of roles and functions, although dressing such a performance does demand an entirely different approach to concept and design. Instead of delineating character, costumes highlight the ensemble and lend an aura of specialness to the theatrical event. They should generate visual excitement and add color and interest to the scene, to movement and to stage pictures. As with all costumes, they must be easy to wear and work in.

Costuming for fragmented, non-linear theatre pieces too often is bland and without interest. Stereotyped "uniforms" — blue jeans and T-shirts emblazoned with the company logo; overalls, sport shirts and tennis shoes, for example — are as stale and uninspired as are ladder-focused neutral settings. Even worse is the non-costume — casual play clothes or street dress. Granted, the actors may be called upon to play anything from a narrator to a dozen characters, trees in the forest, animals, furniture and countless other environmental elements, which precludes definitive costuming, but certainly not visually exciting, theatrically appropriate garb.

Earlier we described the stylized setting for a production of *Golliwhoppers!* and the neutral setting for *Tales from Hans Christian Andersen*, both plays calling for actor transformations from self to characters, animals, and environmental elements. *Golliwhoppers!* has period and folk flavor, so the first decision was to use gingham and calico for the women's skirts, which were full, cut to mid-calf, finished with ruffles, rick rack and eyelet, and gathered on elastic bands for easy removal. The men's shirts, also of gingham and calico, were cut to western style with western detail in piped seams and front closures. Basic garments for both men and women were leotard-tights combinations in bright, clear colors. The women wore no other tops. The men wore narrow cut Levi's. Everyone was shod in black, laced dance slippers. Shirts and skirts were removed and billed caps or close-fitting helmets bearing horns or ears were donned for bird and animal transformations. Aprons, dust caps, bonnets and capes were added where appropriate. Characters in the Indian story wore vests and headbands. To add variety, the men sometimes rolled their sleeves to reveal the leotard, or opened their shirts in front. The whole concept achieved variety and uniformity simultaneously. Scraps of costume fabric were used to cover the single set piece, a decision that was made after the director and set designer decided that paint alone failed to make the desired statement.

A peasant motif was selected for the Hans Christian Andersen stories. Costumes ran to pastels and muted shades of darker colors. Each one was given some individuality through color, cut of sleeves, bodices, vests and trim. The women's skirts were finished inside as well as out so that they could be used to create wings for bird transformations, and ruffled bloomers which were revealed in those transformations added to the effect. Men wore knee breeches, full shirts and a variety of vests. Caps, bonnets and crowns were used to advantage when stories required a hint of character definition in costume. In this production, the narrator maintained that single role throughout. He not only addressed the audience, but the company, who were portrayed as listeners who brought each story to life as the narrator began his sharing. He was dressed as a nineteenth century adult. The costumes communicated a sense of period and place of origin. There was uniformity of style, but sufficient variety to make for interesting images.

These two examples are shared to show that artists need not feel limited when challenged to costume a company unit rather than individualized characters. We hope that all of them will continue to search for fresh and imaginative costume style for ensemble-oriented performances.

Music. Preproduction analysis, research and stylistic investigation undertaken to prepare production concepts for spoken dramas are exactly the same for operas and musicals to the point where decisions must be made about instrumental accompaniment. In making those decisions, the director is faced with a dilemma. Much as he might desire fulsome accompaniment for the singing, he realizes that the young, untrained voices with which he typically works can easily be overwhelmed by instrumental music, even in the most intimate playing space. The problem is compounded when the performance is to be staged in a large theatre. Most musical theatre pieces can be performed quite adequately with piano alone or with piano and some minimal instrumental augmentation. The score will indicate the amount and type of instrumental support the composer deems desirable, but the final decision about accompaniment must be made by the director and musical director as they assess their own needs and problems. In addition, they will have to decide where the musicians will be placed in relation to the action. As productions move out of proscenium theatres and into more flexible spaces, many directors are including accompanists and instrumental musicians in their staging plan, putting them in costume and making their work an organic part of the performance. If there is any possible way to have live accompaniment for an opera or musical, provisions should be made for it. We realize that the circumstances of performance require many groups to have the score taped and that they manage it quite well. However, the ability of live musicians to adjust to the nuances that make each performance slightly different from any other makes their presence highly desirable.

Most directors realize that judiciously interpolated music and sound add a special touch to almost any spoken drama, and many use it extensively in their productions. Playwrights have long recognized the positive effect of music on the young, and they often season their plays quite liberally with songs, dances or stylized movement to musical or rhythmic accompaniment. In fact, some non-musical scripts call for such a number of sound and music cues that it sometimes is difficult to distinguish between what we traditionally define as a musical and the play with music. If the playwright requires songs, the melodic line usually appears somewhere in the script, or, if the musical requirements are extensive, a separate score will be available from the publisher.

Music serves many purposes in productions for young audiences. It can be used to concentrate attention at the beginning of the performance and to lead into the opening scene. It can reinforce the emotional tone of special moments of the play. It is a natural way to bridge scenes. Often a recurring motif will serve to keep the major theme of the play always on the edge of consciousness. In highly stylized and presentational performances, music or percussive rhythms accompanying action sequences make their own comment upon characters. When actions and objects are pantomimed, sound effects created with children's rhythms instruments can be used to heighten the action and make a witty comment at the same time. As with every element in the production, music and sound effects must be chosen or devised to be appropriate to the script.

Music composed to fit precisely into the production scheme obviously is to be preferred to music selected from the existing repertoire. (As an aside, we wonder how many directors are aware that it is not legal to use commercially recorded music for public performance without permission.) The services of a talented composer are invaluable to any producing organization. If one has access to a college or university, it is possible to find budding student musicians who will welcome opportunities to work in the theatre. Sometimes people who appear for auditions have musical talents that can be put to use. If it is possible to commission original music, the director and the composer confer at considerable length and apart from the other artists to set the process in motion. The composer's individual preparation involves script analysis and research just as does the preparation of the rest of the producing team. He participates in production meetings, at least those held during the early stages of conceptualization. It is not unusual for a musician to postpone any serious composing until he has sat in on rehearsals to get a deeper sense of the play and its characters. One of the authors collaborated on several occasions with a composer who approached his work in this manner. He captured vocal nuances and character idiosyncrasies in musical themes that made telling comment on characters. His perception of the text and mood of each scene found its way into musical bridges. His work became so much a part of every play he scored that it is difficult to imagine them without the special touches he contributed.

Interpolated music certainly can be recorded when the talent and facilities are available. In the example just given, the composer assembled the necessary instrumental musicians in a spot suitable for recording and put all the cues on tape. Proper facilities and equipment are essential for good fidelity, however, and they are not always available to a theatre group. Unless the recordings can be of highest quality, they should not be attempted. Amateurish, distorted sound reproduction can do untold damage to the effect of a production.

Interesting music and sound effects sometimes are generated through group explorations in rehearsals. Even when music will be incidental to the performance, many directors include singing ability and the ability to play an instrument among the attributes he seeks in actors, and encourages experimentation in rehearsal. Some very interesting results have come from bringing a collection of rhythms instruments and melody bells into a rehearsal. If one has access to Orff instruments, they can be put to good use. Another good investment for any producing unit is an electronic piano, an amazingly versatile instrument even in its less expensive models.

Consultation and Collaboration

". . . if those creating the theatrical art work do not successfully intercommunicate, there will be neither unity nor art."[8]

Consultation among the director and his artist colleagues begins on an informal basis when he seeks their concurrence with his script choice, and informal exchanges continue as each does his preparatory work. At some point, however, consultation is formalized through a series of production conferences that should be held on a regular basis right up to the opening of the play.

The collaborative process is fraught with potential problems, the main one being that dependence on a team of artists for realization of the production concept can come ". . . dangerously near artistic creation by committee,"[9] with frequently disastrous results. We have all seen confused and confusing productions that appear to have been staged in a vacuum, with visual elements that work against the performance rather than complement and reinforce it and each other. Many designers believe that the solution to this problem lies in the scenographer, a single artist who works under and with the director, but who has authority to preside over the entire visual production. The role of the scenographer can be likened to that of the director in that even as the director has full responsibility for generating a unified performance, so does the scenographer take like responsibility for bringing its visual elements to unified realization. Willard Bellman, a prominent advocate of this system, acknowledges that it is not yet feasible for most producing groups and suggests that the goal of scenography, which is to create a production "that is so single-minded in concept that it appears to be the work of a single artist, can be achieved when the director assumes responsibility for the entire process."[10] We share that point of view.

In the typical producing organization, practical circumstances that have bearing on the production concept are known and taken into account when the script is chosen. If not then, they certainly are established by the time the conceptualizing process begins. The team assigned to the show knows where it will be staged. If it is to be on a proscenium or any other fixed stage, they know its dimensions and equipment, the seating capacity of the auditorium, the distance between the stage and the first row of seats and from the stage to the farthest seat in the theatre. When a flexible theatre will house the production, along with its dimensions and equipment, they know how much latitude it allows for creating interesting seating arrangements and performance configurations and the limitations imposed by the need to accommodate an audience whose size has been predetermined by the budget. If the production is to tour, they will have gathered relevant information about each theatre and stage. If it will be trouping to schools or other sites where it will play in make-shift facilities, that limitation will have been considered before the script was chosen.

The director and his colleagues also will know how much support the production will receive. When they assemble to make their aesthetic decisions, they know what the budget will be, the manpower and shop time that have been allocated them and the amount of time and the space available for rehearsal. They also know whether the play will be cast with adults, young people, children or a mixed age group and have some idea of the strength of their talent and the amount of experience they will bring to the performance. Another important factor will be the number of backstage personnel who will be available to run the show, and their ability and experience as well as the amount of time that can be devoted to their training.

These are some of the realities that will be considered in the conceptualizing process. Earlier, we recommend that practical matters be laid aside in the early stages of script selection. The same recommendation applies to conceptualization, which begins with dreams of the ideal and later adjusts those dreams to the realities of the situation.

While he enters the first production conference with a clear point of view toward the script, the director knows full well how dependent he is on his artist colleagues for the realization of a unified production. His role is not to dictate, but rather to establish a single focal point for all their work. He has let his imagination range as he has dealt with the script and acquired background, but he knows that his forte is working with actors and dealing with words. The visual artist, on the other hand, thinks more in images and sees the pictorial possibilities in the script. Further, he has the skill to translate image into concrete form. Thus the director enters consultation with a mind open to receive and consider the creative ideas of his collaborators. An experienced director has learned that his personal vision can be expanded as well as refined as he shares their thinking. The neophyte will discover that sharing the perspective of visual artists can open expressive avenues he has not yet discovered for himself.

The success of each production can be attributed in large part to the working relationships established in the first production meeting. The director must be sufficiently well prepared to have a sense of conviction about his goals for the production, yet sufficiently open to and nurturing of the ideas of others so that each feels creative stimulation and encouragement to put forth his best efforts on its behalf. In this way, harmonious and successful collaborations are born.

Although the personnel of subsequent meetings will vary according to the purpose of each session, the first production conference includes everyone with any design responsibility, as well as the composer, musical director, choreographer and any assistants the director will be using in rehearsal work. Their primary agenda item is to agree on a stylistic approach, the frame of reference for the production. Having come armed with their individual perceptions of the script and the fruits of their individual study, they look to the director to take the lead in the decision making process.

The conference table probably will be cluttered with books and pictorial materials. There will be much thumbing of the script. The meeting will not be rigidly structured, for it is planned as a time to generate creative ideas, and they do not flow in tidy patterns, Nevertheless, by the time it ends, all the collaborators should have sufficient understanding of what the director hopes to achieve with the production, to serve both the playwright and the audience, so that they can move forward in fulfilling their assignments.

If a specific style has been predetermined, either by the playwright or the director, one basic decision has been taken care of, and the discussion can center on exploration of the most desirable ways to apply the style to the production. Otherwise, the director's interpretation of the script is the stimulus for stylistic discussion. Having analyzed both its surface and sub-surface qualities, he has developed a sense of its pervasive mood and atmosphere and knows the emotional qualities he wishes to capture in individual scenes. He visualizes the performance in space and has ideas about how that space should be shaped and defined as well as what scenic elements he considers necessary to create interesting groupings and stage pictures and to execute unusual and intricate stage business without hindering fluid movement. He has definite ideas about the practical and atmospheric functions the visual elements should fulfill. He has made preliminary decisions about the degree of representation or suggestion, truth to period, and the quality and amount of comment he wishes to convey. He knows when the important moments of the play occur and has ideas about how he wants them focused.

He sees the characters as individuals and as an interacting group related singly and collectively to the plot and theme of the play. At this point he visualizes them as part of the production as well as the performance, and describes the qualities he wishes to convey through costume in a context identical to that established for the scenic elements. If the play is an ensemble piece, discussion centers on how best to costume the actors as a unit. A major decision will be whether the sets and costumes will be equally defining, or whether more reliance will be placed on costume to establish time, place and style.

This is the time to make practical as well as aesthetic decisions. If the play calls for several locales, the artists must decide whether multiple sets will be practical or even worth while, or whether changes can be imaginatively effected through the use of a minimum number of elements shifted by the actors or costumed crew members as part of the stage action. Whatever the concept, practical decisions regarding scenery include how much will be included in the scheme, what function each element will serve, which pieces will be decorative, which must be functional and weight bearing and which will be moved in the course of the action. Although the director may prefer to wait until rehearsals to decide on properties, some preliminary discussion of his anticipated needs is in order.

The costume designer needs at least a preliminary estimate of how many actors are to be dressed. Does the director intend to add chorus characters? Will crew members require costuming? Although production information in a story theatre script usually includes recommendations about the number of actors needed, the director may decide that his concept calls for a different size company, and, in fact, he may wish to keep the number open until auditions have been held. Even when he wants additional time to establish the exact number of costumes, he knows how they will be used and how much stress they must withstand, what physical actions the actors will be called upon to perform. He knows whether characters in the standard play will require costume changes or additions, such as outerwear. He has ideas about how much reliance will be placed on basic costumes to assist in transformations in the ensemble piece, and how many elements he will wish to add for further definition.

All the artists realize that clear communication is difficult at best when aesthetic perceptions are the subject of discussion. Even when pictorial material has been brought in to help clarify thinking, the designers will use a considerable quantity of scratch paper as they attempt to translate words into visual symbols, presenting rough sketches for consideration. "Is this what you mean?" "Is this the way you see it?" are the most frequently-asked questions at early production meetings. By the time the first one is over, stylistic decisions are relatively firm, a general color scheme is established, the rough outlines of the floor plan agreed upon, and the designers are confident that they are sufficiently "in tune" with the director and each other to be able to draft preliminary sketches and a preliminary floor plan for the director's approval.

Thus the process moves from an abstract concept to increasingly precise and detailed graphic renditions of the visual elements of the production. The final floor plan may not be approved until the director has had some opportunity to experiment with it in rehearsal. This, however, is a luxury that may be denied by a tight production schedule. Many problems can be prevented if the scenic designer builds a scale model of the playing space and provides appropriately scaled pieces suggestive of the scenic elements he and the director wish to incorporate in the design, so that the director can determine their exact placement as he works with three-dimensional objects. Ultimately, all design elements are presented in color renderings, and specific plans are drafted to provide all the information necessary to those who will execute them.

The theatre is a prime example of human interdependence. The director cannot block the play without a floor plan, which cannot be finalized without his approval. The shop staff cannot go to work until they have working drawings and elevations, which cannot be drafted until the set design has been approved. Although costumes can be designed and fabric purchased before the play is cast, construction cannot begin without measurements. Costume and scenic designers must interact to ensure that their work is in harmony, and both must interact, individually and in unison, with the director and the choreographer, and, at the proper time, with the lighting designer. His is the important responsibility for putting the final touches on the work of each of his colleagues. While he can conceptualize in a general way after he has studied the script and participated in early production conferences, he cannot create a light plot until the floor plan is available, nor can he finalize it until he has seen the play in rehearsal. Even then, he cannot decide on gel tints until he has actual set and costume colors and textures to work with. No one can make decisions in isolation, and the director must concur in every one that is made. When we consider the incredible complexity of making theatre, we have to be amazed that we can be successful at all.

Communication and scheduling are two important keys to success. It is essential to hold regular production meetings to supplement the informal conferences that necessarily and properly occur through all the steps of the production process, and the larger the number of individuals having responsibility for realizing the production concept, the more important these group interactions become. These meetings not only serve the obvious purpose of keeping track of progress, but they also ensure that every member of the team clearly understands the work of everyone else and that no one is straying from the agreed-upon scheme.

All preparatory work must be carefully scheduled if the production is to reach the stage with minimum confusion and tension. A master schedule is established for all production and management operations (see Chapter VIII), and a rehearsal schedule is drawn up for all work involving the actors. It includes deadlines for introducing technical elements necessary to the rehearsal process. A sample rehearsal schedule, as well as other forms useful for seeking and giving information related to casting and rehearsal will be found in Chapter VII.

COLLECTIVE OR IMPROVISATIONAL THEATRE

Some of the most effective and appealing theatre for children and youth is produced by groups who rely on their own powers of invention rather than on the work of playwrights. The most successful improvisational theatre is generated by established ensembles of skilled and versatile performers who respect themselves, their craft and, above all, their audiences. These companies stay together over extended periods of time and devote themselves quite singlemindedly to their collaborative efforts. When they are successful, their performances have all the qualities we strive for in our work for young audiences, and an artful simplicity that belies the complexity of the process involved in getting them ready for the stage. On the other hand, some of the worst theatre ever presented to the young is staged by companies who apparently believe that group theatre requires nothing more than unleashed imaginations and abundant good will.

In the last chapter we outlined a number of factors the director must take into consideration before choosing to embark on an improvisatory project. While this present chapter assumes that a choice has been made and the conceptualizing process is underway, we cannot proceed without some further exploration of the problems inherent in building a performance "from scratch."

In the typical situation, where each cast is recruited as a separate unit and there may be no overlap of acting personnel from one show to the next, it is extremely difficult to generate an audience-worthy performance unless there is almost unlimited time for group exploration. Even then it is a venture fraught with risks, and we advise the director to be prepared with an alternative if, after a reasonable amount of group experimentation, he sees few signs that the project will culminate successfully. Most of us work in situations where schedules and deadlines have a profound effect on the choices we make, and few of us have the luxury of unlimited time or of working with actors who can devote themselves and their own precious time to endless rehearsal. Clearly, non-scripted theatre is not the ideal choice if the constraints typical of most producing situations cannot be relaxed to accommodate experimentation. In our opinion, the average director in average circumstances is well advised to stay with scripted material. If he wishes to experiment with innovative performance and production styles, he can find scripts written in almost every conceivable mode to satisfy his desire to break with tradition.

Nevertheless, despite its problems and potential pitfalls, this is an immensely popular style. Every director and every company working with improvisation probably has an individualized approach to the process, and no one yet has dared to say that any one method is better than any other. There are, however, a few principles and guidelines that can be applied to collective theatre. First, the performers' goal must be to prepare a viable theatre piece suitable for a young audience and designed to provide an aesthetically valid experience. This goal can be reached only when the performance has focus and shape. Therefore, a single individual, either a director or one chosen from the group to serve in that capacity, must be the final authority and arbiter of choices. In a 1976 interview, the artistic director of the Improvisational Theatre Project of the Mark Taper Forum in Los Angeles, a group noted for the excellence of its work, reinforced this point of view when he said, "Most of our audience have never seen a play before they see us. I want to make sure they've seen one before they leave. It's not television; it's not theatre games; it's a play. . . . You do what has to be done to create some sort of truth. . . . Children recognize honest acting and a commitment and a shaped production just as well as any other audience."[11]

We have seen how two distinct philosophies, one for process-centered participation, the other for play production, have long since merged in the theatre for children and young people. Yet neither has disappeared. When improvisation is to culminate in performance, the director must reconcile what, at base, are conflicting goal structures, one related to the value of the process itself — releasing and channeling the creative resources and energies of participants in a loosely-structured, pressure-free environment; the other, linked to standards that must be applied to theatrical performance. We know from study and experience that the wheels of creativity turn slowly and that they turn best when free of the threat of deadlines. But theatre is product-oriented, and only in the most unusual circumstances can a company work at its own pace until there is general agreement that a show is ready to open. Ready or not, most groups must meet the audience on a predetermined date. The director, then, must be prepared to make some hard decisions about how much intervention is needed to ensure that audience-related goals are achieved. It should be obvious that those decisions always must be made in favor of the audience.

The director who also is a skilled creative drama leader is best equipped to work with collective theatre groups. As a creative drama leader, he knows that pre-preparation is essential. This includes defining goals for the project as a whole and having a plan for each rehearsal session. The individual session plan includes goals and objectives, choice of materials or other stimuli and leadership strategies and techniques. Such planning is necessary to focus and channel the groups' efforts to make best use of time. As a creative drama leader, he also has that special sense that tells him when to step aside and when to intervene, when to make suggestions and when to ask leading questions. As a director, he knows when the work is leading to a theatrical dead end or toward something that has performance potential. It is a difficult dual role. He wants the project to have enough structure to ensure that a production will be ready on time, but he also wants to avoid such heavy-handed imposition of his own ideas that group creativity is stifled before it has had a chance to be released. A number of important decisions about how he will play his role depend on available time and company composition.

We already have warned against attempting to create a performance unless the group has considerably more time than the three to six weeks normally allotted for rehearsing scripted material, suggesting that this approach requires several months' work. Obviously, the more time allotted, the more freedom can be allowed the group to generate and test ideas. If he works with the same company in show after show, the director knows their capabilities, and he also knows that he will not have to devote a great deal of time to establishing the rapport necessary to productive ensemble effort. If, on the other hand, the company is chosen through open casting, he must plan strategies to weld them into an ensemble. In the first case, the company might get right down to work on product-oriented explorations; in the latter, preliminary rehearsal sessions may have nothing to do with the content or shape of the work to come.

Some of these concerns are more appropriately addressed in a discussion of the rehearsal process. For the present, we will concentrate on questions related to conceptualizing the theatre piece as a whole. Some of them relate to content and format, others to recording and shaping material, some to the involvement of design and technical personnel, and others to the role of the director and any assistants he may require.

Content

First, what will be the source and nature of content, and how will the group be stimulated to begin its explorations? Clearly, anything that might inspire a playwright can also light fires in a group of collaborators. In fact, developing a performance improvisationally has much in common with writing a story or play, the difference being that as a rule the playwright works alone and translates images into written language, while performers draw upon their collective consciousness and work as a unit to create images through physicalization and oral language. It is up to the director to set the process on its way.

A playwright-in-residence serving the Improvisational Theatre Project described bringing in a theme or a set of characters, an issue from everyday life or the concept of inanimate objects (guns in one notable instance), taking on human characteristics as the starting point for fully-developed plays.[12] Many companies, of course, develop complete dramas from literary and folk works. One director started with Aristophanes' The Birds and and used its theme and some of its characters and plot elements to develop a full-length production for youth. Another time he had his cast study Plautus' Menaechmi. They then adapted its premise of mistaken identity and improvised a contemporary play, again for youth, entitled "The Twins."[13] Proposing an idea and suggesting an inciting incident can set a company on its way to devising a plot that grows as they devise their own obstacles, or the director imposes them. It is important to remember that all the criteria that apply to the form and content of scripted works also apply to the products of collective collaboration. Whatever material is chosen, it must have sufficient substance to support and sustain itself in a fully-realized performance.

There is no limit to the types of material that lend themselves to fragmentary, episodic works, or to the strategies a director might employ to initiate the company's work. Some directors place their actors in situations where they observe children at play or where they can interact with young people to learn about their concerns. A number of groups have adopted a practice successfully initiated by the Magic Carpet Company, formerly of San Francisco, of collecting children's written work and developing a collage of short scenes and vignettes from it. One director introduced the sturdy giant-size building blocks that ultimately would become set pieces and properties for the finished work, first exploring their potential for creating environments and then introducing stories that would come to life in them. One time he brought in a parachute, which was played with to explore its possibilities for creating impressions and images as well as locales, and then the company did some research as well as some inventing to find the content of their performance. The director may introduce a theme and challenge the company to find related material and situations to weave into a theatre piece. He may have them explore the works of a single author, a given culture, or examine the lives of heroes. He may bring in some material to provide a starting point and set a certain tone and encourage the company to find complementary works. Whatever his approach, the director is mindful of the total circumstances, both practical and aesthetic, that surround the production, and these will have a bearing on his own choices as well as the ones the company makes.

Some rather pervasive misconceptions have grown up around improvisational theatre, and the director should dispel them for himself and for his company before they set to work. One of them is that everything has to be "mod" and updated if it is to appeal to today's audiences. Closely related is the notion that, having been freed from a pre-set script, players are likewise free to manipulate, even distort, story material in the name of relevance or to serve some purpose which may be clear to them, but potentially obscure and confusing to the audience. Story theatre pieces most frequently offend in this regard. Although it is addressed to the playwright, an article entitled, "The Creation of a Folk Drama" contains excellent advice for the improvisational group as well. The author says that the playwright must

> . . . know his subject, both the people he is representing and the history of their culture. He must be completely, not superficially, acquainted with the mores, the ideas, and the inner drives of his characters, and he must above all be faithful in the creation of their expressed thoughts, both to the intent they convey and to the dialect in which they speak. He must have a twofold, almost self-contradictory view. First he must be subjective about his topic, for he must show sympathy for all who appear upon his stage. He cannot, on the other hand, avoid an imperative objectivity. He must stand aside, refuse to comment upon, to caricature, or to demand emotional reaction based on calculated effect at the expense of authenticity. If the writer has been honest with himself, his subject, and his audience, what appears on the stage may be believed as honestly representative of what it assumes to imitate.[14]

Along with presenting the desirable attitudes that should be taken toward folk literature, this advice also underscores the importance of gaining appropriate background information for the same reasons a director does research to enrich interpretation of a playscript.

Another misconception has to do with the importance and treatment of theme in collage pieces. The element of character is often absent from performances that consist mainly of thematic development. Performers become instruments in the thematic workings, even more so than did actors in medieval morality plays. Often they do not even have names to call their own, and they switch function with such alacrity that it is impossible to identify with them as people. Whatever virtues the form may have, empathic involvement with character in dramatic situation is not one of them. The big danger is that these pieces will become exclusively didactic, attractive, entertaining and cleverly contrived as they may be. Some of this problem relates again to notions of relevance and what is important today. Many theme pieces focus on the search for self and for individual identity, which certainly is a worthy idea, but many of them are entirely "me"-centered, focused on self and the individual ego without considering "me" in relation to other people and the world. Other kindred themes reflect upon childhood and youth introspectively, almost sentimentally, looking backward rather than forward and outward. After observing several performances of this type, a critic panel agreed that such thematic treatment probably is more appealing to adults than it is to the young. Such philosophizing is at one extreme. At the other, are company in-jokes, and adult humor that actually takes advantage of the unsophisticated audience.

While the director must allow the company freedom to select and manage material, he must retain the authority to play an editor's role and, when necessary, to exercise veto power. It is very easy for a group of creative and enthusiastic improvisors to get carried away and lose sight of the fact that they are, first and foremost, preparing to share a theatre experience with a young audience. It is the director's responsibility to see that all material is appropriate and that it is handled tastefully. This certainly does not mean that the work should be plodding and humorless, but rather that the company should respect the material, the audience and the occasion.

Format

The director also exercises leadership in determining the format of the performance. The first decision should be whether the group will attempt a fully-realized single-story play or a fragmentary work. To some extent this will depend on the material, but everyone involved also must be aware of the risks involved in group generation of a full-length play. The end products of many of these efforts are unrewarding for everyone, participants and audience alike. Many of them lack substance, structure, focus, character definition, motivation and development — all the important qualities we seek in fine sustained dramatic works. Successful professional companies who create full-length works include writers or script consultants in their number. These people stay with their groups through the entire process and work with their directors to shape and polish the material, sometimes writing complete scripts, sometimes carefully detailed scenarios. These people are chosen for their playwriting talent. Most of us do not have the advantage of such services or are not gifted enough ourselves to handle the assignment. Thus, in typical circumstances, it usually is more sensible to conceptualize the group-created production as an episodic rather than a single-story play.

If the product is a single-story play, it may be presented traditionally, in story theatre or modified story theatre form, as a participatory play (if the performance space lends itself to audience involvement), or in combined story-participatory style. If it is fragmentary, it can take on any of a number of forms, as we observed in Chapter V. Some groups choose not to settle on a single form, such as story theatre or a mood collage, but rather conceptualize each segment in a style appropriate to its content and theme. Taking this approach helps circumvent the problem of monotony that characterizes many improvisational works. No matter how varied the content of each scene or segment may be, a repeated pattern of alternating action and transition, using the same devices again and again, creates an impression of sameness that can have a devastating effect on the audience. If there are stylistic variations from segment to segment, and if each one differs from the others in tone, duration and visual appeal, audience attention and interest will be continually renewed.

Individual scenes are not the only culprits. Repetitive transitional devices can be even worse offenders. They must be conceived to give continuing freshness to the work and to generate renewed interest in each phase of the performance. This requires that they be as imaginative and precisely executed as are the dramatic moments of the piece. If the material is linked to a common theme or subject, good transitions provide a through-line and necessary dramatic progression. They are the unifying element in performances that otherwise have no central thematic, content or stylistic focus. They bridge scenes in a way designed to establish a smooth flow for the performance. Transitions can take a number of forms, ranging from narration to chorus numbers, but whatever form they take, they are the cement that holds the production together.

Recording, Shaping and Refining Material

Collective creations and adaptations must ultimately meet the criteria for structure, character, theme, dialogue and action that apply to comparable scripted works. Group collaborations also require truth to style, period and sources. The director may delegate much of the investigative responsibility to members of the company as the work progresses and needs arise, but however it is handled, the finished work must be given the refinement that is possible only when stylistic decisions are made on the basis of accurate information.

So much that happens in improvisation is ephemeral. An action, a turn of phrase that pops up spontaneously may be as quickly lost unless some provision is made for capturing it. The actor, working in total concentration, may not even be aware of what he has said or done, much less able to recall exact words or the details of a physical effect. Pre-planning, then, must include devising some workable method for recording what the performers do and say.

We already have suggested that a talented writer or script consultant is essential to the success of any company attempting to create a full-length play. The presence of a talented playwright may not be so essential to the group generating a fragmentary performance where the company, guided by the director, can concentrate on shaping and polishing small units, each of which is relatively complete in itself. Nevertheless, some method of recording work in progress must be adopted. If the actors are expected to keep a mental record while simultaneously engaged in creative activity, their attention is necessarily fragmented, a state detrimental to the free flow of ideas. Nor can the director be expected to limit his attention to that single activity.

For many, the solution lies in choosing a knowledgeable assistant who keeps copious notes to serve as reference points and reminders. From them, the company can choose what they wish to retain for further exploration and elaboration. This system works well in the early stages of the process and may even serve to the point where the material begins to take its final form. A tape recorder is profitably used once preliminary exploration is over and the company begins to focus on specifics. For example, the director and his assistant, or even the company in conference can use the notes to devise scenarios for each segment of the performance, then use taped material to refine the scenarios and set dialogue. Sometimes the director and the assistant listen to the tapes outside rehearsal and prepare a detailed scenario including some dialogue that should be consistently spoken, or even a complete script for each scene and, ultimately, the production as a whole.

In addition to deciding how much of the performance will be translated to scripted form, the director's pre-planning includes preliminary decisions about how long he will retain his role as facilitator, and when he will shift to his more traditional function; at what point improvisation will stop, a format be established, transitional material created and worked into the performance and polishing begin; and how much latitude the company will be given to manipulate the performance once it comes to the audience. These matters should be considered in advance to ensure that productive actor-director relationships will be possible once the company is assembled.

Conceptualizing the Production

In directed theatre, all collaborating artists, including the actors, conform to the directorial concept and embark on the project expecting to do so. In the company-generated performance, the physical requirements of the production, the desirability of incorporating music and dance, and the specific needs for technical support emerge with the drama itself. Nevertheless, the production that evolves improvisationally needs the support of collaborating artists as much as the scripted work does. If music is to be incorporated, someone must be responsible for it, just as someone must be responsible for choreography if dance is to be included. The musician and choreographer must be full partners with the company from the inception of the project, lending their expertise as it is required.

Ideally, design and technical artists also are full collaborators from the early stages of the company's work. Then they, too, are involved in shaping the material and so know it well. Having seen the actors at work, they are familiar with their use of space and know what type of environment and material support the production requires. The costumer develops a feeling for the tone of the production and comes to understand the practical requirements costumes must fulfill. In one sense, rehearsals and company discussions take the place of production meetings as director, actors, designers and other supporting artists co-conceptualize the finished production. If designers are caught up in other assignments, their rehearsal participation will necessarily be limited, but they still must come in regularly to observe the emerging product, recording their impressions in sketches and diagrams and conferring with the company until a production concept is agreed upon.

As a rule, the scenic investiture for the group-generated production is simple, economical and non-defining, capable of transforming the environment or space or itself transforming as the space transforms. It usually includes some portable elements that can be manipulated and shifted by the actors to assist in individualizing scenes and to provide variety in movement and picturization. Specific properties can be used, while others may be pantomimed. Alternating between real and imagined hand and stage properties no longer is considered undesirable practice, and most decisions about the presence or absence of properties are made by the actors themselves. Costumes and lighting are conceptualized exactly as they are for a scripted performance. Unless character definition is required, make-up is used merely to heighten and project features.

While the early stages of conceptualization are markedly different from preparation to stage a scripted play, the later phases of the process become increasingly structured along traditional lines until all the elements of the production come together in polished, technically complete form.

WHEN THE ACTORS WILL BE CHILDREN AND TEENAGERS

When we think of productions with children and young teenagers, we think of scripted performances. It is unfair to engage immature youngsters in improvisational activity with the expectation that it will or should culminate in public performance. Sometimes a class or workshop group may reach the point where they want to perform for others, and this is a valid outcome of work in any art form. When their creatively developed dramas are shared, however, it is in a protected and controlled environment where those who watch understand the nature of process-centered drama and appreciate the accomplishment for what it is. Senior high school students can produce effective theatre pieces for young audiences when they have sufficient time and appropriate guidance for their improvisational activity. When they work in this style, the same criteria set forth for adult efforts, attitudes and end products apply. As a general rule, however, high school students as well as their younger peers are more secure in public performance if they work with scripted material.

Although many of our colleagues disagree, our bias is clearly in favor of adult performances for young audiences. We are quite convinced that children's ventures in drama should be free of the inevitable pressures that build around public performance until they are sufficiently mature to withstand them and have gained enough security and technical proficiency to show to advantage on the stage. When children and teenagers are involved in play production, however, we believe that they gain the most value when they can be involved in the entire process. The organizational pattern for production should allow for them to work backstage as well as to act. If we are to give more than lip service to the educatonal purposes of our theatre, producing organizations should offer the young opportunities to discover, through actual participation in all its phases, that theatre involves more than acting. Crew work should be glorified, and opportunities to work backstage should be presented as a privilege. The production, then, is conceptualized to include the fullest possible participation by budding technicians.

Juvenile performers are entitled to the same high levels of technical support accorded adult casts. In fact, while the technical prowess of adults can carry a minimally-staged production, children and teen-agers cannot be expected to be capable of transforming the playing space through imagination, concentration and physicalization alone. Nor can they be expected to project believable characterizations without appropriate costume and make-up. They need all possible support from visual elements to create and sustain the reality of the performance for themselves as well as for the audience.

To play in an environment where things seen in the mind's eye during rehearsal now are literally present draws the young performer more deeply into the dramatic situation and holds his concentration there. Actual properties give definition to action and business. A good costume delineates character for the player as well as the audience. It also helps the actor to feel like the person he is portraying and serves as a constant reminder that he now is transformed into someone else. Although it is unseen by him once he leaves the mirror, make-up, too, contributes to his perception of self as character. The mood and focusing qualities of the lighting affects the performer as well as the performance.

Adult artists responsible for the production concept thus realize that elements must be relatively complete and clear in definition. If they can be designed to capture the innate charm of children's own artistic expression, so much the better. Above all, no scenic or costume element can be allowed to overwhelm the young actor. Everything must be designed to highlight and focus the performance and scaled in proportions that lend convincingness to the actors, their action and the stage pictures they present.

Every production in the theatre for young audiences depends upon the creative vision, literal knowledge and artistic and technical skill of a team of committed individuals who willingly cooperate to realize a common goal. Under the guidance of a director they dream together, consider the practical ramifications of the task, reach agreement and then go about fulfilling their separate assignments. But never do they become independent of each other. True collaboration involves constant and clear communication. The director is responsible for setting the process in motion and for coordinating the efforts of the entire production team. If his concept is clear, or, in the case of a production that grows from improvisation, the company is skillfully led to arrive at its own, the process should be pleasurable and fulfilling.

NOTES

[1]Dorothy Heathcote, "From the Particular to the Universal," in *Exploring Theatre and Education,* ed. Ken Robinson (London: Heinemann Educational Books, 1980) p. 9.

[2]John E. Dietrich and Ralph W. Duckwall, *Play Direction*, 2nd ed. (Englewood Cliffs: Prentice-Hall, 1983) p. 33.

[3]Dietrich and Duckwall, p. 40.

[4]John Allen, *Drama in Schools: Its Theory and Practice* (London: Heinemann Educational Books, 1979) p. 143.

[5]Allen, p. 143.

[6]Constance Schneider, "A Boy Called Tom Sawyer," produced at California State University, Northridge, Christine Parrent, director; Stephanie Schoelzel, costume designer. Unpublished ms. (1980).

[7]Irene Corey, *The Mask of Reality* (New Orleans: Anchorage Press, 1968).

[8]Willard Bellman, *Scene Design, Stage Lighting, Sound, Costume & Make-up: A Scenographic Approach* (New York: Harper and Row, 1983) p. 9.

[9]Willard Bellman, *Scenography and Stage Technology: An Introduction* (New York: Thomas Y. Crowell Co., 1977) p. 11.

[10]Bellman, *Scenography*, p. 14.

[11]Pam Woody, "Interview with the Improvisational Theatre Protect at the Mark Taper Forum," *Children's Theatre Review*, XXVI, 1 (1977) 5-6.

[12]Woody, p. 6.

[13]Describing the work of John Biroc, Assistant Professor of Theatre, California State University, Northridge.

[14] Jordan Y. Miller, "The Creation of a Folk Drama," in *American Dramatic Literature* (New York: McGraw-Hill, 1961).

CHAPTER VII:
STAGING THE PLAY

"O.K., everyone, let's settle down," says the director to a group of young adults scattered about a room noisily chatting or slumped in chairs staring into space. "We have only a couple of hours to get this cast together. Grab a script. We'll start from the top. Who'd like to read first?" There is some movement to the table to pick up playbooks. After a bit of urging enough people are recruited to read the first scene. "Before you read, give me your names, will you?" Names are given and hastily scrawled on a note pad. After a few lines — "That's great. Stick around. Who'll take it from there? Names, please." And so it goes. Later in the evening: "Is there anyone who hasn't read yet?" No response. "Good. Anyone who'd like to read something he hasn't had a chance at?" Some response, and additional readings. "Well, thanks, all of you. Watch the callboard. I'll be wanting to see some of you tomorrow for a few callbacks. We'll have to begin rehearsing the day after that." And the group drifts away, leaving the director to gather the scripts and shuffle through his notes. "Now who was that blonde who read so well? I wonder if that Jones fellow might be interested." He strains to recall individuals, place names with faces and sort out a blur of confused images. Well, it's only a "Kid show." Here is a director who has laid himself open to a lot of difficulty. By contrast —

"Please fill out the audition form. Here's some information you can read before we start. Would you like to look at a script?" A couple of smiling assistants welcome the thirty candidates for audition as they arrive in the theatre for the first of three sessions. From their number, the director will choose a company of twelve to fourteen for a play that first will be performed for young audiences as part of the university theatre season and then troup to neighboring communities for a series of week-end performances. The prospective cast members are students in a theatre department where general auditions have just been completed, a prelude to casting all the semester's productions. They already have passed one test and earlier today found their names on the callback sheet. On the same bulletin board they read a copy of the information material they now hold in their hands. Those who accepted the invitation to bring musical instruments place them carefully beside them. Some thumb through the script, while a few of the less inhibited move to the aisles to flex their muscles in preparation for the work to come. The director's assistants check the audition information forms as they come in and answer routine questions.

The director speaks to them about the theatre for young audiences and about the production to be cast. There is some discussion. A number of questions are answered. Then the musical director summons the candidates to the stage for vocal warm-ups, and the director with some of his colleagues, clipboards in hand, deploy themselves through the theatre to hear short solos. As the actors complete this initial singing audition, they move to the lobby, where the choreographer begins some preliminary movement auditions, which include animal and character walks and movement to specific rhythms. Soon the lobby is crowded and alive with activity. One by one those who wish to be considered as instrumental musicians are invited to play a short selection for the musical director, who also checks on ability to improvise. By and by everyone returns to the stage for vocal and physical improvisation. It is a long evening and a strenuous one, but by the time it ends the director and his colleagues can make their initial assessment of the auditioners, who in turn have been introduced to the kind of work that will follow in rehearsals.

When the actors return to their seats, flushed and perspiring, the director outlines procedures for the next audition sessions, reaffirms the need for commitment and reviews the rehearsal and performance schedule. One or two eliminate themselves from competition, either because the approach is not to their liking, or their other obligations will not permit them to accept this additional one. Those who plan to return are given scripts to read before the next evening. The following two auditions include some readings and numerous improvisations based on script material, vocal and instrumental experimentation and specific movement and choreographic challenges. Some activities involve everyone, but most center on constantly shifting small groups until the actors have worked in every possible combination. By the time the three evenings are over, the director and his colleagues feel they have the information they need, and the actors leave knowing they have had a fair hearing.

In this chapter we trace the steps of the director and performers from casting through post-performance evaluation, presenting formats for auditions, rehearsals and performance organization. At the same time we attempt to clarify and reinforce an ideal philosophy which applies to all play production for young audiences whether the players are adults, children, teenagers or a combination of age groups.

We begin by focusing on the adult cast. Problems unique to working with youngsters will be dealt with at a later point in the chapter.

THE DIRECTOR'S ROLE

Once the production has been conceptualized, the director can devote himself singlemindedly to casting and rehearsing the company. His interactions with the design and technical staff continue, of course, but now his primary job is to assemble a cast and set about bringing a performance to life. In fulfilling this function, he works as he would with any production, following the same procedures, assuming the same responsibilities and working toward the same goals that are set for plays shown to adult audiences. The major difference is that while it is rare for a director, a producing organization or a company of actors to be offhand and slapdash in staging a production for adults, there is danger in the theatre for young audiences that such negative attitudes and approaches will creep in. The director, then, not only must be a thoroughly competent theatre practitioner; he also must have respect for the theatre for young audiences and take pride in the work he does for it. It is the director who sets the tone for the producing group.

His businesslike attitude and attention to detail in preparation and organization set the production process on the right track. He prepares an audition schedule, enlists assistants and plans for each session as he would for a class or business meeting. He establishes the rehearsal schedule and sees that it is observed. He is willing to make decisions and abide by them, an important characteristic, not only in working with actors, but also with his colleagues in the producing organization.

If he works with young and inexperienced actors he must be patient and willing to teach as well as direct. He should be able to achieve a balance between personal warmth and impersonal authority. A desirable rapport will grow in the company in an atmosphere of friendliness and mutual respect, free of extreme permissiveness or unrelenting authoritarianism. The director lets the company know what is expected of them and what they, in turn, can expect of him, and establishes a working relationship which stimulates everyone to put forth his best effort. As part of this climate, the director needs to retain his sense of perspective as well as his sense of humor, remaining an impartial and consistent leader from the first audition through the final performance. The effective director is a diplomat as well as an artist-teacher. Sometimes it is difficult to maintain an even disposition and an impartial attitude when one works with the wide variety of personalities theatre draws into its ranks. However, the director should attempt to understand the unique qualities of each cast member and to discover methods to help each one realize his best potential.

While an attitude of condescension toward the dramatic material and the young audience is not likely to appear in a child cast, it can easily become a serious obstacle in an adult or teenage performance. An actor who feels that he is merely taking part in a "Kiddies' show" rather than a "major production" is not likely to regard his role as a serious acting assignment. Sometimes this attitude reflects the condescension with which the parent organization views the theatre for children and youth, a point of view that can be altered as the excellence of its work proves its value and significance.

The director's own seriousness of purpose and sincerity of approach should help him instill a positive attitude in his company. Whatever the style of the performance, he stresses the idea that the child audience presents one of the greatest challenges the theatre artist is called upon to meet, and he takes pains to prepare the company for their reactions. He must help them sense the presence of an audience and understand the meaning of their reactions. Only in this way will they be able to play to them and gain from their frankly overt responses, adjusting to but never exploiting them.

When it comes to the script or the material that will be adapted for company dramatization, one of the most important things the company must learn is to distinguish between that which is saccharine and patronizing and that which is legitimately childlike in quality and to have high regard for the difference. The director helps his cast look beneath the surface simplicity of the story to find deeper meanings, just as he helps them develop a sincere attitude toward the young audience. J. M. Barrie once suggested "Actors in a fairy play should feel that it was written by a child in dead earnestness and that they are children playing it in the same spirit." The director who can instill this attitude in his company as he simultaneously uses all the artistry at his command to bring them to a technically polished performance is the ideal person to be entrusted with productions for children and youth. His approach to the directing process may differ from show to show — he functions quite traditionally when directing a scripted play, but more as a facilitator-implementer-arbiter, at least in the early stages of preparation of a company-generated work — but his point of view toward the work he and his company are doing never wavers.

ASSEMBLING THE ACTORS

Advance Planning

The fictional director described at the opening of this chapter was ill prepared for his auditions, which even in the best of circumstances are one of the more harrowing aspects of production. Will the right kinds of people present themselves? What if an unmanageable mob shows up? How will he remember who came? Or how various individuals responded and what qualities each exhibited? Director number one might count himself lucky if he could remember anything of value about the people who came to read for him, and the auditioners certainly might feel dissatisfied and negative by evening's end. Director two, on the other hand, ran a carefully planned and organized tryout, which not only helped him gain information he needed, but also began to set a desirable tone for the entire rehearsal and performance period.

Casting never should be a hasty process. Choosing a company is a calculated gamble at best, and it is impossible to do an adequate job of selecting actors in a single tryout session. Whether one is casting children or adults, a series of auditions is an absolute requirement. The second director we described had the advantage of working in an organization which holds twice-yearly general auditions open to everyone interested in being cast in any production to be staged in that half of the season. All the directors, including the director of the theatre for young audiences, participate in this preliminary screening, where each audition consists of a very brief prepared scene. Each candidate completes a detailed form, and provision is made to take a fast-developing photo to attach to it. A sample of the form, which also could prove useful to an individual director, is shown in Figure 7-a.

Needless to say, these auditions can do nothing more than give a general impression of each candidate and a preliminary indication of his interest, but they do help narrow the field. The audition form allows the individual to express particular interest in specific shows, and the director who does not see his title listed can eliminate him on the spot. At the end of each general session the directors confer, and by the time the series is completed, each has established a call-back list. Nothing prevents duplications on these lists, for the individual directors hold simultaneous tryouts, the candidates can move from one site to another, there is regular consultation among directors as they proceed, and no one announces a cast before a final conference has been held. This system has several advantages in addition to permitting the director to control the number of candidates he must deal with in his own auditions. It gives the theatre for children and youth equal status in the season; the director has an opportunity to see more actors than might otherwise present themselves for a single production; and he can eliminate those who give no indication that they could meet the demands of his show.

When auditions for an individual production are completely open, the number scheduled will depend on the type of production to be cast. Some directors rely on three open sessions plus a call-back for the standard scripted play, believing that number sufficient to become acquainted with prospective actors, to note evidence of growth and interest as candidates become familiar with the script and to give a fair hearing to all who wish to be considered. If the play is a musical, or if the director is assembling a company to create its own performance, the pattern may differ, with more sessions scheduled. The sample information sheet, Figure 7-c, shows, among other things, the audition plan for an invitational series following general auditions. The production was a musical that, while scripted, was conceptualized to allow the company considerable freedom to invent movement and business and to depend, to some extent, on company talent to create portions of the score. Each director will plan and schedule tryouts according to his best assessment of what will be fair to candidates and the production itself.

It is helpful if tryouts can be held in the theatre where the production will be staged, and especially desirable for call-backs. It certainly is important to hold them in a room large enough to provide ample space for movement and also for the director to separate himself to check vocal qualities and projection. When the production will include song and dance, some directors set up separate rooms where the music director and choreographer hold their auditions. This arrangement may be desirable only when a large number are auditioning. It may be preferable to incorporate all performance elements in common auditions involving the director and all his collaborators, including the set and costume designers, if possible. While the visual artists do not have a directorial function, they will be working closely with the actors, and their perceptions can prove valuable to the director when casting decisions are made. The additional advantage, of course, is that they gain further insights into the production concept.

The director is well advised to have an assistant director to serve through the entire production process, and he relies heavily on this person during auditions. He also should try to have other assistants to handle routine matters associated with auditions, such as distributing scripts, seeing that audition forms are completed and submitted and answering questions. No director should be expected to handle the mechanics of tryouts. He and his artistic colleagues must be free to give undivided attention to the auditions themselves.

When he is casting adult actors, the director can save much time by duplicating and distributing an information sheet comparable to the one shown in Figure 7-c. Our example does not give a synopsis or individual character sketches, though such information is recommended when a single-story play is being cast. As the sample sheet illustrates, candidates for casting should be aware of the obligations they must assume if they are chosen — when rehearsals will be held, performance dates, touring obligations if the production is booked away from the home theatre. A frank statement of these obligations provides an easy "out" for people whose motives for coming to auditions may be vague in the first place, and eliminates those whose schedules will not permit full participation. When children and young people are being auditioned, however, the information sheet is limited to the synopsis and character sketches, if one is distributed at all. It is better to provide information verbally, lest false hopes be built.

When detailed actor information forms are filled out at general auditions, they usually are kept in a central file where they may be used for reference, and the director does not have them in hand during tryouts for individual productions. This makes it necessary for him to request another, less detailed set for his personal use. Figure 7-b shows a simplified form. Again, the director will devise his own method of record keeping. Some record their reactions directly on the form. Others prefer to keep separate notes, but however they are kept, written notations must be made, since relevant information about candidates cannot otherwise be remembered.

Before starting auditions, the director plans his strategies and selects his material for each session. Even when the play is scripted, he does not rely on readings alone, and he certainly does not run the reading portions of his tryouts by simply starting at the beginning and reading straight through the script, merely changing characters from time to time. Random readings reveal little of the actors' potential. Script scenes in which the characters appear in a variety of combinations and moods should be carefully selected in advance. When the play will be group-created, the director has a detailed plan for

Figure 7-a
Sample Audition Form

(This form is used for general auditions, but it is easily adapted for an individual production. Space is left to answer every question. Two 8½" x 11" sheets of paper are adequate)

PLACE PHOTO
HERE   DATE _____

NAME _____ PHONE NUMBER(S) _____
ADDRESS _____ CITY _____ ZIP _____
MAJOR _____ AGE _____ HEIGHT _____ WEIGHT _____
           (or occupation)

THEATRE BACKGROUND

Performance or backstage work in plays, musicals, concerts, mime, etc.
TITLE   ROLE OR ASSIGNMENT   WHERE   WHEN

ACTING AND DICTION TRAINING

COURSE TITLE   INSTRUCTOR   WHERE   WHEN

MUSIC BACKGROUND

What, if any, musical instruments do you play? _____
Do you read music? _____ What is your vocal range (if known)? _____
Have you had formal singing lessons? _____ If so, how long? _____
With whom? _____ Solo singing experience? _____
_____
Experience with vocal performing groups? (detail) _____
_____

MOVEMENT/DANCE/MIME BACKGROUND

What formal training have you had, and with whom, in:
Movement for the stage:
Dance:
Mime:

REHEARSALS

If you are cast in a show, the rehearsal period will be intensive, involving every weekday evening and week-end days. What obligations do you have that might interfere with this commitment?

If you have a particular interest in a specific show or shows (or role), please indicate here:

Figure 7-b

Sample Abbreviated Audition Form

NAME _____ TELEPHONE(S) _____
ADDRESS _____ CITY _____ ZIP _____
HEIGHT _____ WEIGHT _____ HAIR _____ EYES _____ COMPLEXION _____

EXPERIENCE

Title   Role   Where   When

Play a musical instrument? _____ What? _____ Competently? _____
Read music? _____ Musical training? _____
Vocal range _____ Experience as a soloist? _____
Dance training _____
Indicate any other performance training or special talent (juggling, magic, puppetry, etc.):

Are you interested in working backstage? _____
In what capacity? _____

List any regularly scheduled obligations (classes, work, etc.) that you have during the evening Monday through Friday and at any time of the day Saturdays and Sundays:

Remarks:

Figure 7-c

TALES FROM HANS CHRISTIAN ANDERSEN

This is a scripted version of four Andersen stories which will be played in modified story theatre style with the actors assuming a variety of roles. A storyteller character will provide narrative bridges. The production will rely heavily on ensemble work and will include instrumental music, song and dance. The stories are:

> "What the Old Man Does Is Always Right"
> "The Princess on the Pea"
> "The Ugly Duckling"
> "Numbskull Jack"

It would be helpful if those auditioning have some acquaintance with the stories.

AUDITIONS   are open only to those who have gone through general auditions and whose names appear on the call sheet. If you are called and wish to be considered for the production, you *must* attend all three auditions.

Thursday, 9/7:	Campus Theatre, 7 PM. Be prepared to sing a solo number and to play a selection if you wish to be considered as an instrumentalist. Dress for strenuous movement.
Friday, 9/8:	SD 214, 7 PM. Be familiar with the script. You will read, improvise, experiment with characters and audition for movement and dance.
Saturday, 9/9:	SD 214, 10 AM to noon. Continuation of 9/8 procedures.

A company of 12 to 14 will be selected. We are looking for an equal number of men and women. The cast will be posted the morning of 9/11. Rehearsals begin that evening.

REHEARSALS   start Monday, 9/11, and will be held promptly at 7:30 every evening, Monday through Friday; from 9:30 AM to noon on Saturdays; from 1 to 5 PM on Sundays. There will be some variation in this schedule during technical and dress rehearsals. This is an ensemble piece, requiring full cast attendance at every rehearsal.

PERFORMANCES: On campus in Studio Theatre —

Saturday,	10/14-21-28 & 11/4
	2:00 & 7:30 curtains
Sunday,	10/15-22-29 & 11/5
	2:00 curtain
Friday,	10/20-27 & 11/3
	7:30 curtain

On tour —   El Camino College, Saturday, 11/11; 2:00 curtain
La Mirada Civic Theatre, Sunday, 11/26; curtains at 1:30 & 3:30
Lakewood High School, Saturday, 12/9; 10:30 & 1:30 curtains
Royce Hall, U.C.L.A., Sunday, 12/10; 1:30 & 3:30 curtains
Mid-week brush up rehearsals will be scheduled through the entire run.

Director: (name, office and home phones)
Music Director: (name, office and home phones)
Choreographer: (name, office and home phones)
Theatre telephone, for messages:

theatre games, improvisational challenges and other audition activities he will utilize to give actors opportunities to reveal the qualities he seeks in members of a collaborating company.

Tryout Procedures

When audition time arrives, the director warily surveys the waiting group of hopefuls who have assembled to display their talents. He knows only too well that the best director can make mistakes in casting, and that the most he can expect to discover in tryouts is the possibility of a possibility. He will rely on the judgment of the choreographer and musical director, and ask designers and other theatre personnel who may be present to share their impressions, but the final decision is his to make. No matter how many assistants he has, he has primary responsibility for bringing the performance to life. He certainly must choose actors who meet the tests of musical and dance ability set by colleagues responsible for those aspects of the performance, but otherwise he must be free to choose those who capture the qualities he seeks. In screening actors for productions for young audiences the director applies the same principles of casting observed in the adult theatre.

One problem in selecting an adult cast is that those coming to try out often have no idea what theatre for children or young people is, how it is produced, or even why. They may be both bewildered and skeptical. In this event, the director is responsible for orienting them to this form of theatre and to the specific nature and requirements of the current production. In doing so, he is obliged to communicate his own seriousness of purpose and his belief in the worth of the art of bringing theatre to the young.

Audition strategies are planned according to the style of the performance, giving actors every opportunity to show how they might meet its demands. Even when the play is a traditional scripted work, little can be learned from listening to readings alone. On any age level, oral reading difficulties give an unfavorable initial impression, and ability to give a fluent initial reading does not necessarily indicate acting ability. In fact, the glib reader may lack other qualities which ultimately make for excellence in performance, while those same qualities may be abundantly present in the poor reader.

When there is a script to work with, the director certainly must ascertain whether the actors auditioning are capable of bringing it to life. After they have had some opportunities to read and hear key scenes, the director should attempt improvisation to see what the actors are like when the script is not binding them, to note whether they are feeling their way into the characters, whether they capture the spirit of the scene, and, most important, whether they attempt to play together. During tryouts the director must be especially careful to observe whether individual actors tend to work in a vacuum or whether they seek ways of relating to other characters in a scene. Willingness and ability to fit into an ensemble are primary criteria for choosing each cast member.

As tryouts progress the director can give suggestions about the purpose of a scene, the effect it should create or the meanings it should convey, noting how well candidates are able to assimilate these ideas. Each candidate should be given opportunity to try a variety of roles to see how well he can adapt to different characterizations. If an actor gives the same interpretation to every challenge he is given, he is a poor casting risk. If his portrayals and involvement with the material and his fellow actors do not grow, or if he seems unable to utilize the director's suggestions, it is likely he lacks necessary qualities of imagination, reponsiveness and flexibility.

The director is particularly sensitive to the actors' attitudes as he observes their work and their behavior as they await their turns. A smirking, offhand approach or an air of indifference may change as auditions progress and people are caught up in the material, but those who do not become vital, involved participants should not be given serious consideration, however skillful they may be. Warning clues are found in the content and quality of improvisational work. Self-conscious cleverness, contrived and superficial action and verbalization, double-entendre, a tendency to make jokes at the expense of the material or hints of condescension should give the director fair warning of potential trouble. One of the prime keys to success in the theatre for young audiences is a convincing performance, and no actor can present himself or a character convincingly unless he himself has a positive attitude and is able to become genuinely involved in the make-believe. Rejection or supercilious attitudes in performance lead to audience rejection and the ultimate artistic failure of the production. The director therefore carefully notes any signs of negativism in auditions.

Closely allied to sincerity is the intangible quality we call empathy. This has nothing to do with classic handsomeness or physical beauty. Child audiences often respond to a character the instant he enters the scene; even before he speaks they will decide whether they like or dislike him. In plays where each actor will be assigned a single role, the director looks for positive qualities of warmth in those who will play protagonist characters and qualities in the antagonists that allow the young audience to revel in their downfall. In ensemble pieces where the actors will play many roles, he seeks qualities that will arouse positive identification with every member of the company. Coupled with sincerity, empathic quality adds up to convincingness.

Vitality and physical flexibility and control are obvious factors which can be discovered through objective observation. The actor's physical bearing, facial animation and vocal projection are all indicators of the presence or absence of energy and zest. He may be sincere and eager, but his personality may lack the inner strength to project a believable performance. On the other hand, initial shyness or insecurity may give a false impression of languidness; where this is a possible factor the actor should be given a variety of audition challenges to see whether lack of vitality is habitual.

Today, more than ever before, the play for young audiences requires a great deal of purely physical action and physical transformation. Therefore the actor must be endowed with considerable stamina. A flexible body and the ability to handle it with grace and control are requisite to every performance. Auditions should include sequences that test the actors' ability to meet every possible physical demand the performance will impose.

A sensitive imagination is also essential to acting success, and it certainly is crucial when the group will devise its own drama. Frequently an actor will appear to take on added stature as he discovers meanings and subtleties in the script and gives himself over to its rhythm and mood, or as he moves farther out of himself in responding within an improvisation. Some actors make these connections quite readily. In others several attempts are necessary before these kinds of responses begin to emerge. The only way growth can be tested is through a series of auditions where repeated opportunities for involvement of various kinds provide the director the information he needs about the people who will be entrusted with his performance.

The voice cannot be overlooked during casting. Mere volume is not enough to meet the vocal demands of theatrical production. Pitch, range, vocal quality, flexibility, clear diction, ability to project without evidence of strain and absence of inflection pattern all should be noted. If he is to be believed, the basic quality and pitch level of the actor's voice must suit the character or characters he will portray. Certainly play production is an excellent way to develop good speech habits, but basic voice and speech qualities must be more than adequate to begin with, for the pressures of rehearsals are too great and time is too short for the director to undertake major voice and diction training with his cast.

The director also is well advised to give candidates opportunity to demonstrate any special skills they claim on the audition forms — skills like juggling, gymnastics, acrobatics, special dance forms and the like. It also is very important to check on sensitivity to rhythm and timing, and helpful to note with some care mastery of basic stage deportment and techniques.

At the close of each tryout session the director appraises the possibilities he has discovered. If his auditions are concurrent with those of other directors, he consults with them to determine how much personnel overlap and potential casting conflict they may be facing. While compromises may not be made until all auditions are complete, regular communication can prevent major problems from developing. As he studies his own list of hopefuls, the director finds some who definitely will be eliminated; others are singled out as strong possibilities; some are ranked as questionable. It is frustrating to have a number of truly unqualified people appear again and again at open auditions, but common courtesy dictates that they be given opportunities to participate each time they appear. Often the keen interest that brings them repeatedly to audition can be channeled in other directions, and the director may draw some of his most valuable backstage workers from this group.

Call-Back Auditions

It is difficult to estimate how many candidates a director might see in the course of open auditions. Even when a preliminary screening has occurred in a general audition situation, the director invites a relatively large number of candidates to try out for his show. In either case, at least one closed call-back session must be held to enable the director to concentrate on the actors who are being seriously considered. His goal is to achieve an ensemble approach, whatever the script or production style, and he cannot cast actors in isolation. Evaluated separately, a number of individuals may seem to be completely right for specific roles in the play or functions in the company. However, when they are brought together as a group, the potential cast may be quite unconvincing or out of key. If actors will carry individualized roles from curtain to curtain, physical relationships are of major importance in achieving believability: a family group must be acceptable in terms of relative sizes; Prince Charming cannot be smaller than whichever fairytale heroine he will be matched with; some plays require strong contrasts in size if the roles are to be convincing to young audiences. In transformational pieces where focus is on the company rather than on individual characters, one looks for variety and contrast in size and appearance.

Voice balances also must be considered in assembling the company. While each actor should have a pleasant and distinctive vocal quality which suits his character, the combined voices must blend into a pleasing auditory quality of balance and contrast. Casting actors with similar voices leads to monotony as well as confusion in identifying characters. If unusual vocal demands are to be made, the director has to make sure that actors can produce and sustain as well as give a natural-seeming quality to the voices of giants, monsters, witches and other unusual fantasy characters.

At call-backs, the director concentrates on the ability of actors to relate to one another, as characters and performers. He is especially sensitive to the sincerity with which they listen and respond within scenes and to their willingness to "give" a scene to another actor. An individual's over-all deameanor and behavior in this smaller tryout provide valuable keys to the quality of his commitment.

Before call-backs end, the director makes sure the candidates clearly understand what will be expected of them if they accept roles. He may even ask them to fill out a complete schedule of their classes, work and other obligations which he can examine to ensure that conflicts have not been made light of in the earlier stages of audition. This leaves determination of the seriousness of potential conflict in the hands of the director as well as the actor. All such problems should be resolved before a final cast is posted. When these matters have been settled, the director can announce the cast, reasonably sure that, barring emergencies, he has assembled a company that will remain together, working harmoniously toward a successful theatrical venture.

Special Requirements of Participatory and Transformational Performances

Actors in the theatre for young audiences are called upon to play everything from fully-developed characters to environmental elements. In many productions they are required to create and sustain individual characterizations which might be realistic; human, but one step removed from reality; supernatural beings or humanized animals. All of them vary in age range and personality. In other plays, they may alternate roles, playing a variety of characters as well as environmental elements. Many participation plays require portrayal of individualized characterizations that are sustained even as the performers become creative drama leaders. Then there are plays that combine transformational acting with creative drama leadership. Whatever type of play he is casting, the director seeks actors with the abilities and characteristics we have been discussing. The ability to encompass the audience in performance is not unique to the participatory play. The special nature of actor-audience relationships is common to all theatre for young audiences. Every actor must have a special capacity to communicate and interact with the audience, whether or not the performance includes direct address or overt physical involvement.

Some directors committed to participatory theatre claim that they place less emphasis on the constellation of skills required to perform in the traditional theatre piece than they do on special skills and attitudes related to working with children. Although we certainly agree that child-related skills are essential attributes when the actors will work directly with the audience, the participatory play still is *theatre,* and unless performers are capable of generating and sustaining a convincing, empathy-arousing performance, it can degenerate into nothing more than parlor games. In other words, participation theatre requires that its performers play a dual role — that of actor-teacher.[1] This means that, in addition to their acting skills, they should have had experience working directly with children in creative drama so they have some prior mastery of its techniques. There is hardly time during the normal rehearsal process to teach a course in creative drama as well as to prepare actors for performance.

We agree wholeheartedly with Pat Hale (Whitton), who in listing qualities essential to successful acting in participation theatre, adds that performers must possess the "shaping artistry [of] playwrights in developing a moment set in motion by a child."[2] Children's contributions shape the plot and often determine the outcome of the drama. Actors must be able to rise to meet every possible response, ever alert to handle the unexpected and able to deal with a variety of contingencies for which rehearsal only partially prepares them. Some directors believe that they can gauge the degree of sensitivity, taste and judgment actors will employ in dealing with children and their responses through observing their interactions and handling of material in improvisatory auditions.

The story theatre play and its variants require rich creative ability and an inordinate amount of technical skill. Improvisational tryouts that include rapidly-shifting challenges and instant responses are a critical measure of how well actors can master the art of transformation. The director looks for inventiveness in extracting and presenting essences. He seeks the ability to effect instant and definitive transformations. He values precision and control in movement and pose. He prizes the ability to hold concentration and focus in the face of constantly-shifting stimuli.

The more reliance placed upon the actor to carry the performance, the more skill and background he should bring with him. Participatory and transformational theatre pieces require unique abilities that take time and training to develop. Unless there is more time than is usually alloted for rehearsal, these styles might well be avoided when the director is working with inexperienced companies.

ACTING FOR THE CHILD AUDIENCE

Achieving a performance that captures the charming and geniunely aesthetic qualities of children's own make-believe should be a primary goal of every company producing plays for young audiences. It is not appropriate here to launch a discussion of the complexities of children's "pretend" activities, but it is important to single out several characteristics of juvenile dramatic play that directly apply to the process of acting. First, children are naturally selective in their role playing. They get right to the heart of the matter and portray only those dimensions of a personality that are most striking to them and that have the most telling effect on their fellows. Next, no matter how stereotyped these naive characterizations may seem to the adult observer, they are executed with absolute sincerity. As they "become" adults or animals or fantasy figures living in imagined environments, they truly believe in the persons and events they bring to life.

There is another dimension to this activity, however, for no matter how deep their involvement, a part of them stands aside, knowing that the conflicts and crises they create can be interrupted or terminated at any time. They are experiencing a form of reality. For a moment the literal world is left behind, happily faded into the background, but always there to provide an escape should the pressures of the imagined environment become too great. In dramatic play healthy children never lose their peripheral awareness that it is not actual life they are experiencing.

When actors understand this duality of involvement and objectivity that characterizes children's play, they have gained a valuable insight into their function as performers in the theatre for young audiences, where the suitable acting style is one in which they are sincerely involved with their characters while remaining acutely aware of the presence of the audience. Through their behavior the actors tell young spectators, "We are creating this in your presence, for you. We are totally focused on our work, but we are embracing you in our act simultaneously; but without the embrace contaminating the purity of the act."[3] The relationship here, of course, is one in which the actors and audience remain physically separated, and our discussion now proceeds on that assumption. The special actor-audience relationships established in participatory theatre will be discussed at a later point in this chapter. First, let us consider the two factors that determine acting style: the nature of the material to be communicated and the nature of the audience to whom it is addressed.

The Play and Its Characters

In sharp contrast to many adult dramas, performances for young audiences usually idealize life. Whether the material is scripted or group-generated, it can range from realism to fantasy, from single story to a series of images that have no story line at all. Even when the material is realistic, a high degree of romanticism usually is inherent in its treatment. The dramatic action is based upon wondrous adventures youngsters dream about, and even when the ending is not the traditional happy one, it has idealistic overtones. Deliberate selectivity is exercised in delineating realistic characters, who never emerge as complex psychological studies but rather as people individualized by a rather limited constellation of dominant traits.

Most performances for the young are based on material that is essentially non-realistic in conception. While a youngster might possibly experience a real-life adventure similar to those in the more realistic plays, he will never have direct contact with a fairy godmother, a cruel giant, a witch or a bevy of elves; nor is he likely to encounter animals who behave and talk like human beings. Even when characters are essentially realistic, they are presented in fragmented form in a large body of contemporary dramatic literature and in a vast number of performances that emerge from improvised beginnings. It is impossible to represent a fully-developed character when the nature of the drama itself requires establishment of an essence! In other words, the characters, events and physical action of a play for young audiences do not lend themselves to illusionistic, stage-centered performance where actors represent the characters they portray and attempt to convey a sense of actual life to the spectator. To find an appropriate style, we must turn to the presentational, frankly theatrical audience-centered theatre.

Presentational Acting Style

Presentational acting is frankly acting. Embodying the genuine qualities of children's make-believe, it allows the performer to remain part actor even as he is involved in characterization; it permits him to select those facets which will most clearly define a character for the audience; it lets him comment on his character. Of utmost importance, it allows him to be aware of the audience and its responses as he plays openly and shares his engagement in honest make-believe.

This style is not without its pitfalls for those who do not understand or respect the nature of the actor's dual role and ignore its important inner dimension. The actor must be honestly involved, not with his own virtuosity, but with the content of the drama and the motivations of its characters. Presentational acting frequently has been abused in traditional performances for young audiences, but as we have moved into an increasingly actor-centered theatre we see more abuses than ever in exploitive exhibitions of technique and superficial fun and games that show no regard for substance or character. Genuine presentational acting is anything but this. More than any other acting style, it is designed to provide an aesthetic experience for both actors and audience, but no performance can arouse aesthetic responses in the auditorium unless there is authentic involvement on stage. This requires that the actor remain sincerely in character, concentrating on the dramatic action, while a part of him remains outside the drama, aware that he is acting and equally aware of the audience and its responses. If they do not bring this ability with them, the director must help his actors learn to combine a sense of real life with a sense of the theatrical in their portrayals.

The sense of real life grows out of script analysis and research beyond the script for background information to find the human core of each character in the play and his relationship to its plot and theme. This is an objective, analytical process during which the actor thinks about the character in the third person and as someone about whom he can have an opinion. He justifies the character in terms of its contribution to the unfolding plot and the revelation of the theme and then selects from all that he has discovered the personality traits that will clarify the character's motivations and actions. These he emphasizes in his portrayal.

If, however, the actor never goes beyond a third person relationship with his character, his performance is bound to be superficial. He also must become subjectively involved and think in the first person, finding the source of the character's self-image. In other words, the actor as actor knows things that come through objective observation of his character. The actor as character does not have the same perception, since he is "walking in the character's shoes," rather than standing apart from and having opinions about him. And it is this actor-character relationship that lends credibility to the performance.

The actor establishes a dual relationship with his character, for even as he is identifying with the fictional personality, a part of him remains outside the characterization and has an opinion about the person he is playing. This opinion is expressed through emphasis on selected personality traits, and to some extent it comes through in performance. The actor not only presents a character with human dimension, but he finds subtle means of commenting upon him. The concept of comment in presentational acting is difficult to grasp. For instance, in his third person relationship with a character, an actor may have decided, "This person is an obtuse fool," and limit his portrayal to playing that opinion. Here comment is confused with caricature as the actor makes fun of his character and exaggerates and overplays, concentrating only on externals. Or it can lead to condescension as the actor suggests through knowing winks or other overt signs that he, not the character, is giving the audience an extra treat through sharing his secrets with them. Both approaches are breaches of taste and restraint.

It is valid to hold the opinion that the character is obtuse and a fool, but only when the actor's first person relationship with the character is clear to him and is at the core of the portrayal. In this context, the actor-character thinks, "I am all wise, and everything I say is of earth-shaking importance," never dreaming that the rest of the world barely tolerates him.

Comment can be made through posture, pose, movement, gestural pattern, and, within rigid limits, facial expression. If the play is set in a definite period or culture, typical modes of behavior can be adapted, not only for the obvious reason of giving an aura of authenticity to the performance, but also for character delineation and comment. When a character is individualized and retained through the entire play, costume in itself frequently makes its own comment, and the actor can take a cue from it.

Achieving the proper degree of subtlety and consistency in comment is important to its effectiveness. The actor must avoid overuse of any single mannerism or gestural pattern to the point where it becomes obtrusive and loses effectiveness. Since overuse of these devices can develop without the actor's being aware of the problem, the director must be alert to check on it as well as to see that each character's behavior is consistent.

Good presentational acting is an amalgam of sincerity, belief and excellent technique. It is frank sharing of honest make-believe. It requires broad but precisely controlled physicalization, an open but not overt relationship with the audience and a quality of respectful exuberance.

The Actor and the Audience

We repeatedly speak of the goal of performing for youngsters as "to provide an aesthetic experience." What constitutes an aesthetic experience in the theatre? How do we make certain that such an experience will be provided? To a large extent the answer to these questions lies in establishing a proper actor-audience relationship when the carefully-rehearsed performance comes before the audience.

A rudimentary understanding of the concepts of empathy and aesthetic distance is helpful in assessing the nature of the aesthetic experience. For our purposes, empathy is synonymous with identification, aesthetic distance with the spectator's awareness of the non-actual nature of the art form. To have an aesthetic experience in the theatre the audience must believe in the events and characters on the stage, but in an imaginative rather than a literal sense. In other words, they respond emotionally while remaining aware that they are viewing a performance, a process long described as the "willing suspension of disbelief."

Awareness of performance is almost guaranteed when the actors play a number of roles rather than single, dimensional characterizations. The frankly theatrical nature of most contemporary productions, with their fragmentary, neutral or actor-created environments also provides a certain built-in assurance that aesthetic distance is established and maintained. The necessary empathy rests solely in the hands of the actors, who through their own genuine involvement bring the spectators into the act of sharing. Players who understand the nature of the young audience and are trained to sense its presence and respect its sensibilities are more likely to create an aesthetic experience for youngsters than are those whose performances are either largely stage-centered or blatantly exhibitionistic.

In actual performance the actors alone are responsible for holding attention, preventing boredom, relieving fatigue and controlling tension in the audience. The experienced director knows how impossible it is to predict audience response with any degree of accuracy. However, he should thoughtfully analyze the play or the emerging performance to determine which scenes may pose problems, either planning his direction or guiding the company to help the actors maintain audience control. When the play is scripted, he decides what kind of response each scene should arouse and directs the actors accordingly. When the actors themselves are shaping the performance, they must be led to make the same kinds of decisions about every dramatic segment they create.

Although each scene or segment has a specific response goal, actors should be prepared for the unexpected from the audience. Before they go into performance, the director must warn them of the unpredictable and often overt nature of the responses that come, particularly from young children, and reassure them that variations in audience reception are perfectly normal. Certain lines or action sequences which do not appear to be amusing to the players may prove to be hilariously funny to children. On the other hand, a scene they intend to be comic may be received with deadly seriousness. Something which provokes gales of laughter during one performance may not arouse the slightest chuckle in the next. This unpredictability should keep the players on their toes, ready to hold for a laugh at any point in the performance and unflustered if expected responses do not occur. The actors try to arouse desirable responses and use every legitimate means at their command to prevent undesirable ones. At the same time they should be able to remain composed and retain concentration whatever may happen in the audience.

Children become deeply involved in the tense sequences of a play. It is impossible to know in advance the exact point at which pleasurable spine-tingling suspense or mild fear could become undesirable emotion. Good taste alone can dictate the degree to which any tension response should be prolonged. The same is true of excitement generated by direct conflict between characters, chases, fear that a hiding place will be disclosed, and so on. The actors should be able to sense the moment when tension should be relaxed, and absolutely resist any temptation to carry it to the point of exploitation. Audible responses of any sort may become so gratifying that performers seek to prolong them unnecessarily or even incite them where they are not intended. Such tactics are not to be condoned.

Scenes of direct conflict between opposing forces are usually played at a fairly rapid rate, and there is frequently considerable dialogue in them. If they trigger a noisy response, it is difficult to make the lines audible. While the players always should hold for laughter, topping it with the next line of dialogue just after the laugh has peaked, they should not worry about lines during a fear response. At that point the audience is far more interested in observable action, and holding dialogue will only prolong the scene. The high point should be reached quickly and tension released before audience control is lost.

Fear also can be triggered by antagonist characters. Audiences enjoy disliking and fearing them, but they find little pleasure in being terrified. Through subtle comment, actors playing antagonists can control the level of emotional response they evoke. Sometimes audience response may show the need for some modification of the performance. However, basic characterization never changes, and the performance must never be watered down to the point where it loses strength and meaning.

In today's intimate playing spaces, actors should be wary of approaching the audience too closely or abruptly. All unwitting, the most harmless, likeable character can set off wails that disrupt the performance. Whatever the performance situation, members of the audience must never feel personally threatened by any performer. Keeping the performance open to the audience does not mean mingling with them or approaching them directly, unless, of course, the play is an involvement drama.

We have previously spoken about the importance of rhythm in the structure of any dramatic work. A tension-release cycle gives nuance to the performance and prevents audience overstimulation and fatigue. The actors may notice some restlessness during quiet moments in the action, and up to a point this is perfectly normal and desirable. However, any tension-releasing scene that is prolonged or overly talky can lose the audience. The director and actors should be able to predetermine which segments of the performance might cause this problem and prepare for them by devising interesting movement patterns to retain visual attention and also plan for making sensory appeals to attention through changes in lighting or the introduction of music.

There is no formula for determining the moment when normal restlessness becomes boredom. The actors simply must sense intuitively when they are losing the audience and use honest techniques to hold them. First, they should not allow themselves to become distracted but should retain a high level of inner vitality and be very definite in executing stage movement and business. While the pace of a quiet scene is inherently slower, it never should be relaxed to the point where it seems to drag.

Under no circumstances should actors ever resort to tricks to get or recapture attention. If actors in the theatre for young audiences are thinking, responsible human beings who understand and respect the reciprocal relationship between actor and audience that characterizes this art form, they are likely to have little trouble with audience control.

REHEARSAL

There are almost as many variants on standard rehearsal processes in today's theatre for the young as there are styles of performance. The director plans and organizes the rehearsal period according to the material, the time allotted, the talent he will work with and the goals set for the performance. We frequently have mentioned the critical factor of time and now repeat that from three to six weeks is adequate for an adult cast, depending on the complexity of the script and the demands it makes on the actors to sing and dance as well as play roles. If they will be creating the entire performance or be given a great deal of latitude for experimentation and invention within the framework of a script or scenario, the period will have to be extended. Six weeks is about optimum for the young cast who, we assume, will always be working with scripted material.

Few producing groups have the privilege of holding all rehearsals on the stage where the production will be performed. To ensure rehearsal efficiency the space where early work is done must be large enough to furnish a playing area exactly the size of the stage setting so that movement patterns can be accurately set. Beyond that, it should be large enough and private enough to permit work on vocal projection, as well as to allow the director to get some perspective on the visual effects he is trying to achieve. Action and timing can be completely thrown off if radical space adjustments have to be made as late as technical rehearsals, and continuous practice in a small room or in one where the noise level must be kept to a minimum habituates the actors to playing at low voice levels that are difficult to modify at the last minute.

The Scripted Play

General rehearsal goals for the conventional scripted work are traditionally determined in five stages: reading, blocking, characterization and line, coordination and continuity (polishing), and technical and dress rehearsals. Figues 7-d and 7-e show typical schedules for rehearsing scripted works, one a straight drama, the other a musical adapted from a series of stories.

In organizing the schedule, the director follows the order of the play in reading and blocking rehearsals. Through phase three and into phase four, he divides the script into small scenes in order to plan rehearsals to cover scenes involving the same group of characters, unless the script is an ensemble piece requiring the presence of the entire company at every rehearsal. If the former is the case, the director prepares and distributes a tabular summary of individual script segments and the characters appearing in each so that every player knows without question what his rehearsal obligations will be. While the director has the broad outlines of the rehearsal schedule planned before he meets the company for the first time, he postpones making a final detailed schedule until the cast is assembled. He then can give reasonable consideration to actors with previous commitments and evolve a schedule reflecting a willingness to establish a cooperative working relationship with the company. In the early stages of rehearsal it may be possible to work around busy days if the director knows of individual problems well in advance, but a definite limitation must be placed on such concessions, and last-minute changes simply must be forbidden.

Reading Rehearsals. One, at most two, reading rehearsals should be sufficient for the average script for child audiences. This is the time for general orientation. The director describes his concept of the total production and presents sketches and renderings if they are available. Such aids to visualization are a great help to the cast, for they give a concrete basis for imagining how the completed production will look and allow the actors to keep before them a mental image of the enrivonment in which they will be performing. Furthermore, a well-drawn costume sketch often assists a player in developing his initial concept of the character he will portray.

Although obligations have been outlined at the call-back session, the director reiterates them. He also begins a systematic orientation to the characteristics of young audiences and explains the nature of the playscript and the problems it presents to actors. He is prepared to give any instructions the actors should follow through the rehearsal period. Usually he warns them against learning lines until after blocking is established. Cuts and scene divisions are given and noted in individual scripts. The script is read for continuity and flow. In short, reading rehearsals lay the foundation for a philosophy of theatre for children and youth, prepare the cast for the unique experience of playing for the young audience, and establish the background for character development within a unified scheme.

Blocking Rehearsals. The sooner the cast is up and moving, the better. Actors respond with heightened interest and rapidly developing appreciation of the play as they begin to sense its characters in action. In preparing the typical spoken drama, at least one session should be devoted to blocking each act or major script segment, although more time may be needed if a section is unusually long or involves complicated action or large numbers of characters. The director comes into blocking rehearsals with the basic movement patterns carefully preplanned, and he is well advised to have an accurate ground plan laid out on the floor to orient actors to the size of the playing area and the location of all the set elements.

Blocking rehearsals constitute the most tedious phase of the entire production process, but when they are carefully organized and businesslike, they contribute much to the actors' initial understanding of the play, to their confidence in the director and to their feeling that rehearsals are off to a good start. In setting an over-all pattern for movement, the director's goal is to create a climate of security and free the cast from technical concerns that could hamper their creative development.

As the director and actors work out blocking, the assistant director should accurately note each movement and position in the prompt script. (A simple and workable notation system is suggested in Appendix 6.) Each actor must be responsible for writing his own blocking in his own playbook, always in pencil

Figure 7-d

Sample Rehearsal Schedule for a Traditional Production

TRUDI AND THE MINSTREL

All rehearsals will be held in the Little Theatre. Always bring script and pencil, and wear old clothes. Each rehearsal will begin with warm-up exercises.

REHEARSAL TIMES: Evening   — 7:30 to approximately 10:30 PM.

                          Saturdays — 9:30 AM to noon. Hold afternoons to be scheduled as needed.

                          Sundays   — 1:30 to 5:00 PM.

                          Brush-up rehearsals will be held Wednesday evenings during the run.

Mon.	9/14	Discussion, cutting, read-through	
Tues.	9/15	Character movement, improvisations	
Wed.	9/16	Block Act I	
Thu.	9/17	Work Act I	
Fri.	9/18	Block Act II	
Mon.	9/21	Work Act II	
Tue.	9/22	Block and Work Act III	
Wed.	9/23	Begin scene rehearsals (schedule will be arranged)	
Thu.	9/24	Scene rehearsals	
Fri.	9/25	Scene rehearsals	
Sat.	9/26	Scene rehearsals	
Mon.	9/28	Act I	LINES LEARNED; REHEARSAL PROPS AND COSTUMES
Tue.	9/29	Act II	LINES LEARNED; REHEARSAL PROPS AND COSTUMES
Wed.	9/30	Act III	LINES LEARNED; REHEARSAL PROPS AND COSTUMES
Thu.	10/1	Scene rehearsals	
Fri.	10/2	Scene rehearsals	
Sat.	10/3	Scene rehearsals	
Sun.	10/4	Scene rehearsals	
Mon.	10/5	Act I	POLISHING; ALL CREWS ATTEND
Tues.	10/6	Act II	POLISHING; ALL CREWS ATTEND
Wed.	10/7	Act III	POLISHING; ALL CREWS ATTEND
Thu.	10/8	Entire play	ABSOLUTE DEADLINE FOR ALL SOUND AND PROPS
Fri.	10/9	Entire play	START PHASING IN LIGHTS
Sat.	10/10	Entire play	CAST & CREWS BE PREPARED FOR AN ALL-DAY SESSION
Sun.	10/11	Technical rehearsal	SCENE OPENINGS, BRIDGES, CLOSING, SPECIAL CUES
Mon.	10/12	Technical rehearsal	CURTAIN PROMPTLY AT 7:30. COSTUMES; MAKEUP
Tues.	10/13	Technical rehearsal	at option of the costumer
Wed.	10/14	Dress rehearsal	CURTAIN PROMPTLY AT 7:30. UNINTERRUPTED RUN
Thu.	10/14	Dress performance	INVITED AUDIENCE. 7:30 CURTAIN

TECHNICAL AND DRESS REHEARSAL AND PERFORMANCE CALL TIMES WILL BE POSTED BY THE STAGE MANAGER. OBSERVE THEM TO THE MOMENT. STARTING 10/11, ALL CAST AND CREW MEMBERS MUST SIGN IN ON ARRIVAL. FROM 10/12 ON, THERE IS A MANDATORY GREEN ROOM CALL 15 MINUTES BEFORE EVERY CURTAIN.

Figure 7-d continued

TRUDI AND THE MINSTREL
Scene Break-down

ACT I	Page Nos.
I-1: Countryside (7-9)	
I-2: Sentry (9-13)	
I-3: Baroness (13-21)	
I-4: Passageway 1 (21-22)	
I-5: Cavern (22-27)	
I-6: Passageway 2 (28)	
I-7: Trollheim (28-34)	

ACT II	Page Nos.
II-1: Gypsy Camp (35-46)	
II-2: Baroness (46-48)	
II-3: Gypsy Camp 2 (48-53)	
II-4: King's Head (53-58)	
II-5: Castle Seeblick (58-69)	

ACT III	Page Nos
III-1: Seashore (70-77)	
III-2: Passageway (77-78)	
III-3: Cavern (78-end)	

Characters by Scenes

	I							II					III		
Character	1	2	3	4	5	6	7	1	2	3	4	5	1	2	3
Trudi	X	X	X	X	X	X	X	X		X	X	X	X	X	X
Peter	X	X	X		X	X	X	X		X	X	X	X	X	X
Sentry		X													
Siegfried		X	X						X			X	X	X	X
Baroness			X	X	X				X	X		X			X
Rothbart			X		X	X	X		X						X
Schlafnicht					X										X
Weissbart							X	X				X	X	X	X
Trolls							X	X							
Rom								X		X					
Romola								X		X					
King's Head											X				
Baron Grosskopf												X			
Brother Innocent												X			
Sea King's Daughter													X		

Except when we are working entire acts or running the show top to bottom, we shall try to work scene rehearsals in such a way that no one has to sit around waiting all evening. Every cast and crew member, of course, is welcome to attend all rehearsals. Crew members are expected to follow the progress of the production.

The preliminary rehearsal and performance schedule does not have a complete break-down of time utilization for every rehearsal. We will arrive at that plan when we have gotten started. EVERY MEMBER OF THE COMPANY CHECK THE CALL BOARD EVERY DAY FOR REHEARSAL INFORMATION, COSTUME FITTINGS AND THE LIKE.

TECHNICAL STAFF AND CREWS: Please note that the technical elements of the production are to be phased in through the rehearsal period to avoid last-minute problems. By tech week we should have a complete production going.

Figure 7-e

Sample Rehearsal Schedule for a Musical Story Theatre Production

TALES FROM HANS CHRISTIAN ANDERSEN

GENERAL CALL TIMES: Monday through Friday, 7:15 PM; Saturdays, 9:45 AM; Sundays, 12:45 PM.
Each rehearsal begins with 15 minutes of physical and vocal warm-ups.

Mon.	9/11	Read-through; ensemble improvisation	
Tue.	9/12	Reading and improvisation	
Wed.	9/13	Group songs; instrumental experimentation	
Thu.	9/14	Role assignments; block Story I; work on rhythm and movement	
Fri.	9/15	Block Story II; work on choreography for dance-mime sequences	
Sat.	9/16	Block Story III; concentrate on character transformations	
Sun.	9/17	Block Story IV; group songs	
Mon.	9/18	Story I; character and chorus business	
Tues.	9/19	Story II; dance-mime	
Wed.	9/20	Story III; transformations; ensemble; dance	
Thu.	9/21	Story IV; chases; court characters	
Fri.	9/22	Group songs and solos	
Sat.	9/23	Transitions and dances	
Sun.	9/24	Trial run-through	
Mon.	9/25	Story IV	Scripts down. Music from now on.
Tue.	9/26	Story I	Substitute hand props from now on.
Wed.	9/27	Story II	With dance.
Thu.	9/28	Story III	
Fri.	9/29	Story IV; problem spots in others	
Sat.	9/30	Special attention to transformations, movement, dance and all singing	
Sun.	10/1	Story I and II; polishing	
Mon.	10/2	Story III and IV; polishing	
Tue.	10/3	Run-through, stopping for polishing	
Wed.	10/4	Goals set Tuesday	
Thu.	10/5	Run-through	
Fri.	10/6	Run-through; costume parade	
Sat.	10/7	Technical rehearsal	Curtain at 9:30 AM. Plan on all day.
Sun.	10/8	Technical rehearsal	Curtain at 1:30 PM. Lobby pictures.
Mon.	10/9	Technical rehearsal	Curtain at 7:30 from now on. Costumes from now on.
Tue.	10/10	Technical rehearsal	Make-up at option of costumer.
Wed.	10/11	Dress rehearsal	Uninterrupted; full performance conditions.
Thu.	10/12	Dress rehearsal	

NOTE: The stage manager will post call times for all rehearsals, starting 10/6. All cast and crew sign in on arriving at the theatre. There will be a mandatory Green Room call 15 minutes before curtain for all tech and dress rehearsals and all performances.

During the run, brush-up rehearsals will be held every Wednesday at 7:30 PM.

so that modifications can be noted as they occur in later rehearsals. The director may have to show them how, but he must insist that notes are made. No actor assumes he knows his lines after reading the script a time or two, but some seem to feel that they can remember blocking without taking it down. This is a fallacy that will become apparent the first time a scene is run.

When the play includes dance and chorus numbers, these are handled separately. In blocking rehearsals, action may be plotted up to the point where the number begins, leaving that segment in the choreographer's hands, and planning the action that follows. Separate dance and music rehearsals are scheduled, and these elements are worked into the action at a later time. An opera poses its unique problems, and their resolution will be agreed upon by the musical and stage directors. Sometimes the musical director chooses to prepare the singers to the point of complete musical mastery and then turn them over to the stage director. When this is the plan, the stage director should be present at musical rehearsals so that there is agreement on characterization and interpretation, and the musical director attends blocking rehearsals to help the stage director set action appropriate to the demands of operatic style. Whatever their arrangement, the two directors must coordinate all their efforts to ensure that they are not working at cross purposes.

Characterization and Line Rehearsals. Blocking is by no means complete when rehearsals enter their third phase. As the cast progresses into characterization new motivations and relationships are certain to develop. Increasing familiarity with the situations of the play and growing identification with its characters will lead actors to invent new business, find better ways of carrying out given actions or even feel a need to make major alterations in certain movement patterns or character groupings. The sensitive director notices impulses to move or change position and encourages this type of development.

This does not mean that the director discards all his original plans and allows the actors to reblock the show. However, he should be willing to have them share in the creative process of bringing the play to life, recognizing that their individual actions are an integral part of the imaginative whole. If a change seems necessary to clarify action or meaning, the director works it out with the actors involved; when it is set, the new arrangement is noted in the prompt script. Needless to say, all stage movement, each grouping, every bit of business must be in harmony with the director's conception of the play and its meaning.

Only as characterizations begin to emerge should lines be learned. Once actors begin to sense their characters they will find carrying books a hindrance to further growth. Until they are ready to concentrate on details of action and character development they should work with scripts so that lines and movement are learned simultaneously. Lines memorized in isolation may be delivered mechanically with little thought of their meaning, or they may be interpreted in a manner quite out of keeping with the director's concept. Either pattern is hard to break. A deadline for memorization must be set, however. It is reasonable to require scripts to be down after a week of characterization rehearsals.

Some directors feel that paraphrasing rather than literal memorization of lines is acceptable or even preferable, since it often produces greater spontaneity. In our opinion this is a questionable practice. One reason for literal line reading is purely practical. Actors need dependable cues for lines and action, and technical crews rely to a large extent on line cues to carry out their functions. Consistency in dialogue is one way to ensure a smoothly flowing performance. Furthermore, there is a matter of ethics — if the director has accepted the work of a playwright, he also has assumed an obligation to present it honestly and accurately. Except for the legitimate cuts and minor editorial changes we discussed in the last chapter, the author's dialogue should be learned as he wrote it.

As soon as lines are learned, substitute hand properties should be introduced. It also is well to begin using sound effects and to incorporate any music that will be used in performance. If the production requires period costumes or garments which will make unusual demands on the actors, reasonable substitutes should be provided so that security in wearing and handling their clothing evolves right along with characterizations. If face masks are to be worn in performance, they must be used at every rehearsal to assist in character development and to ensure clarity of vocal communication. We might also add that physical movement is more easily controlled if actors always rehearse in shoes comparable to those they will wear in performance.

Characterization rehearsals include intensive work on both the internal and external aspects of character portrayal as well as on learning lines and setting action. In today's theatre where so much reliance is placed on the actor's ability to create environmental reality in non-defining settings, time must be spent sharpening the senses and perfecting pantomime. More often than not, when actors are called upon to create environments, they also must work with imagined properties. The director must see to it that necessary defining action and business are properly motivated through sensory identification and precisely executed through skillful pantomimic technique.

If the play is a period piece or requires mastery of a specific theatrical style, the director shares his research findings with the cast and helps them master appropriate performance techniques, which include typical poses, attitudes, gesture, movement and general demeanor. He does not require the presentation of a mass of detail, but he does insist upon a faithful suggestion of period and style. Whatever the style of the performance, once it is established it must be followed consistently. However, in mastering externals the director never lets the actors lose touch with the inner lives of their characters.

Broadly defined and readily apparent character traits are likely to lead to hollow, stereotyped characterizations that smack of condescension if the actors' approach is superficial. To prevent this, the director and actors study the script together to discover subtle hints that will lead to a fuller understanding of its characters and their motivations. In addition, they draw on background information gleaned through outside research to flesh out their understanding. This is especially valuable in providing a rationale for events or reactions that are not logically explained in the script. The sensitive actor finds a real challenge to his thought processes and to his art of invention when the director encourages and assists him in doing some independent probing into the various facets of his character.

All rehearsals should include work on voice production. It is good rehearsal strategy to begin each session with physical and vocal warm-up exercises, with special emphasis on physical techniques designed to maintain energy, control tension and ensure adequate projection without vocal strain. The director is especially alert to sense problems with voice and articulation and willing to take time to remedy them. A shrill, vocally strained performance that goes relentlessly on without clarity or nuance not only taxes the actors, it arouses tension in the audience, and in extreme cases causes them to withdraw their attention. The director becomes so familiar with the text of the play that he sometimes loses sight of problems in dialogue communication. He is well advised to have someone not regularly in attendance come to an occasional rehearsal to listen to the play and point out problems the director may be missing.

While the inexperienced director may feel that rehearsal is not in progress until the actors are walking through the action, experimenting with the use of discussion will soon reveal the value of allowing time for thoughtful analysis of character motivations, attitudes, actions, reactions and relationships. Discussion time also should be devoted to filling in details of events immediately preceding the opening of the play, between scenes and the activity of each character when he is not on stage. Reconstructing these events helps each actor develop logical emotion and reaction patterns. This technique should be used with any cast, but it is especially recommended when one is working with young or inexperienced actors.

Improvisation is increasingly used to help deepen character and fill in details of the dramatic situation. In fact, some directors move from reading rehearsal directly into improvisation, feeling that starting with actor-character identification ultimately gives more depth to performance. Only when they are satisfied that the actors are well involved with the characters and the drama do they begin the more technical work of preparing the performance for presentation through set action and focus on acting technique. Whenever improvisation is used it is a valuable means of achieving the emotional tone and reaction patterns the actors must project in performance.

Improvisatory exercises also help the actors in mastering the art of transformation, increasing their ability to make sudden shifts from player to character or object with honesty and precision. Transformational acting is extremely difficult, requiring a high level of commitment and concentration. Plays written in this mode frequently take performers from the scene, but leave them on stage where they have no apparent function until they are next called upon to enter the action. They must be helped to understand that whenever they are on stage they are serving a purpose by helping maintain focus on the performance through their concentration on the scene. No matter what they are doing at any given moment, the players on stage must be fully involved in the event.

When they move into the action of the play, the characters or elements they present must be acceptably defined, both internally and externally. In no other form of performance is the ability to maintain a balance between involvement and detachment so critical to effectiveness. No other form of performance demands a higher level of technical skill. Every transformation, every action, every bit of pantomime must be precise and refined, with perfect timing and clarity. And every moment must be rooted in honest identification with the characters and situations of the unfolding story. When actors handle narration, they still remain in the play, never reverting to casualness, but always maintaining a role. That is to say that in story theatre every line of dialogue is part of the performance, and the narrator is as much a character, though of a different kind, as any other functionary in the unfolding drama.

Polishing Rehearsals. It is difficult to determine at what point the rehearsal process moves from characterization into the polishing phase. As lines are learned and strong characterizations start to emerge, attention begins to shift to detail; and as soon as this happens, polishing begins. Actual polishing rehearsals are usually devoted to coordinating the ensemble and to bringing out subtleties in action and interpretation through careful attention to timing and reactions. Though directors are not likely to permit individual actors to play in a vacuum at any stage of rehearsal, now is the time to integrate the company into a group of believable characters who are meaningfully related to one another and to the dramatic action.

The entire performance is brought together in polishing rehearsals. Scenes which have been worked in isolation are played in sequence, music and dance numbers are put in place and the production is given rhythm and continuity. Timing receives careful attention. Variations of mood and emotional tone develop. Concentration, which involves listening and reacting in character and refining the actor's ability to approach each run-through as if the events of the play were happening to his character for the first time, is especially emphasized. This ensures a quality of believability and spontaneity in performance.

If possible the director should plan to arrange a week of on-stage rehearsal to running the play without any interruptions in the flow of the action, reserving comments for post-rehearsal discussions and spot scene work. Technical crews should be present to become familiar with the continuity of the performance, to get timings and to spot cues. Obviously, all music and sound should be well incorporated into the performance by the end of the polishing period, and many directors encourage the lighting staff to begin experimenting with light cues and levels.

Technical and Dress Rehearsals. Technical rehearsals are less harrowing if various technical elements can be introduced in earlier phases of rehearsal. This, of course, cannot happen unless the company has early access to the stage. When this is not possible, thorough preliminary planning can keep chaos at a minimum. When all members of the producing unit have been well briefed regarding their specific functions and responsibilities and a pattern of organization has been worked out in advance, the technical rehearsal period should proceed without ruffled tempers or undue confusion.

The scenery should be complete by this time, and all properties should be on hand and in place. Lights, sound equipment and special effects should be ready to function as they will in performance. It is advantageous to have actors wear full costume for technical rehearsals. If there are to be scene shifts, they should be executed as they will in performance. The curtain call is carefully rehearsed.

Technical rehearsals with their frequent interruptions to solve problems and make adjustments as well as to set cues can be hard on the actors. Their problems are eased if the first technical rehearsal is simply a walk-through with pauses at key moments to set cues and levels. Even then, minor lapses in characterization are bound to occur in later technical rehearsals as the entire producing unit concentrates on refining the elements so crucial to an effective presentation.

Once the play goes into dress rehearsal, the technical staff "gives the play back to the actors," and barring a major crisis the performance is not interrupted. The director and design artists and all supervisory personnel sit in the house and take notes, then hold discussions with their charges at the end of the run-through. All technical elements are in place, full costume and make-up are worn, the actors remain in their assigned off-stage waiting area and the play is presented as it will be in performance. Some organizations bring in an invited audience for the final dress rehearsal to give the company some idea of the type of response the production will receive. When this practice is observed, the invited group should be chosen to represent a "typical" audience. Some theatres invite groups from special schools or community institutions, children who otherwise would not have an opportunity to come to the play. There is much to recommend this practice.

Dress rehearsal is the time for the director to appraise his work. While he certainly does not withdraw from active participation, he keeps away from backstage. The show now belongs to the cast and crews, and it is too late to make any major changes. His post-rehearsal comments are made with that fact in mind. If he has done his work well, his sole responsibility at this time is to remain calm and to assure the company that it is ready for opening.

Participation Theatre: Preparation for Audience Management

When a participatory play is scripted, the performance aspects are rehearsed just as they would be for any other play.[4] If it is to be developed from improvised beginnings, the work on basic material and performance techniques proceeds as it would if the production were non-participatory. The company must be prepared to present viable characters working as an ensemble in a polished theatre piece so compelling to the audience that they will be motivated to become directly involved in the drama. The major difference, of course, is that actors must not only be prepared to play *for* the audience; they must also be well equipped to play *with* them, performing a double duty on stage. Only with proper background can they execute them both equally well.

If, as we recommend, cast members have prior training in creative drama, time can be spent on the specific challenges they must meet in the context of the play. If they do not, the rehearsal period must be prolonged to allow time for training, and actors must make opportunities outside rehearsal to observe and become involved in children's group activities. Preferably, any participation play is prepared for a specific age level and with a specific audience in mind rather than for a general public audience. When this is the case, the company can focus their observations and study. Directors who have experience in this style of theatre also suggest that preview groups be brought in for at least a week before the play actually goes into performance so that the company can test and adjust their approaches to involvement.

Improvisation is at the heart of the rehearsal process. Here is what several experienced directors have to say about it:

> I find improvisation essential. The spontaneity needed for participation plays can be developed and strengthened through putting actors in open-ended situations. Improvisation becomes increasingly important the more full participation becomes — actors need to be able to handle surprises individually and as a unit — and the more comfortable actors are in improvs, the more they'll enjoy the surprises and deal with them imaginatively.[5]

> Improvisations, sure, but improvisations with an objective, a goal in sight. . . . Always keep your goals and your directives in mind. Are you doing them to improve or to know a little more about the sub-text, or theatre relationships among actors?[6]

Goal-oriented improvisation prepares the actors for the unexpected. Many directors allow the company to improvise, even within the fully scripted play, feeling that the more the actors feel they have invested in the performance, the more secure they will be in dealing with its actualities. Building security and confidence is a primary goal of improvisatory rehearsal, for the more freedom actors have to explore alternatives before performance, the better equipped they will be to respond spontaneously and validly to the audience.

Another facet of rehearsal is preparing motivations for audience involvement that are genuine rather than manipulative, devising control techniques that establish the boundaries for participation, preparing to find alternatives that can be called into use when responses take the play in an unexpected direction, dealing with responses and setting the tone for actor-audience relationships. There is no way of prescribing a method for this type of preparation. No matter how much time is spent speculating about possible responses, the unexpected is bound to occur. Only one thing is certain: performers must be especially sensitive to the audience and well prepared to cope with whatever may happen when they establish the uniquely intimate relationship that characterizes this style of performance and to handle the audience and the material with sincerity, warmth, taste and respect.

The dramatic sequences which are presented to the audience require all the positive qualities of any play in which the audience is only vicariously involved, and the only segments of the performance that are not fully set and polished are those in which the audience will participate.

Rehearsing from Improvised Beginnings

Preceding chapters have contained considerable information about performances developed through improvisation. While the approach to conceptualization and direction may differ, these performances should come to the stage in fully polished form. We have noted several times that this style requires considerably more time to reach performance quality than does the scripted work. In the early stages of rehearsal so much depends on the creative process, which is unpredictable at best, that it is difficult to speculate on just how much time should be allowed, and we reiterate our admonition that the collectively generated performance cannot be perfected in a normal rehearsal period. The only thing that can be said without hesitation is that an absolute deadline must be set for putting the material into final form, and, once that happens, adequate time must be allowed for polishing and for technical and dress rehearsals, which are conducted exactly according to traditional theatre procedure.

Rehearsals that precede the shift from improvisation to standard processes are conducted in much the same way a leader handles creative drama sessions. Each one is goal-oriented, and the pattern includes presentation of challenge, discussion, improvisatory experimentation, more discussion and further experimentation until the company either decides to continue working with the idea or to discard it and proceed to a new one. Overall rehearsal goals are interrelated and not necessarily stressed in isolation, but all must be met at some point before the performance reaches the polishing stage. These goals include:

1. developing a cohesive ensemble;
2. exploring and experimenting with material; investigating background and sources;
3. agreement on material;
4. acting technique and style, including transformations;
5. arrangement of material in sequence; determining a through-line;
6. planning and executing transitions;
7. agreement on a production concept and necessary technical support;
8. experiments with music and sound;
9. setting roles; work on characterizations;
10. setting action and dialogue.

While rehearsals may appear on the surface to be less structured than those that are scheduled to focus on clearly defined segments of a playscript, each one must be planned with especial care so that the company and the director can feel that progress is being made.

PERFORMANCE

Opening day — the time when all the weeks of concerted effort come to fruition! The atmosphere is charged with anticipation as the house staff prepares for the arriving audience and the stage manager, list in hand, guides the technical crews through a final check to be sure that everything is in place and in working order. In the dressing rooms other crew members issue costumes, assist with make-up, arrange hair-dos and help the actors dress. Activity intensifies as the company hear the stage manager's half-hour warning call and hasten to put the final touch on preparations in order to arrive in the green room no later than fifteen minutes before curtain time. After a few brief encouraging remarks from the director, the crews take their stations and the actors are led through a series of warm-up exercises. Time passes quickly, and soon the actors respond to the stage manager's call to take their places for the opening of the performance.

The director joins the audience as the last stragglers are seated. When the stage and house managers agree that all is in readiness, opening cues are called. A hush falls over the theatre as the house lights dim, the overture plays and the performance begins. The routines so carefully set in technical and dress rehearsals are followed precisely. The actors are spirited and play with style, infecting the audience with their enthusiasm. When the final scene has been played and curtain calls taken, the cast, in true Pied Piper fashion lead the audience out of the theatre and mingle with them in the lobby for a few moments of sharing their mutual excitement and pleasure. As the crowd moves on, the cast and crew assemble in the green room for notes. Later, when the stage manager and crew chiefs are satisfied that everything is in order and properly secured, the company is free to leave the theatre, perhaps to continue their post-mortem over coffee at a favorite haunt.

The Company in Performance

The routine of preparation, performance and post-performance review is followed through the run of the play to ensure continuing disciplined involvement on the part of every individual associated with the production. While the designers and technical supervisors usually move on to other assignments once they are assured that the stage manager and crews are fully trained and capable of running the show without further instruction, the director never removes himself from the scene. If rehearsals have provided the right combination of preparation and indoctrination, he can be quite certain that all will be well, but he also knows that his reassuring presence keeps company morale high. Furthermore, he should sit with the audience during every performance to note their reactions and to evaluate the production as a whole. His objective observations are as crucial to his own growth as a director as they are to keeping the company challenged to strive for greater effectiveness each time they play.

Most organizations present several performances of each play for young audiences, some playing daily in a continuous run while others space performances over several week-ends. Either system may give rise to problems. During a continuous run, the director is not concerned with keeping the show together from one performance to the next, but when it plays intermittently he is wise to schedule brush-up rehearsals to keep it at performance quality.

Retaining spontaneity and freshness is probably the greatest problem of the long run. Unless concentration and sincerity remain at a high level, the performance may become mechanical and uninspired, or careless and offhand. The actors may be completely unaware that this is happening. They must be continually reminded that no matter how many times they bring the play to the stage, each audience is new, and the cast is obliged to perform as if the action of the drama is occurring to the characters for the first time. The sense of discipline and professionalism instilled in the company from the very first rehearsal should help them maintain pride in their work.

Fatigue can be a factor in performance quality, and except for avoiding making unreasonable demands on company time for extra rehearsals or technical work and for warning them that a long series of performances is energy consuming and admonishing them to get adequate rest, there is little the director can do about it. Again, self-discipline and professional attitude are the best preventatives. As a matter of fact, fatigue is actually less likely to have an adverse effect on performances than is the relaxed feeling of well-being that comes with overconfidence. The director should be alert to notice signs of indifference and to check for loss of vitality. He must watch for company in-jokes, tendencies toward self-indulgent playing and lapses in precision. In any performance where actors have a measure of freedom to improvise reponses, the director is especially careful to monitor their spontaneous behavior and to call a halt to any breaches of good taste. The minute he senses overconfidence or lack of discipline he should present some new challenges to keep the company alert. Sometimes a session where the actors as characters discuss their relationships with and attitudes toward one another, can be remarkably effective. It forces them to reexamine characterizations and motivations from the perspective of individuals who have "lived" with their characters for a time and gives new insights that can be put to good use in deepening and freshening their portrayals.

Reexamination of characters and their relationship to each other, the plot and the theme also helps actors place focus where it belongs when they show a tendency to pay more attention to the responses they are arousing in the audience than on the business of maintaining the life and vitality of the performance. Any inclination to alter characterizations without consulting the director should be nipped in the bud. Actors must realize that there is a difference between muting or subtly modifying a portrayal to temper audience response and changing it to satisfy a personal whim.

Rehearsals should have prepared the actors for their relationship with the crews. A professional attitude includes respect for backstage personnel and appreciation of the vital role they play as full partners in the production. As rehearsals progress the actors come to realize how much they rely on technical support to complete their own work, and their appreciation of that support grows as technical elements are phased in. When crew members attend rehearsals even before their services are actually needed, their display of interest and concern is valued by the actors, and a feeling of cohesiveness begins to develop. At company meetings the director makes lines of responsibility clear, and during the run of the play he reinforces the authority that has been delegated to the stage manager and crew chiefs.

Company discipline is based on respect and trust. Backstage horseplay, practical jokes, either on or off stage, or any breach of professionalism cannot be tolerated. When a company engages in such behavior it usually is in a spirit of great good will and without malicious intent, but even the most reliable groups have been known to get carried away. Apparently they feel that the young audience cannot detect that things are going wrong on stage. Every company should be forewarned that irresponsible behavior on stage or behind the scenes is indeed detrimental to the production.

Throughout the run the director must maintain high company morale and enthusiasm for the production. He remains calm and impartial in his dealings and senses the proper moments to make suggestions and phrases them in an acceptable way. He should know when to be firm and when to relieve tension with humor and understanding. He must encourage each member of the company to respect the talents and responsibilities of co-workers, and he scrupulously avoids any suggestion of favoritism or rejection in his dealings with individual members of the company.

Performance: A Theatrical Event

While producers and sponsors of productions for children and youth continue to have valid concerns about audience control and response, enlightened organizations have developed more sophisticated attitudes toward young theatre-goers than they once held. We now assume that good house management and excellent, sensitive performances are all the controls that are needed to ensure a positive theatre experience. It is increasingly rare to have a mascot figure or any other person not a part of the performance itself give a pre-curtain speech of welcome and admonition about acceptable audience behavior. The experience can be tarnished by an adult who tells the story from the stage or warns everyone to keep quiet except when something is funny or deserves applause. We believe that didactic speeches about theatre manners are counterproductive. Rather than making young people feel welcome and special, they give an impression that we either fear or undervalue them. We strive instead to prepare the performance environment in ways so intriguing to the arriving audience that they make the transition from the world outside to the world of the theatre without adult intervention. The audience immediately enters the playing environment in many theatres, and open curtains revealing a carefully-lighted setting are common in proscenium houses.

Some companies have the actors on stage doing warm-up exercises as the audience arrives. We do not advocate this practice. In the first place, youngsters entering the theatre may think the play already has begun and will feel upset about having missed part of it. We also believe that such displays of activity normally confined to backstage areas mitigate against the magic that happens when the play begins with proper dramatic impact. Young members of the audience may have difficulty deciding when the play really does start, and, having seen the actors as ordinary people, also find it hard to become identified with the characters they portray.

Preshow company involvement with the audience is legitimate and helpful to prepare them for their involvement in participation plays. This activity is as carefully planned as any other part of the performance, and the actors, fully costumed and made up, wait until most if not all the audience is in, then mingle with them as characters. If only one character will be responsible for soliciting involvement, he alone may work on the preparation. To illustrate this idea, the preperformance plan for *Junkyard,* a play we mentioned earlier in our discussion on conceptualization, might well be reviewed. As the house staff ushered the audience to the "grassy" areas where they would sit, the actors, in character, were playing with the junk that was part of the setting. Just before the performance started, they brought out an imaginary box, went through it, found imaginary balloons and began to blow them up and play with them. In the process of doing so, they "discovered" the audience, and two of the actors began blowing up more "balloons" to distribute to the children. This initial contact was low-keyed and warm, but it indicated to the children that there would be continued interaction with the characters as the play progressed. The additional transitional step from the everyday world to the world of the theatre and then of the play is an important one to orient the audience to their special role in the performance.

In any play, directors frequently have the actors make their initial entrance through the audience. If the play lends itself to this kind of opening, fine. In fact, it has qualities that recommend it when it is as well rehearsed as any other part of the performance and controlled so that it does not stimulate the audience to the point where they cannot settle down once the action begins. We suggest that no direct audience contact or interaction occur during an entering procession.

Since the trend is more and more to having scene shifts occur as part of the action of the play or staging them so precisely that they can be shared with the audience, problems of continuity are less necessary to deal with than they once were. If the play is unusually long, or if the scene shift must be hidden and will take more than a minute or two, it might be wise to plan an intermission. If so, audience control is in the hands of the house staff, and suggestions for management are offered in Chapter VIII. When the hidden shift is brief, light levels and music can help control the audience and keep them in their seats. If an intermission is taboo, as it is in some theatres, a cover scene can be devised and played before the curtain. Such a scene must have clear relationship to the play and forward its action. The director never stages or permits entre'act diversions, and he never permits the audience to be left in a fully-darkened auditorium.

Plays for young audiences frequently end on a note of spectacle with most of the characters on stage, and the curtain call should grow out of the last event in the play. Needless to say, it is taken in character. In a musical, it might include the reprise of a song or even a dance which continues as the actors leave the stage and go in procession through the theatre to meet the audience outside. The curtain call is carefully planned and rehearsed and executed smoothly as an extension of the performance.

Adult actors frequently meet the child audience in the lobby after performances. This experience can be valuable to them, for they learn first hand what children thought of their characters as they frankly share with them their reactions to the play as a whole and to individuals in the drama. They crowd around sympathetic characters, but often avoid the antagonistic ones, staring at them from a distance and hesitating to approach them directly. Often they will speak to the actors as characters, giving little indication that they regard them as having any other identity. The session provides a sense of completion, a chance to touch base with reality, partly reinforcing the knowledge that the performers are human, yet also reinforcing the magic aura surrounding people who become other people on stage. If anything, the mystery of ritual and magic only deepens as children touch and talk with their favorites.

The director always instructs the actors to maintain a sense of their characters and of the performance when they meet the audience and to focus on the children rather than on each other. In many areas these sessions with the audience have become "autograph parties." While some directors react negatively to this practice, it is a festive occasion for the children, and possession of a signed program gives a youngster an important souvenir of his trip to the theatre. Any director who has had a post-performance company meeting interrupted by a parent bringing a disconsolate child back to the theatre in search of that precious sheet of paper, somehow lost along the way, knows that the autograph party is not an empty ritual.

PERFORMANCES WITH CHILD AND TEENAGE CASTS

As we have observed, many organizations producing plays for young audiences outside school settings cast their plays exclusively with children or teenagers. Standard good theatre practices must be applied to any production presented to a public, admission-paying audience, no matter who the cast will be or where it will be performed. If the production is to fulfill its purpose of providing a sound aesthetic experience for those who come to see it, the director seeks the same qualities and characteristics in youthful actors that he hopes to find in adults. This does not mean that he expects them to come to him as technically proficient performers, nor does he expect to make unreasonable demands on them. It does mean, however, that he chooses the best possible cast and then works with them in such a way that participation in play production becomes a worthy artistic experience for them, even as watching the play provides aesthetic benefits for the audience. This is a highly idealistic goal, for no matter how proficient children and young teenage actors are, the audience is far more likely to identify with them as performers rather than as characters, thus changing the nature of the experience they receive. People who regularly produce plays with elementary and junior high school age casts maintain, however, that there is a unique and positive quality in that experience.

Our discussion of production work with young actors emphasizes the special problems of children and early teenagers. Senior high school students, whose in-school involvement in theatre includes performing in plays from the adult repertoire, can be expected to conform quite well to the standards and procedures characteristic of work with adults.

Choosing the Juvenile Cast

All producing organizations must have a definite policy regarding the age of children who may participate in production. We endorse the CTAA suggestion that children below ten years of age should not be in formal plays; at lower age levels they benefit more from creative drama. Some organizations place the lower age limit at the fifth grade level. Casting children younger than this is a questionable practice from two points of view: the developmental benefit to the performers, and the quality of the production as a work of art.

The organizational framework and fundamental purposes of groups producing plays with child casts vary widely. The philosophy of one producer may favor opening tryouts to all interested children in the community. Perhaps a loosely knit organization of several hundred members is involved. Sometimes a play is cast within a single school, youth organization, religious or recreation center. In other cases, a relatively limited group from a drama studio, workshop or community theatre organization is involved. Whatever the organizational pattern may be, we reiterate our position that play production should provide opportunities for children to experience the many facets of theatre in order that they may learn that it involves much more than acting — that actors can function only with the support of a diversified team whose contributions are of equal significance. This philosophy may be difficult to adopt, for it involves a great deal of effort on the part of adults responsible for getting the show on stage, and also on the part of those who must interpret the meaning of theatre to parents, who often think of it only as performance. Nevertheless, it is a worthy goal, and its achievement will be of infinite assistance to the director who faces the problem of dealing with vast numbers of children, all eager to play a part in the upcoming production.

The organizational framework in which he works influences the director's preparation for tryouts. If he works in regular classes or an established situation where he knows how many children are eligible for participation, his work is relatively easy. However, most directors lack the advantage of long acquaintance or of control of numbers. The average director may have to prepare to handle a hundred or more children at an announced audition, in which case he must discover an efficient and time-saving method of judging fairly what each child can do. This involves enlisting a group of adult assistants who are carefully selected on the basis of background and understanding and are fully briefed by the director to share his philosophy of children's theatre and to understand the qualities he seeks in child actors. Each assistant should have a specific assignment covering one phase of the tryout process.

When large numbers of children are expected at an audition, a system of tryout stations is helpful. Such a system might function as follows: as soon as candidates arrive, one assistant helps them fill out tryout cards. Then they move to other stations to participate in various phases of the initial screening. One might involve presentation of a short memorized selection; at another, children might be given a short selection for impromptu reading; at the next, they might pantomime some commonplace activity. After moving through the several stations each child has completed his initial audition and is dismissed.

Some plays lend themselves to a simultaneous three-phase tryout. If there is to be considerable song and dance, the adults who will coach these phases of the performance may each take a third of the children for special auditions while the director holds reading and improvisation sessions for another third. The groups rotate until each child has tried out three times during the first screening session. Any form of mass tryout may be bewildering to children and misinterpreted by their parents unless the director's purposes are made clear. Giving each child a written statement to take home can do much to eliminate misunderstandings and hard feelings. The message should explain that this first tryout constitutes an initial screening and that many children will, of necessity, be eliminated from further tryouts for the current production, reassuring parents that elimination this time should not discourage the child from volunteering for backstage work or from auditioning in the future. It should make clear that backstage assignments are available and important and explain how the child may become involved in them. It also should make clear when and how the child will be notified if he is to be called back for current auditions.

Any children's producing organization should maintain a permanent record of attendance at tryouts and participation in productions. No ethical children's theatre wants to build a star system, and most organizations try to give opportunities to as many children as possible. A card with entries noting attendance at auditions and participation in productions should be kept for each child. A record of consistent interest in the organization certainly should be taken into account when casting decisions are made.

Following mass auditions the director and his assistants confer to decide which children will be called back for subsequent sessions. From then on the director works with more manageable numbers, following the same general procedures he uses in casting adults, except for the final call-back session. Adult actors are usually able to understand and accept elimination from a role, but in selecting a young cast the director must be sensitive to childhood's reactions to false expectations and disappointment, and he should make it a policy never to call back more children than there are roles to fill. A child summoned to the final call-back may then be reasonably certain he will be cast, although he will not know what role he is to play.

One of the guiding principles of theatre with children is that each youngster must be cast in a role in which he has reasonable assurance of success. This means that he must be believable to the audience. When casting is limited to elementary school students, this poses a number of problems, particularly in finding boys who can play adult male roles. If an actor does not fit into the ensemble because of his size and voice, it is a kindness not to cast him. If it is at all possible to mix children and teenagers in the company, this would help solve some of the difficulties that really cannot be resolved otherwise.

When child actors are used, the director may well consider double casting, at least in principal roles, with both children cast in a given role having an opportunity to appear in performance. Fortunately the single performance of a children's play is rather rare, and several performances permit alternating casts to appear. This system allows for the use of more children in the production and, most important, provides insurance against last-minute illness.

To be sure, double casting means extra work for the director, and some feel it is detrimental to the production — an objection that is not necessarily valid. At first the casts rehearse simultaneously and interchangeably, the director taking pains to see that both sets of actors receive equal attention. While he is working with one group, the other observes, not with the idea that both performances will be identical, but to give opportunity to learn through watching. Directors who use this system find that competition between casts can prove stimulating to young performers, and each group is likely to adopt the best features of the other's performance. Final casts are set as rehearsals progress, but in sufficient time to have the program accurately indicate who will play which performances.

The problem of relationships between home and theatre is unique to working with children. Many parents yield to a child's desire to work in a play without realizing what will be involved. Some view with alarm the demands that are made once the undertaking begins; others minimize the importance of faithful rehearsal attendance. Some parents push their children into theatre, seeking a showcase for what they regard as remarkable talents. To counteract these tendencies, the director, with the support of his producing organization, should carefully interpret to parents and children the purposes and goals of the group. Many difficulties can be forestalled if children called to the final casting session are required to bring a schedule of their outside activities. In turn, the director sends home a notice which clearly details dates, times and places of rehearsals, specific information about dress rehearsals and performances, and a reminder of the vital importance of regular and prompt rehearsal attendance. Some directors take the precaution of sending this notice in duplicate, requiring that one copy be signed by the parent or responsible adult and the child and returned to the theatre. The final cast should never be announced until parents have had an opportunity to decide whether they are willing to allow their children to participate and whether they themselves are committed to lending the director full cooperation and support.

Rehearsals

Approximately six weeks should be allowed for rehearsing a performance with juvenile actors. Sessions usually are held after school, limiting the time that can be allocated to each one, and the nature of the teaching and overall preparation that must be given requires considerable time. Though young actors almost always learn their lines very quickly, they must be given a great deal of help with characterization, ensemble work and stage deportment. The overall schedule follows the same steps established for any scripted play, and the goals are the same. The director, however, must be prepared to adjust his expectations without too seriously compromising on quality.

He should establish a general style for the performance and try to bring the young cast as far as he can in achieving it and in perfecting external details of performance, but it is not realistic to demand the level of perfection that adults should reach. It is easy to overemphasize style and technique at the expense of sincerity and concentration on characterization, and this is likely to lead to mechanical movement and gesture and imitative line delivery. The honest, genuine and naive quality which youngsters are capable of bringing to performance should never be sacrificed to an artificial style or preoccupation with stage technique. The director certainly teaches these things and does a certain amount of drill work, but always with the primary goal of assisting the actors to feel comfortable on stage, make them look good to the audience and communicate what they can of period or culture in their portrayals. Sophisticated concepts about acting are never introduced.

The uncomplicated characters found in plays typically chosen for child actors are relatively easy for them to understand and play believably. In working with youngsters the director concentrates on the more obvious means of building characterizations, focusing on the most important dimensions and primary motivations of the central characters and working very hard to help minor and chorus characters achieve a measure of individuality and some very clear motivations. More often than not, one criterion for selecting the script for a young cast is the number of characters it contains so that as many children as possible can appear in the company, and herein lies a major directorial problem. Minor and chorus characters are often brought into the action to serve an immediate purpose; if they then have no further dialogue or easily discernible function in the scene, they may well have difficulty remaining in character. The director must help them find some way to become and remain involved. Probably the best procedure is to determine how they feel about the characters who are actively carrying the scene and how the on-going action affects each character on stage. Youngsters playing minor roles must be helped to feel how important they are to the drama, and when the director pays special attention to their characters, they are encouraged to discover and sustain meaningful reaction patterns.

This technique is equally applicable to members of crowds. The director should carefully attend to blocking scenes involving characters who have only a collective identity, first as a purely technical device to ensure visual appeal. However, even the most attractive groupings are likely to detract from the dramatic action unless the director carries his work one step further. Members of the crowd must know why they enter the scene; they must know what they think, feel and do while they are on the stage. To help them fulfill their function, the director should encourage them to develop definite attitudes toward the other characters on stage and devise appropriate reaction patterns. Frequently this involves a joint study of the script up to the point of entrance to discover a rationale for their attitudes and reactions. Improvisational activities are a wonderful means of helping actors find their way into these kinds of roles. We do not mean to suggest that chorus players should be strongly individualized or permitted reaction patterns which destroy emphasis, but rather to stress the importance of good direction.

Unfortunately, problems of concentration and character retention are not limited to minor and chorus characters. They can cause difficulties in any cast, but they are especially hard to handle when the actors are of tender years. Youngsters tend to be easily diverted, particularly in the unusual surroundings and circumstances of theatrical production. They do fairly well when they have lines to speak, but between lines they may drop character and look around, become interested in the action, not as characters but as themselves or, worst of all, stare out at the audience. More than any other single factor, lack of concentration makes performances by juvenile actors painful to the discerning adult and questionable as a worthy art experience for the child audience. Child actors want to give believable performances, but they need a great deal of assistance in attaining them and constant reminders that audience belief stops at the first sign of breaking character.

The director never stops helping young cast members become fully involved in the make-believe, imagining themselves to be characters in the situations of the play and responding as characters to the events unfolding around them. Once scripts are down, the director should not permit the actors to relax or break character between lines when scenes are being run. He insists that they remain in character, concentrating only on the dramatic action, not upon their own lines, their poses and appearance or upon what they will do next. This discipline not only is one of the best methods of ensuring a believable performance, it also provides a strong creative stimulus for enriching characterizations and refining movement and character business.

All the good work that has been done to prepare young actors for performance can be quickly undone if technical and dress rehearsals provide too many surprises or are conducted in an atmosphere of confusion. While we recommend the gradual introduction of technical elements into any performance, we stop just short of insisting that this must occur when the actors are children and young teenagers. Certainly they must have rehearsal costumes, including footwear, from a very early stage, and any properties they will handle should be on hand as soon as scripts are down. Music and sound must make an early entry into rehearsals. If lighting and scenic elements can find their way into the run-through work done before technical rehearsals, so much the better. It is quite certain that mature actors can recover from any performance lapses that may occur in the technical rehearsal period; it is a gamble to assume that youngsters can. Everything possible should be done to see that proper momentum is maintained as the play nears performance.

Cast Supervision during Performance

The young cast must be carefully prepared to meet the pressures and excitement of performance. However, under the stress of the moment even the best-disciplined group requires the support of adult supervision. They should not be left to their own devices at any time while they are in the theatre. Calmly authoritative adults should make sure that young actors report directly to the locations assigned for make-up and dressing. Prior to the opening curtain they should be assembled in the room where they are to remain throughout the performance except when they are on stage. Actors must never be permitted to stray into areas where the audience may see them in costumes and make-up. Adult chaperones remain in the waiting room where costume and make-up crew members have emergency supplies on hand to make last-minute repairs. While they are not on stage, child actors may be encouraged to read or play quiet games to keep the atmosphere from becoming too tense.

A highly reliable assistant stage manager whose only backstage assignment is to summon the actors should be assigned and trained to give dependable entrance warnings. The routine of performance is carefully observed during final rehearsals so that the young actors have no doubts about what they are supposed to do and where they are supposed to be during the run of the play.

The philosophy of the producing organization or of the director himself will determine whether a curtain call is taken and whether there will be post-performance contact with the audience. Some organizations producing with youngsters emphasize that the actors are only one of several groups responsible for bringing the play to the audience and are no more important than the crews. Since the usual curtain call brings attention to the actors alone, it may tend to break down attitudes which the director has taken great pains to instill in the producing group, and there may be a decision not to stage one. On the other hand, the director may consider audience training important enough to risk the possible sacrifice of other values. When they are taken, these curtain calls should be limited to a straight company front bow, and the crew should be invited to be a part of it.

Casts composed entirely of children generate less identification with performances than do adult companies. The audience tend to identify more with the child actor than they do with the character he portrays, and bringing the child cast out to meet the audience may destroy any illusion that has been created on stage. Children step out of character as soon as they leave the stage. Furthermore, their lack of maturity and experience makes them ill equipped to cope with the reactions and questions they will receive.

The fact that child audience members pay more attention to some characters than they do to others in post-performance meetings and that they even shun some is another good argument for keeping the juvenile cast backstage. The young actors are not likely to understand that the attention they do or do not receive reflects attitudes towards characters in the play, but are more apt to interpret it in personal terms. The sensitive director will immediately recognize that this can be detrimental to the young cast.

We should also mention that in post-show interactions of this kind all attention is lavished on the actors, tending to belie their indoctrination about the equality that should exist among all members of the producing unit.

OBJECTIVE EVALUATION

As directors most of us are inclined to view our productions from a narrow vantage point. All of us conceptualize from a highly subjective point of view despite our efforts to approach each production well armed with background information and the insights we have gained through detailed script analysis. Then we work with actors and watch them grow — only we know how far — through rehearsals. We become so involved with our productions and the individuals who work on them that we find it very difficult to assume an objective stance as we observe them in performance. If we are satisfied that our concept is adequately realized, when no major problems develop and when audiences seem to be "properly" responsive, we tend to view our work with satisfaction. We are pleased to think that the production looked good and ran with apparent smoothness, that the actors really grew and that the audience behaved as if they were having a good time.

Directors who have conscientiously prepared themselves to work in the theatre for children and youth and who keep abreast of the field are well armed with theory, and most are excellent critics — of other people's work. It is far more difficult to take a detached, impartial attitude toward their own. The director who is able to stand aside and view his productions and their effect on the audience with objectivity learns from every performance. When he applies the same criteria to his observations that he applied to every choice he made in the process of bringing the production to the stage, he can measure his success with some accuracy. Sitting among the youngsters at performance, sensitive to their covert as well as their more obvious responses, he can fairly well gauge the nature and quality of their reactions to the production.

In Chapter I, we described audience response studies that employ a team of trained observers who station themselves throughout the auditorium, taking careful note of reactions as they occur. This technique brings best results when observations are recorded objectively with specific notes on exactly what happened. For instance, if the audience screams, the observer should note that they did so and at what precise moment in the performance the response occurred, rather than merely noting that the audience became excited. Inferences about the nature and quality of stimulus-response patterns are drawn *after* the performance, not *during* it.

Believing that immediate "feed back" will help them assess the impact of a production, many companies make a practice of conducting post-performance interviews or of asking patrons to fill out questionnaires as they leave the theatre. We have considerable reservation about this practice. If the audience has been transported from the mundane world into a special realm of make-believe during the performance, some of that magic is carried out of the theatre to be cherished and reflected upon, quietly and at leisure. The satisfying transition from aesthetic experience to everyday life should be allowed to occur without intrusion. As adults we know how difficult it is to objectify a highly subjective experience unless we are given time to contemplate it. How can we expect youngsters to be able to provide considered answers that have any real meaning in arriving at value judgments the instant they leave the theatre? They may feel that they liked the play, but they very well may have not the least idea why, nor are they likely to be able to verbalize their reasons — assuming they have them — when they are still closely involved with the experience.

Producers who only present public performances are at a great disadvantage in their attempts to conduct follow-up studies. Audiences come and go, and there is no easy way to maintain contact with them. Groups performing in schools have established channels for seeking information, and they are well advised to take advantage of their opportunities to utilize ongoing relationships to learn as much as they can about the effects of their work. Organizations of the first type might well consider forming an advisory committee consisting of representative youngsters, teachers, school administrators, parents and directing personnel who meet to share perceptions of each production and of the theatre's youth-oriented program as a whole.

Directors should take advantage of opportunities to receive objective evaluation from colleagues. As we have noted, festivals of theatre for young audiencs typically provide reviewers who offer intelligent and thoughtful comments and suggestions. Lacking the possibility of festival participation, groups of directors and producers might follow the lead of those in one area who took turns inviting each other and students of theatre for children to a "Production, Food and Forum," where all viewed the same performance and then assembled for refreshments and informal discussion. Such interactions are mutually advantageous and are highly recommended.

Many of us have not reached the level of professional trust where we are able either to deal candidly with one another or to take kindly to criticism by our peers. Yet if the theatre for children and youth is to arrive at the stage of maturity where outsiders as well as those deeply involved in it view it with the respect accorded any genuine art form, every director must be receptive to frank and informed evaluation.

NOTES

[1]Pat Hale, ed., *Participation Theatre for Young Audiences: A Handbook for Directors* (New York: New Plays for Children, 1972), p. 18.

[2]Hale, p. 18.

[3]Michael Newell, "Developing an Approach to Actor Training for Children's Theatre," unpublished seminar paper, California State University, Northridge, 1975.

[4]For some of the information in this section, we are indebted to Shelly Raffle, "Participation Theatre: An Inductive Process and Analysis," unpublished seminar paper; California State University, Northridge, 1975, and to Hale.

[5]Page Lee, quoted in Hale, p. 23.

[6]Lon Pressnal, quoted in Hale, pp. 23-24.

REYNARD THE FOX (Fauquez) — CSU-Northridge, 1971-72.

SLEEPING BEAUTY (Shaw) Kabuki Style — Empire State Youth Theatre Institute, SUNY, 1978.

An Unusual Wood God in a Texas ICE
WOLF (Kraus) — University of Texas at
Austin, 1970.

(Top): The Spider from THE BUTTERFLY (Mofid) —
Everyman Players, 1978-80.

(Bottom): RAGS TO RICHES (Harris) — Kansas
University Theatre for Young People, 1978.

Children's Theatre Festivals in Southern California Settings, 1975-77.

201

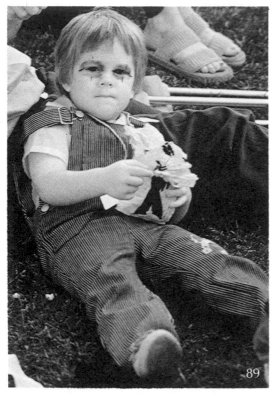

89

Children's Theatre Festivals in Southern California Settings, 1975-77.

90

91

(Top): NO DRAGONS ALLOWED (McKerrow) — San Diego State University at Children's Theatre Festival, CSU-Northridge, 1975.

(Bottom Left & Right): ANDROCLES AND THE LION (Harris) — Kansas University Theatre for Young People, 1968.

95

(Top): Sandy Duncan as PETER PAN, with Marcia Kramer as Wendy — Bufman and Nederlander production, 1979-80.

(Bottom): HEY DIDDLE DIDDLE! (Slater) — The Ensemble of Everyman Players, 1977.

96

204

STEP ON A CRACK (Zeder) —
Kansas University for Young People,
1980.

CHAPTER VIII
TENDING TO BUSINESS

"What did you say your job was in this theatre?"

"Controller," she replied.

She seemed like such an unlikely person to have such a responsibility; so I pressed on.

"Does anyone help you with all this controlling?"

"Don't need any help," she continued. "All you have to do is push the right buttons here on this master panel."

"I don't know many young people's theatres with this kind of layout. Most of them are still operating by hand — lots of hands, in fact." I looked at the blinking signal lights, the rows of small levers, dials and push buttons doubtlessly arranged in meaningful sections, banks, blocks and modules.

"The computer in the basement does the actual work," she admitted. "Everything in this theatre is automated. Lots of smaller terminals here and there for special jobs like setting light cues, but here I control everything that goes on. Stick around. I'll show you."

It was time for the house to open for the performance, but no one else was around. The controller pushed a series of buttons labeled "House Open," "Ticket Reception," "Ushers," "Proctors," "Lavatories," "Ejection," "Psychogalvanometers," "Electroencephalograms," "Eye Tracking." These last three, she explained, were the latest additions to the system, to keep track of the audience's precise attention-giving second by second, all by remote sensing, of course — nothing attached. Another module alerted the actors (still human, I was relieved to find out) that the house was open and the pre-show computer program was in operation.

"When the show begins, I push this." She indicated a master button that set an entire bank of signal lights to flashing sequentially. "That starts the on-stage technicalities all in programmed succession, automatically cueing off the actors' speeches and gestures — it's really very sensitive," she assured me. "No chance for a hitch. Lights, curtains, scene shifts, prop placement — even off stage costume changes — all happen with a system of totally integrated automated technology we developed."

"No crew?" I asked.

"Sure. Crews to put it all together to begin with. But not to run the show. We did have some problems with unions about it at the start, but the facts of life finally won out."

The show was now underway. The audience got to their seats (all preassigned, of course) by individually lighted pathways, called "ushers." During the performance one disruptive child was gently guided to the closest exit by an electronic hand. Another got to the bathroom the same way. And as the whole audience filed out at the end, the controller stepped to a slot in the main panel, withdrawing a detailed printout of the children's moment-by-moment neuromuscular responses differentiated by brain-hemisphere.

"I'll give this to the director so adjustments can be made before the show tomorrow," she said. "Glad you could join us. Oh, maybe you'd like a copy of this." She handed me a complete financial report the computer had just spewed out. "You can see we're over budget on costumes for the next show."

Considering the rate at which space age technology is reaching the open market, the day when this electromechanical wonderland becomes actuality somewhere may not be too far off. In the meantime, we must still work with many hands and often very limited resources to bring productions and audiences together. Formulating the various management systems by which this comes about is the subject of this chapter.

ALLOCATION OF RESOURCES

The efficient operation of a producing organization requires that someone be designated to handle managerial functions. It may be the director, the executive or managing director or the production coordinator. Often the people handling these duties have little or no formal preparation for them, but rather learn through trial and error and often through bitter experience. For most of us the art itself has held the most interest, and we have avoided the business end of things, often according it little respect until life in the cold world makes us realize that art cannot survive, much less prosper, without intelligent management. But with the influx of federal, state and foundation dollars into theatre budgets, the need to increase fiscal responsibility and accountability assumed top priority. As inflation bit ever deeper into fund balances, producing what are euphemistically called "earnings gaps," the need to examine pricing practices and to increase marketing skills became obvious. Specialists in management began to be added to theatre staffs, and a number of exemplary training programs were set up to accommodate a whole new job classification: the arts administrator.[1]

Whatever background this person brings to the job, anyone who functions in the role of manager has but one goal in mind: achieving the optimum balance between what a theatre organization wants to do and what is feasible. He is responsible for the equitable and judicious distribution of the commodities in which we deal: time, space, talent and money. We cannot afford to squander any of them.

Time and Space

An effective managing director or production coordinator has a good working knowledge of the time required to accomplish any of the tasks associated with play production, and his carefully constructed schedule of deadlines will be widely distributed to all those who are responsible for observing them. In formulating the schedule he divides each task into identifiable sub-goals, and his personal checking procedure will be built in at each of these points. Regularly scheduled production conferences enable him to detect troubles in the system early enough to take remedial steps.

One of his first concerns is allocation of rehearsal time and space. The time required to rehearse a scripted production with an adult cast will vary from three to six weeks. Eight weeks or more must be allowed for an ensemble piece to develop improvisationally from the acting company's explorations and experiments. An hour-long straight play requires a minimum of ninety hours in a space roughly comparable to the performance area. If it is a musical, at least another fifteen hours should be added. The level of performers' abilities should also be considered. Actors with developed skills require less rehearsal time than do those whose skills must be developed "from scratch." That applies not only to basic acting, singing and dancing, but to improvisation as well if it will be required to develop the entire performance or participation segments in a scripted work. With a child or teenage cast, a minimum of one-hundred hours should be allowed to rehearse a one-hour script.

Within the overall time allocation, adequate rehearsal must be allowed in the actual performance space to coordinate the technical aspects of the production. As a rule, a minimum of five or six four-hour technical and dress rehearsals are needed to get the production running smoothly under performance conditions. If the cast has not worked on the stage before, this is a critical time for them as they adjust to the performance environment, its acoustics and its psychological ambience. We have earlier mentioned that this process can be enhanced by bringing a trial audience of children into a dress rehearsal. We cannot close this section of the discussion without noting that even as the cast needs time to adjust to the stage and theatre, so does the running crew require time to be acquainted with the show and the people in it. Thus they should be scheduled to attend several rehearsals before the technical phases begin.

If the director of the individual production is not in control of allocating rehearsal time, he must be consulted and be in accord with the arrangement that is made. He then is responsible for carving up the total available hours into segments that will enable the cast to meet its performance deadline. He, too, is responsible for maintaining regular communication with the production coordinator. As a matter of fact, the show's director usually serves as principal coordinator of the various artists working on his production even when a coordinator or manager is in charge of overall program scheduling. In Chapter VI we pointed out the director's concern that all design elements are planned in an ordered sequence that gets the necessary working drawings into the hands of technicians and crews in sufficient time to keep all construction and subsequent planning on schedule. The interrelation of production personnel and their mutual dependence, detailed in that earlier discussion from the director's point of view, is detailed from the production coordinator's vantage point in Figure 8-a. The director outlines his needs. The coordinator sets the dates. The sample Master Production Schedule indicates time intervals normally needed to complete the several tasks of artists, technicians and management personnel.

Several prevailing circumstances will complicate the schedule, forcing the production coordinator to get agreement on priorities for use of the principal rehearsal and performance spaces. If more than one production is in preparation, the one closest to opening has the greatest need for the main stage. If classes are conducted in the same facility, or if theatre shares a multi-use facility with music or athletics, some intricate juggling of rehearsals and noisy construction periods will challenge the ingenuity and patience of the schedule maker and all concerned. Most programs operate under less than ideal conditions, but when the authority of the production coordinator is firmly established as the single person in control and he does his work well, problems can be minimized.

A common scheduling problem emerges when the stage itself is required for scenic construction, drop painting or hanging of lights. If these operations cannot be done at times other than when a show is normally rehearsing, alternate rehearsal spaces need to be provided. A clear plan as well as tolerance of each artist's problems are needed to complete all operations on time.

In the same manner, publicity and ticket office schedules must be set up to bring audiences to the theatre. Tickets for a children's production normally go on sale at least two weeks ahead of the opening. This means that initial promotion giving all pertinent facts and notice that the ticket office is open have to have reached the buying public by that time. Obviously this requires that tickets and promotion materials be designed and ordered to meet distribution deadlines. Program copy must be ready in sufficient time for printers or duplicators to produce the required number in time for the opening. Photographer's services are scheduled well in advance for publicity shots and for the production pictures that will be a highly valued record of the show. If the production record also will include a videotape, special permission must be sought from the copyright owners well in advance.

Talent

Allocation of talented performers, designers and technicians is likely to be necessary only if several productions are being cast or mounted simultaneously, or when a theatre wants to make sure that strength is distributed throughout a season. When a single play is being produced, directors and coordinators assign the best available talent according to the criteria and selection process customary in the organization. But when several are involved, the total image of the theatre is at stake, and allocation of strength to all constituents is a matter of real concern to the managing director.

Elsewhere we have noted that the children's theatre production must be given equal access to available acting talent when several shows are proceeding simultaneously. The same spirit pervades assignments of designers and key technical personnel to the young people's production. While strong design and technical talent is crucial to any production for the young, it is especially so when the show is to tour.

Money

The budget is a statement showing expected income from all sources and the allocation to the various departments of a theatre's operation. Its construction demands great skill on the part of the managing director. Budgets cover a specific period of time, preferably one season; and they are intended to pro-

Figure 8-a
Master Production Schedule

DAY PRIOR TO OPENING

PRODUCTION ACTIVITY

	60	50	45	35	25	20	18	15	10	7	5	3	1	0
Music/Sound: compose	x													
plot-cues					x									
record						x								
integrate								x			x	x	x	
Sets-Props-Special Effects: conceive	x													
design		x												
working drawings			x											
construction				x										
painting							x							
mounting									x					
tech. rehearse											x	x	x	
Costumes — Make-up: conceive	x													
design		x												
construction				x										
fittings						x								
finishing									x					
dress rehearse												x	x	
Lights: conceive				x										
design-plot					x									
mount									x					
tech. rehearse										x	x	x	x	
Cast: chosen			x											
rehearse		x	x	x	x	etc.								
rehearsal props					x	x	etc.							
essence of costumes				x	x	x·	etc.							
coordination rehearsals											x	x	x	
Publicity/Printing: campaign design				x										
poster, handbill distribution								x						
program copy					x									
publicity photos							x							
production photos													x	

vide a blueprint for what the theatre plans to spend to mount its program. As the season progresses, the budget is amended if income is not keeping pace with expectations or if actual expenses deviate from original estimates. In nonprofit organizations the goal of budgeting is to complete the season with accounts showing neither a deficit nor a large surplus; so it is important that the budget be meticulously built on informed estimates rather than on guesswork and wishful thinking.

Anticipated receipts from all sources should be entered on the income side of the budget. If a young people's theatre's resources include a staff whose salaries are subsidized by another budgetary unit such as an arts center, a school or a parent theatre program, those salaries are not normally shown. The same is true if the theatre facility is provided by another organization, such as a municipality, a school or a college. Certainly such items represent an enormous financial contribution to the program, but neither usually appears in the production budget.

At least eight sources of income may appear. The season may be sold as a package, bringing in subscription revenues which usually are somewhat less than the same number of individually sold seats would bring. In most cases individual ticket sales at established prices plus group-rate sales to schools, clubs, and parties provide the bulk of the revenue. Tour fees can be an important source of income, obviously the major one for organizations without a home theatre. Additional revenue may be earned from concession stands, program advertising, and rental of theatre equipment and costumes to other groups according to an established fee schedule. Finally, grants, gifts and contributions may be received from arts councils, foundations, patrons, or interested benefactors.[2] Ticket sales income will reflect generally accepted principles of price structuring, a matter to be discussed at a later point in this chapter.

An organization's planned expenditures directly reflect its stated mission. Expense items to be considered include the following:

Salaries and wages may be the largest single expense in a theatre's budget if it includes payments and fringe benefits to staff and performers. Other labor costs may also be considerable whenever one produces in a union house. Even when performers are not paid, as in community or educational programs, wages of assistants must frequently be accounted for in the costs column.

Facilities payments such as rents, mortgages, insurance, maintenance and utilities must be included in the budgets of all groups that do not have these provided by another body.

Administration costs are those which can be said to apply in a general way to all productions and operations of the season. They include such things as office expenses, telephone and telegraph charges, postage and shipping, duplicating equipment rental, services and supplies.

Ticket Office expenses include season coupons, reserved seat or general admission tickets, and any forms required for its operation.

Publicity and Promotion costs involve paid ads in the media such as newspapers, radio and television, as well as printing costs for season brochures, flyers, posters, and programs. Photography, video tape and display expenses also appear in this category.

The costs of *scripts,* either published or duplicated with permission of the copyright owners, and *royalties* payable in advance of performance form a separate expense category.

Technical production costs form a large single expenditure item when lumped together. Price tags on scenery, properties, costumes and make-up materials are going upward at an astounding rate these days, and the actual total is very difficult to foretell. The previous year's figures for a similar production level, plus the federally announced inflation rate, may be the basis for a reasonable estimate, however. Building supplies, paint, muslin, hardware, welding supplies, costume materials, draperies, lamps and gels, rentals of furniture, props, costumes, special tools, sound equipment or effect mechanisms will all be included in this category of expense. A complicating factor for the budget maker is that designs for the productions are seldom done when the cost estimates must be made; so a series of preliminary conferences involving managing director and the directors and designers assigned to each production is usually required soon after the season is decided and before the budget is constructed.

Touring expenses, difficult to estimate until the exact schedule is finalized, include such items as transportation, *per diem* payments to company, or meals and lodging, separately listed salaries if involved, and miscellaneous. The inflation rate added to the previous year's costs may be used in this category as well, if one can assume a tour of about the same scope.

Capital equipment purchases such as power tools, sound systems, touring light control boards, and special effects mechanisms should form a separate budget category. Many theatres make no provision for such things, or they may include them under the technical production column. Special fund drives to make such purchases are also fairly common.[3]

A *long-range investment* budget category should be provided, assuming there will eventually be need for a substantial sum to update equipment, renovate the building, or expand the program.[4]

If several of the initial estimates of expenditure include an inflation factor, it is clear that the first draft of the budget is likely to show a negative balance. At this point the affected parties confer and reach agreements on a number of questions, including the following: where can we cut without jeopardizing production quality? In what design categories can costs be trimmed by altering a concept, perhaps improving the artistic result? Can advertising costs be reduced without real losses at the ticket office? These and kindred decisions are crucial to the total effectiveness of the theatre's program, since reductions in too many production categories show very quickly in artistic quality. It might be better to think of ways to increase income rather than reduce planned expenditures beyond some predetermined figure.

Before actual spending begins, the managing director provides a working budget for the season as a whole and for each production to all concerned. From then on, all purchasing and ordering is channeled through the one person who exercises control over expenditures. He, in turn, keeps an up-to-date ledger showing the status of all budget categories so that all departments know where they stand, and the managing director can tell at a glance whether troubles are developing anywhere in the production system.

Figure 8-b shows a sample budget for a hypothetical nine-month season at a medium scale young people's theatre that is buying its own building in a community of 300,000 people. The percentage of total appropriation to each category of expense reflects a specific production philosophy and the actual circumstances in which the program operates; but the reader may be able to draw inferences and make modifications appropriate to his own circumstances.[5]

PUBLICITY AND EDUCATION

To a child there is nothing quite so effective as a parade of elephants, beautiful bespangled ladies on horseback and that gorgeous, flamboyant colliope to arouse an irresistible urge to attend the circus. There it goes, right through the center of town with its clear, direct message: buy a ticket and see the greatest show on earth!

Theatre for young audiences sometimes uses the time-honored device of the parade to attract attention, but most usually our promotional efforts today are a little more subtle and perhaps more consciously directed toward the adults who actually make the decisions to send or take the child to the theatre. One of our claims to distinction as a field could be that our persuasion needs to be directed largely toward those who will do the buying, not necessarily to the principal consumers.

Sales campaigns around which publicity and advertising are mobilized will occur at the beginning of a season if several productions will be sold as a package and again near the opening of each show. The first big effort is focused on stimulating subscription renewals and convincing other regular customers to become season subscribers. The experts tell us that costly efforts to convince lukewarm, irregular attendees or the large body of indifferent citizens to subscribe will probably not be productive.[6] For the primary target group, the main thing is to get the necessary information into their hands: who you are, what you offer, what dates are involved, where the events take place, how much it will cost, and how to get tickets. A tasteful, honest brochure linking the programs with artistic excellence and with its patrons' highest motives, proved discrimination and position of cultural leadership, will be coupled with a return

Figure 8-b
A Sample Budget

The theatre for which this budget was prepared is well established in a city of 300,000 people. Ten years ago it purchased a building which was renovated with money raised in a capital fund drive. It has a modified proscenium-thrust stage, and seats 700 people.

The season covered by this budget consists of four productions:
   Jack and the Beanstalk, to be done in experimental fashion, late September through mid October.
   Circus Home, late November through mid December.
   Golliwhoppers!, in February; will tour to 20 area schools (outside city limits) using a paid company of 12.
   Aesop's Falables, late March through mid April.
   Note: all productions perform 28 times, 7 performances each of 4 Wednesday through Sunday periods.
The paid staff consists of an Executive Director whose salary is half paid by a grant from the state arts council; a Designer/Technical Director; a Business Manager; and 10 technical assistants paid hourly. In this budget payment for 4 rock musicians for *Aesop's Falables* is included.

A stock of costumes and standard scenic flats and levels is assumed.

The theatre uses community actors except for the tour to schools in the spring. It also uses volunteer crews. Classes are taught by the paid staff for fees which revert to the teachers in lieu of additional pay. The theatre has a long-standing good relationship with the school of the city.

Income

Season sales	3,300 @ $10.00	$ 33,000
Group rate sales	20,000 @ $3.00	60,000
Individual sales	10,000 @ $4.00	40,000
Tour fees	20 performances @ $800 each	16,000
Theatre rentals	12 nights @ $50 each	600
Concessions	28 eves @ $100 each	2,800
Program advertising	50 ads @ $150 each	7,500
Contributions	25 patrons @ $100	2,500
Grant, State Arts Council	½ Executive Director's salary	12,500
Grants, business, industry	Subsidized productions	32,260
	Total:	$207,160

Expenses

Personnel		
Salaries		
Executive Director	$ 25,000	
Designer-Technical Director	20,000	
Business Manager	18,000	
Benefits (Hospitalization, etc.)	5,800	
Wages		
Technical Assistants (10)	16,000	
Musicians (4) - *Aesop's Falables*	2,000	
		$ 86,800 (41.9%)

Figure 8-b continued

Facilities
    Mortgage payments $ 16,100
    Utilities (heat, light, water)   14,200
    Insurance (accident, liability)   4,900
    Equipment maintenance   1,500

                                               $ 36,700   (17.7%)

Administration
    Office supplies $ 300
    Service contracts   75
    Telephone, telegraph   575
    Duplicator   500
    Postage, shipping   350

                                               $ 1,800   (.9%)

Ticket Office
    Season coupons $ 450
    Tickets (78,400)   2,160
    Complimentary forms   80
    Supplies   150
    Sales tax   260

                                               $ 3,100   (1.5%)

Script and Royalties $ 4,000   (1.9%)

Publicity and Promotion
    Media
        Newspaper ads $ 4,300
        Radio - TV   2,900
        Photographer   700
    Printing
        Season brochures   3,800
        Show flyers   1,000
        Posters   1,150
        Programs   5,700
        Teacher's guides   600

                                             $ 20,150   (9.7%)

Technical Production
    Scenery and props $ 7,200
    Costumes   5,000
    Make-up   700
    Lighting   3,500
    Sound - music   700

                                             $ 17,100   (8.3%)

Touring
    Company (12), $15/performance x 20 $ 3,600
    Per diem, 12 x $15, 20 days   3,600
    Travel: truck and van   2,310
    Royalties: 20 x $35   700
    Miscellaneous   150

Equipment $ 10,360   (5%)
Capital $ 5,600   (2.7%)
Long Range Investment $ 21,550 (10.4%)

                                        Total: $207,160

order form to consummate the action step. Such a campaign is aimed at the parents who are being asked to enroll their children in a regular attendance plan, and they become the core of any theatre's support.[7]

Knowing that parents and other adults are the ones reading and acting on the promotional materials at this point, the publicity director might consider just what motives are operative and how he might subtly appeal to them. Parents normally have their children's best interests at heart. They want to see them happy, to enjoy themselves, to have meaningful and unusual experiences often beyond what the parents had as children. They want them to be well educated and well adjusted socially. But they may also be looking for an inexpensive baby sitting service once in a while, an easy way to fill their turn to entertain the Cub den or Brownie troop, a birthday celebration without too much hassle. There is no harm in suggesting that your theatre provides a perfect answer.

As the time rolls around to put tickets on sale for the first production, a different kind of campaign is begun. If the theatre offers a group rate and sets out to encourage schools, individual classes, clubs, service organizations, churches, or neighborhood centers to bring children to performances by the busload, then a two-pronged campaign is called for. One focus will again by getting the young people's theatre story to the leaders, teachers, administrators and sponsors of such organizations. The other will be to persuade the children of the community that here is something they really don't want to miss. Their action step should be to bring the opportunity to the attention of parents, teachers and others who are in a position to arrange things for them. Even if the schools are not especially cooperative, block parties, birthday parties, church groups, Cub and Brownie troops and neighborhood house groups all are possible customers at the group rate. Flyers in grocery bags, booths at shopping centers, banners on Main Street, library and art center displays, placards inside buses and large signs outside them, spot announcements on radio and TV, bright yellow "I Support the TYP" buttons and t-shirts in department stores and posters everywhere one looks, all will help make members of the community conscious that this is a special time.

Fortunate is the theatre that has full access to the schools. Whether performances are on school time or not, the ability to distribute materials through classes will simplify getting the message to every child in the city. Often a handbill is all that is necessary — something the child can take with him to give his parents, something that gets the necessary facts into every home. Many communities have found the informal social atmosphere of a tea or coffee session with school PTA arts coordinators conducive to effective distribution of tickets for the season. Through these sessions a powerful ally is enlisted in the theatre's cause. School pride, perhaps even a friendly competition among schools, becomes part of the campaign.

Sales to individuals and families may be prompted by any of the mentioned publicity devices or by the more conventional newspaper ads, radio or television spot announcements, reviews that may appear in the press, or perhaps more telling than any of these, good word-of-mouth reports about the show. A theatre's reputation is built step by step, and the best advertising any of us has is the residue of good will left by satisfied patrons who feel they got just value for their investment every time they attended. And we all know parents who keep right on attending long after their children have "outgrown" us.

As the schools become closely interwoven with the theatre's educational effort, the teacher's guide to the production becomes increasingly important. We admit there can be a danger of distortion if too much emphasis falls on theatre-going as a learning experience. We are also aware that artists frequently assert categorically that productions should speak for themselves without help from anyone. Nevertheless, when large groups of children, all of the optimum age, will attend a particular show together, it seems wise to prepare them in ways which should increase their personal involvement. One thing the guide must do is help the children realize they have some obligation to the success of a live performance, that actors respond directly and immediately to their reactions, and that the circular response pattern set up is different from what happens in other forms of viewer experience.

The teacher's guide consists of a page of administrative facts (who, what, when, where, etc.), a plot summary, sometimes without the ending, a discussion of some interesting background to the play, the playwright, the original author, its themes, its style of presentation, any unusual vocabulary or concepts contained in the play, and some things about the people who have worked on the production. The guide may be used to tell children about how theatre is made, what various artists contribute to the total effect, and what special problems they encountered with this show. Often suggestions are made for further study or some things the class may do to enrich the experience: art projects, creative drama explorations, folk dancing, show and tell, or even original writings. It is important that teachers be given options about how much of the guide to use. They can easily be overpowered by a thick booklet that would take all their time for a whole week.

Cast visitations to schools may have begun as a publicity device, but more recently they have been looked upon as part of the total educational effort binding school and theatre. Cast members may or may not appear in costume, but rather than merely stopping by to do a scene from the show, they come to share personal experiences and perceptions about the play and their roles in it. They answer questions and make every effort to acquaint the children with interesting aspects of making theatre that probably are not apparent from the audience side during a performance. The main purpose is to introduce performers as artists and as caring people interested in children. Perhaps if this were done more often, people would not grow to adulthood perceiving all artists as weird, threatening and remote, and the category of adults-indifferent-to-the-arts would begin to diminish.

THE TICKET OFFICE

The Price of Tickets

The past few years have seen ticket prices rising steadily in direct response to inflation and to the need for increased fiscal responsibility in most arts organizations. A few years back one would have been thought insane to suggest that a single seat to a popular family musical on Broadway would cost a child $45 or more. Using that figure as a high point, we can scale our sights down to the community group that stoutly maintains its 50¢ charge, the price established in 1956 when the theatre was founded. Most of us fall somewhere in between. What guidelines can help an organization ascertain a fair figure, one that will recover all or the necessary portion of production costs, one which reflects a realistic view of the total marketplace in any given community, and which reinforces that all-important patron impression of neither underrated nor overrated value?

For many years theatres for young people have used local movie admission prices as a gauge. Now additional and more involved analyses are based in part on patron surveys. It seems that among adults the admission price for some arts events is not actually crucial in making the prime target audience, the "enthusiasts," decide to attend. It doesn't even seem to matter much if a discount is offered them for a season ticket.[8] How true this is for young people's theatre has yet to be tested.

We do know that there is a point on the price scale where purchases do begin to drop off, a point at which an increase in price fails to produce an actual increase in total revenues. Ascertaining that critical point is a difficult management task. The key group is the "sometime purchasers," those who go to some shows but are not season patrons. It is not necessarily a matter of affording the admission price. It is mainly a matter of relative weight given to price plus preference. In other words, where does the occasional purchaser prefer to spend his valuable spare time? The price of a professional ball game could well be many dollars higher; but the choice of which to attend may tip in that direction unless the theatre's ticket price is sufficiently low to make up for the ball game's other attractions.[9] Each theatre really has to construct and test a "demand curve" of its own based on the economics of the community, plus careful assessment of all competing events within the area in order to tell at what level the price of tickets begins to keep a sufficient number of patrons away to affect total income adversely. Whatever the dollar figure, standard price-structuring establishes the individual ticket at the highest price, the season ticket

216

holder's single admission at the lowest, and the group rate in between.

How to make lots of money is certainly not the point of this discussion. We all are interested in increasing our influence in the community in a number of ways. But obviously we cannot accomplish our goals if we are out of business, or if economic factors restrict us in carrying out our mission. For this reason it is wise to set admission prices high enough to produce optimum revenue in the theatre's actual marketplace, and then establish policies for special subsidies for groups of children who otherwise could not attend the theatre. These policies might include an across-the-board offer of complimentary admissions to any children attending with school groups who cannot afford tickets. All the theatre needs is the teacher's word; no questions are asked and no distinctions made anywhere in the distribution system. Groups of special children of many kinds could fall into the same category. The theatre may then pursue outside help to underwrite these comps. Service clubs, business and industry, patrons, a socially conscious student group, a fraternity or sorority may be quite willing to share this economic burden with the theatre.

Once an optimum ticket price is determined, theatres must still face the question of rate differences. Shall there be a price differential between child and adult admissions? Is it advisable to place different value on different seats in the house? Shall there be a difference in the cost of seats to the Friday night performance and the one on Saturday morning? Some theatres avoid the whole matter by setting one price for all seats at all performances, even when they are reserved. The system has the virtue of simplicity, to be sure. And there is no need to ascertain the age at which one is asked to pay the adult rate.

In some communities, however, it is taken for granted that one pays more to sit in the prime seating area, and there is nothing wrong with introducing children to this concept early in life. Obviously, the house cannot be scaled for performances presented to large school groups; but setting a reasonable scale for the house is indeed justifiable for ordinary public performances.

To scale a house, one starts by establishing the optimum price for the category one expects to be most in demand. For instance, a theatre may peg its critical price on the "demand curve" at $4.00. That figure would be assigned the middle seating section, probably the third of the seats just behind the choicest section in whatever configuration the house takes. The top seats, the quarter of the house nearest the stage, would go for $4.50; and all those remaining, for $3.50. The group rate for performances sold completely in class blocks to schools would then be applicable to all seats and set at $3.00.[10] But the group rate set for ten or more attending a public performance would be 20% off the regular price in each seating category; thus $3.60, $3.20 and $2.80. In passing, we should note that in a scaled house, tickets for seats with obstructed views and, for reasons of discipline and safety, the first row of the balcony, might well be pulled, crossed off the seating chart, and remain unsold.

The movies have accustomed us to expect a price difference between adult and child admissions, and some young people's theatres establish a three-level distinction, identifying child, "student" or youth, and adult ticket prices which are tied to elementary, secondary and post-secondary grade levels and obvious adulthood. If the business staff is willing to wrestle with the complicated price structure of the scaled house and group rates, we do not recommend the further complication of age-price differentials. But if age differential is the only one established, a fifty cent interval between categories (i.e., $4.50, $4.00, $3.50) would be reasonable.

Productions in major theatre centers across the country typically are priced higher on nights of greatest demand — normally week-ends; but there seems little justification for theatres in smaller communities to follow suit. It seems to us that the only circumstance in which a young people's theatre production might have a different scale for different performances is one in which the show is part of a regular adult season and is performed for child audiences on a separate schedule as well. Thus *Oliver!* might have several evening performances for family audiences and a simultaneous run of special matinees for children and youth, with separate prices set for each series.

A final suggestion: once a pricing schedule is set, management should resist all requests to reduce rates to accommodate petitioners' charitable causes. Such requests come frequently, but no theatre is obligated to support anyone else's charity.

Operating the Ticket Office

Ticket offices for young people's theatre range in complexity from a table in the lobby where money is exchanged for roll tickets, to the sophisticated system of checks and balances mandated by business managers in larger theatres. Often we find ourselves sharing facilities and operations with other groups in a multi-purpose box office. Whatever its scale, the ticket office serves a single function: channeling patrons into the theatre at prearranged times in exchange for the price of admission. Its importance, however, is underlined by the fact that it frequently provides the most direct contact the patron has with theatre personnel.

Anyone setting up a ticket office for the first time will become acquainted with all the standard procedures which are now well established and widely discussed in sources on theatre business management.[11] These include such matters as physical arrangement of the office, systems for racking or stacking tickets, procedures for reserving or selling them, security of both tickets and money and periodic accounting. Policies about acceptable methods of paying with cash, checks or credit cards, as well as ticket exchanges, refunds and lost tickets need to be clearly defined. Thus far, there is no difference between ticket office procedures for the theatre for children and youth and those followed in all theatre. But we do face certain unique problems in dealing with young audiences and those who buy tickets for them.

When the play is for youngsters, ticket office personnel must be prepared with considerable information about the production. They must be able to summarize the story or explain something about the style, give definite information about its appropriateness for various age levels, including any special cautions that parents may need to decide whether it is appropriate for their children, and to give definite information about running time. If the play calls for audience participation, this should be mentioned in all phone contacts and clearly posted near the ticket window. The age of attendees is very important to the success of the show, and control mechanisms begin at the ticket office. In this circumstance and in circumstances where theatres never allow children below a certain age level in the audience, sales personnel must be especially courteous and well prepared with explanations in order to maintain the theatre's good will.

Certainly children and youth deserve the same courteous, interested attention ticket office personnel traditionally accord adults. It is true that they may be new at ticket buying and more in need of explicit instructions and patient repetition than their elders who normally buy for younger children. But if we adhere to the principle that theatre attendance in childhood prepares one for theatre attendance as an adult, we will remember that ticket buying is the first step of the process and expect ticket office personnel to behave accordingly.

Lost tickets or arriving for the wrong performance are considerably more a problem with youngsters than with older clientele, necessitating some rather lenient bending of the rules. After all, a youngster who has arrived at the theatre only to discover that he has left his ticket at home or lost it, or that he has a ticket for another performance, cannot simply be turned away to wander the streets. In most cases it is safe to assume that there is no intention to defraud the theatre.

To reduce the problem of wrong day arrivals, some managers adopt a system of imprinting a distinctive symbol — a star, crescent or diamond, for example — to distinguish the tickets for each performance. The appropriate symbol then is prominently displayed in the lobby to allow audience members to double check the validity of their tickets. While we have seen cleverly designed tickets which are themselves symbols — cut-out pumpkins, snow men, and the like — we recommend that tickets retain their traditional shape and contain the usual information about date, time and price to facilitate the various audits that are keyed to them.

Every effort should be made to avoid the common problem of long lines waiting to buy tickets just before curtain time. A general policy, frequently announced, that the opening curtain will not be delayed, eventually should persuade regular attendees to exert more effort to purchase tickets in advance. No matter what we do, lines of eager patrons will form to buy tickets to popular public performances, however, and they require special handling. If tickets do not have to be run through a cash register imprint process as they are sold, additional sales stations may be set up in the foyer. While managers might cringe at the suggestion because of the resultant loss of control over the sales process, it will help get the audience into the theatre on time.

After the hubbub has died down, ticket office personnel use the quiet hours to complete the report of how many tickets were sold at what price, balancing the total with actual cash on hand. Mistakes may well occur during hectic, pressurized sales periods. When they do, they present occasions to consider methods for improving accuracy and service.

HOUSE MANAGEMENT

To a large extent the house staff is responsible for making the young people's theatre-going experience a happy one. They greet them getting off the buses or entering the foyer. They set an atmosphere of quiet efficiency, guiding their young charges through the ticket-taking process to their proper seats and giving each one a program if it is theatre policy to provide programs before rather than after the performance. They provide supervision and any necessary assistance during the show, and, at its conclusion, distribute programs (the established practice in many theatres) before helping send the audience on its way. When the cast comes to the lobby to meet the audience after the show, the house staff assists with crowd control. They are alert to spot the stray child whose parents may not have arrived on time to pick him up and turn his problem over to the house manager for resolution. Patrons may not be aware that the house crew is responsible for the attractive lobby displays, for eliminating distractions, for seeing that proper temperature and light control are maintained in the auditorium, and for coordinating house and backstage operations. Contrary to the impression suggested by our computerized wonderland, an effective house staff is one whose personal human interest is consciously bent on making this a very happy occasion in the lives of children.

The House Staff

In larger theatres the house manager may supervise one or more assistant managers, as many ticket takers as are needed to cover the accessways into the theatre, as many ushers as are required to get patrons to their seats in the time allowed, and proctors or chaperones to exert a quieting influence when necessary. Ushers could well perform the chaperone function, though parents and teachers will also be considered adjunct house staff when they attend with their children. If concessions and a coat check service are included as side operations, they usually fall under the house manager's aegis as well. Ideally, of course, each member of the staff is a paragon of tact, a fountainhead of knowledge, and either a pal, a policeman, or a mother/father figure, depending on the need of the moment.

Pre-Show

Preparing for the audience's arrival may involve plans for handling traffic outside the theatre. If special police will be needed to control difficult loading and unloading situations for buses and carpools and for directing vehicles to parking areas, these arrangements must be made well in advance. Keeping disembarking areas clear of other traffic is no small problem, especially in urban centers. Carloads of senior citizens or orthopedically handicapped children may require special greeters who open doors and assist people out of cars. The presence of these groups also requires careful preparation of accessways into the theatre.

Interesting lobby displays centered on the current production should arrest attention and contribute to a sense of occasion as soon as patrons enter the theatre. Displays serve their best purpose when audiences have some free time to wander. Unfortunately, children filing to and from buses get only a cursory glance.

Children are accustomed to finding an open snack bar at movie theatres where the pre-show ritual includes buying popcorn, soft drinks and candy bars. And it is true many young people's theatres make substantial supplementary income from such concession sales. If snack bar service is felt to be essential to the financial solvency of the theatre, then strict rules must be established for its use to prevent distraction and mess that are inevitable when eating and drinking are allowed in the theatre. Items purchased at the stand must be confined to that area, and the house staff should be prepared to confiscate such items at the entrance to the auditorium. If there is a snack bar, it is open only for public performances, never during in-school shows.

A mascot character who is used to publicize, identify and personalize the program and help in its educational effort may be present during the period before the show to circulate among the children, sharing with them the joy of theatre-going and answering questions about the play. It is important to use restraint in these interactions lest the children become so excited by personal contact with the mascot that the show itself becomes an anti-climax. This informal contact, however, is much to be preferred over the practice of having the mascot introduce the performance from the stage, setting up irrelevant expectations.

Seating procedures may range from simply placing children on the floor on their side of an imaginary or actual line demarking the audience from the playing space as in participation theatre, to escorting them one by one down the aisle to a seat reserved by section, row and number. Often large groups will arrive by the busload from every school in the system, and will be seated in predetermined blocks. If the scheme for doing this is carefully worked out in advance, it is amazing how quickly a very large auditorium will reach capacity.

House managers are careful to keep a season-by-season record of seating arrangements for in-school performances, ensuring equitable rotation of seating assignments. Before each scheduled performance the house manager prepares a seating chart which includes traffic patterns for each aisle, thus enabling the house staff to unload and seat several busloads simultaneously with minimum confusion. Ideally, each school receives advance notice of the seating arrangements that have been made for it. When its group arrives at the theatre, it may find an usher carrying a sign bearing the name of the school. Then all they have to do is fall in line and follow the usher to their seating area. Seating within the block is usually handled by principal or teachers who customarily place the smaller children in the group toward the front. The usher stands by to make sure all the seats are filled. As buses are unloaded, the house manager hands each driver a departure schedule so there will be no delays in picking up the children after the performance.

When audience members arrive for public performances, seating is supervised in a reserved seat house, but only loosely supervised if general admissions are sold. In the latter case, adults usually are asked to sit toward the rear of the theatre to leave an unobstructed view for the children. Fewer ushers are needed for open seating, but some are still required to discourage children from racing about to change seats and to help with general house control. Although reserved seating does require more ushers to give individual attention to arriving audience members, few children will violate the strangely authoritative assignment represented by a number on a ticket.

The house manager is directly on the firing line when curtain time comes and the lobby is filled with patrons waiting to buy tickets and the house is buzzing with prompt arrivals who expect the performance to begin. No harm may come if the curtain is held briefly, but a better solution is to take the curtain on time and seat late-comers at the rear of the house where they will not disturb others. We can think of only one circumstance when it might be admissible to delay the curtain: one entire school group whose assigned seating is front center has not yet arrived. A wait will not be disastrous if the audience is told the reason and asked to be patient in helping solve the problem. In any case, the theatre should have a definite policy that no stage manager ever begins a performance without a go-ahead from the house manager.

These days more and more children, and always some fond relative of a cast member, are likely to ar-

rive at the theatre armed with flash cameras ready to take pictures during the show. As in the adult theatre, an authoritative voice on the P.A. system should announce that picture taking is forbidden. since
the sudden flashing of light poses a danger to the performers. If cameras are spotted by the house staff,
they should be confiscated and checked in the front office.

During the Performance

The house staff spends the performance time in watchful waiting. Since it is normally the period of
least activity for ushers, there is always the temptation to leave the area and relax. For young people's
theatre, however, this practice is unwise. Things happen that need attention. Doorways that let in light
should be guarded. Distracting noises should be silenced when possible. Children needing directions to
the restrooms should be guided to the least distracting route and then prevented from bursting noisily
back in, letting in floods of sunlight to destroy the black light sequence in the play. Several people have
noted, incidentally, that the number of children who leave for the restrooms is an inverse measure of a
production's power to sustain interest.

Chaperones keep a watchful eye out for pockets of distraction, for the child who persists in squeaking
his chair to the consternation of all about him, or for those who are deliberately bothering others or
creating a danger. But there is little need for plying the aisles like an overseer ready to strike at any small
miscreant who dares to wiggle. Chaperones need to be especially alert to distinguish between disruptive
behavior and the naturally exuberant responses of children to the performance. The latter are to be encouraged, not put down. Chaperones should be careful they themselves do not become the major
source of distraction in the auditorium.

A director's artistic decision to divide the performance into segments separated by an intermission of
more than a minute or two has obvious implications for house management. The effort to keep children
in or near their seats is aided by keeping house lights dim or out, with lights kept on the curtain during
brief suspensions of the action. Ushers stand by to discourage an exodus. When house lights are brought
up full and stage lights taken out, a clear signal is given that there is time to leave the theatre. Doors
should then be opened to permit free passage to the lobby.

Some theatres encourage the sale of refreshments during intermissions. European young people's
theatres commonly serve tea or fruit drinks. Adult theatres everywhere sell alcoholic beverages. Relax-
ing, chatting, socializing, looking at exhibits and displays are part and parcel of going to the theatre. If
total running time is much more than an hour, such intermissions can give children a needed release
from concentration and prepare them to return with renewed interest. Clear signalling devices such as
flickering lobby lights, chimes or P.A. announcements are needed to get everyone back and reseated. Of
course intermissions extend total performance time. The director's decision on type and length of any
break in the play must take into account the size of the audience, accommodations built into the facility
and a realistic assessment of the house staff's ability to cope. Some sponsors stipulate a no-intermission
policy in their agreements with companies they book.

The house manager uses the performance period to prepare the printed programs for distribution, if
they have not been provided before the play. For in-school performances, programs might be divided
into class-size packets. Each organization will develop its own policy about the time to distribute programs. Many choose post-performance to avoid the almost inevitable distraction they can provide in the
hands of children during the show. Theatres may well decide on pre-show distribution for public performances and have program distribution accompany departure at school matinees.

Post-Show

The play ends and the house lights come up. If it is a public performance, the aisles suddenly fill with
people on their way out. If it is a school matinee, the children know that they stay in their seats until it is

their turn to leave. The house manager goes on stage and names each school in turn, perhaps reinforcing the announcement by holding a sign bearing the school's name. Bus drivers will have been given a coordinated departure schedule to guarantee that vehicles are lined up in proper order so that loading can occur quickly as groups leave the theatre. The system obviously is designed for speed and efficiency. Unfortunately it leaves children little time to savor the immediate aftermath of theatre-going.

As teachers pass the doorways, ushers hand them packets of programs to be given each child on the bus ride back. An evaluation form may also be given to teachers on which to record an assessment of the children's reactions to the performance.

It is not unusual for children who saw the performance as part of a school attendance plan to return for a public performance, partly to take advantage of the autograph party, that popular ritual reserved for unpressured times. We have seen how interactions between cast and audience immediately after the performance benefit the actors. The children, too, benefit from this special extension of the theatre experience. Its logistics usually involve keeping house control until the actors have moved up the aisles and into the lobby, supplying pencils to all of them, and spacing them throughout the area so that they will be easily accessible to the children. At least some of the house staff remain in the lobby to keep the process as orderly and as fair as possible, helping children get their turns to speak to the actors as they sign their characters' names and perhaps pen a brief private message if time allows.

During this happy time other members of the house crew are occupied with clean-up chores and performing the necessary ticket tally. When the report is in and the last stray child accounted for, the job is complete for that performance. Just as ticket office personnel engage in a frank assessment of their effectiveness, the house manager and his staff should constantly evaluate their effectiveness, always seeking ways to improve the important work they do.

TOURING

The decision to tour or not to tour is a managerial one affecting many aspects of a program, whether the young people's theatre exists independently or is a part of a larger operation, and it is made at the highest administrative level. There are advantages and disadvantages to consider before the final choice is made.

Many professional theatres for young people are organized primarily to tour and have, in fact, no home facility. But most groups considering the addition of touring to a local production schedule will look to the additional exposure, good will, income, and opportunity to build an important, even politically advantageous, image through a larger community as reasons for going on the road. An educational theatre will be primarily interested in providing additional learning experiences of a kind not offered in any other way, an aspect of training realistically related to the student's ultimate profession. A community group may choose to add performances in hospitals, nursing homes, centers for delinquent children or prisons in an effort to bring theatre to frequently neglected segments of the population. Countering these pluses will be the additional costs, the enormous commitment of time and energy required of all personnel, and the chance that touring may begin to overbalance the home program in terms of total effort.

Assuming the choice has been made to tour one or more productions for children and youth, the program's administrator will begin to accommodate all aspects of production to that pervasive fact.

Ramifications of Touring

As indicated in Figure 8-b, budgeting a tour must take account of the costs of transporting the company and technical apparatus to all performance sites, any payments to company members, the expense of feeding and housing while on the road — often paid as an inclusive *per diem* allowance — and miscellaneous production expenses or emergencies incurred away from headquarters. Accurate estimates of these costs require that all conditions of the tour be known. How many people will comprise the company? Where will performances take place, and what are the distances involved? How many days will the company be out? What are the daily, weekly or monthly rental or lease rates of all vehicles, and what additional costs must be borne by the renter, such as insurance and mileage? If gasoline is not included in mileage, how many miles-per-gallon does each vehicle get, and what is the cost of fuel in the area? Road and bridge tolls must also be included in transportation. If actual expenses for the company are paid by the company manager, prevailing motel rates and possible group discounts as well as reasonable food allowances for the region encompassed by the tour should be determined. Actors Equity minimums would apply when members are involved.

Royalties for road performances appear separately in Figure 8-b, but there are other administrative and promotion costs related to touring which the manager may prefer to extract from the general categories. A brochure announcing the production to potential sponsors could be a substantial item, especially when postage is added. Extra publicity photos, teacher's guides, and sample posters supplied to sponsors may be separately accounted for. If the company supplies the programs at all tour performances they, too, may be an identifiable extra expense.

These cost items in the tour budget are the ones normally offset by the fees charged sponsors for performances. However, it is well to remember that the show could never tour on this budgetary basis if the initial costs of staging are not covered by the local run. A manager may quite reasonably decide to prorate the total costs of mounting and touring the show over the total number of local and road performances. The practice is justifiable on the grounds that some costs of mounting are incurred because the show is to tour. For instance, the home theatre may have built-in scene shifting devices such as fly lines or a revolving stage that will not be found in the tour theatres. Assuming the production will have some scenery, decisions about design will be conditioned by the fact that shifting devices, if needed, will have to be provided as part of the scenic budget. Variations in stage size encountered on tour, different stage heights, small off-stage spaces, and restricted passageways for loading and unloading, require that scenic units be variable in size, that selected sections must be assembled on the site, and that no single piece is larger than may go through a standard doorway, or fit in the truck to be used. Scenery and prop units need to be more substantial to withstand the loading and frequent set-ups to which they will be subjected. All these conditions involving special construction and additional hardware affect building costs.

Since costumes are not subject to such exigencies, special problems of touring are not so formidible. There may be some additional requirements that costume materials be wrinkle-resistant, that they can be laundered easily to keep them fresh over a long run, or that they be somewhat more substantial in construction because of the extra use. But these differences are not easily translated into additional expense. However, the number and complexity of the costumes may be a serious matter simply because of transportation space.

Lighting may be supplied in full or in part by the host theatre, or carried with the show. Foreknowledge of each plant's lighting installation is needed before the choice can be made. Perhaps the show can be adequately lighted by relying on the local facility for general illumination and on company instruments and controls for special effects. Some standard road houses will be ready to mount the entire light plot using house equipment when the tour manager supplies the plot in advance, but others will supply nothing except power. Most school stages will have some instruments and control units that can be preempted, at least to help light the tour show. If a group elects to tour without carrying any lighting equipment, it agrees to live with a wide range of lighting artistry.

Special effects, such as flying of characters or transformations requiring meticulous light control, should be visualized under realistic tour conditions before deciding to include them. Equipment for special effects, lighting control, instruments, and perhaps even the mounting facilities, such as towers and portals, will occupy considerable truck space, and assembling it all at each tour stop will occupy set-up time the manager will need to account for in the tour schedule.

Touring will also affect casting and the choice of other personnel such as managers and technicians. The total number involved in the company, of course, is decided long before booking the tour, since expense estimates and tour fees are both based to a large extent on that figure; but assembling the company requires recognition of the total job they will be expected to do. Directors accustomed to choosing casts entirely on the basis of talent should be cautioned that compatability and a cooperative spirit are valuable assets much to be cherished when a production goes on the road.

The theatre needs to adopt a "company code" which describes in some detail what is expected of company members. At an unhurried meeting, the code should be distributed and discussed, perhaps with some anecdotal information about how some of the regulations came into being. The code will show the chain of command in each activity the company undertakes. It establishes the company manager as the person fully in charge except when they are on stage or involved in technical work. It specifies members' obligations to make all calls on time and to work under the stage manager to assist with loading, unloading, setting up and striking the show. It assigns drivers, and lays out conditions under which drivers may alternate. It suggests what kinds of clothing to bring, personal luggage limits, and personal equipment such as irons and make-up mirrors. It may even decree matters of decorum in communities visited, such as accepting party invitations, motel behavior, and general cautions about attracting unfavorable attention to the performing group, its parent organization, or its local sponsors. If experience dictates, the code should specify which kinds of infractions will result in dismissal from the company. While such a code may sound unnecessarily restrictive, especially for professional companies, it might be recalled that it was Clare Tree Major, the first full-scale tour producer, who introduced similar regulations to ensure that touring companies present the best possible image to communities they visit.

Bookings and Contracts

Producers use several systems for setting tour performance dates. Bookings may be arranged through a professional agency that, for a fee, contacts potential sponsors and ultimately finalizes a schedule of engagements. Another system, gaining in popularity, is booking through a showcase, a concerted viewing situation where potential sponsors see all or parts of many productions and make arrangements on the spot. (See Chapter I, "Festivals, Showcases and Celebrations.") Still another system is used by Junior Programs of California in which individual sponsoring units are brought together to hear presentations about planned productions, after which they indicate their interest in booking certain ones. Junior Programs then finalizes arrangements for a total itinerary for each producing company. Still other producers book through regional arts councils, such as the Mid-America Arts Alliance, which extensively publicizes organizations selected for special subsidies under their seasonal offerings.

The first step for the individual theatre booking a tour without outside assistance usually is composing and mailing a brochure featuring the production itself and outlining all the conditions that will govern the tour. It will specify the time period the production will be available, geographic restrictions, and note time segments that are tied to specific territories. It will list fees and note whether subsidy is available to sponsors from state arts funds. Over time each organization builds a mailing list which usually includes local and area arts councils, performing arts series, recreation programs, colleges, selected school systems, service clubs and other organizations known to sponsor such events. A reply card on which a respondent may express interest in pursuing a booking will start the process of making arrangements to visit a community.

The reply card asks for a choice of dates on which the production could be performed. The efficient booking of a tour that will encompass a state or region requires the manager to schedule each time block with a minimum of "dead days," but not so tightly that the company must travel all night without rest to make the next stop on time. When a request comes in, the manager will try to fit the community into an already existing time-area circuit; but if this is the first request from an area different from those already blocked out, a date is chosen around which others may later cluster, in hopes that other bookings will augment this new circuit, since a long trip for a single engagement is very expensive. One popular tactic is to contact the sponsor of the single date offering to reduce the fee if assistance can be provided to book a block of additional dates in nearby towns. The manager's experience and his understanding of the tour's economics will help determine how much of a reduction to offer. If this is a prevalent practice it is best to mention block booking rates in the original brochure.

Tour fees are established so that expenses, however calculated, are covered. Each territory of the country will probably have a prevailing rate charged by similar groups with which one is competing; but a fee may be set higher or lower than the average if expenses warrant. A flat rate may be set for all first performances with a reduction for subsequent performances in the same theatre plant, or a zone scheme may be set up which accounts for increasing expenses as the company travels farther from home base. The flat rate would be based on prior knowledge of average expenses within the tour region, and sponsors close by are in effect subsidizing travel to those farther away. The flat rate gives distant sponsors some satisfaction knowing they are not paying a penalty because of their location. In these days of rapidly rising travel costs, however, the zone scheme increases in attractiveness from the manager' point of view.

Some groups may suggest possibilities for reducing the fee if local hospitality is provided — lodging and meals in private homes — or even transportation in sponsors' trucks and cars. We would point out that in such cases the advantage is entirely with the sponsor. There is the possibility the producer will lose all control over tour conditions, sometimes to the point of being unable to fulfill his contractual obligations. Our recommendation is that the company keep a tight hold on its travel arrangements, that the group be housed together in motels, and that established fees be sufficient to cover such expenses.

As soon as arrangements about dates and fees have been finalized, the theatre will issue an agreement or contract in which all understandings are spelled out. The form will contain blanks in which are entered the name of the sponsor group, the city, the name of the facility to be used and its address, the number, times, and dates of performances, and the fee to be paid, usually before the company leaves the premises. There is space for the sponsor's representative to sign along with a contact phone number and address, and a space for the producer's signature as well. Both sponsor and producer keep copies of the agreement.

Attached to and considered part of the agreement may be a statement of division of responsibilities between producer and sponsor. This is a precisely detailed list of the costs and duties to be borne by the sponsor for facilities, publicity and all local arrangements, and those production, travel, and company duties and expenses to be borne by the producer. Sample agreement and division of responsibility forms will be found in Appendix 10.

The Publicity Packet

Once an agreement has been concluded, the producer and sponsor share a desire to get substantial community response. At least five or six weeks in advance of the engagement, the theatre will send out a publicity packet containing promotional and educational materials that can be used or modified as the sponsor sees fit to spark the local promotional effort.

The packet should contain sample handbills and poster designs, a teacher's guide that can be adapted for local conditions, several black and white glossy prints of scenes from the production with characters, performers, and situations clearly identified, short biographies of company members, reviews of earlier performances, and ideas for feature stories on the production, the playwright, the director, the company, or the play itself. Sponsors should be able to select from these materials to create the kind of publicity that will produce the best results in each community.

Business Arrangements

Making sure the necessary arrangements have been made to conduct a tour is the job of the company manager. Specifically, the vehicles for transporting the company and equipment must be scheduled, borrowed or leased. Motel, hotel or other lodging has to be booked. Cash and credit cards need to be made available to cover expenses on the road. All orders and contracts may have to be handled by one person authorized to conduct the theatre's business affairs. Some producers may be bound by state, county or municipal fiscal policies which strictly control how and for what purpose funds can be spent or committed, and under what conditions payments can be made. Naturally such policies and regulations affect the way the company manager operates to finalize arrangements for touring, and they certainly extend the time required for preparation.

If the theatre owns or has access to vehicles which can be assigned to it the company manager simply schedules their use. Most groups, however, solicit competitive bids from commercial leasing firms, specifying time period, size and type of truck and required capacity of buses or other passenger vehicles. Each bid must specify associated costs, including driver compensation when applicable, insurance, mileage and fuel charges and discounts for weekly or monthly use. Before any bid is accepted, all vehicles should be inspected to ascertain their suitability. This is especially important for the truck, which must have an unobstructed bed and lift gate and loading doors in top operating condition. Once a firm is selected, the responsible representative of the company executes all necessary agreements. Thereafter, the drivers are charged with accounting for all vehicular expense. Fuel normally is charged to the company credit card. Incidental expenses, such as tolls, are paid from the cash carried by the company manager.

The company manager should keep an evaluative record of all motels the company encounters on its yearly itinerary so that it can return to the best ones and avoid the bad. If a new community is involved, he can seek recommendations from local sponsors or consult any of the numerous directories issued by automobile clubs and motel chains. Direct contact with motels will be the best source of comparative prices and availability of group discounts. It also is important to ascertain whether an overnight facility will accept credit card payment or require cash, so that plans can be made accordingly. It is best to guarantee every reservation either with a deposit or a credit card number. The important thing to remember is that the company must have a firm reservation for every overnight stop.

Day-to-day accounting procedures place a heavy burden on the company manager. His task will be simplified if the theatre business manager allows each company member a daily food allowance, releasing the company manager from the onerous task of spending every evening deciphering a sheaf of barely legible cash register tabs, hoping the while that their total will balance with cash actually spent. When accounting procedures require restaurant receipts for individual meals, this is just what he must do. If he is able to book lodging with motels which allow meals to be charged to rooms, thus providing accurate accounting, he is released from that onerous task.

No matter how well obvious touring expenses can be covered by credit cards, the company manager still must carry sufficient cash to cover contingencies — broken equipment, emergency medical treatment, an endless list of unforeseen problems that are bound to plague any company on the road. Only experience will tell how much should be allowed. But one thing is certain. It is easier to turn back cash at the end of the tour than it is to be caught without it in time of need.

Tour Equipment

The tour stage manager must know a number of things about each theatre plant where the production will be shown. Therefore it is essential that a theatre information form be devised and sent to each sponsor as soon as an engagement is set. Couched in layman's language, this form asks for all pertinent dimensions of the playing area and offstage spaces, a description of the fly system, location of permanently hung curtains and cyclorama, the presence of traps, locations of light mounting positions and detailed descriptions of the lighting control board, the instruments that are permanently connected to it, the number of uncommitted dimmers, accessibility of extra instruments, and the location of an electric power tap suitable for connecting a portable control board. A sample form constitutes Appendix 9.

Any tour is likely to encounter a wide variation in the type and quantity of equipment to be found in various plants. Completed theatre information forms will reveal to what extent the production can depend on local equipment to mount the show satisfactorily. In most cases it will be quite evident that even minimum effectiveness will require the tour to carry considerable equiment and plan to spend the time necessary to mount it. This need may even extend to such items as masking drapes, but it is almost certain to indicate that special lighting equipment must be included in the company's gear.

Groups that perform extensively on the road usually assemble a tour light system that is both artistically responsive and quickly mounted. The heart of it is a portable SCR control board containing twelve 2 KW dimmers which can be mastered in flexible combinations. The board draws power from a nearby source of 220-volt current. Portable trees or towers are set up in front of the curtain at the sides of the apron, out on the house floor or in the balcony, and highly efficient spotlights are mounted on them, connected by preassembled cabling to the control board and focused on the acting area. Since distances can be kept relatively stable from stage to stage, original light cues will produce a consistent light design at every performance. Special carrying cases should be constructed to fit the equipment, keeping it secure in transit and helping ensure that delicate instruments are functional at every stop.

Tricks of the touring trade are learned through experience. Property boxes or cases should be custom fabricated to safeguard especially fragile pieces. To save space, other props can be packed inside any set piece or large property that can serve as a container. Rostra, pedestals and boxes may be designed to nest for transit. Some companies use large wicker hampers for props and costumes. These containers have the advantages of sturdiness and light weight, and, for costumes, the additional advantage of ventilation. It is wise to carry collapsible costume racks, and, since facilities for making up are notoriously unreliable, each performer must carry an appropriate mirror.

The local theatre can usually be counted on to supply any needed amplification for performers' voices from the stage; but an independent system of tape deck, mixer, and speakers must be carried to reproduce the show's sound track if one is needed. A spare tape of music and sound effects is also recommended to cover that one-in-a-hundred performance emergency.

The Company Manager

Throughout this section we have described the multitude of duties assigned to one of the key figures in any touring organization, the company manager. Fortunate indeed is the production director who has in that job a person of unlimited stamina, honesty, foresight, resilience, patience and drive — in short, one who possesses all the qualities necessary to guide a disparate group of artists and technicians through a tour with their spirits intact. The extent of the company manager's duties and authority varies considerably from group to group, but his tasks will include, but not necessarily be limited to, the following.

All correspondence related to booking dates, completing contracts (except probably the ultimate signature), filing theatre information forms, and all subsequent dealings with sponsors may advantageously be channeled through the company manager so that details of all engagements are thoroughly known before the company arrives. Keeping track of arrangements for transportation is also a good idea, so possibilities of breakdown in the plans can be spotted. It may be the company manager who requests authorization from whatever administrative agency grants permission for the group to travel. Assembling and mailing publicity packets, booking motel and hotel space, planning itineraries and issuing tour schedules to all concerned usually fall into this person's bailiwick. As the time approaches for the tour to begin, the job of establishing the company manager's authority starts when a meeting is called to explain the company code and the expectations that will prevail during the period.

The long-awaited time has arrived, the truck is loaded, the log-keeper assigned, and proof of effective planning is about to be revealed. The company manager may be at the wheel of a vehicle, but even if he is not, he is truly ensconced in the company driver's seat, clearly in charge except when the group is directly responsible to the stage manager. The fact that he dispenses all cash and is directly responsible for their bed, board and general well-being, establishes his authority, prestige and power. The importance of the presence of such a figure must not be underestimated.

A natural or acquired maturity is an advantage in dealing with the day-to-day personal problems that are sure to arise. Individuals will need "stroking" or discipline, sympathy or a firm hand, depending on circumstances and personalities. The longer a group is out, the more likely it is that interpersonal problems will develop. Factions may form, a company scapegoat may emerge, or one person may obviously be getting on everyone's nerves. The company manager must understand the complexity of the personalities with which he deals in order to decide on appropriate techniques to apply to each problem situation that may arise. He must be able to understand the human issues involved, evaluate them and make wise decisions, never losing sight of the fact that "the play's the thing." However, should an individual display a consistent pattern of ignoring the ground rules and showing contempt for the common good, the company manager may wish to recommend that that person be replaced. The final decision on such matters rests with the director of the production, who never takes such a drastic step without giving the offender opportunity to mend his ways.

It is more likely that some emergency — an injury or illness — will bring about the need to replace someone temporarily in the cast. The company manager then decides on the spot who the replacement will be: a technician, himself, or perhaps even one of the other actors whose role can then be filled by someone outside the existing cast. To forestall the necessity for such action, however, the company manager keeps a close watch on the health and well-being of all members, discouraging late night partying and raucous, throat-straining vocalization.

The company manager is considered the producer's representative to the sponsors, school systems, auditorium managers and any others the group encounters. The job has important public relations connotations, and the success of the touring program could well rise or fall depending on the effectiveness of the person holding it.

The work is done when the company log is brought up to the final hours and handed over to the director, when all business transactions are passed on to the next person in the system for completion, and when financial accounting is made. A complete financial report may not be possible immediately, but balancing out the tour cash with receipts should be done quickly while details are fresh in mind.

When a tour is over, only the good memories should remain.

Sponsor Relations

Often a tour company's awareness of sponsors and what they do is surprisingly vague unless specific efforts have been made to educate them. As the person who no doubt has handled all prior arrangements with the sponsors, the company manager continues to be the primary contact throughout the tour, and performers may have very little interaction with them.

If a sponsor representative is not on hand when the troupe arrives at the tour site, the company manager checks in by phone to ascertain that everything is under control. Depending on the time of day or night, some of the sponsors may arrive with refreshments, watch the show being set up and get acquainted with the company. Just as frequently, however, they are not present at this time, and the stage manager makes necessary contacts with technicians and other personnel connected with the theatre facility. If sponsors are in the theatre, the company manger is the one who answers their questions, introduces them to other members of the company and accepts any social invitations that might be offered. He remains with them through performances, helping in house matters, garnering their responses to the show and collecting copies of all local publicity and reviews for the tour report.

The company manager must be especially alert for any effort by members of the sponsoring group to go backstage and give directorial advice to performers. They have been known to demand alterations that range from individual words to massive cuts in order to shorten running time. The company manager should stand ready to absorb such suggestions, take them under advisement, and either decide to make the adjustments in performance or pass the problem back to the production director by phone. Performers should be instructed that if a sponsor starts giving advice they should listen politely but suggest the matter really should be taken up with the director's representative.

Sponsors should be perceived as hard working, dedicated partners in the business of bringing theatre to young audiences, not as adversaries. Usually they are excited about the company, the show, and the prospect of making an important impact on the cultural life of their community. Relationships with them are usually very pleasant and productive, and whatever problems emerge do so largely because clear procedures and lines of authority are not established to begin with. Producers and sponsors both have indispensable jobs when a production tours. An effective harmony between them should be the goal of any touring program.

FESTIVALS OF THEATRE FOR CHILDREN AND YOUTH

Managerial experience garnered in the course of their everyday professional lives serves children's theatre people well as the basis for performing the complex organizational tasks of producing a festival. Many of the same skills of thorough, imaginative planning, making diversified community contacts and developing an affinity for unconventional logistics that are part of the normal experience of mounting and touring productions for children and young people will be called upon in bringing together a heterogeneous group of producers and an unspecified public in a common festival bond. While festivals of this kind have not been part of the contemporary scene much more than a decade, there are now enough of them around to permit some general observations.

Sponsorship and Festival Parameters

Festivals are sometimes undertaken by single colleges, universities or theatres as part of an extension commitment, but more likely they will be sponsored by a state chapter or regional affiliate of CTAA or of the parent body, ATA. While the organization provides the initial impulse, the institution hosting the festival is in effect a co-sponsor, since the scale, logistics and character of it are shaped by the facilities and personnel at its site more than by any other single influence. The decision to hold a festival at all is tied realistically to the presence of an institution — a university, an extension service, a theatre — willing to undertake the job.

First festivals in any area are the trial runs. Sponsor committees dream, experiment, tabulate the results, and pass on to the next year's group the record of accomplishments and failures. Soon the association files are bulging with valuable documents to be digested by all subsequent committee heads and the procedures are improved with each trial.

The sponsors decide the basic parameters of any festival. The purposes usually stated or assumed are:

1. to provide a fun, festive occasion, an experience with theatre art in all its diversity, for children and families in the area;
2. to give producers and performers a chance to see each other's work, to share with others the joys and problems of making theatre for young audiences; and to receive evaluations from qualified responders;
3. to enhance the image of young people's theatre as an art form by exposing examples of it to professional critical examination and public review;
4. to showcase the best of the area's theatre for young audiences for potential sponsors; and

5. (not yet operative) to serve as a step in the selection process leading to a national festival.

Festival scale depends largely on the limitations of the facility to be used and on the number of possible entries. If several theatres or performing spaces are available on the site, simultaneous showings can be scheduled, as in the Southern California format, and invitations to perform over two or three days can be issued to a number of groups.

When purposes are clear and the realities ascertained, the sponsors decide the basis on which companies or individuals will be invited to perform. Some festivals are composed from responses to open invitations sent to all producers in the affected area, others on the basis of a screening process undertaken by the sponsoring organization. Yet another system is that of the direct invitation or commission to selected groups known for their exemplary work. Whether or not to pay the expenses of those who perform at the festival will probably be tied to which of these invitation systems is adopted and how much money the festival is expected to clear through ticket sales or other funding.

Organizing the Festival

With an *Executive Director* or *Producer* at the helm, various committees are formed to undertake separate aspects of staging the festival. If it will be a small affair the Executive Director is able to handle many duties independently, but even so it is best to have others involved. The functions that need to be covered are listed below; however, it must be emphasized that each committee needs to be perfectly aware of what every other committee is doing, so closely are their functions intertwined. It is the Executive Director's primary task to call rather frequent meetings at which these plans are shared.[12]

A *Rules and Registrations* committee (or perhaps separate committees if the job is complicated), focusing on the recruitment of company or individual performer entrants in the festival, and on scheduling their appearances, begins the process by formulating the exact conditions under which performances will take place, writing them up in clear unambiguous language and distributing them to likely producers.

The dates and festival location will be stated first. The rules may include such things as the maximum length of performance; casting restrictions, such as number and age of performers; available physical facilities and ground rules for assigning them; on-site technical support and the company's obligations for its own technical personnel and equipment; set-up time; application deadlines and deadlines for submitting floor plans, technical data and publicity materials; entry fee structures and conditions governing reimbursement of company expenses. Rules may also include notice of post-performance sessions with responders. The Southern California festival has found it necessary to stipulate the kind of production that will be acceptable and that certain standards of taste and artistry will be applied by those who preview the work. They also require each company to sign over a liability waiver to the sponsor.

A reply form may ask for expression of interest in taking part and request that the entrance fee be sent with the application. It will ask for the company's own restrictions on its involvement, such as dates, times and absolute need for a specific playing space, the need for expense reimbursement if such is available and times when the performance may be previewed if the festival requires screening.

When the committee assesses the responses to its initial mailing, the chairman may decide to follow up with phone calls to especially promising companies to encourage applications. Some may resent the necessity to be previewed or evaluated. Others may have discarded the idea initially as too much bother. The phone call is a good way to explain the point of the festival and the need to display the best that exists in the area. Reply forms enable the committee to communicate previewing information to those who will make an initial assessment and certify that minimum standards are met by potential performers. Previewers may not be formally organized, but merely a number of qualified people who agree to see productions and certify their acceptability to the Rules and Registrations Committee. After certification, the group's registration is processed. If for some reason the production is denied entry, the registration fee is returned with a suitable explanation. Such an eventuality is, of course, fraught with unpleasant possibilities for all concerned, but the committee must have the courage to stand by its regulations.

Construction of a schedule of events is the ultimate task of this committee. It will reflect as wide a variety of production styles as possible and, ideally, present a good cross-section of the best work being done in the area. Even if the festival consists of only a few productions, an effort should be made to construct the program with sequential variety so that those who attend only part of it will see as many different kinds of performances as possible.

The chairman of *Program* shapes the schedule into attractive printed form. From it, celebrants and participants will be able to locate all events on a detailed map, get important information about each performance, including age level appropriateness and running time, and learn from the credits who is who among the many individuals responsible for staging the event. Often the program is given special treatment to serve as a momento of the occasion, in which case a small charge is not out of order. Probably the biggest problem for this committtee is getting all the necessary information in time to meet a printer's deadline.

The *Publicity* committee will use every available means to call attention to the event by educators, the public, the press, civic officials, local, state, regional and even national arts representatives. Local newspaper reviewers and feature writers should be in on early plans and alerted for the presence of noted performers, companies, evaluators and distinguished guests. If possible, radio and TV personalities should be enlisted to serve on committees to ensure their coverage, especially on the local news. Any tasteful device concocted to let everyone in the area know that something special is happening will be fair game. Good photos showing performers in action before child and family audiences not only provide material for publicity, but also provide an invaluable record of the event.

It is virtually essential that the festival *Technical Director* be on the staff of the host institution, for he really is the key to festival success once the event is underway. He works out all logistics of arrival, unloading, setting up, tech rehearsing, running and striking. He supplies accurate details of the assigned facility on floor plans, elevations and a specifications list to each producer in ample time to allow for adjustments in the production. He encourages personal visits to the site and may even schedule a producers meeting. The technical director recruits and trains whatever local backstage help is needed, assigning stage managers and crews who will supply a minimum work force to get the shows in and running. Each producer must know how much manpower the company must supply and be aware of any local regulations that restrict their operation of equipment. It is easy to see that the TD and his staff are really the heartbeat of the festival.

The *Responders* or Reviewers committee will have the job of lining up enough qualified evaluators so that a minimum of three can be scheduled to see each show and hold an oral critique with the performers within a brief time afterward. Responders may also be asked to submit written comments to each group within a specified period. The Southern California festival has sometimes used an additional group of carefully selected children to serve as "junior reviewers," a practice that gives a unique perspective on performances. It is common practice to ask directors of festival productions to respond to some of the other productions, but the full complement of reviewers is usually assembled from many sources if the festival is a large one. Instead of scheduling a panel, some festivals bring in one or two prominent authorities to critique productions, but most are aware of the advantages of many points of view. While most responders are not asked to pick a "winner," a few festivals are set up to produce one first choice plus an alternate to go on to the next step in a fesitval hierarchy. This practice may increase as state and regional festivals become stairways to a national event. Most responders, by the way, appreciate some "gestation time" after a show to organize their thoughts before meeting with a company. Even a ten minute break is helpful. They also need time to prepare the written evaluations which later will be given each company. Most festivals develop a standard form for this purpose, and responders generally are asked to leave them in the Reviewer committee's hands.

A *Hospitality* committee may be hard at work during both the planning stage and the festival period, seeing to the well-being of special guests and performers. Its members make sure that everyone receives advance information about housing, eating arrangements on site, locations of nearby restaurants, availability of snacks, parking arrangements and maps of the area as well as the festival site. This committee may also be charged with maintaining a lost and found facility. Obviously, an efficient, conscientious staff must be recruited to fulfill the numerous assignments associated with hospitality in order that the festival may be a pleasurable experience for everyone.

Festivals taking place at a distance from commercial fast food stores may need to appoint a *Concessions* committee to make arrangements for the public to buy lunches or snacks. Occasionally a catering service or college cafeteria will agree to make box lunches available at a central location on the site, or perhaps the cafeteria itself can be persuaded to remain open to the public on festival days. The best answer may be to set up food stands where snacks, hot dogs, packaged sandwiches and canned soft drinks can be dispensed. An ambitious committee may elect to sell festival t-shirts. The scope of their undertaking will depend on whether scheduling of events mandates on-site food service, what local regulations govern the sale of food and other items, and the general budgetary structure of the event.

Just as any theatre operation needs a *Business Manager,* so too does a festival. This person sets an admission price and formulates a budget which shows income from participants' registrations, public admissions, concessions, program sales, and any grants or subsidies balanced against anticipated expenses for facilities, hired labor, food, hospitality, honoraria to guests and evaluators, printing, and presentation expenses. Designing and supervising an admission process, whether certified by a ticket, a hand stamp, a pin or neck pendant, will be something of a challenge to the Business Manager's staff, since large festivals are likely to spread out and present fewer opportunities for control than the average theatre performance. The Business Manager will have the usual duties to pay bills and present a final accounting to the sponsors.

Participating in Festivals

Taking a production to a festival is very much like taking it on any other tour. All the same arrangements must be made for transporting and sustaining the company and paying royalties. One big difference is that the group is not likely to be paid for this engagement. Either the producer looks upon it as a promotional effort which might lead to future bookings or as an educational experience for the company. There also is the advantage of being identified with significant efforts to upgrade the profession. On these bases the administrator of the theatre program might apply for special grants from schools or local businesses, or simply include an item to cover festival participation in the season production budget.

Festival participation may call for some adjustments in the production itself. An imposed limit on running time could entail some trimming. If the show customarily tours, adjusting to the host facility should pose no problem; but if the production has been played only on its home stage it may have to be modified to fit the prescribed physical limitations. Special account will have to be taken of time available to set up and tech rehearse, and some simplification of technical demands may be worth considering. Foresight in these matters is essential. The alternative is panic if the show is not ready to perform at the scheduled time.

The noncompetitive festivals being staged across the land are doing much to focus favorable attention on the art form. They are both a celebration and a learning experience for everyone involved. Good companies cannot really afford to stand aloof from them. If they have pride in their work and in their profession they will be there in the spirit of sharing, not expecting to "win" as if one were entering a contest, but to receive evaluation from knowledgeable people in the field and to come away with renewed perspective and commitment.

NOTES

[1]Management and arts administration programs into which various levels of NEA and other federal funding have been committed presently exist at the Graduate School of Business Administration, UCLA; Harvard Summer Institute; Community Arts Management Program at Sangamon State University; Graduate School of Business, University of Wisconsin-Madison; Yale University School of Drama; the Certificate Program in Arts Management, under University Extension, University of California (Berkeley), given at San Francisco; and the Public Management Institute Seminar, University of Colorado, Boulder.

[2]John E. Clifford, *Educational Theatre Management* (Skokie, Ill.: National Textbook Co., 1972), p. 100. Fund raising possibilities are discussed above in Chapter I.

[3]Groupings to some extent are based on Clifford, p. 109, modified by Nat Eek, TS to author, 23 October 1980.

[4]Category according to Eek.

[5]Budget figures suggested by Nat Eek and Terry Raison, College of Fine Arts, University of Oklahoma.

[6]Roger A. Strang and Jonathan Gutman, "Promotion Policy Making in the Arts: A Conceptual Framework," in Michael P. Mokwa, William M. Dawson, and W. Arthur Prieve (eds.), *Marketing and the Arts* (New York: Praeger Publishers, 1980), p. 231; Mokwa, p. xiv.

[7]Arts management books devote much attention to the importance of subscription campaigns and how to conduct them effectively. An admittedly controversial, flamboyant plan is one possibility. See Danny Newman, *Subscribe Now!* (New York: Theatre Communications Group, 1977).

[8]Christopher Lovelock and Phillip Hyde, "Pricing Policies for Arts Organizations: Issues and Inputs," in Mokwa, p. 243.

[9]Lovelock and Hyde, pp. 247, 251.

[10]Clifford recommends a 50% discount for educational groups, but our sample price structure suggests only a 25% reduction.

[11]See especially Clifford and Lawrence Stern, *School and Community Theatre Management* (Boston: Allyn and Bacon, 1979), for details of setting up a ticket office.

[12]Readers are referred to Chapter Four, "Festivals," in Lawrence Stern's book, especially pp. 113-135 where he supplies reproductions of many of the organizational forms used in the 1976 Southern California Children's Theatre Festival at California State University, Los Angeles.

CHAPTER IX
ON BEING A SPONSOR

"I was amazed at its power. I was actually moved — and the children were spellbound! Never thought a play for children would ever treat that kind of subject!"

The speaker was one of a small group of ladies congregated over coffee in the lobby of the largest of several theatres taken over for this event. They constituted the selection committee charged by their peers with finding three excellent productions to bring in for their city's performing arts series next season.

What could be neater? Here in one square block in a city at the cultural center of the state, the third regional festival of theatres for children and youth was underway. The fare at the festival was so rich the group was obliged to split up into couples to cover everything, and they would have to rely on only two recommendations on each event to get a comparative judgment; but since these ladies were experienced, knew each other's preferences, and were knowledgeable on the subject of what to look for in such works, a comparison was possible. They expounded virtues and shortcomings, and already some strong possibilities were beginning to emerge.

Festivals, of course, are only one means of finding excellent theatre to sponsor, albeit one of the best. But for the moment let us go back farther in the story to see why all this was happening.

RATIONALE AND STRUCTURE

Any person or group deciding to bring in outside art events to present to the young people of a community becomes a sponsor. Other acts of sponsorship include underwriting the costs of mounting a production by a local group or one from a nearby community — perhaps a community or college theatre — in exchange for the right to present performances under the sponsor's banner, underwriting the costs of transporting a production to a particular audience or bringing a designated group of young people to a place of performance. As we noted in Chapter I, all these meanings of sponsorship are operative in the contemporary scene.

To begin constructing a viable sponsorship organization, the initiators must make both idealistic and pragmatic assessments. The first of these will culminate in a statement of goals, a rationale for doing what they intend to do; and the second will produce a blueprint for an organizational structure capable of realizing the established objectives.

Goals of Sponsorship

As we review the purposes that underlie all activity in theatre for young people, we find many of them espoused by sponsors. Their primary goal, of course, will be to provide worthwhile entertainment for young citizens of their communities. A group may also wish to include in its stated objectives a desire to bring the city's children an enrichment dimension not provided otherwise — a program specifically focused on increased awareness of theatre art and the contributions it makes to education, to the psychological well-being of young people, and to aesthetic awareness.

In some cases, sponsoring theatre events for children proceeds from other kinds of motives. For some community service groups, sponsorship simply is a means of fulfilling a charter commitment. We also have noted how it sometimes is tied to promotional or business operations, sometimes simply to fund raising. While any motive for bringing theatre into a community may seem to be worthy enough, the fact is that the reasons for doing it affect the way the sponsor committee approaches the job, how well they prepare themselves for it, and how deeply they feel an obligation to explore beyond the most obvious philosophical bases, functions and levels of accomplishment.

The rest of this chapter is addressed to sponsoring bodies that recognize the enormous potential and importance of bringing children into contact with theatre, and who have the motivation to find out all they can about what they are doing. Their commitment must be every bit as strong as that of the best producers.

Organizing for Action: The Single Group

An individual functioning alone to bring in a theatrical troupe will have a formidible task, but the fact that for many years a single person was often the sponsoring committee proves it is not impossible. Today, however, with the complexity of agencies that should interact, it is best that a group of people be involved. This is not to lessen the importance of the highly motivated individual. Certainly not. In fact it is usually this person who undertakes a survey of the needs and resources of the community in order to put together a structure to do the job.

The "prime mover" may be a member of a service club, say the AAUW. While visiting a large city she happened to see a production for children, and was reminded that as a college student some years back she actually appeared in a small role in just such a play. The idea struck her: why can't productions like that be done for the children of my own town? As far as she was aware, nothing like this was given during all their elementary school years. Why doesn't our community theatre do a production for children once in awhile? Or maybe the high school drama club? One morning she got on the phone to find the answers to some of her questions, and at the next AAUW meeting she got her proposition put on the agenda.

Having become a "prime mover," she spent some time before the meeting lining up support from several close friends who were soon convinced of the practicality of her plan, and who shared her enthusiasm. Her argument was well documented. The community had not presented a theatre production for children since the Kiwanis brought one in from Dallas ten years ago. The club had lost money so they never tried again. Besides, no one seemed to care one way or the other. The community theatre director was up to his ears right now getting ready to open *Plaza Suite,* but he would think about the problem when he had a moment. The high school drama teacher did not think she had the background necessary to undertake anything specifically for child audiences; however, she offered to help by serving on any committee that came out of this meeting. Finally, a frank discussion with the superintendent of schools produced an agreement that if the AAUW were to bring in a worthy production for the children, he and the schools would cooperate fully.

Others at the meeting wondered what the club would be getting itself in for. A project of this magnitude was somewhat beyond their experience, and what about the financial obligation of the members if it failed? How much time would each person be expected to contribute? Where would such an event take place? It was a lively session, and as questions were directed to the one who was already being perceived as an expert, it became clear that there was considerable interest and even some enthusiasm — enough so that the newly appointed chairwoman of an *ad hoc* committee — our "prime mover," of course — was urged to dig around some more to get a sense of potential community response. One month later there were some answers and still more questions; but the chairperson was ready with a set of goals that sounded much like the ones we recently described and a plan of action to present for approval.

Thus an AAUW chapter became the sponsor of a theatre for young audiences. On recommendation of the chairwoman, subcommittees composed of AAUW members were appointed to take charge of:

Production Selection, a group with whom the chairperson would work very closely;

Publicity, Promotion and Education, responsible for relations with the public and with the schools;

Ticket Sales, responsible for operation of ticket offices wherever sales would be conducted;

Facilities, responsible for all arrangements for the theatre plant and associated labor;

Transportation, responsible for arranging busing for local school children;

Hospitality, providing for the visitors' creature comforts;

House Management, arranging for ticket takers, ushers and chaperones;

Business Manager, one person to pay all bills and keep accounts.

All chairmen would function as a final evaluative body charged with reviewing the event and making recommendations for future efforts.

From the time they organized until they held their evaluation session, the AAUW would go through the processes described in this chapter.

The Representative Community Agency

The structure set up by this AAUW might continue for many years. On the other hand, the group might soon recognize a need to go beyond its own membership to perform certain jobs better, that the time had come to branch out to include other community organizations. For instance, a minority minister ought to be appointed to the Production Selection subcommittee, a radio announcer to Publicity, a retired bank cashier as House Manager, and the owner of the local bus company to Transportation. The idea takes shape. It is time to form a sponsoring body independent of any one group, yet fulfilling the commitment of several.

Thus our AAUW would make overtures to the Junior League, the Soroptimists, the PTA Council, the Lions, Rotary, Kiwanis and other groups to form a joint community young people's theatre board. Its constitution would reflect the various groups' contributions to the effort but stress the particular mission of the independent organization.

By a natural evolutionary process that has been demonstrated over and over in this country the independent board may increase the scope of its operations, undertaking a total arts series for children, including symphony concerts, chamber music, solo performers in all idioms, ballet and modern dance, in addition to a wide variety of theatrical events. All this would develop slowly, to be sure, expansion building upon success. Such a sponsoring organization might undertake a fund drive to build or buy a local performing arts center, or exert sufficient political pressure to have the municipality provide one. From its experienced membership may come the beginnings of a local arts council, following up on previous contacts with the state arts agencies to the benefit of the total cultural life of the community. No matter how diversified the sponsoring organization becomes, it still needs to perform the necessary operations that make for a pleasant and productive experience for all.

PRELIMINARY OPERATIONS

The chairwoman of the sponsor's young people's theatre committee confidently delegates to subcommittee heads the responsibility for completing their assigned jobs on time; but she also schedules meetings at which progress can be checked and plans shared.

The operations discussed in this section all fall under one or another of the subcommittees mentioned earlier. The general chairperson may work more closely with some than others, but it is not wise for her to give the impression that she really prefers to do the job herself. Some marks of an effective leader are an ability to keep an eye on progress while seeming to trust completely, giving praise generously, and making it seem as if all the good ideas originate with someone else.

Constructing a Balanced Season

In constructing a season it is best for sponsors to decide first to what age range of children the series will be directed. When only one production constitutes the season there is obviously no problem since a publicity campaign can stress the primary appeal of the show, whether it is general family fare or is geared for a particular age. But if the community is small and two or more productions in a series will need to appeal to nearly all children, then family theatre titles — those that attract a broad age span from preschoolers to grandparents — probably should be chosen. Sponsors that schedule productions very specifically geared to a given age level, and then sell them as a series to the entire age range, do themselves and the community a serious disservice. In this respect Selection subcommittees will find the audience profiles contained in Chapter III helpful, and they will need to be thoroughly familiar with the content, dramatic form, and style of the actual productions to make appropriate choices.

Within this framework of age appeals, most sponsors will try to put together a season of theatre that reflects some of the different styles and performance idioms presently available. Traditional plays in a wide range of subject matter, musicals, operas, ensemble pieces, story theatre, ethnic dramas, participation plays all have their place in a greatly expanded field of production and performance styles which are described elsewhere in this book. Since there are so many, and fashions change so rapidly, no single season can contain them all. But over a period of several years the children of the community ought to experience many different genres in a way that will provide a basis for future enjoyment of theatrical art.

If theatre is part of a performing arts series, the complexities of scheduling sometimes lead to locking in a limited range of production choices year after year. This tendency should be resisted. Sponsors need to take the leadership role in a community to explore beyond comfortable, familiar patterns and limited perceptions, and make every effort to identify their program with the living dynamics of a vital art form.

Selecting the Company

Perhaps the most critical decision the sponsor will make is that of choosing the right company to perform. Production Selection subcommittees have many more methods open to them today than ever before. The system used by one sponsor to preview possible companies for a performing arts series was described at the beginning of this chapter. Attending a regional festival would enable subcommittee members to see and compare the work of several, perhaps many, of the area's producers, all performing under comparable conditions away from home base. If the festival is an invitational one based on a screening process, potential sponsors have assurance that the groups they see represent the better ones in the area. Having taken advantage of the opportunity to view a number of productions in the convenient circumstances of a festival, the subcommittee then can determine the availability of groups through personal contact.

While festivals are not usually organized specifically to provide screening opportunities for sponsors, various showcases now emerging in this country are designed to do just that. We refer the reader to Chapter I for information about some of the presently available showcases. Any sponsor wishing to take advantage of their convenience and efficiency, needs only keep informed about those events and budget for sending a delegation. If such travel is impractical or if festivals are not available, bookings can sometimes be handled through a professional agency.[1]

Needless to say, not all companies doing meritorious work travel to present themselves at festivals or showcases, nor do they aspire to representation through a professional agency. For some, budgetary limitations preclude taking advantage of these obviously beneficial opportunities. At any rate, until large numbers of companies participate in festivals and showcases across the length and breadth of the country, other systems will have to be exploited in the search for touring groups.

In former days an informal communication network was the principal means of exchanging recommendations and advice, and a good deal of this type of exchange continues to go on. However, significant efforts are being made to formalize it. Today, a new sponsor's request for help from a veteran is likely to produce an invitation to attend the next sponsorship workshop hosted by the state association of community arts councils. Sponsors seeking this type of interchange should become members of their own state association and plan to take part in such workshops as well as to take advantage of the many related services it makes available.

Some state arts commissions are setting up "touring arts programs" through which endowment money is automatically available to sponsoring groups that book one of the approved touring productions during the specified time period. Up to fifty percent of tour fees may be paid by the commission for such bookings; so no sponsor can really afford not to investigate. They need merely to get themselves on the mailing list for the arts commission's yearly brochure naming the companies and support conditions. Since listing is granted only after screening, sponsors have assurance of quality in the choices. Regional arts alliances support sponsors in much the same way by publishing an approved list of arts events each season and underwriting a share of sponsorship costs. Their selection of events can be national, even international, in scope, but with the subsidy they provide, the fees remain in the possible range for many sponsors. An application time frame is always involved for both state and regional programs of this kind; so sponsors need to plan many months in advance.

However they conduct their search, the files of the Production Selection subcommittee soon will bulge with brochures and information about the various groups available for bookings. Much of this promotion will consist of hyperbole, of course, for that is the nature of publicity materials. Nevertheless, brochures at least provide a starting point for investigation. It is wise to check with others who may have signed the company in recent seasons, but even with that information in hand a group should make every effort to send its best critics to watch a performance in the presence of children. Before making a final decision, those doing the screening also should bear in mind that the "chemistry" of a company may be just right for one community but quite wrong for another, including their own. They also should check with the state arts commission to find out if previous sponsors have registered complaints. Our advice is to avoid being completely swayed by other people's opinions. Inquiries certainly should be made, but it is only fair to be cautious in interpreting replies.

The chance to increase the impact of a first-rate company's visit by scheduling workshops or residencies with teachers and children has strong appeal these days when extra federal and state money may be available to finance them. Certainly, extending and intensifying the drama/theatre experience in this way is an advance from the old "play and run" pattern we have lived with so long. But the sponsor's decision to augment the performance with a two-hour workshop in creative drama with elementary teachers or a two week residency in playmaking, improvisation or mime with children in one of the schools does complicate the selection process.

In essence, the sponsor must try to determine in advance of booking not only the company's performance quality, but also the personal maturity, breadth of experience and professional stature of company members to estimate their likely effectiveness as teachers. These are difficult qualities to ascertain from a distance on the basis of very limited information. The fact that producers quite readily offer such adjunct services as workshops and residencies does not automatically make them experts at it by any means. Apart from general "grapevine" reactions a sponsor might pick up from others, state arts commissions may be in possession of assessments recorded by former sponsors, or of evaluations made by their own investigative panels to help in this regard. In the future, state arts agencies may be persuaded to provide such badly needed assessments in a more systematic way, even though quality would most certainly be tied to the actual personnel comprising a company in any given season.

Facility Selection

Sponsors will want to examine all possible sites for the production they are bringing in. Initial contacts with the producing company will establish the essential characteristics of the performance facility needed for the best effect. If it is a full-scale proscenium production, then the best standard theatre will be desirable with its stage equipped with standard mechanisms, its adequate lighting system, its dressing rooms with lighted mirrors, its installed sound system, and conventional loading doors near the stage area. If it is a participation play or another kind of intimate presentation, then an arena or open stage facility will be necessary, not a proscenium theatre. If the production is of a scale somewhere between these two, still other possibilities for performance sites should be sought.

Comparative costs will certainly need to be considered. Some municipal auditoriums may be rented for a token fee, others for hundreds of dollars a day plus accompanying mandatory charges for union labor. A high school auditorium may be had for a medium fee that includes janitors, skeleton crew and utilities. The community theatre has a set rental schedule for other community groups that is quite modest, but all other costs are extra. And a Scottish Rite cathedral might be available free of charge if a member of the Masons requests it; but there will be charges for custodians' overtime and for utilities. So the list would be built with rentals and other charges ready to be balanced against factors of suitability, location and evaluated quality.

If traffic access is good, the theatre nearest the geographical center of the population being served will have an obvious advantage over other facilities. But even more important than location will be the presence of features that contribute to the best possible performance conditions.

What is spoken on stage should be heard easily from every seat in the house. Sight lines should be open to all parts of the stage area. Theatre for young audiences plays best in a facility small enough to create a sense of intimacy between actors and audience and where the subtleties of performance can be communicated. We have all sat miserably in theatres, hearing and understanding about half of what was being said because of excessive reverberation or acoustically dead spots, seeing nothing that occurred in any of the upstage areas because the seating extended far beyond the proscenium width, or being so far away up in the top balcony that all the actors looked like toy people miles away. Ideally, audience size should be limited to six or seven hundred children per performance. Troubles with control of audience attention can be expected when sponsors plan to exceed this maximum, especially in theatres with poor acoustics and sight lines. Participation plays can be performed effectively only when the producer's stipulated attendance figure is honored.

The ideal facility — one which is centrally located, available any time and without charge (including free labor, of course), with about seven hundred seats, all with perfect sight lines and acoustics, plus a stage equipped to handle any show from *Peter Pan* to *Dig 'N Tel* — may not readily reveal itself on the list the sponsors compile, but at least they can test each plant against these guidelines and make a final choice after all the features of each facility have been balanced against each other. All most of us can hope for is a reasonable compromise.

Educating the Community

The theatre for young audiences is a new idea in this town. Hardly anyone has heard of it before, but the local newspaper has carried a story about an upcoming production for children. Realizing that details must be provided for as many people as possible in a limited time, the sponsors set up a speakers bureau ready to send a knowledgeable representative to tell about the plan, talk about the production and the company presenting it, and explain why it is time for the children to be exposed to entertainment other than television. If invitations for this service do not come in, the sponsors will ask to be booked into upcoming meetings of clubs and community organizations. Any group concerned with the well-being of the community and its children should welcome such presentations.

Educating the adult public is an extremely important matter. Sponsors need to feel that the community understands and is supportive. Only they know the community and its predispositions well enough to undertake a campaign of this sort. They will sense where opposition is likely to emerge, and a little special preparation in these spots will pay big dividends as time goes on.

Naturally the overall coordinator of the project will be a key member of the speakers bureau, but it is wise to hand-pick the speaker for each scheduled session. Few people are equally effective with all audiences, and a poor choice will not do the cause much good. If possible, each speaker should bring good visual material. Given sufficient notice, most producers will make special efforts to supply whatever they can to assist in the sponsor's crucial promotional campaign. In addition to these personal contacts, word of the new program also should be spread through the more traditional channels with feature stories in the press, and interviews and community service features in the broadcast media.

Relationships with Schools

In our illustration of the development of an AAUW sponsorship we suggested that all it took was one brief phone call for the school superintendent to agree to cooperate fully with the group in presenting a production for the school children. Actually such instantaneous capitulation is extremely rare. Looking at things from the school's point of view, we must realize that society places almost limitless demands on their doorsteps. When something new comes along the first question from teachers and principals is likely to be: how much time will it take, and what will have to be sacrificed to make room for it? Some instantly recognize the value of the proposal, but there will be many others for whom it will be just one more interruption, one more demand on an impossibly full schedule.

If the school administrator's initial reply to a request for cooperation was a polite but definite no, a sponsor may decide that at least as long as this person occupies the position there will be no change, that plans for the theatre program will have to account for this fact and develop in completely independent ways. If, on the other hand, there was some encouragement, the sponsor may hope for an eventual integration of educational efforts and begin to develop strategies to achieve it.

If sponsors operate without the functional cooperation of the schools during the early years of the program, they should concentrate on proving the program's worth as a community cultural resource. As it flourishes without their help, notice will gradually be taken by school personnel. Things about productions will begin to crop up in classes, and teachers will be the first to be aware that something is going on that they should know about. Some will begin to attend, and they will talk with other teachers. Sponsors may encourage their attendance by offering special prices. Certain teachers and principals may be singled out to help the sponsor's subcommittees in significant ways, thus getting them involved and encouraging them to have an individual stake in the success of the venture.

And, of course, efforts continue to be focused on the superintendent's office. Persistence, good will and excellent productions eventually should produce results. The first opening will probably be permission to distribute publicity materials through classes. With this kind of indirect endorsement the next step is to provide teachers with guides to the production so they can answer questions about it if asked. If the doorway opens a little farther, it may be permissible for the sponsors to sell tickets in the school entrance or a hallway at recess or lunch hour. With performances after school hours, low attendance from schools some distance from the theatre may be due almost entirely to a transportation problem for the children or their parents, in which case service clubs might be persuaded to underwrite the cost of one or two buses from each of these schools. Or perhaps the PTA's of the affected schools would agree to share bus costs with a service club. If many groups are willing to contribute, the cost would be very low for each one of them.

Another method of working on the periphery of the schools involves the cooperation of PTA's if these groups are operating strongly in the community. With some kind of profit sharing agreement with the sponsors, or perhaps with the sole motive of assisting in an important cultural enterprise, PTA's may actually take over ticket sales in the schools. PTA arts coordinators meet with the sponsor's Promotion and Ticket Sales people at a working coffee or tea session where they receive carefully audited blocks of tickets. They, in turn, distribute them to room mothers or fathers, and coverage of the entire school system is complete in a manner that exerts subtle pressure on every parent in town to support two worthy causes at once.

A final step toward integration comes when the school system, on mandate from the superintendent's office, buys out performances scheduled during school hours, collects the money and brings the children by busloads in the same manner it does for any other field trip. When this occurs, other sorts of interaction become possible. We suggest a number of them in the next chapter. As sponsors join hands with the schools, laypersons and educators alike are cautioned to remember that theatregoing must retain its essential entertainment function and never be allowed to become just another kind of lesson.

Arranging the Fee

The price quoted in a producer's tour announcement may be firm and non-negotiable, but sponsors have additional options open to them if they seek assistance in funding performances. We have previously referred to several sources of subsidy, either partial or full, that may be available. State and regional "touring arts programs" provide support for importing specific companies to perform and conduct workshops. State arts commissions may also finance other groups as well, if the sponsor submits a timely grant application. To do this, plans must be made nine months to a year in advance. The application process is time consuming, but well worth it when it may result in a fifty percent reduction in the support revenues a sponsor must raise. The same time frame is required when the sponsor seeks financial support from local business or industry. Commercial organizations must follow prescribed procedures in such matters, and their regulations may well determine the planning pattern of the entire sponsorship operation.

Sometimes a producer's quoted fee can be reduced through negotiation and offers of additional services. Although producers generally are unwilling to relinquish control of transportation, in rare instances the sponsor might absorb that expensive item by providing member-driven passenger vehicles and trucks to carry the show and its personnel. A better possibility is to offer to provide meals and lodging during the visit. Again, most producers will insist on keeping the company together, but others are perfectly agreeable to this time-honored means of reducing tour costs and passing the savings on to the sponsor. The Hospitality subcommittee can often arrange to have individual members of the organization provide dinner, bed and breakfast for houseguests from the company, and the entire subcommittee assumes responsibility for bringing lunch to the theatre between performances. The block booking system outlined in Chapter VIII is the best way to effect substantial savings for a number of sponsors in adjacent communities.

Negotiating Contracts

As we have noted in Chapter VIII, it is customary for a producer to issue a formal contract or written agreement at the close of negotiations with a sponsor. In some instances, especially when the sponsoring organization is a large one, that group issues its own contract as well. This should pose no problem as long as the two documents do not work at cross purposes. The amount of detail included in a contract will depend on the past experience either party has had encountering disagreements and misunderstandings. If there is any feeling that such problems might arise between the negotiators, the contract may be very specific indeed about areas of responsibility.

A simple agreement form comparable to the one shown in Appendix 10 and briefly described in the preceding chapter usually will suffice. If a more detailed document is drawn, it could include any or all of the following stipulations affecting the producer: deadlines for providing publicity materials and program copy; time limits for set-up and strike, and a requirement that the performing area be restored to its prior condition; assurance that all paraphernalia conform to local fire regulations; a punctual opening curtain and adherence to a prescribed running time; the number of complementary tickets available to the company; and, in some cases, a clause forbidding competing performances within a certain distance and time period.

Although the standard agreement will show that the producer agrees to provide a performance, the contract may add that the group is obligated to pay all expenses of mounting the show and all salaries, wages and other payments associated with the process, including royalties and licensing fees and the cost of insurance on its own equipment and personnel. If the company wants to retain quality control over the printed program, the contract will stipulate that it must provide a sufficient number for each performance.

The sponsor may require the producer to provide a copy of the script and agree to conform strictly to it. The sponsor may also want assurance that the play does not infringe on anyone's rights, that it is in good taste, and that it is suitable for children within a specific age range.

The most obvious duty of the sponsor is to pay the required fee in the manner stated in the contract. In addition to those duties shown on the sample agreement form, the sponsor's contractual obligations may include paying for the electric power required for stage lighting; providing a skeleton crew familiar with the stage and its facilities; and supplying sound amplification if house acoustics require it. The sponsor also is responsible for all promotion, publicity, ticket printing and sales, and other local arrangements, including front-of-house operations before, during and after the performance. The sponsor is given the right and the obligation to duplicate and distribute promotion and publicity materials provided by the producer, and to reproduce programs when they are not supplied by the company. Sometimes use of the host theatre's lighting system, and payment of any required union labor emerge as gray areas which are subject to negotiation. As a rule, however, the sponsor assumes those costs.

Whether the contract is issued by the sponsor or the producer, it should not be finalized until each is certain that all matters of importance to a felicitous and effective working relationship have been included. In closing this section we must suggest that both parties to the contract will want to include an "out clause" which provides for dissolution of the agreement without obligation on either side if some external condition beyond the control of either of them forces cancellation of the planned performance.

FUNCTIONS OF SPONSORSHIP

Necessary as it is, the contract does not reflect the warmth and mutual regard that should characterize producer-sponsor relationships. These complementary agencies must consider themselves partners in all they do, since both presumably share an interest in achieving a common goal. Cold and businesslike as it may seem, the contract provides a set of guidelines for the sponsoring group as each of its subcommittees charts the course of action it must follow to ensure a successful culmination of its efforts.

While all matters of business covered in the preceding chapter were presented from the producer's point of view, they are equally applicable to the sponsor, and we urge anyone in that position to apply all the information provided in that section to the work he does. Some matters of business, however, uniquely relate to sponsorship, and we now shall concern ourselves with them.

Publicity

As we have seen, the community promotion campaign begins long before the producer's publicity packet arrives, as the sponsor establishes contact with key organizations, community opinion setters and the local press and broadcast media. But the Publicity subcommittee chairperson shifts into high gear when the producer's materials arrive five to six weeks in advance of the performance.

The first order of business is to prepare all materials that must be locally printed or duplicated and get them to the appropriate firm to ensure that they will be ready in good time. These include program copy, if the sponsor is responsible for the playbill, teacher's guides, posters and handbills. Then the guides must be distributed to the schools, and posters and handbills placed in every location that will post or circulate them. Photographs are delivered to the newspaper office to be run along with locally composed news and feature stories about the play, the production, and the people involved, both the visitors and the local sponsoring committee. If the company includes a person from the area, that fact should be exploited. If the subject or theme of the play has special relevance to the community, another idea presents itself. If the performance coincides with some other significant local event, the tie-in should be emphasized.

While costumed members of the performing company will not be available for school visits, the sponsor's mascot might visit classes to discuss the program, supplementing the efforts teachers make to utilize the teacher's guide. Broadcast interviews, displays of all kinds — virtually all the promotion and publicity devices suggested in Chapter VIII — apply to sponsors as well as producers. The sponsor is urged to try every one of them.

Facilities

The importance of the theatre information form to the producer's plans already has been noted. The sponsor will receive it immediately after the contract has been signed, and the chairperson normally will turn it over to someone on the theatre staff who is familiar with the plant, and with standard theatre terminology. Appendix 9 provides a sample form showing the information a producer must have in order to prepare for the company's visit. It is important that this form be returned to the producer as quickly as possible.

The Facilities subcommittee will prepare for the company's arrival by making sure that everyone concerned is informed of all the requirements for setting up and running the production. If the company has sent a light plot to be executed by local personnel using house equipment, it must be delivered to the theatre stage manager who will be charged to have all instruments mounted and connected and ready to be focused when the touring crew arrives. The Facilities chairperson must also make doubly sure that both the principal and the drama teacher at a high school auditorium are aware of the company's requirements. Sometimes "in house" communication between principals and teachers is not one hundred percent effective, and the day the production arrives is no time to find out that the junior class play is in dress rehearsal with its set already pegged down on the stage!

A responsible individual should be scheduled to meet the company on its arrival at the theatre to make sure they can get into the building and find their way around, to explain any local rules that must be observed, to help locate anything the company cannot readily find and simply to be accessible to answer questions as they may arise. This person may also be in charge of locking and unlocking doors, securing equipment and the front of the house. Usually a custodian is assigned this responsibility, and his services are indispensable. Arrangements for his services as well as for personnel to assist with setting up and running the show, and others the facility's management may require to serve as doormen, ticket takers, security and custodial staff must be arranged in advance by the sponsor's Business Manager. The organization must expect to be billed for these services. In its negotiations with the managerial representative, the sponsor Business Manager will determine what functions can be performed by volunteers and will plan to use them wherever permissible in order to reduce expenses.

Transportation

Transporting children to and from the theatre may not pose a problem in towns where they may simply walk from school or be transported in their parents' cars. Elsewhere, however, the Transportation subcommittee may assume a tremendous responsibility as they arrange buses or car pools to handle large numbers of youngsters. The coordinator may work through the school system, which often contracts with bus companies for a given number of field trips at a fixed rate. If this is not feasible, every possible avenue of transport will be explored and the most efficient and reasonable one chosen. Special arrangements may have to be made to transport orthopedically handicapped children and to accommodate them once they arrive at the theatre. The special problems associated with handling traffic are outlined in Chapter VIII, where they appear as a responsibility of house management.

Ticket Sales

Again, ticket office systems discussed in detail in the preceding chapter are applicable to sponsors as well as to producers, especially if there is access to an established facility at the theatre where the performance will be shown. We know, however, that sponsors' Ticket Sales personnel usually are not permitted use of the theatre's ticket office until the day of performance, necessitating some special planning for pre-sale of admissions.

Whatever the system, tickets must be printed as soon as dates, times, admission price and seating plan are decided. If reserved seats are to be sold, portable ticket racks are highly desirable. If there is to be more than one performance, a rack should be provided for each. They may be set up in the home of a member who is willing to handle phone orders, or they may be set up each day in a donated commercial location, such as a bank or department store. Establishing several centers complicates the Business Manager's accounting, but careful coordination can keep all locations supplied with a mixture of available seats. Equally careful plans will have to be made for keeping track of cash and ticket racks for each change of volunteer sales personnel in order to achieve an accurate accounting of all transactions.

Selling general admission simplifies and speeds the process somewhat, but either seating plan requires essentially the same mechanical arrangements. If sales take place at tables in school hallways, racked or stacked tickets and cash boxes will be necessary. Many sponsors who conduct sales this way have an attractive portable ticket booth which serves its necessary practical function and has the added advantage of being a good advertising device. If the sponsor mascot can be on hand when tickets are sold, so much the better.

Ticket Sales personnel are responsible for enforcing any policy regarding the lowest age limit at which children will be admitted. If there is a contract provision specifying a lower age limit, the sponsor is obliged to respect it. A very narrow age range is essential to the success of a participation play. Even when the contract or the type of material being presented does not call for specific age level limitations, the sponsor may wish to exclude children below the age of four or five. Others in their eagerness to fill the house, or to share the pleasure of playgoing with everyone who wants to buy a ticket, make no provision for drawing the line. If age limits are established, however, the ticket booth must carry a sign giving that information, and sales personnel are responsible for informing everyone who makes a purchase that these rules will apply.

House Management

House management procedures for sponsors are virtually identical to those set forth for producers in Chapter VIII, with a single exception. House Management subcommittee members have no responsibility for outside traffic and parking. These duties belong to the Transportation subgroup. The two bodies will work together to make all necessary arrangements to accommodate the arrival and seating of handicapped children.

The ultimate responsibility for enforcing age restrictions lies with the house crew. However diligent the ticket sellers may be, people will succeed in getting tickets for very young children, and one by one they appear before the ticket takers, pasteboard in hand, ready and eager to see the show. With each of these arrivals comes a moment of truth. If a limitation has been set and generally observed through the sales process, it must be enforced at the door or dissolve in shambles. A single exception will produce untold ill-will. When admission is denied, the ticket office must make a refund, or perhaps issue a voucher for a future admission. Needless to say, any action of this sort must be taken most courteously.

The House Manager needs to check with the show's Company Manager to determine whether the actors will enter or exit through the house, whether the aisles will be used during the performance, and whether performers wish to begin their interactions with the children from the moment they enter the playing area. This latter circumstance is likely to be true in ensemble productions where the actors meet children at the door and place them in a definite arrangement in seats or on the floor. At the end of more conventional performances company members may wish to station themselves at the door, distributing programs and chatting informally with the children as they leave.

A house staff that is concerned with fulfilling its obligations will never leave the immediate theatre area while a performance is going on. It is during the show that they will be able to display their fullest professional commitment as they try to make the experience as comfortable and distraction free as possible.

Changing the Production

Dissension between sponsors and producers most frequently centers on efforts by members of the sponsorship committee to effect changes in the production during its local run. At the time a production was chosen it satisfied local performance standards and expectations, but when it appears on the home stage one or another of the group may feel it has changed or has not transported well. Certainly companies may not be entirely blameless in the matter. Away from home base and the director's watchful eye, small changes sometimes creep into even the most professional productions without anyone's being aware of them. The appropriate representative of the sponsor group, usually the general chairperson, is quite right to call specifics of deterioration to the Company Manager's attention and to insist on restoration of the original performance quality. But creative ideas to improve the production passed directly to performers by various committee members — anything from changing minor stage business to making major cuts or character modifications — are out of line and are properly ignored or turned aside. All such suggestions must be channeled to the director through the Company Manager, since only the director or his surrogate has authority to institute any changes in performance.

A request to cut five minutes from the running time may seem simple enough and perfectly justifiable from a sponsor's point of view when bus drivers are threatening to take the children out before the show is over. But actually, a five-minute cut could entail the elimination of thirty or forty lines of dialogue or several short action sequences, all with ramifications for characterization, story line, motivations, and the rhythmic structure of the work itself. Hastily and unskillfully made without the director's guiding hand, such cutting could result in a thoroughly disintegrated show. It is far better to have specified an absolute maximum running-time when the contract was negotiated than to attempt a patch job after the fact.

If a sponsor wishes to exercise a contractual right obligating a producer to make stylistic or substantive changes in the production, the request must come immediately after previews, not during the run. Local performances will be much better if changes have time to be assimilated and the fabric of the production knit back together.

Hospitality

Unless everything is one hundred percent business, there is much to recommend a warm interchange between sponsor and company. Even though the Hospitality subcommittee may not have to arrange overnight lodging and regular meals for a visiting company, they are largely responsible for a feeling of welcome and concern which can develop over coffee and rolls during set-up or between performances. Sometimes a lunch prepared at home and brought in to the backstage area will be a virtual necessity because of the short interval between a morning and an afternoon show. The sponsor may actually be under no obligation to provide lunch, but it would be very much appreciated in such circumstances.

Hospitality subcommittees in smaller communities seem especially alert to recognize that company members might enjoy a break in their performance-to-motel routine by taking a sight-seeing expedition to historically interesting places they might otherwise miss. They may even decide to give a gala dinner party at a member's home, inviting the company, sponsors, other project workers, and the arts and political leaders of the community. An occasion of this kind does much to celebrate the partnership of community and cultural arts which is exemplified in sponsorship of theatre for young audiences.

The show is over. The company has loaded up the truck and left town. Members of the sponsorship committee meet over coffee at the "prime mover's" home, put their feet up, and relax, enjoying the quiet and the calm in contrast to the frenetic afternoon's activity. Well, maybe we didn't do everything right, but undoubtedly we made a splash the town will not soon forget! Half the city's child population must have been there. And the show itself was a real crowd-pleaser. We'll have to go some to beat that! But to think we took a chance and really put it over the top! We have every right to feel proud.

Now how many of you would like to serve on next year's committee?

NOTES

[1]Some professional booking agencies handling programs of various kinds for young people are the following:

Briggs Management	Frances Schram 36 Park Street Montclair, New Jersey 07042
The National Theatre Company	Fran Weissler/Andria York 165 West 46th Street, Suite 1202 New York, New York 10036
Producers Foundation, Ltd.	John Peel/John Smith 800 Third Avenue New York, New York 10022
Raese Management Co.	855 Deer Park Court Deerfield, Illinois 60015
Sheldon Soffer Management, Inc.	Sheldon Soffer 130 West 56th Street New York, New York 10019
THEATREWORKS/USA	Charles Hull 131 West 86th Street New York, New York 10024

Our thanks to Mickey Miners of the Detroit Institute of Arts Youtheatre for this list.

CHAPTER X
JOINING HANDS WITH THE SCHOOLS

We are about to visit two schools which could be located in any section of the country. Both are typical elementary schools with the usual complement of classrooms and a staff of teachers dedicated to their profession. Their administrators believe that pupils should receive a well-rounded education and a variety of experiences that go beyond the fundamentals.

As we stand in the corridor of the first building, we cannot help being captivated by a group of third graders whose faces seem unusually bright and whose chatter is particularly animated. As they come nearer we notice that they are wearing their Sunday best. Some even sport new shoes. Each one carries a dog-eared slip of paper to hand to the teacher. "These are trip slips," an excited little girl tells us. "We are going to see a play!" And she skips merrily off to her desk. The teacher makes a valiant effort to introduce the first lesson of the day. "The bus won't be here for a long time. First there's work to be done." The lesson does not go well. These theatre trips certainly do disrupt the routine. Of course it's wonderful to provide enrichment, but it does cut into class work, and this reading lesson is so important. Well, another day lost.

Finally the bus arrives. The children try to form an orderly line, but they are deaf to all reminders that they are supposed to be quiet during the ride. The teacher sighs with resignation and settles in her seat. When we get to the theatre our children march through the lobby in pretty good order and find their way to their assigned places. During the performance they are enthusiastically responsive, but never rowdy. As a reward they are allowed to join the lines of young theatregoers eager for a chance to meet the cast. This always prolongs the trip, of course, but the children do get a kick out of seeing the costumes and make-up and exchanging a word or two with the actors. After all, it really doesn't happen all that often. For the children the time is all too short, but they obediently troop back to the bus where there's no stopping the chatter; and it's very hard to settle down in the classroom. They don't want to stop talking about the play, so they might as well get it out of their systems. But there is work to do. Let's get back to the business of teaching. They can talk to each other during lunch and recess, and they'll enjoy sharing their experiences with their folks this evening. So much for that. Back to the books.

Across town, we join a group of parents filing into an elementary school auditorium, the typical all-purpose room with its small elevated stage. This morning it is filled with neat rows of folding chairs. As we take our places at the back, the front rows fill with children filing in from their classrooms. Today it's the second grade's turn to do a play. Backstage the teacher dabs rouge on already flushed cheeks, adjusts the make-shift costumes and turns once again to page twenty of her dog-eared instructional magazine so that the script will be handy in case anyone forgets a line. At least she can help them that way, but will they remember everything else they've been told?

The parents look at their watches, chat aimlessly with their neighbors and await the appearance of their own children. Only at those moments are they really interested and involved. The children wait to be amused. It's always fun to see other kids on the stage. They laugh heartily when someone trips over his own feet and almost falls down. They tense with sympathy when someone else forgets a line, but later they will be quick to taunt him. The performers walk through their parts and speak their lines loudly and clearly, but their eyes keep straying toward the audience. One little girl can't see her mother out there. Something goes out of her performance. The teachers keep a sharp eye on the audience. The principal leans against the wall, taking stock of the entire situation. As soon as the play is over, he returns to his office and more important things. The parents are politely enthusiastic in their applause and in their congratulations to the cast, the teacher and each other. How wonderful the children were!

The teacher feels a sense of relief. Her colleagues think with apprehension about the next time. Who will have to go through all this in a month or so? The young actors return to their classroom so heady with excitement that it is difficult to concentrate on the day's normal activities. Those who did not forget lines or stumble are warm with triumph. Those who did are warm with embarrassment. The little girl whose mother did not come has her own private feelings to deal with. But the arithmetic lesson goes on.[1]

Our two school visits present a rather grim picture of drama and theatre in the educational setting. Of course this sort of thing does not occur everywhere, but even in an era of burgeoning interest in, and study of the vital role of the arts in education, comparable practices are more prevalent than we care to believe. Too many schools perpetuate archaic and discredited uses of drama. Despite the efforts of theatre professionals, the cooperation of a significant segment of the educational community and the support of government and prestigious public figures and institutions, drama and theatre are far too frequently kept out of the mainstream of public education. Occasional attendance at performances in school time, but with no classroom preparation or follow-up has been described as "kids going bump-in-the-night with theatre."[2] While it certainly is better than no theatre at all, it continues to define the art as something peripheral to education.

An increasing number of teacher preparation programs include creative drama as a requirement or recommended elective, and a number of states have developed curricular frameworks and courses of study in drama/theatre for all grade levels. Even so, dynamic involvement in drama/theatre processes continues to lurk on the fringes of classroom life in too many schools. It is difficult to break down a pervasive misapprehension that play production is the only way to involve children in dramatic activity. It is unfortunate that so many educators are not cognizant of the values that are lost, or indeed the damage that may be done when children are put on public display in a situation that is in no way a logical extension of classroom study. At the elementary level, formal play production often is imposed upon teachers who have no training for it, and children are used to achieve some ill-defined goal that bears little relationship to valid educational philosophy and practice.

THE THEATRE EXPERIENCE IN EDUCATION

Today a number of channels are open to enable children and young people to experience theatre in conjunction with their work in school. They can be taken to a theatre, a large auditorium or a university campus to join with students from other schools in a shared viewing of a production. Or a play can be brought to them and performed in their own school environment. This might be a more traditionally staged performance or one in which they actively participate. In recent years the in-school performance might be the product of mutual involvement, where a group of theatre professionals takes up residence in the school and includes students in the entire production process, from inception through performance.

The practice of taking busloads of youngsters to a central location to see a play is as old as the theatre for children. In the days when the fully-mounted production of a traditional script was virtually the only style acknowledged by the field, this was the single practical way to link school and theatre. It remains a viable system. Despite the unquestioned merit of newer production and performance styles, a well-rounded acquaintance with theatre requires that students have opportunities to view the elaborately staged, fully-realized work of art as well as to see or participate in more simply produced performances. Theatre educators long have held that exposure to exemplary models not only increases appreciation of the art, but, of singular importance in education, it sets standards toward which students may strive in their own playmaking and production activities. Add to these the potential the great works of the theatre or the classics of literature translated into dramatic form have for enhancing the study of literature, history, the allied arts and the humanities, and there is no need to seek further justification for theatre attendance on school time.

Theatre attendance in this context has the greatest impact and most lasting value, however, when it occurs within a framework that extends far beyond the time spent traveling and seeing the play. Sometimes the framework is provided quite coincidentally when an astute teacher discovers that a production of a drama being studied in his class will be shown at a theatre in the city. What an advantage it is for a high school English class to be able to see the Shakespeare play they have been struggling to comprehend, suddenly come to clear and vivid life! How exciting it is for children to experience a favorite story, often seen in the mind and sometimes the subject of a reading lesson, fully fleshed out and vibrant with magic!

Long before producers began to distribute teacher guides for post-performance activities and discussions, educators took advantage of the enrichment opportunities opened by theatre attendance. Many a file cabinet contains folders of paintings and essays done by classes whose teachers encouraged personal responses to the playgoing experience. Many a teacher returned to school inspired to attempt informal dramatic activities based on the play — with the full cooperation of students filled with ideas about how they would like to recreate the experience. These were the venturesome ones who were willing to use intuition, trial and error and a great deal of common sense to capitalize on the extraordinary stimulation theatregoing provided their students.

Whether it came about because teachers expressed a desire for ideas from producers, or whether producers decided without prompting, the teacher's guide was developed to assist the process of making playgoing integral to education. Each company has its own style and content for the guide. Some simply contain factual information about the play, its source and the style of the production. Others are far more elaborate, outlining strategies for stimulating anticipation before the performance and providing detailed instructions for post-performance activities and discussions. The idea is to inspire and encourage teachers to use the theatre experience as a means of expanding student creativity as well as using the play as a springboard for studying ideas and backgrounds. The extent to which these guides are used is, of course, a matter of speculation. Nevertheless, their potential value is unquestioned, and they are especially helpful when contact with the producing unit occurs only when classes go away from campus to see a play or when the company comes to the school, sets up, performs and departs with no direct interaction with students or faculty. Recognizing that the educational values of this somehow impersonal theatre experience are not as fully realized as they might be, many companies performing for bused-in groups invite the audience to remain in the theatre for a question and answer discussion with the cast. Some also encourage teachers to arrange post-performance backstage tours so that the students can see the stage, construction areas, dressing rooms and control booths. This unveiling of the mysteries adds a new dimension to theatre appreciation.

The Theatre Comes to the School

More and more often these days performances are brought into the schools as part of a program of arts education and curricular enrichment, and each performance becomes a focal point for classroom activities in which the actors themselves may be deeply involved. A significant number of producing units have added in-school performances to existing programs, and any number devote themselves exclusively to this work. Many groups are professional. Others are associated with college or university theatre programs. They offer a variety of services in addition to performance. These may include teacher workshops and post-performance sessions in individual classrooms with actors leading the students in their own dramatic activities as an extension of the performance.

Teacher workshops are not necessarily designed to orient participants to the play itself, although there is value in sharing the production concept and goals and, when there is something of unusual interest about the style of the performance, providing background information that the teachers can use with their classes. Most importantly, workshops should present some of the basic tools of drama leadership that can be effectively and simply applied to preparatory and post-performance classroom activities. They might include demonstrations with children. They always should include involvement. Activities should be designed to make teachers comfortable, both as participants and as leaders, and be sufficiently uncomplicated to give them confidence that they will be able to adapt them to their own classes and personal teaching styles. A well-designed teacher's guide can serve as the point of departure for workshop activity as well as provide tangible material which the teacher can use in the classroom. Some workshops and the guides prepared for them go beyond drama activities into story creation, visual art, music and simple puppetry, giving concrete ideas about extending the theatre experience through other media of expression.

A popular form of performance follow-up is the actor visit to the classroom. After the in-school performance, members of the company fan out into individual rooms where they may simply hold a question and answer session with the youngsters, or as a logical extension of the play, engage them in dramatic activities. The theatre and drama experience meld when the actor poses "what if?" questions regarding characters and events in the play, stimulating the class to think through and enact alternatives to what they actually saw. There is little value in this actor-student contact unless the material used to stimulate creative thought and activity relates to or grows directly out of the play itself.

Teacher orientation through workshop experiences and/or printed guides, and the extension of the theatre experience through classroom visitation, are planned and implemented by sponsors and producers alike to eliminate the "play and run" aspect of so much in-school theatre. All of these strategies are designed to give real educational value to encounters with the performing arts. Values run in both directions, however, for when they take full advantage of their contacts with students, performing artists gain as much as those they have come to serve. Classroom interactions provide instant and honest responses of a very special kind.

When companies request evaluation sessions with faculty members at the end of a performance day, another avenue of enlightenment is opened to them. Sponsors also profit from such follow-up activities to such an extent that they may wish to complete the collaborative process by establishing an advisory committee of educators. Both producers and sponsors may also supplement face-to-face sessions with teachers by sending a questionnaire which allows further opportunity to evaluate a performance in light of their perception of its effects on the audience. Some groups limit their follow-up to the questionnaire.

Theatre artists who play in school have an advantage denied companies performing only for public audiences in that they know exactly who saw their work. The opportunities this provides for ongoing evaluative study are almost limitless. Producers who systematically seek the cooperation of the educators with whom they have contact gain valuable insights into the quality and impact of their work. When they share their findings with others, they contribute to the growth of the entire field.

Residency Programs

Far more elaborate and comprehensive in scope than even the most highly organized programs of in-school performances are projects where members of a producing unit take up residence in a school for an extended period. The patterns of activity for these programs vary widely, but the universal goal is to provide some sort of in-depth experience in the art of the theatre. Some groups come into a school with a performance already in process and involve students in its completion.

One such project, described by Gillette Elvgren of the University of Pittsburgh, began with his company's decision to create a play with a circus motif that had structure, a theme that would challenge elementary age children and that would also provide opportunities for meaningful involvement with the theatre process. As the script evolved, so did plans for a series of workshops designed to achieve the latter goal. Mime exercises recreating typical circus performance activities, creative drama sessions in which children learned the rudiments of characterization through becoming circus participants, both human and animal and devising conflict situations for them, music workshops where circus sounds and rhythms were explored and various art workshops where murals were painted, collages created and slide projections produced, all were structured to culminate in products that eventually were incorporated into the production. This extensive and comprehensive involvement occurred over a period of several weeks' residency in a single school.[3]

Not all residencies include a student production, but what one program of the Children's Theatre Company of Minneapolis termed a "model class," in which participants presented a demonstration of dramatic material developed improvisationally by workshop participants. Programs of this sort have been offered on both the elementary and secondary levels and might run from one to several weeks.

Another residency program was reported by the Bear Republic Theatre of Santa Cruz, California. During a two-month stay in a secondary school a ten-member company developed a multi-ethnic, bilingual play based on stories and legends from the various cultures represented in the community, holding open rehearsals to make the process of creating a play accessible to students and teachers. Adjunct activities included classroom workshops in creative drama and improvisational theatre techniques, in-service training in the use of theatre to teach other subject matter, and special interest workshops in puppetry, set design, dance and voice.[4]

These examples suggest a few of many approaches followed by theatre companies in their working relationships with schools. However diverse methodologies may be, most companies involved in residency programs maintain a focus on the art of the theatre, espousing a common goal of involving children and youth in theatre processes and audience-related activities to teach the values inherent in the art form. To that end, there is more emphasis on the aesthetic than the utilitarian dimension.

Theatre in Education (TIE)

Although there are some apparent similarities between theatre-school collaborations in the United States and the Theatre in Education program, a British innovation which goes back to the mid-1960's, the resemblance is superficial and limited to certain commonalities in organization and strategy. American companies bring *theatre education* to the schools, showing students and teachers how theatre works, what it is, how it is performed and, ideally, how to appreciate it. The philosophical difference is manifest in the British insertion of *"in"* between "theatre" and "education." The universally-expressed goal of TIE groups is "to harness the techniques and imaginative potency of theatre in the service of education."[5] Gordon Vallins, a pioneer in the movement, describes an early project for secondary schools. At its center was a "deliberately didactic piece of theatre based on (a disaster) . . . and presented in the style of documentary theatre with sound effects, folk songs, projected pictures, a giant map and a number of props." This presentation was used as a stimulus for improvisation and thought as the actors held post-performance sessions with classes to explore the subject of responsibility.

Vallins goes on to say that the company was primarily concerned with comprehension of moral dilemma. "How well the story had been told in terms of theatre was a secondary consideration. The objectives of theatre were subordinate to the objectives of the classroom. We were attempting to use techniques of theatre in the service of specific educational objectives. We were not in the business of creating tomorrow's audience."[6] This philosophy is echoed in Eileen Murphy's introduction to *Sweetie Pie*, a TIE play on women's liberation, in which she describes the TIE method:

> It is not actors from the local rep going into schools to dramatise passages from examination texts and advertise their current production. It isn't commercial children's theatre or drama teaching, though it can include some techniques from both. It is a group of actors, in character, and a group of children (or young people or adults) exploring and living through a situation in which they are physically and emotionally involved.
>
> It can include scripted dialogue between actors, but most of the "script" is improvised by the actors and by the individuals with whom they are working,

and results directly from their reactions to the situation which has been created. The programmes can have a set ending or be open-ended depending upon the subject matter and the age of the people for whom they are devised. The actors are both a focus of attention and a stimulus for the children's involvement, and they use their combined talents to encourage the children to express and work out their involvement as individuals and as part of the group.[7]

Tony Jackson attributes the rise of TIE to a number of developments, among them ". . . the theatre's search for a useful and effective *role* within society and an exploration especially of its potential both as an educational medium and as a force for social change . . . and, in educaton, the recognition in recent decades of the importance of the arts (and drama particularly) in the school curriculum, together with the increasing stress now given to the *functional* role that the arts have to play in helping children to understand, and operate in, the world in which they live." He asserts that the fully conceived "programme of work" that surrounds the TIE performance ensures a more potent "central stimulus for a deeper and richer learning process than the 'one-off' play ["play and run" performance] . . . could hope to provide." He says,

> The TIE programme is not a performance in schools of a self-contained play, a 'one-off' event that is here today and gone tomorrow, but a co-ordinated and carefully structured programme of work, usually devised and researched by the company, around a topic of relevance both to the school curriculum and to the children's own lives, presented in school by the company and involving the children directly in an *experience* of the situations and problems that the topic throws up. It generally combines elements of traditional theatre (actors in role and the use of scripted dialogue, costume and often scenic and sound effects); educational drama (active participation of the children in improvised drama activities in which ideas are explored at their own level); and simulation (highly structured role-play and decision-making exercises within simulated 'real-life' situations).[9]

Virtually every account of TIE programs stresses this utilitarian application of theatre with a heavy emphasis on the immediate relevance of its content. We find descriptions of programs designed to join history lessons with arousal of political awareness, others illuminating the women's movement or problems in interracial understanding. Some deal with mathematical concepts or other strictly curriculum-related subjects. Descriptions of the use of costumes, properties and set pieces and of the actor-teachers working "in role" indicate that the aesthetic dimension is not totally ignored. Nonetheless, the primary focus is on the use of theatre techniques to convey subject matter and influence social thought and action.

Performers involved in TIE refer to themselves as actor-teachers, ". . . double-timers, people with two closely-related skills" — proficiency in performance and the ability to work with all types of students and within a vast spectrum of subject matter and social issues. Tony Coult calls them "thinking" actors who see "theatre and education as different arrangements of the same tune," and whose guiding principle is that children are "to be helped to take some control over their lives by increasing their understanding of the world about them, and their confidence in affecting it." He sees their function as feeding into the classroom teacher's work "a kind of intense stimulus to educational process."[9] Vallins, whose team originated the actor-teacher designation, insists that TIE personnel must have enthusiasm for and experience in both acting and teaching, that they must either be actors who can teach, and preferably have had some teacher training — or teachers who can act. Whatever their background, they must have a fundamental interest in the process of learning.[10]

TIE has aroused considerable interest on this side of the Atlantic, and a number of American groups have begun to experiment with the method. The Creative Arts Team (C.A.T.) of New York University has been in the vanguard of this movement. Although their program encompasses a number of approaches, their repertoire has included a number of polished productions of issue-oriented plays designed to entertain audiences as well as to serve as springboards for discussion and action. In program notes for "Tower of Babble," an allegorical play dealing with communication problems, they describe their goals:

> Our integrated arts team's aim is to provide theatrical presentations for audiences of all age levels, and to develop innovative programs incorporating a variety of artistic, educational and entertaining experiences.[11]

C.A.T. has been notably successful in developing performances that stand alone as viable theatre pieces with messages presented in a genuinely entertaining format. Such efforts are not always that felicitous. More often than not, important aesthetic values are sacrificed when theatre is used strictly in the service of education. Almost invariably the doctrinaire and the didactic take precedence over art and, at its worst, theatre used for moral and utilitarian purposes can be so heavy-handed and offensive to aesthetic sensibilities that it fails to communicate its message. Companies must avoid at all costs distorting or misusing the art form to serve a purpose that has nothing to do with art.

STANDARDS FOR IN-SCHOOL PROGRAMS

The best theatre-school interactions occur in an atmosphere of mutual understanding and respect. Neither producers nor sponsors can impose theatre programs on the schools. Administrators must be convinced of their value, and teachers must want them. And, having experienced in-school theatre, educators must see a clear connection between the program and the goals they have for educating the young. They may not have sophisticated criteria for evaluating theatre *per se*, but they certainly are capable of assessing its effects.

Theatre practitioners often go into the schools lacking even the most rudimentary understanding of educational goals and processes, and, unfortunately, with the attitude that they are capable of teaching children and young people far more effectively than professional educators. To make valid connections, artists going into schools must know what education is about, and all collaborations must make sense, not only to them, but especially to the schools.[12] There can be no hint of arrogance or condescension, nor can the motives espoused seem so lofty that teachers are overwhelmed.

This does not mean that companies "water down" their work or compromise artistic standards when they go into schools, whether it is for a single performance or for an extended residency. It simply means that they also must develop informed standards and strategies for relating to young people and those who educate them. In an address to ATA, Bernard Rosenblatt urged every in-school performing group to find answers to a number of questions related to theatre, young people, respect for self and for education. His questions about education bear repeating:

> Do we love and respect educational processes? Do we view education as foe or ally? Do we believe in the finest quality of educational experiences? Do we consider how performances, workshops, residencies, and educational materials can be coordinated for the most effective and qualitative impact? Do we know enough about schools and schooling? What kind of specialized training is needed for theatre artists working in the schools? What is the appropriate training for educators? Do we care about and respect teachers?[13]

Rosenblatt reminds theatre artists that confidence in their own artistic worth is crucial to their interactions with educators. Feeling thus secure, each one can then say, "I would like to enter into a *partnership* with you — I accept you as a professional and you accept me as a professional and together we will discuss what each of us can and wants to accomplish and then [decide] how we can work *together* to help these young people to grow."[14]

In this climate, teacher workshops are presented from the educator's point of view, not from one imposed by an actor who is not cognizant of life in the classroom. Post-performance classroom sessions with students occur in a context that extends beyond the day and moment. Theatre becomes more than a diversion. It becomes an integral part of the educational process, functioning importantly to enhance the aesthetic and personal growth of youngsters and of their teachers as well.

We recognize that theatre artists, both by nature and training, are not necessarily prepared to establish effective relationships with school personnel or, in fact, with children in the educational setting. This problem has plagued artist-in-residence programs across the country. Some arts organizations have found it beneficial to band together and hold training sessions designed to acquaint artists with learning processes, curriculum guidelines and educational objectives, objectives for the arts in education, and appropriate communication skills. Such sessions are more likely to occur in metropolitan areas, of course, but when they are available they provide excellent opportunities to gain necessary background and understanding.

Theatre groups have an advantage over artists who go into the schools as individuals in that they include a number of persons who can be chosen, not only for their artistic and leadership skills, but also for their background. Any group with ties to the schools does well to have at least one individual who is well versed — preferably experienced — in educational process to serve as liaison, to prepare supplementary materials for distribution, to have primary responsibility for teacher workshops and to conduct in-service training for members of the company in preparation for classroom encounters.

DRAMA/THEATRE IN THE CLASSROOM

Recall if you will the experience of the second grade play described at the beginning of this chapter — but do not dwell on it. Come with us instead to another elementary school where a group of parents is assembling in another typical all-purpose room. All the chairs are adult-size this time, and there is a large empty space between the first row of seats and the small stage which dominates the area. The walls are lined with murals — desert and mountain scenes and some skylines reminiscent of ancient desert cultures — vividly executed in Tempera paint on large sheets of white butcher paper. No children join us. This is a program for adults. The parents know that something exciting has been going on in the sixth grade classroom, and they have had hints that one day they would be invited to see a play. But they have not seen a script, nor have they been asked to hear lines or to dig through closets and storage boxes in search of costume possibilities.

Soon the teacher appears and explains that today's program is the culmination of a unit of study that began after a formal reading lesson about David and Goliath aroused student interest in this historical event of heroism. It has been shown several times to other classes in keeping with the school's tradition of holding assemblies whenever a group has something very special to share. It is entirely the product of student investigation and creative activity. Having learned that in olden times ballads were written to celebrate the lives and deeds of heroic figures, they studied the form and wrote their own "Ballad of David," for which they also composed music. After that, one thing led to another until the class was deeply involved in an interdisciplinary arts project. And we now are privileged to see the results.

The teacher moves aside, takes up a guitar and checks it for tune as her students enter and deploy themselves in the playing area. One seats himself at the piano as a group clusters around him. Some take positions in the open area below the stage. Others begin to unfurl a large roll of paper to provide a pictorial background for the first scene. Soon we see a pantomimed dramatic interpretation of the epic tale of a humble shepherd boy who became a powerful king. The ballad sometimes is sung, sometimes spoken, either by individuals or by a speech chorus. With each new scene, a fresh pictorial background comes into view as the youthful artists who created it manipulate their continuous cylinder of paper with professional precision.

The entire program is presented with poise and vitality. Nothing extraneous has been imposed upon it. If a crown is needed, it appears, a simple child-created object that is integral to, never imposed upon, the performance. Every word, every melodic strain, every action, every production element obviously is part of a totally class-generated project. We are not aware of any self-conscious playing for the audience, but we are happily aware of total involvement combined with prideful and exuberant sharing. The teacher is as deeply involved as anyone else as she provides guitar accompaniment, following the lead of the student at the piano. When the program ends, we know we have had a theatre experience, and we are reluctant to let go of the moment. On reflection, we realize that we have seen an exemplary demonstration of drama, the perfect catalyst for multi-arts experiences and dynamic exploration of subject matter.[15]

This is a book about theatre, and inclusion of an extensive discussion of creative or informal drama is beyond its scope. The subject is thoroughly covered in a number of excellent texts, several of which go into considerable detail about classroom activities culminating in demonstration performances. We do wish to emphasize, however, that engagement in improvisational drama provides in-depth experience with the processes of theatre. This experience can either be an end in itself, or it can be extended to encompass an audience other than members of the participating group. The decision rests with the teacher, who will make it after carefully assessing what is fitting and salutary for the class.

We join with a majority of our colleagues in advocating that younger children be spared the pressures of working in formal, scripted plays in any setting, but especially in schools where the average teacher has no preparation as a director or any informed set of criteria for choosing scripted material, and the children themselves are not yet ready for the experience. John Allen reinforces our point of view in a description of a play done in a school with seven- and eight-year-olds:

> The problem encountered by these children was that a precise and formal structure which is highly comprehensible in narrative terms is intensely constricting in dramatic. At an age when they had not learnt in any way to discipline their speech to the formal requirements of so tightly structured a story they had to act in a most constrained manner even though the material was well within their comprehension.

He continues by describing another performance by a small cast of eight- and nine-year-olds, who enacted a story "that is not at all the stuff of drama. . . . and the opportunities for that open-ended free-flowing use of the imagination that is characteristic of children of this age did not exist," since the story imposed too many limitations. Of both performances he writes, ". . . only a small number of children from each class were involved, and I suspect the parts went to the children who were the best 'actors.' . . . at seven to nine they were a little young to be subject to extreme selectivity . . ." Finally, he warns against imposing a sense of form on younger children "before they [have] worked through the stage of applying their creativity specifically to drama."[16] A logical extension of this philosophy would include an admonition to all educators to avoid putting students at any level into public performances of scripted plays until they have had both developmental and technical training as actors.

A valid program of theatre *as* education is based on the presumption that all children are endowed with creative imagination and deserve equal opportunities to develop it through participatory experiences in the art form. The *Drama/Theatre Framework for California Public Schools* and the *Visual and Performing Arts Framework* that superceded it define three process clusters: originating and performing, producing, and responding and evaluating. Within each cluster, activities and teaching strategies are designed to provide experiences of increasing challenge until students reach a level of security and sophistication which prepares them to engage in performance activities for audiences other than themselves to the mutual benefit of both groups.[17] It is assumed that all activities exclusive of formal play production can and will be handled by non-specialist classroom teachers, but that the latter aspect is clearly the province of appropriately trained teacher-directors.

At the lower levels of education, experiences in drama/theatre should be available to all children, both as viewers and participants. Beyond the elementary school, a process of selection begins as students plan individual programs of study which may or may not include courses in theatre or any of the arts. Theatre study then becomes a matter of choice, and performance activities likewise are voluntary and generally limited to those students whose inclinations and talents lead them to seek continuing experiences in the art form. This course of events should not exclude the general student body from exposure to theatrical performance, however. The production program should be geared to serve the cultural needs of the entire school community.

While young people are free to choose whether or not they will engage in play production, children at the elementary level are not. In addition to the discussed and implied weaknesses of the scripted performances described elsewhere in this chapter, another negative aspect is that almost invariably such projects are imposed on rather than generated by the children. In contrast, "The Ballad of David" was performed because the students were eager to share the fruits of their learning, and appropriate arrangements were made for them to do so. It is both natural and fitting that a class project of this kind should come before an audience. It should be noted, however, that the project was not originally conceived with performance in mind. The desire to put it in polished form arose after the students and their teacher agreed that they had achieved something worthy of showing.

For most classroom drama, involvement in process for its own sake is sufficiently rewarding to children and teachers alike. In a sense it is unfortunate that the field has adopted its narrow definition of performance as showing to others, when the word also is synonymous with achievement. John Allen reminds us that performance, in this less confining definition, means "the right of a young person to be helped to do whatever he wants to do to the very best of his ability, and this applies to work in primary as much as secondary schools."[18] In this statement, Allen sets a standard for the informal classroom experience in improvisation. To elaborate: "A child when improvising is indeed in one respect exploring an area of experience; but he is doing so not only because it is fun but because he is trying to embody that feeling in form."[19] As he is helped to find an appropriate form for his expression, he is learning about theatre.

Considering performance in its narrower definition, Allen observes:

> . . . it is a natural instinct that having discovered or demonstrated skill in a particular activity the 'performer' should look for a certain appreciation or even acclamation. While it is absolutely proper that drama teachers should resist the tendency as long as possible, they must recognize the close relationship that inevitably exists between achievement, communication, and emotional response.[20]

When conditions are right, and this means that the children are at an appropriate stage of personal as well as artistic readiness, there is nothing wrong with inviting their peers or adults who are capable of understanding and appreciating creative achievement to share in their accomplishments. The emphasis, however, is on *sharing*, as if to say, "This is a play we have made for ourselves, but we have enjoyed it so much we have decided to bring you here to see it. We have not invited you here to watch us show off, but rather to involve you in our work."

Unquestionably the "model class" or demonstration-performance is the preferred way to give children the experience of working before an audience. To orient in-school drama/theatre activities too heavily toward a shared culmination, however, places focus where it should not be and diminishes the value of the experience in much the same way formal play production mitigates against the real benefits of theatre as education. Performances for outsiders are at their best when they come about almost accidentally, when a classroom project becomes so engaging that the youngsters themselves feel a compulsion to bring it to a spectacular and fitting climax.

NOTES

[1]Grace Stanistreet, "Quiet — Children at Work," *Children's Theatre News* (Region 14), Oct. 1970, pp. 4-5.

[2]Gillette Elvgren, "Children's Theatre and the Workshop Experience," *Children's Theatre Review,* XXVI, 4 (1977), 6.

[3]Elvgren, 7 & 10.

[4]*Bear Republic News,* Winter '81 Edition. P.O Box 1137, Santa Cruz, CA.

[5]Tony Jackson, ed., *Learning through theatre: Essays and Casebooks on Theatre in Education* (sic) (Manchester: Manchester University Press, 1980), p. viii.

[6]Gordon Vallins, "The Beginnings of TIE," in Jackson, p. 13.

[7]Eileen Murphy, "Introduction," *Sweetie Pie* (London: Eyre Methuen, Ltd. 1975), p. 5.

[8]Jackson, pp. viii-ix.

[9]Tony Coult, "Buried Glories," *Plays and Players,* Sept., 1977, pp. 18-19.

[10]Vallins, in Jackson, p. 12.

[11]Notes from the program for "Tower of Babble," a production by the Creative Arts Team of New York University, commissioned by the Education Program of the New York Urban Coalition, 1978-79.

[12]Bernard Rosenblatt, "Ethics and Excellence: A Challenge to Producers of Theatre for Children and Youth," American Theatre Association Convention, San Diego, August, 1980.

[13]Rosenblatt.

[14]Rosenblatt.

[15]This is an account of an actual project at Knollwood Elementary School, Granada Hills, CA. The teacher was Beth Rogers, the Principal, Angelene Kasza. It occurred in 1970.

[16]John Allen, *Drama in Schools: Its Theory and Practice* (London: Heinemann Educational Books, Ltd., 1979), p. 52.

[17]*Drama/Theatre Framework for California Public Schools* (Sacramento: California State Department of Education, 1974), p. 3. *Visual and Performing Arts Framework for California Public Schools: Kindergarten Through Grade Twelve* (Sacramento: California State Department of Education, 1982), p. 38.

[18]Allen, p. 113.

[19]Allen, pp. 114-115.

[20]Allen, p. 115.

APPENDICES

APPENDIX 1

The following article is reprinted from the *Children's Theatre Review*, XXVII, 1 (1978), 10-11, by permission of the Children's Theatre Association of America and its authors.

TERMINOLOGY OF DRAMA/THEATRE WITH AND FOR CHILDREN:
A Redefinition

by
Jed H. Davis and Tom Behm

INTRODUCTION

In 1956 a special committee of what was then called the Children's Theatre Conference of the American Educational Theatre Association published "*Drama With and For Children: An Interpretation of Terms,*"[1] While that committee's report accounted admirably for aspects and views of the field prevalent at that time, continued development in children's theatre and creative dramatics ultimately left practitioners without a comprehensive statement on terminology.

In December, 1975, Children's Theatre Association of America President, Coleman A. Jennings, appointed twin committees, charging them to undertake a reexamination of terminology in the allied fields with the ultimate goal that of producing a set of new definitions which would more accurately reflect what is being done today.[2] The groups deliberated between February, 1976, and August, 1977, with an open session at the 1976 Annual Meeting provided to give an opportunity for the membership to respond to preliminary reports. Both committees presented their findings to the Governing Board of CTAA in August, 1977, and they were accepted.

This article represents the essence of the two committee reports.

THE DRAMA/THEATRE CONTINUUM

Drama and Theatre by and for children was seen to exist on a continuum that could be represented thus:[3]

Drama in its natural state	Guided Drama	Participation Theatre/Drama	Theatre
	Creative Drama or Child Drama	Audience members alternately watchers and participants	Strictly prearranged art form; Clear distinction between actors and audience

This spectrum of activities involving children and the drama/theatre is established on the classic definitions of *drama* (a thing done) and *theatre* (to gaze on). The natural dramatic propensities of children, located at the far left on the continuum, are seen to be the bases of, and to infuse, all the forms of drama and theatre. The two committees, however, limited their definitions to those terms that involve consciously applied leadership and direction.

DEFINITIONS

Creative Drama

"Creative Drama" is an improvisational, non-exhibitional, process-centered form of drama in which participants are guided by a leader to imagine, enact, and reflect upon human experiences.[4] Although creative drama traditionally has been thought of in relation to children and young people, the process is appropriate to all ages.[5]

The creative drama process is dynamic. The leader guides the group to explore, develop, express and communicate ideas, concepts, and feelings through dramatic enactment. In creative drama the group improvises action and dialogue appropriate to the content it is exploring, using elements of drama to give form and meaning to the experience. The primary purpose of creative drama is to foster personality growth and to facilitate learning of the participants rather than to train actors for the stage. Creative drama may be used to teach the art of drama and/or motivate and extend learning in other content areas. Participation in creative drama has the potential to develop language and communication abilities, problem solving skills, and creativity; to promote a positive self concept, social awareness, empathy, a clarificaion of values and attitudes, and an understanding of the art of theatre.

Built on the human impulse and ability to act out perceptions of the world in order to understand it, creative drama requires both logical and intuitive thinking, personalizes knowledge, and yields aesthetic pleasure.

Children's Theatre

"Children's Theatre" is a nonspecific, global term indicating the general field of theatre as applied to children.

While it is recognized that the term is used in a variety of academic, literary, and bibliographic contexts, the use of more specific terms such as those which follow should be encouraged for situations where exactness of meaning is important.

Theatre for Young Audiences

"Theatre for Young Audiences" is a term encompassing "Theatre for Children" and "Theatre for Youth," the distinction being the age range of the intended audience. Even though adults frequently attend Theatre for Young Audiences, either as teachers accompanying classes, as parents with their children, or merely as interested patrons, the focus of the performance remains on the young people in the audience as defined below.

"Theatre for Children" indicates theatrical events specifically designed to be performed for young persons typically of elementary school age, five to twelve.

"Theatre for Youth" indicates theatrical events specifically designed to be performed for young persons typically of junior high school age, 13 to 15.[6]

"Theatre for Young Audiences, consists of the performance of a largely predetermined theatrical art work by living actors in the presence of an audience of young people, either children or youth as defined above.[7] It embraces the following characteristics:

The performance may be based on written scripts of traditional form, or adapted, devised, or developed improvisationally by directors, directors and actors in cooperative effort, or by actors working in ensemble.

The dramatic material of the performance may be a single story line designed to engage the full empathic commitment of the audience in a succession of events, or it may be a series of shorter, separate, or thematically related stories or sketches. In either case the product is constructed to communicate emotionally and intellectually with the audience members, individually and collectively, and to provide an entertaining and meaningful theatre experience.

Preferably highly skilled adult actors are engaged for the performance, with especially talented child actors in child roles.

The full spectrum of theatrical arts and crafts may be called upon to enhance the actors' performance: costumes, make-up, lighting, scenery, properties, sound, and special effects. It must be noted, however, that many successful performances make only minimal use of these elements of production.

The audience may be assembled in any configuration utilizing a variety of spaces described by any number of theatrical forms, from proscenium to open field. Since all theatre strives for communication among all parties, an intellectual and emotional participation by the audience is essential. Participation may extend to limited direct physical and vocal involvement from their seats.

"Participation Theatre" is the kind of "Theatre for Young Audiences" consisting of the presentation of specially written, adapted or devised drama with an established story line constructed to include limited and structured opportunities for active involvement by all or part of the audience. Participation may range from simple verbal responses to an active role in the outcome of the drama. In the participation segments, adult actors function as creative drama leaders, guiding the audience. The seating configuration is determined by the kind and degree of participation expected. While such theatrical events can be constructed for any age child or youth, they are, at present, most usually performed for children five to eight years old. Strict control over audience age grouping and special leadership training for the adult actors are advisable for success.

"Theatre by Children and Youth" is a particular variant of "Theatre for Young Audiences" in which the performers are children and/or teenagers rather than adults.

Preferably the performers are no younger than ten years old and have been well schooled by a director in their primary task of bringing the dramatic material to life for the audience. Organizations engaged in "Theatre by Children and Youth" ordinarily plan their productions to focus on audiences of children younger than the performers plus interested adults. They generally do not use people below 8th grade level to perform scripted roles in "Participation Theatre" because of the demands of effective creative drama leadership.

CONCLUSION

The above definitions are intended to be sufficiently comprehensive to accommodate both existing practices and innovative developments in creative drama and theatre for young audiences as they may occur. While some values and standards are implied in these definitions, the exploration of them in fuller form is left to other committees. The definitions themselves were felt to be the first essential step.

NOTES

[1] Ann Viola, "Drama With and For Children: An Interpretation of Terms," EDUCATIONAL THEATRE JOURNAL, VII, 2 (May, 1956), 139-142. Members of the committee were Isabel Burger, Kenneth L. Graham, Mouzon Law, Dorothy Schwartz, Sara Spencer, Winifred Ward, and Ann Viola, Chairperson.

[2] Members of the Committee to Redefine Terminology in Creative Dramatics were Lynn Bradley, Courtaney Brooks, Donald Doyle, Ruth Heinig, Coleman A. Jennings, Elizabeth Kelly, Mary Kerr, Nellie McCaslin, Robert Petza, Milton Polsky, Laura Salazar, Dorothy Schwartz, Ann M. Shaw, Geraldine Siks, Julie Thompson, Anne Thurman, Patricia Whitton, and Tom Behm, Chairperson.

Members of the Committee to Redefine Terminology in Children's Theatre were Gayle Cornelison, Mary Jane Evans, Margaret Faulkes, Moses Goldberg, Kenneth L. Graham, Jeanne Hall, Claire Jones, Judith Kase, Marsha Evans McGee, Margaret McKerrow, Kenneth R. McLeod, Raymond Picozzi, and Jed H. Davis, Chairperson.

Each committee arrived at its conclusions independently of the other, and there was no procedure for approval of the combined report by personnel of both.

[3] For this idea, we are indebted to Donald Baker, "Defining Drama: From Child's Play to Production," THEATRE QUARTERLY, V, 7 (1975), 61-71.

[4] Based on the definition developed by Ann M. Shaw, Frank Harland, and Anne Thurman for the 1972 Congress of the International Association of Theatre for Children and Young People.

[5] Some other terms used to describe this form of drama include improvisational drama, informal drama, educational drama, drama with children, developmental drama, child drama, and drama.

[6] The committee acknowledges the difficulty of ascribing any specific upper age limits to a dynamic field such as this. How to account for the increasing involvement of senior high school students (age 15 to 18) in productions geared for older children and an extended "youth" audience which might, indeed, include senior high ages, took considerable committee energy. Since such productions are still relatively rare, the committee preferred to keep the upper limit of "Theatre for Youth" at 15 and recognize the variant in this way. Also of note in this connection is the European as-

sumption that Theatres for Youth encompass an age range extending into the early to mid 20's. These concerns overlap with those primarily under the aegis of the Secondary School Theatre Conference, and may one day be defined jointly by both CTAA and SSTA.

⁷This definition is understood to include pup-

petry performed by living puppeteers in the presence of audiences of young people.

Jed H. Davis is professor of Theatre, University of Kansas; Tom Behm is director of Theatre for Young People, University of North Carolina, Greensboro.

APPENDIX 2

On November 9, 1976, an important series of workshops culminated in issuance of the following report known as the "Attleboro Conference Working Paper on Theatre and Drama for Children." It is reproduced here with permission of the conference organizers and its principal writer, Pat Hale Whitton.

DEFINING CHILDREN'S THEATRE AND CREATIVE DRAMA
A WORKING POSITION PAPER FROM THE ATTLEBORO CONFERENCE

I. A POINT OF VIEW.

We are concerned with creative drama and children's theatre as dramatic experiences which are designed to lead to the growth and pleasure of children. What do we include under growth? New perceptions, new images, clarification of thoughts or feelings that lead to change or understanding, new identifications. It could be a gasp of delight at a wonderful new image of the possibilities of the human body; it could be an insight into a new way for a group to solve a problem.

Attempts to define either term often end up as attempts to defend, to prove one or the other better, in the mistaken notion that we must choose one in favor of the other.

Though children's theatre and creative drama are often thought to be separate categories of experience, they have at heart two commonalities:

1. Children — and a concern for their growth and development

2. Drama — we define drama as a metaphorical representation of concepts and people in conflict in which each participant is required either to project imaginatively into an identity other than his or her own or to empathize, through enactment, with others doing so. Drama has a structure, occurs in real time and space and typically demands intellectual, emotional and physical engagement to yield its fresh insights into the human condition.

Despite the wide variety of tools and techniques that we use, creative drama and theatre can be considered as representing the ends of a continuum. Each of the elements of drama is there, in different degree. The balance of emphasis on any one element within the continuum — the amount of pre-planning, for instance, or the role of the adult in designing the experiences — may vary widely. Indeed it may vary widely in any two examples of either children's theatre or creative drama; the important thing to remember is that the differences are differences in degree and style. As long as the drama experience is well done (and we are talking about the best) we do not have to make judgments about which is more important or valid or memorable to the child. Whatever forms they may take, experiences in creative drama and children's theatre reach the child in a way that only drama can, providing a catalyst for growth, delight, learning and change. Both have a valid and valuable role to play in the life of the child.

II. A DESCRIPTION OF THREE DRAMATIC EXPERIENCES.

Differences do exist between creative dramatics and children's theatre, making the experiences recognizably distinct from each other. These distinctions range from the type of involvement to the amount of organizational framework. Audience participation theatre, which overlaps both children's theatre and creative drama, makes up yet another category of experience.

In *Creative Drama* children with a trained leader engage in dramatic play which is process-oriented and non-presentational. In guided improvisations children develop ideas through physical enactment, problem-solving and decision-making. The purpose is to foster growth and development of the child and provide group interaction and fun.

In *Children's Theatre* performers and director work together for a child audience to present a dramatic enactment. The performance is planned and rehearsed to create a selective and heightened experience around a theme shaped by a playwright in order to enlarge a child's perception of the world, awaken feelings and provide pleasure.

In *Participation Theatre* children interacting with performer/teachers share a dramatic enactment involving spontaneous interaction within the structure of a play. The performer/teacher initiates improvisation with children to create a play in which both children and performers take roles and may make decisions and create dialogue. The purpose is to provide an informal theatre experience in which the children share physically and vocally with the performing artist.

III. A NEW WAY OF LOOKING AT PROCESS AND PRODUCT.

A frequently heard dichotomy is that creative drama deals with process and children's theatre with product. Actually, process and product are inextricably entwined in each and it might be more helpful, for developing rule-of-thumb distinctions, to look instead at the cast of characters, the setting in time and place, the plot and the purpose. See the chart on the next page for a summary of these distinctions.

The key differences that emerge in the chart are differences in *convention*. The term convention covers the codified assumptions that we make about the *means* (such as the materials and structure) we use to achieve a particular activity in relation to the arts. They are based on commonly understood and accepted manners of doing things. Theatre has its conventions of time, place, structure, identification with the characters, manner of shaping the material, language, etc. So does creative drama. By examining their conventions at their most absolute — at the opposite ends of a continuum — (with the awareness that dramatic experience is rarely represented in its "pure" form) we may gain insight into the key differences between creative drama and children's theatre and the way that participation theatre often (but not always) occupies a pivotal position between the two.

For instance, in the area of the allied theatre arts — scenery, lighting, sound effects, costumes, music, etc. — the continuum can range from a bare room or stretch of lawn to a theatre complete with every technical effect imaginable. We normally think of children's theatre at one end of the line, with lighting scenery and costumes; and creative drama at the other end, making use only of the children's bodies and voices and perhaps a few home-made props. We think of participation theatre as somewhere in between with selected props and costumes to enhance effects, but with very little scenery. Yet we can all think of wonderful theatre which took place on a bare stage or no stage at all as well as creative drama making use of sound effects, music and scenery.

	Creative Drama	Children's Theatre	Participation Theatre
WHO	Children with a trained leader concerned with child development	Playwright Director Performers; adults, children or both Usually designers and technicians Child Audiences	Writer who provides structure Children partaking with performer/teachers
WHERE	Space not specific; classroom, open space, outdoors . . .	Stage or open space Outdoors	Classroom or open space Outdoors
WHEN	Anytime; during or after school hours. No duration limits fixed	Pre-arranged special event that happens once, at a specific time for a specific duration	A largely pre-arranged event that happens once, at a specific time for a flexible duration
WHAT	Process-oriented dramatic play. Freely structured exploration, self directed and self-motivated. A non-presentational enactment, group activity	Product-oriented, presentational art form; a finished product in a finished framework; selected and heightened experience shaped by a playwright. Dramatic entertainment; as a celebration	Dramatic enactment involving spontaneous interaction between performer/teachers and children. Structure of the play flexible enough to allow choice and diversity among the participants
HOW	In guided improvisation that may be informally rehearsed children develop ideas through physical enactment, through problem-solving and decision-making. Dramatic enactment through activities and group interaction related to age levels and development	The performance of a scripted play is planned and rehearsed, shaped to elicit audience response. Costumes, scenery, lighting, etc. may be used	Within a planned structure performers initiate improvisation with children. Characters interact with children to create a play. Children take roles, make decisions, may create dialogue or make sound effects
WHY	To develop freedom of physical expression and language skills. To enhance self-confidence, self-awareness, self concepts. To free creative potential in individual. To foster the growth of the child, provide pleasure and awaken feelings	To develop appreciation of an art form. To expose children to a range of ideas and values and to enlarge their perceptions of the world. To provide pleasure and awaken feelings	To provide an informal theatre experience that develops appreciation of the theatre process. To provide an opportunity for children to share physically and vocally with the artist in creating a play and to foster interaction between children and adults. To awaken feelings and provide pleasure

267

Here are some other lines on the continuum which can be examined fruitfully.

Source of the material

At one end is the child creating; "let's do a play," out of his or her own experience. At the other end is a completed script in which the ideas, characters, events and actual language are all provided by the writer. In between, we may have creative drama in which children improvise a story that has been originally written by an author, *The Three Bears*, for instance, using the characters and events but creating new dialogue and modifying scenes. Or we may have improvisational theatre in which the actors accept ideas or characters from the children but give them their own language and gestures. In participation theatre the children may add dialogue or individualize actions but the basic action, character and theme have been shaped in advance from a written story or one created by the performing company.

Nature of Child's Identification

In theatre the child's identification takes place imaginatively; mind and feelings are involved as he or she empathizes with the character or characters. In creative drama the child's identification with the character he or she plays is kinetic and physical; response is vocal and active as well as imaginative. In participation theatre the child identifies physically with the role he or she plays and also projects self imaginatively into the parts of the characters played by the performer/teachers.

Degree of Structure

The dramatic structure can range from the very loosest, a barely structured play scene in which the children spontaneously interact on the basis of their own ideas, to a tightly designed structure in which every part, every word has a preplanned time and space. Most dramatic experiences fall somewhere in between. In creative drama the teacher often has planned the experience with a certain outcome in mind; in even the most formal theatre the actor will vary his performance and pace in response to his interaction with the audience. Many children's theatre experiences are planned to allow a great deal of variance. In participation theatre part of the structure is open to allow for the input of the child but the overall shape of the experience is fixed.

Language

In creative drama language is spontaneous — whatever happens to serve the need of the moment in improvisation. At the other extreme, using a written script, the language has been artfully designed to achieve its intended effects.

Goals for the Children

Several lines might be woven together in this continuum. For instance, one line showing group experience at one end and individual experience at the other; or a line showing orientation toward development of skills — problem-solving, decision-making, verbal expression — on the one hand and emphasis on growth through concept formation on the other. The goal might be to introduce children to the process of drama through making their own plays; or it might be to introduce children to the art of drama through enjoying a play made by artists.

IV. WHY A CHILD SHOULD HAVE ALL THREE EXPERIENCES.

The most striking thing to us at Attleboro was that as we tried to express these ideas visually, the lines of these continuums did not go up or down (this is at the bottom; this is at the top) but rather in and out from each other, sometimes in intertwined circles. They represented a range of experiences that we believe all children should have. The continuum is not a one-way journey; you meet yourself and others coming and going at various levels.

The choice of which kind of learning experience you choose to offer a child at a given time will depend on many factors, not least of which is the personal style of the leader. A leader may like the immediate feedback children give in creative dramatics, or he or she may value more the vividness of experience that formal theatre provides through its ordered visual and sensual elements. People working in participation theatre speak of the importance of being able simultaneously to share in creation and yet stand outside the story.

Children too have different styles. Some respond better to the opportunity for release of physical energies that creative drama gives; others need the opportunity for personal relationship between adult and child that participation theatre offers. Still others need the opportunity for intense identification without risk that children's theatre can provide. Some children learn better visually; some verbally or tactilely and yet others through active participation. A hyperactive child might be better served by creative dramatics; a severely handicaped child by children's theatre.

The nature of the material we want to share also helps determine the kind of learning experience we choose. Certain kinds of material work better in one mode than in another. Is the vividness of the experience more important than the quiet, reflective moment? Is active exploration of ideas the goal of the experience or do you wish to share the playwright's analysis and synthesis? Is it important for the child to work at his or her own pace or is your goal for the moment to extend the ability to listen?

Most children can benefit most from having the full range of experiences in drama. In music education one does not ask whether the child should choose between playing an instrument or listening to live music in performance. In art education the child is expected to learn both through making images and observing those made by artists or, in the best of instances, those in the process of being made. In dance education the child choreographs his or her own movement and sees the dancer perform, if not on stage at least on the screen or the television tube. Should we not act to insure that every child will have opportunities to enjoy and to benefit from an equally full range of experiences in drama and theatre?

APPENDIX 3

The following report of the CTAA Wingspread Conference on Theatre Education for Public Schools is reprinted here from the *Children's Theatre Review*, XXVII, 2 (1978), by permission of the Children's Theatre Association of America and its author.

CTAA AT WINGSPREAD

by Lin Wright

A "symbol of soaring inspiration" well describes Wingspread, the site of the Children's Theatre Association of America Conference on Theatre Education for Public Schools. Thirty-five selected specialists in creative drama and children's theatre from throughout the United States[1] met from August 9-11, 1977, at this educational conference center of the Johnson Foundation in Racine, Wisconsin. They exchanged ideas on pre-determined topics and found a deeper understanding of what each was doing and a new sense of solidarity.

The areas of discussion were: 1) how children's theatre and creative drama can enhance education as a unique discipline and as a process/tool within today's school curriculum; 2) how the generalist and specialist can meet the needs of education through drama and the theatre in schools today; and 3) how CTAA and other concerned national associations can implement recommendations made by the conference participants.

Prior to the conference, each participant had read a series of articles and books related to the Conference topics (see Appendix) and had developed lists of areas of agreement. At the conference a series of small group meetings followed by plenary sessions led to the drafting of two position papers.[2] Both papers received consensus support at the final plenary session.

The idea of such a conference had long been the dream of CTAA leaders. A conference on theatre education was suggested at the ATA Wingspread meeting in 1975. Judith Kase, president of CTAA, wrote the proposal to the Johnson Foundation for this 1977 conference. With the help of Tom Behm, Orlin Corey, Jed Davis, Ann Hill, Ann Shaw, Joe McCarthy, Bart O'Connor, and Ann Haggerty Wright, she designed the schedule of activities and chose the preconference readings.

This conference was a beginning step in fulfilling the ATA request for a theatre education conference. Regional "Wingspread" meetings can lead to the refinement of the position papers and to a plan to implement theatre/drama in the school curriculum. With such a document, mutual support and dreams of high quality theatre education for all children can come closer to realization.

Following is a synopsis of the paper developed from the first discussion topic.

CREATIVE DRAMA/CHILDREN'S THEATRE: ARTS TO ENHANCE EDUCATION

Aesthetic development (learning to perceive, judge and value that which is beautiful) must be as central to the educational curriculum as intellectual development. Involvement in the arts is a particularly effective way to heighten the child's capacity to recognize, analyze, and experience the aesthetic qualities of his or her world.

The Arts, Education and Americans Panel report, *Coming to Our Senses,* supports this view. "Educators at all levels must adopt the arts as a basic component of curriculum deserving parity with all other elements . . . The fundamental goals of American education can be realized only when the arts become central to individual experience in or out of school and at every stage of life."[3]

Drama and theatre should be central to the arts, for dramatic imagination is natural to the human being. Children learn by pretending to be a part of the adult world; this natural power is particularly important to the child because the mental act of transformation is a major mode of learning. In school the child should be guided from the pretending of drama in its natural state to involvement in the entire drama/theatre continuum. This continuum has been defined by the CTAA Redefinition Committee as being established on the classic definitions of *drama* (a thing done) and *theatre* (to gaze on). The continuum moves from "drama in its natural state to guided drama, to participation theatre/drama, to theatre."[4]

As with all of the arts, drama/theatre adds form in a non-discursive mode to complex human perceptions and experiences. As with all of the performing arts, theatre involves interaction between performer and audience. But drama/theatre is a unique discipline that is particularly important to education.

THE DRAMA/THEATRE CONTINUUM AS A TOOL/PROCESSS

The unique qualities of drama/theatre lead to skills and attitudes that a child can apply to the arts and to general living. Involving the child in the drama continuum enables the teacher to work with the child in diverse ways and to enrich the curriculum.

Individualization. In the drama continuum the child can be actor and creator as well as observer and evaluator. Through drama activities, the teacher can include alternative styles of learning in the classroom. The content and activities of drama can center the educational process on the child and allow the teacher to be more sensitive to individual differences.

By expressing ideas and emotions in his/her own unique manner in constructive verbal and nonverbal ways, the child can realize some measure of individuality and success.

Cooperation. Interaction is basic to the drama/theatre process. Through theatre experiences the teacher can help the child value the interaction between audience and actor.

Within the drama process the teacher can give individuals an opportunity to work collaboratively rather than competitively. Students of varying abilities can work together. Discussions evolving from the drama process can foster an awareness of the importance of the individual's and group's contributions to the process. Thus the value of and skills in cooperative behavior can be learned.

Finally, by leading drama activities the teacher may develop more techniques for large group management.

Motivation. Drama and theatre are exciting. By including these activities in the curriculum the teacher can arouse the curiosity that comes from direct involvement and motivate in-depth learning.

Involvement in drama activities can help exercise the senses, increase spatial awareness, and strengthen body awareness for the child. Increased ability to concentrate may help the child develop constructive behavior changes. The strong motivation to solve problems can lead the child to find analogies, develop new ideas, elaborate on ideas, and seek closure with the group.

By using a variety of techniques to include the child in the drama continuum the teacher can facilitate the creative use of and response to verbal and nonverbal symbols. This can lead to the acquisition of skills in spoken and written language and the development of expressive and imaginative skills.

Integration. Drama is a form of communication and interaction which is implicitly verbal and includes motivation, thought processes, and actions. It fosters the integration of the cognitive, affective, and psychomotor domains. The child can personalize and internalize information by connecting abstract and symbolic thought and concrete experience.

Values clarification. Drama/theatre deals with people in action, making decisions and living with the consequences of their choices. It deals with questions which people must ask but for which there are no definite or absolute answers. In presenting a format through which individuals can find personal answers to universal questions, drama and theatre both clarify and influence value structures.

Through empathy, the child participant or viewer becomes partisan, and, through drama, partisanship can be influenced and the child stimulated to examine his/her values. This empathic response can help the child clarify values by expanding knowledge of life in other cultures and at other times.

The interaction within the drama process can help the child to value classmates' ideas and contributions as well as his or her own.

Appreciation. Experiencing theatre and drama as participant and viewer is the best means for the child to achieve an understanding of the art form.

THE UNIQUE PROPERTIES OF THEATRE AND DRAMA

Role identification. Drama and theatre present and represent human life symbolized through live persons engaged in live action. The dramatic situation is revealed through human motivation, action, reaction, and interaction occurring in real time and space simultaneously portraying imagined time and space. Thus drama can be a "rehearsal" for the act of living. It also allows direct exploration of human experience not always within one's direct experience. The enacted experiences become immediate and personalized. At the same time the drama process provides for opportunities to reflect upon life. The child creator can image and enact the lives of others, expanding his/her personal role repertoire.

Through having real actors symbolizing the imagined characters, the audience of a theatrical performance can also safely explore the life of another. The intensity and immediacy of the experience arouses individual identification, empathy, and discovery. The experience is inherently educational and entertaining.

Symbolic action. Through selectivity, distillation, and focus of the human experience, drama and theatre create a form for action with the illusion of more real than real. The entire action becomes symbolic and the actors and audience use their humanness to express, interpret and intuit the symbol/metaphor.

Collaboration. Drama/theatre encompasses sound, music and speech, movement and dance, visualization and the visual arts, identification and assumption of character, symbolic and concrete representation, appreciation and evaluation of performance. It involves a collective exploration of human ideas, human dilemmas, and human conflicts. It demands a cooperative, collaborative effort between and among all participants: among players, among audience members, between audience and players.

TRAINING FOR THE GENERALIST

The sequencing and specifics of this course of study for the generalist may be handled in diverse ways according to particular needs, but three program areas are seen as essential.

Exploration in aesthetic education. The student

should be engaged in the *process* of the various art forms in order to enhance his/her aesthetic sensibilities and to gain an understanding of how arts elements are transformed through the creative process into whole works of art.

The learner should also be engaed in the *perception and analysis* of the sensory qualities of the environment and of works of art. Relationships of the sensory qualities and whole works should be analyzed and the emotional effects of aesthetic experiences discussed. The impact of works of art and performances from immediate and distant cultures should be analyzed. Knowledge of how to analyze art forms, development of critical language of the arts, and increased confidence in valuing and making aesthetic judgments should be goals for this process. Finally, the generalist should gain a perspective on the relationship of drama and theatre to the other arts and the importance of the arts to education.

Exploration of drama and theatre as an art form. The learner should study the various forms of dramatic literature as well as analyze the elements of drama within improvisation. Attendance at the theatre is also important.

Simultaneously, the student should be using his/her powers of imagining and enacting to create drama, exploring the elements of drama. Creative drama processes such as theatre games directed improvisations, and small group work would allow participants to use and internalize the elements of drama that they are investigating. Individual reflection and group discussion after these activities should synthesize the total experience.

Study of specific methodologies of creative drama as a process/tool. Through the *study* of creative drama theory the generalist should examine drama as a process/tool, identify the potentially dramatic elements in the general curriculum, and design ways to use it in implementing that curriculum. Through *guided practical experience* with children, the learner should develop skills in leadership.

PREPARATION FOR THE SPECIALIST AND GENERALIST TO MEET THE NEEDS OF EDUCATION THROUGH DRAMA IN THE SCHOOLS

A synopsis of the paper developed from the second discussion question included the following points:

If the potential of drama for education is to be realized, training in drama/theatre must be designed to prepare the classroom teacher, support personnel, and specialists to meet the needs of the children as well as to fulfill the demands of the job. For the generalist[5] this program should include an exploration of aesthetic education as well as experience with drama/theatre.

The specialist[6] training should be designed to fit the needs of the individual as new jobs are created.[7] It is assumed that the required generalist preparation will be previous to or concurrent with the specialist training.

TRAINING FOR THE SPECIALIST

Specific course descriptions and requirements

have limited future value for specialist programs since the field is growing and job descriptions change radically. To avoid these limitations, a model to predict needs and define educational experiences was designed.

To use the model, a job description should be developed. From this, *functions* of the specialist in this role should be determined and listed on the vertical axis of the model. Next, the various kinds of *learning experiences*, including formal course work, competency-based training programs, and informal life experiences should be listed on the horizontal axis. Finally the level of competency/expectation (high, medium, low) should be entered on the grid.

An example of the model follows.

GRID FOR DETERMINING SPECIALIST FUNCTIONS AND COMPETENCIES

SPECIALIST FUNCTIONS	THEATRE				OTHER ARTS				THEATRE EXPERIENCE		PHILOSOPHY			EDUCATION					INFORMAL LIFE EXPERIENCES			
	STUDIO	APPRECIATION	HISTORY	CRITICISM/THEORY	STUDIO	APPRECIATION	HISTORY	CRITICISM/THEORY	AUDIENCE	PERFORMANCE	PERSONAL	ARTISTIC	EDUCATIONAL	ADMINISTRATION	TEACHING METHODS	LEARNING THEORY	INSTRUCTIONAL DESIGN	PSYCHOLOGICAL DEV.	CROSS CULTURAL AWARENESS OF FIELD	CHANGE AGENTRY	LIBERAL ARTS	OTHERS
SUPERVISE AND ADMINISTER		H				M			H		H	H	H	H	H	H	H	M	H	H	M	
PROVIDE THERAPY	L	L		L	L	L		L	L		H	H	H		H	H	L	H	H		M	
COUNSEL (CAREER/PERSONAL)																						
COORDINATE ARTS ACTIVITIES																						
FOSTER TRANS ARTS RELATIONSHIPS																						
DO PUBLIC RELATIONS WORK																						
DESIGN CURRICULUM																						
INTEGRATE THEATRE WITH OTHER CURRICULUM AREAS																						
PROVIDE PROFESSIONAL DEVELOPMENT FOR TEACHERS																						
PRODUCE ART																						
FOSTER CRITICAL SKILLS																						
FOSTER APPRECIATION																						
FOSTER AESTHETIC DEVELOPMENT																						
FOSTER ART SKILLS																						
FOSTER INTELLECTUAL DEVELOPMENT																						
FOSTER SELF-DISCIPLINE																						
FOSTER SOCIAL DEVELOPMENT																						
AND MANY OTHERS																						

LEVELS OF COMPETENCIES/EXPECTATIONS
KEY: H HIGH
M MEDIUM
L LOW

EVALUATION OF THE CONFERENCE AND FUTURE PLANS

The goal of achieving final papers for all three areas of discussion was unrealistic. In a three-day conference there was not enough time for the reflection needed to produce a finished product. The conferees could spend only one session on the third discussion topic: how CTAA and other concerned national associations could implement recommendations made by conference participants. A committee (Barbara Salisbury, Orlin Corey and Carole Huggins) was created to formulate goals arising from the position papers and to develop plans to implement these recommendations. They expect to have reportable results at the 1978 American Theatre Association convention.

The process at Wingspread was so valuable and inspirational for those attending that there are plans to use the drafts of the position papers from this conference as a basis for future "mini-Wingspread" meetings across the county.

Judith Kase at the opening sessions called for assessment of areas of theoretical agreement and necessary disagreement so that mutual support could grow. Large areas of agreement were found and bonds for mutual support were cemented. Wingspread was indeed a success.

NOTES

[1] A planning committee selected the participants who came to Racine at their own expense. A list of those attending the conference and the Johnson Foundation Staff follows this article.

[2] "Conversations from Wingspread," three tapes on creative drama and the education of children were also recorded at this time. Program No. R-421 with Carol Halsted, Program No. R-422 with Barbara Salisbury and Ann Shaw and Program No. R-423 with Orlin Corey and Jed Davis are available from the Johnson Foundation, Racine, Wisconsin 53401.

[3] David Rockefeller, Jr., Chairman, *Coming to Our Senses* (New York: McGraw-Hill Book Company, 1977), p. 248.

[4] Jed H. Davis and Tom Behm, "Terminology of Drama/Theatre with and for Children: A Redefinition," *Children's Theatre Review*, XXVII, 1, 1978, pp. 10-11.

[5] The term "generalist" applies to elementary, middle school and high school subject oriented teachers as well as such support personnel as curriculum advisors, guidance counselors, school librarians, media specialists, special needs staffs, the administrators of the elementary and middle school systems and college professors of education.

[6] The term "specialist" applies to high school drama teachers and department chairpersons, district drama supervisors, elementary school drama specialists, theatre pedagogues, artists in residence, materials and curriculum developers, children's theatre artists, state department of education and special education drama specialists, arts team members, college professors of child drama.

[7] It is important for those in theatre education to act as "change agents," within the system and help create new jobs in the area.

APPENDIX
LIST OF PARTICIPANTS

Tom Behm, NC; Orlin Corey, LA; Shirley Corey, LA; Jed Davis, KS; Ruth Denny, TX; Mary Jane Evans, CA; Moses Goldberg, NY; Jeanne Hall, CA; Carol Halsted, WI; Brian Hansen, DE; Ruth Beall Heinig, MI; Ann S. Hill, TN; Carole C. Huggins, DC; Anna May Hughes, MD; Coleman A. Jennings, TX; Thomas C. Kartak, TN; Judith B. Kase, FL; Elizabeth F. Kelly, OH; Carol Korty, MA; Virginia Koste, MI; Lynne Kramer, NJ; Jack Morrison, DC; Bart O'Connor, MA; Helane Rosenberg, ND; Bernard S. Rosenblatt, MO; Barbara Salisbury, WA; Jane Schisgall, MD; Dorothy Schwartz, AL; Ann Shaw, NY; Wallace Smith, IL; Patricia Snyder, NY; Anne Thurman, IL; Jearnine Wagner, TX; Patricia Whitton, CT; Ann Haggerty Wright, RI; Lin Wright, AZ. *Observer:* C.A. Edington, WI. *The Johnson Foundation Staff:* Leslie Paffrath, President; Henry Halsted, Vice President-Program; Rita Goodman, Vice President-Area Programs; Richard Kinch, Program Associate; Kay Mauer and Penny Deming, Coordinators for the Conference.

LIST OF PRECONFERENCE READINGS
Published Books and Articles:
Davis, Jed H. and Tom Behm, "Terminology of Drama/Theatre with and for Children: A Redefinition," *Children's Theatre Review*, XXVII, 1,

1978, pp. 10-11.

Kelly, Elizabeth, "Dramatics in the Classroom: Making Lessons Come Alive." Bloomington, Indiana: The Phi Delta Kappa Educational Foundation, 1976.

Rockefeller, David, Jr., Chairman. *Coming to Our Senses.* New York: McGraw-Hill Book Company, 1977.

Sharpham, John, Chairman. "Report: Drama in Eduation," *Theatre News,* Summer, 1977.

Siks, Geraldine Brian. *Drama with Children.* New York: Harper & Row, Publishers, 1977.

Wagner, Betty Jane. *Dorothy Heathcote — Drama as a Learning Medium.* Wash., D.C.: National Education Association, 1976.

Unpublished Articles and Papers:

Goldberg, Moses. "Aesthetic Development: A Position Paper," New York.

Kase, Judith. "Cleveland Seminar Report." Tampa, Florida

SCA/ATA. "Competency Models in Communication and Theatre for Preparation and Certification of Elementary and Secondary School Specialists and Non-Specialists."

Siks, Geraldine, Chairman. "Statement of Standards for Children's Theatre Association of America." CTAA Committee Report.

Whitton, Pat Hale, ed. "Attleboro Conference Working Paper on Theatre and Drama for Children."

Lin Wright is CTAA's Vice-President for Research and teaches at Arizona State U., Tempe.

Note: This report has been augmented by the published deliberations of subsequent Wingspread and other conferences held from 1983 to 1986. See *Philosophy, Scope and Sequence for a Model Drama/Theatre Curriculum,* a National Theatre Education Project sponsored by the American Association of Theatre in Secondary Education, and the American Association of Theatre for Youth, 1986.

APPENDIX 4

A GLOSSARY OF ACRONYMS AND OTHER SHORTHAND TERMINOLOGY

AACT	American Association of Community Theatre
AACT/FEST	Festival of the American Association of Community Theatre
AAE	Alliance for Arts Education
AATSE	American Association of Theatre in Secondary Education
AATY	American Association of Theatre for Youth
ACTF	American College Theatre Festival
AITA/IATA	Association Internationale du Theatre Amateur/International Amateur Theatre Association
ANTA	American National Theatre and Academy
ASSITEJ	Association Internationale du Theatre pour l'Enfance et la Jeunesse (International Association of Theatre for Children and Young People). ASSITEJ/U.S.A. is the United States Center for ASSITEJ.
ATEJ	Association du Theatre pour l'Enfance et la Jeunesse (Association of Theatre for Children and Young People)
ATHE	Association for Theatre in Higher Education
BCA	Business Committee for the Arts
BCTA	British Children's Theatre Association
CEMREL	Central Midwest Regional Education Laboratory (now defunct)
CTR	Children's Theatre Review
DIE	Drama in Education
DOE	Department of Education; formerly the Office of Education (OE) of the Department of Health, Education and Welfare (HEW)
ITI	International Theatre Institute (agency of UNESCO)
JPTA	Job Placement and Training Act; successor to the Comprehensive Employment and Training Administration (CETA)
KC	John F. Kennedy Center for the Performing Arts, Washington, D.C.
NAST	National Association of Schools of Theatre
NCAH	National Committee, Arts with the Handicapped (now Very Special Arts)
NEA	National Endowment for the Arts
NEH	National Endowment for the Humanities
NIE	National Institute of Education (agency of DOE)
NRPA	National Recreation and Parks Association
PACT	Producers Association of Children's Theatre (New York City)
PTA	Parent-Teacher Association

276

TIE	Theatre in Education
TIUZ	Theatre for Young Spectators (USSR)
TJ	*Theatre Journal;* formerly *Educational Theatre Journal* (ETJ)
UNESCO	United Nations Educational, Scientific, and Cultural Organization
UNIMA	Union Internationale de la Marionnettes (agency of UNESCO)
USITT	United States Institute for Theatre Technology
Wingspread	Conference Center of the Johnson Foundation, Racine, Wisconsin
YMCA	Young Men's Christian Association
YM-YWHA	Young Men's and Young Women's Hebrew Association
YTJ	*Youth Theatre Journal*
YWCA	Young Women's Christian Association

These acronyms indicate divisions and programs of the American Theatre Association (ATA) which is now inactive. They are included here because they may still be encountered in the field, and are used occasionally in this book.

ACTA	American Community Theatre Association (Division of ATA)
ATA	American Theatre Association
CTAA	Children's Theatre Association of America; formerly Children's Theatre Conference (CTC), Children's Theatre Association (CTA) (Division of ATA)
FACT	Festival of American Community Theatre (program of ACTA)
SSTA	Secondary School Theatre Association (Division of ATA)
UCTA	University and College Theatre Association (Division of ATA)

APPENDIX 5

SAMPLE PROMPT BOOK PAGES

Following is an exerpt from the closing story of *Tales from Hans Christian Andersen,* a musical by Mary Jane Evans, Deborah Anderson and Ed Archer. Adapted from four Andersen tales, it is played in modified story theatre style. One character, the Storyteller, handles all narration, and others emerge from the ensemble to assume characterizations as the stories unfold. Those not playing individual roles are spectators and members of the singing and dancing chorus.

The premiere production was staged to perform in a variety of proscenium theatres as well as in three-quarter arena. The set consisted of solidly constructed units built to resemble books. The central unit was the only non-weight bearing structure. It was open at the top, and its spine opened to provide a doorway. The 6″ platform immediately to its left and the 6″ platform shown protruding from the 1′6″ platform on the right of the set were moveable.[1]

The sample prompt book pages are included to demonstrate a simple and practical method of recording basic blocking as it evolves and finally is set. Members of the ensemble are designated by capital letters, A through K. The Storyteller is abbreviated ST. Actor A becomes Jack (JA); actor G, Harold (HA); actor H, Olaf (OL); actor J, Squire (SQ). Standard abbreviations are used for specifying stage areas — DRC for down right center, for example. Other standard abbreviations inlcude X for cross, ∧ to mean rise and ↙ to indicate that an actor sits. A circle with an arrow — ⟲ — indicates the direction an actor faces.

If the director elects to use the blocking suggested in the script, it should be underlined; if not, it should be crossed out. Each movement is designated by a number at the appropriate place in the script and is detailed on the facing page in an entry carrying the corresponding number. Each script page is numbered separately. This is only one of many possible systems that may be used. Every director will develop a method for blocking notation best suited to his purpose. The system is not as important as the need to have one and to follow it consistently. It also is essential that the cast and all directorial assistants understand it.

[1]This production was directed by Mary Jane Evans. The setting was designed by Owen W. Smith, costumes by Cathy Susan Pyles, all of California State University, Northridge.

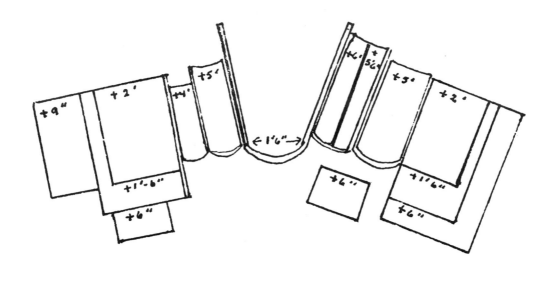

(1) ST squatting; others sitting, leaning, kneeling; Focus on ST.

(2) H becomes OL; ∧ X UR, Gets stool, X DR, ↙ ⟲.

(3) G becomes HA; ∧ X UL, Gets stool, X L, ↙ ⟳; A becomes JA, X DR to OL, hold C, bewildered; ST X UR onto 2' platform; E, K, F, C + B exit over R platForms; F, D, I exit over + around L platForms

(4) JA X L To HA, Then URC To ST.

(5) JA X Toward DL, DR, C, bowing.

(6) JA ↙ C ⚲.

(7) ST ↙ 4' book UR.

(8) JA ∧, X R above + L oF OL.

(9) OL ∧, X above stool, below JA, To DC area. Figure 8 pace pattern

(10) JA Follows OL. Dance Fills C area.

280

TALES FROM HANS CHRISTIAN ANDERSEN

Story Four: "Numbskull Jack"

<u>ENSEMBLE gathers around the STORYTELLER.</u> Music of opening song plays under the narrative. [(1)]

STORYTELLER: Somewhere in the country there was an old manor house, and in the old manor house there lived an old squire. He had two sons, and those sons were brainy as could be. One knew the Latin dictionary by heart. [(2)]His name was Olaf.

OLAF: <u>(Separating from the group. Music out.)</u> Books, pencils, papers, pens . . .

STORYTELLER: The other, whose name was Harold, was a brilliant mathematician.

HAROLD: [(3)]<u>(Separating from the group)</u> Measures, slide rules, formulas, fancy clothes . . . What have I forgotten?

JACK: [(4)]Me!

STORYTELLER: Oh, yes, There was a [(5)]third brother, though nobody thought he counted for very much, for he was not as clever as the other two. In fact, they forgot about him more often than not. But when they thought of him at all, they called him [(6)]Numbskull Jack.

Now this was a very special day. You see, the Princess had announced that she would take for her husband the man who was never at a loss for an answer. Olaf and Harold both decided to propose to the Princess, and felt quite equal to the task. They had prepared themselves for a whole week, and that was plenty of time, for they were clever and well schooled. [(7)]

<u>(HAROLD and OLAF are thinking and rehearsing,</u> unaware of anything around them. [(8)] <u>JACK approaches OLAF.)</u>

JACK: What are you doing?

OLAF: [(9)]Never mind! Sum-es-sunt; sumus-estes-sunt; eram-eras-erat; eramus-eratus-erant.

<u>(JACK imitates OLAF's gestures and movements. Music for a tap dance comes in, and JACK begins to dance. OLAF, without thinking, joins in and creates a lively dance as he continues his conjugations.)</u>

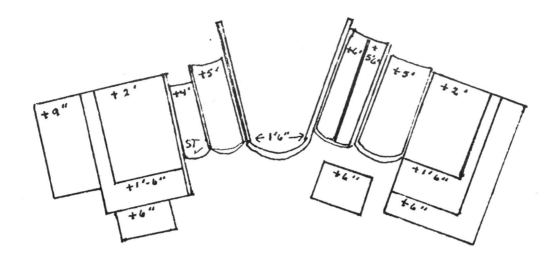

(1) OL stops dance; JA continues a beat; OL pushes JA ULC; OL x to stool R, ↙.

(2) JA x Toward OL, then L above & R of HA.

(3) HA ∧ ⊘; plays L & DL area.

(4) JA x DC ⊘. Ensemble enters:

      B from UL; stand DL corner of 6" & 1'6"

      C through C door w/ white hobby-horse; stand L of dock on 6".

      D over R platforms w/ billy-goat; ↙ DR corner of R 1'6".

      E over R platforms; stand DS on R 9"

      F Through C door w/ black hobby horse; stand R of door.

      I over L platforms; stand on L 2'

      J over R platforms; stand middle of R 2'

      K over L 9"; stand at its DS corner

(5) HA pushes JA Toward RC & goes to L stool, ↙.

(6) JA x to UR of HA.

(7) OL ∧, starts Toward HA; JA starts Toward OL; JA, between OL & HA, is pushed back & forth LC Toward URC; JA Falls DLC. Fight continues.

(8) JA ∧.

(9) OL & HA stand RC, HA R of OL.

(10) JA x RC, drives OL & HA DR to LL below platforms. JA ends C.

(11) SG enters from UR platforms; x to JA; pushes him R. JA Falls. SG x to OL & HA LL.

OLAF: Amo-amas-amat; amamus-amatus-amat. Hic-haec-hoc; huius-huius-huius. Fui-fuis-tis-fuit . . . E. Pluribus Unum!

[1](OLAF realizes what is happening and comes to an abrupt halt.)

What's going on here? Out! Go! Scat!

JACK: [2]Just tell me what you're doing!

[3](HAROLD has been unaware of all that has happened. Now he begins to do sums in the air, gesturing vigorously. [4]JACK turns to him and begins to imitate his movements until they become those of an orchestra conductor as academic music swells. The ENSEMBLE enters and hums the melody.)

HAROLD: When executing the construction of our popular parallelogram, please note that an important observation must be made. Being four-sided more often than not, this structure bears a striking resemblance to our common square. To put this formula into effect, one must divide the sum total of the length times width by the density of the parallelogram's interior. Let me see . . . six thirds times four plus . . .

[5](HAROLD becomes aware of JACK. Music stops abruptly.)

What's happening here? Out-out-out!

JACK: [6]Just tell me what you're doing!

HAROLD: Preparing to win the Princess for my bride.

OLAF: [7](Moving menacingly toward HAROLD) For *my* bride!

(OLAF and HAROLD tussle, both physically and verbally. JACK for a moment is caught in the middle, then is pushed aside.)

JACK: [8]I'm coming, too!

BROTHERS: (United) [9]Over my dead body!

[10](JACK draws an imaginary sword and drives them across the stage. [11]SQUIRE enters.)

SQUIRE: Out-out-out! And now, my brilliant, witty and charming sons . . .

(The horses are hobby-horses, brought forward by members of the ENSEMBLE. Each horse movement is accompanied by clopping sounds made on rhythm instruments.)

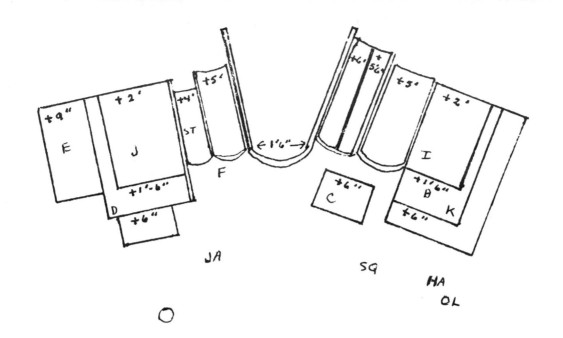

(1) C brings horse to R of SQ; returns to place.

(2) F brings horse to R of SQ; returns to place

(3) HA & OL gallop DR.

(4) JA ∧

(5) JA X LC to SQ.

(6) SQ X RC & on to HA & OL.

(7) HA & OL X figure & DR to LL & exit DR. SQ x DR to wave.

(8) SQ starts LL; JA stops him C

(9) SQ continues LL

(10) JA follows SQ, who stops.

(11) JA X R to stool; ∠

(12) SQ x to JA, then to DL stool; takes stool & exits LL.

(13) D ∧, edges LC, jingling bells on billy-goat. JA ∧.

(14) D gives goat to JA & takes R stool off UR.

(15) JA gallops, zig-zag counterclockwise course around stage. Ensemble points DR.

(16) JA exits L.

284

SQUIRE: (1)(To HAROLD) A white horse for you, all saddled and ready. (To OLAF) (2) A black one for you. What a beauty it is!

(3)(HAROLD and OLAF gallop aside.)

JACK: (4)Where is my horse? Haven't you forgotten something? (Ignored) (5)Your're forgetting someone!

SQUIRE: (6)(Brushing JACK aside) Enough of that! (To the BROTHERS) Now be off. And may the best man win.

BROTHERS: (7)(Riding off, *ad lib* argument, as they go) I will! No, *I* will! ...

JACK: (Above the din) (8)I'm going, too! (9)(SQUIRE laughs) (10)All of a sudden I feel like getting married. If she takes me, she takes me. And if she doesn't, (11)I'll take her anyway!

SQUIRE: (12)Stuff and nonsense! You'll get no horse from me! Why, you've never had a sensible answer to anything. But take your brothers now . . . that's a different matter. They're a couple of bright sparks with answers to spare.

(SQUIRE exits, laughing. (13)An ENSEMBLE member comes forward with a billy-goat fashioned like a hobby-horse. Its movements are accompanied by a cow bell.)

JACK: (14)I don't need a horse. I'll take the billy-goat. It's my own, and quite strong enough to carry me.

(Music for JACK's ride. He gallops about the stage, trying to decide which way to go. Despite the fact that the entire ENSEMBLE point in the right direction, he takes off in the wrong one, calling as he goes until his voice grows faint.)

STORYTELLER: (15)So Jack seated himself astride his billy-goat, dug his heels into its sides, and galloped away down the highroad.

JACK: (16)Whee! I'm off! Hey-ho, out of my way!

APPENDIX 6

TEACHER'S GUIDE
TO THE K.U. THEATRE FOR YOUNG PEOPLE PRODUCTION OF

RAGS TO RICHES

by Aurand Harris

Produced by special arrangement with
The Anchorage Press, New Orleans

Performances of *Rags To Riches* are scheduled as follows:

Wednesday	September 27	1:00 PM	Reserved for County Schools
Thursday	September 28	1:00 PM	Reserved for children in grades 4, 5, and 6 of Lawrence Unified
Friday	September 29	1:00 PM	School District 497 and St. John's School.
Saturday	September 30	10:30 AM	This performance is open to the public.

TICKETS FOR THE 4TH, 5TH AND 6TH GRADERS ONLY will be available at the schools according to the schedule announced by the Director of Fine Arts for the Lawrence Unified School District.

COMPLIMENTARY ADMISSION will be available to children in grades 4, 5, and 6 unable to pay the admission price, and to all teachers and administrators of the attending schools. Requests for complimentary admissions are filed by the teachers with the District. Complimentary tickets are also available to the teachers throughout the system regardless of grade taught.

TICKETS FOR 1ST, 2ND, AND 3RD GRADERS will be available only through the Murphy Hall Box Office. These children, their parents, and others may attend only the Saturday performance. All seats are reserved and the admission price is $1.50. No complimentary tickets will be available to those children not included in the in-school attendance plan.

COUNTY SCHOOLS AND THOSE OUTSIDE THE LAWRENCE UNIFIED SCHOOL DISTRICT. We have reserved for them the Wednesday, September 27, 1:00 PM performance. Children will attend in class groups, and the admission price is the same as that applied locally. Complimentary tickets are available for teachers and administrators. Reservations should be made in advance of the performance.

THE IN-SCHOOL ATTENDANCE PLAN is designed to provide an optimum theatre-going experience for the elementary school child. With this in mind, the K.U. Theatre for Young People and the Director of Fine Arts for the Lawrence Unified School District 497, Gary Kroeger, have designed this guide to aid the teacher with in-school preparation. It is hoped that this will help make the theatre experience educationally, as well as culturally enriching.

The Story of the Play

Richard Hunter, more commonly known on the streets of New York as Ragged Dick, plies his trade as a shoe shine boy, making a modest living for himself since becoming an orphan at age seven. But he is a stalwart lad who, as we shall see, will rise in the world and become a success. The first step up the ladder for this poor but honest 14-year-old is provided by Mr. Greyson, who stops for a shoe shine on his way to work and asks Dick to change a $2 bill. Dick is glad to do this little extra service to get the promised 60¢ tip from the rich banker when he delivers the change; but when he tries to get Mickey Maguire, a dishonest acquaintance, to change the bill, Mickey tries to cheat him by claiming the money is counterfeit. A friendly Policeman and Mr. Greyson expose Mickey's trick, and Mickey vows revenge. With his profits, Dick buys apples from kindly old Mrs. Flanagan for his breakfast. As Dick leaves to pursue further business in shoe shines, evil old Mother Watson, as villainous a villain as there ever was, comes in looking for her ward, Mark, the Match Boy, whom she keeps with her in order to use his meager income to keep herself supplied with whiskey. Brandishing her little whip, Mother Watson scolds Mark for spending one of his few pennies to buy a piece of bread for his breakfast, takes his matches from him and orders him to beg in the streets if he can't earn money otherwise. Reluctantly, Mark tries to beg from passers-by; but he is ill and heartsick at having sunk so low. As Mrs. Flanagan sadly sings "Poor Little Orphan Laddie," Mark trudges on down the street.

Meanwhile, Ragged Dick returning the change from the $2 bill, has arrived at the Fifth Avenue mansion of Mr. Greyson, where the banker's lovely young daughter, Ida, is having tea. Admitted into the sitting room by the pert French maid, Mimi, Dick finds himself ill at ease in these rich surroundings; but with the understanding and sympathy of the considerate Ida, he soon relaxes into the friendly atmosphere of the Greyson home. In fact, Ida offers to give the unschooled shoe-shine boy lessons in numbers, grammar, etiquette and social graces. When her father returns, Ida and Mr. Greyson are so impressed with Dick's honesty they give him a new suit of clothes and retain him as a special detective to locate a long lost boy, a relative who had been disowned by his grandfather and has now become heir to a large fortune. "If he is in the streets," declares Dick with determination, "I will find him."

Back on the cold, friendless street, Mark the Match Boy holds his mother's faded photo in his hands and sings of his misery since she died and left him alone in this cruel world. Mickey Maguire, the bully we saw earlier, emerges from the shadows to force Mark to yield up his few pennies; but fortunately Dick arrives just in time to take on the bigger boy and return Mark's money. Sensing Mark's desperate straits, Dick offers to let him stay in his own sparsely furnished room; but before they can leave, Mother Watson, drunk as usual, returns to chide Mark, beat him, and bring him back into her service. Dick stands up to her bravely, taking Mark's part and wrenching away the old hag's whip; and just as they are about to engage in real battle, the Policeman arrives to send Mother Watson on her way. And she, too, vows revenge against this interfering do-gooder. The Act ends with a rousing Finale describing the American ideal of climbing the ladder of success from a humble but honest beginning.

Act II begins with a scene depicted on countless Christmas cards. The snow is falling, carollers are singing under the lamp post, shoppers are hurrying to and fro along the New York Street. And Mark the Match Boy, trying desperately to sell his matches, collapses in the snow, ill with fatigue and fever. Up in Dick's room, Dick tries to find a way to get Mark badly needed doctor's attention. His prayer is answered by the arrival of his tutor, Ida, who offers the Greyson family physician to minister to his sick friend. But as Mark lies helpless, Mother Watson and Mickey conspire to cheat him out of his rightful inheritance. Yes, word has gotten around that "they're looking for a lost boy" who is heir to a fortune. His name is John Talbot, says Mickey to Mother Watson. But Mother Watson knows that John Talbot is really Mark the Match Boy, and she contrives a way to steal the photograph of Mark's real mother and pass Mickey off as the long-lost grandson. The plan almost works, but for the timely arrival of Dick at the Greyson mansion; and he has no trouble identifying Mickey Maguire as his old street acquaintance and not John Talbot at all. Just then, a fire alarm sounds, and the street is filled with firemen, panicky onlookers, and frantic tenants. Mrs. Flanagan, flustered and terrified, announces that Mark the Match Boy is trapped on the top floor of the burning building. The tenement is a blazing inferno, says a fireman; no one could go in there now. But who is this just arriving on the scene? It is Dick, our hero. "I will save him!" cries Dick;

and he plunges into the burning building. The saga of his daring rescue is told in song and mime by the excited onlookers. Against incredible odds and untold perils, Dick brings his friend, Mark, safely through the flames to the street below where he is proclaimed a true hero. And to make things come out even better, Greyson immediately recognizes his long-lost nephew, proclaiming Mark the Match Boy heir to a fortune, and offering Richard Hunter, formerly Ragged Dick, a well-paying situation in his own bank.

"We've made our fortune, Mark. We've come from rags to riches," says Dick proudly, and the entire company joins the two heroes in a stirring tribute to the possibilities America offers to all her industrious citizens.

About the Play

Aurand Harris, one of America's most prominent playwrights for young audiences, wrote *Rags to Riches* in 1966. It was selected by Coleman A. Jennings as one of the plays to be included in *Six Plays for Children by Aurand Harris* (Univ. of Texas Press, 1977). The K.U. Theatre for Young People has previously done Harris' *Androcles and the Lion, Steal Away Home* (just last Fall), *The Brave Little Tailor,* and *Punch and Judy.* His work is honored by many awards, and his writings about the children's theatre playwriting field are highly regarded. Harris often serves as guest professor at some of our leading universities, and is said to be "America's most produced children's theatre playwright."

The Sources

Harris based his play, *Rags to Riches,* on two novels by Horatio Alger, Jr.: *Ragged Dick* and *Mark the Match Boy.* Both of these famous "dime novels" were written and published in 1868, originally appearing as serialized episodes in the popular boys' magazine, *Student and Schoolmate.* Alger's novel, *Ragged Dick,* is cited today in the Grolier collection as one of the hundred most significant books published before 1900. The publishing firm of Collier-Macmillan brought out an edition of the two novels in a single paperback volume in 1962, and it has been consistently reprinted since then, even as late as 1973. This fact may attest to some sort of resurgence of popularity of Alger's most famous works.

In this connection, it is interesting to note that, far fetched as Alger's situations appear now to be, they were based on actual fact, in most instances. If not a great literary artist, Alger was at least an accurate chronicler of his times — the post Civil War urban readjustment period. Homeless, fatherless Drummer-boys, mustered out of the Union Army, descended en masse on the streets of New York. They plied lowly occupations such as shoe shine boys (like Dick), match sellers (like Mark), newspaper vendors (like Mickey), messengers, beggars, street musicians, and errand boys. They made a marginal living in most cases, and were grateful to seek a clean bed and breakfast (each for 6¢) at the Newsboy's Lodging House, the upper two floors of the *Sun* Building, founded by philanthropist Charles Loring Brace in 1853. The publication of *Ragged Dick* in 1868 brought Alger to the Lodge where he lived most of the rest of his lonely life and where he became friends with and gathered the stories of hundreds of actual street boys to use in his novels.

The World of Horatio Alger

The man who gave his name over a hundred years ago to the prototype of the American Dream himself never really achieved his highest ambition to become an author of literary stature comparable to the giants who were his contemporaries: Charles Dickens, Mark Twain, or Hans Christian Andersen, all of whom wrote classics of children's literature still regarded at the top of the charts. Yet Alger's works were enormously popular in his time. It is said his 120 novels sold some 17 million copies, though some have estimated the sale as high as 120 million copies! They were read, at any rate, by many more boys (and girls, too) than bought the books, either in serial or bound form. Through these rather unimaginatively written pages, they were introduced to the wonders of New York City life (he was a most accurate guide to the sights of the great wicked city). And his thin plots, full of most improbable coincidences, were a constant reassurance that if:

> one is virtuous and deserving;
> one is honest and sober;
> one is industrious and thrifty;
> one has a strong religious faith;
> one takes advantage of educational opportunities;
> one stands for decency and honor;

and

> despite a deprived background;
> despite poor beginnings;
> despite dirty clothes (if it's honest dirt);

and

> with a little bit of luck —

then

> one may rise to the very pinnacle of financial success in this land of opportunity.

Alger, of course did not invent this philosophy. He had good help from William Penn and Benjamin Franklin (Poor Richard). And he had living, or recently living, examples of the very truth in Andrew Carnegie, the poor immigrant boy from Scotland who later built half our country's libraries, and in Abraham Lincoln, who changed his address from log cabin to White House.

The strength of the Alger pattern of respect for those who rise from humble beginnings to fame and fortune, can be seen daily on television and in the newspapers. A recent advertisement in a local newspaper placed by a candidate for public office chronicled this gentleman's rise from a humble farm background through adversity and poverty and, by way of superhuman efforts to gain an education, his emergence into the world of big business, big agriculture, and big politics.

The Horatio Alger success story never fails to stir our hearts. And its strength is as formidible today as it was in 1868 when *Ragged Dick* first appeared in print.

Melodrama in the Theatre

Rags to Riches is called a musical melodrama for children. While a less sophisticated age may have provided a theatre full of adults enthusiastically cheering the hero or hissing the villain, such behavior shows up today mostly at productions designed to spoof the venerable old melodrama form. We do, of course, experience such behavior to some extent from child audiences quite regularly.

In melodrama there is no doubt which characters are good and which are bad. To make things even clearer, actors adapt an acting style that is best described as "pointed," or perhaps "declamatory." Speeches are delivered almost always directly front; and "asides" are given to the audience which most of the time are not supposed to be "heard" by the other characters on stage. Melodramas are full of plot complications and surprising coincidences. They also tend to exploit theatrical spectacle in such scenes as the burning tenement, or the grandeur of the Greyson mansion. In this case singing and dancing become an integral part of the play's theatricality. Familiar to the children will be such tunes as "Oh, Suzannah," "Here We Go Round the Mulberry Bush," "Glow Worm," and "Sidewalks of New York."

Traditionally supporting this kind of production is a scenic scheme that uses painted perspective on backdrops almost exclusively. This aspect of *Rags to Riches* may be a somewhat new experience for the children since we have not used the painted drop in this way in our productions in recent years. There may be some surprises in store as various "realistic" effects are depicted in this style. Such drops are regarded in the theatre as supreme triumphs of the scene painter's art. Also the children may be told to expect that each major musical number will have some additional "signature" piece added to the basic scene. For instance, when Mark the Match Boy is singing about his loneliness, a large portrait of his departed mother is lowered into the scene; or when the ensemble sings of climbing the ladder of success in this land of opportunity, a large American flag descends to grace the scene. Lighting, too, will play an important role in the spectacle. Footlights will be used prominently throughout the show, and a "follow spot" will highlight the solo performers in musical numbers.

Suggested Classroom Activities

Rags to Riches offers unusual opportunities for classroom enrichment. Alger was meticulous in providing details of money transactions — the rents charged for rooms of various degrees of luxury, the price of suits of clothes, costs of meals at various restaurants, trolley fares, interest rates, tips, and mortgage terms.

From this perspective, children could be encouraged to explore old newspaper and magazine advertisements to discover prices of things of interest to them (such as automobiles, clothes, refrigerators, appliances of all kinds); then compare these prices with prices for similar items today. It will be a good exercise in perceiving effects of inflation, but mainly it will provide an index to changing times. Such a study can, of course, lead many directions other than the monetary ones.

Along this same line, children might bring in and explain their games of Monopoly, Acquire, or Life — all of which have monetary concerns at their base.

Some of the children may have coin collections, or stamp collections. They might like to explain how the value of the coins or stamps has increased over their face value, and what factors contribute to their value.

Another investigation might be made by some interested children into the lives of some of America's "self-made" persons: Andrew Carnegie, Henry Ford, Thomas Alva Edison, etc. Or they might be encouraged to keep an eye out for reports of "Alger-like" success stories appearing in papers and magazines. And, of course, if any one has a collection of Alger's novels, it would be an interesting thing to share with the class. (One of our cast members has inherited almost a complete set of Alger dime novels from her grandfather. And the Spencer Research Library on the K.U. campus has a formidible collection in its "rare books" section.)

On still another level, children might discuss what they would save up their money for if they lived in Ragged Dick's time.

Since he lived in a period when there were no effective child labor laws, what kinds of jobs might they try to get to earn money with? How much could they expect to get paid for their work?

And if they had no mother or father, no home, and very little money except what they could earn, what would their lives be like? What personal resources would they draw on in order to survive?

Such questions as the above suggest many possibilities for exploration in creative drama ways.

And, of course, the personnel of the K.U. Theatre for Young People would, as always, be most interested in hearing from you and and children what thoughts were generated by the play, in written form or as art work.

APPENDIX 7

TEACHER'S PRODUCTION EVALUATION FORM

This form may be distributed to teachers following a production. Teachers record on an opinion scale of 1 to 10 their subjective observations of the class' response to the occurrences on stage. (Form used by the KU-Theatre for Young People.)

TO: Teachers
Please indicate your answer to the following questions by ranking on a scale of 1 (low) to 10 (high) using your best subjective judgment; or answer appropriately:

1. Did the children in your class appear to understand what was happening in the play?

    1   2   3   4   5   6   7   8   9   10

2. Would you identify the portion(s) that seemed to confuse them?

3. Did the children in your class seem attentive most of the time?

    1   2   3   4   5   6   7   8   9   10

4. What segment(s) appeared to lose their attention?

5. To what extent was an undesirable level of excitement generated by the production?

    1   2   3   4   5   6   7   8   9   10

6. What incidents caused excessive excitement?

7. To what extent was an undesirable level of fear generated by the production?

    1   2   3   4   5   6   7   8   9   10

8. What incidents appeared to cause an excessive fear response?

9. Did the children discuss the play freely after it was over?

    1   2   3   4   5   6   7   8   9   10

10. Do you think the experience was a meaningful one (in an educative sense) for the children?

    1   2   3   4   5   6   7   8   9   10

11. How do you think this production ranks with the others in the TYP series that you have seen?

    1   2   3   4   5   6   7   8   9   10

12. Please indicate the level at which you prepared the children for seeing the play.

1	2	3	4	5	6	7	8	9	10

i.e.:   10   extensive preparation, including telling or reading the synopsis of plot, discussing background and thematic concepts, and engaging in some related activities.

      4   told or read the story

      2   told them the title of the play

      1   none

APPENDIX 8

THEATRE INFORMATION FORM

A sample "Theatre Information Form," completed by sponsors and supplied to the producing company's stage manager.

UNIVERSITY OF KANSAS
THEATRE FOR YOUNG PEOPLE

THEATRE INFORMATION FORM

Name of Theatre_____

Theatre Location_____. _____ , _____
                         (street)   (city)   (state)

Sponsoring Organization _____

****

I. HOUSE

How many seats?   main floor _____   Is the house floor sloped?   yes _____
                          mezzanine _____   no_____
                          balcony_____   Are there steps from   yes _____
                          total_____   house to stage?   no_____

Is the seating best described   as a standard auditorium?   _____
                                      a gymnasium floor   _____   (If none please describe
                                      a "cafetorium"?   _____   on the back of this sheet)
                                      a bleacher section?   _____

Would you say that the acoustics in the auditorium are   good? _____
                                                      fair?   _____
                                                        poor? _____

Are sight lines to the stage   good? _____   Can outside windows be
                              fair?   _____   blacked out?   yes _____
                              poor?   _____   no _____

II. ACCESS

Is there a *loading door* (easily accessible) having direct access from the driveway to the stage? _____

If there is *no* outside loading door, please describe how scenery, etc., can be brought from the truck to the stage, including sizes of intervening doors and hallways:

III. STAGE

Please fill in the dimensions requested. The numbered questions refer to the numbers on the diagram.

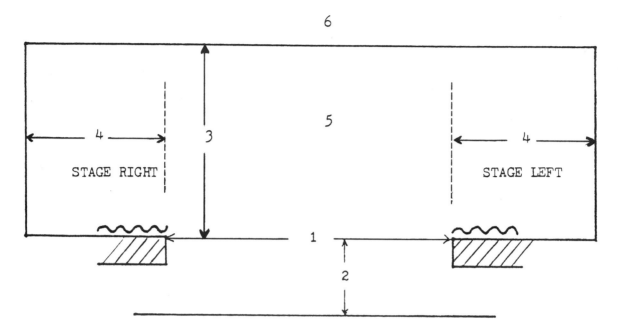

1. *proscenium opening* (distance between curtains when fully opened) _____ feet.
   proscenium height (height of the opening through which the audience sees the stage) _____ feet.
   Is there an adjustable teaser to control the height of the proscenium opening? _____

2. *apron depth* (usable acting space in front of the closed front curtain) _____ feet.

3. *depth* of stage (from proscenium to rear wall) _____ feet.
   height of stage (how many feet of free space above the stage floor before encountering a permanent obstruction?) _____ feet.

4. off stage wing space to the *right* of an actor facing an audience _____ ft.
   off stage wing space to the *left* of an actor facing an audience _____ ft.
   Are the off stage areas right and left the same height as that above the acting area? _____ If not, what are their heights? _____R; _____L

5. Is the stage equipped with a system for flying scenery? _____ If yes, is it a rope line _____, or a counterweight system _____? How many sets of lines are available? _____
   Indicate the position(s) of any *permanently hung curtains* other than the front curtain. (use diagram above)
   Is there a *sky cyclorama permanently hung* or available for use? _____
   Distance of each set of lines from the proscenium opening. Please indicate these distances on the above *diagram*.
   Does the stage contain traps (removable sections in the stage floor)? _____. If yes, how many? _____ What are their dimensions? ___ by ___. What is their location in relation to the proscenium? _____

6. *cross over* (with a setting in place that extends to the rear wall of the stage, is it possible to get from one side of the stage to the other without being seen by the audience?) _____

IV. LIGHTING

This company travels with a portable minimum lighting set-up which can be self-sufficient *(except for electrical power)* or can be used to supplement existing installations. The lighting effects for the production are designed in accordance with our "minimum lighting set-up" but the answers to the following questions will facilitate the mounting of our prepared "design" in your theatre.

POWER SUPPLY:

Is there a 110 volt, 100 ampere power supply within 50 feet of the

"behind the front curtain area"? _____

If *over* 50 feet, how far? _____

Do local regulations stipulate that the connection to the main power supply be made by a local man (school electrician, contractor, etc.)? _____ If so, please furnish _____ and _____. name

phone

LIGHT INSTRUMENT CONNECTIONS:

What type of connectors are used in your lighting system?

_____ pin connector, _____ twist lock, or _____ household.

Are there positions (architectural supports such as pipe battens or a balcony rail) for the hanging of spot lights out in the auditorium?

_____

Are there positions for hanging spot lights behind the front curtain?

_____

LIGHT CONTROL:

Describe the location of the light control board in relation to the front curtain or to the back stage area.

How many circuits are connected to this board? _____

How many dimmers, not permanently connected to lights, are there? _____

What wattage are the dimmers? _____

Someone, a drama student perhaps, familiar with the light board circuits should be present at the time the production is mounted. If such a person is available would you please supply the name and phone so that we can make contact on our arrival?

APPENDIX 9

A Sample "Agreement" form and "Division of Responsibilities" for Touring Programs

AGREEMENT

A signed copy of this form will indicate that an agreement exists between

_____
(name of sponsoring group)

_____
(address)

_____
(city, state, zip)

and the University Theatre of the University of Kansas, Lawrence, Kansas 66045

* * * * * * * * * * * * **

The University Theatre, or subdivision thereof, agrees to present _____ (no.) performance(s) of its pro-

duction of _____
(title)

in _____   _____
(auditorium)   (street)

_____ , at _____ on _____
(city)   (time)   (date)

under the sponsorship of the above named organization, in return for a fee of $_____.

The attached "Division of Responsibilities: Producer and Sponsor" is understood to be part of this agreement.

While every reasonable effort will be made by both parties to keep the terms of this agreement, it is understood that an engagement can be cancelled because of circumstances beyond control.

_____   _____
(signed: representing sponsor)   (signed: representing U. Theatre)

_____   _____
(date)   (date)

1. Please sign and return one copy of this form to the KU Theatre.
2. Payment in full should be made to the Company Manager before the company leaves the premises, unless other arrangements are made prior to arrival. Make check payable to KU — THEATRE FOR YOUNG PEOPLE.

DIVISION OF RESPONSIBILITIES:
PRODUCER AND SPONSOR

The Producer (The University of Kansas Theatre) agrees to:

1. Supply a production of the play named in the Agreement; both actors and technical crews will form the company which will be responsible for the effective mounting and running of performances. All costs of production, including royalties, scenery, costumes, properties, make-up, sound and lighting equipment (other than that supplied by the performance auditorium) will be borne by the producing group.
2. Adhere to the performance schedule as specified in the agreement.
3. Supply sample materials for local publicity and promotion.
4. Supply the company's meals and lodging during the period of the engagement.
5. Allow local students (high school or junior high school) to watch the set-up, strike, and loading processes. Company members will be available within reasonable limits to talk with students on theatrical matters and to assist local teachers with making the company's visit a significant part of an educational program.

The Sponsor agrees to:

1. Provide a suitable auditorium for the mounting of performances, bearing the costs of rental and necessary personnel for the use of the facilities. (Custodians, stage manager, electrician, ushers, ticket takers, ticket sellers, etc.)
2. Handle local publicity and promotion, ticket sales, and house management. In the case of a production for children, adequate chaperoning of the audience should be provided, as well as arrangements to transport the children to and from the place of performance.
3. Make the auditorium available to our stage manager and crews a minimum of _____ hours before announced performance time to permit set-up of scenery and lights.
4. Provide adequate dressing rooms (with mirrors) for a cast of _____ women and _____ men.
5. Provide microphones and sound amplification for the performance(s) if the acoustics of the auditorium make them necessary. (Producer will provide sound to be integrated with the production itself.)

The sponsor and others interested in this agreement are hereby notified and understand that any agency of the State of Kansas is immune from liability and suit on any implied contract, or for negligence, or any other tort pursuant to K.S.A. 46-901, and the parties agree that no provision herein, expressed or implied, special or otherwise, directly or indirectly shall be deemed to constitute a waiver of this immunity, notwithstanding any such provision to the contrary.

APPENDIX 10

PUBLISHERS OF PLAYS AND MATERIALS: THEATRE FOR CHILDREN AND YOUTH

ANCHORAGE PRESS, INC., P.O. Box 8067, New Orleans, LA 70182

BAKER'S PLAYS, 100 Chauncy Street, Boston, MA 02111

BOOSEY & HAWKES, P.O. Box 130, Oceanside, NY 11572

CENTERSTAGE PRESS, 4638 E. Shea Blvd., Suite B-150, Phoenix, AZ 85028

I.E. CLARK, INC., St. John's Road, Schulenburg, TX 78956

COACH HOUSE PRESS, INC., P.O. Box 458, Morton Grove, IL 60053

CONTEMPORARY DRAMA SERVICE, Box 7710-T, Colorado Springs, CO 80933

DAVID MCKAY CO., INC., 2 Park Ave., New York, NY 10010

DRAMATIC PUBLISHING CO., 4150 No. Milwaukee Ave., Chicago, IL 60641

DRAMATISTS PLAY SERVICE, INC., 440 Park Ave. So., New York, NY 10016

CARL FISCHER, INC., 56 Cooper Square, New York, NY 10003

HEINEMANN EDUCATIONAL BOOKS, INC., 4 Front Street, Exeter, NH 03833

INVOLVEMENT DRAMATICS, University Theatre, Oklahoma City University, Oklahoma City, OK 73106

MODERN THEATRE FOR YOUTH, 2366 Grandview Terrace, Manhattan, KS 66502

MUSIC THEATRE INTERNATIONAL, 119 West 57th Street, New York, NY 10019

NEW PLAYS, INC., Box 273, Rowayton, CT 06853

ON STAGE! P.O. Box 25365, Chicago, IL 60625-0365

PICKWICK PRESS, Midland Community Theatre, 2000 Wadley, Midland, TX 79701

PIONEER DRAMA SERVICE, 2171 So. Colorado Blvd., Denver, CO 80222

PLAYERS PRESS, P.O. Box 1132, Studio City, CA 91604

PLAYS, INC., PUBLISHERS, 8 Arlington Street, Boston, MA 02116

PLAYWRIGHTS UNION OF CANADA (PLAYWRIGHTS CO-OP), 8 York Street, 6th Floor, Toronto, Ontario, Canada M5J 1R2

READERS THEATRE SCRIPT SERVICE, P.O. Box 178333, San Diego, CA 92117

RODGERS AND HAMMERSTEIN LIBRARY, 598 Madison Ave., New York, NY 10022

SAMUEL FRENCH, INC., 45 West 25th St., New York, NY 10036; 7623 Sunset Blvd., Hollywood, CA 90046

G. SCHIRMER, INC., 40 West 62nd Street, New York, NY 10023

TAMS-WITMARK MUSIC LIBRARY, 757 Third Ave., New York, NY 10017

TELOS PRESS, Department of Sociology, Washington University, St. Louis, MO 63130

THEATRE ARTS BOOKS, 153 Waverly Place, New York, NY 10014

VIKING PRESS, 625 Madison Ave., New York, NY 10022

For information about unpublished playscript services of the American Association of Theatre for Youth, contact Roger Bedard, Executive Secretary, AATY, Theatre Arts Department, Virginia Tech, Blacksburg, VA 24061.

For catalogues of operas and musicals for young audiences, contact Opera for Youth, Box 219, Route 2, Athens, OH 45701.

APPENDIX 11

PLAY LIST

In this listing we present the basic facts on three hundred fifty playscripts, most of them available for production. Many of these have been cited in the preceding chapters in one context or another, but some are included to make their existence more widely known. A few are here merely to provide some historical information. For each playscript we provide title, category (if other than a straight drama), author(s), translator, and composer(s), agency controlling the rights and royalties, date(s) of composition or copyright, if known, cast requirements, sets, and a brief statement of its subject matter. We have tried to keep the summaries as clear of judgmental bias as possible, assuming each potential producer would wish to make up his own mind about the script's value after reading it in complete form.

Playscripts from the international repertoire which have not found publication in the United States are documented either according to Michael Pugh's "International Bibliography of Plays in Translation Recommended for Performance to Children and Youth," or Patricia Whitton's *Outstanding Plays for Young Audiences: International Bibliography* (see Chapter IV). Translators are not designated in either source.

Anthologies in which some of the playscripts appear are cited in shortened form. The anthologies referred to, plus others of interest, are:

Bedard, Roger, ed. *Dramatic Literature for Children: A Century in Review.* New Orleans: Anchorage Press, 1984.

Birner, William B., ed. *Twenty Plays for Young People:* New Orleans: Anchorage Press, 1967.

Donahue, John Clark. *The Cookie Jar and Other Plays.* ed. Linda Walsh Jenkins. Minneapolis: Univ. of Minnesota Press, 1975.

Donahue, John Clark, and Linda Walsh Jenkins, eds. *Five Plays from the Children's Theatre Company of Minneapolis.* Minneapolis: Univ. of Minnesota Press, 1975.

Doolittle, Joyce, ed. *Eight Plays for Young People: Prairie Performance II.* Edmonton: NeWest Press, 1984.

Hughes, Ted. *The Tiger's Bones and Other Plays for Children.* New York: Viking Press, 1974.

Jennings, Coleman A., and Gretta Berghammer, eds. *Theatre for Youth: Twelve Plays with Mature Themes.* Austin: Univ. of Texas Press, 1986.

Jennings, Coleman A., and Aurand Harris, eds. *Plays Children Love: A Treasury of Contemporary and Classic Plays for Children.* Garden City, NY: Doubleday and Co., Inc., 1981.

Jennings, Coleman A., ed. *Six Plays for Children by Aurand Harris.* Austin: Univ. of Texas Press, 1977.

Jonson, Marian. *Timblewit and Other Plays.* Chicago: Coach House Press, 1973.

Lifton, Betty Jean, ed. *Contemporary Children's Theatre.* New York: Avon, 1974.

Mamet, David. *Three Children's Plays.* New York: Grove Press, 1986.

Moe, Christian, and Darwin Reid Payne, eds. *Six New Plays for Children.* Carbondale: Southern Illinois Univ. Press, 1971.

Morton, Miriam, ed. and trans. *Russian Plays for Young Audiences.* Rowayton, CT: New Plays Books, 1977.

Moses, Montrose, ed. *Another Treasury of Plays for Children.* Boston: Little, Brown & Co., 1926.

Moses, Montrose, ed. *A Treasury of Plays for Children.* Boston: Little, Brown & Co., 1921.

Swortzell, Lowell, ed. *All the World's A Stage.* New York: Delacourt Press, 1972.

Swortzell, Lowell, ed. *Six Plays for Young People from the Federal Theatre Project (1936-1939).* New York: Greenwood Press, 1986.

Walker, Stuart. *Portmanteau Adaptations.* Cincinnati: Stewart & Kidd, 1921.

Zipes, Jack, ed. and trans. *Political Plays for Children.* St. Louis: Telos Press, 1976.

AN ADVENTURE OF BABAR, by Leon Chancerel and Jean de Brunhoff
A.T.E.J., 98 Boulevard Kellermann, Paris, France (Pugh) (n.d.); 7m, 3w, 1 puppet; 6 ext. Babar, the elephant, has adventures with an ostrich, a centaur and a tamer.

THE ADVENTURES OF BRER RABBIT (Musical), by Pat Hale; music by Paul Spong
New Plays, 1962. 8 m or w, 4 extras; 1 ext. Brer Rabbit's successes and near-failures when he encounters the other animals in the Briar Patch are depicted without the active participation of the Uncle Remus character.

ADVENTURES OF COYOTE, by Wendy Gray
Unpublished; information from Marie Starr, Dept. of Dramatic Art, Univ. of California, Santa Barbara, CA 93106 (1978); Company of 24 play many roles; open stage. Coyote loses his shadow and while trying to find it has several adventures in which he tricks others or is tricked by them.

THE ADVENTURES OF TOM SAWYER, by Charlotte B. Chorpenning
Coach House Press, 1956; 9m, 5w, 6 children, extras; 1 int., 3 ext. Boyhood adventures of Tom and his friends who test their mettle in dangerous antics, pitting their courage against forces of nature and the evils of men.

AESOP'S FALABLES (Musical), by Ed Graczyk; music by Shirley Hansen; lyrics by Marty Conine and Ed Graczyk; Anchorage Press, 1969; 13 people play 15 animals, a boy, and a Jack-in-the Box; neutral set with props. Sir Wilfred Wolf maintains he has been much maligned in fables and so he "reinterprets" several in a rock idiom.

ALADDIN, by William Glennon
Coach House Press, 1965; 10m, 8w; 2 ext. Some new twists on the familiar tale of the poor boy who acquires a magic lamp with its genii and, through difficulty, wins fortune and a princess.

ALADDIN, by Moses Goldberg
Anchorage Press, 1977; 3m, 2w, 1 mime; open stage with props. Peddlers become actors to present the story of Aladdin who, with the help of a genii of the lamp, acquires wealth and a princess, all with audience participation.

ALADDIN AND THE WONDERFUL LAMP, by James Norris
Anchorage Press, 1940; 8m, 4w, extras; 2 int., 1 ext. Geniis of the Ring and Lamp help a poor boy face the diabolical opposition of the greedy Magician to acquire great wealth and status, including the Sultan's daughter for his bride.

ALICE IN WONDER, by Virginia Koste
New Plays, 1971; 14m, 3w, 2 children, Cat, Dormouse, extras; 11 locations suggested, all exteriors. Alice follows the White Rabbit down the hole and encounters a succession of strange creatures who are rude and make insane demands on her.

ALICE IN WONDERLAND, by Charlotte B. Chorpenning
Coach House Press, 1956; 13m, 4w, 1 child, extras; draped stage, suggestively modified. The familiar scenes of Carroll's original are focused in plot as the fantastic characters of Wonderland work their bewildering magic on Alice.

ALICE IN WONDERLAND, by Alice Gerstenberg
Longman, 1941; 16m, 5w, 4 int., 3 ext. Favorite Victorian fantasy involving Alice's encounters with many strange creatures in the land beyond the rabbit hole.

ALICE IN WONDERLAND, by Eva LeGallienne and Florida Friebus
Samuel French, 1932; 50 speaking parts, extras; 7 int., 11 ext. Elaborate combination of Lewis Carroll's *Through the Looking Glass* and *Alice's Adventures in Wonderland*.

ALICE IN WONDERLAND, by Madge Miller
Anchorage Press, 1953; 2m, 4w, 7 animals; bare stage, suggestively set. Meandering Carroll plot is given focus around the theft of the Queen's tarts by the Knave, culminating in his trial.

AMAHL AND THE NIGHT VISITORS (Opera), by Gian Carlo Menotti
G. Schirmer, 1952; 4m, 1w, 1 boy, chorus, dancers; 1 int. Three kings on their way to Bethlehem stop to rest in the cottage of Amahl's mother and stay long enough to see the crippled boy's miraculous cure as he offers his crutch to the Christ child.

THE ANALYSIS OF MINERAL #4, by Moses Goldberg
Anchorage Press, 1982; 3m, 3w; 1 int. While searching for the composition of a sample meteor as part of a chemistry final, Aline, a high school girl, reaches conclusions about her unique self.

ANDROCLES AND THE LION, by Aurand Harris
Anchorage Press, 1964; 5m, 1w; 1 ext. (commedia dell'arte stage). A humble slave extracts a thorn from a lion's paw, beginning a friendship that so astonishes the Emperor that he grants them both freedom.

ANGEL OF THE PRISONS, by Brian Way
Baker's Plays, 1977; 4m, 4w play 24 roles; open stage. In the context of making a film, the life's work of Elizabeth Fry, an English prison reformer, is explored with audience help.

ANTELOPE BOY, by Joy Harvey
Arequipa Press, c/o, Guidon Books, 83 W. Main St., Scottsdale, AZ 85251; 1968; 4m, 2w, 1 boy, 1 girl, extras, 1 int., 1 ext., 1 combination int.-ext. An Indian boy is tricked by Coyote to go into the kiva of the Antelope people to kill them; but instead he becomes an Antelope, joining with them to bring about Coyote's downfall.

APPLESEED, by Ed Graczyk
Anchorage Press, 1971; ensemble of 7m, 4w play many roles; unit set with modifications. Johnny carries a message of peace and productivity along with his appleseeds when he sets off to cover the west with trees.

THE ARABIAN NIGHTS, by Lowell Swortzell
Dramatic Publishing Co., 1977; 8m, 9w, extras; 1 int. The Sultan's new wife, Scheherazade, is spared death each day so she can continue her engaging tale; and in the process, the Sultan's anger is calmed and happiness restored to the kingdom.

THE ARKANSAW BEAR, by Aurand Harris
Anchorage Press, 1980; 1m, 1 girl, 2 bears, a mime, Star Bright, 2w voices; 1 ext. An old circus Dancing Bear, frantically trying to escape death, gradually comes to accept the idea of ensuring continuation of his art through Little Bear, thereby providing an object lesson for Tish whose Grandpa is also dying.

BABAR THE ELEPHANT (Opera), by Nicolai Berezowsky
Carl Fischer, 1953; 5m, 5w, dancers; 1 int., 1 ext., 1 int.-ext. A young elephant, Babar, is captured by hunters and sent to France where the Old Lady gives him an education and prepares him to take his place as King on his return home.

BAMBOOZLED, by Michael Brill
Anchorage Press, 1985; 8m, 1w; platform stage with backdrop. In traditional commedia fashion, the clowns outwit their miserly masters and unite the young lovers.

BEAUTY AND THE BEAST, by William Glennon
Coach House Press, 1966; 4m, 4w; 1 int., 1 ext. A Prince is turned into a Beast, but through the loving attention of Beauty he is at last changed back to his former self.

BEAUTY AND THE BEAST, by Nicholas Stuart Gray
Samuel French, 1951; 3m, 3w, 1 baby dragon; 3 int., 3 ext. An absent-minded wizard forgets he has imprisoned a rude Prince; and when he finds out the Prince has turned into a Beast, he contrives to bring Beauty into his life to restore his humanity.

THE BEAUTY OF THE DREAMING WOOD, by Marian Jonson
Coach House Press, 1973; 10m, 12w, 1 boy, extras; 1 int. The princess is promised death by her six-

teenth birthday, but her own willingness to face the trials of growing up and Prince Honore's courage succeed in thwarting the curse.

THE BELL, by Brian Way
Baker's Plays, 1977; 2m, 2w; open stage. A bellman named Tom is asked by a strange man to make the Bell of Happiness; and with the children's help, utilizing the senses, he accomplishes the task.

THE BEEPLE, by Alan Cullen
Anchorage Press, 1968; 12m, 6w; 2 int., 2 ext. In the Bee queendom, Humble aspires to marry the Princess who is betrothed to another, but events finally turn his way.

BIG KLAUS AND LITTLE KLAUS, by Dean Wenstrom
Anchorage Press, 1966; 6m, 1w, extras; 4 ext., 1 int.-ext. Little Klaus is bullied by Big Klaus who resents all Little Klaus' good fortune; but finally Little Klaus gets rid of his adversary once and for all.

THE BIRTHDAY OF THE INFANTA, by Stuart Walker
In *Pormanteau Adaptations,* 1921; 5m, 2w; 1 int. In this Oscar Wilde story a hunchback boy is brought to entertain the Princess on her twelfth birthday but dies when he discovers the truth about why people laugh when he dances.

BIZZY, DIZZY, DAFFY AND ARTHUR, by Dagmar Dorsten, Uli Gressieker, Volker Ludwig, Stefan Ostertag, Carsten Kruger and the premiere cast; trans. Jack Zipes
In *Political Plays for Children,* 1976, written 1971; 4m, 2w, Voices; Neutral stage with props. Four children find a place to play in an abandoned building, until police run them out; but they finally convert the building into a youth center.

THE BLUE BIRD, by Maurice Maeterlinck
Dodd, Mead, 1907 (Samuel French); 10m, 12w, 24 children, extras; 5 int., 4 ext. The classic journey of Mytyl and Tyltyl to find the blue bird ends with their finding it at home.

BLUE HORSES, by Kathryn Schultz Miller
Coach House Press, 1982, 1984; 2m, 2w; 1 ext. Four children explore their fuller potentials through imaginative play.

THE BOY WHO STOLE THE STARS, by Julian Wiles
The Young Charleston Company, 1981 (133 Church St., Charleston, SC 29401); 1m, 1w, 1 boy, 1 girl, 2 m or w; open stage. The boy, Nicholas, has lost his best friend, and furthermore, his grandfather is acting distant and irritable. As he comes to accept the trauma of separation whether through Alzheimer's disease, growing up, or just moving away, Nicholas finds there are compensations if you don't shut them off.

THE BOY WHO TALKED TO WHALES, by Webster Smalley
Anchorage Press, 1981; 5m, 2w, 1 boy, 1 girl, 1 whale (heard only as a girl's voice); 1 ext. A boy proves he can communicate with whales and contrives to save them from extinction at the hands of greedy whale hunters.

THE BRAVE LITTLE TAILOR, by Aurand Harris
Anchorage Press, 1961; 3m, 3w; 1 int., 2 ext. A Tailor brags that he has killed seven (flies) at one blow, but most people prefer to think he has killed giants, especially the two silly Queens and their maid-of-all-work who are beset by giants and need such a hero to rescue them.

A BRIDE FROM PLUTO (Opera), by Gian Carlo Menotti
G. Schirmer, 1982; 2m, 2w, extras, dancers; 1 int. In order to marry the exotic visitor from Pluto, Billy, the tailor's son, must have his heart replaced with an electronic device to make him immortal; but he and his earthly fiancee conspire to bring in a substitute bride for the Plutonian.

BUBBYLONIAN ENCOUNTER, by Gene Mackey
Unpublished; information from author: Theatre for Young America, 7204 West 80th St., Overland Park, KS 66204 (1980); 1m, 2w; open stage. Bub, a voyager from the planet Bubbylonia, comes to Earth to explore the sense of touch, but discovers she needs to learn ways to forestall "forced sexual touch." As she learns, the children in the audience are also taught.

BUFFALO BILL, by Aurand Harris
Anchorage Press, 1954; 13m, 1w, 3 children, extras; 5 ext. Bill Cody makes use of early training provided by his Indian friend to become a scout and carry mail by Pony Express.

THE BUTTERFLY, by Bijan Mofid
Anchorage Press, 1974; 6m, 3w; 1 int. A Butterfly captured by a Spider is unable to fulfill her bargain that she would find a substitute insect for his meal; but the Spider frees her anyway.

BYE, BYE BIRDIE (Musical), by Michael Stewart; music by Charles Strouse; lyrics by Lee Adams
Tams-Witmark, 1958, 1960, 1961; 10m, 13w, 1 boy, extras; 6 int., 7 ext. Rock star Conrad Birdie is about to be inducted into the Army and his agent has arranged a "last kiss" ceremony in a small midwest town to be telecast nationwide.

CANTERBURY TALES, by Bernice Bronson
New Plays, 1971; 5m, 4w, musicians; 1 int. On their way to Canterbury, a group of pilgrims stops at an Inn, and they entertain themselves with wonderful tales while the audience helps in selective ways.

CAPTAIN BILLY (Musical), by Frank Leary; music and lyrics by Hank Beebe
New Plays, 1970; 4m, 4w, extras; open stage. A young boy with dreams of becoming an astronaut takes off to the moon and gets the help of a space mouse, monkey, and chicken in returning to earth.

CAPTAIN JOHN PEOPLEFOLKS, by Dusan Radovic and Mirslav Belovic
Unpublished; information about English version from Sharon Ellis, Dept. of Speech and Drama, Southwest Missouri State Univ., Springfield, MO 65802; 16m, 2w, extra women; 3 ext. set by crew. In a parody of the "heroic" pirate tradition, Captain John outwits and slays the seven-headed monster of the China Seas and reestablishes his reputation for gallantry.

LA CENERENTOLA (CINDERELLA) (Opera), by Giaochino Rossini; libretto by Jacopo Fernetti
Tams-Witmark (1852); 4m, 3w, chorus, ballet dancers; 4 int. Instead of a step-mother, Cinderella is in the care of the Baron, her stepfather; and the Prince recognizes her after the ball not by means of glass slippers but by twin bracelets.

CHANTICLEER (Opera), by Seymour Barab; libretto by M.C. Richards
Boosey & Hawkes, 1964; 2m, 2w; 1 ext. Operatic version of the Nun's Priest's Tale from Chaucer's *Canterbury Tales* in which a prize rooster almost loses his life at the hands of a wily fox because of his own vanity.

CHARLOTTE'S WEB, dramatized from E.B. White's story by Joseph Robinette
Dramatic Publishing Co., 1984; 7m, 9w; unit set. As the girl, Fern, watches, a barnyard drama unfolds in which Wilbur the humble pig is saved from the butcher by Charlotte, literature's most remarkable spider.

THE CHEST OF DREAMS, by Max Bush
Coach House Press, 1979; 3m, 4w; 1 int. With some audience help, Lili makes use of the materials and costumes in an old chest bequeathed to her by her grandmother to subdue a mysterious hypnotist who inhabits her playroom and tries to control the imaginations of herself and her playmates.

CHINOOK, by Paddy Campbell
Playwrights Co-op, 1973; 2m, 2w, 1 m or w; open stage (story circle). With the help of the children in the story circle Chinook rescues the Old Man from the home of the Ice Woman and ensures the return of spring.

CHRISTMAS ALL OVER THE PLACE (Musical), by Judith Martin; music by Donald Ashwander
Anchorage Press, 1977; 3 m, 6w; bare stage. A short sketch in which the Huffenpuffs go south and the Wigglebees go north to visit each other for Christmas is staged in the familiar Paper Bag Players' fashion.

A CHRISTMAS CAROL, by Martha Bennett King
Anchorage Press, 1941; 14m, 6w, 8 children; 4 int., 1 ext. Dramatization of the Charles Dickens story in which the miserly Scrooge is transformed overnight by a series of ghostly vistors.

A CHRISTMAS CAROL, by Brian Way
Baker's Plays, 1977; 16m, 8w play 80 roles; open stage or simultaneous set. Participation theatre version of Dickens' story of Ebenezer Scrooge who changes his personality from miser to philanthropist in a single night.

CINDERELLA, by Charlotte B. Chorpenning
Anchorage Press, 1940; 4m, 7w, extras; 1 int., 1 ext. Prototype of fairy tales in which the persecuted but lovely girl is helped by her fairy godmother to go to a ball where she finds her true love.

CIRCUS HOME, by Joanna Halpert Kraus
New Plays, 1979; 11m, 4w, 3 boys (doubling recommended); 1 ext. A grotesquely large boy tries vainly to find acceptance in normal family surroundings, but finds he is most comfortable among his circus friends.

THE CITY WITHOUT LOVE, by Lev Ustinov, trans. Miriam Morton
In *Russian Plays for Young Audiences*, 1977; 7m, 2w, 1 boy; 1 int., 1 ext. A Clown and an Urchin team up to defeat the powers that keep the city enslaved without love, kindness or laughter.

THE CODE BREAKER, by Pauline C. Conley
Anchorage Press, 1983; 2m, 2w, 1w voice; 1 multiple section int. The computer-controlled lives of four teenagers are upset when Pete discovers the great, free outdoor world beyond the Orb.

COURAGE! adapted from Stephen Crane's novel by Ed Graczyk
Pickwick Press, 1973; 12m, 1w, extras; unit set plus projections. A young man recalls his transition to maturity during the Civil War as he battled the enemy and his own cowardice.

CREATION, by Saphira Barbara Linden and Ira Rosenberg
New Plays, 1970; 9 to 12 players; open playing space. Children in the audience help the players construct environments free of polution.

CROSSROADS, by Brian Way
Baker's Plays, 1977; 3m, 3w; open stage. A Tramp experiences adventures when asked by a mysterious stranger to help him solve some conflicts involving other people and creatures.

CRYING TO LAUGH, by Marcel Sabourin
Le Theatre de la Marmaille (42 Ouest, Avenue des Pins, Montreal, Quebec H2W 1R1), 1980; 1m, 2w; open stage. Moa's dog has died and Toa, an admired acquaintance, has told her she must not cry or she'll not grow up. With her mirror image's urgings Moa learns to express her emotions without shame.

THE DANCING DONKEY, by Erik Vos
Anchorge Press, 1965; 3m, 2w, 1 donkey; 1 ext. Two scoundrels steal a Friar's pet donkey in order to exhibit his dancing talents for profit; but when the donkey will not dance for them, they try to sell him back to the Friar.

DANDELION (Musical), by Judith Martin; music by Donald Ashwander
Paper Bag Players, 1978 (distrib. by Baker's Plays); 2 m, 2w, 2 musicians, play many roles, bare stage, cardboard props. In the familiar Paper Bag Players' style the performers play nine brief episodes on the evolutionary ladder, from early earthquakings and fish to the origin of human communication.

THE DECISION, by Brian Way
Baker's Plays, 1977; 2m, 2w; open stage. The audience helps the people of Xavia decide whether to continue in their simple, isolated and untroubled ways or to adopt a materialistic culture.

DIG 'N TEL, by Flora Atkin
New Plays, 1979; 7 or 8 m or w; open stage. Archaeologists unearth artifacts in their Israeli excavations from which the company is stimulated to enact stores from Jewish folklore and literature.

A DOCTOR IN SPITE OF HIMSELF, by Aurand Harris
Anchorage Press, 1968; 9m, 10w; 1 int., 2 ext. Adaptation of the Moliere classic tells the story of Sganarelle, a woodcutter, who is forced by his wife into the role of a doctor, in which capacity he "cures" a young woman and unites her with her lover.

DON QUIXOTE OF LA MANCHA, by Arthur Fauquez; trans. Margaret Leona
Anchorage Press, 1967; 8m, 2w, extras; 1 int., 5 ext. Adaptation of the Cervantes classic about a Spanish don who, with a faithful servant, sets out to prove that chivalry is not dead in this cynical age.

DON'T COUNT YOUR CHICKENS UNTIL THEY CRY WOLF (Musical), by Carol Lynn Pearson; music by J.A.C. Redford
Anchorage Press, 1979; 8 players minimum; bare stage with blocks. Contemporary view of several Aesop fables told in story theatre techniques by a versatile ensemble.

DOORS, by Suzan Zeder
Anchorage Press, 1985; 3m, 1w; 1 int. Jeff's parents are heading toward divorce, and he tries to drown the sound of bitter quarrels in the next room by playing the TV and stereo loudly and by retreating into a fantasy world where all is harmony, only to discover the problem is best faced openly.

DRACULA'S TREASURE, by Dudley Saunders
Anchorage Press, 1975; 5m, 3w; 1 int. The Boone family's house has an extra and unwanted occupant who sets about entrapping Nancy, almost succeeding in his diabolical attempt.

THE DRAGON, by Eugene Schwartz; trans. Elizabeth Reynolds Hapgood
Theatre Arts Books, 1963; 18m, 6w, 1 boy; 2 int., 1 ext. Lancelot comes to a city dominated by a Dragon who is about to take his annual "bride," kills the Dragon in a spectacular aerial fight, only to find the townspeople submitting to a new tyranny.

THE DRAGON OF NITT, by Phil Grecian
Coach House Press, 1986; 6m, 2w, 4 m or w; extras; neutral set suggests 5 ext. The timid Abercrombie, with much outside help, retrieves the silver box of happiness from the lair of witch Hecate and dispels the myth of a vicious dragon.

A DREAM OF SKY PEOPLE, by Isabelle Foord
Playwrights Co-op, 1969; 5m, 3w; open stage. A Cree Indian creation myth in which Nazabo and his wife, Nacha, come to earth and elect to share with all creatures the joys and sorrows of life.

ELECTRIC FOLDEROL (Musical), by Ed Graczyk; music by Gerry Pyle
Pickwick Press, 1971; 6m, 7w, unit set. Sequel to *Aesop's Falables* in which Sir Wilfred Wolf is involved with characters much like those in Lewis Caroll's works, all to a rock rhythm.

THE ELVES AND THE SHOEMAKER, by Nora Tully (McAlbay) and Charlotte B. Chorpenning
Anchorage Press, 1946; 1m, 9w, 3 elves; 1 int. With the Shoemaker away at the wars, Heckla is about to succeed in evicting his impoverished wife and daughter when three good elves intercede and restore their prosperity.

THE EMPEROR'S NEW CLOTHES, by Charlotte B. Chorpenning
Samuel French, 1938; 7m, 4w, 1 child, extras; 1 int., 1 ext. Mischievous adventurers Zar and Zan find themselves in an Oriental kingdom where they save the Royal Weavers from banishment at the hands of Han, wicked minister of the Emperor's robes.

THE EMPEROR'S NEW CLOTHES, by Judith B. Kase
Anchorage Press, 1979; 5m, 1w, 4 m or w, 2 girls; Kabuki platform stage. Two venerable opportunists earn the vain Emperor's gratitude for exposing hipocrisy in his court and helping him perceive his own shortcomings.

THE EMPEROR'S NEW CLOTHES (Opera), by Douglas Moore; libretto by Raymond Abrashkin
Carl Fischer, 1949; 4m soloists, 2m and 2 boys speaking, chorus; 3 int., 1 ext. Two scoundrels pretend to weave a special cloth for the Emperor's robes which anyone unfit for office cannot see.

THE EMPEROR'S NEW CLOTHES (Musical), by Ruth Perry, based on Arnold and Lois Peyser's adaptation, lyrics by Paul Francis Webster, music by Allan Jay Friedman
Dramatic Publishing Co., 1969; 8m, 7w, extras; 7 int., 2 ext. A prince and his attendant pretend to weave special material for the vain Emperor's birthday suit, bringing about restitution of the Emperor's sanity and the union of two estranged kingdoms.

ESCAPE TO FREEDOM, by Ozzie Davis
Viking Press, 1978; 3m, 2w, 2 boys, open stage. Early life of Frederick Douglass is shown in vignettes of plantation and Baltimore life until his escape to New York.

EVERYBODY, EVERYBODY (Musical), by Judith Martin, music by Donald Ashwander
Elsevier/Nelson Books, 1981; 4 or more m or w; open stage, with cardboard props. Brief musical sketches of everyday events in children's lives are enacted in a humorous vein by dancer/actors in the well-known Paper Bag Players style.

THE FIREBIRD AND TRIXIE THE VIXEN, by Jan Jilek
DILIA, Theatre and Literary Agency (Vysehradska 28, 128 24 Prague 2 Czechoslovakia), 1968; 7m, 7w; 3 int., 2 ext. With the help of Trixie the Vixen, the youngest son of a king is able to overcome all obstacles, achieve wisdom and maturity, find the firebird that has been stealing apples, and restore his father's health. In the process, he finds his bride.

FIVE LITTLE PEPPERS, by Rosemary G. Musil
Anchorage Press, 1940; 2m, 4w, 9 children; 2 int. Adaptation of the Margaret Sidney story of the Pepper children's home life, their mischief-making, and their affection for each other.

FIVE MINUTES TO MORNING, by Mary Melwood
New Plays, 1965; 2m, 1w, 5 animals (mimes); 1 int., 1 ext. Agrubbing environment spoiler is thwarted in his efforts to foreclose on the ruined old school house inhabited by a remarkable retired school teacher.

FLASHBACK! (Musical), by Alice Wilson
Anchorage Press, 1981; 3m, 3w; bare stage. A small ensemble company romps through a succession of familiar childhood experiences in a total theatre fashion.

THE FLYING PRINCE, by Aurand Harris
Anchorage Press, 1985 (originally Samuel French, 1958); 7m, 5w, 1m or w, extras; 1 int., 3 ext. A prince of India leaves his body behind as he takes the form of a bird to rescue his betrothed from a bandit. In his absence, an ambitious servant has usurped his body; but with the help of a magic sword he restores order.

FOOL OF THE WORLD, by John Urquhart and Rita Grossberg
Anchorage Press, 1986; company of 2m, 2w play several roles; open stage with props. Children help Dmetri prove he is not a fool but instead clever enough to invent a flying machine and bring the heart of a cloud to the Czar and win the princess.

THE FOREST RING, by William C. DeMille and Charles Bernard
In A Treasury of Plays for Children, 1921; 4m, 6w, 2 boys, 1 girl; 2 ext. A girl with the help of a fairy princess rescues a mother bear's cubs from a cruel trapper who wants to sell their fur.

THE FORGOTTEN DOOR, by Gregory A. Falls, from the book by Alexander Key
Anchorage Press, 1986; 7m or w play 18 roles; multiple locations either depicted or suggested minimally, with actors becoming scenic and prop elements. Jon, a boy accidentally transported from another world, uses his supernatural abilities to reveal earthlings' not-so-admirable qualities before finding his way home.

THE GHOST OF MR. PENNY, by Rosemary Musil
Anchorage Press, 1939; 4m, 4 children; 2 int. Sally and her friends who play in the coach house of the abandoned Penny estate mistake a tramp for the owner who disappeared years before; and together they prove Sally is the rightful heir.

THE GOLDEN APPLES, by Arthur Fauquez
Unpublished; information from author: Maleves, Ste. Marie, 11 Rue d'Orbais, Belgium (Pugh); 5m, 2w, 1 boy; 2 ext. "A train driver tries to graft a new strong apple tree for the use of his friends, who scorn him for his efforts."

THE GOLDEN FLEECE, by Alan Cullen
Anchorage Press, 1971; 10m, 5w play many roles; bare stage, props. The fisher folk of a Greek village decide to play out the epic of Jason's search for the golden fleece to appease Poseidon and calm the raging seas.

GOLLIWHOPPERS! (Musical), by Flora Atkin
New Plays, 1973; 7 to 9 players enact many roles; neutral playing space. Story theatre versions of four American tall tales that stretch credulity and reflect an indomitable spirit.

GOOD GRIEF, A GRIFFIN (Musical), by Eleanor and Ray Harder
Anchorage Press, 1968; 7m, 5w, 1 ext. A Griffin visits the village to admire his likeness carved on the local church, becomes involved in the efforts of the Canon to change the villagers' ways, then returns to the Dreadful Wilds with a promise of their reform.

THE GREAT CROSS-COUNTRY RACE, by Alan Broadhurst
Anchorage Press, 1965; 14m, 6w (possibly reduced to 7m, 5w); 1 basic set, modified. While racing the tortoise in a cross-country challenge, the hare is diverted sufficiently to allow the tortoise to win.

THE GREENFIELD CHRISTMAS TREE (Opera), by Douglas Moore; libretto by Arnold Sundgaard
G. Schirmer, 1963; 4m, 1w, 1 boy, 2 girls, chorus; 1 int.-ext. A stern Puritanical grandfather is finally persuaded that his orphaned grandchildren's Christmas tree can remain in his barn for the holiday.

GREENSLEEVES' MAGIC, by Marian Jonson
Coach House Press, 1951; 6m, 5w, extras; 1 ext. The arrival of Greensleeves triggers Princess Miranda's determination to learn the secret that will rid her father's kingdom of the evil Grand Duchess.

GRINDLING GIBBONS AND THE PLAGUE OF LONDON, by Brian Way
Baker's Plays, 1977; 8m, 4w play 40 roles; open stage. A London air raid is the excuse for telling the story of Grindling Gibbons, a wood carver who survived fire, plague and subterfuge to become an assistant to Christopher Wren.

HANSEL AND GRETEL, by Charlotte B. Chorpenning
Coach House Press, 1956; 2m, 5w, 11 children, extras; 3 ext. Two children are abandoned in the forest when their parents can no longer support them, but manage to overcome the witch who captures them.

HANSEL AND GRETEL, by Moses Goldberg
New Plays, 1972; 3m, 3w; open stage. Some child participation helps commedia dell 'arte players perform the story of Hansel and Gretel who get lost in the forest and are captured by a child-eating witch.

HANSEL AND GRETEL (Opera), by Engelbert Humperdinck; libretto by Adelheid Wette
Schott & Co., London, 1895; in the U.S., G. Schirmer or Boosey & Hawkes; 1m, 6w, children's chorus, 14 angels ballet; 1 int., 2 ext. A desperate mother sends her two starving children into the woods to gather strawberries, but before she and her husband can find them again they have managed to kill a witch and release a spell on the Gingerbread children.

HANSEL AND GRETEL, by Madge Miller
Anchorage Press, 1951; 1m, 3w, 3 children, extras; 3 ext. Hansel and Gretel are helped by an enchanted cat to defeat the wicked witch and free the Forest Fairy, all in addition to the more traditional elements of the story.

THE HAT, by Brian Way
Baker's Plays, 1977; 2m, 2w; 2 int. When Peter's mother makes a special hat for Mr. Hump, Peter is obliged to deliver it, and this leads to problems the audience children help solve.

HAVE A GRUMPISH HOLIDAY, by Claire Jones and Robert Varga
Involvement Dramatics, 1970; 2m, 2w; 1 int. (open stage). The Queen and her Grand Grump are helped by the children to discover the secret of happiness in the neighboring land ruled by a charming Princess and her chief troubadour.

THE HEADLESS HORSEMAN (Opera), by Douglas Moore; libretto by Stephen Vincent Benet
E. C. Schirmer, 1937; 3m, 1w, chorus; 1 ext. Operatic version of Ichabod Crane's encounter with Brom Bones' imitation of the lengendary Headless Horseman.

HELGA AND THE WHITE PEACOCK, by Cornelia Meigs
Macmillan, 1922; 2w, 3 children, West Wind, Grey Goose, Peacock; 1 int., 1 ext. With the vain peacock's guidance and the Grey Goose's piloting, Olaf reaches the House of the Trolls to rescue his sister from eternal bondage.

HELP, HELP, THE GLOBOLINKS! (Opera), by Gian Carlo Menotti
G. Schirmer, 1969; 5m, 3w, 12 children, Globolinks (indefinite number); 1 int., 2 ext. A school bus of young musicians is captured by Globolinks, creatures from space; and when their forgotten instruments are provided to them, the children are able to drive off their celestial enemies.

HEY, THERE — HELLO! by Gennadi Mamlin; trans. Miriam Morton
In *Russian Plays for Young Audiences*, 1977; 1m, 1w, 4 mimes; 1 int., 6 ext., 1 int.-ext. Masha and Valerka, both 14-year-olds, gradually come to know love founded upon respect for each other's unique personal qualities.

HIAWATHA, PEACEMAKER OF THE IROQUOIS, by James Norris
Anchorage Press, 1953; 14m, 2w, 1 girl, 1 rabbit puppet, 1 raccoon puppet; 1 int., 2 ext. Historical account of how Hiawatha wins the confidence of all five Iroquois tribes and convinces them to live in peace together.

THE HIDE AND SEEK ODYSSEY OF MADELINE GIMPLE, by Frank Gagliano
Dramatists Play Service, 1970; 4m, 1w, extras; 1 ext., modified. In a series of game contexts Madeline learns to face not only her fears but the truth about her being an orphan.

THE HOBBIT, by Patricia Gray
Dramatic Publishing Co., 1968; 24 Hobbits, dwarves, trolls, elves and goblins; suggestive locations under and above ground. Dramatization of part of the Tolkien vision of the doings in Middle Earth where Bilbo Baggins goes in search of treasure.

THE HONORABLE URASHIMA TARO, by Coleman A. Jennings
Dramatic Publishing Co., 1972; 3m, 3w, 6 boys, 5-person Sea Scorpion, 4 Seasons, extras; formalized exteriors above and under water. Taro, a poor fisherman, is taken to the kingdom below the sea to save the inhabitants from the deadly Sea Scorpion, and when he returns to the shore he finds he has been gone many years.

HUCKLEBERRY FINN, by Frank M. Whiting
Anchorage Press, 1948; 9m, 5w, 4 children; 1 int., 5 ext. Huck escapes from a cabin where he has been imprisoned by his ne'er-do-well father and travels down the Mississippi River with Jim, a runaway slave, encountering friends and foes along the way.

THE HUNTERS AND THE HENWIFE, by Nicholas Stuart Gray
Samuel French, 1954; 6m, 2w; 2 int., 1 ext. An ogre captures a baron and his servants who wander into an enchanted forest, but he is defeated by them and the henwife's daughter.

HURRICANE ISLAND, by Rosemary Musil
Unpublished; information from author, c/o Anchorage Press (n.d.); 4m, 3w; 1 ext. The arrival of the well-mannered orphan boy, Pilgrim, upsets life on the island, especially that of Adolph who feels displaced in his mother's affections, until Pilgrim proves his fortitude in a hurricane.

I BELIEVE IN MAKE BELIEVE (Musical), by Carol Lynn Pearson, music by JAC Redford
Anchorage Press, 1984; 12 or more m or f; open stage. Using story theatre form, transformational acting and the framework of the "Princess Who Could Not Laugh," performers enact five Grimm fairy tales.

THE ICE WOLF, by Joanna Halpert Kraus
New Plays, 1963; 8m, 7w; 2 ext. Anatou, a fair-haired Eskimo girl, is banished from the clan after her parents die, and she spends her life seeking revenge as an ice wolf until she is hunted down.

THE IMPERIAL NIGHTINGALE, by Nicholas Stuart Gray
Samuel French, 1957; 9m, 4w; 2 int., 2 ext. An Emperor chooses a mechanical nightingale over a live one because of appearances; but at the hour of his death it is the real bird that sings him back to life.

THE INCREDIBLE JUNGLE JOURNEY OF FENDA MARIA, by Jack Stokes
In *Contemporary Children's Theatre*, 1974 (play copyright 1973); 5m, 4w, 1 m or w, chorus; bare stage permitting audience involvement. African tale about how the girl, Fenda Maria, defeats the witch and reunites the divided person of the Prince.

THE INDIAN CAPTIVE, by Charlotte B. Chorpenning
Anchorage Press, 1937; 3m, 3w, 5 children; 2 ext. A pioneer girl is captured by Indians and is adopted into the tribe when she proves her bravery.

IN ONE BASKET, by Shirley Pugh
Anchorage Press, 1972; 3m, 3w perform many roles; unit set. Twelve short tales (or any portion of the total) are presented in story theatre style.

INOOK AND THE SUN, by Henry Beissel
Playwrights Co-op, 1973; 2m, 1w, 4m spirits, 3w spirits, 9 animals; 3 int., 2 ext. Inook is an Eskimo boy whose determination and stamina bring him to the land of the dead where he releases the sun from captivity to warm his land and people once again.

IN OTHER WORDS, by Sharon Doyle
Anchorage Press, 1979; 4m, 2w ensemble; bare stage with title in letter blocks. Improvisationally derived depiction of the development of human communication in challenging transformation acting.

IN THE BEGINNING, by Bernice Bronson
New Plays, 1971; 6 players; open staging with props. Tribes of children, each with an adult leader, enact nature myths from several ethnic cultures.

I THINK I CAN (Musical), by Kathryn Schultz Miller and Barry Miller, music by Bruce Bowdon
Pioneer Drama Service, 1975; 2m, 2w; open stage. With the help of the audience Becky is finally convinced that she can do anything she really wants to do.

JACK AND THE BEANSTALK, by Charlotte B. Chorpenning
Anchorage Press, 1935; 7m, 5w, 1 child; 1 int., 2 ext. Jack's trade of his mother's cow for a bag of beans does not seem advantageous until the beans sprout and lead him to the Giant's kingdom in the sky where he amasses a fortune and gains maturity.

JIM THORPE, ALL-AMERICAN (Musical), by Saul Levitt; music by Harrison Fisher
Anchorage Press, 1980; 7m; unit set. Jim's life is traced from his early rejection of formal education in various Indian schools to finding a place in athletics and his ultimate disillusionment.

JOHNNY MOONBEAM AND THE SILVER ARROW, by Joseph Golden
Anchorage Press, 1962; 2m, 1 boy, 3 gods; 1 ext. An old trapper narrates an Indian boy's mimed passage to maturity which includes taking water, fire, and corn from the gods who hold these elements, and learning to share them.

JUNKYARD, by Isabelle Foord
Playwrights Co-op, 1971; 2m, 1w, 2 m or w; 1 ext. Three children contrive to save their favorite playground, a junkyard, from conversion into a parking lot.

JUST SO, by Jan Silverman
New Plays, 1981; 7 or more m or w; open stage with movable blocks. Rudyard Kipling himself introduces this adaptation of several *Just So Stories told* in story theatre style by a versatile company of actor-singers.

JUST SO STORIES (Musical), by Aurand Harris
Anchorage Press, 1971; 5m, 4w, extras; unit set. Musical adaptation of three Rudyard Kipling stories of "when the world was young and all" and a social structure was just being formed.

KAP THE KAPPA, by Betty Jean Lifton
In *Contemporary Children's Theatre,* 1974; permissions from Curtis Brown, Ltd., 60 E. 56th St., N.Y., NY 10022; 7m, 2w, 1 boy, 1 girl; open stage, projections, props. Kap is a mythological Japanese mischief maker who spends some time with humans but eventually returns to his natural home under water.

KING ARTHUR'S SWORD, by Margery Evernden
Coach House Press, 1959; 6m, 2w; 1 int., 2 ext. Heroic legend of young Arthur who is able to withdraw the magic sword, Excalibur, from the stone, proving his right to the throne of Britain.

THE KING OF THE GOLDEN RIVER, by Margery Evernden
Coach House Press, 1955; 4m, 2w, 2 children; 1 int., 1 ext. Southwest Wind Esq., punishes Hans and Schwartz for their greed by drying up their valley; but Gluck, their kindly brother, restores its fertility with the help of the King of the Golden River.

KING PATCH AND MR. SIMPKINS, by Alan Cullen
Anchorage Press, 1964; 8m, 3w, 1 dog; basic set, modified to suggest 1 ext. and 4 kingdoms. A jester named Patch becomes king of a land in desperate condition; but after a series of improbable adventures he is able to bring order out of chaos with the help of his sheepdog, Mr. Simpkins.

THE LADDER, by Brian Way
Baker's Plays, 1977; 2m, 2w; 1 ext. A ladder on top of a mountain is tended by a Keeper who grants wishes of those who make the climb.

THE LAND OF THE DRAGON, by Madge Miller
Anchorage Press, 1946; 5m, 5w, 1 dragon; 1 basic set (Oriental stage). Princess Jade Pure is set upon her rightful throne by Road Wanderer despite the conspiracies of her wicked guardians and jealous relatives.

THE LAND OF OZ, by Elizabeth Fuller Goodspeed
Samuel French, 1928; 6m, 5w, 1 girl, 2 creatures, 2 monkeys, extras; 4 int., 1 ext. Early adaptation of

the L. Frank Baum story about Tip who encounters many strange creatures and has many adventures before being transformed into Ozma of Oz.

LEE BOBO, DETECTIVE FOR CHINATOWN, by Rose Hum Lee and Charlotte B. Chorpenning
Anchorage Press, 1948; 6m, 3w, 6 children; 1 int., 1 ext. Lee Bobo takes pleasure in the excitement of trapping a thief who has been plaguing shops in Chinatown.

THE LEGEND OF SLEEPY HOLLOW, by Bernice Bronson
New Plays, 1982; 5m, 6w; arena modified with props and blocks. Washington Irving's familiar story of Ichabod Crane and the headless horseman is enacted by an ensemble company with participation by the children in the audience.

THE LEGEND OF SLEEPY HOLLOW, by Frederick Gaines
In *Five Plays,* 1975; rights and royalty information from Children's Theatre Co., 2400 3rd Ave. So., Minneapolis, MN 55404; 5m, 3w, school children, extras; unit set. Washington Irving's famous tale of colonial New York, told in fluid style, involves Ichabod Crane's futile attempts to deny the truth of the Headless Horseman superstition.

LIFE, HERE WE COME, by Miloslav Stehlik
DILIA, Vysehradska 28, Prague, Czechoslovakia (Pugh) (n.d.); 13m, 5w; 1 ext. Burun, a ruffian in a Soviet colony for homeless and delinquent children, runs away but returns to live with the only friends he has.

LI'L ABNER, by Norman Panama and Melvin Frank; music and lyrics by Johnny Mercer and Gene de Paul
Tams-Witmark, 1957; 22m, 8w, extras; 6 int., 4 ext. Mammy Yokum's secret tonic interests the U.S. government enough to delay Dogpatch's destruction by atomic tests; but ultimately it is General Cornpone's statue that saves the town.

THE LION, THE WITCH AND THE WARDROBE, dramatized from C.S. Lewis' story by Don Quinn
Dramatic Publishing Co., 1968; 7m, 3w, 2 boys, 2 girls, extras; simultaneously 1 int., variable ext. Four children go through the wardrobe in the spare room into the fantasy world of Narnia where they help Aslan, the king, defeat the White Witch.

THE LITTLE ANIMAL HOUSE, by Samuel Marschak
Soviet Center for ASSITEJ, 16/2 Gorky St., Moscow, U.S.S.R. (Pugh) (n.d.); 6m, 3w; 1 int., 2 ext. A mouse, a frog, a rooster and a hedgehog defend themselves from the bigger animals by sticking together.

THE LITTLE HUMPBACK HORSE, by Pyotr Ershov; trans. Lowell Swortzell
Anchorage Press, 1984; 7m, 3w, extras; unit set. Ivan, a simpleton third son, proves himself more worthy than his clever brothers, and with the help of the Humpback Horse he becomes Tsar and marries the Daughter of the Moon.

LITTLE LORD FAUNTLEROY, by Frances Hodgson Burnett
Samuel French, 1889, 1913; 8m, 3w; 2 int. Young Cedric Erroll is taken by his widowed mother to England where he succeeds in humanizing his irascible grandfather while learning to become the next Earl of Dorincourt.

THE LITTLE MERMAID (Musical), by Pat Hale; music by Al Bahret
New Plays, 1974; 5m, 8w; 3 ext., 2 under the sea. A young Mermaid falls in love with a human Prince and exchanges her tail and voice for feet to share his world; but he marries another, and the Mermaid becomes foam on the ocean when she refuses to kill his bride.

THE LITTLE PRINCESS, by Frances Hodgson Burnett
Samuel French, 1911; 5m, 5w, 11 Children; 3 int. Romantic tale of Sara Crewe, a Victorian girl who falls from great wealth and position to poverty and menial status in Miss Minchin's boarding school, only to be raised again by a mysterious neighbor.

THE LITTLE PRINCESS, SARA CREWE (Musical), by Nancy Seale; music by Melissa Sweeney
Anchorage Press, 1981; 5m, 18w (12 are pupils of the girls' school); 3 int. Musical version of Frances Hodgson Burnett's novel and play.

LITTLE RED RIDING HOOD (Opera), by Seymour Barab
Boosey & Hawkes, 1965; 2m, 3w; 2 int., 2 ext., or bare stage. A comic Wolf, susceptible to sweets, tries to capture Red Riding Hood at her Grandmother's house but is repelled when the two victims describe a variety of rich desserts.

LITTLE RED RIDING HOOD, by Eugene Schwartz; trans. George Shail
In *All the World's A Stage,* 1972 (Dramatic Publishing Co.); 6m, 4w, extras; 1 int., 4 ext. Friendly birds bring the Forester to Grandmother's cottage in time to rescue Red Riding Hood and Grandmother from the Wolf's stomach.

LITTLE WOMEN, by Marion DeForest
Samuel French, 1911; 5m, 7w; 1 int., 1 ext. Early version of the Louisa May Alcott story about the New England family of girls who support each other while their father is away fighting the Civil War.

LITTLE WOMEN, by Sara Spencer
Anchorage Press, 1940; 2m, 10w; 1 int. Jo March takes her first steps to becoming a writer in the restricted atmosphere of mid-Nineteenth Century New England small town life.

LIVIN' DE LIFE, by Ed Graczyk
Anchorage Press, 1970; 5m, 4w; unit set. Brer Rabbit has come down with a bad case of "de mopes" after prankin' and caperin' with Brer Fox and Brer Bear, and Aunt Mammy Bammy effects a special cure.

THE LOST AND FOUND CHRISTMAS (Musical), by Judith Martin; music by Donald Ashwander
Anchorage Press, 1977; 5m, 5w minimum; neutral stage, cardboard set pieces brought on by actors. The Paper Bag Players' story of Josephine Kindly who lends her presents to bus passengers only to have them returned in a gala Christmas party.

MAGGIE MAGALITA, by Wendy Kesselman
Unpublished; information from James Howe, Lucy Kroll Agency, 390 West End Ave., N.Y., NY 10024 (1980); 1m, 5w, 1 boy, 1 girl, extras; 1 comb. int., 7 suggested locations. When Maggie's grandmother arrives from their native country, Maggie is embarrassed and grandmother is afraid; but gradually their understanding and love grow.

THE MAGIC HORN OF CHARLEMAGNE, by Anne Nicholson and Charlotte B. Chorpenning
Coach House Press, 1951; 5m, 5w, extras; 2 ext. Young Roland is revealed to be the true hero capable of rescuing the Emperor's sword from the power of the evil Falerina.

THE MAGICIAN'S NEPHEW, by Aurand Harris from the book by C.S. Lewis
Dramatic Publishing Co., 1985; 3m, 3w, 4 m or w; 2 int., 2 ext. Digory, a young boy, and his friend Polly travel by means of magic rings to a fantasy land where a witch threatens to become supreme ruler; but by following Aslan, the Lion King's, instructions, Digory subdues the witch and brings back an apple that restores his mother to good health.

THE MAGIC ISLE (Musical), by Wesley Van Tassel; music and lyrics by Mark Ollington
Modern Theatre for Youth, 1967; 7m, 2w; bare stage (commedia dell'arte). The stock characters are shipwrecked on an island where the Captain exercises an inept magical control, and the time is divided between finding food and each other.

MAGIC JOURNAL: THE ALCOTT FAMILY AT FRUITLANDS, by Marie Starr and Lisa Merkl
New Plays, 1981; 6m, 6w; unit set with multiple locations. Entries in Louisa May Alcott's journal come alive as she, her family and friends become part of a utopian community experiment in New England of the mid-1800's.

THE MAGIC POUCH, by Claire Jones and Robert Varga
Involvement Dramatics, 1968; 2m, 2w; open stage. Tobey, assistant to a magician with declining powers, asks the help of the audience to prevent the Witch of Itch from getting possession of three magic symbols.

MAGIC THEATRE, by Saundra Mathews-Deacon
Dramatic Publishing Co., 1977; 7m or w (or more); neutral playing space modified with props. Stressing songs, transformations and theatre games technique, an ensemble explores familiar childhood concerns in a succession of brief sketches.

MAGIC THEATRE II (1981)

MAGIC THEATRE III (1983)

THE MAKE BELIEVE DOCTOR (Musical), by Wesley Van Tassel; music and lyrics by Mark Ollington
Modern Theatre for Youth, 1971; 6m, 3w; 1 int., 1 ext. Musical version of Moliere's *A Doctor in Spite of Himself* in which a woodcutter is "persuaded" by his wife's accomplices to enter the medical profession, which he likes so well that he chooses to remain a doctor.

THE MAN IN THE MOON, by Alan Cullen
Anchorage Press, 1964; 8m, 5w; 6 ext. Professor Plum and his daughter go to the moon in a balloon, but Gremlins force them to get help of the Man in the Moon to return.

MAN OH MAN, by Volker Ludwig and Reiner Lucker; trans. Jack Zipes
In *Political Plays for Children,* 1976; written 1972; 4m, 2w; neutral stage, props. The mother of two children remarries, and together they combat insidious sexism, injustice, and job discrimination.

THE MAN WHO KILLED TIME, by Arthur Fauquez; trans. Margaret Leona
Anchorage Press, 1964; 5m, 4w; 1 int., 1 ext. The inn-keeper, Ambrosio, destroys all clocks to free his friends from time's tyranny over their lives; but he creates chaos in the process which is eventually righted.

MANY MOONS, by Charlotte B. Chorpenning
Dramatic Publishing Co., 1946; 5m, 3w, 2 children; 3 int. While the king's learned courtiers seek to fulfill Princess Lenore's ardent wish for the moon, the little Jester suggests a simple way to gratify her and restore her to health.

MARCO POLO, by Geraldine Brain Siks
Anchorage Press, 1941; 11m, 4w, extras; 1 int., 2 ext. Young Marco stows away with his uncles on a trading voyage to the distant court of Kublai Khan, encountering harrowing adventure along the way.

MARCO POLO AND THE PRINCE TIMUR, by Marie Starr and Lisa Merkl
New Plays, 1983; 5m, 4w, 1 m or w, extras as ensemble and shadow puppeteers; open stage with backdrop and added props. Prince Timur, heir to the throne of China, accompanies Marco Polo on a journey to Persia to deliver a bride to the king, and a scheming general pursues them to promote his own ambitions for the throne of Kublai Khan.

THE MARTIAN CHRONICLES, by Ray Bradbury
Dramatic Publishing Co., 1985; 24m, 12w; open stage with scrims for projections of exteriors. A series of expeditions to Mars by earthmen results in extinction of the Martian race.

THE MARVELOUS ADVENTURES OF TYL, by Jonathan Levy
New Plays, 1973; 4m, 3w; unit set. The rogue, Tyl, demonstrates his contempt for customary social values in comic encounters with the establishment that lead eventually very close to the headsman's block.

THE MARVELOUS STORY OF PUSS IN BOOTS, by Nicholas Stuart Gray
Samuel French, 1955; 8m, 3w; 1 int., 4 ext. A very clever cat puts on a pair of boots made for the

Princess' doll and saves her from the ogre's enchantment and his master from the ogre's dinner table.

THE MASQUE OF BEAUTY AND THE BEAST, by Michael Brill
Anchorage Press, 1979; 4m, 3w, 5 Groteques; unit set with modifications. Beauty voluntarily goes to the Beast's castle to save her father from certain death, but remains to see beyond the Beast's ugliness and find love.

MEAN TO BE FREE, by Joanna Halpert Kraus
New Plays, 1967; 9m, 4w, 1 boy, 1 girl; 3 int., 3 ext. Harriet Tubman, the "Moses of her People," leads two Black children out of bondage to freedom in Canada.

MEDEA'S CHILDREN, by Per Lysander and Suzanne Osten
Folmer Hansen (Teaterforlag Lundag 4, S-17163 Solna, Sweden), 1975; 2m, 3w; 1 ext. The story of Medea's revenge against her husband, Jason, for his infidelity and ungratefulness, is told through the eyes of her children who, in the classic Greek play, have only two lines.

THE MEDICINE SHOW, or HOW TO SUCCEED IN MEDICINE WITHOUT REALLY TRYING, by Virginia Glasgow Koste
Anchorage Press, 1983; 6m, 3w; open stage with neutral blocks. In this short adaptation of Moliere's *Doctor in Spite of Himself,* Sganarelle, a woodcutter, is forced to pretend he is a great doctor; and, in spite of himself, he is responsible for "curing" the miser's daughter and making possible her marriage to the man of her choice.

THE MEN'S COTTAGE, by Moses Goldberg
Anchorage Press, 1980; 2m, 1w, 1 boy, 1 girl; unit set, various locations. Gini Kanwa, a boy who undergoes the rituals of his tribe which accompany the passage from childhood to adulthood, realizes the changes in him are more than symbolic.

MERLIN'S TALE OF ARTHUR'S MAGIC SWORD, by Keith Engar
Anchorage Press, 1982; 13m, 5w; 3 int., 3 ext. Merlin, the magician, relates how the boy, Arthur, squire to the proud Sir Kay, was the one who was able to pull the magic sword out of the anvil and prove he was the rightful heir to the throne.

METRICS CAN BE FUN, by John Baldwin
Pioneer Drama Service, 1977; 4m or w minimum; open stage. Using total theatre techniques in a story theatre format, a small company explores the world of metric measurements.

THE MIRACLE WORKER, by William Gibson
Samuel French, 1956; 7m, 7w; 1 int.-ext. Annie Sullivan arrives at the Keller home to tend their blind, deaf and mute daughter, Helen; and how she breaks through to reach Helen's active mind is one of the most miraculous of modern miracles.

THE MIRRORMAN, by Brian Way
Baker's Plays, 1977; 2m, 2w; 1 int. Toyman introduces his new doll, Beauty, who, with the audience's help, can walk and talk; but trouble in the land behind the mirror involving Mirrorman and a Witch complicate Toyman's and Beauty's lives.

MOLLY WHUPPIE (Musical), by Joella Brown
New Plays, 1980; 4m, 8w; 2 int., 1 ext. In her fantasies, Molly creates a world in which she is brave enough to confront the Giant in his home, only to find a real-life need for her discovered bravery.

MONKEY, MONKEY, by Charles Jones
Anchorage Press, 1986; ensemble of 7m, 3w plus selected children; a jungle gym set is modified with props, drapes and scrolls. The Handsome Monkey King, a roguish Oriental diety, proves his cleverness and bravery by erasing his subjects' names from the scroll of death and robbing the Sea Dragon of his magical weapons, only to be summoned by the Jade Emperor to lead his Dragons of Sunrise and Sunset forever across the sky.

A MOON BETWEEN TWO HOUSES, by Suzanne Lebeau
Le Carrousel (556 Mercille, St-Lambert, Quebec J4P 2L7), 1981; 2w; open stage. Plum and Taciturn own adjacent houses. Plum attempts to make connections with her neighbor while Taciturn counters them with increasing indications of fear and suspicion. But the same moon shines down on both houses.

THE MOONCUSSER'S DAUGHTER, by Joan Aiken
Viking Press, 1973; 8m, 2w, 1 bird; 3 int., 3 ext. The mooncusser's (wrecker's) daughter, Sympathy, prevents a criminal gang from recovering treasure from a sunken ship.

THE MOST POWERFUL JUJUS, by Bernice Bronson
New Plays, 1974; 6 to 9 players; 1 ext. A young girl, Iyabo, is thrust from the Yoruba village accused of thievery; but she returns after a time among the animals to reclaim her rightful place at the King's side.

MOTHER HICKS, by Suzan Zeder
Anchorage Press, 1984; 4m, 4w portray 3 principals and 5 support and chorus roles; one basic set is modified to suggest several locations in and around a southern Illinois town. Girl, an unnamed orphan, uses Mother Hicks' healing powers to cure both physical and emotional illnesses, discrediting the widespread belief that Mother Hicks is a witch.

MRS. McTHING, by Mary Chase
Dramatists Play Service, 1954; 6m, 7w, 1 boy, 1 girl; 2 int. A wealthy woman learns to discover true human worth when her son is replaced by a stick and she herself is forced to earn her keep in a pool hall.

MUGNOG, by Rainer Hachfeld; trans. Jack Zipes and Pamela Bro-Harrison
In *Political Plays for Children*, 1976; written 1970; 4m, 2w perform 14 roles, guitarist; neutral stage, props. Two children drive adults in town to distraction with a box they have named "Mugnog" which gives them sensible advice.

MY DAYS AS A YOUNGLING: JOHN JACOB NILES: THE EARLY YEARS (Musical), by Nancy Niles Sexton, Vaughn McBride, and Marsha Harrison Jones; songs by John Jacob Niles
Anchorage Press, 1982; 7m, 6w, 3 children, plus singing chorus if desired; open stage. A company of actor-singers recreates events in the early life of the folk song composer-singer, John Jacob Niles.

MYSTERY AT THE OLD FORT, by Rosemary G. Musil
Anchorage Press, 1944; 6m, 2w, 2 children; 2 int. Old Fort Niagara becomes the focus of a World War II spy plot involving the Bishop family and other characters.

THE NAKED KING, by Eugene Schwartz, trans. F.D. Reeve
In F.D. Reeve (ed.), *Contemporary Russian Drama* (New York: Pegasus Books, 1967); 4m, 4w, a pot, extras; 3 int., 3 ext., 1 int.-ext. A Princess is betrothed unwillingly to a vain, foolish King; but when the King's stupidity is revealed by his appearing naked in a parade, the Princess is free to marry her true love, the Swineherd.

THE NEAR-SIGHTED KNIGHT AND THE FAR-SIGHTED DRAGON (Musical), by Eleanor and Ray Harder
Anchorage Press, 1977; 5m, 2w, extras; 1 int., 1 ext. The kingdom is controlled by a wicked Duchess; and the Knight looking for a job, the Princess looking for a career, and the Dragon looking for peace all team up to bring about the Duchess' downfall.

NEW CLOTHES FOR THE EMPEROR, by Nicholas Stuart Gray
Samuel French, 1957; 11m, 3w; 3 int., 2 ext. Piers and Perkin are the roguish "weavers" of magic cloth for the Emperor's robes which no one can see; but their prank lands them in the stocks.

NEWCOMER, by Janet Thomas
Anchorage Press, 1987; 2m, 3w play 10 roles; open stage. Mai Li, arrives at an American high school from Vietnam unable to speak English. With some sympathetic help from teachers and, eventually, from Benny, a boy of Chinese ancestry, she starts to find her way into a new and strange world.

NICCOLO AND NICOLLETTE, or THE PUPPET PRINCE, by Alan Cullen
Anchorage Press, 1957; 7m, 3w, extras, dancers; 3 int., 2 ext. Prince Niccolo has been turned into a puppet by Magnus, the magician; and his "niece," Nicollette, who tends the toy shop, is the one who leads the effort to release the enchantment.·

NIGHTINGALE, by John Urquhart and Rita Grossberg
Anchorage Press, 1983; company of 3m, 2w play several roles and musical instruments; open stage with props. Story theatre retelling of Andersen tale of an Emperor who learned to look beneath glittering surfaces for true values.

NOAH AND THE GREAT AUK, by Bix Doughty
Anchorage Press, 1979; 4m, 2w; 1 int. When the Hyena tries to lead a revolt against Noah aboard the ark, the Great Auk sacrifices herself to bring the other animals to their senses.

NO DOGS ALLOWED, or JUNKET, by Aurand Harris
Anchorage Press, 1959; 2m, 2w, 3 children, 1 dog; 1 ext. Even though father has forbidden dogs in their new country home, Michael, Montgomery, and Margaret are somehow adopted by a large airdale.

NOODLE DOODLE BOX, by Paul Maar; adapted and translated by Anita and Alex Page
Baker's Plays, 1979; 3m or w; bare stage with two large boxes and backdrop. Two quarrelsome clowns learn to cooperate when their domain is threatened by a militaristic drum major.

THE NUREMBERG STOVE, by Geraldine Brain Siks
Anchorage Press, 1956; 4m, 1w, 4 children, extras; 3 int. Story of young August who hides in the magnificent Hirschvogel stove when his family is forced to sell it to a Munich art dealer.

THE ODYSSEY, by Gregory Falls and Kurt Beattie
Anchorage Press, 1980; ensemble of 6m, 2w play many roles; unit set. Homer's epic of Odysseus who is lost with his men while returning from the Greek victory over Troy, and who battles natural and unnatural forces in his efforts to reach home.

OLD SILENT MOVIE, by Marie Starr
New Plays, 1980; 9m, 8w; 1 int. A day at a 1920's movie studio turns into farcical chaos as actors, directors, and technicians scramble to make a film.

OLIVER! by Lionel Bart
L. C. Quinney, 1962 (Tams-Witmark); 8m, 6w, 1 boy, 1 girl, extra boys and adults; 6 int., 2 ext. Charles Dickens' story of an orphan boy, Oliver Twist, begins with his miserable childhood in a workhouse, follows him through trials in Fagin's clutches, and ends with his finding a happy home with his real grandfather.

ONCE UPON A CLOTHESLINE, by Aurand Harris
Samuel French; originally Row Peterson, 1945; 2 clothespins, 2 birds, 9 insects; 1 ext. Pinette, a clothespin, is captured by the Black Spider and rescued with the help of the other creatures.

ONE TO GROW ON, by Brian Kral
Unpublished; information from the author, c/o Anchorage Press; 3m, 1w, 4 boys; simultaneously set in several locations. Timmy learns to adjust to the divorce of his parents and the death of his grandfather.

ONLY A MIRACLE (Opera), by Seymour Barab
Unpublished; information from composer, 1225 Park Ave., N.Y., NY 10028; 3m, 1w; unit set (ext.). A comedy version of the story of King Herod's abortive effort to discover the whereabouts· of the Christ child.

ON TRIAL, by Brian Way
Baker's Plays, 1977; 2m, 2w; open stage. An epidemic in an African village sends an expedition to a

distant area in search of a special herb; and audience members accompany the leaders in four teams.

O.P.Q.R.S., ETC., by Madge Miller
Anchorage Press, 1983; 3m, 3w; 1 ext. Otto the Official decrees that the alphabet begin with O and that everything be orange in color because that is his favorite, until an artist arrives in town demonstrating the virtue of freedom of choice.

THE OTHER CINDERELLA, by Nicholas Stuart Gray
Samuel French, 1958; 5m, 5w; 1 int., 5 ext. In this version, Cinderella, a disagreeable girl with delusions of persecution, is paired with her father's valet, while her two sweet stepsisters end up with the Prince and his chief captain.

OTHER DOORS, by Suzan Zeder
Anchorage Press, 1987; 2m, 3w; 1 int. Jeff's parents are in the final stages of getting their divorce and all parties face many readjustments in their lives, especially the need for openness and honesty.

THE OUTLAW ROBIN HOOD, by Moses Goldberg
Anchorage Press, 1980; 16m, 4w; 5 locales in a unit set. Robin's defiance of the Sheriff's law is shown against a background of injustice and greed within the ruling powers.

OZMA OF OZ: A TALE OF TIME, by Suzan Zeder
Anchorage Press, 1981; 5m, 4w, 6m or w, extras; 4 int., 7 ext. Dorothy's adventures with the Wheelers, Princess Languidere and Roquat of the Rocks convince her that Uncle Henry's advanced age does not lessen his value.

THE PADRONE, by Robert Landy
New Plays, 1983; 7 to 9m, 2w; simultaneous set with a balcony and spaces for int. and ext. scenes. Horatio Alger's *Phil the Fiddler* is modified in a Brechtian style to highlight the evils of the 19th century Padrone system in which boys were bought for a few dollars from their Italian parents and turned into New York beggars and street musicians for the profit of their owners.

THE PALACE OF THE MINOTAUR, by Helen Avery
New Plays, 1978; 10m, 7w, 12 m or w; 1 w voice; 4 int., 1 ext. Theseus kills the Minotaur, ending the annual sacrifice of Athenian youths to the man-eating monster; and in the process he is united with Ariadne, his predestined bride.

PEACE CHILD, by David Woollcombe (adapted from *The Peace Book,* by Bernard Benson), music and lyrics by David Gordon
The Peace Child Foundation, P.O. Box 33168, Washington, D.C. 20033, 1983; 12 to 100 children, either m or f, choruses; back curtain and open stage, with props added to suggest several locations. In the year 2035, a Peace Day celebration recreates the "historic" events of the mid-1980's when an American boy and a Russian girl persuaded their presidents to abolish nuclear weapons and live in harmony.

PEACH BOY, by Marie Starr and Larry Jorgensen
New Plays, 1973; 8m, 4w, extras; Oriental stage, locales set with suggestive pieces. A Prince found floating in a peach stone is brought up by his aged foster parents and eventually returned to his rightful place in court.

PECK'S BAD BOY, by Aurand Harris
Anchorage Press, 1974; 3m, 3w, 1 boy; 1 int. Henry's energetic mischief-making puts his father on the road to heaven and captures a thief.

PEOPLE AND ROBBERS OF CARDEMON TOWN (Musical), by Thorbjorn Egner
Anchorage Press, 1968; 8m, 2w, 3 children, extras; 6 int., 1 ext. Kidnapping Aunt Sophie to keep house for them leads to the undoing of three robbers when she makes them toe the mark and become really useful.

PETER PAN, by James Barrie; musical version, music by Mark Charlap, lyrics by Carolyn Leigh
Samuel French, 1928, 1956; 12m, 3w, 10 children, dog, ostrich, crocodile, mermaids, pirates, Indians (musical version: 28 principals plus extras); 1 int., 4 ext., 1 int.-ext. The classic story of the boy who refused to grow up tells of his adventurous life in Never Land.

PETER, PETER, PUMPKIN EATER, or BEAN BLOSSOM HILL, by Martha Bennett King
Anchorage Press, 1945; 2m, 6w; 1 ext., modified. Peter's efforts to pursue his own life style with a girl of his choice leads him to build a house from a spectacular pumpkin.

PHILLIS, by Martha Hill Newell
New Plays, 1987, 1981; 11m, 7w, extras; 7 int., 3 ext. minimally suggested. The life and career of the noted black poetess, Phillis Wheatley, is traced from Africa to colonial Boston, to her triumph in the great houses of London.

THE PIED PIPER, by William Glennon
Coach House Press, 1967; 7m, 5w; neutral set. A piper offers to rid the town of Hamelin of its rats, but when the officials renege on their bargain he leads off all the children, returning them when his terms are met.

THE PIED PIPER OF HAMELIN, by Madge Miller
Anchorage Press, 1951; 3m, 3w, 3 youths, extras; 1 ext. Dirk, a crippled boy, learns to play the Piper's tune on his pipe and bring the children of Hamelintown back from their mountain entrapment when the town officials make good on their bargain with the Pied Piper.

THE PINK SIAMESE (Opera), by Seymour Barab; dialogue and lyrics by Susan Otto
Boosey & Hawkes, 1960; 5m, 5w, 2 boys, acrobats, extras; 1 int., 1 ext. A Siamese cat, born with pink fur, joins a circus as a freak where he remains until a red haired boy convinces the crowd neither of them is a real freak and gives the cat a loving home.

PINOCCHIO, by Madge Miller
Anchorage Press, 1954; 2m, 1w, 2 children, cricket, cat, fox; 2 int., 4 ext. A puppet created by a woodcarver, Gepetto, learns many difficult lessons on his way to becoming a real live boy.

PINOCCHIO, by Brian Way
Dennis Dobson, 1954 (Baker's Plays); 10m, 5w, extras; open stage, designated areas. Gepetto, the puppet-maker, is surprised when his wish is granted that his latest creation could come to life; but it is many experiences later that the mischievous Pinocchio becomes a real boy with some help from the audience.

PIPPI LONGSTOCKING (Musical), by Wesley Van Tassel; music and lyrics by Mark Ollington
Modern Theatre for Youth, 1973; 8m, 4w; 1 int. An adaptation of the Astrid Lindgren stories about Pippi, a girl of nine, who is able to control adults through magic.

THE PLAY CALLED NOAH'S FLOOD, by Suzan Zeder
Anchorage Press, 1984; 12 to 30 m and w play 49 roles; unit set. Villagers of Frodsham, England, in 1491, discover they prefer their version of the mystery play of Noah's flood, and decide to begin their own festival.

THE PRINCE AND THE PAUPER, by Charlotte B. Chorpenning
Anchorage Press, 1951; 13m, 16w; 2 int., 4 ext. Mark Twain's story of how look-alike boys changed places for a lark and a London pauper was almost crowned King of England.

PRIVATE HIGH, by Thomas Martin
Anchorage Press, 1986; 2m, 3w; open stage. When five actors come to a high school to present an alcohol-abuse assembly program, events take a sudden turn when one breaks character, forcing the others to drop the pretense and work informally and improvisationally in terms directly relevant to the actual audience. The tragedy of homicide in DWI situations is emphasized.

THE PUSHCART WAR, by Gregory A. Falls
Anchorage Press, 1985; 8m or w play 44 roles; open stage with "brick wall" background. In the framework of a future TV news show, the story of the war between pushcart owners and truck drivers for supremacy of the streets of New York City is played out by an ensemble company.

THE PRINCE, THE WOLF, AND THE FIREBIRD, by Jackson Lacey
Anchorage Press, 1972; 8m, 5w, Firebird, 4 horses, extras; 5 int., 9 ext. Prince Ivan, third of the King's sons, joins the others in a race to capture the Firebird who has been stealing golden apples; and his journey leads him to the far corners of Russia and into the very jaws of death.

THE PRINCESS AND THE SWINEHERD, by Nicholas Stuart Gray
Samuel French, 1952; 4m, 6w; 3 int., 2 ext. A Swineherd with an eye for beauty and true worth reveals his princely identity when he wins the heart of a haughty Princess.

THE PRINCESS AND THE SWINEHERD, by Madge Miller
Anchorage Press, 1956; 3m, 5w; 1 int., 1 ext. A fairy tale Princess is at first contemptuous of her suitor, but disguised as a Swineherd he is able to help her find true life values.

PROFESSOR FILARSKY'S MIRACULOUS INVENTION, by Erik Vos
Anchorage Press, 1980; 4m, 2w; 1 ext. A comic professor has invented a machine which doubles things and people that go near it; and before its powers are fully understood it is responsible for some bizarre occurrences.

PUNCH AND JUDY (Musical), by Aurand Harris
Anchorage Press, 1970; 8m, 1w, dog, 2 ghosts, 2-person horse; a puppet stage. Punch battles his wife, the law, conventions, death, and finally the Devil to keep himself unfettered in this human level adaptation of traditional puppet plots.

PUSS IN BOOTS, by Madge Miller
Anchorage Press, 1954; 3m, 2w, cat; 1 int., 2 ext. A miller's son inherits a cat who proves to be instrumental in earning for his master a noble title, an estate, and a bride.

PUSS IN BOOTS (Opera), by Douglas Moore; libretto by Raymond Abrashkin
Carl Fischer (rental only) (n.d.); 4m, 1w, narrator, crier, chorus; 1 ext. A cat teaches himself to talk and helps his master win a kingdom and a princess.

RACKETTY-PACKETTY HOUSE, by Frances Hodgson Burnett
In *Another Treasury of Plays for Children*, 1926; 12m, 14w, extras; 4 int., 1 ext. A girl receives a "Tidy Castle" doll house as a gift, but its inhabitants are reluctant to establish warm personal relationships with their humble neighbors who live in "Racketty-Packetty House."

RAGS TO RICHES (Musical), by Aurand Harris
Anchorage Press, 1966; 6m, 3w, extras; 2 int., 2 ext. Ragged Dick, the shoe shine boy, starts up the ladder to success while protecting Mark the Match Boy from the evil exploitation of Mother Watson.

THE RANSOM OF RED CHIEF (Opera), by Seymour Barab
Unpublished; information from composer, 1225 Park Ave., N.Y., NY 10028; 3m, 1w, 1 child; 2 int. An imaginative boy is kidnapped, but he so disconcerts his kidnappers that they offer a reward to the parents to take him back.

REASONS TO BE CHEERFUL (Musical), by Judith Martin, music by Donald Ashwander
Paper Bag Players, 1985 (Baker's Plays); 4 or more m or w; open stage with cardboard props. Eleven brief musical sketches explore a variety of moods and familiar human conditions.

REYNARD THE FOX, by Arthur Fauquez; trans. Marie-Louise Roelants
Anchorage Press, 1962; 6m, 1w (all animals); possible extras; 1 ext., changes with seasons. The trickster, Reynard, lives up to his reputation by turning the other animals' greed and vanity into their own misfortunes, but he saves them all from the hunters at the end.

THE RIDDLE MACHINE, by Beth Lambert

In *Contemporary Children's Theatre,* 1974; information from the author; 3m, 2w, 1 robot, 1 dove; 1 int. A group of children, under the care of a dictatorial robot, is enroute to settle a new world; but before the group arrives the power structure aboard the space ship is rearranged.

RIDDLE ME REE, by Martha Bennett King

Anchorage Press, 1977; 8m, 5w; 1 int., 1 ext. The King's penchant for playing serious riddle games leads him into a trap set by the wicked Astrologer to cheat one of the King's courtiers out of his estates.

RIDE A BLUE HORSE, by Aurand Harris

Anchorage Press, 1986; 6m, 3w can play 19 roles; a bare stage is modified with props and small set pieces. James Whitcomb Riley narrates and plays happenings of his youth in Indiana which provided material for his famous poems.

ROBIN GOODFELLOW, by Aurand Harris

Anchorage Press, 1977; 4m, 2w; 2 ext. Segments of Shakespeare's *Midsummer Night's Dream* are connected to emphasize Puck's fun and games with Rustics and Oberon's feud with Titania.

ROBIN HOOD, by James Norris

Anchorage Press, 1952; 11m, 2w; 1 int., 2 ext. Dramatization of the medieval English legend in which Robin fights injustice from the sanctuary of Sherwood Forest during the King's absence until a contrived archery contest almost brings him to a surprise defeat at the Sheriff's hands.

ROBIN HOOD: A STORY OF THE FOREST, by Timothy Mason

In *Five Plays,* 1975; rights and royalty information from Children's Theatre Co., 2400 3rd Ave. So., Minneapolis, MN 55404; 9m, 3w, 1 boy, extras; 1 ext. Robin's life in the forest with Marion, his men, and Much, the Miller's son, is shown largely as an exercise in patient waiting.

ROBINSON CRUSOE, by Madge Miller

Anchorage Press, 1954; 5m, parrot puppet; 1 ext. Crusoe, shipwrecked on a tropical island, rescues a native from cannibals, and together they contrive ways to survive without benefit of civilization.

RUMPELSTILTSKIN, by Charlotte B. Chorpenning

Anchorage Press, 1944; 6m, 7w, extras; 1 int., 2 ext. An evil dwarf helps a simple miller's daughter to become Queen in exchange for her first-born child, but the Queen manages to foil his plot by discovering his real name.

RUMPELSTILTSKIN (Musical), by Wesley Van Tassel; music and lyrics by Mark Ollington

Modern Theatre for Youth, 1970; 5m, 2w, simultaneously 1 int., 2 ext. In addition to the basic story of the miller's daughter who promises her first-born to a dwarf in exchange for spinning straw into gold, this musical version includes other antagonistic forces that complicate the conflict.

RUNAWAY (Musical), by Ed Graczyk; music by Gerry Pyle

Anchorage Press, 1977; 7m, 4w, voices; neutral set with props. In the company of many runaway young people, Jed discovers the thing he was really searching for was available very close by.

THE RUNAWAY PRESENTS (Musical), by Judith Martin; music by Donald Ashwander

Anchorage Press, 1977; 2m, 2w, presents, extras; neutral set, large cardboard box. Christmas Presents run away from Mrs. Hurryup and almost ruin her party until the guests discover they can have a good time without expensive gifts.

SACRAMENTO FIFTY MILES (Musical), by Eleanor and Ray Harder

Anchorage Press, 1969; 4m, 2w; 1 ext., 1 int.-ext. Two inept robbers are chased from their adopted home by four animals who have banded together against the inhumanities of mankind in this Old West version of the Brementown Musicians.

SAINT GEORGE AND THE DRAGON, by Esther Porter Lane

Anchorage Press, 1985; 10 to 25 m or f; open stage. A troupe of mummers presents in song and pageantry the play of St. George and the Dragon in celebration of the Christmas season, much in the medieval tradition.

SCHOOL WITH CLOWNS, by Friederich Karl Waechter
Verlag der Autoren (Staufenstrasse 46, D 6000 Frankfurt/Main, Germany), 1975; 4m, 1w; 1 int. Four clownish children give their strict teacher a hard time in this parody of ultra-strict German school life.

THE SECRET GARDEN, adapted from Frances Hodgson Burnett's novel by Helen P. Avery
Anchorage Press, 1987; 4m, 4w, 1 boy; 3 int., 2 ext. When her parents die, Mary moves to her uncle's mansion in England where she changes the lives of her cousin, Colin, and her uncle by reviving life in an abandoned, locked garden.

THE SEVEN LEAGUE BOOTS, by Aurand Harris
Baker's Plays; originally Row Peterson, 1948; 5m, 6w; 1 int., 2 ext. Hop o' My Thumb has boots in which he can step seven leagues at once, a skill he uses to save some children from the Ogre and transform him into a flower.

THE SHADOW, by Eugene Schwartz; trans. F.D. Reeve
In F.D. Reeve (ed.), *Twentieth Century Russian Plays* (New York: Norton Library, 1973); 11m, 5w, extras; 2 int., 2 ext. A Scholar's Shadow separates from him and assumes the Scholar's place as groom of the Princess, only to discover he cannot survive the Scholar's execution.

SHAMAN, by Isabelle Foord
Playwrights Co-op, 1973; 2m, 2 "naked newts;" neutral set. With the help of the children in the audience the kindly old Shaman prevents the evil Dark Shaman, Ooktah, from becoming King of the Arctic.

SHINING PRINCESS OF THE SLENDER BAMBOO, by Sylvia Ashby
I.E. Clark, 1987; 15m, 3w, 1m voice, extras; 1 ext. Princess Moonbeam, daughter of the Moon King, spends some years as a mortal, bringing joy to an old couple, until suitors and the Emperor try to make her choose her future husband. Her love for the Emperor is short-lived as her father, the Moon King, calls her back into his own palace.

THE SILVER THREAD, by Constance D'Arcy Mackay
Henry Holt, 1910; 9m, 4w, 6 goblins, extras; 4 int. Cubert, a miner lad, rescues the Princess from goblins with the aid of a special ring that sends out a luminous silver thread showing the way to safety.

THE SILVER WHISTLE, by Patrick B. Mace
Anchorage Press, 1985; 3m, 3w, 7 m or w, extras; multiple locales in and around a town, both interiors and exteriors, minimally suggested with props in an arena playing area. A soldier, a conjuror and a princess all learn that possession of the silver whistle with its magical powers is more troublesome than beneficial, and agreee that neutralizing its powers is in everyone's best interests.

SIMPLE SIMON, or SIMON BIG EARS, by Aurand Harris
Anchorage Press, 1953; 6m, 2w, 3 children, 3 garments, extras; 1 ext. Simon chances upon a country tyrannized by a dictatorial queen and innocently demonstrates the greater strength of truth and freedom.

SINBAD AND THE EVIL GENII, by Jack Melanos
Anchorage Press, 1986; 7m, 3w and 2 m or w; 1 int./ext., 2 ext. A mischievous boy and a willful princess use their fellow prisoner, Sinbad, as a model to learn true values as they attempt to outwit an Evil Genii whose island holds rich treasure.

SIR GAWAIN AND THE GREEN KNIGHT, by Dennis Scott
Anchorage Press, 1978; company of 4m, 2w play many roles; open stage. A Conteur tell the story of how Sir Gawain met the tests of character presented to him by the Green Knight and Lady Alison, with characters and natural forces enacted in a total theatre framework.

SKUPPER DUPPERS (Musical), by Flora Atkin
New Plays, 1975; 7 to 9 players enact many roles; neutral stage. Story theatre treatment of four tales of American ports of call: Alaska, Virgin Islands, Hawaii, and Puerto Rico.

THE SLEEPING BEAUTY, by Charlotte B. Chorpenning
Anchorage Press, 1947; 3m, 8w, 1 boy; 2 int., 1 ext. The Princess Beauty's parents try vainly to protect her from the curse of death at her sixteenth birthday; but Prince Elano's bravery and perseverance enable him to awaken her after 100 years of sleep.

SLEEPING BEAUTY, by Richard Shaw
In *Five Plays,* 1975; rights and royalty information from Children's Theatre Co., 2400 3rd Ave. So., Minneapolis, MN 55404; 3m, 3w, 1 boy, 1 girl, 3 spirits, 20 extras; unit set with modifications of one segment. As Grandfather tells his children the story of the Princess who awakens from the Ogress' curse of death after a sleep of 100 years, the events are enacted in Kabuki style.

SLEEPING BEAUTY, by Brian Way
Baker's Plays, 1977; 8m, 4w play 21 roles; open stage. Princess Carol is promised death at her eighteenth birthday by an evil godmother; but after 100 years of sleep, Simple, now a Prince, is able to awaken her.

THE SNOW QUEEN, by Suria Magito and Rudolf Weil; based on the play by Eugene Schwartz
Theatre Arts Books, 1960; 9m, 10w, extras; 4 int., 2 ext. When Kay is captured by the Snow Queen his little friend Gerda endures many hardships to rescue him.

THE SNOW QUEEN AND THE GOBLIN, by Martha Bennett King
Coach House Press, 1956; 3m, 2w, 2 children, 1 goblin, extras; 2 int. Some original twists of plot mark this adaptation of the Andersen tale, but essentially it remains the story of Gerda's attempts to rescue Kay from the Snow Queen's palace.

SNOW WHITE AND ROSE RED, by Madge Miller
Anchorage Press, 1954; 3m, 3w; 1 int., 1 ext. A Bear and a Fish are released from their enchantment by the persistence and courage of Snow White and Rose Red.

SNOW WHITE AND THE SEVEN DWARFS, by Judith Baker Kase
Anchorage Press, 1984; 2m, 2w, 7 m or w; 2 int., 1 ext. Princess Snow White is protected from the wicked queen by seven dwarfs; and when the queen almost succeeds in killing her, the jester-turned-prince brings her happily back to life.

SNOW WHITE AND THE SEVEN DWARFS, by Jessie Braham White
Samuel French, 1912; 5m, 11w, 7 dwarfs, 3 cats, extras; 3 int., 1 ext. Snow White's stepmother, the Queen, is impelled by jealousy to seek the death of the fair princess; but the love and faithfulness of the 7 dwarfs and the Prince restore her life.

SPACE HARP, by Martha Bennett King
Coach House Press, 1969; 2 boys, 2w; 3 int., 2 ext. Johnny spends much of his time trying to communicate with anyone out there in space, and is surprised with a visit by a boy from another world.

SPECIAL CLASS, by Brian Kral
Anchorage Press, 1981; 6m, 8w; 1 int. A class of children with developmental handicaps demonstrates in relationships the same needs and problems as those of other children.

THE SPECTACULAR SPECTACLES OF ALEXANDER JONES (Musical), by Deborah Anderson
Unpublished; information from author: 452 21st Street, Santa Monica, CA 90402. (1978); 12 ensemble performers; a game environment. Alexander tries many pathways in search of his real self, finally realizing he has to find his own way without copying others.

SPRIDITIS (Musical), by Anna Brigadere, lyrics and English version by Vilnis Baumanis, music by Andrejs Jansons

Coach House Press, 1984; 13m, 9w, extras; 2 int., 1 ext., 2 int./ext. This Latvian operetta tells the story of Spriditis, a small 13-year-old boy, who sets off to seek his fortune, encounters life-threatening adversaries, and returns home much wiser.

STARMAN JONES, by Douglas L. Lieberman
In *Contemporary Children's Theatre,* 1974; copyright 1972; royalty information from Lurton Blassingame, 60 E. 42nd St., N.Y., NY 10017; 8m, 3w, 1 boy, 1 girl; unit set suggesting parts of a space ship and 1 ext. Max, the boy stowaway on an interplanetary voyage, proves his worth and takes his place as the ship's astrogator.

STAR SPANGLED MINSTREL, or STAR SPANGLED SALUTE (Musical), by Aurand Harris
Anchorage Press, 1975; ensemble of 4m, 1w minimum; open stage. Patriotic musical revue in the old minstrel show format with interlocutor, endmen, and specialty numbers.

STEAL AWAY HOME (with music), by Aurand Harris
Anchorage Press, 1972; 9m, 4w, choir; bare stage, suggestive sets. Adaptation of the Jane Kristof novel relating the adventures of Amos and his little brother, Obie, on a trip north to Philadelphia on the Underground Railroad in the 1850's.

STEP ON A CRACK, by Suzan Zeder
Anchorage Press, 1976; 2m, 2w, 1 girl, Voice; 2 int., 1 ext. Ellie's father has remarried and her feelings about stepmothers lead her to extended fantasies with imaginary playmates and rejecting behavior that reaches dangerous proportions.

STORY THEATRE, by Paul Sills
Samuel French, 1971; 5m, 3w; bare stage, projections. The original production which passed its name to all subsequent scripts of the genre features stories from Grimm and fables from Aesop in a fluid structure that mixes song, dance, mime and narrative connections.

STRIKING OUT, by Michael Bigelow Dixon and Valerie Smith
Anchorage Press, 1983; 8m, 6w, 1m voice; 1 ext. A school baseball team battles the potential humiliation of a shut-out by a superior opponent while discovering things about the game and themselves.

THE STRUGGLE, by Brian Way
Baker's Plays, 1977; 4m, 2w; open stage. Adam is a present-day Pilgrim as he explores ways of living and experiences the temptations and pleasures available at every turn.

THE SUN KING, THE MOON KING AND THE WIND KING, by Jan Jilek
DILIA, Vysehradska 28, Prague 2, Czechoslovakia (Pugh) (n.d.); 9m, 5w; 5 int., 5 ext. The Kings of Sun, Moon, and Winds help Prince Silomil defeat a wicked witch and the King of Fire and win his Princess.

SUNSONG, by Saphira Barbara Linden
New Plays, 1976; 12 players; open playing area. Children participate in the problems experienced by a family in conflict and suggest solutions.

TAKE ME TO THE TREASURE, by Claire Jones and Robert Varga
Involvement Dramatics, 1970; 2m, 2w; open stage. Bad Bart pursues Princess Telmeetru to get her to reveal the whereabouts of the Indian tribe's treasure; but Teddy, with the children's help, foils his efforts.

TALES FROM HANS CHRISTIAN ANDERSEN (Musical); book by Mary Jane Evans and Deborah Anderson; lyrics by Mary Jane Evans; music by Ed Archer
Anchorage Press, 1983; ensemble of 7m, 5w; neutral stage. Ensemble engages in song, dance, mime and transformations to play four Andersen tales.

TARRADIDDLE TALES AND TARRADIDDLE TRAVELS, by Flora Atkin
New Plays, 1971; 6 to 8 players enact many roles; neutral stage. Published together but possibly played separately, TALES and TRAVELS each presents 4 stories from folk and ethnic literature in story theatre form.

THIRTEEN BELLS OF BOGLEWOOD, by Max Bush
Anchorage Press, 1987; 4m, 3w; 1 ext. Brian, a young man, is hired by a greedy man to help him find the legendary gold treasure hidden in his forest—a treasure, they discover, protected by Hiddeous Spriggans and needed to sustain the lives of forest fairies. When the greedy Bogle joins the search, Brian changes sides and helps the forest creatures retain their treasure and change his employer into a Bogle.

THREE TALES FROM JAPAN, by Robin Hall
Anchorage Press, 1973; company of 6m, 6w play many roles; Oriental stage. A troupe of Japanese actors performs three stories under the watchful eye of the Stage Manager: "The Magic Fan," "The Princess of the Sea," and "Little Peach Boy."

THE THWARTING OF BARON BOLLIGREW, by Robert Bolt
Samuel French, 1966; 21m, extras; bare stage, props. Sir Oblong Fitz Oblong is sent on a quest to kill the dragon of the Bolligrew Islands in this mock-heroic epic.

TIMBLEWIT, by Marian Jonson
Coach House Press, 1971; 11m, 2w, 1 girl, extras; 1 int., 1 ext. Timblewit, a young star, comes to earth to learn to be human and falls in love with a Fool, the wisest of humans.

THE TIGER'S BONES, by Ted Hughes
Viking Press, 1974; 7m, 1 m or w, extras; 1 ext. A muddled scientist convinces a primitive society to change its economy base, with disastrous results.

THE TINDER BOX, by Nicholas Stuart Gray
Samuel French, 1951; 7m, 4w, 7 creatures, extras; 5 int., 3 ext. A witch fools a soldier into retrieving a treasure from a hollow tree, but the soldier uses the magic tinder box to win himself a princess and a kingdom.

THE TINGELARY BIRD, by Mary Melwood
New Plays, 1969; 2m, 2w; 1 int. An old man and old woman are visited by a strange bird who brings a new dimension to their chaotic lives.

THE TIN SOLDIER, by Sasa Lichy
DILIA, Vysehradska 28, Prague, Czechoslovakia (Pugh) (n.d.); 10m, 1w, extras; 2 int. The son of a toymaker disguises himself as a tin soldier, helps the King defeat his enemy, and teaches the King's daughter not to treat human beings as toys.

TO BE (Musical), by Ed Graczyk; music by Gerry Pyle
Pickwick Press, 1971; 7m, 4w; unit set. Jason, a teenage young man, is propelled many directions by parents, peers, and his own desires in this rock musical version of Shakespeare's *Hamlet*.

A TOBY SHOW, by Aurand Harris
Anchorage Press, 1978; 3m, 4w, extra vaudeville entr'acts; 1 int. Toby, the countrified American folk hero, is again triumphant as he straightens out the tangled romance of Cindy and the Prince in a story much like Cinderella.

TOM EDISON AND THE WONDERFUL "WHY," by Faye Parker
Coach House Press, 1961; 2m, 2w, 1 boy, 4 girls; 1 int., 2 ext. The inquisitiveness and inventiveness of the young Tom Edison are demonstrated in a series of episodes.

TOM SAWYER (Musical), by Sara Schlesinger; music by Michael Dansicker
New Plays, 1967; 8m, 7w; 3 int., 6 ext. Musical version of Tom's adventures while growing up in a small Missouri town in the 1850's.

TOM SAWYER, by Sara Spencer; also available with music
Anchorage Press, 1935; 10m, 3w, 12 children; 5 int., 3 ext. Small town mischief-maker and adventurer shows his true character by testifying about a murder and saving his old friend.

TOM THUMB (Musical), by Tadeusz Kierski and Julia Hartwig
Unpublished; information from Jed Davis, Univ. Theatre, Murphy Hall, Univ. of Kansas, Lawrence, KS 66045 (1964); 15m, 11w, 1 boy's voice, horse, lion, fox; 2 int., 3 ext. Tom, who is so small he is invisible, sets off to find the magic herb that will help him grow to normal height, and has many adventures before he finds it.

THE TOWN MOUSE AND THE COUNTRY MOUSE, by Vicky Ireland
Anchorage Press, 1987; 2m, 2w; book set with pages revealing 11 locations. William, the country mouse, accepts his cousin's invitation to visit the city and inspect the new house (a hunting boot) he has inherited. After numerous and harrowing adventures, he decides that town life is not for him, and he returns to the country.

TREASURE ISLAND, by Jules Eckert Goodman
Samuel French, 1915; 22m, 1w, 1 boy, 1 parrot; 2 int., 6 ext. Jim Hawkins' adventures in search of treasure in the South Seas after he gains possession of a pirate map; elaborate stage version of the Robert Louis Stevenson novel.

TREASURE ISLAND, by Aurand Harris
Anchorage Press, 1983; 12m, 1w; 1 int., 3 ext. Jim Hawkins' possession of a treasure map leads him and his friends on a voyage to the South Seas in search of pirates' plunder; but a crew of cut throats, led by Long John Silver, has the same goal.

TREASURE ISLAND, by Brian Way
Baker's Plays, 1977; 13m, 1w minimum to play 21 roles; open stage. An old pirate's treasure map leads the boy, Jim Hawkins, to a South Sea island where the crew's treachery almost costs the lives of Jim and his friends.

THE TRIAL OF TOM SAWYER, by Virginia Glasgow Koste
Anchorage Press, 1978; 18m, 8w; 3 int., 4 ext. Mark Twain narrates and comments on the events of Tom's summer adventures involving whitewashing a fence, a graveyard murder, trial of the town drunk, and his near escape from Injun Joe.

TRIBE, by Barbara Linden
New Plays, 1970; 9 players; open playing space. Audience children are members of three tribes whose life-patterns are disrupted by the coming of White men.

THE TROLL AND THE ELEPHANT PRINCE, by Max Bush
Anchorage Press, 1985; 3m, 3w; 1 ext. Citizens of Trolltown dutifully pay tribute to a wicked troll for protection from really harmless Zanies until Jack, a peasant boy with a toy elephant, discovers the treasure of his heritage and sets them free.

TRUDI AND THE MINSTREL, by Alan Cullen
Anchorage Press, 1966; 10m, 4w, extras; 6 int., 5 ext. The peasant girl, Trudi, teams up with a minstrel, and together they seek their fortune, which includes encounters with a Baroness and her son, a dragon, trolls, a mermaid, and a Baron who arranges Trudi's marriage.

TWELVE MONTHS, by Samuel Marschak; trans. Alexander Bakshy
In Alexander Bakshy (comp. and ed.), *Soviet Scene: Six Plays of Russian Life* (New Haven: Yale Univ. Press, 1946); 22m, 5w, 5 animals, extras; 2 int., 2 ext. A Stepdaughter is sent into the woods in January with instructions to gather snowdrops the Queen wants and is willing to pay handsomely for; and with the Twelve Months' help she not only brings back the flowers but is able to teach the Queen, her cruel stepmother and stepsister some important lessons.

THE TWO MAPLES, by Eugene Schwartz; trans. Miriam Morton
In *Russian Plays for Young Audiences*, 1977; 3m, 2w, Bear, Cat, Dog, mice; 1 ext. modified. Vasilisa-the-Hardworker more than fulfills the impossible tasks set for her by the witch, Baba Yaga, and thereby frees her two sons from enchantment as maple trees.

TWO PAILS OF WATER, by Aad Greidanus
Anchorage Press, 1965; 4m, 2w; 1 ext. Dophilius and Alfonso trade names, homes, occupations and social status, confusing their respective fiancees and the girls' father in this dramatization of the Dutch folk rhyme.

UMIAK, THE COLLECTIVE BOAT, by Francois Camirand, Yves Lauvaux, Monique Rioux, and Michel O. Noel; English translation by John Van Burek
In *Canadian Theatre Review* 46 (Spring 1986), 72-94; information from Theatre de la Marmaille, 42 Ave. des Pins, Ouest, Montreal, Quebec H2W 1R1, Canada; 5 m or w play multiple roles using masks and puppets; open playing space with raised area. Children in the audience are directly involved in the roles of parents, grandparents and children of an Inuit village, deciding appropriate actions and facing crises of Eskimo life such as shortage of food and ice break-up.

THE UNWICKED WITCH, by Madge Miller
Anchorage Press, 1964; 2m, 4w; 1 int. Winona is the youngest of the witches living in the old house, but her inability to make witchery work remains frustrating until her real identity is discovered.

VASALISA, by Joanna Halpert Kraus
New Plays, 1973; 4m, 7w, 1 cat; 2 int., 2 ext. Vasalisa is forced by her stepmother to do all the dirty work around the house; and when she is captured by the witch, Baba Yaga, she performs several "impossible" tasks with outside help, resulting in her release from both witch and stepmother.

THE VELVETEEN RABBIT, adapted from Margery William's story by James Still
Unpublished; information from Emmy Gifford Children's Theatre, 3501 Center St., Omaha, NE 68105 (1986); 2m, 1w, 1 boy, 4 m or w, extras; 1 int., 1 ext. A legless toy rabbit becomes real through being loved by its four-year-old owner.

THE VIOLIN OF PASSING TIME, by Aristide-Christian Charpentier
Anchorage Press, 1972; 4m, 1w; 1 int. Jacques, a young shoemaker, and his friend, Pierre, are helped to find the course of their lives when an ornate chest is delivered without its keys.

WHAT DO YOU CALL LOVE HERE? by Helma Fehrmann, Jurgen Flugge, and Holger Franke
Verlag der Autoren (Staufenstrasse 46, D 6000 Frankfurt/Main, Germany), 1976; 2m, 2w; open stage. Two teenagers make their first explorations into a loving relationship, learning to respect each other and relate their feelings to the larger context in which they live.

THE WHEEL, by Brian Way
Baker's Plays, 1977; 2m, 2w; neutral stage. A magic wheel is used as a stimulus for the performers to enact stories with the help of the children of the audience.

WHERE THE WILD THINGS ARE (Opera), by Maurice Sendak and Oliver Knussen
Faber Music of London (G. Schirmer), 1982; 5m, 4w; 2 int., 2 ext. Max, an imaginative boy, is sent to his room as punishment; but he transforms the room into a forest, then into the mysterious island where the Wild Things live, are tamed and crown Max "the wildest of them all."

WHERE TO, TURULU? by Henri Degoutin, Jeanine Vedienne, and Yves Hugues; trans. Miriam and Lewis Morton
New Plays, 1980; 2m, 3w; 1 ext. The young innocent Turulu joins up with three companions, and together they cope with the worldly evils introduced by MacBluff.

WHO AM I? (Musical), by Seymour Barab
Unpublished; information from composer, 1225 Park Ave., N.Y., NY 10028 (1980); 2m, 3w; 2 int., 1 ext. Grimms' story of "The Goose Girl" concerns a lovely Princess whose place is usurped by her Waiting Woman and she is forced to serve as a tender of geese until the truth of the deception is discovered.

WIGGLE WORM'S SURPRISE (Musical), by Judith Martin; music by Donald Ashwander
Anchorage Press, 1977; 7 m or w minimum; 1 ext. Wiggle Worm saves the trees in the forest to celebrate their own Christmas, in the familiar style of the Paper Bag Players.

WILEY AND THE HAIRY MAN, by Jack Stokes
Coach House Press, 1970; 2m, 1w, chorus; open stage. The tale of Wiley, whose father was eaten by the Hairy Man and who fears the same monster will get him, too, fosters self reliance and courage.

WILEY AND THE HAIRY MAN, by Suzan Zeder
Anchorage Press, 1978; 1m, 1w, 1 boy, dog, 4 or more chorus; 1 int.-ext. Wiley is helped to conquer the object of his greatest fear by a combination of Mammy's conjure spells and his own ingenuity.

WILLIAM TELL, by W. Vosco Call
Coach House Press, 1963; 8m, 3w, 1 boy, 1 girl, 1 child; 2 ext. William Tell and his son challenge the despotic rule of the tyrant, Gessler, in their Swiss village; and Tell is forced to shoot an apple off his son's head with an arrow.

WIND IN THE WILLOWS, by Moses Goldberg
Anchorage Press, 1974; 2 humans, 8 to 10 animals; unit set. Toad carries his passion for speed and danger to ridiculous lengths; and his friends, Rat, Mole and Badger, use their ingenuity to protect him from his worst impulses and recapture Toad Hall from the Weasels.

WINNIE-THE-POOH, by Kristin Sergel
Dramatic Publishing Co., 1957; 1 boy, 1 man's voice, 11 or more animals; 3 ext. A.A. Milne's famous stories about Christopher Robin's toy animals who have problems when Kanga comes to live in the forest.

WINTERTHING, by Joan Aiken
Samuel French, 1972; 3m, 5w; 1 int., 1 ext. Five children come to Winter Island with their peculiar Auntie and in the six years of the island's invisibility discover strange facts about their background.

THE WIZARD OF OZ (Musical), by Frank Gabrielson; score by Harold Arlen and E. R. Harburg (from the MGM film)
Tams-Witmark, 1938, 1978; 4m, 3w, extras; 2 int., 4 ext. Dorothy is transported by a tornado from Kansas to Oz where she meets some friends who accompany her on the Wizard's charge to rid the country of the Wicked Witch of the West.

THE WIZARD OF OZ, by Adele Thane
Anchorage Press, 1957; 6m, 7w, dog, extras; 1 int., 6 ext. The only way Dorothy can get back home to Kansas after being blown to Oz by a tornado is to get the Wizard's help; but he demands she and her friends rid Oz of the Wicked Witch of the West in return for his help.

THE WIZARD OF OZ, by Camilla Wolak
New Plays, 1962; 5m, 4w, extras; 2 int., 5 ext. With the help of a Scarecrow, a Tin Woodman and a Lion, Dorothy is able to convince the powerful Wizard of Oz to let her return to her home in Kansas.

YANKEE DOODLE (Musical), by Aurand Harris
Anchorage Press, 1975; 12-person ensemble plays many parts; unit set. Musical revue celebrating the U.S. bicentennial with highlights of people big and small who have made the country what it is.

YOUNG BEN — FRANKLIN'S FIGHT FOR FREEDOM, by Faye Parker
Coach House Press, 1958; 5m, 1w, 1 boy, 1 girl, extras; 1 int.-ext. A youthful Franklin displays early signs of patriotic zeal in his struggle with authorities in a matter of freedom of the press.

YOUNG DICK WHITTINGTON, by Alan Broadhurst
Anchorage Press, 1964; 12m, 5w, extras; 3 int., 3 ext. Cook's helper Dick is leaving London in contrived disgrace when his talented cat persuades him to return; but the cat is the one primarily responsible for making Dick's fortune in the Orient trade.

THE YOUNG GRADUATES, by Victor Rosov; trans. Miriam Morton
In *Russian Plays for Young Audiences*, 1977; 6m, 4w; 2 int. A group of young people face the need to pass examinations admitting them to their preferred schools or failing them and selecting alternative careers.

THE YOUNG GUARD, by Anatoly Aleksin; trans. Miriam Morton
In *Russian Plays for Young Audiences*, 1977; 19m, 14w, 1 boy, extras; 1 ext. modified. A Nazi Gestapo General interrogates teenagers about the sabotage activities of the Russian Young Guard while their exploits are reenacted.

YOUNG STEPHEN FOSTER (Musical), by Faye Parker
Coach House Press, 1968; 3m, 3 boys, 3 girls; 1 int., 1 ext. The famous composer's early life is spent assimilating the folk music of the area and preparing him for his ultimate recognition.

YOU'RE A GOOD MAN, CHARLIE BROWN (Musical); book, music and lyrics by Clark Gesner
Tams-Witmark, 1967; 4m, 2w; 1 ext. Charles Schultz' comic strip characters romp through a series of episodes depicting usual and unusual crises of childhood.

¡ZAS!, (Musical), by Virginia A. Boyle, musical arrangements by Virginia A. Boyle and T.M. Scruggs; translation by Roberto Lopez
Coach House Press, 1979; 3m, 4w, plus 9-piece band if desired; simultaneously set 1 ext., 2 flexible spaces. An exploitative bear is taught a lesson in human rights and decent employee relations in this bilingual (English and Spanish) urban allegory.

BIBLIOGRAPHY
Theatre for Young Audiences

Published Works

Broadman, Muriel. *Understanding Your Child's Entertainment.* New York: Harper & Row, 1977.

Burbank, P. Donna, ed. *The First Twenty Years: 1943-1963.* Baltimore: Children's Theatre Association, 1963.

Chorpenning, Charlotte B. *Twenty-One Years With Children's Theatre.* Anchorage, KY: Children's Theatre Press, 1954 (now New Orleans: Anchorage Press).

Corey, Orlin. *Theatre for Children — Kid Stuff, or Theatre?* Anchorage Press, 1974; now New Orleans.

Cornelison, Gayle, comp. and ed. *A Directory of Children's Theatres in the United States.* Washington, D.C.: American Theatre Association, 1980.

Davis, Jed H., and Mary Jane Larson Watkins. *Children's Theatre: Play Production for the Child Audience.* New York: Harper & Row, 1960.

Doolittle, Joyce, and Zina Barnieh. *A Mirror of Our Dreams: Children and the Theatre in Canada.* Vancouver, B.C.: Talonbooks, 1979.

Evans, Dina Rees. *Cain Park Theatre: The Halcyon Years.* Cleveland: The Halcyon Press, 1980.

Fisher, Caroline E., and Hazel Glaister Robertson. *Children and the Theatre.* Rev. ed. Stanford: Stanford Univ. Press, 1950.

Fordyce, Rachel. *Children's Theatre and Creative Dramatics: An Annotated Bibliography of Critical Works.* Boston: G. K. Hall & Co., 1975.

Forkert, O.M., ed. *Children's Theatre That Captures Its Audience.* Chicago: Coach House Press, 1962.

Goldberg, Moses. *Children's Theatre: A Philosophy and a Method.* Englewood Cliffs, NJ: Prentice-Hall, 1974.

Hale, Pat, ed. *Participation Theatre for Young Audiences.* New York: New Plays for Children, 1972.

Heinig, Ruth Beall, ed. *Go Adventuring! A Celebration of Winifred Ward: America's First Lady of Drama for Children.* New Orleans: Anchorage Press, 1977.

Heniger, Alice Minnie Herts. *The Children's Educational Theatre.* New York: Harper & Bros., 1911.

Kennedy, Carol Jean. *Child Drama: A Selected and Annotated Bibliography, 1974-1979* (a project of the Theatre Department, Arizona State University). Washington, D.C.: Children's Theatre Association of America, 1981.

Johnson, Richard C. *The Theatre Student: Producing Plays for Children.* New York: Richards Rosen Press, Inc., 1971.

Latshaw, George. *The Theatre Student: Puppetry, The Ultimate Disguise.* New York: Richards Rosen Press, Inc., 1978.

Morton, Miriam. *The Arts and the Soviet Child.* New York: Free Press, 1972.

_____, ed. and trans. *Through the Magic Curtain: Theatre for Children, Adolescents, and Young Adults in the U.S.S.R.* New Orleans: Anchorage Press, 1979.

Motter, Charlotte Kay. *Theatre in High School: Planning, Teaching, Directing.* Englewood Cliffs, NJ: Prentice-Hall, 1970.

McCaslin, Nellie. *Act Now!* New York: S.C. Phillips & Co., 1975.

_____, ed. *Children and Drama.* 2nd ed. Lanham, MD: University Press of America, 1985.

_____. *Shows on a Shoestring: An Easy Guide to Amateur Productions.* New York: David McKay Co., 1979.

_____. *Theatre for Children in the United States: A History.* Norman, OK: Univ. of Oklahoma Press, 1971.

_____, ed. *Theatre for Young Audiences.* New York: Longman, Inc., 1978.

Power, Thomas A., and Donna Sincyr, eds. *Children's Theatre Directory: 78-79.* Portland, ME: Univ. of Southern Maine (1979).

Rodenberg, Ilse, ed. *Kinder-und Jugendtheater der Welt*. Berlin: Henschelverlad, 1978; U.S.A. distributor, Anchorage Press, New Orleans.

Rosenberg, Helane S., and Christine Prendergast. *Theatre for Young People: A Sense of Occasion*. New York: Holt, Rinehart and Winston, 1983.

Siks, Geraldine Brain, and Hazel Brain Dunnington, eds. *Children's Theatre and Creative Dramatics*. Seattle: Univ. of Washington Press, 1961.

Spolin, Viola. *Improvisation for the Theatre*. Evanston: Northwestern Univ. Press, 1963.

Swortzell, Lowell, ed. *Six Plays for Young People from the Federal Theatre Project (1936-1939)*. New York: Greenwood Press, 1986.

Van Tassel, Wesley, ed. *Children's Theatre Bibliography*. Washington, D.C.: American Theatre Association, 1975.

Ward, Winifred. *Creative Dramatics in the Upper Grades and Junior High School*. New York: Appleton-Century-Crofts, 1930.

_____. *Theatre for children*. 3rd rev. ed. Anchorage, KY: Children's Theatre Press, 1958.

Watson, Charles M., ed. *Theatre Resources Handbook/Directory*. National Endowment for the Arts, Artists-in-Schools Program. Washington, D.C.: GPO, 1979.

Way, Brian. *Children's Theatre and Audience Participation*. Manchester, NH: Theatre Center America, 1977. (Baker's Plays)

Whitton, Patricia, ed. *Outstanding Plays for Young Audiences: International Bibliography*. Vol. I. New York: ASSITEJ/USA, 1984.

The Wichita Children's Theatre: The First Thirty Years. Wichita, KS: The Wichita Children's Theatre Guild, 1975. (Anchorage Press)

Wood, Ronald. *The Magic World of Brian Way's Theatre*. Boston: Baker's Plays, 1977.

Wright, Lin, ed. *Professional Theatre for Young Audiences*. Vol. I (1984), Vol. II (1986). Tempe, AZ: Department of Theatre, Arizona State Univ.

Unpublished Works

Aldrich, Dorothy Edna. "A Study of Child Audience Reaction to a Controversial Character in a Children's Play." Thesis Pittsburgh 1965.

Allen, Darlene Kaye. "A Procedure for Directing a Sign-Language Theatre Production for a Child Audience." Thesis California State Univ.-Northridge 1977.

Bedard, Roger L. "The Life and Work of Charlotte B. Chorpenning." Diss. Kansas 1978.

Beger, Lois Lee Stewart. "The Theory and Practice of the Children's Theatre Company and School of Minneapolis, Minnesota." Diss. Florida State 1981.

Behm, Thomas. "Elements of Style in Scene Design." Thesis Kansas 1967.

Bethea, Sara Kathryn. "Opera for Children: An Analysis of Selected Works." Diss. Kansas 1971.

Cornelison, Gayle. "Death and Childhood: Attitudes and Approaches in Society, Children's Literature and Children's Theatre and Drama." Diss. Kansas 1975.

_____. "Preferences of Children for Saturated Colors and Tints." Thesis Kansas 1965.

Crenshaw, Clayton. "Color Association in Costume Design." Thesis Kansas 1967.

Davis, Jed H. "The Art of Scenic Design and Staging for Children's Theatre." Diss. Minnesota 1958.

Gamble, Michael W. "Clare Tree Major: Children's Theatre, 1923-1954." Diss. New York University 1976.

Goldberg, Moses. "A Survey and Evaluation of Contemporary Practices at Selected European Children's Theatres." Diss. Minnesota 1969.

Graham, Kenneth L. "An Introductory Study of the Evaluation of Plays for Children's Theatre in the United States." Diss. Utah 1947.

Green, Elizabeth. "Female Gender Role Representation in Children's Theatre." Thesis Kansas 1975.

Guffin, Jan A. "Winifred Ward: A Critical Biography." Diss. Duke 1976.

Kilmer, Paulette. "Theatre and Self Esteem in Teenagers." Thesis Kansas 1980.

Kingsley, William H. "Happy Endings, Poetic Justice and Strength of Characterization in American Children's Drama: A Critical Analysis." Diss. Pittsburgh 1964.

Kraus, Joanna Halpert. "A History of the Children's Theatre Association of Baltimore, Maryland from 1943-1966." Diss. Columbia 1972.

Machiach, Sellina. "Allegory in Children's Theatre and Drama." Diss. Kansas 1975.

Melody, Patricia. "Children's Interests in Story Content for Children's Theatre." Thesis Kansas 1967.

Regan, Frederick Scott. "The History of the International Children's Theatre Association from its Founding to 1975." Diss. Minnesota 1975.

Rhea, Martha Hershey. "A Comparison of Children's and Adults' Attitudes Toward an Imperfect Protagonist in a Children's Play." Thesis Kansas 1970.

Rodman, Ellen. "Edith King and Dorothy Coit and the King-Coit School and Children's Theatre." Diss. New York University 1979.

Rubin, Janet E. "The Literary and Theatrical Contributions of Charlotte B. Chorpenning to Children's Theatre." Diss. Ohio State 1978.

Scoville, Sharon L. "The Rogue as a Children's Theatre Protagonist." Thesis Kansas 1963.

Woodruff, Marci. "Feminine Sex-Role Models and the Socialization of the Child Audience." Diss. Florida State 1980.

Zeder, Suzan L. "A Character Analysis of the Child Protagonist as Presented in Popular Plays for Child Audiences." Diss. Florida State 1978.

Play Production

Adix, Vern. *Theatre Scenecraft.* Rev. ed. New Orleans: Anchorage Press, 1981.

Barton, Lucy. *Historic Costume for the Stage.* Rev. ed. Boston: Walter H. Baker, 1961.

Bay, Howard. *Stage Design.* New York: Drama Book Specialists, 1974.

Bellman, Willard. *Scene Design, Stage Lighting, Sound, Costume & Make-up: A Scenographic Approach.* New York: Harper and Row, 1983.

_____. *Scenography and Stage Technology: An Introduction.* New York: Thomas Y. Crowell Co., 1977 (Harper and Row).

Benedetti, Robert L. *The Actor at Work.* Englewood Cliffs, NJ: Prentice-Hall, 1970.

Blunt, Jerry. *The Composite Art of Acting.* New York: Macmillan, 1966.

Boleslavski, Richard. *Acting, The First Six Lessons.* New York: Theatre Arts Books, 1934.

Brook, Peter. *The Empty Space: A Book About Theatre.* New York: Atheneum, 1968.

Burris-Meyer, Harold, and Edward C. Cole. *Scenery for the Theatre.* Rev. ed. Boston: Little, Brown & Co., 1971.

Chaikin, Joseph. *The Presence of the Actor.* New York: Atheneum, 1972.

Chekhov, Michael. *To the Actor.* New York: Harper & Row, 1953.

Clifford, John E. *Educational Theatre Management.* Skokie, IL: National Textbook Co., 1972.

Clurman, Harold. *On Directing.* New York: Macmillan, 1972.

Coger, Leslie Irene, and Melvin R. White. *Readers Theatre Handbook.* Rev. ed. Glenview, IL: Scott, Foresman, 1973.

Collison, David. *Stage Sound.* New York: Drama Book Specialists, 1975.

Corey, Irene. *The Mask of Reality.* New Orleans: Anchorage Press, 1968.

Corson, Richard. *Stage Make-up.* 5th ed. Englewood Cliffs, NJ: Prentice-Hall, 1975.

Crawford, Jerry, L. and Joan Snyder. *Acting in Person and in Style.* Dubuque, IA: Wm. C. Brown Co., 1976.

Dean, Alexander, and Lawrence Carra. *Fundamentals of Play Directing.* 3rd ed. New York: Holt, Rinehart & Winston, 1974.

Dietrich, John E., and Ralph W. Duckwall. *Play Direction.* 2nd ed. Englewood Cliffs, NJ: Prentice-Hall, 1983.

Dolman, John, and Richard K. Knaub. *The Art of Play Production.* 3rd ed. New York: Harper & Row, 1973.

Gillette, J. Michael. *Designing with Light: An Introduction to Stage Lighting.* Palo Alto: Mayfield Publishing Co., 1978.

Grotowski, Jerzy. *Towards a Poor Theatre*. New York: Simon & Schuster, 1969.

Gruver, Bert. *The Stage Manager's Handbook*. New York: Drama Book Specialists, 1972.

Guthrie, Tyrone. *On Acting*. New York: Viking Press, 1971.

Hagen, Uta, and Haskell Frankell. *Respect for Acting*. New York: Macmillan, 1973.

Healy, Daty. *Dress the Show: A Basic Costume Book*. Rev. ed. Rowayton, CT: New Plays Books, 1976.

Hodge, Francis. *Play Directing: Analysis, Communication and Style*. Englewood Cliffs, NJ: Prentice-Hall, 1971.

Langley, Stephen. *Theatre Management in America: Principle and Practice*. New York: Drama Book Specialists, 1974.

Lessac, Arthur. *Use and Training of the Human Voice*. New York: Drama Book Specialists, 1967.

Linklater, Kristin, and Douglas Florian. *Freeing the Natural Voice*. New York: Drama Book Specialists, 1976.

Miller, James Hull. *Self-Supporting Scenery for Children's Theatre...and Grown-Ups' Too*. Shreveport, 1976. (Anchorage Press)

Mokwa, Michael P., William M. Dawson, and E. Arthur Prieve, eds. *Marketing and the Arts*. New York: Praeger Publishers, 1980.

McGaw, Charles. *Acting is Believing: A Basic Method*. 4th ed. New York: Holt, Rinehart & Winston, 1980.

Newman, Danny. *Subscribe Now!* New York: Theatre Communications Group, 1977.

Oxenford, Lyn. *Playing Period Plays*. London: J. Garnet Miller, 1958 (Coach House Press)

Pektal, Lyn. *Designing and Painting for the Theatre*. New York: Holt, Rinehart & Winston, 1975.

Reiss, Alvin H. *The Arts Management Handbook*. 2nd ed. New York: Law-Arts Publishers, Inc., 1974.

Rizzo, Raymond. *The Total Actor*. New York: Odyssey Press, 1975.

Rubin, Joel W., and Leland H. Watson. *Theatrical Lighting Practice*. New York: Theatre Arts Books, 1954.

Russell, Douglas A. *Period Style for the Theatre*. Boston: Allyn and Bacon, 1980.

_____. *Theatrical Style: A Visual Approach to the Theatre*. Palo Alto: Mayfield, 1976.

Schechner, Richard. *Environmental Theatre*. New York: Hawthorn, 1973

Selbie, Robert. *The Anatomy of Costume*. Crescent Books, 1977.

Stanislavsky, Constantin. *Building a Character*. Trans. Elizabeth Reynolds Hapgood. New York: Theatre Arts Books, 1949.

Stern, Lawrence. *School and Community Theatre Management*. Boston: Allyn & Bacon, 1979.

Strickland, F. Cowles. *The Technique of Acting*. New York: McGraw-Hill, 1956.

Wilfred, Thomas. *Projected Scenery: A Technical Manual*. New York: Drama Book Specialists, 1965.

Creative Drama, Arts and Education

Allen, John. *Drama in Schools: Its Theory and Practice*. London: Heinemann Educational Books, 1979.

American Council for the Arts in Education. *Coming to Our Senses: The Significance of Arts for American Education* (A Panel Report). New York: McGraw-Hill, 1977.

Arnheim, Rudolf. *Art and Visual Perception*. Rev. ed. Berkeley: Univ. of California Press, 1974.

Bruner, Jerome S. *The Process of Education*. Cambridge, MA: Harvard Univ. Press, 1962.

Burger, Isabel B. *Creative Play Acting*. 2nd ed. New York: Ronald Press, 1966.

Clark, Kenneth B. *A Possible Realty*. New York: Metropolitan Applied Research Center, 1972.

Courtney, Richard. *The Dramatic Curriculum*. New York: Drama Book Specialists, 1980.

_____. *Play, Drama and Thought*. New York: Drama Book Specialists, 1974.

Davis, Jed H., comp. and ed. *Theatre Education: Mandate for Tomorrow*. New Orleans: Anchorage Press, 1985.

Drama/Theatre Framework for California Public Schools. Sacramento, CA: California State Dept. of Education, 1974.

Gallagher, Kent G., ed. *Drama Education Guidelines: A Curriculum Guideline for the Theatre Arts in Education in the State of Washington*. Olympia: Dept. of Public Instruction, 1972.

Heinig, Ruth Beall, and Lyda Stillwell, *Creative Dramatics for the Classroom Teacher*. 2nd ed. Englewood Cliffs, NJ: Prentice-Hall, 1981.

Jackson, Tony, ed. *Learning Through Theatre: Essays and Casebooks on Theatre in Education*. Manchester Univ. Press, 1980.

Kase-Polisini, Judith, ed. *Children's Theatre, Creative Drama and Learning*. Lanham, MD: University Press of America, 1986.

_____. ed. *Creative Drama in a Developmental Context*. Lanham, MD: University Press of America, 1985.

King, Nancy. *Giving Form to Feeling*. New York: Drama Book Specialists, 1975.

Klock, Mary E., ed *Bibliography in Creative Dramatics*. Washington, D.C.: American Theatre Association, 1975.

Koste, Virginia. *Dramatic Play in Childhood: Rehearsal for Life*. New Orleans: Anchorage Press, 1978.

Landy, Robert, *Handbook of Educational Drama and Theatre*. Westport, CT: Greenwood Press, 1982.

Madeja, Stanley, and Sheila Onuska. *Through the Arts to the Aesthetic*. St. Louis: CEMREL, Inc., 1977.

McCaslin, Nellie. *Creative Drama in the Classroom*. 4th ed. New York and London: Longman, 1984.

McGregor, Lynn, Maggie Tate, and Ken Robinson. *Learning Through Drama*. London: Heinemann Educational Books, 1977.

Moore, Raymond S., and Dorothy N. Moore, et. al. *School Can Wait*. Provo, UT: Brigham Young Univ. Press, 1979.

O'Toole, John. *Theatre in Education (New Objectives for Theatre - New Techniques for Education)*. London and Toronto: Hodder and Stoughton, 1976.

Philosophy, Scope and Sequence for a Model Drama/Theatre Curriculum. A National Theatre Education Project. Blacksburg, VA: American Association of Theatre for Youth and American Association of Theatre in Secondary Education., 1987.

Polsky, Milton. *Let's Improvise: Becoming Creative, Expressive and Spontaneous Through Drama*. Englewood Cliffs, NJ: Prentice-Hall, 1980.

Postman, Neil. *The Disappearance of Childhood*. New York: Delacourt Press, 1982.

Robinson, Ken, ed. *Exploring Theatre and Education*. London: Heinemann Educational Books, 1980.

Rosenberg, Helane S. *Creative Drama and Imagination*. New York: CBS College Publishing, 1987.

Salisbury, Barbara T. *Theatre Arts in the Elementary Classroom, Fourth Grade Through Sixth Grade*. New Orleans: Anchorage Press, 1986.

_____. *Theatre Arts in the Elementary Classroom, Kindergarten Through Third Grade*. New Orleans: Anchorage Press, 1986.

Schattner, Gertrud, and Richard Courtney, eds. *Drama in Therapy*. Vol. I: Children. New York: Drama Book Specialists, 1980.

Schwartz, Dorothy T., and Dorothy Aldrich, eds. *Give Them Roots. . . And Wings!* New Orleans: Anchorage Press, 1985.

Shaw, Ann M., and CJ Stevens, eds. *Drama, Theatre, and the Handicapped*. Washington, D.C.: American Theatre Association, 1979.

Singer, Jerome L. *The Child's World of Make-Believe*. New York: Academic Press, 1973.

Siks, Geraldine Brain. *Drama With Children*. 2nd Ed. New York: Harper and Row, 1983.

Slade, Peter. *Introduction to Child Drama*. London: Univ. of London Press, 1958.

Spodek, Bernard, ed. *Early Childhood Education*. Englewood Cliffs, NJ: Prentice-Hall, 1973.

Visual and Performing Arts Framework for California Public Schools: Kindergarten Through Grade Twelve. Sacramento: California State Department of Education, 1982.

Wagner, Betty Jane. *Dorothy Heathcote, Drama As A Learning Medium*. Washington, D.C.: National Education Association, 1976.

Ward, Winifred. *Playmaking With Children*. 2nd ed. New York: Appleton-Century-Crofts, 1957.

_____. *Stories To Dramatize*. Anchorage, KY: Children's Theatre Press, 1952; now New Orleans: Anchorage Press.

Way, Brian. *Development Through Drama*. London: Longmans, 1967. (Baker's Plays)

Webster, Clive. *Working With Theatre in the Schools*. London: Pitman & Sons, Ltd., 1976 (Baker's Plays)

Child Studies

Almy, Millie. *Young Children's Thinking*. New York: Teachers College Press, 1966.

Bandura, Albert. *Social Learning Theory*. Englewood Cliffs, NJ: Prentice-Hall, 1977.

Beard, Ruth M. *An Outline of Piaget's Developmental Psychology*. New York: Basic Books, 1969.

Bettelheim, Bruno. *The Uses of Enchantment: The Meaning and Importance of Fairy Tales*. New York: Alfred A. Knopf, 1976.

Brearley, Molly, and Elizabeth Hitchfield. *A Guide to Reading Piaget*. New York: Schocken Books, 1966.

Carmichael, Leonard, ed. *Manual of Child Psychology.* New York: John Wiley & Sons, 1974.

Feshbach, Seymour, and Robert D. Singer. *Television and Aggression: An Experimental Field Study*. San Francisco: Jossey-Bass, 1971.

Friedrich, Lynette Kohn, and Aletha Huston Stein. "Aggressive and Prosocial Television Programs and the Natural Behavior of Children." Monographs of the Society for Research in Child Development, Serial No. 151, 38 (Aug. 1973), pp. 56-63.

Fromm, Erich. *The Anatomy of Human Destructiveness*. New York: Holt, Rinehart & Winston, 1973.

Graham, Douglas. *Moral Learning and Development*. London: B.T. Batsford, Ltd., 1972.

Himmelweit, Hilde T., A. N. Oppenheim, and Pamela Vince. *Television and the Child*. London: Oxford, Univ. Press, 1958.

Joseph, Stephen M. *Children In Fear*. New York: Holt, Rinehart & Winston, 1974.

Kohlberg, Lawrence. "Development of Moral Character and Moral Ideology." in *Review of Child Development Research*. Eds. Martin L. Hoffman and Lois Wladis Hoffman. New York: Russell Sage Foundation, 1964, pp. 383-431.

Longstreth, Langdon E. *Psychological Development of the Child*. 2nd ed. New York: Ronald Press, 1974.

Lorenz, Konrad. *On Aggression*. Trans. Marjorie Kerr Wilson. New York: Harcourt, Brace & World, 1963.

Lowenfield, Viktor, and W. Lambert Brittain. *Creative and Mental Growth*. 6th ed. New York: Macmillan, 1975.

Menninger, Karl. *The Crime of Punishment. New York: The Viking Press, 1969.*

Piaget, Jean. The Language and Thought of the Child. Trans. Marjorie Gabin. New York: New American Library, 1974.

Pickard, P.M. *I Could a Tale Unfold*. New York: Humanities Press, 1961.

Plummer, Gordon S. *Children's Art Judgement*. Dubuque, IA: Wm. C. Brown Co., 1974.

Skinner, B.F. *Beyond Freedom and Dignity*. New York: Alfred A. Knopf, 1971.

Stein, Aletha Huston, and Lynette Kohn Friedrich. *Impact of Television on Children*. Chicago: Univ. of Chicago Press, 1975.

U.S. Public Health Service. *Television and Growing Up: The Impact of Televised Violence*. Report to the Surgeon General from the Scientific Advisory Committee on Television and Social Behavior. Washington, D.C.: GPO, 1972.

Wohlwill, Joachim F. *The Study of Behavioral Development*. New York: Academic Press, 1973.

Wolfenstein, Martha. *Children's Humor*. Glencoe, IL: The Free Press, 1954.

PHOTO CREDITS

(1) - Page 25
THE DREAM FISHER, by John Clark Donahue (unpublished).
The Children's Theatre Company and School, Minneapolis
Director: John Clark Donahue
Sets by John Clark Donahue and Donald Pohlman
Costumes by John Clark Donahue and Gene Davis Buck
Lights by Jon Baker
Music by Steven M. Rydberg
Photo by Paul Hager

(2) - Page 25
REYNARD THE FOX, by Arthur Fauquez (Anchorage Press)
Everyman Players
Director: Orlin Corey
Designer: Irene Corey
L to R: Randolph Tallman, Allen Shaffer
Photo by Jerry Mitchell

(3) - Page 25
CIRCUS MAGIC, original company creation (unpublished)
University of Wisconsin-Madison
Director: John Tolch
Sets by Charles Erven
Costumes by Marla Jurglanis
Lights by Chris Deignan
Photo by Zane Williams

(4) - Page 26
THE ICE WOLF, by Joanna Halpert Kraus (New Plays)
California State University, Hayward
Director: Jeanne L. Hall
Sets by Thomas Hird
Costumes by Judy Governor

(5) - Page 26
A LANCASHIRE LAD, by Adrienne Kennedy
Empire State Youth Theatre Institute-State University of New York
Director: Joseph Balfior
Sets by Richard Finkelstein
Costumes by Elaine Yokoyama
Lights by Lloyd S. Riford III
Music by George Harris
Photo by Fred Ricard

(6) - Page 26
THE ARKANSAW BEAR, by Aurand Harris (Anchorage Press)
University of Texas-Austin
Director: Coleman A. Jennings
Sets by Charles Beyer
Costumes by Paul D. Reinhardt
Lights by Jeff Zucker
Photo by Marty Bass

(7) - Page 26
THE ARKANSAW BEAR, by Aurand Harris (Anchorage Press)
University of Texas-Austin
Director: Coleman A. Jennings
Sets by Charles Beyer
Costumes by Paul D. Reinhardt
Lights by Jeff Zucker
Photo by Marty Bass

(8) - Page 27
THE PIED PIPER, by Melvin Bernhardt (Coach House Press)
California State University, Hayward
Director: Jeanne Hall
Sets by Gloria Fricke
Costumes by Richard Barulich
Photo by Earnest Jaco

(9) - Page 27
A MEMORABLE ACCOUNT OF MARK TWAIN IN THE SANDWICH ISLANDS, by Michael Colwell (unpub.)
Honolulu Theatre for Youth
Director: Kathleen Collins
Sets and costumes by Joseph Dodd
Lighting by Gerald Kawaoka
Photo by Pepi Nieva

(10) - Page 27
JACK AND THE BEANSTALK, by Charlotte B. Chorpenning (Anchorage Press)
The Gallivanting Inspiration Group, San Jose State University Theatre
Director: Robert Jenkins
Sets by Fredrick Jefferson
Costumes by Ellen T. Briggs
Lights by Jerry Enright

(11) - Page 27
THE ODYSSEY, adapted from Homer by Gregory A. Falls and Kurt Beattie (Anchorage Press)
A Contemporary Theatre/The Young ACT Company, Seattle
Director: Gregory A. Falls
Sets by Shelly Henze Shermer
Costumes by Sally Richardson
Actors: (from UC on boat) Robert John Zenk, James W. Monitor, Richard Hawkins,
    John Michael Hoskings, Richard Lee, (DR) Maria Mathay; (DL) Marritt Olsen
    Photo by Chris Bennion

(12) - Page 27
STEAL AWAY HOME, by Aurand Harris (Anchorage Press)
Kansas University Theatre for Young People
Director: Jed H. Davis
Sets by Ed Kirkman
Costumes by Chez Haehl
Lights by Charles Lown
Photo by Andrew Tsubaki

(13) - Page 28
WILEY AND THE HAIRY MAN, by Susan Zeder (Anchorage Press)
Everyman Players
Director: Marilee Hebert-Slater
Designer: Irene Corey
Photo by Karl Stone

(14) - Page 28
REYNARD THE FOX, by Arthur Fauquez (Anchorage Press)
Theatre for Children, California State University, Northridge
Director: Mary Jane Evans
Sets by Owen W. Smith
Costumes by John S. Furman
Masks by Betsy Brown
CSU-N staff photo

(15) - Page 28
THE MAN IN THE MOON, by Alan Cullen (Anchorage Press)
Children's Theatre, Goodman School of Drama
Director: Kelly Danford
Sets by Alan Traynor
Costumes by Al Tucci
Lights by Lymon Dunning

(16) - Page 28
MOBY DICK - REHEARSED, adapted from Herman Melville (unpublished)
Nashville Academy Theatre
Director: Tom Kartak
Designed by Ken Parks
Photo by Ken Parks

(17) - Page 28
TWO PAILS OF WATER, by Aad Greidanus (Anchorage Press)
Theatre for Children, California State University, Northridge
Director: Mary Jane Evans
Sets by Owen W. Smith
Costumes by John S. Furman
Photo by Gilman W. Rankin

(18) - Page 29
PETER PAN, musical based on James Barrie's play by Mark Charlap and Carolyn Leigh
  (Samuel French)

Zev Bufman and James M. Nederlander Production
Director: Rob Iscove (after original production by Jerome Robbins)
Production designed: Peter Wolf
Costumes by Bill Hargate
Lights by Thomas Skelton
Flying by Foy
L to R: Sandy Duncan as Peter, Jonathan Ward as Michael, Marsha Kramer as Wendy
Photo by Martha Swope

(19) - Page 29
A CHRISTMAS CAROL, adapted from Charles Dickens by Barbara Fields (unpublished)
The Guthrie Theatre, Minneapolis
Director: Richard Remos
Sets by Jack Barkla
Costumes by Jack Edwards
Lights by Neil McLeod
Jake Dengel as Scrooge
Photo by Boyd Hagen

(20) - Page 29
THE MEN'S COTTAGE, by Moses Goldberg (Anchorage Press)
Stage One, The Louisville Children's Theatre
Director: Moses Goldberg
Sets and costumes by Ken Terrill
Lights by Moses Goldberg
Kirk Davis as Gini Kanwa, John Youngblood as the Witch Doctor
Photo by Richard Trigg

(21) - Page 29
GOLLIWHOPPERS! by Flora Atkin (Anchorage Press)
Theatre for Children, California State University, Northridge
Director: Mary Jane Evans
Sets by Owen W. Smith
Costumes by John S. Furman
CSU-N staff photo

(22) - Page 30
BEANS, by Buddy and David Sheffield (unpublished)
Sheffield Ensemble Theatre
Directors: Rita and Buddy Sheffield
Designer: Buddy Sheffield
Photo by David Sheffield

(23) - Page 30
JOHNNY MOONBEAM AND THE SILVER ARROW, by Joseph Golden (Anchorage Press)
Kansas University Theatre for Young People

Director: Jed H. Davis
Sets by James Harrington
Costumes by Chez Haehl
Lights by Charles Lown
Photo by James Harrington

(24) - Page 30
TALES FROM HANS CHRISTIAN ANDERSEN; book by Mary Jane Evans and
    Deborah Anderson; lyrics by Mary Jane Evans; score by Ed Archer (unpublished)
Theatre for Children, California State University, Northridge
Sets by Owen W. Smith
Costumes by Cathy Susan Pyles
Photo by Cathy Susan Pyles

(25) - Page 31
THE SNOW QUEEN, adapted from Hans Christian Andersen by Michael Dennis Browne (unpub.)
The Children's Theatre Company and School, Minneapolis
Director: John Clark Donahue
Sets and costumes by Dahl Delu
Lights by Karlis Ozols
Music by Steven M. Rydberg
Photo by Paul Hager

(26) - Page 31
THE CLOWN OF GOD, adapted from Tomie dePaola by Thomas E. Olson
The Children's Theatre Company and School, Minneapolis
Director: John Clark Donahue
Sets by Don Yunker; design consultant Tomie dePaola
Costumes by Judy Cooper
Lights by Robert S. Hutchings, Jr.
Muisc by Steven Rydberg
Photo by George Heinrich

(27) - Page 31
TREASURE ISLAND, adapted from Robert Louis Stevenson by Timothy Mason
The Children's Theatre Company and School, Minneapolis
Director: John Clark Donahue
Sets by Dahl Delu
Costumes by Rae Marie Pekas
Lights by Andrew Sullivan
Music by Hiram Titus
Photo by Patrick Thomas Boemer

(28) - Page 31
THE 500 HATS OF BARTHOLOMEW CUBBINS, adapted from Dr. Seuss by Timothy Mason
The Children's Theatre Company and School
Director: John Clark Donahue

Sets by Jack Barkla
Costumes by Judy Cooper
Lights by Karlis Ozols
Music by Hiram Titus
Photo by Gary Mortenson

(29) - Page 32
ALICE IN WONDERLAND, adapted from Lewis Carroll by Robyn Flatt
Dallas Theater Center MimeAct
Director: Robyn Flatt
Designer: Irene Corey
Photo by Brimstone Films, Karl Stone, Larry Gerbrandt

(30) - Page 32
ALICE IN WONDERLAND, adapted from Lewis Carroll by Robin Flatt
Dallas Theater Center MimeAct
Director: Robyn Flatt
Designer: Irene Corey
Photo by Irene Corey

(31) - Page 32
ALICE IN WONDERLAND, adapted from Lewis Carroll by Robyn Flatt
Dallas Theatre Center MimeAct
Director: Robyn Flatt
Designer: Irene Corey
Photo by Irene Corey

(32) - Page 84
MAGICAL FACES, by Brian Way (Baker's Plays)
University of Wisconsin-Madison
Director: John Tolch
Sets, costumes and lights by Alan Wolf
Photo by Zane Williams

(33) - Page 84
THE LEGEND OF SLEEPY HOLLOW, adapted from Washington Irving by Frederick Gaines
    (University of Minnesota Press)
Eastern Michigan University Theatre Of the Young (TOY)
Director Virginia Koste
Sets and lights by George Bird
Costumes by Katherine Holkeboer

(34) - Page 84
THE 500 HATS OF BARTHOLOMEW CUBBINS, adapted from Dr. Seuss by Timothy Mason (umpub.)
The Children's Theatre Company, Minneapolis
Director: John Clark Donahue
Sets by Jack Barkla
Costumes by Judy Cooper
Lights by Karlis Ozols
Music by Hiram Titus
Photo by Gary Mortenson

(35) - Page 85
THE ICE WOLF, by Joanna Halpert Kraus (New Plays)
California State University, Hayward
Director: Jeanne Hall
Sets by Thomas Hird
Costumes by Judy Governor

(36) - Page 85
RIP VAN WINKLE, by Grace Ruthenburg (Anchorage Press)
Arizona State University
Director: Lin Wright
Sets by Douglas Scott Goheen
Photo by John Barnard

(37) - Page 85
THE BUTTERFLY, by Bijan Mofid (Anchorage Press)
Everyman Players
Director: Marilee Hebert-Slater
Designed by Irene Corey
Tom Hayes as the Grasshopper
Photo by Irene Corey

(38) - Page 86
TOM SAWYER, adapted from Mark Twain by Vern Adix (unpublished)
University of Utah, Summer Theatre for Young People
Director: Vern Adix
Sets by Vern Adix
Costumes by Peggy Freeman
Photo by Robert Clayton

(39) - Page 87
MAGGIE MAGALITA, by Wendy Kesselman (unpublished)
Carole C. Huggins production for the John F. Kennedy Center for the Performing Arts Programs for
    Children and Youth
Director: Wallace Chappell
Sets and lights by Charles H. Vaughan III
Costumes by Ken Holamon
L to R: Trina Alvarado, Teresa Yenque
Photo by Jack Buxbaum

(40) - Page 87
STEP ON A CRACK, by Suzan Zeder (Anchorage Press)
University of Wisconsin-Madison
Director: John Tolch
Sets by Kurt Sharp
Costumes by Carol Dietmeyer
Lights by Peter Reader
Photo by Zane Williams

(41) - Page 87
MAGGIE MAGALITA, by Wendy Kesselman (unpublished)
Carole C. Huggins production for the John F. Kennedy Center for the Performing
  Arts Programs for Children and Youth
Director: Wallace Chappell
Sets and lights by Charles H. Vaughan III
Costumes by Ken Holamon
Trini Alvarado (on couch), Teresa Yenque
Photo by Jack Buxbaum

(42) - Page 87
THE MIRACLE WORKER, by William Gibson (Samuel French)
Empire State Youth Theatre Institute, State University of New York
Director: Patricia B. Snyder
Sets by Douglas W. Schmidt and Russell Christian
Costumes by Patrizia von Brandenstein
Lights by Michael J. Cusick
Photo by Fred Ricard

(43) - Page 88
ARM IN ARM, adapted from Remy Charlip by Zero Weil and the Metro Theatre Circus (unpublished)
Metro Theatre Circus, St. Louis
Directors: June Ekman and Zaro Weil
Sets by Branislav Tomich and Nicholas Kryah
Costumes by Branislav Tomich
Photo by Scott Dine

(44) - Page 89
CARNIVAL OF THE ANIMALS as interpreted by Betsy Brown Puppeteers
Los Angeles Festival (1976)
Photo by Julie Kay Davis

(45) - Page 89
PETER PAN, by James M. Barrie (Samuel French)
Theatre for Young People, University of North Carolina- Greensboro
Director: Tom Behm
Sets and lights by Dennis C. Maulden
Costumes by Zoe Brown
Photo by W.C. Burton

(46) - Page 90
THE HUMBLE KING, collaboratively adapted from "King Thrushbeard" by the Yellow
  Brick Road Shows (unpublished)
Directors: Rita Grossberg and John Urquhart
Photo by Julie Kay Davis

342

(47) - Page 90
THE BIRDS, adapted from Aristophanes by John Biroc (unpublished)
Theatre for Children, California State University, Northridge
Director: John Biroc
Costumes and Masks by Van Doh
CSU-N staff photo

(48) - Page 90
FOOL OF THE WORLD, by John Urquhart and Rita Grossberg (Anchorage Press)
Yellow Brick Road Shows
Directors: Rita Grossberg and John Urquhart
Photo by John Urquhart

(49) - Page 90
NIGHTINGALE, by John Urquhart and Rita Grossberg (Anchorage Press)
Yellow Brick Road Shows
Directors: Rita Grossberg and John Urquhart
Photo by John Urquhart

(50) - Page 91
GOOD MORNING, MR. TILLIE, by John Clark Donahue (unpublished)
The Children's Theatre Company and School, Minneapolis
Director: John Clark Donahue
Sets by Don Yunker
Costumes by Rae Marie Pekas
Lights by Karlis Ozols
Photo by Patrick Thomas Boemer

(51) - Page 91
KID'S WRITES devised by James Mairs
The Magic Carpet Theatre Company of San Francisco
Los Angeles Festival (1976)
Photo by Julie Kay Davis

(52) - Page 91
A BOY CALLED TOM SAWYER, by Constance Schneider (unpublished)
Theatre for Children, California State University, Northridge
Director: Christine Parrent
Sets and lights by Don Rohrbacker
Costumes by Stephanie Schoelzel
Photo by Jeff Levy

(53) - Page 131
THE RABBIT WHO WANTED RED WINGS, by Nellie McCaslin (Coach House Press)
California State University, Hayward
Director: Jeanne L. Hall
Sets by Ivan Hess
Costumes by Alice Harchell
Photo by Earnest Jaco

(54) - Page 131
HAPPY BIRTHDAY US, a company creation (unpublished)
University of Wisconsin-Madison
Director: John Tolch
Sets by Laura Maurer
Costumes by Sue Christensen
Lights by Gary Cleven
Photo by Zane Williams

(55) - Page 131
ANDROCLES AND THE LION, by Aurand Harris (Anchorage Press)
Theatre for Children, California State University, Northridge
Director: Mary Jane Evans
Sets and Costumes by John S. Furman
CSUN staff photo

(56) - Page 131
A CHRISTMAS CAROL, adapted from Dickens by Barbara Fields (unpublished)
The Guthrie Theatre, Minneapolis
Director: Richard Remos
Sets by Jack Barkla
Costumes by Jack Edwards
Lights by Neil McLeod
Actors: L to R: Jake Dengel, T.R. Knight
Photo by Boyd Hagen

(57) - Page 132
THE GREAT CROSS-COUNTRY RACE, by Alan Broadhurst (Anchorage Press)
Everyman Players
Director: Orlin Corey
Designed by Irene Corey
David Kingsley as Mr. Fleet
Photo by Orlin Corey

(58) - Page 132
THE THWARTING OF BARON BOLLIGREW, by Robert Bolt (Samuel French)
Young People's University Theatre (YPUT), University of Minnesota-Minneapolis
Director: Jeffrey S. Miller
Sets, Costumes, Lights by Nan Zabriskie

(59) - Page 132
THE ICE WOLF, by Joanna Halpert Kraus (New Plays)
Kansas University Theatre for Young People
Director: Jed H. Davis
Sets by Harry Silverglat, Jr.
Costumes by Chez Haehl
Lights by Marilyn Bernstein
Photo by Andrew Tsubaki

(60) - Page 132
EVERYBODY, EVERYBODY, by Judith Martin ("Big Country")
Paper Bag Players
Director: Judith Martin
Production design by Judith Martin
L to R: Irving Burton, Judith Martin, Douglas Norwick, Adrienne Doucette
Photo by Martha Swope

(61) - Page 133
STEAL AWAY HOME, by Aurand Harris (Anchorage Press)
California State University, Hayward
Director: Jeanne L. Hall
Sets by Thomas Hird
Costumes by Sharon Fong
Photo by Earnest Jaco

(62) - Page 133
JOHNNY MOONBEAM AND THE SILVER ARROW, by Joseph Golden (Anchorage Press)
Young People's University Theatre (YPUT), University of Minnesota-Minneapolis
Director: W. Hyrum Conrad
Sets by Rolfe D. Bergsman
Costumes by Robert W. Jones
Lights by Jacob Haagsman

(63) - Page 134
OLIVER! by Lionel Bart (Tams-Witmark)
Cabrillo Theatre, Oxnard, CA
Director: Mara Lysova
Sets by Larry Parker
Costumes by Mara Lysova
Lights by Loren Burton
Photo by Julie Kay Davis

(64) - Page 134
BEAUTY AND THE BEAST, by Nicholas Stuart Gray (Samuel French)
Kansas University Theatre for Young People
Director: William B. Birner
Sets by William Henry
Costumes by William B. Birner and Chez Haehl
Lights by Patrick Prosser

(65) - Page 134
THE HONORABLE URASHIMA TARO, by Coleman A. Jennings (Dramatic Publ. Co.)
University of Texas-Austin
Director: Coleman A. Jennings
Choreographed by Mel Freeland

Sets by Rachel Garland Goode
Costumes by Paul D. Reinhardt
Lights by Charles Lown
Photo by Tom Bayne

(66) - Page 135
A CIRCLE IS THE SUN, by John Clark Donahue and Frederick Gaines (unpublished)
The Children's Theatre Company and School, Minneapolis
Director: John Clark Donahue
Sets by Donald Pohlman
Costumes by Gene Davis Buck
Lights by Jon Baker
Music by Frank Wharton
Photo by George Heinrich

(67) - Page 136
THE LITTLE HUMPBACK HORSE, by Pyotr Ershov; trans. by Lowell Swortzell (unpublished)
Program in Educational Theatre, New York University
Director: Lowell Swortzell
Sets by Gary Speziale
Costumes by Lillian Pam
Lights by Marty Chafkin and Kathy Kauffman
Photo by Lowell Swortzell

(68-71) - Page 136
PUNCH AND JUDY, by Aurand Harris (Anchorage Press)
Kansas University Theatre for Young People
Director: Jed H. Davis
Sets, costumes and puppets by Terryl Asla
Lights by Tom Rowe
Photos by Andrew Tsubaki

(72) - Page 137
A WRINKLE IN TIME, adapted from Madeleine L'Engle by Gregory Falls (unpublished)
A Contemporary Theatre/The Young ACT Company, Seattle
Director: Gregory A. Falls
Sets by Shelley Henze Schermer
Costumes by Julie James
Lights by Donna Grout
Actors: L to R: Nina Wishengrad, Richard Hawkins, Peter Kelley, David Calacci
Photo by Chris Bennion

(73) - Page 137
PETER PAN, by James Barrie (Samuel French)
Arizona State University
Director: Don Doyle
Sets by Douglas Scott Goheen
Costumes by David Rhinders
Photo by John Barnard

(74-79) - Page 138
Montage of autograph party shots, California State University, Northridge
(74) Crowding around.
(75) Even the Baroness is "safe" in an outdoor setting.
(76) An eager public
(77) ANDROCLES AND THE LION, lobby of Schoenberg Hall, UCLA.
(78) TRUDI AND THE MINSTREL.
(79) PUNCH AND JUDY characters meet their fans.
Photos by CSUN staff

(80) - Page 198
REYNARD THE FOX, by Arthur Fauquez (Anchorage Press)
Theatre for Children, California State University, Northridge
Director: Mary Jane Evans
Sets by Owen W. Smith
Costumes by John S. Furman
Masks by Betsy Brown
CSUN staff photo

(81) - Page 198
SLEEPING BEAUTY, by Richard Shaw (Univ. of Minnesota Press)
Empire State Youth Theatre Institute, SUNY-Albany
Directors: Joseph Balfior and Adrienne Posner
Sets by Marsha Louis Eck
Costumes by Patrizia von Brandenstein
Lights by Lloyd S. Riford III
Caren McGee-Russell as Beauty (foreground), Paul J. Villani as the King and Jeanne
Vigliante as the Queen (on inner stage).
Photo by Joseph Schuyler

(82) - Page 199
THE ICE WOLF, by Joanna Halpert Kraus (New Plays)
University of Texas-Austin
Director: Coleman A. Jennings
Sets and Costumes by Tomy Matthys
Lights by Rachel Garland Goode
Photo by Dale K. Kennedy

(83) - Page 200
THE BUTTERFLY, by Bijan Mofid (Anchorage Press)
Everyman Players
Director: Marilee Hebert-Slater
Designed by Irene Corey
Ronlin Foreman as the Spider
Photo by Orlin Corey

(84) - Page 200
RAGS TO RICHES, by Aurand Harris (Anchorage Press)
Kansas University Theatre for Young People
Director: Jed H. Davis
Sets by Gregory Hill
Costumes by Chez Haehl
Lights by Charles Lown
Photo by Andrew Tsubaki

(85-91) - Pages 201 & 202
Montage of Festival shots, Southern California Educational Theatre Association
Photos by Julie Kay Davis

(92) - Page 203
NO DRAGONS ALLOWED, company derived under director (unpublished)
San Diego State University (1975)
Children's Theatre Festival at Northridge
Director: Margaret McKerrow
Photo by Julie Kay Davis

(93-94) - Page 203
ANDROCLES AND THE LION, by Aurand Harris (Anchorage Press)
Kansas University Theatre for Young People
Director: Jed H. Davis
Sets by Robert Chambers
Costumes by David Blackwell and Chez Haehl
Lights by Charles Lown
Photo by Herb Williams

(95) - Page 204
PETER PAN, musical adaptation of James Barrie's play by Mark Charlap and Carolyn
   Leigh (Samuel French)
Zev Bufman and James M. Nederlander Production
Director: Rob Iscove (after original production by Jerome Robbins)
Production designer: Peter Wolf
Costumes by Bill Hargate

348

Lighting by Thomas Skelton
Photo by Richard Braaken

(96) - Page 204
HEY DIDDLE DIDDLE! The Rhymes and Riddles of Mother Goose, devised
   by Marilee Hebert-Slater (unpublished)
The Everyman Players
Director: Marilee Hebert-Slater
Designed by Ken Holamon
Clockwise from center floor: Holly Shelton, Bates Brooks, Thomas Hayes,
                                  Jerry A. Confer, Marilee Hebert-Slater,
                                  Richard Hauenstein, Ronlin Foreman, Mary-
                                  Beth Confer
Photo by Patricia Moore

(97-99) - Page 205
STEP ON A CRACK, by Suzan Zeder (Anchorage Press)
Kansas University Theatre for Young People
Director: Jed H. Davis
Sets by Mark Riley
Costumes by Chez Haehl
Lights by Tom Swift
Photos by Andrew Tsubaki

INDEX

Jed H. Davis, Professor Emeritus, University of Kansas, and formerly Director of the K.U. Theatre for Young People, traces his interest in children's theatre to the period of his own childhood in Stillwater, Minnesota, and a seemingly endless round of melodramatic plays written and produced with friends in local barns and vacant lots. Later as a University of Minnesota undergraduate he met his future wife when both trod the boards in a Kenneth Graham production of *The Emperor's New Clothes*. The World War II years brought service as a radio operator in Europe after which he returned to complete a degree, marry, and start a family ultimately numbering three children. While a young instructor at Macalester College in St. Paul, he was urged to direct a children's play as part of the season, a charge that sent him back to the University for a whole new focus to his career.

All three of his academic appointments included designer obligations — the area of his initial specialization; and this interest is reflected in both master's and doctoral thesis topics. During the seven years he headed the children's drama program at Michigan State University, he began his collaboration with Mary Jane (Watkins) Evans. Their first book, *Children's Theatre: Play Production for the Child Audience* (Harper and Row, 1960), was highly praised and widely adopted as a basic text. A combined appointment at the University of Kansas in 1960 was soon changed to expedite his efforts to establish Kansas as a major center for graduate studies in children's drama. In addition to the production of more than forty-five plays, the Kansas years yielded *A Directory of Children's Theatres in the United States* (AETA, 1968), *Theatre Education: Mandate for Tomorrow* (Anchorage Press, 1985), and numerous other publications in the field.

His first association involvement was as chair of exhibits for the 1950 Children's Theatre Conference (CTC) convention in Minneapolis. The excitement surrounding those early expansive years led to increased activity on CTC's committees and projects, culminating in election as Director (president) in 1963. A natural expansion into concerns of AETA led to the presidency of the parent body as it changed its name to the

American Theatre Association in 1972.

He was elected to the National Theatre Conference while serving a nine-year tenure as Director and Head of Theatre at Kansas. During this time he was instrumental in founding the Association of Kansas Theatre, furthering the work of the U.S. Center for ASSITEJ as a board member, and serving the Children's Theatre Foundation as Treasurer. Appointments to the Theatre Advisory Panel of the Kansas Arts Commission and to the Lawrence Arts Commission provided valuable state and local perspectives.

With biographical listing in several regional and specialized *Who's Who* editions, he takes pride in his election as a Fellow of both the ATA and the Mid-America Theatre Conference, his Edwin Strawbridge Award and the Marijane Morgan Medallion for service to national and regional children's theatre, the AMOCO Gold Medallion for contribution to the American College Theatre Festival, and in his selection as a charter inductee of the Kansas Theatre Hall of Fame. As he approached retirement, he was given the University of Kansas Chancellor's Club Career Teaching Award; and in his final semester, the Kansas Conference on "Theatre for Young Audiences: Principles and Strategies for the Future" gave testimony to his years of service to the profession.

Mary Jane Evans had her first experience with children's theatre when, as a student at Northwestern University, she was assigned to the costume crew for a production of *Treasure Island*. Subsequently she was easily lured into the circle of confirmed disciples of Winifred Ward. The day after receiving her degree she traveled to Cain Park Theatre where Dina Rees Evans became her first employer. It was there that she met Dr. Evans' nephew, Robley, who later became her husband.

Her career as a theatre educator includes initiating an experimental drama program at Sunbeam School for Crippled Children in Cleveland and employment as director of the Junior Civic Theatre of Kalamazoo, Michigan. She held a graduate assistantship and later a faculty position at Michigan State University where she earned her M.A. and became a colleague of Jed Davis. She has done additional graduate work at the University of Minnesota, Western Reserve University and the University of Wisconsin at Eau Claire.

In 1959, she moved to California to join the faculty of the newly-established San Fernando Valley State College, now California State University, Northridge, where she was given responsibility for developing a program in creative drama and theatre for children that gained a national reputation for excellence. The CSUN Theatre for Young Audiences, which she coordinated until her retirement in the summer of 1985, was the 1981 recipient of the Sara Spencer Award, the most prestigious accolade for quality theatre bestowed by the Children's Theatre Association of America. Northridge productions regularly tour for Junior Programs of California, and Mrs. Evans' production of *Reynard the Fox* was named an alternate for the 1972 ASSITEJ Congress in Albany, the only college or university theatre to be so honored.

Because of her Northwestern-Cain Park ties she was among the fortunate who attended the founding meeting of the Children's Theatre Conference. She was involved in the development and operation of the Children's Theatre Association of America as an officer, member of numerous committees, Governor of several regions, hostess to the 1968 Conference held at Northridge and participant in the 1977 Wingspread

Conference. She regularly appeared on convention programs.

A Fellow of the American Theatre Association, she saw service on its Board and Executive Committee, as chair of its Task Force on Governance and as a member of various committees. As recorder for the Commission on Theatre Education, she assisted in the preparation of the 1978 ATA Wingspread Conference Report.

On the state level Mrs. Evans has held several vice-presidencies in the Southern California Educational Theatre Association and has been a producer of its Festival of Theatre for Young Audiences. She chaired a state-wide committee that developed curricular materials for the *Drama/Theatre Framework for California Public Schools,* and was named consultant to the Framework Committee. Subsequently she was a member of a state-wide interdisciplinary group charged with preparing the *Visual and Performing Arts Framework* which now is the basis for arts instruction in the California public school system. A Past President of the California Educational Theatre Association, she is actively involved in its programs.

Her publications include co-authorship with Jed Davis of *Children's Theatre: Play Production for the Child Audience;* an essay, "Theatre for Children: Art Form or Anarchy," in Nellie McCasln's *Theatre for Young Audiences;* her "In Response to Anita Silvers," in *Children's Theatre, Creative Drama and Learning,* edited by Judith Kase-Polisini; co-authorship of *Tales from Hans Christian Andersen,* a play for young audiences; and numerous articles and reviews.

Now an Emeritus Professor, she served the last three years of her tenure at California State University, Northridge, as Chair of the Department of Theatre. In 1985, the Southern California Educational Theatre Association presented her its Award for Outstanding Contributions to the Theatre for Young Audiences. She is the 1987 recipient of the California Educational Theatre Association Outstanding Theatre Educator Award.

Mrs. Evans lives in Sepulveda, California, with her husband, a retired Administrative Law Judge.